BENEFITS
and Beyond

BENEFITS
and Beyond

A Comprehensive
and Strategic Approach
to Retirement,
Health Care, and More

THOMAS E. MURPHY
Miami University, Ohio

Los Angeles • London • New Delhi • Singapore • Washington DC

For information:

SAGE Publications, Inc.
2455 Teller Road
Thousand Oaks, California 91320
E-mail: order@sagepub.com

SAGE Publications Ltd.
1 Oliver's Yard
55 City Road
London EC1Y 1SP
United Kingdom

SAGE Publications India Pvt. Ltd.
B 1/I 1 Mohan Cooperative
   Industrial Area
Mathura Road, New Delhi 110 044
India

SAGE Publications Asia-Pacific Pte. Ltd.
33 Pekin Street #02-01
Far East Square
Singapore 048763

Printed in the United States of America

Library of Congress Cataloging-in-Publication Data

Murphy, Thomas E.
  Benefits and beyond : a comprehensive and strategic approach to retirement, health care, and more / Thomas E. Murphy.
     p. cm.
  Includes bibliographical references and index.
  ISBN 978-1-4129-5088-6 (cloth) — ISBN 978-1-4129-5089-3 (pbk.)
  1. Employee fringe benefits—United States. 2. Postemployment benefits—United States. 3. Health planning—United States. I. Title.
  HD4928.N62U6524 2009
  658.3'25—dc22

                              2008037598

This book is printed on acid-free paper.

09 10 11 12 13 10 9 8 7 6 5 4 3 2 1

Acquisitions Editor:	Lisa Cuevas Shaw
Editorial Assistant:	MaryAnn Vail
Production Editor:	Belinda Thresher, Appingo Publishing Services
Copy Editor:	Lisa Allen
Typesetter:	Amanda Sylvester
Proofreader:	Sandy Livingston
Indexer:	Linda Buskus
Cover Designer:	Ravi Balasuriya
Marketing Manager:	Jennifer Reed Banando

Contents

Preface

About two years ago, several colleagues at Miami University and I were discussing our employee benefits course that they had taught in the past and I had been teaching for the previous two years. We lamented the fact that there were no textbooks available that adequately supported the course, even though it was becoming increasingly popular among our finance, management, and accounting students. We opted instead to use a combination of Web sites, articles on our respective Blackboard sites, and a series of case studies we developed in lieu of a textbook. At some point my colleagues suggested that I should write a textbook. Long story short, I was intrigued. Shortly thereafter I prepared the requisite prospectus and contents. It was sitting on my desk when, as luck would have it, Al Bruckner, an editor from SAGE, stopped by my office and asked if I had any interest in writing a text on benefits. I hesitated, but only for the few moments it took to produce my materials. The book you are reading is the "rest of the story."

I have found that teaching benefits and demonstrating their strategic potential is exciting and fun, and would tell my students to "strap on their seat belts" because today's lesson on actuarial concepts and their relationship to pensions was going to be a thrilling experience. And I wanted my textbook to impart the same rich and fundamental understanding of benefits to students that I was trying to accomplish in my class.

The book is, by design, pedagogical, often simplifying complex topics, offering opportunities to apply concepts and principles, and encouraging an analytical approach to the study of benefits. It covers employer- and government-sponsored and mandated benefits, metrics, and global benefits. As pointed out in the book, benefits are "in the news," and they impact everyone and every institution. What I have tried to accomplish is not just to demonstrate how benefits work, but to illustrate how they can be an effective part of an organization's strategy.

There are many individuals I would like to acknowledge and thank for their contributions and encouragement: my wife, Janet, read every word of the text, making helpful suggestions, and her perseverance, insights, and attention to detail were absolutely essential to the completion of the book; Susan Hurst, business librarian at Miami University, spent many hours with my graduate assistants and me, helping us navigate the endless research opportunities and sources that we needed; Lisa Wintersheimer Michel, partner at the law firm of Keating Muething & Klekamp, for her excellent edit of the chapter on legal compliance; Michael Stoll, vice president, benefits, The Kroger Co., for his continual help and direction; Francis Ille, professor at the International University of Monaco, for his insights into the French health and retirement systems; my graduate assistants, Jim Lewis (MBA), Paul Spiller (MS, Economics), and Sarah Simeone (MBA), for their great help in developing figures and tables and finding data and research sources; my colleagues at Miami, professors Joshua Schwarz, Rebecca Luzadis, Jim Brock, and Kay Snavely, for their support and inspiration; John Flynn, of The Kroger Co., and Jim McKeogh, actuary and benefit consultant, for their excellent ideas and case examples; Al Bruckner and MaryAnn Vail, editors at SAGE, for their insights and support; as well as the eight anonymous peer reviewers, who provided outstanding suggestions to improve the book. Finally, I wish to thank Lisa Allen, copy editor at Appingo Publishing Services, who not only found the errors but also found a way to make much in the text read better.

This is the first effort. For those of you who read it and use it, I welcome your ideas for making it better. Writing, teaching, and being a student are all learning experiences.

Introduction to Benefits[1] 1

Rarely a day passes without some news on benefits appearing regularly in a number of venues—journals, newspapers, books, and television. Health care, the uninsured, the Social Security crisis, saving for retirement, stock option backdating, and an assortment of other contemporary benefit topics are grabbing the attention of the American public. Even as this textbook is being published, the benefits information highway is jammed with news. For example:

"Health insurance gap surges as political issue."[2]

Should the government take over the administration of the entire U.S. health care system? Or should the problem of the 47 million uninsured in the United States be solved by a targeted expansion of health care? Perhaps market-based solutions can be used to make health care more affordable. If it were more affordable, would the problem of the uninsured be solved?

"Can today's workforce accumulate sufficient funds to finance their retirement?"[3]

Employer sponsors of retirement plans are shifting from defined benefit plans, where the sponsor processes lifetime retirement income to the

---

1. In the interest of word efficiency, throughout this text the author has chosen to use "he" instead of "he or she" or "he/she" as the pronoun to describe an unnamed person.

2. Solomon, D., & Wessel, D. (2007, January 19). Health insurance gap surges as political issue. *The Wall Street Journal*, A1.

3. Clements, J. (2007, January 17). How to survive retirement even if you're short on savings. *The Wall Street Journal*, D1. See also Ghilarducci, T., & Jeszeck, C. (2006). Retirement, pensions, and managing one's own money. In D. Lewin (Ed.), *Contemporary issues in employment relations* (pp. 223–249). Champaign, IL: Cornell University Press

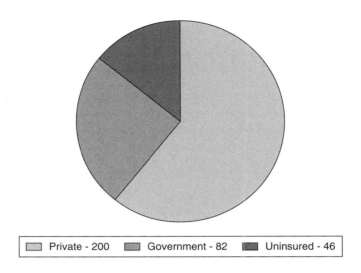

Figure 1.1   Sources for Americans' Health Insurance in 2007 (numbers
                  represent millions)

SOURCE: U.S. Bureau of the Census (2007).

participant, to defined contribution plans, which depend on employee
contributions. This has created a new and heavy reliance on employee savings. It also has shifted the longevity, investment, and inflation risks of
retirement from the employer to the employee. This comes at a time when
there is a funding crisis in the U.S. Social Security system.

   *"What should U.S. policymakers be doing to deal with the potential
underfunding of Social Security and Medicare?"* [4]

   Are these plans ready to embrace the large number of baby boomers
about to join the ranks of the retired, or will they become "bankrupt"?
Figure 1.2 shows the timetable for Social Security Administration and
Medicare insolvency.

The Plan Sponsor's Dilemma

Benefits that we have taken for granted are in jeopardy. Both employer
and government sponsors are concerned they may not be able to continue to offer benefits without making major changes, and those changes
do not bode well for participants. More of the burden of financing benefits is being shifted to employees. Rising benefit costs threaten the

---

4. Government Accountability Office (GAO). (2007, March). *Social Security
Reform. U.S. GAO, Report to Congressional Committees.*

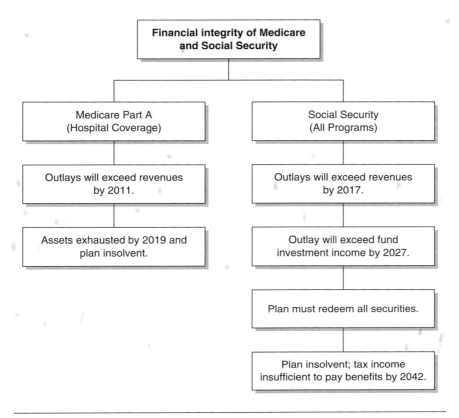

Figure 1.2   Financing of Social Security and Medicare

employer sponsor's ability to remain competitive in the global market-place. Government sponsors face the prospects of seeking higher tax support for benefits or cutting entitlements. Meanwhile, the general population faces serious lifecycle events that require government- and employer-sponsored benefits. Reliance on the fiscal soundness of these benefits, however, is undergoing a wave of change and creating anxiety and doubt among participants.

Benefits Infrastructure

Why do employers sponsor benefits? Why do governments? And what are the essential ingredients of benefit offerings? Employers offer a variety of benefits in order to recruit and retain qualified employees. They look to their external competitors to see what benefits they are offering and then determine whether they want to meet, lead, or lag behind them. Their decision ultimately relates to their business strategy and how choosing certain benefits can help support that strategy.

Governments sponsor benefits that usually fill the gaps left by employer sponsors. What happens when people cannot work or are too poor to contribute to the costs of certain benefits? In these instances, long-time government-supported programs such as Social Security, Medicare, and Medicaid provide a broad safety net of health, retirement, and disability income to those who otherwise would not be protected.

In the United States employers are well suited to offer benefits because of the favorable tax treatment they receive. Their benefit expenses are deductible and either tax-exempt or tax-deferred for the employee. They have the advantage of a higher level of design expertise, better information systems, and optimal use of capital markets to invest benefit funds. Size alone affords them an advantage to using their purchasing leverage to buy benefits at more competitive costs than individuals; and from an economic perspective, they are able to offer benefits more efficiently than individual purchasers.

Furthermore, the employer or government sponsor is in a better position than the individual to assume the longevity, inflation, and investment risks that are inherent in assuring retirement income. In the case of longevity risk, if the plan sponsor promises a benefit at retirement, and periodically funds an account that will be used to pay income for the life of the participant, it assumes the obligation to pay a retirement annuity regardless of the participant's life expectancy. If the promise to pay retirement income is coupled with an agreement to increase the benefit based upon cost of living changes, then the sponsor also assumes the inflation risk. If the employer invests the funds set aside to pay the retirement benefits, he must pay them regardless of the market performance of his investments.

The actual cost of the benefit for the employer or government sponsor is often less than its value to the participant because the cost to the individual to acquire such a benefit would be substantially higher.[5] It is important to understand that employer- or government-sponsored benefits are awarded on a tax-favored basis. If the individual were to buy such a benefit, it would be with after-tax dollars, meaning the employee would have fewer dollars to spend.[6]

One can understand from the news excerpts above that economic reality and attitudes among sponsors toward benefits are changing. Sponsors no longer refer to their benefit offerings as "fringe" benefits, a term that

---

5. This assumes the participant needs and wants the benefit, in which case there is real value to him.

6. Similarly, an insured health care plan will protect the participant against significant financial risks arising out of the treatment for acute or chronic health care conditions that could cost in the hundreds of thousands of dollars.

implied their minimal impact on the organization. Instead, benefit plan sponsors are looking for different retirement plan designs that shift the longevity, investment, and inflation risks to the participants, largely because of rising benefit costs, changing demographics, and the extended life expectancy of our national workforce. With respect to other benefits, they are slowly transferring the financing costs directly onto the participants.

Employers and the Business Strategy

A key element in the employer's decision to sponsor benefits is the business strategy and the human resources practices that drive it. For example:

Ted Jones' father owns and operates a large grocery warehouse in Boston. The 80,000-square-foot facility was leased 30 years ago and is now in need of significant repairs. Located in a heavily congested area of Boston, the warehouse lacks simple access to the interstate. The landlord has no interest in upgrading the facility and has made threats to increase the rent significantly. Ted has persuaded his father to close this facility and move to a new location with lower real estate costs and better interstate access. He has purchased property in a small Vermont town and started construction on a new 200,000-square-foot grocery warehouse and two contiguous frozen food and perishable warehouses, which will provide the opportunity to fully serve the needs of supermarkets up and down the east coast. Since the new warehouse is a considerable distance from the previous facility, Ted believes he will have to hire a new workforce that would include about 225 warehouse employees, 75 truck drivers, and 50 salespersons, buyers, management, administrative staff, and clerical employees.

He has rethought the compensation and benefit strategy currently in place at the Boston facility. Taking into account the new capital expenses related to the construction of the warehouse and the need to generate sufficient cash flow to service the debt incurred, he knows he will have a tight budget and must find ways to keep his labor costs low. Accordingly, he has decided on a simple human resources compensation and benefits strategy—to offer cash compensation at labor market levels together with more cost-effective benefits. If possible, he will base some of the cash compensation and benefit entitlements on company results. Long-term employee retention is not an absolute goal at this point; nevertheless, he needs highly productive, enthusiastic, and committed associates.

Before we focus exclusively on Ted's plan, let's look at some of the principles and issues affecting his decision.

Benefits and cash compensation are part of a total rewards system. Depending upon the demographics of the workforce and the business strategy of the employer, compensation and benefits can include fixed cash compensation, bonuses based upon individual or company performance, stock ownership, retirement plans, life insurance, and health care plans. Each of these can be fully or partially financed by the employer. Depending upon the plan design, the employer can allocate a certain amount of the cost of the benefit, as well as the inherent risks, to the employees. For instance, he can provide a retirement plan that will replace a high percentage of final pay at retirement age and a first dollar health plan that covers just about every medical condition without requiring any financial contribution by the employee.

The opposite is true as well. Employers can peg their benefits below those offered by their competitors. They can place a large share of the benefit financing on the employees, provide health care plans that only cover catastrophic conditions, and design retirement plans wherein the employee will receive a lower percentage of final pay. They can even shift the investment, longevity, and inflation risks to their employees.

Why someone chooses to work and stay at a company may depend upon a variety of total rewards—everything from company training and development opportunities to career advancement, work experiences that enable migration to other employers, free parking, casual dress, international assignments, life insurance, pension, health care, good pay, and a positive and collegial work atmosphere. Typically, however, employee benefits have usually included some of the following:

- Pension plan
- Health insurance
- Life insurance
- Disability protection
- Paid time off

- Equity benefits
- Work/life benefits
- Unemployment insurance
- Workers' compensation insurance
- Long-term care insurance

As Ted reflects upon which benefits to offer and their respective design features, he must first examine each component of his business and his human resources strategy to determine how benefits might relate to and positively affect or support these functions. How will the company design various jobs? What competencies will it look for in recruitment and selection? How will its benefits facilitate recruiting and job tenure? What are the expected demographics of the workforce, and how will they perceive total rewards, including benefits? Can the benefits be designed to enhance the productivity of the workforce? Should benefit entitlements be related to length of service, employee performance, employee level or status, or business success? Should benefits be designed to enhance long- or mid-term service?

Ted's compensation and benefits strategy—to pay cash compensation at labor market levels, to provide additional income and possibly benefit enhancements based upon company and individual performance, and to optimize the sharing of benefit costs among his employees—should enable him to recruit employees who, while they may not be with him for the long term, will be highly productive and engaged in the success of his warehouse company.

With respect to benefits, Ted has decided to offer a tax-qualified retirement savings plan that will be financed by employee contributions. While the employees will assume the longevity, investment, and inflation risks, the company will match a percentage of the employee's contributions to the plan based upon company results. To encourage some reasonable tenure, Ted's plan will increase the level of matches based upon years of service. With some disciplined and regular savings by the employees, in addition to the matches, he believes the employees will be able to accumulate savings that, together with their Social Security benefit, may yield retirement income of about 60 percent of final pay. Further, this plan gives him sufficient financial flexibility to meet his business plan goals.

He also has chosen a health care plan that requires cost sharing by the employees. It will cover large-scale medical expenses, leaving the routine care to be paid by the employees. The plan is designed to encourage preventive and certain diagnostic care that, over time, will serve to mitigate the possibilities of catastrophic medical events.

He believes that offering either a bonus or some type of gain-sharing plan that pays cash to the employees based upon the attainment of significant business or unit results might attract productive employees to his company. He also intends to offer a relatively inexpensive term life insurance policy to each employee that will provide some income security in the event of premature death.

In summary, developing the connection between a well-designed compensation, benefits, and total rewards program and the business strategy is an important first step for the employer. Depending on the company's size, demographics of its workforce, maturity, industry, location, and the price elasticity of its products and services, the employer has a number of alternatives. Small employers who may be strapped for cash, for example, can look at more efficient retirement plans such as the savings incentive match plan for employees' individual retirement accounts (SIMPLE IRA). Here both employee and employer contributions are placed in an IRA, minimizing administrative and legal compliance costs and placing the longevity, investment, and inflation risk on the employee. The employer who is experiencing high health care insurance costs could choose to convert to a high deductible plan, placing the obligation to pay the first $3,000 of annual medical expenses, for example, on the employee. Also, he could establish a pretax health savings account (HSA) that can be funded by employer or employee dollars and used to pay some of the employee's out-of-pocket health care expenses. Finally, in trying to recruit and retain better candidates without significantly affecting his labor costs, the employer also could offer performance-based stock awards. All of these approaches provide the employer with more flexible labor costs, while still giving employees retirement income and basic protection against health risks.[7] That said, however, with compensation and benefits, one size does not fit all.

Companies that are more mature and established may decide to lead the market in total rewards, perhaps, enabling them to hire and keep the best. Accordingly, they will design their compensation and benefits packages with features that encourage extended service.

Others may choose to design total rewards in order to attract a workforce with the requisite competencies. For example, offering piece rates instead of hourly rates to warehouse employees coupled with a profit-based employee savings plan, such as a 401(k), may facilitate the recruitment of highly competitive, self-assured, and productive candidates. Offering potential ownership interest through stock options and other equity plans could be an effective recruitment tool that encourages productive employee behaviors and causes employees to remain with the company.

In this book we look at compensation and benefits as value propositions, not just costs to be absorbed and tolerated. When carefully designed and aligned with the company's business strategy, they can help drive the factors that generate sales and profits and create new and significant financial returns to the enterprise.

Learning Objectives

The overall learning objective of this book is to provide you with an understanding and working knowledge of the principles and factors that support the offering of benefits. It is not intended to be a desk reference or loose-leaf service manual describing all the recent changes in benefit designs or legal regulations. The author does not teach to memorize the latest restrictions on pension income or current 401(k) limitations on contributions. You should know that such restrictions exist and be in a

---

7. The U.S. Labor Department produces statistics on labor costs. Their 2007 report shows that benefits represent about 30.2 percent of total labor costs. Discretionary benefits include pension, health care, life insurance, paid leave; legally required benefits include Social Security, Medicare, Unemployment, and Workers' Compensation. U.S. Department of Labor. (2007). *Employer costs for employee compensation summary.* Release No. 07 1434.

position to question whether one needs to do the research and find out what the limitations are. It is the author's intent, however, to teach to understand, to distinguish, to evaluate different approaches, to solve problems, and to innovate. Further, it is to have you routinely apply an analytical process using data and metrics to enhance the benefit decision-making process, and to calculate the financial value that benefits can return to the sponsoring enterprise.

Fundamental benefit designs, their underlying principles and concepts, as well as their evolution and effects, represent the core teachings of the chapters that follow. Understanding them will enable you to comprehend, analyze, and evaluate benefit plans offered today and in the years to come. The exercises following many chapters offer additional opportunities to engage and improve problem-solving skills.

Employees and their dependents, and others who participate in benefit plans, need them to respond to important lifecycle events. How well benefit plans respond should be an ongoing, important consideration of the sponsoring entity.

Topics Covered

The foundation and building blocks of benefits are covered in Chapter 2, Human Resources Economics, Principles, and Actuarial Concepts Applicable to Benefits, where we will examine a variety of labor economic theories such as the agency theory, tournament theory, efficiency wage theory, and adverse selection. The benefits model will be introduced, providing an important template for the design and evaluation of any benefit plan. Understanding these will allow you to comprehend the underlying concepts that shape benefit designs and objectives, and see how benefits can be aligned with business objectives.

We will analyze common assumptions about certain benefit designs to see if they are accurate. For instance, does a typical defined benefit retirement plan really encourage long service? If one's service continues to a certain point, does the present value of such a benefit decrease? Do employer matches in a 401(k) plan encourage higher contributions by the participant? Does a 401(k) plan sort more productive employees? What does an actuary do and how do actuarial concepts apply to benefit plan designs and administration? What are longevity, investment, and inflation risks, and how are they allocated among sponsors and participants?

Lifecycle events are the "raison d'être" for benefits. They include everything from adoption, childbirth, marriage, and divorce to sustaining a disability or serious health problem, saving for retirement or a child's college education, and more. How well do employers and government sponsors understand the particular needs and wants of their participants? Some employees, for example, may not want to retire completely at the normal retirement age, opting instead to phase into this stage of their life. Do current benefit designs and the supporting infrastructure respond to this choice? Others would prefer higher cash compensation to offered benefits. Should the sponsor assess how well its benefits are valued by its participants? In Chapter 3, Lifecycle Events, we delve deeply into these events and explore a methodology to determine which benefits to offer and how they should be designed to enhance their value to both participants and sponsors.

What is retirement and how can those who wish to change or reduce the demands of their work life ensure a sufficient stream of income? In Chapter 4, Retirement Plans—Evolution and Design, the evolution of a variety of employer-sponsored retirement income systems is discussed. Beginning with the defined benefit plan (DBP), where the sponsor promises a formula or unit based annuity for life, and moving on to the defined contribution plan (DCP), where certain risks and financing responsibilities are shifted to the participants, you will examine the various strategic purposes and designs of such plans. Next, you will explore profit sharing plans and employee stock ownership plans (ESOPs). In profit sharing plans, the employer contributes money to the employee's retirement account based in part on the company's profits. In ESOPs, the employer's contribution is made in company stock and can be financed by borrowing. The learning objective here is to facilitate the student's understanding of how retirement plans have evolved and to recognize alternative design features of specific plans and how they can be linked to the sponsor's business strategy.

Chapter 5 covers retirement plans that are more suitable for smaller employers who do not have the economic support or administrative capacity to sponsor the traditional plans. Recent changes in the law have allowed these employers to offer retirement plans that are designed to simplify administration and minimize legal compliance costs.

The Number[8] is a bestseller, discussing the life-defining issue of how much money is needed to secure the rest of your life. It is a firsthand account of a former corporate executive who details how to calculate "the Number" and what to do with it. In Chapter 5, a variety of approaches and calculators that can be used for retirement planning are introduced. How much do I need to retire comfortably? How do you determine if a prospective retiree has enough to last for his lifetime? What are the

---

8. Eisenberg, L. (2006). *The number.* New York: Free Press. Clements, J. (2007, January 17). How to survive retirement—even if you're short on savings. *The Wall Street Journal,* D1. The article describes some new ideas on the importance of aggressive saving for retirement; the use of income annuities to guarantee retirement income for life and minimize the longevity risk; tactics on how to disaggregate investments, retirement funds, and savings after retirement; and suggestions on why a delayed receipt of Social Security payments is a good idea.

appropriate strategies as the participant goes through the stages of accumulation, investment, and disaggregation of retirement assets?

Chapters 6 and 7 focus on health care. What are the life events that create a need for employer- or government-sponsored health care? Following a brief history on health insurance, we trace the evolution of health care plan designs beginning with the indemnity plan (or major medical plan), move on to a variety of plan designs called managed care, and finish up with the new consumer-driven plans. We will examine the design features of all plans, as well as the economic and market factors underlying each step in the evolution. You will learn about wellness approaches to health care and be able to redesign health care plans based upon the changing needs of the employer or government sponsor.

What is wrong with our country's health care system? Why are so many people uninsured, and why is health care becoming so expensive? How can we make our health care system more accessible and affordable? Should we reform our health care system and, if so, how should it be done? Chapter 8, Improving Access to Quality Health Care—Do We Need Reform?, explores everything from introducing more market-based features into the system to broad government interventions that will ensure universal health care coverage.[9]

The teaching objective is to enable a clear understanding of the underlying causes of our health care challenges in the United States and, in particular, the problems of health care affordability and the uninsured. We will take a look at the drivers of health care inflation in the United States and learn how they contribute to the problem of the uninsured and lead many participants in employer-sponsored plans to pay more for their health care insurance. We will identify a range of possible directions and try to establish the analytical framework that can best lead us to an optimal solution. These are important contemporary issues and everything from filling the gaps in coverage to introducing more market-based reforms, mandating employer health care coverage, and requiring health care insurance among our residents, to creating a national or single-payer health care system are considered. Further, we will discuss the fundamental

9. Porter, M., & Teisberg, E. (2006). *Redefining health care–Creating value-based competition and results* (p. 18). Boston: Harvard Business School Press. This is a recent bestseller about restructuring health care by introducing real market features such as assessing clinical outcomes of hospitals and physicians and relying on performance-based provider reimbursements. It supports the argument that such changes will reduce health costs and transform U.S. health care into an affordable, vibrant, and high-quality system accessible to all Americans. The book points out that, while the United States spends more on health care than a number of developed nations, it has the largest percentage of persons with health problems who did not get treatment or medication due to cost.

organizational changes in the health care system that should be made to accommodate such reforms.

The Pension Protection Act of 2006 (PPA), a major revision of the historic 1974 Employee Retirement Income Security Act (ERISA), clarifies a host of ambiguities and compelling issues relating to the employer's sponsorship of pension plans.[10]

What are the basic laws applying to benefits and how do we ensure compliance? In Chapter 9, Benefit Legal Compliance, we will explore the various provisions of ERISA and the Internal Revenue Code (IRC) that control the design and administration of pension and health care plans. We also will see how the PPA resolves pension plan design issues and pension plan funding, as well as new methods to enroll a broader group of employees into 401(k) plans. This chapter also reviews reporting and disclosure obligations by the sponsor, minimum participation and coverage requirements of pension plans, the employer sponsor's fiduciary obligations, IRS limitations on benefit amounts, vesting and break-in-service rules, plan terminations and plan freezes, pension insurance, and a variety of other statutory rules.[11] Compliance with these laws will ensure the sponsor that his plan is tax qualified and, thereby, entitled to the tax-favored status and creditor protections of the U.S. code.

More and more chief financial officers (CFOs) are looking at health care as an opportunity to create value.[12] Chapter 10 introduces a fairly new approach called benefit metrics. The working assumption is that benefits can create financial value and should not be considered simply as an unavoidable expense driven by an employer's desire to be competitive in the recruitment of new employees. Health care plans can reduce absenteeism and increase productivity, and do so on a cost-effective basis. Similarly, retirement plans can improve the quality of recruitment, affect employee retention, and positively affect participant behaviors. Stock plans can create a strategic alignment between owners and employees and enhance sales and profits. We will learn how you can use data and metrics to calculate the prospective return on investment (ROI) or net present value (NPV) of such benefits.[13]

---

10. Bronstad, A. (2006, October 6). Pension law to spur legal work. *The National Law Journal*. Retrieved November 14, 2008, from http://www.law.com/jsp/law/index.jsp

11. The U.S. Bankruptcy Act and how and when it applies to benefits is addressed briefly.

12. Parry, T., & Molmen, W. (2003, March 18). CFOs take a fresh look at health care and productivity. *Managed Health Care Executive*. Retrieved November 14, 2008, from http://managedhealthcareexecutive.modernmedicine.com/

13. For example, in Chapter 10, we explore the case of a company considering a proposal to offer a daycare center for the children of employees. An approach to calculating the financial returns is explained.

Some time ago, PepsiCo. introduced a broad-based stock option plan that awarded options to most of its workforce. The intent of the plan was to align employees with the interests of the shareholders. Some said the plan would not work because lower-level employees did not understand how their work on the plant floor had any effect on the price of the stock. Pepsi began an ingenious communication program to help all employees understand how their work does link to the driving forces of stock price appreciation.

Equity benefits are covered in Chapter 11. We will review of a variety of equity benefits from stock matches in 401(k) plans to stock options, restricted stock, stock appreciation rights (SARs), and stock purchase plans, as well as a variety of new performance-based criteria being applied to equity plans. We will discuss vesting, how grants are allocated among the workforce, the risks associated with equity plans, tax and accounting treatments, a variety of design features and alternatives, and the various approaches to calculate the cost of certain equity awards. We also will examine ways to measure the impact of such awards on employee productivity. Using Pepsi's approach, we will describe various communication methods that might help create an ownership mentality in the workforce that will link employees' work behaviors to improved company performance and increased stock value.[14]

Chapter 12 covers government-sponsored and mandated benefits. We will look at Social Security, Medicare, Medicaid, Worker's Compensation Laws, and Unemployment Benefit entitlements. We also look closely at laws that require employers to provide certain benefits, such as medical leaves covered under the Family Medical Leave Act (FMLA), and to continue health care coverage after a major life event (COBRA).[15] We will study laws limiting the employer's ability to preclude health care coverage of pre-existing conditions (HIPAA),[16] as well as laws that establish the rehire and benefit continuation rules for employees who take military

---

14. But see Forelle, C., & Bandler, J. (2006, March 18). The perfect payday. Executives get bonuses as firms reprice options. *The Wall Street Journal*, A1. This Pulitzer Prize-winning article uncovered the practice of backdating options among U.S. corporations. The purpose of backdating was to revive the value of options that had become worthless because of a price decline in the stock.

Rosen, C., Case, J., & Staubus, M. (2005). *Equity: Why employee ownership is good for business.* Boston: Harvard Business School Press.

15. The Consolidated Omnibus Budget Reconstruction Act of 1986.

16. The Health Insurance Portability and Accountability Act of 1996.

leaves (USERRA).[17] The learning objective is to become familiar with these laws, how and when they apply, and when to raise the red flag as benefit plans are designed and administered.

"The U.K. commits to resolving its criticized long waits for health care services and to reforming its National Health Care plan. Italy struggles with the financing of its Social Security retirement plan hurt by low birth rates and inadequate tax revenue." [18]

Chapter 13 is about global benefits. The educational objective is to increase awareness of global labor costs and benefits as noteworthy competitive issues. As companies extend their competitive reach and begin selling products, supplies, and services abroad, or find new foreign locations for their operations, it becomes essential for them to understand the benefits and labor costs of businesses within those countries. Likewise, it is important to understand the potential advantages in labor costs their foreign competitors might have when they sell their products and services to the United States.

We will discuss the differences in benefit offerings, which in the United States are largely employer sponsored while in other countries they are government financed and administered. How does health care work in the United Kingdom, Germany, or China? We will identify a series of health care benchmarks among our global market competitors and provide a basis to evaluate their effectiveness, comparative costs, and competitive impact. We will do the same for Social Security and pension plans.

We also will look at the basic compensation and benefit issues facing expatriates whose home country is the United States. Companies with international operations frequently develop a corps of managers and professionals who work abroad for several years. We will discuss various approaches to their compensation and, equally important, how the company extends its benefit plans to these employees.

In Chapter 14, Collective Bargaining and Benefits, we will focus on several unique features of benefits that arise in collective bargaining relationships. The dynamics of bargaining over benefits has become increasingly important as organized employers attempt to trim their purported uncompetitive benefit and legacy costs.[19]

---

17. Uniformed Services Employment and Reemployment Rights Act of 1994.

18. BBC News (2006, August 24). Long waits for NHS tests revealed. Retrieved November 14, 2008, from http://news.bbc.co.uk/. Brugiavini, A., & Peracchi, F. (2003). Social Security wealth and retirement decisions in Italy. *Labour – Review of Labour Economics and Industrial Relations,* 17(Supp), 79–114.

19. Legacy costs refer to pension and retiree health care benefits that continue for many years after employees retire. These, together with the benefit costs that are higher among organized employers, create tensions for the collective bargaining relationships. The obligation to financially report the future costs of such benefits has led employers such as General Motors to propose that all of its future benefit

You will learn about the National Labor Relations Act (NLRA)[20] and the employer's obligation to bargain with a union over benefits, as well as the requirement to create benefit trust funds that are jointly managed by union and employer representatives. We will discuss a unique approach to funding benefits that involves the employer's responsibility to contribute an agreed-upon amount of money to the health, welfare, and pension trust that is obligated to buy a certain level of benefits. Other topics such as maintaining existing benefit levels in the joint trusts, the co-administration problems arising from the union-management control of such trusts, as well as the portability of benefits among industry employers will be reviewed. Further, we will explore the economic value of benefit parity among industry employers, in addition to the obligation of an employer that is discontinuing participation in a multi-employer fund to pay withdrawal liability to the fund under the Multi-Employer Pension Plan Act (MPPA).[21]

"Many seniors (citizens) are being confronted with a variety of retirement products such as lifetime annuities, long-term care insurance, reverse mortgages, living trusts, and life settlements."[22] How do these work? Should an employer sponsor them for its employees or should the employer facilitate their purchase by employees?[23]

Life and disability insurance and paid time off are the subjects of Chapter 15. Employer-sponsored or procured-life and long-term care insurance as well as annuities are discussed. The learning objective is to identify how, when, and why employers sponsor or facilitate the purchase of such insurance by their employees. We will discuss the tax consequences to the employer, employee, and beneficiary(s) of employer-sponsored insurance and look at the economic principles underlying these programs as well as

---

health care liabilities for retirees be transferred to a jointly trusted plan for fair and adequate consideration. UAW might assume Ford, GM retiree health care liabilities. (2007, January 25). *Medical News Today.* Retrieved November 14, 2008, from http://www.medicalnewstoday.com/

20. 29 USC §151 et seq.

21. 29 USC §1381 et seq.

22. Opdyke, J. (2007, January 13). Smart retirement shopping. *The Wall Street Journal*, B1. A life settlement occurs when one sells his life insurance for more than the cash value but less than the face value. This provides additional cash during the remaining years of life when the person really does not need a life insurance policy but needs the cash.

23. McQueen, M. (2007, January 23). The shifting calculus of workplace benefits. *The Wall Street Journal Online.* Retrieved November 14, 2008, from http://www.careerjournal.com/. The author explores a number of benefits that are "for sale" at the workplace, including disability and life insurance, long-term care, homeowner insurance, critical illness health policies, and limited benefit health insurance. Employee assumptions that these benefits are cheaper because of the employer's purchasing leverage and having been "vetted" and evaluated by the employer are not always valid.

the processes used to calculate their costs. We will identify which life events and life status conditions exist that would make life or disability insurance worthwhile, as well as the use of insurance as a funding vehicle for other corporate programs.

Sometimes just offering simple, low-cost benefits can be highly regarded by workers. Referred to as convenience or accommodation benefits, they can include anything from casual dress to flexible work schedules. In Chapter 16, Convenience and Accomodation Benefits, Benefit Administration, we will examine a genre of low-cost benefits that enable the employee to deal with certain life events while maintaining his focus on work. For example, some employers might offer a concierge service that could include laundry and dry cleaning pickup and delivery for employees, grocery shopping plus delivery, video rental, and a variety of other tasks that could otherwise distract the employee from his work. Employee assistance plans (EAPs) are free counseling services made available to employees going through significant life events such as divorce or death in the family. Similarly, respite care provides regular but limited relief for workers who have elder care or home care responsibilities of family and loved ones. A few other convenience benefits that rank high on the worker's wish list are flexible work schedules, telecommuting, and pay-for-time not worked. Employers cannot discount the importance of such benefits to the employees and the execution of their business plan.

Finally, in this same chapter, we will explore the benefit plan sponsor's process of benefit administration and planning. This includes the role of corporate governance in benefit administration, trust management, and investment strategies, and the importance of employee benefits communications. We will examine various management information systems that facilitate cost-effective administration of benefits, and explore the recent trend of participant self-enrollment and benefit management through Web-based systems. The learning objective is to cause awareness and appreciation of how efficient administration of benefit plans can lead to higher satisfaction levels among participants and enhance the strategic impact of a plan and its overall cost-effectiveness.

Conclusion

Increasingly, employer sponsors are dealing with the high costs and insufficient funding of their benefit offerings. The same problems exist among government-sponsored plans and, ultimately, impact the lives of the general public and the competitiveness of employers. The teaching objective is to facilitate a fundamental understanding of the competitive, financial, legal, and management strategies relating to benefits, which, in turn, will enable you to manage benefits now and in the future; hence, the basis for the book's title, *Benefits and Beyond*.

Business Strategy Illustration

In this chapter we emphasized the importance of linking the business strategy to all elements of the human resources strategy, particularly benefits. The following analytical template and exercises will provide an opportunity to apply the principles discussed.

BENEFITS ANALYTICAL TEMPLATE

When we develop a new or revise an existing business strategy, we must determine how the employees of the organization can assist in its implementation. Such strategies can include an increase in market share, improvement of customer service, increased quality products, cost reduction, productivity improvements, pursuing strategic business relationships, or simply improving sales, cash flows, and profits. There are a number of management practices that should be considered when making this assessment. All or some, including compensation, benefits, and other rewards, could prove most helpful. Managers should implement those practices that are particularly related and aligned with the new strategy. A series of steps should be followed to ensure the selection of optimal management practices, including the choice of benefits that will best serve the new strategy.

1. Articulate the new strategy.

2. Identify the business operational drivers that can positively affect the new strategy.

3. Specify the quantifiable goals expected.

4. Review and assess every human resources practice that, if modified, could have a positive effect on the operational drivers. These would include the organizational structure of the business, job designs, employee recruiting practices and selection criteria, employee training, performance management and employee development, total reward systems including pay and benefits, and legal compliance.

5. Identify one or more new management practice(s) most likely to support an improvement of the business drivers.

6. Take baseline measures of the drivers that affect the new goals.

7. Implement the new management practice(s).

8. Compare the results of your plan by measuring the differences in baseline measures over time.

9. Calculate the return on investment (ROI) or net present value (NPV) of your plan.

EXAMPLE OF THE ANALYTICAL TEMPLATE

A retail employer with a chain of stores is experiencing a serious problem with poor customer service that is seriously affecting his sales. He is taking steps to implement a new program to better serve the customer and to incorporate his new vision of becoming the best in the market with respect to service. First he wants to create a customer service index in order to measure the perceptions of service by his customers, and commits to improve the index by 20 percent each year. He has identified the drivers of good customer service as low prices, friendly and helpful service, and excellent product selection and choice. Next he examines a variety of business drivers that would reduce his operational costs, thereby creating an opportunity to offer lower prices. He also studies how to effectively procure and maintain a better product variety. His solutions will involve some new employee training and enhancements in worker productivity. He focuses on how to improve friendly and helpful service by examining the complete list of management practices from organizational and job design to compensation and benefits to see what might be changed to achieve his goal. After making some assessments, he decides that changing employee selection criteria will introduce more service-oriented employees into the workplace and resolves that better training and development will further enhance the focus on friendly and helpful service. He also decides that a gain-sharing plan, in which cash awards are given to the workforce when the company achieves targeted customer service improvements, would help in furthering his goal. He changes his benefits plan to basic low-cost health care and performance-based company stock awards for both part-time and full-time employees, which he believes will enable him to widen his applicant pool and attract more emotionally mature workers who are comfortable in a service environment. Since his business does not require long-term service among workers, he will offer a basic contributory retirement plan, whereby workers can defer a percentage of their income into the plan and invest it on a tax-deferred basis. The company will retain the flexibility to match the employees' contributions when business results permit. The employees will have the opportunity to take their retirement funds with them when they leave. By following a disciplined approach, the retail chain can better ensure that the solutions selected will improve customer service.[24]

---

24. See Chapter 10, Employee Benefits and Metrics, which examines this process and how to evaluate such solutions in more depth.

Chapter Exercises

An important point with respect to benefits planning and which benefits to offer relates to the employer's business strategy. How can compensation and benefits help drive the intended results of the business strategy? The following cases illustrate how this might be done. Put yourself in the role of internal consultant and prepare a brief report that answers the questions listed, applying a relevant analytical framework.

1. You are the operations manager of a new start-up airline that will serve Chicago, Cleveland, and Newark. It will be a no-frills airline, offering customers low-cost, on-time service. You want to recruit pilots and other support personnel who will be willing to work long hours, be flexible in their assignments, assume some risk with respect to the company's future success, have a team orientation and strong customer service values, and appreciate and value their time with your company. The major airlines offer a wide range of comprehensive and expensive benefits to their employees, but you cannot afford them. Given all this, what should your compensation and benefit strategy be? How will it link to the business strategy? What assessments should you make? Who, most likely, will be attracted to your company as a new pilot, flight attendant, mechanic, or other staff employee? Why would they come? Are there elements of total rewards that are more attractive to some prospective employees? Structurally, how will you organize your company? What specific benefits would best support your strategy? How would you evaluate them?

2. Your company, a chain of retail food stores in Ohio, is organized by the United Workers Union. Your collective bargaining obligations result in an hourly total, average compensation cost of $30 per hour, which includes benefits of about $10 per hour. Benefit costs have been increasing an average of 12 percent per year. Indications are that your costs exceed the hourly labor costs of your competitors by $2.50 for every hour worked. Your CEO has asked you to conduct an analysis of this issue and make some recommendations. Analyze and describe a range of possible solutions to the problem of higher labor costs, and then select one solution and support it with an analysis and action plan. Identify how you would evaluate its effectiveness.

Human Resources Economics, Principles, and Actuarial Concepts Applicable to Benefits

2

There are a number of incentives, tax policy considerations,[1] microeconomic principles and theories, as well as human resources strategy issues that affect the employer's decision to offer benefits. These factors also impact how the benefits should be designed and funded. In this chapter we will see how the employer might use them to make optimal choices in his benefit decision-making process. In addition, we will introduce briefly the actuarial principles that determine how benefit plans should be funded and how certain plan designs affect the rate at which benefits are distributed.

Total Rewards

Two entrepreneurs are starting a new airline to provide service to three cities situated about 400 miles from each other. Their strategy is to fill a void that currently exists for business travelers who are looking for a low-cost, no-frills, and dependable commuter airline. One of the first issues the owners confront is how to compensate their workforce, especially the pilots. They cannot afford to match the high salaries and rich benefit levels of the large airlines, they have no stock or equity benefits to offer at this point, they will not be profitable for several years, and a cash-based profit sharing plan is not feasible. How will they attract pilots? The answer is that they must look at total rewards, not just salaries and benefits.

---

1. As we pointed out in Chapter 1, the U.S. government's policy supports the offering of employer-sponsored benefits by making many benefits tax deductible to the employer and tax deferred or even tax-exempt to the beneficiary.

Long-term retention is not a priority. If they can find competent pilots who need flight hours and are excited about working for a new airline, the company will succeed. By offering flight hours in the cockpit, the company provides new pilots with a valuable opportunity and the possibility of moving on to a bigger airline in the near future. So, while the new airline is limited in what it can pay in terms of salaries, it can offer a bonus based on company results, the promise of future equity when the company goes public, moderate retirement and health care benefits, and plenty of flight hours. The benefit package might include a defined contribution plan (DCP) funded by tax-deferred employee contributions and a high deductible health care plan that imposes significant cost sharing on the employee but extends protection in the case of serious and costly medical occurrences. The salary and benefits would be well below that of the major airlines, but would allow the company to compete effectively in its markets. Its total compensation would be both affordable for the company and attractive to its particular workforce.

One of many decisions an employer must make is how much he can pay his employees. The decision is based on profitability, cash flows, labor intensity of the business, and the price elasticity of a company's products and services. If the product or service is price sensitive, then the employer must control his labor costs carefully or run the risk of losing customers and sales. Business operations that are labor intensive will affect profitability adversely if they allow labor costs to be excessive. How an employer divides up his total compensation is based on other factors.

With respect to the pilots, the total rewards include the opportunity to increase flight hours. In other employment venues, the employer must assess how to define and allocate his total rewards within his financial limits so as to attract productive employees. In many instances, this will be determined by the demographics of the employer's prospective workforce and which rewards would be the most important and valuable at their particular stage of life or circumstances.

The total rewards package can include an infinite number of features such as salary or wages, bonuses, health care, pensions, profit or gain sharing, equity awards, paid time off, favorable working conditions, telecommuting, flexible schedules, time off during summer months, education and tuition assistance, training and development opportunities, internal promotion policies, free parking, and casual dress. As we consider the total rewards package, we should examine the monetary value of benefits.

Monetary Value of Benefits

All elements of compensation and benefits have a monetary value.[2] Take flextime, for example. What is its precise monetary value?[3] It depends, in part, on what workers are willing to give up in exchange. In the case of the pilots, the reward of flight hours compensates for the lower salary and benefit costs they are willing to accept. With flextime, if workers are willing to accept a lower wage in order to have flexible hours, its value to the employer is the difference between the external market wage rates the employer would otherwise pay and the wages actually paid minus the transactional costs of flextime.

We hear schoolteachers remark that their salaries are low, but their benefits are great. Apparently, schoolteachers and, for that matter, many public employees are willing to accept more generous benefits over higher wages and bonuses that are available in business sector jobs.[4] These benefits would include employer-funded pension and health care plans with minimal risks and cost sharing to the participants. The value to the employer is the opportunity to pay lower cash compensation offset by the higher costs of the benefit plans. The employer can limit his total labor costs to affordable levels. The particular mix of total rewards in the educational sector creates acceptable rewards and costs for both teachers and their employers. They are not, however, necessarily equal.

A fairly common question with respect to benefits is why not just give employees cash and let them buy their own? The answer is an employer can use his size and expertise as leverage to purchase or provide benefits at a lower cost than what an individual employee would pay.[5] For example,

---

2. Lazear, E. (1998). *Personnel economics for managers* (pp. 377–407). New York: John Wiley & Sons, Inc. Professor Lazear's text is an innovative and relevant textbook in human resources economics. He explores a variety of principles involving compensation, health and pension plans, the use of teams, training, equity awards, output-based pay, worker-owned firms, and outsourcing.

3. Using activity-based costing, an employer can determine the economic value or cost of flextime versus traditionally scheduled work time. See http://www.valuebasedmanagement.net/methods/.

4. There are a variety of attributed reasons why this situation exists, including the fact that teacher pay is usually set, in part, by public officials who find it more expedient to agree to long-term benefit rewards than immediate and liberal salary increases. Public officials are very sensitive to taxpayer reactions that are likely to occur when more obvious incremental labor expenses are incurred.

5. There is an additional value to the employer in offering a benefit instead of cash. With an employer-sponsored benefit such as health care or a "wellness program," the employer can control how the money will be spent and can better ensure improved health and productivity of its workforce than if it simply gave its employees the cash to buy the benefit. See Lazear (1998), p. 391.

assume an employer's actual monthly cost for health care per employee is $600, whereas an employee would pay $1,200 in after-tax dollars to buy the same benefit, further increasing the cost of the purchase.[6] The monetary value of the employer-sponsored health care is $1,200 and, under the tax law, it is not imputed income to the employee.

Not all benefits are perceived to have value. Younger employees, for example, may place very little value in an employer's pension plan. Unless the employer is able to effectively communicate the terms, conditions, and value of his benefit offerings, it might be difficult to rationalize a trade-off of pension plan in lieu of higher cash compensation. Targeted communication can enable employees to better understand and appreciate the employer's sponsored benefits.

There is a finite amount of total compensation an employer can offer. How does the employer allocate total rewards and present choices to his workers? Moreover, when the costs of the benefit are rapidly rising, the employer has the choice to either absorb the costs or pass them along to the employees in the form of lower wages or higher benefit contributions. This scenario is playing out more often as employers develop their total rewards program or negotiate with a union over wages and benefits.[7]

From an economic standpoint, the employer should be neutral with respect to how total compensation is allocated. But it is not always so easy. For example, rapid inflation in health care costs is not easily offset by lower wages if the employer's labor competitors continue to offer generous health care plans or if there is a labor contract and an obligation to bargain wages and benefits collectively. Often the employer must find ways to increase the limit on affordable labor costs. This can be achieved through increasing sales and profits, increasing profit margins by changing the mix of products or services sold, reducing operating costs, or taking labor out of the business by replacing it with technology or cheaper substitutes. The employer also can search for new benefit designs that will mitigate the inflation, but this usually involves a reduction in both the cost and value of the benefit and could have an unintended result of diminished

---

6. This represents the underlying rationale why employers offer benefits versus simply giving the employees the cash to buy them. For an interesting exploration concerning under what circumstances employees would be willing to buy their own insurance, see Fronstin, P. (2006, June). *The tax treatment of health insurance and employment-based health benefits.* Employee Benefit Research Institute, Issue Brief No. 294.

7. This is called the Principle of Compensating Differentials and is attributed to early writings by Adam Smith. Today, economists argue that employees pay for the full costs of all their benefits because the employer must allocate a limited amount of labor expense in order to remain competitive and profitable, and must trade off all costs against wages and salaries. See Butrica, B., Johnson, R., Smith, K., & Steuerle, E. (2004, November). *Does work pay at older ages?* (p. 4). Center for Retirement Research at Boston College, http://www.bc.edu/crr/.

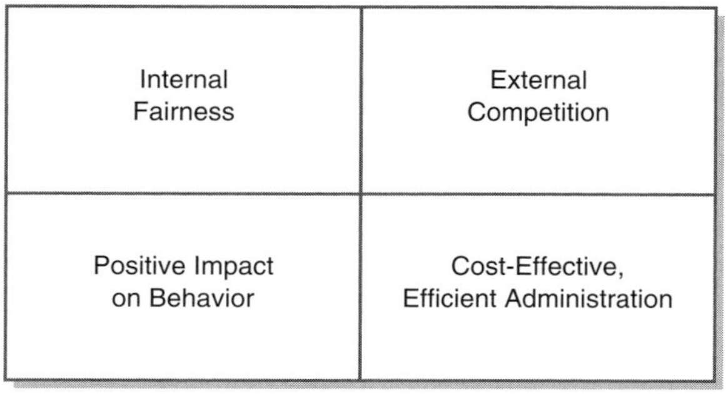

Internal Fairness	External Competition
Positive Impact on Behavior	Cost-Effective, Efficient Administration

Figure 2.1   Benefits Model

employee commitment, lower productivity, or difficulty in recruiting and retaining the workforce.

As in the case of our start-up airline, the employer must adjust his compensation and benefit strategy and find a way to remain competitive in his labor market. This requires a disciplined approach and an application of an important analytical template called the benefits model.

The Benefits Model

The benefits model is an analytical template that can be used to design and evaluate a benefit plan. It comprises four elements that, if followed, ensure the efficacy and affordability of a benefit and enhance its potential to create value. They are: internal fairness, external competitiveness, positive impact on participant behavior, and cost-effective and efficient administration.[8]

INTERNAL FAIRNESS

The benefit plan must adhere to the principle of internal fairness and not favor one group of employees over another. For instance, an employer provides life insurance only to employees with two or more dependents, perhaps in the belief that this group needs life insurance more than persons with fewer or no dependents. The excluded group would conclude that persons with two or more dependents are being paid more. Their

---

8. The author has adapted the benefits model from the pay model developed by Milkovich, G., & Newman, J. (2005). *Compensation.* New York: Irwin McGraw-Hill. The pay model has similar components but is applicable to cash compensation.

conclusion is justified because life insurance has monetary value and, therefore, it would be unfair to offer it to a selected group.

On the other hand, if the employer offers life insurance to employees who wish to purchase it, there is less chance that employees would regard the offering as unfair. This is true even though the employer is offering something of value, because the employer has the ability to purchase insurance at lower costs and on a tax-favored basis. Let's say the employer offers a life insurance benefit to all employees who have worked more than one year. The employees would probably perceive this as internally fair since the benefit is available to all who have completed the required year of service, and job tenure has some rationale as an eligibility requirement.

The issue of internal fairness becomes more apparent when one looks at exclusive benefits being offered to select employees. For example, the employer's human resources strategy is to use his benefit plans to sort[9] a certain demographic group in order to better ensure the selection of highly productive workers. Many young university graduates searching for jobs will look favorably on firms that offer tuition subsidies for postgraduate education such as an MBA. This benefit can have the effect of sorting highly motivated candidates who are attracted to the idea of an employer-financed MBA. The problem with this strategy could be the older workers who have no interest in pursuing a degree. Because the tuition subsidy only has significant monetary value to a limited group of employees, the employer's argument that such a benefit enhances recruitment and the overall productivity of the workforce[10] would not satisfy older employees who see it as inequitable. Some adjustment in the benefit offerings should be made in order to ensure that the plan does not collide with this important principle.

Internal fairness is intertwined with other benefits such as health care. When one considers the age of the workforce, it is generally true that older workers utilize more health care resources and, as a result, cost the employer sponsor more than younger workers. Similarly, younger workers with more dependents, all of whom are enrolled in the employer's

9. We use this term in its labor economic context. Employers choose a particular compensation or benefit plan that has the effect of attracting a certain type of worker. Essentially, the workers self-select the employer because a certain benefit has a different value to them. Lazear, E., & Shaw, K. (2007, Fall). Personnel economics: The economist's view of human resources. *The Journal of Economic Perspectives, 21*(4), 100, 103.

10. The theory of Efficiency Wage holds that employers with more generous wages and rewards can effectively recruit better and more productive workers. Neilson, W. (2007). *Personnel economics* (p. 127). Upper Saddle River, NJ: Pearson Prentice Hall. Recent research on the theory can be found in Uwe, J. (2006, July). A note on efficiency wage theory and principal/agent theory. *Bulletin of Economic Research, 58*(3), 235–252.

health care plan, receive a higher benefit value than those single employees who have no dependents. The disparate value of benefits between young and old employees, with dependents and without, creates an internal fairness issue.[11] Should the employer apportion and reduce the wages of those employees who are receiving the higher valued benefits, or should these favored employees pay more to receive the benefit?

There are several approaches to consider. One is to calculate the additional cost or value that an employee is receiving and allocate all or a significant portion of that cost to the employee. Thus, the employee with more dependents incurs a higher deductible or pays a higher premium for the benefit. Those participating in the tuition plan for advanced degrees can either pay for the education or be given a loan by the company to pursue the degree. This solution has some negative consequences, however, and might reduce the desired impact of certain benefits on recruitment, retention, and productivity.

Another approach is that the employer can offer his employees a choice. If the employer wishes to take advantage of tax-favored benefits treatment, then the employee or employer can deposit pretax dollars in an account. Typically, this is called a cafeteria benefit plan, wherein the employee can choose the type of benefit to be funded—health care, dependent care, or life insurance.[12] Similar tax-preferred treatment can include tuition reimbursement but, in this instance, it must be established in a separate plan and not be part of an assortment of benefits from which an employee can choose.[13] If the employer wishes to forgo tax-favored treatment, he can designate a maximum monthly cost for several benefits other than health, dependent care, or life insurance. The benefits would be considered

---

11. Since the employer is paying more for the one group's benefits without any apparent additional productivity from this group, it is essentially giving away incremental value and receiving nothing in return. See Lazear (1998), p. 412. However, there are some legal restraints applicable which would make it difficult for employers to charge older employees more for health care or to reduce the pension benefits of women employees because they live longer. See *Erie County Retirees Assn. v. County of Erie*, 220 F. 3d 193 (2000). This was an Age Discrimination in Employment (ADEA) action against an employer who had reduced retiree benefits for those who were eligible to receive Medicare. The court ruled the employer's action was unlawful. The EEOC, however, has approved and ruled specifically authorizing retiree health benefit plans to coordinate plan benefits with Medicare or comparable state-sponsored health benefits without violating the Age Discrimination in Employment Act (ADEA). The U.S. Circuit Court of Appeals for the 3d Circuit upheld the EEOC's position. *AARP v. EEOC*, 489 F.3d 558 (3d Cir. 2007).

12. §125, the Internal Revenue Code (IRC).

13. §127 et seq., educational assistance plans (EAPs). The IRC includes a dollar cap on the total amount of reimbursement and also prohibits the plan from favoring highly compensated employees.

Table 2.1   Cafeteria Plan

Total Monthly Allowance: $400

Benefit	Monthly Costs
High deductible health care plan with health savings account	$220
Traditional (PPO) health care plan (single coverage)	$360
Pre-school day care allowance (per child)	$280
Life insurance for spouse or dependent (1x salary of $100,000)	$30
Long-term disability – 70% salary	$120
Dental insurance (single coverage)	$35

NOTE: The employer's contribution probably would be made to a tax-favored flexible spending account (FSA) and not be taxable to the employee, provided it is spent on the specified benefit. See §125, IRC. The health care plan involves single, not family, coverage.

taxable income to the employee. In either case, pretax or taxable plan, the employee is given the opportunity to choose and the employer provides the most value to the employee for a fixed amount of benefit dollars.[14] The company is indifferent about which benefit is chosen.

Suppose a company offers its executives special benefits such as company cars, additional life insurance, paid country club dues, and security systems for their homes to protect against kidnapping or extortion. In addition, they are awarded large numbers of stock options, paid a supplemental pension, given special life insurance plans, and allowed to defer their compensation and the concomitant taxes beyond the limits imposed on other employees who are participating in the company's defined contribution plan. On top of all that, they get a corner office. Does the lure of such benefits help drive the internal job market and increase the productivity of the lower-level employee who aspires to climb the corporate ladder and become an executive? Some would argue that it does.

The concept is called the tournament theory[15] and the analogy is to a tennis tournament. If the winner gets $400,000, second place $395,000,

14. Lazear (1998), p. 414.

15. Lazear (2007), p. 94. See also DeVaro, J. (2006, Fall). Internal promotion competitions in firms. *Rand Journal of Economics, 37*(3), 521–542. This author conducted a study validating the connection between wage spreads and optimal performance levels.

third place $390,000, and the loser $300,000, what is the likelihood of having a highly competitive and aggressively contested tournament? The answer is, probably not likely. If, on the other hand, there were big differences in the prizes, there might be more intense competition among the players.

The tournament theory would imply the same holds true for total rewards in the business enterprise.[16] It justifies an apparent infraction of the principle of internal fairness because it stimulates increased competition for career advancement that results in higher productivity.[17] There are factors, however, that might warrant extra benefits for certain executives.

First, a ranking of jobs (internal job evaluation system) within the enterprise merits differences in salaries and bonus potentials.[18] Should there be a difference with respect to benefits? It depends. If certain benefits are available because of the unique status of the executive and have no appeal or relevance to nonexecutives, perhaps they might be justified. For

---

16. The author has some anecdotal experience with the tournament theory. While serving as senior officer and chief human resources executive of a Fortune 26 company, he eliminated company cars, country club memberships, and other executive perquisites, arguing that such benefits serve no purpose, cost too much money, and help to widen the gulf between lower-level employees and the executive group. Executives called him a populist, and managers pointed out how much they had looked forward to the day they became executives and would have the cars and club memberships. They were willing to put in long hours and hard work to attain this status. This is not exactly empirical research, but it does bear credence to the tournament theory. The author, however, was unmoved by the comments and the perks were eliminated.

17. Compensation and benefit managers who endorse the concepts of the tournament theory might want to validate its effectiveness by using metrics as set forth in Chapter 10, Employee Benefits and Metrics.

18. Most employers have some type of internal job evaluation system that ranks positions (not people) within the company on the basis of certain relevant factors that are important to the overall business strategy. For example, positions can be evaluated based on such factors as skill, effort, responsibility, and working conditions. The Equal Pay Act uses these criteria in evaluating claims of pay discrimination. 29 USC §206(d). Another scheme ranks and evaluates management positions based on accountability, know-how, and problem solving. This is the Hay System. See http://www.haygroup.com/. Still others, like The Kroger Co., use financial impact, customer service, and leadership as criteria to evaluate and rank jobs in their companies. Whatever factors are used, if the system works, so that employees perceive there is a rationale or fairness underlying the ranking of jobs and that pay levels are based on such differentiations, then the employer will have achieved the objective of having an internally equitable compensation system.

Table 2.2   Tournament Theory

By increasing reward differentials (RD) among various levels within the organization, one can increase aspiration levels of employees resulting in higher productivity (P).

Level	1	2	3	4	5
Total Reward	$100,000	$150,000	$220,000	$290,000	$410,000

example, it is doubtful an hourly employee would defer his entire salary to a non-tax-qualified executive salary deferral plan where the deferred salary is not protected against creditors.[19]

Second, performance-based bonus plans and stock option plans are often used in place of higher fixed executive compensation. As managers move up the corporate ladder, often more of their compensation is dependent on the achievement of corporate results. Thus, the executive's potential to enhance his overall compensation is at risk. This assignment of risk at higher levels ordinarily is not compatible with the lower-level employee group where total compensation is less, and placing a large portion of total compensation and benefits at risk would be unacceptable.

Third, as we will see in Chapter 4, Retirement Plans—Evolution and Design, some supplemental pension plans available to executives involve a restoration of the pension amount attributable to the plan formula. The Internal Revenue Code (IRC) precludes payments of pensions from defined benefit plans (DBPs) that exceed certain amounts,[20] so the company pays the difference between the benefit calculated and the benefit allowed by way of a supplemental, non-tax-qualified plan.

There are competing theories that must be considered as employers wrestle with the principle of internal fairness. Compensation and benefits are, in part, based on what the competition in the employer's product or service market is doing for its employees. Similarly, external competition becomes very relevant in determining which benefits an employer should include in his total reward plan.

---

19. See 29 USC §1056 (d)(1), and the 2005 amendments to the Bankruptcy Act that extended the protections to additional types of retirement plans. See 541(c)(2) of the Act.

20. See IRC §415.

EXTERNAL COMPETITIVE REWARDS

While internal fairness helps determine which jobs get the highest pay and benefits, the actual salaries, bonuses, and benefits associated with those jobs are determined, in large part, by examining external competitive compensation and benefit practices. When comparisons are obtained from the employer's own product or service market, assumptions can be made that the comparators have similar cost structures and margins and compete in the same labor market. Thus, their compensation and benefit levels are relevant.[21]

After the employer determines what others in his market are including in their total reward package, he must choose a compensation and benefit strategy that is linked to his business and overall human resources strategy. Does he want to meet, lag, or exceed competitions' levels? Benefits can be an important element in making this determination and can have a significant impact on the employer's ability to attract and retain the right employees.[22]

Going back to our new commuter airline, the two entrepreneurs will survey the external competition. Since the new company cannot compete in total rewards with the big airlines, their compensation and benefits strategy will be to lag behind the competition and offer other rewards that will attract good employees. Their total rewards package will include the opportunity to accumulate flight hours, maybe some flexible work opportunities, and the challenge and excitement of starting up a new airline.

By getting data on the total rewards plans of his competitors and establishing a compensation and benefits strategy, the employer can design a set of benefits that are affordable and, based on the probable demographics of the prospective workforce, enable him to attract energized and committed employees. Since their strategy will not guarantee retention, they must deal with the eventual turnover that will occur as the pilots amass flight hours and experience and leave to work at the bigger airlines.[23]

---

21. The maturity of the company, the industry, the state of unionization, size, and location, as well as cost structure and price sensitivity of the industry also are relevant to the process of understanding and analyzing a comparator's reward package.

22. For example, Lazear (2007), p. 103, points out that by offering a pension plan, the employer can attract those who are more likely to remain in service for a longer period of time. So, if the firm values loyalty, it can offer a pension plan.

23. There are benefit designs that can have a positive effect on turnover; we will discuss them in this chapter. In this case, however, the value to the employer of offering rewards below labor market levels might be offset by the increased costs of higher turnover.

Through benefit offerings, the employer has the opportunity to attract employees whose demographics and characteristics fit his business and human resources strategy. A carefully planned benefits package can attract the desired workforce and actually cause individuals with the relevant competencies to self-select or sort themselves to work for this particular employer, as illustrated in the following.

An upscale coffee bar chain decides that it wants to hire a more mature workforce. The company wants to send a clear signal to prospective applicants that it is looking for mature, responsible people who understand and appreciate good customer service. It faces a number of challenges: (1) Entry-level positions usually do not require any special skills, experience, or education. (2) Customer flow indicates that most positions should be part-time; with more flexible labor, varying customer service levels can be met. (3) Part-time employees usually are not offered any significant benefits. So, what is the signal?

The company decides to offer health care to part-time workers, a 401(k) plan, and stock options. In addition, hourly rates will be slightly above competition. Clearly, the benefit package far exceeds that offered by the competition. The anticipated result is the benefits will attract a significant number of the targeted audience, including single mothers who need health care and a part-time job for the next five to six years. The part-time status is attractive to them because of family and, particularly, child care obligations. And most in this unique group will appreciate the importance of customer service in light of their own life experiences. The stock options and 401(k) plan serve to underscore the employer's interest in a committed, aligned, and longer-term employment relationship, as opposed to a weekend job for a high school student. Overall, the employer's benefit offering serves to preselect or sort workers with the desired characteristics, causing them to self-select themselves for the coffee bar.

Where does one find competitive data that includes detailed benefit descriptions of the comparators in a specific market?[24] It is not enough to

---

24. Some surveys are available at the Bureau of Labor Statistics, U.S. Department of Labor Web site at http://www.bls.gov/. One also can find comparative compensation and benefits data in publications of the Employee Benefits Research Institute at http://www.ebri.org/. Management consulting firms publish various compensation and benefit surveys and will custom design a survey for a particular industry; for example, see the Web sites of Towers Perrin (http://www.towersperrin .com/) and Mercer (http://www.mercerhr.com/).

learn that your competitors have a pension or a health care plan. The employer needs to know the design details to determine where he wants to be on the competitive scale—meet, exceed, or lag the levels of his competitors' plans. Examples of some of the information the employer needs are: Does the competition offer a 401(k)? Do they offer a match in their 401(k) and, if so, how much? Do they offer health care and, if so, what are the eligibility requirements, cost sharing arrangements, and premiums? Many surveys simply do not provide these kinds of details even though benefits can have significant cost impact and possibly affect recruitment of a productive workforce. Thus, very detailed comparative data is absolutely necessary as an employer develops his compensation and benefit strategy.[25]

Can benefits help to retain workers? Can they be designed to positively affect behavior in the workplace? Can they be an important factor in executing the business strategy? This brings us to the third element of the benefits model.

POSITIVELY AFFECTS EMPLOYEE BEHAVIORS

A very important element of the benefits model is how a benefits plan can cause certain positive behaviors among participants. For example, a woman covered by her employer-sponsored health care plan visits the pharmacy with a prescription. The pharmacist informs her that if she chooses a generic drug instead of the prescribed patented drug, her co-pay will be only $5 instead of 20 percent of the cost ($25) of the patented drug. Assured by the pharmacist that the generic has the same chemical content and effect as the patented drug, she chooses the generic and saves $20 of her own money. Here, the design of the prescription plan changes the behavior of the participant to make more cost-effective choices for herself and her employer sponsor.

As we will see in Chapter 6, Health Care, many plans utilize participant co-pays for doctor visits, deductibles, and even plan premiums to affect the utilization of health care resources in a positive manner. The ultimate plan design, the health savings account (HSA), uses a high deductible to cause participants to behave more like consumers in a real health care market. The benefit plan sponsor should design plans with incentives that cause employees to make choices consistent with their company's business and human resources strategies. Do these incentives really work?

---

25. As we will discuss in Chapter 13, Global Benefits, it is important for employers who trade in global markets to obtain international, external, competitive total reward data so they can understand the competitive cost advantage or disadvantage it might have in such markets, and appreciate the consequences of locating its operations in such venues.

Some plans depend on the achievement of certain results in order to trigger an entitlement. These include profit sharing plans, employer profit matches for participants in a defined contribution plan such as a 401(k), stock plans that are contingent upon the attainment of certain performance results, and gain sharing plans where employees share in the financial gains attributable to certain operational targets such as reductions in lost-time accidents. When properly designed, these plans can generate positive employee behaviors.[26] In the case of a 401(k) profit match,[27] employees are motivated to take action to lower operating costs, improve productivity, and enhance customer service and sales. Similarly, equity plans where stock options or restricted stock are awarded can create an alignment between the workforce and the shareholders. One possible obstacle that could prevent employees from thinking and behaving like owners is the lack of a connection between what the worker does and how it impacts the intended result. The principle is called "The Line of Sight."[28]

For example, can an employee stocking grocery shelves see any connection between his work and the price of the company's stock? If not, should the employer reward him with stock options that provide increasing benefit value as the stock price increases? One could argue the line of sight is too long and that options are more appropriately granted to executives. By

---

26. Even, W. E., & MacPherson, D. A. (2005, July). The effects of employer matches in 401(k) plans. *Industrial Relations, 44*(3), 525–549. Research indicates that the size of the employer's match does affect the rate of participation among employees in a 401(k). Also, there is some evidence that participation in a 401(k) does affect productivity positively. Do co-pays and employee cost sharing features in health care plans really reduce health care resource utilization? Yes. Do they adversely affect the health care for the average person? The research says no. See Gruber, J. (2006, October). *The role of consumer copayments for health care: Lessons from the Rand health insurance experiment and beyond.* Kaiser Family Foundation, Publication No. 7566, http://www.kff.org/insurance.

27. A profit sharing retirement plan works in a similar manner and requires effective employee communication if the employer expects to affect employee behaviors positively. A Web site devoted to profit sharing issues and design, as well as related DCPs, is http://www.psca.org/.

28. Milkovich, G., & Newman, J. (2005), p. 63. The Line of Sight is an important consideration in designing plan features intended to cause positive employee behaviors among participants. See also Colvin, A., & Boswell, W. (2007, March). The problem of action and interest alignment: Beyond job requirements and incentive compensation, *Human Resource Management Review, 17*(1), 38–51. The authors studied the issues of employee line of sight to organizational strategy and shared mind-sets within the organization.

shortening the line of sight, however, an employer can offer a variety of broad-based benefits that can result in positive employee behaviors. When properly designed and effectively communicated, there are a variety of performance-based benefits that can reduce the gap between management and hourly employees, support the principle of internal fairness, and promote productivity improvements.

Take the stock option plan. Combined with a comprehensive communication program, a stock option plan can help employees recognize and appreciate the connection between their work and the price of the stock. PepsiCo had such a program.[29] It offered stock options to a broad spectrum of its workforce. Employees were regularly reminded which activities at their work stations could have an impact on reducing costs, enhancing sales, and improving profits. They informed employees that sales and profit improvements frequently have a positive impact on the stock price. Management pointed out that reducing waste, turning off lights, adhering to quality outputs, saving on packaging expense, and improving customer perceptions of service could all add value to their stock option plan. As a result, the offering of stock options had the desired effect of positively motivating employees at all levels to enhance productivity. Similarly, a company's comprehensive communication effort on its matching contribution to the 401(k) plan, based on achieving targeted profit or sales levels, can have a positive effect on the behavior of employees at the executive, management, and hourly levels.

Since all benefits involve costs to the employer sponsors, they should test the presumed behavioral impacts of their benefit plans. This can be done with a variety of metrics tools, as discussed in Chapter 10, Employee Benefits and Metrics. For now, suffice it to say, a stock option plan generally creates an interest in the stock price among its participants. If these same participants can be shown how they can influence the drivers of

---

29. PepsiCo called its program "Share Power." Employees at all levels were eligible to receive stock options. There were signs and posters everywhere in the plants and distribution centers reminding employees which activities impacted costs and sales. PepsiCo was shortening the line of sight between the work activity of its employees and the stock price. They saw the link, realized the potential value of their benefit, and changed their behaviors. PepsiCo continues Share Power, but has modified it slightly to account for higher employer matches to the company 401(k) and to respond to the new accounting changes with respect to the expensing of options. See PepsiCo press release (2004, December 2). This is discussed in Chapter 11, Equity Benefits. Other companies, mirroring the PepsiCo approach, have successfully communicated the links between stock value and employee behaviors. Covel, S. (2008, February 7). How to get workers to think and act like owners. *The Wall Street Journal,* B6.

higher stock prices—namely, good operational results—then the benefit will have achieved a positive change in employee behavior.[30]

While some might argue that gain sharing plans are not benefits, their design can provide important insight with respect to affecting employee behaviors positively with benefits. The typical gain sharing plan can include a number of performance measures such as reducing lost time due to accidents, improving customer service levels, reducing downtime on the production line, improving the ratio of labor costs to sales, and achieving high production or predictable yields from raw materials in a manufacturing plant. In most cases, employees see and appreciate the connection between what they do and these operational measures. Further, the measures are inextricably linked to sales, or cash flow, or earnings before interest, taxes, depreciation, and amortization (EBITDA),[31] or profits. When specific goals are met, the employee team, department, or entire workforce receives a share of the gain. It is usually paid in cash and on a quarterly or semiannual basis.[32] When an employer pays a benefit based on financial results, it is the improved performance that is funding the benefit. The lessons here are obvious. In order to capitalize on the opportunity to affect employee behavior positively with benefits, one must shorten the line of sight, require financially based performance achievements, and

---

30. The author's experience is that, at the very least, profit- or output-based benefits, or a broad-based stock option plan, give the employer an opportunity to communicate with lower-level employee participants about the competitive challenges of the company and its external market threats, and share with them the opportunities for improvements. The communication can enhance better alignment between the workforce and the business strategy, as well as employee motivation. The stock option plan is also a less expensive form of reward because it involves variable, noncash compensation. Even with the new Financial Accounting Standards Board (FASB) accounting changes for options that must be reported on the employer's financial statements, there is considerable savings to the employer. This savings is represented in the time value of money because option exercises or payouts are deferred pending vesting and market developments and because, in many cases, the employer pays less cash compensation when options are granted. See Chapter 11, Equity Benefits. See Pfeffer, J., & Dee, T. (2007). *Hard facts, dangerous half-truths, and total nonsense: Profiting from evidence-based management.* Boston: Harvard Business School Press. They argue there is no evidence to support that stock options positively affect employee behavior.

31. EBITDA is a more practical way to measure profits without consideration to certain accounting and financing issues.

32. The payoff must be sufficiently generous to motivate, and frequent to maintain focus among the workforce. A powerful complement to the gain sharing plan is a problem-solving process in which employees' views, ideas, and contributions are solicited in order to improve work processes that will better ensure gain sharing results. With the possibility of significant reward, these employee activities can be galvanized and effective.

effectively communicate the program, making it an integral part of the company's culture. Let's see how this might apply to other benefit plans.

Results-based employer contributions could be included in a variety of benefit plans such as defined contribution retirement plans, supplemental health care plans that expand coverage or benefit levels, added life insurance coverage, employee medical or dependent care accounts, and vacation entitlements. The results-based approach can serve as a catalyst to stimulate employee behavioral changes that result in improved business results. Making sure there is a short or shortened line of sight is important in designing plans that affect employee behaviors. This is the challenge of the plan designer.

Some retirement designs can have positive effects on participant behavior. Most plans include vesting requirements that obligate the employee to remain in the sponsor's employment for a given period of time before he has a nonforfeitable interest in the benefit. When the full vesting requirements are met, the employee will be considered to be 100 percent vested in the benefit, and his accrued benefits will not be subject to forfeiture. These requirements have the intended effect of enhancing employee retention and rewarding longer service. The link to the business strategy is to support an objective of enhancing employee loyalty.

Retirement plans that use pay (particularly final average pay) and years of service in the formula to calculate one's pension also encourage longer service and motivate employees to seek progressive career moves that will enhance their earnings. When bonuses are included in the earnings portion of the pension calculation, there is an added incentive on the part of the employees who are nearing retirement to perform well, achieve a high bonus payout, and increase their pension.

Years ago, most defined benefit plans made retirement at age 65 compulsory. Changes in the law, however, made this practice illegal and now most employees can continue to earn pension credits as long as they are working, and they can work as long as they want. Does the typical defined benefit plan begin to discourage retention after certain ages? The answer is, probably yes, and here is why.

A defined benefit plan prescribes a benefit to the retiree as long as he lives. In some cases, there are survivor benefits paid during the life of certain spouse or contingent beneficiaries. For the participant, however, the shorter the life expectancy, the less benefits he receives. In other words, the present value of the retirement income under a defined benefit plan declines as the participant ages, or remains working at the company, or defers receipt of his pension. This is so even though the participant continues to accrue years of service credit. At a certain point, this becomes reality and the participant will terminate his service because of the pension plan. This is explained in some detail in Chapter 4.

Conversely, when one compares the present value of a defined contribution plan (DCP) to a defined benefit plan (DBP), the former increases in value as the participant gets older. The participant's continued contributions to a DCP result in an increase in the present value regardless of his age or life expectancy. This is because the benefits in the DCP do not expire with the death of the participant. The benefits comprise the participant's aggregated retirement contributions and employer matches, and they continue to earn interest on a compounded and tax-deferred basis until the participant elects to begin receiving payments from the fund. Thus, while a defined benefit plan encourages longer service, at some point based on the pending mortality of the participant, it also encourages retirement, whereas the defined contribution plan does not lead to retirements because of pending mortality.

DBPs generally are not portable, while DCPs are. When a benefit is not portable and an employee does not remain at one company, the net effect is a reduction in retirement income from the defined benefit plans. This is discussed further in Chapter 4. Including portability as a design feature facilitates movement and turnover of employees among firms.[33] Employers who offer such features, however, must understand there is a cost[34] involved and they should measure that cost against the returns such features have on improved recruiting and productivity of the workforce. Let's continue to explore retirement plan design features that can impact participant behavior.

In some cases the employer uses the retirement plan as an incentive to reduce the size of the workforce. Early retirement incentives take the form of artificially adding years of service to the formula, giving large amounts of separation pay, or agreeing not to actuarially reduce the benefit because of the participant's early retirement.[35] Usually, there are age and service requirements that determine eligibility for the program.

The incentives may work if the added benefits included in the package are significant. Typically, the employer will predict how many will take the plan and what the labor cost savings in reduced wages will be. This must be contrasted against the real cost of the plan, including the added benefits as well

---

33. There is some interesting research pending publication that indicates workers who actively participate in 401(k) plans have a greater propensity for saving for the future and tend to have higher goals and render superior performance. The conclusion is that a 401(k) plan can result in higher productivity among participant workers. Burham, K. (2007). *401(k) as strategic compensation: Align pay with productivity and enable optimal separation.* Doctoral dissertation, Notre Dame University, Department of Economics.

34. Defined contribution plans and hybrid plans such as cash balance plans typically permit portability and, thus, do not encourage long service.

35. There are some ERISA and IRC restrictions on the employer's ability to modify the pension by adding such incentives. In general, employer sponsors must comply with the specific terms of their plan documents. The funding of supplemental benefits, therefore, often comes from financial sources outside the plan.

as the temporary loss of productivity that will occur due to the loss of experienced employees. Essentially, the employer is modifying a number of retirement plan features that were designed to encourage employee retention, and using the plan to encourage separation. Obviously, careful attention must be paid to legal issues, but the employer must carefully examine the return on the investment or payback period of its retirement incentive. This is discussed in some detail in Chapter 10, Employee Benefits and Metrics.

A related issue involves enhanced utilization of older workers and the concept of phased retirement. This has become an important issue as we experience worker shortages and new perspectives among employees on what activities they wish to pursue when they retire.[36] Here again, incentives and resultant behaviors can be observed. For instance, Employee A is approaching 65 and wants to retire, but would like to remain with the company on a part-time basis. The company wants to retain his experience and knowledge for several years and offers a possible solution: phased retirement. It is a win–win proposition; however, there are several considerations:

- Should the employee receive the entire pension amount when he goes on part-time, semiretired status, or should the benefit be proportionately reduced and, if so, by what amount?

- Should the employee, where he is a participant in a defined benefit plan, continue to accrue service credits during semiretirement?[37]

- When he finally retires completely, should a new pension calculation be made using his lower, part-time earnings?

What reasonable and fair incentives can the employer make that would encourage an older worker to remain employed on a semiretirement basis? How would you design such a program? The Pension Protection Act of 2006, discussed in Chapter 9, Benefit Legal Compliance, has relaxed some barriers that made it difficult for employers to offer phased retirement. The above questions are discussed in Chapter 9.[38]

In addition to coordinating the pension issues, are there special benefits the employer can design to induce employment of older workers who are

---

36. See Peterson, S., & Spiker, B. (2005). Establishing the positive contributory value of older workers: A positive psychology perspective. *Organization Dynamic, 34*(2), 153–167.

37. In the Social Security system, persons seeking benefits at age 62 or before the prescribed normal retirement date are subject to benefit reductions if they earn money in a postretirement position. Similarly, portions of the Social Security benefit are subject to ordinary income tax if the person earns wages above certain levels. See Chapter 3, Lifecycle Events.

38. There are new legal issues here. The Pension Protection Act of 2006 has provided some relief to this dilemma by allowing some pension distribution during a phased retirement. See §905 of the Act and Sammer, J. (2006). Pension law makes way for phased retirement. *HR Magazine, 51*(11), 28.

already participating in Medicare and, perhaps, receiving Social Security retirement benefits? The ordinary package of employer-sponsored benefits may not be particularly relevant to their needs. This worker does not need health care or a pension plan. Should the employer tailor a benefit program that will enhance his ability to recruit and retain older workers? Would they be more interested in financial counseling, contributions to a college education fund for their grandchildren, long-term care insurance, longer vacations, or flexible schedules? With some research and innovation, and by offering choices to workers, special benefit designs can assist employers who want to improve utilization of older workers.[39]

In some cases, employers design output-based benefit plans to foster cooperation among a number of departments within the company. For example, a company offers a special restricted stock benefit to its employees provided certain corporate objectives are achieved. The expressed intent is to encourage a unified effort throughout the company to find ways to reduce overhead and to develop effective, efficient management systems. The expectation is improved corporate profits. The cost of the restricted stock benefit is projected to be far less than the potential return. This type of plan can be very effective in changing a company's smokestack mentality[40] and, indeed, positively affecting the behavior of its participants. When merging companies look for ways to better integrate their operations, they often will resort to using benefit plans to encourage cooperation.

Some benefits by design have built-in incentives that produce counterproductive results. For example, paid time off, sick pay, and other similar programs generate significant costs to the employer and often produce incentives for workers to take full advantage of the benefit. When paid time off is offered on a "use it or lose it" basis, which normally covers a one-year period, the employee will take it. If they are permitted to carry it over into the next year and accumulate their sick days, they will do that. Finally, the employee is permitted to take the paid time off as part of his retirement benefit or add the income value of the benefit to his retirement calculation.

The question is, do we have the right incentives? Does the worker really value the paid time off? In cases where it is accumulated, the intended value is not apparent. From an economic standpoint, it might be better to simply pay the worker the extra sick pay each year and encourage him to work instead of taking the time off.[41] Employees can decide whether to be absent or to work and receive extra pay. The latter arrangement would be

---

39. There are IRC and other legal issues here, but there are practical approaches that could be effective. See Peterson, S., & Spiker, B. (2005).

40. Smokestack is a common term used to describe a company that recognizes business unit performance without regard to the success of the enterprise as a whole.

41. Lazear (1998), p. 436. A similar analysis could be applied to vacation or holiday pay.

Table 2.3   Example of Performance Criteria Applicable to the Vesting of 1,000 Shares of Restricted Stock

1,000 Share RS Grant	2009	2010	2011	2012
Percentage of shares vesting if annual profit goals are achieved	20%	20%	30%	30%
Shares received after restrictions lapse on percentage of shares vested	200	200	300	300
Total number of shares received over four-year period				**1,000**

better for the employer since no replacement workers or overtime costs would be incurred. It also would appear to be better for the employee who receives the extra pay. Using this approach is more economical to the employer than including unused sick pay in the pension calculation, because the added income would be multiplied by years of service and the pension replacement percentage and incremental amount would be paid for the life of the annuitant.

As the employer sponsor of a benefit plan, one must be aware of the importance of the third element of the benefits model—does it positively affect employees' behavior? How do you determine this? There are some behavioral theories that might be helpful in assessing the issue of functionality of benefit plan incentives.

The agency theory assumes that certain compensation designs can cause an executive to think and behave like an owner. Absent this design, the interests of the executives and owners may diverge.[42] For example, executives may want to acquire companies in order to create a corporate empire, while owners may be interested more in the anticipated financial returns of strategic relationships. Risk perceptions also may be different. Owners often have diverse portfolios of company stocks, while executives have most of their eggs in one basket and, therefore, may be more risk averse with respect to company strategies and ventures. Finally, executives are employees and have a shorter time horizon than owners. They may work for several companies during their career and, in order to maximize

42. For a basic description of the agency theory, see Milkovich, G., & Newman, J. (2005), pp. 264–265.

the return on their current employment relationship, may take too much of a short-term perspective with regard to business activities. Owners, on the other hand, are invested for the long term.

It is incumbent on a well-managed company to design compensation and benefit plans that align the interests of the executives and their subordinates with those of the owners. A common perception is that equity benefits, such as stock options or restricted stock,[43] can achieve this objective because owners would have a shared interest with executives—both would own company stock. In the case of a stock option plan, however, what risk is the executive taking when he accepts a tranche of options priced on the date of grant?

Unlike the owner, he has not invested any of his own money, though he accepts stock options as a substitute for additional cash compensation. He is risking the value of a higher salary or bonus in exchange for the potential gain in the value of his options. The value to the option holder, unlike the real shareholder, is the time value of money. The option recipient does not have to invest his money initially to purchase the stock.[44] If the options turn out to be worthless, the executive's risk, unlike the owner's, is the value of additional cash compensation he would have received in lieu of the options. The benefit plan design challenge is apparent. Can the stock option plan include sufficient risk to the executive so that he will share risks similar to those of the owner and, thus, behave like an owner?[45]

---

43. The design features of stock options and restricted stock can be found in Chapter 11, Equity Benefits. Basically, however, stock options involve rights of option holders to purchase the company stock at the price applicable on the date the option was granted, while restricted stock confers ownership rights on the grantees as soon as the restrictions, such as the passage of time, lapse.

44. From an economic standpoint, since one does not know whether the price of the stock will increase at the time of the grant, the real value to the agent is that it allows him to invest in the stock without advancing any money to buy the stock. The value is essentially the time value of money. Some would argue the agent could exercise his options when they are vested and as soon as a spread between the price at the time of the grant and the current market price occurs. This is true. But the principal can sell his stock when there is an available short- or long-term gain as well.

45. A number of institutional shareholder groups have long complained about excessive grants of options to executives that generate the large accumulation of wealth with only modest stock price appreciations. Unlike shareholders whose total shareholder returns might fall far below the alternative investments in the market, the executive with a very large tranche of options whose price has only appreciated negligibly still enjoys a risk-free and quite sizable return. With the latest scandal over the backdating of options by executives, institutional shareholders have asked for full disclosure. See Testimony of Russell Read, California Public Employees Retirement System, Senate Banking Committee, U.S. Senate, September 6, 2006.

The best approach is to attach performance-based incentives to the option award that align with the interests of the owners.[46] For example, the options do not vest unless certain business results are achieved, or do not vest until the market price of the stock increases above industry levels or above analysts' expectations. This would place the option recipient closer to the risk status of an owner. Positive behaviors of owners would be encouraged, resulting in improved operating results that drive stock price increases.

> A large manufacturing company wants to improve profits, grow sales on a global basis, and provide shareholders with a competitive total return. The company's total reward plan is designed to include base salaries pegged at about the 50th percentile of its external competitors. It offers a short-term annual bonus to its executives that will be payable depending on the return on operating assets. It also provides for a long-term bonus that is payable based on the attainment of certain economic value-added requirements similar to shareholder value propositions. Finally, it awards participants with traditional, nonqualified stock options. Overall, the plan puts important compensation features at risk and blends short-term and long-term perspectives among executives. The design of the plan places the agents on par with the owners and achieves alignment within the various units of the organization.

As we see in this vignette, the short-term perspective of the executive and his subordinates is a problem that can be addressed through a thoughtful, total reward design. Profit sharing retirement plans have long-term perspectives, since the value accrues to the executive and other participants when there is a consistent, long-term record of profit making by the enterprise. Similarly, setting profit, free cash flow, or operating cash flow goals[47] that require consistent, year-by-year attainment of aggressive

---

46. These could include stock options, restricted stock, stock appreciation rights plans (SARs), long-term bonuses, and other benefits that are dependent on real business results.

47. Many corporations use earnings before Interest, Taxes, Depreciation, and Amortization (EBITDA) as a better indication of their performance than accounting-based profits. EBITDA is different from free cash flows or cash flows because it does not include the cash requirements for replacing capital assets. See Higgins, R. (2001). *Analysis for financial management* (pp. 5–6, 44–45). New York: Irwin McGraw-Hill.

performance targets can trigger the vesting of a variety of benefit entitlements among executives and their subordinates. This achieves better
alignment and drives positive behaviors.[48]

Sometimes incentives encourage negative motivation, as in adverse
selection. Suppose a firm has a contingent beneficiary provision in its
defined benefit plan that allows employees, prior to retirement, to select
one or more beneficiaries should the employee die while receiving benefits. The beneficiaries would receive a percentage of the employee's benefit for their lives, but the cost of this choice is an actuarial reduction of
the benefit for the employee. Now, suppose this employee is about to
retire and discovers that he has an incurable disease and will die within
two months. Just before retiring, he decides to choose the contingent
beneficiary option so his children will get his benefit. The employee's
decision is adverse to the financial interests of the employer, since it will
cost the employer more to pay pension benefits to his beneficiaries.
Because his death is so near, he will not incur the actuarial cost normally
associated with choosing this option. How does an employer address
this issue? Are there plan provisions that might mitigate the impact on
the employer? Yes. Typically, they involve time limits for making certain
benefits choices. For example, the plan may require that a participant
must choose his beneficiaries one or more months before retirement. In
a health care plan, adverse selection might arise when an employee
learns that he has a serious illness and, as a result, wants to choose a
more generous health care plan. Most plans limit plan changes to specific annual enrollment dates.

For instance, Company A has a rich health care plan and Company B
pays higher wages but has no health care for its employees. Suppose a job
applicant has two children and one has an acute health care problem.
Which firm is he most likely to choose for employment? Obviously,
Company A, which would raise its health care costs significantly. This

---

48. Other theories that are relevant to considering behavioral implications
of compensation and benefit plans include the reinforcement and expectancy
theories. The reinforcement theory holds that superior performance followed
by special rewards will reinforce future high performance levels. Could this
apply to a wellness program, for example, where the attainment of certain
weight reduction goals results in a financial reward from the employer? The
expectancy theory focuses on the effects of compensation as an incentive to
increase employee motivation. In this case, the employee perception of the
link between behavior and compensation is an important consideration. See
Gerhart, B., & Milkovich, G. (1990). Organizational differences in managerial
compensation and financial performance. *Academy of Management Journal,
33*, 663–691.

is adverse selection,[49] and it requires employers to be mindful of their plan designs.

There are a number of principles that relate to employee incentives and total rewards; however, the overriding consideration in effective plan design is to make sure that it conforms to the four elements of the benefits model. The employer should never lose sight of the important opportunity it has to affect employee–participant behavior positively. An effective and efficient benefits plan can generate real value instead of just another cost that must be assumed. Let's examine the fourth and final element of the benefits model.

COST-EFFECTIVE AND EFFICIENTLY ADMINISTERED

Perhaps you have seen periodic articles on the best places to work, saluting companies that offer the best to their employees in terms of benefits, working conditions, amenities, and so forth. They often enjoy a brief moment of glory and, thereafter, disappear only to surface in the business section some time later as having experienced financial difficulty and, perhaps, even destruction. Benefits should be regarded as strategic elements of a total reward plan that helps to achieve the business strategy. They must be cost-effective and efficiently administered.

As with the start-up airline mentioned earlier, some benefits are simply too costly for the employer to fund and sponsor. One must look for other solutions and determine their efficacy. Do they really support the human resources and business strategy and will the predicted outcomes occur? Does the investment in benefit costs produce quantifiable results? Are there alternative designs? Should the employer shift some of the cost and risk elements of the plan to the participants?

If benefits are perceived as investments with the potential of generating real and positive financial returns instead of levying costs, the employer will be in a better position to assess their cost-effectiveness. The employer sponsor must challenge and ask himself a number of revealing questions. For example, does a retirement plan really provide adequate retirement income, positively impact productivity, improve recruitment and retention, and encourage employee savings? Does a health care plan reduce absenteeism, improve productivity, and deliver a healthier workforce?

---

49. Lazear (1998), p. 418. See also Nelson, W. (2007), pp. 189–201. Nelson points out that among the uninsured persons who believe the cost of the health care plan is far less than the cost of a known health care risk will buy health insurance. Since the insurance company is unaware of the risk, the decision to buy the insurance amounts to adverse selection.

Does an employer-sponsored fitness center enhance the overall health of the workforce and improve productivity? Can these and other benefit plans really improve sales, profits, and total shareholder return?

A benefit cannot be cost-effective if it is not effective.[50] Employers spend a lot of time looking for the right health care bargain from third-party administrators (TPAs) and examining requests for proposals submitted by vendors seeking to manage their 401(k) plans. They also must be sure they invest as much time in research to determine whether the plan supports the overall objective of keeping employees healthier, reducing illness-related absenteeism, and detecting early medical conditions that could create catastrophic health care problems later. Furthermore, they must examine the hidden costs of administration, looking closely at the returns of the investment choices included in the vendor's package, and analyze how the benefit plan helps to achieve the business strategy.

In general, employer sponsors need to be sure they are offering the most cost-effective benefit plans[51] that are designed to be efficiently administered. Selecting simple and easy-to-understand benefit designs is a first step. Then employers must look for ways to achieve efficiencies. For example, they could introduce electronic, system-based benefit information, which facilitates and tracks enrollment and other participant activities; or they could place a large portion of the administrative work on the participant and then follow up on a regular basis to evaluate the system's effectiveness. Do employees understand the benefit? Do they value it? Are they making the right decisions? There are quality and consistency programs such as Six Sigma the employer can utilize to achieve an efficient benefit system.

One more resource with which we should become familiar before launching into the specific benefits is actuarial principles. How does the employer sponsor know how to fund his benefits, and what factors might be relevant to adjusting certain benefits?

Actuarial Principles

What does an actuary do? Some time ago I organized a conference for our company's benefit managers. I decided they should know a little about actuarial principles and invited an actuary from a leading benefits consulting firm to speak. She described her job by talking about saving for college.

---

50. When the benefit design includes output-based incentives, the employer should require operating results that drive sales and profits and not simply reward activities. Activity does not fund benefits; results do. Whatever benefit design is chosen, the output must involve drivers that directly contribute to sales and profits.

51. The administration of benefit plans is discussed in Chapter 16, Convenience and Accommodation Benefits, Benefits Administration.

John and Mary recently married and Mary is pregnant with their first child. In the United States, a major concern of parents is how they will pay for the university education of their children. John and Mary sit down to discuss the issue and agree they must start saving now. The question is, how much should they put aside each month in order to adequately finance their child's education? After doing some research on their own and speaking with their financial consultant, they came to realize the answer depends on several factors:

- How much they can afford to save
- The age of their child (or children) and how many years they have to save
- How much interest they can earn on their savings
- An estimate of how much the education will cost when their child is ready to go to university
- What the duration of their child's university education will be—four years for a baccalaureate, five years for a master's degree, or seven or eight years for a doctorate

These same factors come into play when an employer sponsor is deciding how much should be put aside in order to fund the defined benefit retirement plan.

- How much can the employer afford to put aside in a trust to fund a defined benefit plan?

- When will employees under the plan begin to retire? How many years of savings can be anticipated?

- By investing the funds in stocks and bonds, what are the expected earnings of the fund account?

- What will the value of the benefits be, as employees retire over the years? If benefits are based in part on final pay, what rate of income inflation can the actuary expect over the next years?

- Since defined benefit plans are paid for the life of the participant, what are the various life expectancies of the participants? Longevity is, of course, the underlying driver of retirement risk and, in the case of a DBP, the risk is on the employer.[52]

52. See *Key findings and issues, longevity: The underlying driver of retirement risk.* (2006, July). Society of Actuaries. It should be noted that longevity is the major risk for retirees who are saving for retirement and wondering about the adequacy of their accumulated accounts. Will they outlive their retirement? The report finds that in the face of increasing longevity, retirees may prematurely deplete their assets if they do not plan properly.

As you can see, the actuary uses the same factors as parents, but also looks at employee turnover rates to determine how many employees will work long enough to be entitled to pensions. He works with investment advisors on how expected versus actual returns can affect funding obligations of the employer and constantly assesses the adequacy of funding for accrued vested benefits.

Let's look at a few scenarios. Suppose the employer has been overestimating the investment returns of his retirement assets. In actuality, they have been somewhat disappointing. The employer will examine new investment strategies to shore up his returns and avoid facing a funding shortage requiring a large, one-time contribution to the plan. Worst-case scenario, the disappointing returns could lead to a termination of the plan altogether, or cause the employer to reduce benefits on a prospective basis to better align earnings with benefits.

In another example, the employer's DBP fund is producing exceptional investment returns far above those expected, leading to an overfunding of the plan. Because investment returns in the plan are not taxed, the employer could decide to do nothing with the overfunding and simply realize the extra gains earned from the tax-deferred investments. Or he could decide to forgo additional contributions to the plan and allow the market to fund it for the next several years, thereby saving cash and actual pension expense. In some cases the employer might decide to terminate the plan, use the excess funds to finance new capital projects, and reestablish the pension fund with the remaining plan assets.

Pension actuaries who use mortality tables must accurately assess life expectancies of the DBP participants so the proper funding rates of the plan can be achieved. People are living longer and some have a desire to retire earlier. The actuary must consider these trends and constantly assess funding rates for the plan.

Actuaries also consider how to reduce a benefit based on a participant's choice to elect certain options in the plan. For example, suppose a participant decides to take advantage of the defined benefit plan's option to retire at 55 instead of the normal retirement age of 65. Should the retiree receive a full benefit, or should it be reduced based on the fact that he will receive the benefit for ten additional years? The answer is, the benefit will be actuarially reduced based on the additional ten years. Similarly, suppose a participant in the same plan chooses to name a beneficiary who would receive a portion of his benefit in the event he dies after retiring. Again, the benefit would be reduced based on the age of the beneficiary and the amount of benefit to be received. The younger the beneficiary, the longer the benefits will have to be paid out, so the initial benefit to the participant is actuarially reduced to reflect this potential obligation on the part of the plan sponsor.

Inflation is another key component of the actuarial process. For defined benefit plans, which base the pension calculation on final average pay, wage inflation is a critical part of the anticipated pension-funding obligation. Inflation after retirement also becomes relevant in order to assess the adequacy of either the defined benefit plan or the defined contribution plan. How much of final pay does the company's plan replace at retirement? Should the employer consider changing the benefit formula or offering additional plans? What is the inflation rate after retirement and can retirees cope with the added expenses? Will employees have enough to pay for higher medical expenses, housing, fuel, and energy utilities?[53]

Similar factors apply to other benefits such as health care plans, where the employer sponsor tries to determine future health care risks, the adequacy of its reserves to pay for higher unanticipated health care utilization, and the future rate of health care inflation. All of these assessments may lead, for example, to the introduction of more cost-effective health care plan design, increased contributions to the plan, or more effective wellness programs. There is a demographic development that weighs heavily on the actuary's perspective—the aging population.

In the United States in 1950, the ratio of persons aged 25–60 to 65 and older was seven. In the year 2020, it will be about four; and in 2050, less than three. In Europe, the situation is graver. In 1950, the same ratio was six to one; in 2020, it will be under three; and in 2050, under two.[54] This means there will be fewer workers paying payroll taxes and funding public benefits, and more retirees needing health care and employer-sponsored benefits. Some estimate that retirement will have to be delayed significantly in order to accommodate this new gray world, and there will be even more reliance on individually funded benefits.

This comes at a time when the ratio of work years to retirement years is declining.[55] When people used to work 47 years, retired at 65, and had five years' life expectancy, the ratio was over nine to one. Today, prospective workers spend more years getting an education, consequently delaying their entry into the workforce, and also have a significantly higher life expectancy.

53. See *Consumer spending by older Americans, 1985–2005.* (2007, September 24). Congressional Research Service Report to Congress.

54. Siegel, J. (2006, September 20). Gray world. *The Wall Street Journal,* A26. See also Webb, A. (2005). *The dependency ratio.* International Longevity Center—USA, http://www.ilcusa.org. This ratio measures the ratio of persons under 18 and over 65 who are presumably out of the workforce to those between the same ages. In most developed countries, including the United States, the ratio is increasing due to a demographic transition caused by increased population over the age of 65, increased longevity, and lower birth rates. It portends problems for retirement plans, particularly those funded on a pay-as-you-go basis. More of this issue will be discussed in Chapter 12, Government-Sponsored and Mandated Benefits.

55. Pollock, A. (2006, September). *Retirement finance: Old ideas, new reality,* American Enterprise Institute for Public Policy Research, http://www.aei.org.

Table 2.4   Dependency Ratio

The Ratio of those younger than 18 and older than 65 compared to those between the ages of 18 and 65.

Country	2000	2025
Italy	.267	.406
Japan	.252	.490
Germany	.241	.390
United Kingdom	.244	.328
United States	.186	.293
France	.245	.328

SOURCE: Webb, A. (2005). *The Dependency Ratio.* International Longevity Center—USA, http://www.ilcusa.org.

Therefore, a college graduate may not begin full-time work until age 25, and would like to retire at age 55, when his life expectancy is perhaps 27 years. As a result, the work to retirement years ratio is 1.1 to 1.

It is important to note that the number of employers in the United States who offer defined benefit plans is declining. More are offering defined contribution plans, placing the risks and saving obligations on employees.[56] If an employee's retirement income is based in substantial part on his contributions to a pension plan, the prospect of saving sufficient funds to retire early will be less likely. This could mean that retirement would be delayed to a point where the remaining retirement years would outpace the increase in life expectancy. Employees might find they cannot afford to retire until there are only a few years remaining in their lives. There are ideas circulating that purport to address this global issue.[57] They range from totally redesigning publicly and privately sponsored benefits to changing the capital flows between developed and developing countries where populations are increasing.[58] It is a serious issue that

56. See *Trends in retirement plans.* (2007). Employee Benefits Research Institute, Chapter 10, Data Book, http://www.ebri.org/.

57. Milken, M. (2006, September 19). The boom generation, seventh decade. *The Wall Street Journal,* A26, http://webreprints.djreprints.com/1552621259811 .html. The author argues that with increased life expectancy persons in their sixties will change careers, but continue to earn money instead of selling their assets to survive.

58. Ibid.

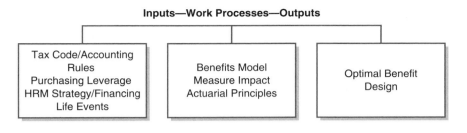

Figure 2.2   Workflow of Benefits

deserves worldwide focus, creative public policy changes, and a great deal of actuarial attention.

Conclusion

On a microeconomic level, as employers assess the demographics and characteristics of their employees and choose which benefit plan is the most responsive to the lifecycle needs of their workforce, it is important for them to pay close attention to the benefits model. Does the plan provide internal fairness, and how does it measure up to that offered by external competitors seeking to recruit and retain from the same market? Does it contain design features that motivate employees to behave in a manner consistent with the employer's business and human resources strategies? Is the plan cost-effective, based on the employer's ability to fund, and does it produce its intended effect? Does the employer sponsor understand the behavioral theories and principles that underlie the incentives included in the plan? What are the actuarial concepts relevant to the employer's obligation to fund the benefit? The answers to all of these questions are necessary, as the employer searches for the optimal plan design that best fits his needs and better ensures the selection, retention, and motivation of a highly productive workforce. Figure 2.2 is a workflow of benefits table that shows how and when certain factors apply to the offering and design of benefits.

Chapter Exercises

The following will help to enhance your understanding of the underlying concepts in this chapter. You will be required to do some independent research to answer the questions.

1. Go to http://www.savingforcollege.com/. Using the calculator, see how much you need to save to finance a child's college

education. What are the relevant factors in the calculation? Check out a §529 Plan. How does it work? What would be an ideal investment strategy for a newborn whose parents are saving for college?

2. Go to Northwestern Mutual Insurance at http://www.nmfn.com/ and click on "Learning Center" and then "Calculators." There are many interesting calculators on this site, including saving for college, doubling your money (Rule of 72), power of tax deferral, and the longevity game. Explore each one and draw some conclusions about their relevance to some of the principles concerning retirement plans. Also, make sure to determine your life expectancy, making special note of the variables that can affect your life span.

3. What would the consequences be if the U.S. Congress changed the current tax treatment of health care plans by making all employer-sponsored benefits taxable to the employee but allowing the employee to deduct all of his nonreimbursed health care expenses? Explain the possible changes and impacts in the employer-sponsored benefit system.

4. Go to http://www.payscale.com/ and select a job and region to compare total rewards. What elements of compensation are included in total rewards? How would you use this information to develop your pay and benefit strategy?

5. Cafeteria plans often are used to overcome problems with internal fairness. Check the IRS Web site and review the IRS rules with respect to cafeteria plans. Which benefits are excluded from these plans? For example, can an employer include financial assistance to join a health club? How about educational assistance? Are some benefits taxable as income to the recipient? Are there limits to the amounts that can be offered in a cafeteria plan? See http://www.irs.gov/publications/, Publication 15-B.

6. Suppose a health care plan pays the first $3,000 of a participant's health care expenses, and the participant pays the next $2,500 of covered health care expenses. Thereafter, the plan covers 100 percent of any additional medical expenses incurred during the year. What impact, if any, do you think this delayed deductible will have on the participant's behavior?

7. Go to the U.S. Department of Labor's Bureau of Labor Statistics at http://www.bls.gov, and identify the current percentage of labor costs attributed to benefits in a given industry or region. How would you use this information in operating your own business?

8. Check Peterson, S., and Spiker, B. (2005). Establishing the positive contributory value of older workers: A positive psychology perspective, *Organization Dynamics, 34*(2), 153–167, as well as recent legislation in the Pension Protection Act of 2006 dealing with phased retirement, and determine whether there are sufficient incentives to accomplish the goal of higher utilization of older workers. What barriers have been adjusted or removed? Also, what are the tax consequences to persons over 65 who continue working? Read Butrica, B., et al., (2004, November). *Does work pay at older ages?* Center for Retirement Research at Boston College, http://www.bc.edu/crr/

9. Can you reconcile the tournament theory with the agency theory? Are there some relevant lessons in the headlines where, allegedly, excessive compensation has been awarded to certain chief executives? Do some research and organize a discussion of this issue.

10. With respect to external competition, how might an employer inadvertently distort his labor expense by comparing his total rewards to a labor competitor instead of his product or service competitor?

11. Some economists argue that mandated benefits required by the Family and Medical Leave Act (FMLA), such as unpaid leaves, are paid for by employees. This is based on the principle of compensating differentials. Check the principle and be prepared to discuss the claim.

Lifecycle Events 3

Benefits Respond to Lifecycle Events

Benefits, whether provided by an employer or a state sponsor, are designed to respond to the specific needs of the beneficiary as he confronts lifecycle challenges. As we described in Chapter 2, the benefits model requires the employer to consider benefits as a means to recruit and retain workers and, if possible, to motivate them to enhance productivity. To do this, the employer should sponsor benefits that are linked to the unique characteristics of his workforce and the particular lifecycle events they encounter.[1]

For example, workers approaching retirement hold different views regarding when to retire and what activities, including work, they might pursue in retirement. Similarly, not all employees share the same plan for vacation with respect to how long they want to be gone or what they intend to do. From a personal standpoint, I have worked with colleagues who felt five days were sufficient to visit China, and that included travel time, whereas others valued a longer period away from work and carefully planned extended trips with their families. People also have varying perspectives on everything from health care to life insurance. As the demographics of the workforce change, with more women, older workers, Asians, Blacks, Latinos, and people with various religious beliefs entering the workplace, employers must recognize the need to provide benefits that

---

1. Some employers survey their employers to determine which benefits they value most. By asking whether the employee would rather have life insurance or dental insurance, a pension plan or retiree health care, employers can assess which benefits employees most value and make choices as to which they will offer. The Ford Motor Co. recently did this when they surveyed their employees in an attempt to assess their affinity to various benefits. See Hoffman, B. (2006, July 29). Benefits survey shakes up Ford staff. *Detroit News.*

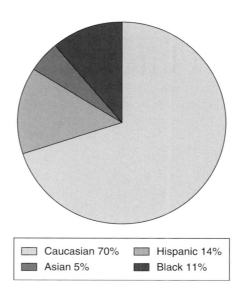

Figure 3.1   Demographic Allocation of U.S. Workforce
SOURCE: U.S. Department of Labor, Bureau of Labor Statistics. (2008, September). The Labor Force Characteristics by Race and Ethnicity, 2007, Report #1005.
NOTE: Females represent 36 percent of the total workforce.

are responsive to their unique lifecycle events. Age, sex, race, religion, national origin, geographic location, personal characteristics, and culture all impact the types of life events occurring within a workforce and the respective attitudes and expectations of workers.

In this chapter we will discuss specific lifecycle events, briefly describe the relevant public laws that mandate or regulate benefits, and identify some ways an employer might devise a set of benefit plans that align with the requirements of his own workforce.[2] In many cases where there is a law mandating benefits, such as the Family and Medical Leave Act (FMLA),[3] the employer can choose to supplement the law with special benefits. In the case of the FMLA, the employer can elect to extend an employee's leave or continue his salary during the leave. This type of discretion can serve to maximize the opportunities of the benefits model.

---

2. There are a variety of both federal and state laws that impose either the offering of a particular benefit or regulate how benefits must be offered. COBRA (42 USC §300bb-1, et seq.), for instance, does not require the employer to offer health care, but if the employer does it must allow employees and their dependents who experience certain life events to be offered the right to temporarily continue coverage at their own cost under the health benefit plan.

3. The Family and Medical Leave Act of 1993, 29 USC §2601.

Health

Sickness, disease, disability, and injury due to accident are lifecycle events usually provided for under an employer's health care plan, which is substantially financed by the employer. Health insurance coverage for dependents may be offered as well, provided the employee shares in the extra cost.[4]

An employer's decision on how far to extend benefit coverage can have positive sorting implications to the recruiting process.[5] By covering part-time workers, an employer may be compensating above competitive levels but attracting a special segment of the population. For example, a single parent who only can work part-time might be attracted to an employer who offers health care benefits to part-timers. She also could have the advantage of being more mature and service-oriented than someone younger.

If women occupy a significant percentage of an employer's workforce, the employer should consider covering selected diagnostic procedures and preventive care measures applicable to them in his health care plan. Obviously, this should be done for both men and women. In doing so, the employer enhances his ability to recruit and retain both sexes, and also ensures higher productivity and fewer catastrophic health care incidents.

What happens when an employee does not want health insurance or wants it in a different format?[6] This could happen when someone is covered by another's health care policy. The employer can elect to offer any number of designs and options in his benefits plan, including giving his employees the power to choose which qualified benefits are important to them. For example, some may select a low deductible health care plan with

---

4. In fact, some health care plan sponsors provide special help to participants to navigate the health system particularly when the participant or his dependents suffer from chronic or acute conditions that require high utilization of health care resources. In such cases, the participant runs the risk of reaching the lifetime maximum benefits available under the plan. See the Disease Management Association of America, http://www.dmaa.org/. This organization promotes the empowerment of individuals with chronic diseases and their care providers to effectively manage their diseases and prevent complications through adherence to medication regimens, regular monitoring of vital signs, and healthy lifestyles.

5. For an interesting study of how health insurance can be used in sorting groups of employees, see Lehrer, S., & Pereira, N. (2007, September). Worker sorting, compensating differentials and health insurance: Evidence from displaced workers. *Journal of Health Economics, 26*(5), 1034–1056.

6. The employee might be covered by a policy offered by the spouse's employer, or may be covered by Medicare, or may simply not see the need for such insurance.

minimum cost sharing but high premiums, while others may prefer a plan that has more cost sharing but lower premiums.

There is evidence the MTV, or millennial, generation is more comfortable with higher deductible, consumer-driven policies that require more cost sharing but lower premiums. The health savings account (HSA), funded with pretax dollars, is an attractive benefit to this age group. They live in the moment and maximize efficient and effective utilization of the health care resources being offered.[7] Certainly, the presence of a younger workforce should cause the employer to be cognizant of these special preferences.

With respect to special health needs of employees, employers need to decide just how far they will go to protect the long-term vitality of their workforce. Today, a disproportionate number of Americans are overweight.[8] Suppose an employer has a large number of employees who are significantly overweight, or smoke excessively, or are reluctant to take control of their cholesterol or hypertension problem. The employer's objective is to make his health care benefits more cost-effective by enhancing the health status of his workers—also, healthy workers, presumably, are more productive. The workforce stands to gain a better quality of life through the benefit support received from the employer. In this example, the employer could elect to sponsor wellness programs that reward healthy lifestyles, or design his health care plans to encourage preventive care.[9] What if the employee is disabled?

Disability

An employee's illness or injury could lead to time lost at work and even a short- or long-term disability. During this period the employee may have several needs, including an accommodation that would facilitate his ability to continue working, or a continuation of income. In the former, the

---

7. Bridgeford, L. (2006, December). Life-stage benefits. Wooing the MTV and Internet generations. *Employee Benefit News*, http://www.benefitnews.com.

8. *Statistics Related to Overweight and Obesity*. (2008). U.S. Department of Health and Human Services, National Institutes of Health, http://win.niddk.nih.gov/statistics/.

9. Sometimes compliance with healthy lifestyles, such as improving body mass indices, smoking cessation, or controlling chronic health conditions, can be offered to employees or require higher cost sharing. Conlin, M. (2007, February 26). Get healthy—or else. *Business Week*, 58–69. This is a story about Scotts Miracle Grow Co. and its aggressive wellness program that mandates compliance with various wellness directives. It includes an episode where a probationary employee declined to quit smoking and was discharged.

Americans with Disabilities Act (ADA)[10] may require the employer to provide a reasonable accommodation. In the case of income continuation, this need could be fulfilled informally by an employer's policy or financed by an insurance policy paid for by the employer, the employee, or both. If the disability is permanent and substantial, the employee can apply for benefits under the Social Security Administration.[11] The employer may choose to supplement that benefit. For example, the employer-sponsored defined benefit retirement plan might provide a disability retirement benefit under such circumstances. The business rationale behind the employer providing sickness or disability benefits is to retain workers during short-term incapacities, and to present a reasonable mechanism to replace those with permanent impairments who have no reasonable prospect of being productive. Overall, reflecting on the benefits model, the employer who offers such benefits can attract and retain good workers, and enhance productivity.[12]

Employee Counseling

> Frank is going through a difficult divorce. He and his estranged spouse are contesting almost everything, including child custody. He is emotionally involved in the litigation and it is obvious to his fellow employees that he is very distracted and somewhat unproductive at work. He knows he needs some help and would like to see a psychologist. Unfortunately, this is not an eligible benefit in the company-sponsored health care plan.

Certain life events, such as death or divorce or some other traumatic incident, can impede a worker's productivity and create a need for psychological counseling. Frequently, while this is not covered by a traditional health care plan, the employer will subsidize professional counseling to

10. 42 USC §12112.

11. Social Security protection if you become disabled, Social Security Administration, http://www.ssa.gov/.

12. In some cases, accrued sick leave may be converted to cash at retirement or be added to the service element of the pension formula. The employer also may want to coordinate the disability plan with the Social Security disability benefit provisions. In certain instances of long-term disability, the Social Security system will provide lifetime income for permanently disabled persons.

the employee in the form of Employee Assistance Plans (EAPs). When properly designed, EAPs can be very effective in addressing the psychological, emotional, and physical effects of these kinds of events. In considering such a benefit, the employer must assess the link with his business and human resources strategy and reflect on what the potential returns would be in sponsoring such a benefit. Is it important to extend the benefit to the employee's dependents? Should the employee be required to partially finance the benefit, or should it be free? Is it appropriate to limit the duration of the benefit? It is up to the employer. In most cases, the employee has access to the EAP benefit over a limited period of time or is confined to a certain number of visits. The employer should also consider whether the benefit could be offered in a nonclinical setting, such as over a dedicated 1-800 line. Providing unilateral access to the EAP protects privacy concerns of the employee, and there is no requirement to go through a company representative or supervisor. In general, companies that offer a professional counseling benefit to their employees can reduce emotional obstacles to workplace productivity.

Childbirth and Adoption

The birth of a child is a life event that creates another opportunity to provide an employer-sponsored benefit. Covering the medical costs and allowing for a leave of absence are essential to meeting the needs of an employee who is having a baby. Federal law requires, in most instances, that at least 12 weeks of unpaid leave be provided.[13] It is at the discretion of the employer, however, to provide for a continuation of income during such a leave. The issue of leaves and compensating leaves also extends to adoption and to male employees who are involved in the care of a new arrival.[14] Under the law, benefit participation must be continued on the same basis as though the employee were actively at work. Generally, the Pregnancy Discrimination Act[15] prohibits any discrimination on the part of an employer with respect to the hiring or the continuation of employment and working conditions of a pregnant employee or prospective employee.[16]

An employer whose recruiting demographics include a large number of professional women can independently respond to this life event by doing

---

13. The Family and Medical Leave Act of 1993, 29 USC §2601.

14. The Family and Medical Leave Act of 1993, 29 USC §2601.

15. The Pregnancy Discrimination Act of 1978, 42 USC §2000(e)(k).

16. 29 USC §1185. The health care plan for employees or their dependents must allow a minimum 48-hour hospitalization for the delivery of a newborn.

more than what the law requires and perhaps more than what his competitors are doing. By compensating mothers and fathers for this leave, or by extending the leave term, the employer can enhance his ability to recruit and retain highly qualified candidates.

Daycare

When the new parent wishes to resume work, he or she may have a need for daycare services. This may be an apparent issue in a company with a large number of younger female employees. Preschool daycare can be an extremely important benefit for working mothers that serves to attract and retain productive employees. Should the employer provide it? What would the returns be?[17] There are a number of alternatives the employer could consider. For example, he could use his purchasing leverage to contract with daycare providers, but require the employees to pay for the service. He could subscribe to a service that provides ratings or research pertaining to daycare providers. He could use the tax law by offering a flexible spending account (FSA) that uses an employee's pretax contributions to finance the daycare expenses.[18] This format will mitigate a problem with the internal fairness element of the benefits model by structuring a cafeteria-type plan that provides for employer contributions to support several alternative benefits. Some employers simply build daycare centers for their employees or just buy a service. Could an FSA approach be used here? Would or should the employees using the center be obligated to finance their benefit? Regardless, the issue of internal fairness still exists because older or single employees without preschool children have no use for daycare services. There are also other benefit issues relating to education.

Educational Assistance

What are the needs of parents who are thinking ahead about their child's education? This is a major life event and can be a substantial financial

---

17. For example, would providing such a benefit be cost-effective? Would it reduce turnover or decrease absenteeism and distractions at the workplace?

18. The Internal Revenue Code, §125, permits the employer to allow employees to make pretax contributions to a Flexible Spending Account. These contributions can be used by the employee to pay for dependent care; however, they are limited in amount and must be used during the year the contribution is made or will be forfeited.

burden. What type of benefit might fulfill the needs of employees who are saving for their child's college education?[19] An employer might design a special scholarship fund for the children of his employees. Contributions could be based on the child's achievements in precollege work or on the basis of financial need. The employer could also help by providing financial counseling on how parents can use tax-favored savings mechanisms, including their own 401(k) funds, to finance higher education or how they can navigate the various university scholarship, fellowship, and loan schemes available.[20] By offering this kind of assistance, the employer can enhance his ability to attract and retain better workers, and can minimize the productivity-consuming distractions caused by the employees' concern over how they will afford to send their kids to college.[21]

General educational opportunities might be appropriate for certain segments of the workforce. For example, for employers with large numbers of Latino or entry-level workers, offering English classes, special classes on family finance, facilitating General Educational Development (GED) programs, and providing healthy living programs might be appropriate. Certainly this could help attract and retain certain workers, as well

---

19. The Internal Revenue Code permits individuals to contribute to a college fund and deduct the amount from their earnings under a state income tax system, IRC §529. Provided the funds are used for education, the earnings and contributions are not subject to any state or federal income tax. The employer has no role in this program but as with 401(k) or individual IRA accounts it can educate and encourage the use of such methods.

20. Under the IRC, and in accordance with the design of the defined contribution retirement plan such as a 401(k), the employee can borrow funds from his own account in the event of an emergency or significant financial need, provided the employee reimburses his account with the full amount plus interest, IRC §414(i). If the employee is prepared to meet the income tax consequences, he can argue that he needs the money due to a hardship and simply withdraw it from the defined contribution plan with no intention of replenishing the account. If the employee does not meet the hardship criteria of the Code, or the amount exceeds certain statutory limits, then an excise tax of 10 percent in addition to the income tax must be paid, IRC §417.

21. The employer must be careful to avoid any preferential loans or credit extensions to its highly paid managers or executives. Some large employers have created credit unions that facilitate easier savings and loan opportunities for their members. According to state and federal law, these credit unions must maintain a high degree of independence from the sponsoring organization. Often, they grow into larger banking institutions, affiliating with employee groups of many larger employers. See the National Credit Union Administration for a history, description, and review of the laws pertaining to employer-sponsored credit unions at http://www.ncua.gov/.

as open opportunities for advancement within the firm and enhance their productivity.[22]

Employees interested in career advancement are often eager to complete the requirements for an undergraduate degree, obtain an advanced degree such as an MBA, or participate in some form of continuing professional education. The employer may decide to fund this educational benefit, provided it meets certain tax law requirements and is linked to the special interests of its workforce.[23] In offering such a benefit, the employer must determine whether it will help to recruit and retain and also whether the enhanced education will improve the work performance of the participants. Once again, however, there are internal fairness issues when a benefit has no particular relevance to other workers, as discussed in Chapter 2. Let's look at the problem of aging parents of employees.

Caring for Sick Dependents

> Ramon is a 20-year employee of a large electronics retail chain. His father suffers from memory lapses and Ramon fears he may be experiencing the beginning stages of Alzheimer's disease. Ramon wants to accompany his father for a series of neurological evaluations. He is considering having his dad move into his house so he can be assured of his safety and good care, but is concerned about how this will impact his job. Among his immediate concerns are: Will his employer allow him to take off work periodically for his dad's treatments? How will his commitment to home care his father affect his ability to focus on his job? If his father eventually required skilled nursing care, how would Ramon pay for it?

It is estimated that over 16 million full-time workers are providing this type of care to their parents.[24] The loss in work and productivity is estimated to cost over $2,000 per employee, or $34 billion annually.[25] Being placed in a

---

22. Marriott Hotels and Resorts has been recognized over the years for offering such programs.

23. IRC §127.

24. Companies increasingly offering workplace benefits for employees who provide eldercare. (2006, July 27). *Kaiser Daily Health Policy Report*, http://www.kaisernetwork.org.

25. Ibid.

skilled nursing facility can wipe out a lifetime of savings.[26] Should the employer design a benefit that might support employees who are experiencing this challenge and, if so, what kind of return might mitigate this burden? There are a variety of approaches the employer can take.

The employer can offer long-term care insurance as a voluntary benefit, financed by the employee to cover his parents, his spouse, or himself. Or the employer could sponsor it as a paid benefit. The employer should assess the demographics of his workforce to determine the relevance of such a benefit. He also must determine whether the benefit would affect employee behaviors positively by reducing distractions at the workplace. The life events that lead to a need for long-term care are bona fide and provide the employer with an opportunity to respond with a meaningful benefit.

Another approach would be for the employer to allow special leave over and above that mandated by the Family and Medical Leave Act to care for dependents.[27] It could include paid leave, intermittent leave, or extending the statutory leave period beyond 12 weeks.[28] An employer also could provide information or services that help the employee navigate through the complex system of elder care.[29] Some employers are offering emergency

---

26. Nursing home costs are currently averaging about $63,000 per year, but only 14 percent of people over age 65 have long-term care insurance. In most instances, provided they qualify, this insurance can be purchased by active employees for their parents. Premiums for long-term care vary depending on the age of the insured, services covered, coverage amounts, and length of coverage. Currently, premiums range from $1,000 to $9,000 annually. Purchasers must be careful to avoid inflation riders that increase premiums as retirement age nears. Premiums for qualified long-term care insurance are considered unreimbursed medical expenses and can be deducted to the extent they and other medical expenses exceed 7.5 percent of adjusted gross income, IRS Publication 502 (2006). Also see Bernhart, M. (2006, December). Future caregivers have stake in long-term care. *Benefit News*, http://www.benefitnews.com.

27. The FMLA also requires leaves for employees who are caring for their seriously ill parents; The Family and Medical Leave Act of 1993, 29 USC §2601.

28. The FMLA allows for intermittent leave for birth or adoption with the approval of the employer. It also allows intermittent leave to care for a seriously ill family member or when the employee is seriously ill. This does not require the approval of the employer and is limited to a total of 12 weeks, 29 USC § 2601, et seq.

29. Some plans provide for a geriatric care specialist to visit the employee's ailing parent and draw up a complete care plan. Other plans will help the employee locate emergency caregivers for the elderly. A variety of approaches are discussed in McQueen, M. (2006, December 27). Employers expand eldercare benefits. *The Wall Street Journal Online*, D1, http://online.wsj.com/.

home care for the elderly parents of employees, thus mitigating the need for episodic absences from work.[30]

Caring for elderly parents can be physically and emotionally exhausting for the caregiver. The Respite Care Act[31] provides for temporary relief to family care providers. Family members deliver 80 percent of long-term care provided in the United States. The respite law offers federal funding to expand state and local programs designed to access relief for family caregivers. For example, respite care could allow family providers to enjoy a one- or two-day-a-week break from their care obligations for an invalid family member. The Act also funds programs designed to help families navigate the existing programs for custodial care. Since family care reduces the costs of government-sponsored long-term care programs, the respite care concept is an economically sound approach that helps ensure caregivers can continue to offer this important service. There could be an opportunity here for employers to improve employee productivity by offering a similar or more generous benefit to their employees who are bearing some burden of care for a family member. This benefit could take the form of providing flexible work schedules, work-at-home opportunities, or volunteer worker substitutes.

Retirement

Alex has worked at a market research company for the past 30 years. He is 62 years old and wants to have more time to spend with his grandchildren and also enjoy his vacation cabin in Michigan's Upper Peninsula. He is concerned about whether he has accumulated enough savings under his company's plan that, together with his Social Security benefit, must provide retirement income for the remainder of his life. He plans to ask his employer if he could work part-time for several years instead of leaving work altogether.

Employers with relatively large numbers of older workers who are approaching retirement age face special issues that often arise at this important lifecycle event. For instance: (1) At what age do your employees

---

30. Ibid.

31. Lifespan Respite Care Act of 2006 (HR 3248); 42 USC §201 et seq. (2901).

want to retire?[32] (2) Does this comport with normal retirement age in your pension plan? (3) What is the earliest date an employee can retire? (4) What impact does the actuarial reduction have on an employee's decision to choose early retirement?[33] (5) Does the employer have an advantage when older employees retire because it allows the substitution of hours worked by employees with higher labor rates with those worked by employees with lower pay? (6) Does an early retirement prerogative open up career opportunities for younger workers who might otherwise leave the organization? In answering these questions, the employer should use this information to design his plan so it properly influences behaviors that serve both his interests as well as those of his workers.

Some employees might be interested in a phased retirement.[34] For example, does the employer's retirement plan allow an employee to continue to work on a paid, part-time basis while collecting retirement benefits? Are there legal issues here? About 23 percent of employers have programs permitting phased retirement.[35] Over 50 percent of them,

32. An individual can receive Social Security benefits as early as age 62. The benefits are actuarially reduced, however. See http://www.ssa.gov/retire2/agereduction.htm/. On average a participant will receive about 20 percent less than the amount he would have been paid at normal retirement age. If the early retiree under Social Security earns income over $13,560 at age 62 (for 2008) and up to $36,120 for the year at full age retirement, for each $2 in income over these amounts the benefit is reduced by $1. Also, outside earnings in excess of $25,000 to $34,000 can result in up to 50 percent of one's Social Security benefits being subject to federal income tax. Earnings above $34,000 can result in up to 80 percent of the benefit being subject to income tax. See http://www.ssa.gov/planners/taxes.htm.

33. In most cases there is not a full actuarial reduction for early retirement and the employer sponsor is, in effect, providing a subsidy to those who make the choice. The early retirement subsidy provides workers with an incentive to retire early. As life expectancy increases, however, and as worker shortages increase, some employers are finding ways to reduce this incentive and lessen the encouragement to retire early. See *Taking the subsidy out of early retirement.* (2007). Watson Wyatt, http://www.watsonwyatt.com/.

34. Armarks, J., Fergusson, H., Madamba, A., & Utkus, S. (2007). *Six paths to retirement.* The Vanguard Center for Retirement Research. This new study shows the conventional view of retirement involving a precipitous cessation of work is not accurate. The study describes a variety of approaches among recent retirees with respect to retirement: never retire; downshift to reduce hours at work; never work again after retirement; retire and take on a new career or part-time work; retire early but, for financial reasons, later return to full-time work; individuals with lower work histories peg their retirement to that of their spouse.

35. Hutchens, R. (2007, February). *Phased retirement: Problems and prospects.* Center for Retirement Research, Boston University, Series 8.

however, indicate that employees on phased retirement could lose their health care coverage.[36] This could be a dramatic impediment to such a program. The legal issue of whether an employee who is on phased or part-time continuation can receive retirement benefits has been clarified by recent legislation to some extent. Congress has modified the Internal Revenue Code provisions that penalized such choices.[37] Age 62 early retirement Social Security benefits, however, can be both reduced and subject to income taxes based on continued earnings.[38] Phased retirement could be beneficial for the employer who wants to hold on to the experienced, productive employees in order to share their knowledge with newcomers.[39] An employer should assess the interests of his workforce and the potential advantages to the company before making any plan design changes, but such an approach could have significant relevance to an employer's aging workforce.

Do employees wish to delay or defer their retirement and continue working full-time indefinitely beyond normal retirement age? Some employees would choose never to retire, while others depend on their spouse's retirement plan or other external events to determine the timing and income sources of their own retirement. Should the employer facilitate this trend by changing the normal retirement age in his defined benefit plan? There are advantages here for both the employee and the employer. When an employee continues to work beyond retirement age, he continues to receive full compensation and benefits from the employer. Similarly, the employer can realize higher productivity by retaining older workers. These workers, however, incur penalties in the form of higher tax on their Social Security benefits.[40]

---

36. Hutchens, R. (2007). Ordinarily, this is due to not being able to meet the full-time eligibility requirements for health care included in many plans.

37. Generally, the law has prohibited a pension plan from paying benefits before retirement, §401(a)(36) of the IRC. The Pension Protection Act of 2006, however, in §905, provides that a pension plan would not fail to qualify under §401(a) solely because an employee who has attained age 62 receives benefits even though he has not separated from employment. The Treasury Department is currently studying possible rules on phased retirement and receiving benefits before full separation from employment.

38. Refer to http://www.ssa.gov/ and footnote 26, supra.

39. Hutchens, R. (2007).

40. While there are apparent labor shortages, and researchers have assumed a real demand for the continued employment of older workers by the firm, a recent study has indicated there is not an overwhelming desire among employers to facilitate this option. Eschtruth, A., Sass, S., & Aubry, J. (2007, May). *Employers lukewarm about retaining older workers.* Center for Retirement Research, WOB #10.

In addition, the employee who delays retirement must continue to pay FICA and Medicare taxes and, while making more income from his employer, will probably pay income taxes at a higher marginal rate. Further, if the employer continues to offer health care, his employee Medicare benefit that is supported through a payroll tax becomes a secondary or supplemental (gap) benefit to his employer-sponsored plan. There are some advantages to delaying the receipt of Social Security benefits. A person born on or after 1943 who delays retirement beyond his full-age retirement can increase his Social Security benefit by 8 percent for each year up to age 70.[41] A similar actuarial increase could be offered by the employer-sponsored retirement plan. Also, one can add additional years of potentially higher income to both the Social Security benefit calculation and the employer-sponsored final average pay formula in such cases.[42]

Finally, is retirement an opportunity to stop working altogether or to pursue another career, passion, or entrepreneurial opportunity?[43] Should the employer be involved in helping future retirees determine their retirement income from all sources and match it against their future expenses? If so, the employer could offer a retirement planning benefit to facilitate his employees' understanding of when they can retire and pursue their passion.[44] He could also facilitate and encourage educational programs that will make his employees' retirement a more fulfilling experience. In this case, the employer meets the interests of his workers and generates a potential value for the enterprise by facilitating the departure of higher paid workers.

A note of caution: The employer must be careful in offering counseling and financial planning advice to his employees, since there are possible

---

41. Delayed retirement credits, http://www.ssa.gov/retire/.

42. It can be a duel-edged sword, however, since an employee who delays his retirement and continues to work after reaching normal retirement age reduces the present value of his employer-sponsored defined benefit. This is because his life expectancy is growing shorter and the years he will receive his annuity are becoming fewer. See Figure 4.2 in Chapter 4.

43. Greene, K. (2008, February 16). Twelve people who are changing your retirement. *The Wall Street Journal,* R1. This is an interesting story of people, many retired, who are providing new insights and help with respect to retiree issues.

44. McDonald, I. (2007, January 22). Here's to a long life. *The Wall Street Journal,* R6. Many employees are concerned they may outlive their retirement income. Do employees need professional counseling with respect to this important life event? The longevity risk is very real to those who are age 65 and have a 50 percent chance of living until they are 85. There are products the employer could offer such as guaranteed lifetime income annuities that, for a price, shift the longevity risk to a third party.

conflict of interest issues and liabilities.[45] The Pension Protection Act provides incentives for employers to facilitate some types of counseling that will help their employees plan for retirement.[46]

Retiree Health Care

> Yousef has worked for 30 years as a mechanic for an airline company. Because of the physical demands of the job and the frequent requirement to work overtime, he wants to retire at age 55. He is concerned, however, because his company has discontinued offering retiree health care and wonders if he can afford to purchase it until he qualifies for Medicare at age 65. Also, he has learned that even with Medicare, one must pay for a gap policy in order to cover medical expenses not reimbursed by Medicare. His company's former retiree health care policy used to take care of this, but it is no longer offered. Perhaps he should try to find a job at another company that offers health care and where there are less physical demands. As Yousef contemplates his future, he continues to wonder if he can achieve his dream of retiring at 55.

With respect to expenses and the impact of inflation in retirement, health care coverage is a major concern.[47] This is especially true for those retiring before being eligible for Medicare at age 65. Do employees need some

---

45. The employer in a 401(k) plan must be careful not to tout his own stock as an investment option. Zweifach, L. (2002, January). Current developments and issues in the criminal prosecution of federal securities law violations. *Securities Reform Act Litigation Reporter, 12*(4), 547–577. Employers have been sued for encouraging overpurchasing or requiring the anchoring of company stock, making it difficult to sell. A large amount of company stock in a pension plan is a critical problem when the company stock price is declining, thereby devaluing the accumulated retirement savings of the employees. *How well do 401(k) plans work and who benefits most from them?* (2002, November 20). Research at University of Pennsylvania, http://www.upenn.edu/researchatpenn/. The article describes the events at Enron when the stock price tumbled, but reports that most employers are less likely to encourage employee ownership of company stock.

46. The Pension Protection Act of 2006.

47. *Consumer spending by older Americans, 1985–2005.* (2007, September 24). Congressional Research Service, Report to Congress. This report showed seniors' payments for health care expenses rose by 40 percent during the period 1985–2005.

form of retiree health care? Who should pay for it? Many employers are discontinuing the retiree health care benefit.[48] This includes retiree health care that applies to the pre-Medicare eligibility period, ages 55–65, and health care that extends beyond Medicare and serves as a supplement or gap to Medicare coverage. Without health care, the early retiree must consider either finding a way to purchase his own health care plan, which is usually cost prohibitive, finding a new job that offers health care, or remaining at work until he is eligible for Medicare.[49] According to the Employee Benefits Research Institute, a couple that retires at age 65, is covered by Medicare, and lives to normal life expectancy will pay $295,000 for health care expenses.[50] The EBRI estimates that Medicare by itself only covers about 51 percent of the costs of health care.[51] This is a daunting prospect that creates a dilemma for elder workers. Will we have a generation of baby boomers who grudgingly remain employed simply to retain the employer-sponsored health care? Again, the employer must consider not only the expense of offering retiree health care in some form,[52] but also, depending on the demographics of his workforce, the cost of retaining older workers who are simply hanging on for the health care coverage.

---

48. Many employers have discontinued the benefit because of its excessive costs, which has been made more "transparent" as a result of accounting changes, particularly the Financial Accounting Standards Board (FASB) Rule 106 requiring the inclusion of current and future retiree health care expenses in a company's financial statements. In 1997, 22 percent of U.S. employers offered retiree health care; in 2003, the number had declined to 13 percent. Fronstin, P. (2006, July). *The savings needed to fund health insurance and health care expenses in retirement.* Employee Benefits Research Institute, Issue Brief No. 295.

49. Friedberg, L. (2007, March). *The recent trend toward later retirement.* Center for Retirement Research at Boston University, Series 9.

50. Fronstin, P. (2006).

51. Since the expenses incurred for Medicare eligible are $295,000 over a 17-year life expectancy, and Medicare pays about 51 percent of the total cost, a safe assumption is that health care expenses would be more than twice the above amount over a ten-year period. It would probably be more. This also assumes lower health care resource consumption because of the lower ages of the early retirees. One should also note that as an employee defers or delays the retirement benefit, the present value of the benefit declines with age because the benefit is paid over the participant's lifetime, which is getting shorter for each year of delay or deferral. Lazear, E. (1998). *Personnel economics for managers* (p. 422). New York: John Wiley and Sons.

52. Some employers consider a type of DCP where they procure a policy for their retirees but limit their financing to a set amount of dollars per month. This avoids the burden of health care inflation costs.

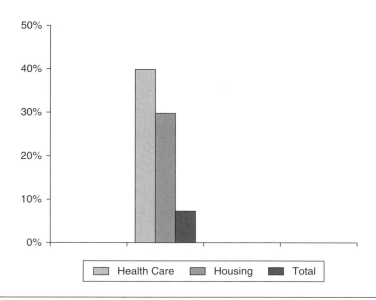

Figure 3.2   Percentage of Increases in Expenditures for Health Care, Housing, and Total Among Persons Between the Ages of 55 and 64 From 1985 to 2005

SOURCE: *Consumer spending by older Americans, 1985–2005*. (2007, September 24). Report to Congress, Congressional Research Service.

Marriage

What happens when an employee marries? Should the spouse participate in the employer's various benefit plans? Usually, spouses and children of the employee are considered legal dependents and, therefore, are included in health care plan coverage and designated as beneficiaries in retirement and life insurance plans. How should the cost of this coverage be allocated? In most plans the employee will pay an additional amount to provide spousal or dependent coverage, and also will have a higher deductible to pay. The extra cost is consistent with the benefits model calling for internal fairness. Without requiring such additional payments, some employees would be receiving higher benefits than others without spouses or children.

Should domestic partners be afforded the same treatment as spouses or other employee beneficiaries? What purpose would this serve for the employer and how could he determine eligibility? A number of companies have considered domestic partners the same as married dependents and extended health care, retirement, and other coverage accordingly. Currently, 20 percent of Fortune 500 companies extend dependent status to domestic partners.[53] While only a handful of states mandate the offering of benefits to domestic partners,[54] there are some tax issues that present complications.

The IRS considers the value of most health care benefits to be tax-exempt to the employee and his dependents. This position is based, however, on the legal status of dependency that includes lawfully recognized marital status.[55] Since the domestic partner does not fit this category, the benefit cost offered by the employer sponsor would be considered taxable income. Similarly, an extension of health care under COBRA to dependents would not be available to persons who are not lawful spouses.[56] Employers have begun offering benefits to domestic partners because the policy enhances recruitment and retention, and it recognizes the reality of a new family structure.[57]

In the case of the employee undergoing a divorce,[58] this life event raises a number of potential benefit needs. First, how should the benefits of the nonemployee spouse be continued or divided as a result of the divorce? Should health care be continued for the nonemployee ex-spouse? What about other benefits such as employer-sponsored life insurance plans? Should these be extended to a nonemployee ex-spouse?

---

53. Domestic Partner Benefits, http://www.salary.com/, 2007. Also, *Companies offering domestic partner benefits increase despite economic challenges,* Human Rights Campaign, http://www.hrc.org/, 2004.

54. Massachusetts currently allows and recognizes same-sex marriages, while Connecticut, New Jersey, California, Maine, Hawaii, the District of Columbia, and Vermont recognize civil unions between same-sex partners. See http://marriage.about.com/ and http://en.wikipedia.org/.

55. For an interesting explanation showing how institutions that offer domestic partner health care benefits deal with the possibility of the benefit values being taxable to the partner under IRS rules, see http://www.smith.edu/hr/documents/.

56. 29 USC §1161 et seq. and 42 USC §300bb-1, et seq. Consolidated Omnibus Budget Reconciliation Act of 1986 amends ERISA, the Internal Revenue Code, and the Public Health Service Act.

57. Employers who offer domestic partner benefits in states where such status is not given legal recognition usually require an affidavit of domestic partnership signed by the employee. See Indiana University's affidavit at http://www.indiana.edu/~uhrs/pubs/forms/affidavits/hrm/.

58. For domestic partners the issue is somewhat problematic because most states do not recognize a same-sex relationship as marriage; therefore, divorce is not a viable opportunity for dissolving the relationship. The Defense of Marriage Act, 28 USC §173C, allows states and the federal courts and agencies the right not to recognize a marriage between persons of the same sex, even though it was previously recognized by another state.

There are state and federal laws that pertain to some of these issues. First, in many state jurisdictions, nonemployee ex-spouses are entitled to a certain portion of the accrued or current retirement benefits of the employee at the time of the divorce. Federal law accommodates such an alienation[59] of retirement benefits by permitting the employer to allocate the accrued retirement benefits in accordance with the divorce decree, commonly called a Qualified Domestic Relations Order (QDRO).[60] In a traditional defined benefit plan this would entitle the nonemployee spouse to receive a pension benefit after he reaches retirement age as defined by the plan. The amount is based on the accrued benefit at the time of the divorce. In the case of a defined contribution plan, there is no prohibition against alienation. The employee owns that portion of the account vested. Therefore, divorce decrees can mandate a division of the employee's retirement account or joint property without any special federal statutory provision.

From an employer's standpoint, having efficient and current systems[61] to manage the benefit implications of divorce will minimize the inevitable employee distractions arising from this life event.[62]

Separation From Employment

Is there a need for a benefit when an employee is involuntarily separated from employment? Most employers are required to help fund, through tax payments, state-mandated unemployment benefits that provide a percentage of income to the employee who is furloughed, laid off, or separated from employment. Although unemployment benefits are controlled

---

59. ERISA prohibits any alienation of vested retirement benefits to creditors or others. This is one exception to this prohibition, 29 USC §1056(d)(1).

60. Refer to http://www.dol.gov/ebsa/, an electronic copy of a booklet describing the obligations of benefit plans to recognize domestic relations orders that call for an alienation of the benefit.

61. Referencing the benefits model's fourth element, the effective and efficient administration of benefits.

62. 29 USC §1161, et seq. and 42 USC §300bb-1, et seq. Consolidated Omnibus Budget Reconciliation Act of 1986 amends ERISA, the IRC, and the Public Health Service Act. See Regulations promulgated by the IRS at 26 CFR Part 54. COBRA provides for the continuation of employer-sponsored health care benefits for the nonemployee ex-spouse for up to 36 months. No more than 102 percent of the employer's cost of the health care benefit can be required to be paid by the COBRA beneficiary. Since there are no statutory mandates with respect to life insurance, it is up to the Domestic Relations Court or the employer's benefit policy to fashion a continuation of this benefit.

by the various states, the maximum benefit is usually around 50 percent of the worker's weekly pay and extends for a period of 26 weeks.[63] Should the employer offer more?

Some voluntarily provide for severance pay and an extension of benefits in such instances. This is usually calculated on the basis of length of service, income level, and possibly age. For example, the employer could provide that a person who is involuntarily separated for performance reasons, or due to a downturn in the business, will be eligible to receive severance pay of from one month's pay to one year's pay based on years of service. He also could be entitled to all unused vacation, and a continuation of health care and life insurance from one month to one year depending on length of service. The employer who offers such benefits must consider how they support the human resources strategy.[64] Employee assessments could show they enhance overall employee commitment and loyalty. Should all employees be covered, or just certain levels, such as top executives?[65] The principle of internal fairness leads to the conclusion that a broad program would be better.

If the cause of the layoff is due to a merger, acquisition, or change in corporate ownership, the employer might choose a slightly different and more generous approach. Providing a robust severance package, including pension upgrades, one year of severance pay, a continuation of health care for one year, life insurance, and outplacement assistance for a wide group of employees serves several purposes. First, it can act as a type of poison pill, requiring the new owner to sustain some significant expenses and, perhaps, diminishing his interests in the takeover. Second, it provides some peace of mind for employees during a potential change of ownership period, permitting them to focus on the business and not worry about potential job loss. They take some comfort in knowing that if they lose their jobs, they have significant protection and will get help finding new ones.

Outplacement services typically involve helping the employee organize his job search, and providing intense counseling on how to develop a new career search. The employer usually finances this type of benefit, and different levels of expense are allocated based on the level of the employee

---

63. Refer to the Economic Policy Institute's Web site at http://www.epinet.org/ for a good summary as well as a benefit calculator.

64. In most instances the severance benefits would not be offered for gross misconduct.

65. In some cases senior executives are given employment contracts that guarantee certain large severance payments and an extension of benefits in the event of job loss. These are often referred to as golden parachutes. Some companies offer similar benefits called tin parachutes to all employees who are affected by job losses resulting from a merger, acquisition, or change of ownership. See The Kroger Employees Protection Plan, http://www.kroger.com/.

before the loss of job. This differential is based on the increased difficulty experienced by higher-level employees in finding new positions.

There are several related benefit issues here. What happens to an employee's benefits when the employee voluntarily or involuntarily leaves employment and is reemployed elsewhere? Can health care coverage be continued?[66] What happens when the employee encounters the second employer's decision to exclude preexisting conditions? How are pension assets transferred?[67] These questions are answered by several laws that will be discussed in some detail in Chapter 12, Government-Sponsored and Mandated Benefits.

Death of the Employee

Death of an employee or his dependent is a life event that can create significant problems. Primary among them in the case of an employee's death is the loss of income to the dependents. The benefit that typically links to this event is life insurance.[68] The employer can choose to finance this benefit or simply use his purchasing leverage to facilitate the purchase by his employees. Or, he could do both by financing a certain level of life insurance and allowing his employees to finance the remaining desired face amount.[69] Should the employer extend life insurance coverage to the employee's dependents? Generally, if the employer's workforce is younger and many have new families, life insurance can be an important and relevant benefit. Life insurance is vital in the case of those who die young and

---

66. 29 USC § 1161, et seq. and 42 USC §300bb-1, et seq. The law here is HIPAA. Waiting periods for eligibility are permissible and are unique to the new employer, but there are protections, especially for health insurance. For an excellent summary of HIPAA, which will be covered in more depth in Chapter 12, see http://www.dol.gov/ebsa/faqs/faq_consumer_hipaa.html/. HIPAA can be found at 42 USC §§300gg-11, and 300gg-91(e) 4, and 29 USC §1161, et seq.

67. Portable retirement benefits, usually limited to those in a defined contribution plan, can be rolled over to the new employer's defined contribution plan or to an IRA, thus preserving the compounding and tax-deferred advantages of the benefit. This rollover must be completed no later than 60 days from the date he has ceased participation in the plan. Refer to http://www.irs.gov/ and Chapter 1, IRS Publication 590.

68. In many cases, DBPs provide for a small death benefit to the spouse when a retiree dies. Social Security also pays a death benefit of $255, see http://www.ssa.gov/.

69. As we will see in Chapter 15, Life and Disability Insurance, Pay for Time Not Worked, there are legal limitations on the amount of life insurance an employer can provide on a tax-favored basis.

having dependents makes the loss a serious financial problem. Thus, the employer with this demographic, who offers a robust life insurance program, may be able to better recruit and retain his workforce.

When an employee leaves employment or retires, the employer can allow a life insurance policy to be convertible. This permits the employee to pay for but continue life insurance, protecting his family against economic loss in the event of his death. What human resources strategy elements, if any, are satisfied in such instances? When offered in the case of retirement, providing some assurances against premature death offers retirees comfort to better enjoy a fulfilling retirement and adds perceived value by the employee for the overall retirement process. If employees value the employer-sponsored benefit, their perceptions of the total rewards can militate against discontent and poor commitment and loyalty. Finally, the employer can partially fund certain benefits with life insurance policies. Corporate-owned life insurance can be a powerful financing mechanism and provide significant tax advantages.[70]

Time Off From Work

Providing paid time off for leisure or other pursuits allows employees to better balance their work and personal lives. Vacation can accrue on an hourly or weekly basis, depending on the employee's length of service. Typically, vacation can be taken the year after it is earned; it is accrued in one year and taken in the next. The employer's vacation entitlements are dependent on the culture of his company and the practices of his competitors. The length of vacation offered can be an important recruiting tool.

Vacations are expensive. The employer is paying double compensation for the hours worked. Companies that offer significantly more generous vacation than their peers, typically, must have more employees to cover the longer vacation periods.

Vacations, sabbaticals, and the opportunity to bank or carry over vacation are discussed further in Chapter 15.[71] Depending on the structure and demographics of the workforce, how time off is treated by the employer can be a big factor in the company's recruitment, retention, and, ultimately, productivity. Again, the employer must assess how this benefit

---

70. See Chapter 15 where we discuss insurance approaches.

71. In many cases, the employer awards increased vacation entitlements as certain service benchmarks are achieved. For example, after one year and up to five years of service, vacation is two weeks. Between six and ten years, the entitlement is three weeks. In the eleventh year, the employee can begin to take four weeks; and after twenty years of service, vacation becomes five weeks. Keep in mind, for most companies the entitlement is five workdays of pay for each week of vacation.

might impact the company's human resources strategy and business plan. Will the workers' productivity be enhanced?[72] Will the employer be able to attract and retain better employees?

Some employers are dispensing with the idea of vacation, holidays, sick days, and other nonwork time awards with a new generic category called paid time off. The employee accrues so many hours off for each week worked, and can take it in time off or receive the equivalent in pay. All paid time off is lumped into one category. This has a certain attractiveness and simplicity for many employees who feel in control of their time off.

Some employees have difficulties in balancing their work and personal lives. For them, concierge or convenience benefits, as discussed in Chapter 15, may be very relevant. Similarly, employees with significant family responsibilities, such as working mothers, may find flexible work schedules, telecommuting, and shared work opportunities to be very relevant to their lifestyles. Offering them convenience benefits may aid in recruitment, retention, and productivity on a cost-effective basis.

Many employers also recognize that all work does not necessarily have to be performed at the office or during traditional work hours. Eligible employees have personal and family needs that can be met by offering this type of opportunity. Networking and functional opportunities available with home-based computer and electronic workstations have become apparent.

Companies like Deloitte[73] have received high marks for their acceptance of flexible job designs, and have indicated their efforts have had a direct and positive effect on their ability to recruit and retain highly productive associates.

---

72. Should the employee be allowed to forgo or bank his vacation if he cannot or does not want to take earned vacation in a given year? Or should the benefit be offered on a "use it or lose it" basis? If so, in what form will it be awarded to the employee? Is the idea of giving employees relief from the pressures of work undermined by facilitating the banking of vacation? What if an employee needs more time off than that accrued for vacation? Should the employer accommodate this need by offering unpaid time off? Should the employer allow a leave of absence or a sabbatical, whereby the employee can fulfill some important nonwork need by pursuing a passion or community interest?

73. Deloitte & Touche USA, LLP, has been a recognized leader in providing flexible work schedules for its employees with special family obligations, and supporting women's careers and professional development. See Badal, J. (2006, December 11). To retain valued women employees, companies pitch flextime as macho. *The Wall Street Journal Online,* http://online.wsj.com/. For eight consecutive years, Deloitte has been named one of Fortune magazine's top 100 companies to work for. It also has a nondiscriminatory policy that includes sexual orientation. 100 best companies to work for. (2007, January 22). *Fortune,* http://www.fortune.com/.

Once again, employers need to assess the company culture when considering such programs. Face time, the time one actually spends in the office, may be an overriding cultural value at certain workplaces. If so, then telecommuting and nontraditional work schedules are not embraced, and those who participate in them are not taken seriously. In those instances, the company's leadership has to work either to change attitudes or to abandon the idea of implementing flexible work opportunities, a decision that could be vital to attracting the right workforce.

Cultural and Global Perspective

The need for benefits in response to lifecycle events is fundamentally dependent upon the culture of a particular country. In many European countries, for example, it appears there is more balance between one's work and personal life.[74] Accordingly, benefits are often mandated by law, sponsored by government, or financed by taxes. For example, Social Security retirement benefits in many European countries replace a higher amount of final income than the U.S. Social Security pension program.[75] Many European Social Security systems, however, are in jeopardy as low birth rates and extended life spans threaten their financial integrity.[76] This problem will probably lead to some reduction in benefits or significant increases in taxes.

Other benefit comparisons show similar results. Vacation entitlements in Europe are often legally mandated and, generally, are more generous and available earlier in the employee's work history than those in the United States. Many European countries mandate extensive pregnancy leave with full or partial pay. Only a small percentage of U.S. employers choose to supplement the FMLA leave by offering compensation and leave beyond the 12 weeks.[77] Similarly, the employment laws in Europe specify

---

74. Sunil, J. (2002). *Work-life balance: A case of social responsibility or competitive advantage?* http://www.worklifebalance.com/. Reid, T. (2004). *The United States of Europe: The new superpower and the end of American supremacy.* New York: The Penguin Press. Global benefits are discussed in some detail in Chapter 13.

75. In some European countries the benefits are so generous they encourage early withdrawal from the workforce. See Gruber, J., & Wise, D. (2004). *Social Security programs and retirement around the world: Micro-estimation.* Chicago: The University of Chicago Press.

76. Siegel, J. (2006, September 20). Gray World, *The Wall Street Journal Online*, http://online.wsj.com/.

77. 29 CFR 825.825.207 that allows employers to substitute paid leave, such as vacation time, for FMLA. However, the issue of whether the employer should be required by law to provide compensation during the FMLA leave is hotly

certain wages, hours, benefits, and working conditions, while in the United States, major employment law focus is on discrimination; very few benefits are mandated.[78]

How long-term care is offered to aged and disabled family members differs widely among countries. In the United States, this life event is heavily dependent upon the use of nursing home facilities. The expense of such care is skyrocketing and affecting a number of public benefit plans such as Medicaid.[79] In other countries, many elderly stay with their extended families, and the demand for nursing home care is not as apparent. Law and economics also play a role in shaping the private or public scheme of offering benefits.

In Western European countries, leaves of absence are more extended than in the United States and the employer, in many instances, has a legal obligation to continue all or part of the salary during the leave period.[80]

The tax system in the United States provides financial incentives for employers to offer benefits in response to lifecycle needs. Contrast that to European countries where a heavier tax burden on the employee and the employer serves as the financing mechanism for public benefits. In the United States, a large percentage of pension and health care benefits are related to employment. In Europe, with some notable exceptions,[81] benefits such as health care are not linked to employment, but instead are government entitlements. Similarly, capital markets and investment opportunities are vital factors in the financing of the U.S. employer-sponsored system, while such markets in Europe, with its publicly financed benefits, are largely irrelevant.

Thus, when examining lifecycle events and relevant benefits, one must consider the distinct variations among countries. There are very different and distinct perceptions, expectations, and cultural perspectives that affect the type of response to lifecycle events in European countries and the

---

debated in the United States. Most employers do not. There are recent legislative proposals offered in Congress to require such compensation. See Brady, R. (2007, February 16). Employer paid FMLA leave: Good idea? Bad idea? Whose time has come? *HR Daily Advisor, Business and Legal Reports*, http://hrdailyadvisor .bir.com/. Also, some states provide for paid leave in such instances.

78. Blanpain, R. (2002). *European labor law*. London, New York: Kluwer Law International, The Hague.

79. Gleckman, H. (2007, April). *Medicaid and long-term care: How will rising costs affect services for an aging population?* Center for Retirement Research at Boston College, No. 7-4.

80. Blanpain, R. (2002). *European labor law* (pp. 428–432). London, New York: Kluwer Law International, The Hague.

81. For example, Switzerland requires persons to acquire health care. Some others mandate employer coverage. These issues are fully explored in Chapter 13, Global Benefits.

United States. As more and more U.S. companies do business abroad and compete with foreign companies doing business in the United States, it is important for them to take these differences into consideration. Keep in mind, however, that in the United States the decision to offer employer-sponsored benefits such as pensions and health care is largely voluntary. Once offered, however, these benefits must comply with certain federal and state laws.

Conclusion

Employee needs are changing. In times past, the number of years a person worked compared to the years he was retired—work to retire ratio—was quite high.[82] One started working at age 16 or 18, continued until 65, and then retired and lived another five or ten years. The ratio was 47:10. Today, workers go to college, start work at age 22, and work until they are 60, with a life expectancy of 22 years. The ratio is 38:22. Thus, the years during which an individual works and earns pension benefits and saves for retirement are declining. This presents a new challenge for employers and policymakers. The lifestyle expectations of the workforce are changing and traditional assumptions about work are eroding.[83]

It is important for any employer sponsor to understand a basic principle—there are many lifecycle events that give rise to a possible need for benefits.[84] In making the decision as to which benefits to offer and how they should be designed, the employer sponsor must assess carefully the demographics and specific needs and perspectives of his workforce. It is no longer sufficient to simply conclude we must have health care, pension, and life insurance, and where can we buy the cheapest plans? Employees' lives and deep linkages to work require more detailed analysis by the employer sponsor. Moreover, assessing how particular benefits might help drive the business strategy and add value to the enterprise is very important. Workforces comprise diverse people with complex needs and aspirations. The employer must understand this diversity and find the best fit for his workforce. There are some basic steps to follow.

---

82. Pollack, A. (2006, September). *Retirement finance: Old ideas, new reality,* American Enterprise Institute for Public Policy Research, http://www.aei.org.

83. Milken, M. (2006, September 19). The boom generation, seventh decade. *The Wall Street Journal Online,* http://online.wsj.com/.

84. During his years of experience at corporate headquarters, the author discovered that one of the employees' most valued benefits offered was business-casual dress, five days a week.

The employer should determine the relevance of any publicly mandated or sponsored benefit to his workforce. He must understand his labor market and how other employers are competing for labor and talent, how price sensitive his product or service is, and how the choice and design of benefits will impact the company's sales and market share. Life expectancy and other lifecycle changes can significantly impact the need for and the specific design and cost of a benefit. The employer must measure and assess this in his workforce. Employers should also consider how they might use capital markets to fund benefits. The investment returns, however, are no longer as rich as in the previous decade. Finally, the employer must understand that as he expands his operations into new global markets, he will confront even more diverse cultures that generate varied lifecycle events and perspectives. Different laws, economics, and tax systems can have a major effect on which benefits an employer might offer.

The question of which benefits to offer can have a dramatic effect on the success of the enterprise. Recruiting, selection, retention, employee development, and productivity can be profoundly affected by the decision. No dollars should be spent on any benefit unless one can demonstrate how it will help the enterprise succeed and if it will do so in a cost-effective manner. Examining closely the lifecycle needs of a specific workforce is the first and most important step in making this decision.

Chapter Exercises

1. The Ford Motor Co. recently surveyed a number of its employees, seeking to assess how they value certain benefits and the degree of affinity they have for each. See Footnote 1, supra. Develop a list of possible questions you might ask employees to determine whether they value certain benefits typically offered in large companies, and whether these benefits affect their behavior in the workplace, or positively affect the recruitment and retention of good workers.

2. How would you calculate the potential financial returns of offering a three-month sabbatical for certain employees after 15 years of service? How should such a benefit be designed in order to optimize such returns?

3. If life events drive the perceived need for benefits, brainstorm a list of possible benefits that might be especially attractive to female workers, young workers, Hispanic, Asian, male workers, African American employees, and older workers. How would you assess the link these might have to the business and human resources' strategies?

4. Do employees over age 65 need a basic health care benefit? Explain. If some do not, what alternative benefits, if any, might you offer this group that would respond to their interests and meet the four requirements of the benefits model?

5. You are the HR director of a large heavy manufacturing company with 12,000 employees located in a major midwestern city. Your CEO has asked you to do some research on Employee Assistance Plans that might be a good fit for the company. Benchmark the best plan designs found in the literature and outline a range of possible plan features your company should consider.

6. How would you calculate the potential financial returns to an employer who offers GED assistance to its workforce?

Retirement Plans— $\quad$ 4
Evolution and Design

Ajax Steel Products has sponsored a defined benefit pension plan for the last 30 years. Ajax has financed the plan and promised its employees a lifetime benefit when they become eligible for retirement. Until the late 1990s, the plan had been more than fully funded, with assets well invested and market returns largely responsible for funding the plan. The plan actuary even told Ajax executives they would not have to contribute to the fund for many years because of the investment returns.

Last year, following two years of a down market, Ajax was informed that the plan was underfunded. To be in compliance with legal minimum funding requirements, a substantial contribution was necessary. They also were advised that the funding holiday was over and regular contributions would be required for the future. Meanwhile, the company's business has been declining. The effect of these financial problems resulted in management's decision to freeze the retirement plan benefits of its employees, to discontinue accruing any future benefits, and to switch over to a defined contribution plan (DCP) that relied on employee contributions that Ajax would match. This result has not gone over well with Ajax employees.

Harry Mitchell, a veteran employee, complained to the HR department, indicating that he had wanted to retire after 30 years with the company, but now was not sure he could. After tallying his retirement benefits, which included Social Security, the remainder of accrued benefits in the Ajax frozen plan, and the amount he might accumulate in the new plan, Harry tells the HR director that he does not believe he will have enough to retire at a comfortable standard of living after 30 years of service at Ajax. He may have to work elsewhere after he retires, or he may have to stay on at Ajax an additional ten years.[1] The HR director shrugs his shoulders. It seems like overnight, things have changed.

1. Munnell, A., & Sass, S. (2008). *Working longer—The solution to the retirement challenge.* Washington, DC: Brookings Institution Press. In the book, the authors indicate that increasing the average retirement age from 63 to 66 can make a big difference and employers should consider encouraging longer service.

Introduction

A significant life event among employees in the United States, as in most developed nations, is their retirement. In 1935, the United States introduced Social Security, a publicly funded system intended to provide a retirement benefit for workers and their dependent spouses after reaching a certain age, originally 65 years. Eligibility for the benefit is, in part, based on a minimum, qualifying employment history, while the benefit itself is calculated based on a history of earnings. The plan is funded on a pay-as-you-go basis with tax contributions made by the employee and the employer.[1]

In 1875, the American Express Company offered its employees a privately sponsored retirement plan.[2] Although there was no legal obligation on the part of an employer to provide a retirement plan to its workers,[3]

1. In 1956, Congress amended the Social Security Act to provide income benefits for disabled workers and their dependents. In 1965, Congress added Medicare that provides health care benefits for retirees, and in 2006, it added a therapeutic drug benefit to Social Security. We will discuss Social Security in more detail later in this chapter.

2. *Employee benefits in the U.S.* (2005). Employee Benefits Research Institute Data Book on Employee Benefits, Chapter 1, Washington, DC, http://www.ebri .org/publications/books/.

3. Even though there is no legal obligation to offer a retirement plan, if one is offered it must comply with various legal rules, in particular those outlined in the Employee Retirement Income Security Act (ERISA) and the Internal Revenue Code (IRC). As we will discuss in Chapter 9, these laws and their supporting

over the years more and more employers began to sponsor them. Typically, they involved defined benefit plans (DBPs) in which the employer promised a calculable benefit at retirement age for the remaining life of the participant. There were several motivating reasons for employers to do this.

Defined benefit plans provide for an orderly and predictable progression of employees through the organization, from date of hire to a time when they no longer can or wish to work. They instill employee loyalty to the firm by encouraging them to remain there for a relatively long period of time. And, since many employers had begun offering retirement benefits, they allowed the employer to compete effectively in the labor market and to recruit and retain good workers. Provided they are internally fair and cost-effective, DBPs generally meet the basic elements of the benefits model. Employers who offer these plans are afforded favorable tax treatment.[4] For example, money used to fund plans that meet tax-qualified requirements is tax deductible, the investment returns are tax deferred, and there is no taxable income attributed to the employee until he retires and receives retirement benefits.

In the collective bargaining arena, unions have bargained for employer-sponsored plans to supplement Social Security. In the case of medium to higher income workers, the benefits under Social Security are often insufficient to sustain a worker's lifestyle after retirement.[5] Initially, union efforts to secure pension plans for its members met with some resistance by employers who argued there was no obligation to bargain over such benefits. The courts clarified this issue and pension plans were found to be a mandatory subject of bargaining, requiring employers to bargain with their respective union representatives.[6] In the United States today, both private and public employers, whose employees are represented by unions, are likely to offer their employees a defined benefit plan.

Employer sponsors of DBPs typically base their benefit amounts on years of service and income. Unlike Social Security's pay-as-you-go approach, employers fund the plans as indicated by actuarially based calculations. They invest their contributions in the capital markets, thus allowing the markets to help finance their retirement income obligations.

---

regulations provide for certain requirements and restrictions with respect to reporting and disclosure, vesting and eligibility, prohibited transactions, benefit distribution, the fiduciary responsibility of pension administrators, minimum participation, funding, and coverage tests, maximum salary and benefit limits, and control disproportionate participation among higher paid employees.

4. *Employee benefits in the U.S.*, 2005.

5. Munnell, A. (1982). *The economics of private pensions* (p. 77). Washington, DC: Brookings Institution Press.

6. *Inland Steel Co. v. National Labor Relations Board*, 170 F.2d 247 (7th Cir. 1948).

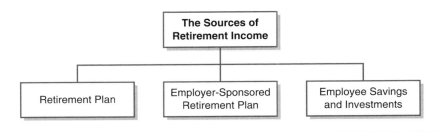

Figure 4.1   Sources of Retirement Income

This chapter will describe the design features of the defined benefit plan and also outline the evolution of new employer-sponsored plans that have developed over recent years. We will discuss the turmoil that has occurred because some employer-sponsored DBPs have failed or been terminated due to lack of sufficient funds to pay future benefits. In their absence, retirement savings programs, commonly called defined contribution plans (DCPs), and other less costly plans requiring more significant financing and investment risk on the part of employee participants, have become increasingly popular.[7] How do these programs come together?

In general, total retirement income is derived from three sources: employer-sponsored plans,[8] individual savings, and Social Security. As we review various retirement plans, the question that comes up most frequently is, will these three sources provide sufficient income for the individual to retire comfortably? This is usually expressed as a percentage of replacement income (retirement income ÷ average final pay) the plans will generate for the retiree. In examining the evolution of employer-

7. A recent Mercer survey of 316 employers reported that 24 percent indicated they had terminated their traditional benefit plan and had changed over to a DCP. Of the remaining employers, about 50 percent were considering making such a change. Aglira, R. (2006, July 17). *To freeze or not to freeze: Observations on the U.S. pension landscape.* Mercer Human Resource Consulting. There also has been a new interest in less costly plans, called hybrids, which include cash balance plans. These will be explained later in this chapter. Katz, D. (2006, August 23). Pension act tilts to cash balance plans. *CFO.Com,* http://www.cfo.com.

8. About 65 percent of all full-time employees in the United States participate in some retirement plan sponsored by their employer. About 33 percent are participants in a DBP while nearly 50 percent participate in a DCP. *Participation in employee benefit programs.* (2005). Employee Benefits Research Institute Data Book on Employee Benefits, Chapter 4, EBRI, http://www.ebri.org/publications/books/.

sponsored plans, one finds there has been more reliance placed on the individual savings of the employee in recent years as a funding source for retirement.[9] First, however, we will look at the design features of DBPs to gain a better understanding of how they can be adjusted to fit certain business strategies of the sponsoring employers.

Factors Affecting Retirement Plan Design

The employer sponsor of a DBP typically views long service as an important part of his human resources strategy; however, they must be mindful as well of the life expectancy of their workforce.[10] Life expectancy determines how long the employer will be obligated to pay the retirement benefit. The current ages and sex of the workforce also play a part in determining how long the employer can expect to fund his company's retirement plan before the employees embark on their retirements.

Tax incentives are important. An employer who wishes to take advantage of the deductions and income deferrals must design his plan to comply with the Employee Retirement Income Security Act of 1974 (ERISA) and the Internal Revenue Code (IRC). In such cases the plan will be considered tax qualified. Failure to design a tax-qualified plan could result in legal actions being brought under ERISA, a loss of fund protection against creditors, and a loss of the tax advantages provided by the IRC.[11] Accordingly, the law drives certain design features of many retirement plans. We will discuss these requirements in detail in Chapter 9, Benefit Legal Compliance.

Financing of Retirement Plans

There are a number of questions for the employer sponsor concerning the financing of plans: (1) Should the employer be the only source of funding? (2) Should the employer assume the sole risk of providing the stated benefit or should this be shared in whole or in part with the employee

9. *Aggregate trends in defined benefit and contribution plans.* (2005). Employee Benefits Research Institute Data Book on Employee Benefits, Chapter 10, EBRI, http://www.ebri.org/publications/books/.

10. *Longevity: The underlying driver of retirement risk.* (2006, July). American Society of Actuaries, http://www.soa.org/.

11. IRC §Section 401 et seq., and ERISA, 29 USC §1001–1461 (2006).

participant?[12] (3) Can the investment of retirement funds in various capital markets be used as a funding source and a means to grow the pension fund? (4) How aggressive or conservative should the investment strategy be? (5) Is it possible to fund a retirement plan by other types of assets, such as the employer sponsor's stock, life insurance, or company profits?

For the most part, DBPs are financed 100 percent by the employer. The exceptions typically involve teachers' and some state employees' DBPs, which require financing by both employers and employees.[13] Intrinsically, DBPs guarantee to pay an annuity for the lifetime of the participant; therefore, it is the employer who assumes the longevity risk. This focuses attention on the investment risk assumed by the employer sponsor who must manage the pension assets and make choices with regard to appropriate investment strategies. There are other types of retirement plans in which the employer funds the plan with company stock or a share of profits. We will learn more about those later.

Fund Protection

The employer sponsor must secure his promise to fund the retirement plan by placing assets of the plan beyond the reach of creditors or others. Provided that the plan complies with the relevant provisions of ERISA and the IRC and is considered tax qualified, plan assets are insulated from fiscal incursions. Creditors of the employer sponsor, for example, cannot claim the assets of a tax-qualified plan, even in the case of bankruptcy.[14] Furthermore, under the Pension Benefit Guarantee Act, employer sponsors pay a per-capita insurance premium to the Pension Benefit Guarantee Corporation, a federal agency, to insure the continuation of at least a percentage of the retirement income promised to the beneficiaries under the plan.[15]

---

12. *Annual 401(k) benchmarking survey*, 2006, Deloitte Consulting Group LLP, showed increases in employee participation in 401(k) plans in recent years. At the end of 2005, the proportion of 830 employer-sponsored plans, which were surveyed with more than 70 percent of eligible employees participating in a DCP, rose to 67 percent from 63 percent last year. See also *Employee benefits in the U.S.* (2005).

13. Many state and local pension plans for public employees, teachers, and university professors require contributions from employees and sponsors. See Munnell, A., et al. (2008, April). *The miracle of funding by state & local pension plans.* Center for Retirement Research at Boston College (No. 5).

14. §522 of the Bankruptcy Act.

15. ERISA §4001, et seq.

Employers have some flexibility to terminate a plan as long as accrued benefits are guaranteed. They can use excess assets to sponsor more cost-effective plans or change the design of a plan in order to accommodate the benefit integration strategy caused by a merger or acquisition.[16] This will be covered in Chapter 9, Benefit Legal Compliance.

The Benefits Model

The design features of the employer sponsor's retirement plan should be compatible with his values and strategies. These features should follow the basic principles of the benefits model—provide internal fairness, consider the rewards of external competitors, include features that positively affect productive behaviors, and ensure the plan is cost-effective and well administered. The employer must decide how generous the pension will be in terms of replacement income, for example, should the plan maintain the employee's preretirement standard of living?[17] The employer must choose a pension formula that meets his goals with respect to replacement income for the average retiree. Remaining issues the employer sponsor must manage include shared risk, funding, and protection of the employee in the event of certain life events in addition to retirement, such as long-term disability or premature death, and the security of his dependents. Specific plan features can address the employer's intentions, but should his plan be equal to, less than, or better than that provided by his key competitors? Is offering a better plan than one's competition enough to ensure being able to recruit and retain a highly qualified and committed workforce? Does the plan encourage loyalty and long service? Do these features help drive productivity in the workplace? Will the plan be tax qualified and in compliance with ERISA and the IRC?[18] What can best ensure this outcome? Can the employer sponsor afford to pay the benefit? Are there more cost-effective plan designs available? Is it administered so as to generate a high degree of satisfaction among its participants? Is it taking advantage of the optimal and most cost-effective administrative services? These represent issues and questions that employer sponsors should raise as they design and evaluate their retirement plans.

---

16. ERISA §4041, et seq.

17. *Measuring income adequacy: Calculating income replacement rates.* (2006). Employee Benefits Research Institute (EBRI), Issue Brief No. 297.

18. All the important details of ERISA, the Internal Revenue Code, and the Pension Protection Act of 2006 will be discussed in detail in Chapter 9, Benefit Legal Compliance.

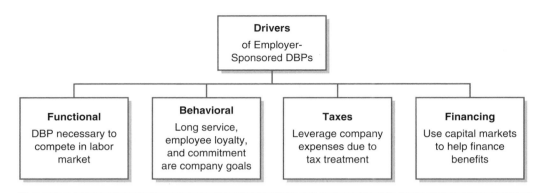

Figure 4.2   Drivers of Employer-Sponsored DBPs

Basic Design Features of a Defined Benefit Plan

Suppose you own a laundry and dry cleaning chain consisting of 20 retail outlets, a large facility plant, pickup and delivery service, and an accounting and management office. You employ 200 full-time and 20 part-time workers, and they are putting pressure on you to institute a retirement income plan. You decide to investigate the issue and begin to look at various plan design alternatives. What type of plan would be best for you, and how do you go about determining this? What are the design features and choices?

Let's look first at the design features of a DBP that is funded by the employer and includes a promise to pay a specific benefit when the participant fulfills the requirements to retire. Most often this entails years of service and age. The formula for calculating the DBP benefit usually involves age and income.

COVERAGE AND ELIGIBILITY

An employer must consider coverage. What facility and which employees should be covered under the plan? Should it include any or all of the following: part-time workers, office workers, and management? ERISA will control some of these issues, as we will see in Chapter 9; however, employer sponsors do have some discretion in making coverage decisions.

The employer sponsor must consider eligibility requirements that include minimum age and service required for participation. ERISA requires the employer to count vesting service after age 18 and participating service after age 21. Vesting renders the benefit nonforfeitable and participating service is used to calculate the amount of the benefit. For example, if an employee was hired at age 18 and worked until age 23, and the defined benefit plan provided that the retirement benefit is 100 percent vested after five years of service, the employee's accrued benefit would be nonforfeitable. But how much is this benefit? If service after age 21 were used to calculate his accrued benefit, at age 23 only two years of service would be used in the benefit formula.[19]

Since years of service are important in calculating a benefit, one must determine how much service is required to participate. Minimum service also is controlled by ERISA. Where the employee has worked at least 1,000 hours in a plan year, that year must be recognized as a year of service. In such instances, a part-time employee can achieve the minimum amount of service required to be a plan participant.

VESTING

Under ERISA, the employer sponsor of a DBP has several choices with respect to vesting. He can use a five-year cliff approach, meaning that after the fifth year the employee is fully vested. He can also elect a seven-year graded vesting schedule. Graded means that a certain percentage of the benefit is vested after the passage of each year until the seventh year has been attained, in which case the employee will be 100 percent vested.[20]

BENEFIT CALCULATION

Calculating the amount of benefit in a DBP can be done in several ways. The most common is the formula approach where the employee's income, usually referred to as final average pay, is multiplied by years of service, adjusted if necessary by actuarial considerations,[21] and then multiplied by a percentage chosen by the employer sponsor. The percentage, which we call the replacement percentage, is typically 1, 2, or 3 percent, depending on the employer's benefit strategy. It has a major impact on the percentage of final pay the pension plan will replace when the employee decides to retire.[22] In using a formula, the employer is revealing his values; in this

---

19. ERISA §203 and §204.

20. The employer can elect a schedule requiring less time for vesting. See ERISA §203.

21. If, for example, a person wants to retire early, the pension amount will be reduced.

22. A generous DBP, for example, might target a 70 percent replacement rate of average final pay as its goal for employees who complete a significant amount of service, say 30 years, and retire at the normal retirement age, usually 65. This target will be affected by the replacement income percentage the employer chooses for his pension formula and how he determines final average pay. See EBRI, Issue Brief #297 (2006). The brief discusses the importance of final pay replacement calculations.

Table 4.1   Minimum Vesting Schedules for DBPs

DBP	Year 1	Year 2	Year 3	Year 4	Year 5	Year 6	Year 7
5-year cliff	0	0	0	0	100%		
7-year graduated	0	0	20%	40%	60%	80%	100%

case, that retirement should be a function of long service and have some relationship to one's final, average compensation. The longer one stays, the more salary one makes, and the higher one's retirement benefit will be. Thus, with respect to the benefits model, participants are encouraged to work hard, get promoted, earn pay increases, and pile up the years of service. In doing so they can directly affect the pension amount they will receive. Using final pay in the formula takes into consideration wage inflation by applying the highest years of pay as a basis for calculating the final retirement benefit.

Typical Final Average Pay Formula

The formula plan provides for the calculation of the average high three out of the last five years of pay just before the retirement date. The result is multiplied by the number of years of service, which then is multiplied by a replacement income percentage; if necessary, actuarial adjustments are made. For example, an employee's average pay for the high three out of the last five years is $60,000, multiplied by 30 years of service, and then multiplied again by what the employer considers to be a reasonable replacement income percentage of 2 percent. The employee is retiring at normal retirement age (65), therefore, there are no actuarial adjustments. The calculation of DBP using this formula, $60,000 \times 30 \times 2\% = \$36,000$. The employer's apparent objective is that the DBP on average will replace about 60 percent of final pay.

What if the employee's average pay included a large bonus in one of the high three years, raising the high three out of the last five years' average pay to $75,000, and the employee worked 35 years instead of 30?[23] What if the employee wanted to retire at age 55 instead of 65 and the employer's plan permits early retirements? If final average pay increases, so will the retirement benefit. The employee who leaves ten years before the normal

23. Often employees who are considering retirement will give consideration to future bonuses or pay changes and calculate their impact on the benefit calculation. In such cases the expectation of changes in their income may control the timing of their retirement.

retirement age of 65, theoretically, would receive benefits for an extra ten years; however, the benefit calculation will be actuarially reduced to reflect this longer stream of payments.

Tax policy has some relevance here. The government puts limits on tax-favored treatments of benefit amounts. Hence, the IRC limits the maximum amount of final average pay that can be included in the formula and also the amount of pension that can be received in one year by a participant.[24]

Not all DBPs use the formula approach. In a collective bargaining agreement where there is significant uniformity in pay, typically the DBP benefit is determined using either a unit or a flat benefit form of calculation. In the case of a flat benefit, once the employee reaches the years of service or retirement age requirements, he is paid a flat amount, for example, $500 per month or a percentage of pay, such as 40 percent. The monthly unit benefit is calculated by multiplying a set amount of dollars times years of service. If the unit benefit is $10 per month, multiply that times years of service, 30 for example, and the monthly benefit will be $300 per month.

FUNDING

The employer sponsor, with assistance from his actuary and reference to minimum funding rates mandated by ERISA,[25] must decide at what rate the promised benefits should be funded.[26] The employer must determine the targeted replacement income of his plan as well as the features that will support this goal. And, he must be mindful of external competitors' plans,

---

24. §415 IRC. The amounts for 2008 are $185,000 maximum pension and $230,000 maximum compensation that can be used in the formula to calculate the pension. The amounts are indexed each year. These maximum limits have led employers to offer supplemental or excess benefit retirement plans (SERPs) to higher paid executives so their full pension entitlements under the formula plan will be received. Variations of these executive plans are sometimes called Top Hat plans. Ordinarily, these plans are not tax qualified and are subject to the claims of creditors in the event of employer insolvency. They can be exempt, however, from certain provisions of ERISA and the Internal Revenue Code. If the deferral of income earned by the employee is not "constructively received," the amounts deferred will not be subject to the income tax until the amount is actually distributed to the employee. See Chapter 9.

25. It has been noted that the Pension Protection Act of 2006, which among other things tightens up the minimum funding standards of employer-sponsored DBPs, may cause more employers to freeze their plans and move toward some form of DCP. Quinn, J. (2006, June 28). A requiem for pensions. *Newsweek*, http://www.msnbc.msn.com/.

26. In this text we do not explicitly discuss pension accounting, although we will mention, occasionally, some related issue.

and not overextend himself with pension expense. The actuarial assumptions should include the following factors: when various cohorts of employees reach retirement age, their life expectancy, the inflation rate for wages, the employee turnover rates that will affect the number who will qualify to retire, and the benefits retirees will receive. In addition, the actuary calculates the investment returns on the funds put aside for retirement, because the employer sponsor of a DBP can use the capital markets or other financial investments to partially fund his pension obligations.[27] Let's look in more detail at the additional design features of a DBP.

BENEFICIARIES

Should the sponsor provide for beneficiaries in a DBP? The law requires that the spouse, as a survivor of the participant, must be guaranteed 50 percent of the participant's benefit unless the spouse specifically waives this right.[28] This is important because, ordinarily, a DBP provides for a benefit only as long as the participant is retired and living.[29] The plan also can allow the participant to name other beneficiaries, frequently called contingent annuitants, to receive a percentage of the participant's annual benefit. The plan sponsor is not legally bound to include such a provision. The designation of a beneficiary, whether it is the spouse or a contingent annuitant, will often result in an actuarial reduction depending on the age and sex of the beneficiary. If the beneficiary is younger than the participant and has a longer life expectancy, the plan has an obligation to make benefit payments for a longer period. Thus, there will be a reduction in both the participant's and beneficiary's benefit amount.

A related plan design feature involves benefit restoration. Let's say a retired participant selected a beneficiary and his current retirement benefit has been actuarially reduced. While the participant is receiving the reduced

---

27. This is especially relevant when the employer has promised a specific benefit. As new plans such as DCPs utilize employee funding, there should be some educational effort on the part of the plan sponsor to help participants understand what their own rate of contributions to the fund should be in order to provide sufficient retirement income. The new Pension Protection Act of 2006 provides some guidelines on how employers can provide this. See Chapter 9.

28. Why would a spouse waive this benefit? In order to avoid receiving actuarially reduced benefits for the remainder of their lives, there are a variety of circumstances that might ameliorate the risk inherent in choosing the waiver. See Johnson, R., Ucello, C., & Goldwyn, J. (2003, September). *Single life vs. joint and survivor pension payout options: How do married retirees choose?* The Income and Benefits Policy Institute at The Urban Institute.

29. That is, unless an optional form of benefit is chosen by the participant. This will be discussed further.

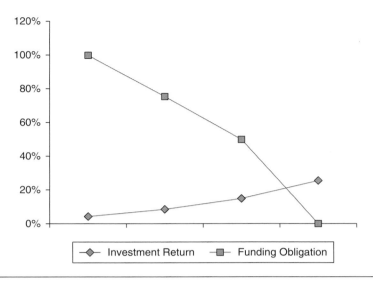

Figure 4.3   The Inverse Relationship Between the Investment Return of a
DBP and the Funding Obligation

NOTE: Investment return assumptions are 5 percent, 9 percent, 15 percent, and 25 percent and funding obligations are 100 percent, 75 percent, and 50 percent, and zero respectively.

benefit, the beneficiary dies. In this case a plan feature called restoration benefit can be provided that will cancel on a going-forward basis the actuarial reduction and will restore the participant's retirement benefit to the full amount.

PARTICIPATING SERVICE

Another DBP plan feature involves how the plan calculates years of service, commonly called participating service. The law mandates when service should begin, but sometimes employers put a cap on the years of service that can be counted and used in the benefit formula. For example, an employer's DBP can apply a maximum of 40 years of service in the benefit formula. This could have the effect of discouraging long service and, of course, would save the employer money because it limits one important multiplicand in the benefit formula—years of service.

AGE AT RETIREMENT

Should the employer sponsor allow his employees to elect early retirement? What is the human resources strategy behind this? In referring to the benefits model, it may be appropriate if other employers provide this opportunity. It also might help to open career opportunities for younger workers who could decide to leave the firm if promotions are not apparent. If there is a full actuarial reduction for early retirement, then there should be no added cost to the employer in providing this benefit. At what age should the employer allow early retirement? Typically, the age is set at 55. If the employer wants to encourage later retirements among his workers, he may choose not to offer early retirement or offer it closer to normal retirement age. The employee considering early retirement must understand that he is forfeiting added years of service, which would be used in the retirement formula, and possibly higher compensation he would have received had he stayed on until normal retirement age.

Employer sponsors often peg normal retirement age at 65, wherein an employee who is fully vested will be entitled to a full, unreduced benefit. Simply by identifying a normal or full retirement age does not mean an employee must retire at that age. The Age Discrimination in Employment Act (ADEA) does not permit a covered employer to mandate termination at a certain age.[30] While some employers allow an unreduced benefit at earlier ages, such as age 60 or 62, in light of current life expectancies and advances in health care, one could argue that using age 65 as the full retirement age is unrealistic and should be raised.

Generally, DBPs can be effective in both providing worker efficiency and loyalty and inducing timely retirements.[31] In choosing the retirement ages, particularly for early retirement, the employer must be cognizant of the potential loss of productivity as workers with higher levels of skills are induced by plan designs to leave the firm. This is especially true during periods when there is a shortage of labor skills in the sponsor's market.[32] As we note in our discussion of Social Security in Chapter 12, Government-Sponsored and Mandated Benefits, a plan can actuarially increase benefits for persons who elect not to retire at the normal, full-age retirement and continue working. The obvious purpose for the Social Security Administration is to reduce pension costs, because its participants will receive fewer benefits over their remaining lifetimes. Could this be done where a private

---

30. There are exceptions for commercial pilots and certain law enforcement and fire personnel.

31. While DBPs are generally considered to encourage longer service, once an employee reaches a certain age and chooses not to retire, the present value (in 1,000s) of his pension declines. Why? The number of annuity payments he will receive declines as death nears. This concept is based on the analysis in Lazear, E. (1998), pp. 422–428.

32. Gokhale, J. (2004, September 9). *Mandatory retirement age rules: Is it time to re-evaluate?* The Cato Institute, testimony before the U.S. Senate Special Committee on Aging.

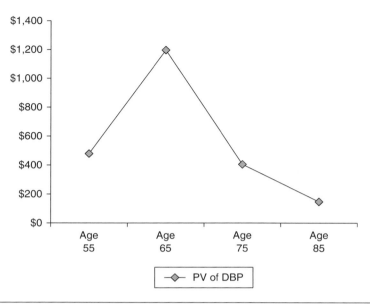

Figure 4.4   Present Value of DBP and Age

plan sponsor wants to maximize the utilization of its older workers? Are the same principles applicable?

PENSION ADJUSTMENTS AND DISTRIBUTIONS

For most DBPs the payment of a lifetime annuity is the typical means by which the benefits are distributed. Thus, the employer assumes the longevity risk in that he promises a benefit regardless of the life span of the participant. What about inflation risk? Who assumes the risk that the amount of the pension will be outpaced by inflation and over time will not be sufficient to meet the retiree's expenses? Should there be an adjustment to the annuity? The most obvious design feature to ameliorate this inflation risk for the participant is to include cost of living adjustments (COLA) in the plan. This is a design choice the employer can make. He can decide either to lock in the benefits at the time of retirement, allowing some discretionary ad hoc increases in later years, or to provide systematic and regular cost of living adjustments to the retiree's benefit amounts. In the latter case, usually some public index of consumer prices is used to make the adjustment. The employer sponsor may agree to pay 100 percent of the increase recorded by the index, or a certain percentage thereof. In view of the fact that people are living longer, while a cost of living adjustment adds expense to the employer's retirement plan cost, it does avoid the potentially devaluing effect inflation can have on a pension amount that was calculated when the retiree departed the company a number of years ago.[33] The employer should look to his competitors' plans to see if such features are included in their plans and also assess the cost impact of adding a COLA to his DBP.

With a DBP the benefit ends upon the death of the participant, unless he has designated beneficiaries. Are there other design features that could ameliorate this potentially harsh consequence? Yes. If the plan sponsor provides, a participant can choose several years, a period certain, of benefits that will be paid to his estate, in the event he dies before the period elapses. Usually, this involves either a 10-year or 15-year certain option, meaning that if the person dies before the selected period has elapsed, the annuity will be paid to his estate for the years remaining under the period certain. For example, the participant chooses a 10-year certain option and dies after only 5 years of receiving retirement benefits; the remaining five years of annuity payments will be made to his estate. There is an actuarial charge for choosing this option.

There are other pension distribution choices an employer sponsor can make. Should benefits be paid as an annuity for the participant's lifetime or should they be paid as a lump sum when the participant retires?[34] In most cases, the plans provide for an annuity. There are some, however, that offer a lump sum distribution where the accrued benefit is small or where the plan sponsor decides for human resources reasons simply to offer a lump sum alternative. The lump sum is calculated using the participant's expected annuity at retirement, factoring in his expectancy based on relevant mortality tables, aggregating the payments, and then applying a discount rate to determine the present value of the benefit.

---

33. For example, if a person retires in year one with a DBP pension of $50,000 per year, and for the following ten years there is annual price inflation of 3 percent, the real versus nominal pension will be $38,461. This means the lower pension is the actual purchasing value that existed in year one (Nominal Pension ÷ 1.00 + Accumulated Inflation = Real Value of Pension in base year).

34. A study by EBRI indicated that the increased number of employees participating in DCPs has led to an increase use of lump sum cash-outs paid by the plan sponsor to the participant at retirement. Although there was some fear that participants would use the money for consumption, this has not proven to be the case. *Lump sum distributions: An update.* (2005, July). Employee Benefits Research Institute Notes, 23:7, http://www.ebri.org/. AARP reported more discrete patterns relating to the use of lump sum distributions. It found that rollovers of lump sums to tax-qualified retirement accounts increased with age, education, and family income. Lichtenstein, J. (2006, July). *Pension lump sum distributions.* AARP Public Policy Institute, Issue Paper No. 2003-10.

Sometimes there is a point of contention over the calculation of the lump sum; in particular, the employer sponsor's choice of a discount rate.[35] For example, an expected stream of annuity payments over the life of a participant (20 years) amounts to $500,000. We predict that investing this money can earn 5 percent annually. The present value (or lump sum) would be $188,000. This means that $188,000 invested over the period of the participant's remaining lifetime (in this case 20 years) at 5 percent would generate the same amount as the sum of his annuity, $500,000.

What if the employer is an optimist and wants to use a higher discount rate to determine the present value? Will the amount be smaller or bigger than that which occurs when a larger discount rate is utilized?[36] The rule is that the higher the discount rate, the lower the lump sum. The lower rate will result in a higher lump sum. The discount rate, of course, should accurately reflect a realistic interest return available in the market.

What happens if an employee participant leaves employment before reaching retirement but after becoming vested?[37] He is commonly referred to as a separated-vested employee. In this case, ERISA will require the plan to include a feature that allows this person to claim benefits at retirement age. With shortened vesting requirements and the increased mobility of the workforce, many employees leave an employer with a small, vested accrued benefit that they cannot claim until they reach retirement age. Often these vested accrued benefits represent an administrative burden on the plan. Keeping track of former employees, and knowing where they will be when they reach retirement age and claim their benefits, can be problematic to pension administrators.[38] Accordingly, separated vested employees are often encouraged or compelled to receive a lump sum

---

35. For a helpful and interesting explanation of present value, see Economics Interactive Tutorial, Discounting Future Income and Present Value 2005, University of South Carolina, http://hspm.sph.sc.edu/.

36. This is often a contentious issue and many urge the use of a more uniform and predictable investment rate assumption, perhaps blending a long-term bond rate assumption with an equity investment rate. The new Pension Protection Act of 2006 allows the use of longer-term corporate bond rates in calculating present values. Would this be more or less conservative than using government bond rates? See Chapter 9.

37. For those employees leaving the employer sponsor's employment before vesting, their accrued benefits are forfeited and can be credited to the funding obligation of the employer.

38. This benefit is usually quite small because final pay for this group is calculated based on lower earnings recorded at the time of their departure and their years of service are often limited. If the participant chooses to receive benefits at his early retirement age, there also will be an actuarial reduction.

distribution at separation. In that way, they are out of the system and no longer need to be tracked and monitored. The amount of the cash out is the accrued benefits as of their separation date reduced to present value by applying a market discount rate.

What happens when a DBP participant dies before retiring, but is vested and has reached retirement age? In the case of death before retirement, typically DBPs provide for the payment of an actuarially reduced benefit to the surviving spouse or to the designated beneficiary. The assumption is the participant retired the day before his death, and the calculation of the benefit is made on that basis. If the participant dies after vesting, but before reaching minimum retirement age, then he will be considered separated vested, and the spouse can claim survivor benefits when the participant would have attained the requisite age.

COVERED COMPENSATION

Plans normally consist of all earned income in the final average pay formula used to calculate the pension amount. This includes bonuses, premium pay, overtime, and other extra pay. It also could include the accumulation of unused sick time pay, although in some cases unused sick time is simply added to years of service in the benefit formula.[39] In some cases, the application of these factors can have a significant impact on the participant's decision as to when to retire.

Frequently in a final pay DBP, participants who have reached retirement age will consider past and possible future variations in their covered compensation in order to determine the most opportune time to retire. (See Chapter Exercises, No. 6, infra.) If they are expecting some large bonuses or hefty pay increases in the next year, they may decide to postpone retirement in order to take advantage of these higher pay amounts that will be used to determine their pension.

Unused vacation normally will not be added to the benefit calculation but, instead, will be taken by the retiring employee at the commencement of his separation from work. After the vacation time is exhausted, retirement benefits will commence.

SOCIAL SECURITY OFFSETS AND ADJUSTMENTS

Should the employer, who has contributed to the employee participant's Social Security benefit in the form of a 6.2 percent wage tax, take

---

39. See, for example, the University of California plan in Chapter Exercises Nos. 7 and 8 at the end of this chapter.

some credit for this contribution? This is normally accomplished in a DBP by proportionately reducing the benefit of the employee. Such a plan design alternative is legally permitted and is called Social Security offset or integration.[40] Here is an example of how this works.

An employer's DBP formula is based on years of service, the average of the high three out of final five years of pay, and a 2 percent income replacement factor. The employee works 30 years with a final pay average of $100,000; there is no actuarial reduction. The plan defines the Social Security offset formula as 1.25 percent, for example, of the primary Social Security benefit. Let's say the employee will receive $20,000 from the Social Security Administration as his primary Social Security benefit. The total retirement benefit from the employer-sponsored plan would be ($100,000 × 30 × .02) − (.0125 × $20,000) = $60,000 − $250 = $59,750 per year. Another way to calculate this is to offset the retirement benefit by multiplying the employer's proportion of Social Security covered earnings;[41] for example, $45,000 × .0075 (which is the employer's representative share of the wage tax paid to Social Security), or $337.50. This amount would be deducted from the annual retirement benefit paid by the employer.

LEVEL INCOME OPTIONAL BENEFIT

A benefit design feature for a person retiring under his DBP before he is entitled to Social Security benefits is called the level income option. Here, the employee wants to keep his total retirement benefits relatively constant before and after he begins to receive his Social Security benefit. The DBP can provide a level income option that increases the employer-sponsored benefit before the Social Security benefit is received and then reduces it thereafter. As one might expect, there is an actuarial cost to provide this option. The overall benefit from the DBP, though providing a stable and a higher benefit in the pre-Social Security period, is less than the long-term annuity that would have been received from the plan were the option not chosen. There is a price one pays for predictability.

BREAKS IN SERVICE

Employee mobility is becoming quite common in the current employment landscape. What happens when an employee leaves the employer,

---

40. Some would argue that this offset has a disproportionate impact on the lower paid retiree since their DBP benefit is smaller and the Social Security benefit as a percentage of final pay is larger than higher income participants.

41. Covered earnings are those earnings of the employee subject to the tax.

Table 4.2   Hypothetical Example of a Level Income Option

- Employee A retires at age 62 and his benefit is $2,000 per month from his final average pay DBP.
- His Social Security (SSA) benefit at age 65 (full age retirement) will be $1,000, giving him a total retirement income of $3,000 per month at age 65.
- He chooses to receive a total of $2,700 from his DBP in order to maintain a semblance of level income up until he qualifies for full-age, unreduced Social Security benefit.
- At age 65, he will receive the full $1,000 from SSA, but $1,900 from his DBP giving him a total of $2,900 per month for the remainder of his life.
- There is a $100 actuarial charge imposed by his company's DBP for receiving the higher-level income payment.

ceases participation in the retirement plan, and then returns? Should the employee's past service under the plan be added or bridged to his future service? While an employer could be more generous in providing design features that would allow for this, the bridging of service is largely controlled by ERISA's break in service rules, which stipulate: (1) A break in service cannot exceed five years; if it does, the accrued benefits earned in the prebreak period are forfeited. (2) Accrued benefits that are vested under the plan prior to a break in service are not forfeitable, regardless of the length of the break. (3) If the years of the break in service exceed the years of prebreak service, the employer is not obligated to bridge the previous service with the current. The prebreak accrued benefits are forfeited.[42] (4) An employee must work at least one year after the break in order to qualify for bridging his service.

Now that we understand the importance of years of service in the typical DBP final average pay formula, bridging prior service can add significant value to the employee's eventual retirement income.

Keeping track of breaks in service is an administrative burden for employer sponsors. As a result, there are added administrative costs. Persons who leave the plan and are no longer entitled to benefits add some financial value to the plan because their accrued benefits are forfeited. Plan actuaries typically estimate turnover rates and the resultant

---

42. Breaks in service can occur if the employee works less than 500 hours in a 12-month period. If an employee were 100 percent vested prior to the break in service, this service must be added to his post-break years even if the break was five years or more, 29 USC 1053 (2006).

forfeiture of accrued benefits in determining appropriate funding rates for the plan.

DISABILITY RETIREMENT

What happens when an active employee suffers an acute and disabling health event and cannot work? Can the DBP be used to provide a disability benefit? The answer will often depend on whether the employee's disability is short term or permanent. In the case of a short-term disability, usually defined as lasting less than six months, an employer can provide a full or partial salary continuation benefit. The benefit is expressed as insurance and is either self-insured by the employer or purchased by the employer.

A long-term disability, defined as a permanent physical or mental impairment that renders the employee unable to continue gainful employment, presents another set of challenges for the employer. Often there is some reference to the individual's ability to generate a percentage of his predisability income. For example, a person who is unable to earn more than 50 percent of his previous pay would be considered eligible for a disability retirement. In many instances the source of the long-term disability benefit is the DBP. Provided the employee is vested, the DBP will pay a disability benefit to the disabled employee. The issue is the employee may have limited service and income that makes using the final average pay formula somewhat problematic. In this case, DBP sponsors often provide a limited percentage of pay depending on years of service that will be paid to the long-term disabled employee until he reaches retirement age. At that point, a nonactuarially reduced pension is paid to the participant.[43] Since the employee may also qualify for a Social Security disability pension, the employer sponsor may offset the pension benefit as described earlier.[44]

Some employers choose to use long-term disability insurance instead of the DBP as the means to pay long-term permanent disability benefits until the person reaches retirement age. The insurance can be funded by employer or employee contributions, or by both. If the employee pays the premiums, the benefits received will not be taxed as ordinary income. As with the special disability retirement, when the employee reaches retirement age the benefit will be paid out of the DBP. Typically, long-term disability insurance also pays a fixed percentage of pay until retirement age is reached.

---

43. Since it was the disability that affected the employee's ability to continue working and accrue years of service, the benefit is not actuarially reduced.

44. Disability insurance will be covered in Chapter 15. In 1956, the SSA was amended to provide a disability benefit that can continue through the life of the participant and also be available to his or her dependents.

NONPORTABILITY OF DBP BENEFITS

Should the employer sponsor of a traditional DBP allow a departing vested employee who is under retirement age to take his account with him? Normally, a DBP benefit is not portable, so the answer is no.[45] A participant in a DBP has a benefit accrual, not assets, in a real or nominal account. If an employee leaves vested, he can come back and claim the benefit when reaching retirement age. There is a penalty for leaving early and a reward for rendering long service. Because the DBP is designed to encourage long service, offering portable benefits would be at odds with that objective. Employees covered by DBPs will actually lose retirement benefits if they move from employer to employer, even if the employers have identical DBPs, as illustrated in the following.

Employee A works for Company #1 for 30 years and retires. Company #1 has a 2 percent final average pay DBP. Employee B works for Company #2 and participates in the same DBP; however, he leaves Company #1 after 10 years and goes to work for 20 years at Company #2, which has an identical DBP and formula. He then retires at the same age as Employee A. Figure 4.3 shows the projected total retirement benefit of Employees A and B, both of whom worked under identical plans. The amount of total retirement for Employee B is significantly less than for Employee A, because the final average pay formula generates larger benefits when two of the significant factors, service and pay, are also high.

ALLOCATION OF RISK IN DBPs

There are three risks we often consider with retirement plans: longevity, investment, and inflation. In a DBP, the sponsoring employer promises a specific annuity benefit based on the participant's income and years of

---

45. The movement of accrued benefits from one plan to another can become an issue in mergers and acquisitions when the employers want to offer past service credits to the acquired company's employees as if they participated under the acquiring company's plan. This involves choosing the right human resources practice. Unless sufficient assets from the acquired company's plan are transferred to the acquiring company's plan, so as to provide funding for past service credits, the acquiring company will not be able to offer them.

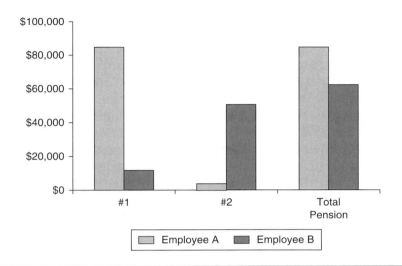

Figure 4.5   Aggregate Pensions of Employees A and B

NOTE: In this example we used the same DBP formula for both companies: years of service x final average pay x 2 percent. This demonstrates how the design features of a typical DBP encourage long service.

service for the remainder of his life.[46] What happens if an employee participant lives longer than expected? The employer remains liable to pay and, if applicable, continues to pay the employee's beneficiaries. The employer assumes the longevity risk.

The employer sponsor also invests his funds in various markets in hope that the returns will be sufficient to fund his benefits plan. If they are not, the employer sponsor may have to increase his contributions to the plan. Thus, the employer sponsor assumes the investment risk.

In the case of a final average pay DBP, the benefit has a built-in inflation factor because the compensation used to calculate the benefit includes accumulated pay increases and inflation. Thus, some inflation risk for the participant is ameliorated. However, postretirement, the inflation risk is assumed by the retiree unless the plan includes a viable COLA. As living expenses increase, a DBP retirement benefit without a COLA shrinks in value. As newer approaches to retirement plan designs are developed, the allocation of risks change somewhat dramatically.

---

46. Of course, if the DBP is terminated or frozen, the sponsor's risk is diminished. There were 2,700 DBPs (10 percent) frozen in 2003. In most cases the cause was underfunding. Van Derhei, J. (2006). *Defined benefit plan freezes.* Employee Benefits Research Institute, Issue Brief 291.

Defined Contribution Plans

In the early 1980s, some employers wanted to supplement their DBPs with a plan that relied more on employee financing. They also wanted to increase employee stock ownership.[47] Others, many small and medium sized employers, found the risks associated with the DBP too lopsided, and wanted to shift these risks and associated costs to a different plan.[48] They discovered a better fit called a defined contribution plan (DCP). The employer migration to DCPs was accelerated with the stock market decline in the early 2000s. The stock slide exposed the very real investment risks inherent with sponsoring a DBP, many of which became seriously underfunded.[49]

> Corporations were happy to offer rich retirement plans to their workers . . . but now the game is up. . . . During the previous decade, when it seemed that every pension promise could be fulfilled by a rising stock market, employers overpromised or recklessly underprovided—or both—for the commitments they had made. [50]

So the pension evolution continued.[51] Based on the section of the Internal Revenue Code authorizing the creation of qualified deferred compensation

---

47. Since contributions to DCPs are often invested in company stock, the potential to create better linkages and common interests between workers and owners did not go unnoticed by employers who were considering changing from a DBP to a DCP.

48. Between 1985 and 1998, there was a substantial shift among small and medium sized employers from defined benefit plans to defined contribution plans. *Aggregate trends in defined benefit and defined contribution plans.* (2006). Employee Benefits Research Institute, Chapter 10, Chart 10.1, http://www.ebri .org/publications/books/.

49. Lowenstein, R. (2006, October 23). The end of pensions. *New York Times Sunday Magazine*, 58–59. The economic recession and stock market stagnation, together with increasing employee longevity, caused many employer-sponsored DBPs to be underfunded. The choices some employers had were: (1) pay a large amount of money to restore the proper funding status of their plan; (2) freeze the accrued benefits as is, and discontinue counting future service under the plan; and (3) change to a more cost-effective plan design, particularly one that involves employee contributions and financing. Aglira, R. (2006, July 17). *To freeze or not to freeze: Observations on the U.S. pension landscape.* Mercer Human Resource Consulting.

50. Lowenstein, R. (2005).

51. The use of evolution is more than a metaphor. Although some of the time periods overlapped, and we cannot identify precise dates when new designs appeared, there was a sequenced progression of retirement plans.

plans, the new DCP was called the 401(k) plan. It is a retirement plan that relies more extensively on employee contributions for funding,[52] and, as such, shifts our three key risks from the employer sponsor to the employee participant. There were other factors driving the change.

From a human resources standpoint, assumptions about the workforce were changing and employers and employees no longer saw long-term employment as a critical element in the work relationship.[53] The DCP did not provide incentives for long tenure, and younger employees were more comfortable with the idea of investing in capital markets. Key design elements of DCPs responded to the changing demographics and their needs and preferences.

RATIONALE OF A DEFINED CONTRIBUTION PLAN (DCP)

The major feature of the new DCP, which found its genesis in §401(k) of the Internal Revenue Code, was the retirement benefit was based on a defined contribution and not a benefit. Both employee and employer could make contributions. The contributions would be tax deferred and could be invested among a variety of options, including the employer's stock. Since no specific benefit was promised, the account comprising the employee and employer contributions was portable, allowing a departing employee to take his balance with him to the new employer, or place it in a tax-qualified instrument such as an individual retirement account (IRA). The employee assumed all the risk of investment performance, interest rate changes, and longer life expectancy.

Employers who offered a DCP as a supplement to a DBP saw it as serving several new strategic objectives: (1) It would relieve the cost pressure on the employer to increase the benefit levels, or to introduce COLAs into his existing DBP. (2) It offered an efficient mechanism to increase employee stock ownership of the sponsoring employer, thus enhancing alignment and productivity—the employees would think and behave like

---

52. Declining stock market returns in the late 1990s and the early 2000s exacerbated the expense issue. Aglira, R. (2006). These returns had been funding a number of large plans for several years. Also, the added years of life expectancy affected the employer's DBP expense, but had little impact on a 401(k). For an excellent discussion of the implications of freezing DBPs, see *Defined benefit freezes*. (2006, March). Employee Benefits Research Institute, Issue Brief No. 291, http://www.ebri.org/.

53. There are 401(k) income deferral-type plans that are offered to state and local public educational employees, called 403(b) plans, and for other state and local employees, they are called 457 plans. In most cases these plans are offered in addition to a traditional Defined Benefit Plan, but in the case of a 457 plan, it is not considered a tax qualified plan that protects assets from creditors.

owners.[54] (3) Its portability allowed employees more freedom to move to another employer without losing this retirement benefit. The 401(k) design did not encourage long-term employment and retention. (4) The risks were reallocated—they were all borne by the employee.[55] (5) The simplicity of seeing one's account balance and investment returns and being able to project future values was more attractive to the participant. Thus, employers felt that DCPs provided them with a benefit that was more valued by their workers than a DBP. (6) Generally, the cost of sponsoring a DCP was lower than a DBP.

401(K) DESIGN FEATURES—COVERAGE AND VESTING

The 401(k) plan design includes a number of features to consider. First, there is coverage. Which facilities or groups of workers will be covered by the plan? Then, the plan must establish some eligibility or participation requirements. The law establishes minimal requirements: employees must begin participation after attaining age 21 and completing one year of service,[56] which includes part-time workers who work the minimum number of hours per year as mandated by ERISA.

Vesting is another design feature of a DCP. Since it is the employee's pretax earnings that are contributed to the plan, all of the employee's contributions are immediately vested. The typical 401(k) may provide for employer contributions called matches, which are also tax deferred. Matches are made in response to an employee's contribution to the plan, thereby increasing the amount in the 401(k) account. Studies have shown

---

54. After introducing the 401(k), many employers experienced an increase in employee ownership. The Kroger Co., for example, increased employee ownership from less than 1 percent to 33 percent shortly after introducing its 401(k). A number of studies discuss the link between 401(k) plans and employee productivity. Mitchell, O., Blitzstein, D., Gordon, M., & Mazo, J. (2003). *Benefits for the workplace of the future.* Pension Research Council, University of Pennsylvania Press; Brown, J., Lang, N., & Weisenberger, S. (2006, August). 401(k) matching contributions in company stock, *Journal of Public Economics, 90*(60), 1315–1346.

55. Between 1985 and 1998 there was a substantial shift among small and medium sized employers from defined benefit plans to defined contribution plans. *Aggregate trends in defined benefit and defined contribution plans.* (2006). Employee Benefits Research Institute, Chapter 10, Chart 10.1, http://www.ebri.org/.

56. In order to encourage employee saving, many employers are eliminating the one-year rule and allowing employees to participate in their 401(k) at the time of employment. See Smith, L. (2005). *Annual 401(k) benchmarking survey.* Deloitte Consulting, LLP.

Table 4.3 Current Minimum 401(k) Vesting of Employer Matches

401(k)	Year 1	Year 2	Year 3	Year 4	Year 5	Year 6
3-year cliff	0	0	100%			
6-year graduated	0	20%	40%	60%	80%	100%

NOTE: Employee contributions are 100 percent vested immediately. There were other vesting schedules in effect prior January 1, 2002, that apply to matches made before this date.

that matches encourage employees to contribute to their 401(k).[57] By encouraging more savings, the DCP can become a more attractive plan for recruiting purposes and provide a better mix of funding sources.[58]

EMPLOYER CONTRIBUTIONS (MATCHES)

Frequently matches are discretionary and, unlike the DBP, give the employer significant financial flexibility.[59] They are defined usually as a percentage of the employee's contribution, but with a maximum cap expressed as a percentage of the employee's income. For example, the employer will match 100 percent of the employee's contribution up to a maximum 3 percent of the employee's annual earnings. The employer's match can be subject to the standard vesting rules, such as cliff vesting of three years or graduated vesting of up to six years.[60]

Some 401(k) plans offer profit matches, which are based on the profit performance of the company for a given period. With respect to the benefits model, this involves an effort by the employer to enhance productivity

57. Even, W., & Macpherson, D. (2005). The effects of employer matching in 401(k) plans, *Industrial Relations, 44*, 525–549. A recent TIAA-CREF Institute study, *The employer match and participant behavior,* http://www.tiaa-crefinstitute .org/research/, July 2006, concluded that employer matches boost employee participation but have little effect on increasing contributions unless there is a significant (more than 25 percent) increase in the match.

58. TIAA-CREF Institute, 2006.

59. There is sometimes an issue as to the timing of the match. If the employer chooses to make the match at the end of the plan year, there is some savings to the employer in the form of the time value of money. If, on the other hand, matches are made at the time of the employee contribution, there is added cash cost to the employer.

60. Employee contributions are typically deducted from their payroll checks.

of the participant group. Matches contingent upon attaining certain profit levels also give more financial flexibility to the employer. The profit match can be made in addition to the traditional match or can be the sole criterion for an employer's contribution to the employee's account. As with other incentives, there is the issue of line of sight. How does the employer communicate the connection between the work of the participant and the attainment of profit goals? When compared to the ordinary personal investment and savings activities of an employee, the 401(k), with its tax-deferred status, compounding of savings and their returns, and the possibility of employer matches, represents a powerful tool to accumulate retirement income.[61]

OWNERSHIP VERSUS PROMISE TO PAY

Monies contributed to a 401(k) are placed in trust and are not subject to creditors in bankruptcy. Unlike a DBP, death of the participant does not extinguish the benefit. With or without selected beneficiaries, the 401(k) account is the property of the participant and can pass to heirs in accordance with the appropriate state laws of testate or intestate succession. Accordingly, unlike the DBP, the present value of a DCP increases with age and service, and is not affected by the life expectancy of the participant.

The classic DBP actuarial reductions do not apply to the savings in a 401(k). It does not matter how long the participant or the beneficiaries will live. Longevity and investment risks are on the participant. The employer has no fixed obligation to pay a benefit. For example, if a 65-year-old participant in a 401(k) marries a 20-year-old, who becomes his beneficiary, there is no reason to apply an actuarial reduction in order to take into account the spouse's longer life span and resultant stream of payments. What about early retirement under a 401(k)? Should any actuarial principles apply that would affect the calculation of the benefit? The answer, of course, is no.

LIMITS ON CONTRIBUTIONS

How much can the employee and the employer contribute to the 401(k) each year? Who would have the key interest here? The answer to the latter is the government. The IRS allows favored tax treatment, but to avoid being too generous it has placed limitations on these contributions, called §415 limits. In essence, this places limits on employee deferrals to a 401(k) as well as on the aggregate contributions. The limits are indexed to

---

61. To see how these dynamics work, go to the Chapter Exercises at the end of this chapter.

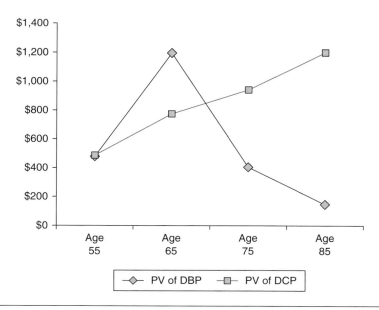

Figure 4.6   Comparison of Present Values of DBP and DCP

NOTE: This is a hypothetical graph that compares the present values of an employee's 401(k) savings plan (DCP) and a DBP (in $1,000s) and age of retirement. This concept is based upon the analysis in Lazear, E. (1998), pp. 422–428.

increase each year.[62] Also, in order to encourage a higher degree of participation and retirement savings among those who perhaps have not saved sufficiently in their early years of employment, the law permits additional catch-up contributions for those over 50 years of age.[63]

INVESTMENT CHOICES

Since there is an employee ownership feature with respect to the 401(k), the participant must now be given the opportunity to self-direct the investments of his account. In most cases the decision to change investments or choices can be made at any time.[64] The employer provides

62. For example, the §415 limits for 401(k) plans in 2008 are $15,500.

63. The catch-up for over age 50 participants for 2008 is $5,000.

64. §The PPA of 2006 requires the sponsor to allow employee investment direction. In some cases there are restrictions as to when an investment can be changed. This typically occurs when a participant is an insider (usually a senior officer of the company) or someone who has inside information, which has not been released to the public, and is forbidden by SEC rules to trade in the company's stock.

a number of investment options for the participants that may include the opportunity to purchase company stock, if it is publicly traded, as well as other assorted mutual funds with specific investment characteristics ranging from fixed income to higher risk equity plans. Perennial issues pertaining to investment options are how many investment choices to offer, and what educational assistance should be provided to the participants to enhance appropriate choices. Many 401(k) plans now include lifestyle investment choices, whereby the participant can elect a fund that identifies the fund's degree of risk, the potential returns, and the remaining years the participant has to save before retirement. This facilitates the participant's choices.

The early experiences of many 401(k) plans found participants[65] with heavy concentrations of company stock and insufficient balance in their portfolios.[66] Maybe it was too convenient to choose the company's stock, or investment inertia caused participants to pay little attention to the financial planning issues. For many, perhaps, it was naivete—employees had faith in their company's management and a strong loyalty to their company, so they chose the company stock. Employers perceived the investment in company stock as a means to generate higher productivity, thinking their employee shareholders would fulfill the objectives of the agency theory, acting and behaving like owners.

While careful not to tout their own stock as an investment choice, many employers did offer additional matches of 10 to 20 percent, if company stock were chosen. In exchange for offering the match, the employer wanted the employee to retain the stock for a given period and anchored the purchased stock so it could not be sold or exchanged within the 401(k) plan for a given period of time. Anchoring has fallen into disfavor among many employer sponsors. Requiring employees to hold their company-matched stock created a significant investment risk. In reality, the concern that employees would receive their match and quickly dispose of it in favor of another investment option in the plan did not often materialize. Today, most employers offer numerous investment choices[67] in addition to company stock, and allow employees

---

65. In the mid-1980s, most participants were managers and executives. Mid-level and lower paid employees did not earn sufficient income to make contributions, and others were covered by collective bargaining agreements that did not include such a plan.

66. Even, W., & Macpherson, D. (2004, June). Company stock in pension funds. *National Tax Journal, 57,* 299–313.

67. There is some evidence, however, that some 401(k) plans do not offer adequate choices. Elton, E., Gruber, M., & Blake, C. (2006, August). The adequacy of investment choices offered by 401(k) plans. *Journal of Public Economics, 90*(6/7), 1299–1314.

who invest in company stock to sell and exchange it without any special limitations.[68]

Heavy concentration of company stock in the portfolios of many 401(k) participants, as well as the company stock anchors, created the perfect storm in cases like Enron, where the stock plunged in value and many participants either did not or could not sell their stock and minimize their losses. In such cases participants lost all or most of their 401(k) savings. This has led to reform legislation and proposals, most of which are directed at improving the education of participants, blocking stock trades inside or outside the 401(k) by senior officers when ordinary participants cannot trade the company stock in their own 401(k) accounts, and essentially eliminating the use of anchors.[69]

LOANS AND WITHDRAWALS

Some 401(k) plans allow for hardship withdrawals and loans.[70] Provided statutory guidelines are followed and a genuine hardship is shown, the employee who removes all or part of the contents of his 401(k) amount will be taxed at ordinary income rates. There will be no other penalty. As for loans, they are extended based on statutorily described needs and without tax consequences; the loan must be repaid to the 401(k) with interest. Of course, the debtor is essentially paying the principal and the interest back to his own account.

These design features add considerable administrative expense to the 401(k) and are paid for by the participants. The features made some sense when employers offered both DBPs and DCPs; the latter was simply a supplement to the former. But as more employers move to offering just a DCP, it seems inappropriate to allow withdrawals and loans from the

---

68. Section 901 of the Pension Plan Amendments Act requires employers to provide at least three choices of investments and prohibits requirements to retain company stock, provided the employee has three years of service. See also Deloitte Consulting LLP 401(k) Annual Benchmarking Survey 2005–2006, which describes trends in investment choices, participation rates, fees and expenses, participant education and communication efforts, and new design features, at http://www.deloitte.com/.

69. See Section 901 of Pension Protection Act of 2006. The 2003 Enron situation was exacerbated by frequent blackout periods. These occur when the administrator of the plan needs an interval of electronic inactivity in trades in order to update the recordkeeping system. Also, during the period when the Enron stock price was declining, some executives who held company stock outside the 401(k) were able to sell and minimize their losses.

70. See IRS guidelines on Retirement Plans and FAQs Regarding Loans and Hardship Withdrawals at http://www.irs.gov/retirement/.

exclusive retirement plan. From a participant's standpoint, however, knowing he can withdraw money from his account in case of an emergency does enhance the ability of the employer to enroll 401(k) participants.

ADMINISTRATION

Employer sponsors have found that outsourcing the fund administration can increase efficiency and reduce costs. In terms of economies of scale, third-party administrators (TPAs) have expertise, software, and equipment to handle vast amounts of information, including the records of all participants' earnings, deferrals, and investment choices.[71] Frequently, the administrator is a mutual fund company that sponsors a number of individual funds. In this case, their own funds are usually among the investment choices available in the 401(k). This type of arrangement can result in lower administrative and transaction fees for the employer sponsor and his participants because the administrator receives transaction fees when his own investments are chosen by participants. Often, the fund administrator will assume the role of investment educator as well, offering information about retirement strategies to the participants.

Normally, participants pay administrative and transaction fees for their 401(k) plans. When they examine the investment returns of their 401(k) funds closely, they can see the impact these fees have on their account balances. When one considers the potential investment returns of a particular fund within a plan that might average 3 to 6 percent annually, the seemingly minimal administrative fees of 1 to 2 percent could significantly reduce these returns. Plan fees have become an important consideration in the design of 401(k) plans.[72] To mitigate the fee problem, as mentioned earlier, plan administrators often will offer lifecycle funds and index funds that track the performance of a discrete group of stocks or bonds. These formatted choices help simplify investing decisions by the participant and also serve to limit the expense of 401(k) funds because there are fewer individual fund transactions and lower brokerage fees.[73]

---

71. See *LaRue v. DeWolff Boberg & Associates*, 2008, 128 S.Ct. 1020, involving a breach of fiduciary duty by the 401(k) plan administrator who did not follow the investment direction of the plaintiff participant.

72. There has been a spate of class action lawsuits against plan sponsors for allowing excessive plan costs and not properly monitoring charges against services received. The U.S. Department of Labor is also targeting investigations on this issue. See AON Consulting Alert, October 23, 2006.

73. See Deloitte Consulting LLP 401(k) Annual Benchmarking Survey 2005–2006, which describes trends in investment choices, participation rates, fees and

DISTRIBUTION

The distribution of a 401(k) account to a departing or retiring employee is usually made in a lump sum. Some plans offer to convert the lump sum to an annuity and, here again, the investment or interest rate assumption becomes very important. What can an invested lump sum earn and how much can it distribute in periodic payments to the retiree? Typically, the higher the expected investment rate assumption, the larger the annuity. What is the life expectancy of the retiree and what happens if he dies earlier than expected? What if he lives longer than expected and outlives the planned distribution payments? These are typical annuity issues that will be discussed later in this chapter when we cover retirement planning. The motive for including an annuity option in a 401(k) plan, however, is based on the concern that a retiree receiving his entire savings account as a lump sum may choose underachieving investment strategies or engage in spendthrift activities. Or, he may not roll it over into a tax-favored account, but instead use the money for nonretirement expenses.[74] There is some evidence to suggest that a large number of DCP participants do not roll over their lump sum payment into a tax-qualified account.[75]

Since 401(k) funds are not taxed to the participant until he receives payment(s), one who is not interested in using the funds at the time of withdrawal must take appropriate steps to preserve their favorable tax treatment. This is called a rollover process, where the withdrawn funds are quickly placed in a similarly situated tax-deferred account, such as another DCP or an individual retirement account, called an IRA.[76]

There are IRS rules that control early distributions of 401(k) funds to participants and also mandate distributions when the participant reaches a specific age.[77] Once again, the IRS wants to complement its favorable tax policy with clear limits. Unless the plan provides for a specific early retirement age, any distributions before age 59.5 years will result in both

---

expenses, participant education and communication efforts, and new design features, at http://www.deloitte.com.

74. There is some evidence that offering a lump sum instead of an annuity allows for leakage of the retirement income because the retiree uses it to pay for nonretirement expenses. Lichtenstein, J. (2006).

75. See *Pension lump-sum distributions: Do boomers take them or save them?* (2003). AARP Public Policy Institute.

76. Ordinarily, the participant is given 60 days to perfect the rollover. See IRA Online Resource Guide—Information about Rollovers at http://www.irs.gov/retirement/.

77. For a comprehensive guide, see Retirement Plans FAQs Regarding the Required Minimum Distributions at http://www.irs.gov/retirement.

taxation of the account as ordinary income as well as a 10 percent penalty. Similarly, participants at age 70.5 must begin taking a required minimum distribution of their 401(k) account funds.[78] What important factor do you believe the IRS would consider in determining the actual minimum distribution amount?[79]

BROAD PARTICIPATION AND DISCRIMINATION TESTING

A major problem among employers who sponsor 401(k) plans is the lack of participation among lower paid employees. This creates legal compliance issues for the employer sponsors since the IRS closely monitors the rate of participation and savings by all employees. The process is called discrimination testing[80] and is discussed in Chapter 9, Benefit Legal Compliance. Since preserving favorable tax treatment in the 401(k) design and administration is vital to both the employer sponsor and the participants, it is important for the employer to maximize the rate of participation. The concerns here are important to consider. The IRS wants to make sure there is full participation among both higher and lower compensated employees, and that the 401(k) does not become a private tax shelter for highly paid managers and executives. The employer wants to make sure that employee deferrals are not reversed and, thereby, subject to taxation due to noncompliance with discrimination testing. The employer also must deal with the reality that many lower paid employees do not enroll in the 401(k). A solution seemed elusive until a new design feature appeared in the workplace.

---

78. For a summary of the discrimination testing and other compliance rules, see EP Compliance Risk Assessments—401(k) Report at http://www.irs.gov/retirement/.

79. The life expectancy of the participant based on mortality tables is a critical factor in determining the annual amount of the required minimum distribution. This can provide a good estimate of the number of payments that will be made over the remaining life of the participant. The account balance is divided by the remaining years in the lifetime of the participant. See Treasury Regulations §1.401(a)(9)-9, A-2.

80. The IRS offers an opportunity to present a 401(k) without considering the issue of discrimination testing. The design is called a Safe Harbor 401(k). It is illustrated in the John Murray vignette. One issue with respect to automatic enrollment is how the employer should invest the funds. The Department of Labor will issue guidelines on this, but there is some fiduciary responsibility on the employer to invest prudently until the employee takes charge of the investments in the account. More on this issue can be found in Chapter 9, Benefit Legal Compliance.

For the last six years, John Murray has been a manager at Burlington Drug Stores, a 300-store chain. Currently, he participates in their defined benefit plan and is 100 percent vested. Today he received an announcement from the company's benefits office that a new retirement plan, called the New 401(k) Savings Account Plan, was available. The brochure states that Burlington will automatically enroll him in the new plan and contribute annually an amount equal to 1 percent of his compensation, up to $1,000, if he has less than five years of service. They will contribute 2 percent, up to $2,000, if he has more than five years of service. Then, if he contributes some of his own salary to the plan, the company will match his contribution 100 percent up to a maximum equal to 3 percent of his salary and 50 percent up to a maximum of 2 percent of his pay.

To help facilitate a broader participation in 401(k) plans, some employers are automatically enrolling all eligible employees as participants. It is called a nonelective participation. The employer can make the contribution of its own funds, as we see in the above case, or he can unilaterally defer a portion of the employee's compensation. In the latter case, the employee can affirmatively opt out if he does not wish to participate.[81] Alternatively, in order to encourage more participation and avoid the problem of discrimination testing, employers guarantee certain levels of matches to the employee's contributions and vest them immediately. The problem with nonelective enrollment, however, is it does not by itself really change an employee's participation in his retirement planning. This takes effective communication. In order to use nonelective enrollment as a springboard to activate a real savings plan by employees, employers and their TPAs must communicate with employees about retirement planning and use calculators to show the ultimate results of specific savings and investment strategies. In some cases, auto enrollment and aggressive communication strategies have caused both an increase in the participation and contribution rates of employees in the lower pay ranges.[82]

81. The Pension Protection Act of 2006 now explicitly permits this involuntary enrollment. The 2005–2006 Deloitte Consulting, LLP, Annual 401(k) Benchmarking Survey found that of the 830 employer sponsors responding, 23 percent were auto enrolling their participants versus 14 percent in 2004.

82. Marquez, J. (2006, August 28). Retirement benefits: Getting employees in the game. *Workforce Magazine*, 27–33.

Table 4.4   Three Types of Safe Harbor Designs Using Nonelective and Elective
                  Enrollments

Employer auto enrolls (nonelective) employee into a 401(k) and contributes an
amount equal to at least 1 percent of the employee's earnings. The amounts are
immediately vested. The employer also can match using standard vesting.

Employer auto enrolls employee into a 401(k) and defers up to 3 percent of the
employee's compensation. The employee can opt out.

Employer matches 100 percent of an employee's voluntary deferral up to 3 percent
of his compensation and 50 percent of the next 2 percent of compensation.
The match vests immediately.

SOME PERSPECTIVE

A fundamental question remains: Are those who are eligible to participate in a 401(k) really saving enough for retirement? The general answer
is no. Later we will provide retirement calculators and statistics that are
useful in answering this question more fully. Obviously, the issue becomes
very significant when the employer chooses to offer only a 401(k).[83]

A 401(k) plan can be a powerful tool to accumulate wealth and to
finance one's retirement. Studies have indicated that a 401(k) can, theoretically, outperform a typical DBP as a source of retirement income.[84]
Also, younger employees do not plan to stay at a single employer for their
entire working career; therefore, they prefer the portability, ownership,
and the flexibility to direct their own investments.[85] As more and more
employers drop their DBPs, offering a DCP represents an externally competitive move.[86] In some cases where the matches are based on company

83. See Chapter Exercises at the end of Chapter 5 to determine what annual benefits a lifetime savings will generate.

84. The calculation involves comparing the present values of a unit plan DBP with
identical years of service and salaries. Comparisons at various retirement ages
showed the DCP with significantly higher present values than the DBP. Lazear
(1998), pp. 418–428.

85. For an excellent discussion of financial education and pension plans, as well
as other policy pension issues, see *Private pensions and public policies*, edited by
Gale, W., Shoven, J., & Warshawsky, M. (2004). Washington, DC: Brookings
Institution Press.

86. Some employers are offering Roth 401(k) plans that provide for after-tax savings to be placed in the account. The earnings are tax deferred and, if distributed in
accordance with IRS rules, the entire distribution will not be subject to taxation.

results, there may be an opportunity to affect the behavior of employees positively. Nevertheless, current U.S. employee savings rates are sufficiently inadequate to consider the 401(k) as a suitable retirement nest egg for many employees.[87] We will await the data to determine whether the new forms of nonelective plans will make a difference.

The Evolution Continues

A new species of retirement plan appeared in the 1980s and slowly began to capture the interest of some employers. In between a DBP and a DCP, it was called a hybrid plan. Employers were looking for a plan that was more cost efficient, avoided the employer's promise to provide a specific benefit, and minimized the longevity and investment risks. They also were looking for something that included features favored by employees, such as accounts and portability. The pension consulting firm Kwasha Lipton in New Jersey came up with such a design and called it a cash balance plan (CBP).

HYBRID CASH BALANCE PLAN DESIGN FEATURES[88]

Certain demographics and business strategies set the stage for the introduction of the cash balance plan. Where the employer is satisfied with

87. A recent Vanguard study among those actively saving for retirement showed four in ten households would need to save more than they do currently. *Vanguard retirement outlook for 2006.* (2006, August). Vanguard Center for Retirement Research, 25. Many workers close to retirement age have meager savings. *Working after retirement: The gap between expectations and reality.* (2006). New York: Pugh Research Center. Also, the General Accountability Office has reported that workers born in 1990 who will participate in a DCP will generate about 22 percent of their final average pay. The lowest income workers will have zero percent replacement income, while the highest will have income replacement rates of 34 percent. The current median balance among workers between the ages of 55 and 64 who participate in DCPs is now $50,000. See *Low defined contribution plan savings may pose challenges to retirement income security, especially for low-income workers.* (2007, November). GAO, Private Pensions. See also Munnell, A., Webb, A., & Golub-Sass, F. (2007, September 20). *Is there really a savings crisis?* Center for Retirement Research at Boston University. This report indicates that 45 percent of U.S. persons at age 65 who annuitize all their retirement assets will be at risk of being unable to maintain their standard of living at retirement.

88. U.S. Department of Labor, Frequently Asked Questions About Cash Balance Plans, 2006, Employee Benefits Security Administration, http://www.dol.gov/ebsa/. Cahill, K., & Soto, M. (2003, December). *How do cash balance plans affect*

medium instead of long service benefit incentives and is looking for a lower cost retirement plan, the CBP was a welcomed creation. Its key design features are:

1. The employer calculates a benefit annually and credits it to an employee's nominal account.

2. The amount of the credit is based on the employee's annual earnings multiplied by some percentage such as 1, 2, or 3 percent, depending on how generous the employer wishes to be.

3. Each credit earns interest based on a rate set by the employer annually.

4. The employee can view his account balance and easily understand its current value.

5. Both contribution and earnings are tax deferred.

6. The employee balance is portable.

7. A three-year, cliff-vesting rule applies.

8. The benefit can be paid in a lump sum or in the form of an annuity.

9. As with the 401(k) plan, actuarial reductions are not applicable because the employee has a nominal account, not a promised annual benefit that would be affected by longevity risks.

10. The employer can pool the accruals and leverage his investment by generating yields in excess of the interest rate promised to employee participants.

11. The risk with respect to investments is on the employer. However, it is based on short-term projected returns.

The major advantage to the employer is the accrual is based on annual earnings instead of final average pay. This design feature usually results in a lower pension expense to the employer, particularly compared to the pension costs of long-service employees participating in a DBP.[89] The CBP does not rely on employee contributions and, because it is portable and available in a lump sum, it is quite attractive to the new workforce.[90]

---

the pension landscape? Center for Retirement Research at Boston College, Issue Brief, Number 14. The authors conclude that, while CBPs have a high appeal among a mobile workforce and reward median instead of long service compared to a DBP, they yield lower benefits for longer-term employees.

89. See, however, Schieber, S. (2003). *The shift to hybrid pensions by U.S. employers: An empirical analysis of actual plan conversions.* Pension Research Council Working Paper 2003-23. Philadelphia: The Wharton School. This paper indicates that cost savings have been negligible to employers who convert, especially since employers converting their DBP to a CBP allowed substantial "grandfathering" of benefits.

90. Cahill, K., & Soto, M. (2003).

Notwithstanding, there have been some legal problems with cash balance plans that arise as a result of the employer's action to convert his workers from a DBP to the new CBP.

If an employer grandfathers his existing workforce in a predecessor plan and then applies a CBP to his new hires, there is usually no legal problem. The legal problem arises when the employer attempts to convert his existing participant group who is in a DBP, for example, to a CBP. The question becomes, which employees must transfer and what will the opening balance of their CBPs be? Logically, the opening balance should be the accrued benefit of the employee participant's DBP. Several lawsuits were filed by participants whose plans were converted, and they argued the method of calculating the balance is unfair and adversely affects participants protected by the Age Discrimination in Employment Act (ADEA).[91] Employers, typically, used several approaches in converting to the CBP and in calculating the opening balance.

First, they allow those participants over a certain age to maintain their participation in the DBP, a practice called grandfathering. Younger participants, in such cases, were required to transfer. At least for a period of time, the employer could be operating with two pension plans. Some employers, in calculating the opening balance of the CBP account, decided to first determine what the balance would have been had the employee participated in the CBP from the inception of his work experience. If the account balance, consisting of the accrued benefits from the DBP, were more than this hypothetical account, the employer did not add any new contributions to the account until the two amounts were equal. This technique was called *wear away* and essentially consisted of permitting the transferred accrued benefit amount to wear away in the new CBP until it equaled the hypothetical CBP amount. Sponsors of the new CBPs that were replacing a DBP were accused of improperly using disparate interest rate assumptions when they calculated the value of the future stream of

---

91. In the case of *Cooper v. IBM Personal Pension Plan*, 274 F. Supp. 2d. 1010 (S.D. IL 2003), the Court held that certain practices used by employers, as discussed in the text above, to establish the opening balance violated the ADEA. The Court held that older employees under a CBP would accrue lower account balances than younger employees because of lower interest compounding on their accounts. Since DBPs are not affected by interest compounding but, instead, final average pay, the Court found that such a practice violates the ADEA. The legal controversy of the CBPs is abating. The U.S. Court of Appeals (7th Cir. 2006) overruled the Cooper case. *Cooper v. IBM Personal Pension Plan*, 457 F3d 636 (7th Cir. 2006). Moreover, the Pension Protection Act of 2006 affirmed the legality of CBPs, prospectively, but did outlaw the wear away and the whipsaw process of calculating lump sums. In spite of the favorable legal ruling by the circuit court and the change in the law, the IBM decision slowed the spread of CBPs among cautious and prudent employers who were concerned about whether they would pass legal muster.

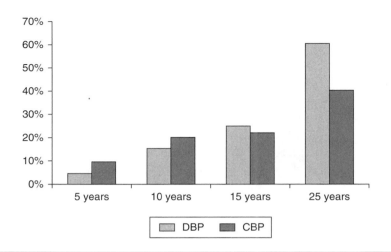

Figure 4.7   The Long-Term Difference in Final Pay Replacement
                  Percentages Between a CBP and DBP

NOTE: Figure 4.7 involves a general comparison on the replacement
income generated by both plans. You will note that in the early years, the
CBP outpaces the DBP, but for long-term employment, the replacement rate
is higher for the CBP. These are hypothetical numbers used for illustration
purposes only.

annuities under the DBP and discounting it to a lump sum. This was
called *whipsawing.*

   These practices, as well as the general proposition that older workers who
were converted to a CBP would have fewer years to accumulate their annual
account balances with resulting lower compounding of their accounts than
younger workers, led some to believe that the CBP was inherently violative
of the ADEA. These legal problems inhibited the popularity of CBPs for
several years. Most legal issues, however, have been resolved in the courts
and by the passage of the Pension Protection Act of 2006.

   Cash balance plans do have some inherent attraction to employers. For
one thing, they fit comfortably into an employer strategy that seeks some
reduction in pension expense and risk. And they assist recruitment
because they meet the special needs of the new, mobile workforce. By
offering portability and the opportunity for employees to see and better
understand their account balance, many employers are convinced that
CBPs are highly valued by employees.[92]

   Some employers, however, have changed their CBP designs to encourage more mid-level and even longer service.[93] This can be done by

92. Cahill, K., & Soto, M. (2003).

93. Another hybrid plan that is not frequently found among sponsoring employers is a Pension Equity Plan. This is a defined benefit plan that provides an

increasing the annual contribution or the annual interest rate earned on the account balances as the years of service increase. It can stimulate longer service, but does add cost to the plan. In the end, however, by using annual earnings to calculate a benefit instead of final average pay, longer-service employees typically will earn lower pensions than they could have earned under a traditional DBP.

PROFIT SHARING RETIREMENT PLANS

The evolution of pension plans has taken some twists and turns as new business models and human resources strategies have emerged. A special type of DCP, called a profit sharing retirement plan, maximizes employer flexibility by relying on profits to finance the plan. It has a long history. First introduced among many large employers in the 1940s, these plans continue today. Basically, they send a message to employees: If we do well, you will do well. Company results are used to fund this type of retirement plan.

> Pomodoro Pasta Products, Inc., a manufacturer of pasta sauce, has employed Art Carey for 20 years. The firm offers a profit sharing retirement plan to its workers. It is the exclusive retirement benefit and is totally paid for by Pomodoro. Art contributes nothing. Each year Pomodoro has put the equivalent of a percentage of Art's pay into this plan, where it is then converted to company stock. As Art's service has increased, so has the contribution to his account. This year it will be 20 percent of his compensation. The stock price has doubled about every six years. From time to time, Art has thought about retiring early; he already has over $2 million in his account. But it is difficult to leave when the employer's contribution and the stock price keep going up. Perhaps he will stick around a few more years.

A profit sharing retirement plan allows the employer to establish a portion of earned profits to be allocated to the retirement accounts of its

---

annuity or lump sum at the termination of an employee's employment. There is no actuarial reduction for early retirement, but an employee earns an increasing percentage of final pay with age. Thus, a person who works in the later years could earn a higher portable benefit than one who is younger, even though they both worked the same number of years and had equal final pay. For an interesting description of a Pension Equity Plan, see Green, L. (2003, October 29). *What is a pension equity plan?* U.S. Department of Labor, Bureau of Labor Statistics, http://www.bls.gov/.

participating employees.[94] All the basic design features of a DCP—eligibility, vesting, coverage, various retirement ages, and insulation from creditors—are part of the design. If there are no profits, there is usually no contribution.[95] In the case of a profit sharing retirement plan, no monies are distributed until the employee reaches retirement age. Since employers sponsoring these types of plans and employees participating in them are given favored tax treatment,[96] the Internal Revenue Code limits the amount of profits that can be allocated to them. Currently, this amount is 25 percent of compensation, or $46,000 per participant in 2008.[97] In most cases, the employee's profit share is allocated to his account by dividing the employee's earnings by total employee earnings and multiplying this amount times the total profit allocated for the plan. In other plans, the allocation is based on a percentage of compensation that increases with years of service. Table 4.5 illustrates some examples.

Typically, profit sharing allocations to the participants are immediately converted to company securities. As the stock appreciates in value and dividends are paid, the account balance will increase. Conversely, if there is a price drop and no dividends are earned, the value of the account will decline. Unlike a DBP where company stock cannot exceed 10 percent of fund assets, profit sharing retirement plan accounts can comprise 100 percent of company stock. The employer sponsor, however, must allow the participant to gradually diversify his account portfolio, and sell the company stock in exchange for other equity after reaching age 55.[98] Distributions are normally made in lump sums.

---

94. In some cases, profit sharing plans are not retirement plans but, instead, distribute cash annually to its participants. Also, it is possible to have a profit sharing plan in a nonprofit enterprise. In such a case, contributions can be made when there is an operating surplus.

95. The IRS does, however, allow a limited profit sharing distribution in nonprofit years. See Choosing a Retirement Plan: Profit Sharing Plan at http://www.irs.gov/retirement.

96. The employer can take a deduction and the allocation and appreciation are tax deferred to the employee. Ibid.

97. See §415 of the Internal Revenue Code. The $46,000 limit will be subject to cost of living adjustments in future years. The employee can be permitted to make after-tax contributions to a profit sharing plan, and the plan can be integrated with Social Security. Also, 25 percent of total compensation represents the limits on the employer's deductions for profit sharing plans. The early distribution penalties (pre 59.5 years of age) and mandatory distribution rules (post 70.5 years) are applicable to profit sharing plans. Similarly, all of the same rules are applicable to other defined contribution plans such as the ESOP that is discussed infra.

98. ERISA and the IRC require profit sharing plans funded with company stock and employee stock ownership plans (ESOP) to allow participants who are at least 55 years old and have ten years of service to diversify over a five-year period

Table 4.5   Three Formulas Used to Allocate Annual Profit Sharing Retirement Plan
Amounts to Employees

Formula 1: (profit sharing plan allocation) × (individual employee compensation ÷
total employee compensation) = individual's profit sharing amount for the year.

Formula 2: 25% × (individual employee's total compensation) = annual profit sharing
allocation. (The amount cannot exceed Section 415 limits.)

Formula 3: Using Formula 1 above, the employer can provide additional credit for
years of service, provided the amount does not exceed 415 limits and does not
improperly favor highly compensated employees.

NOTE: For a concise explanation of profit sharing plans see Employee Benefits Research
Institute (2005). *Fundamentals of Employee Benefit Programs, Profit Sharing Plans,* Chapter 6, http://www.ebri.org/.

   With respect to risk, these plans place the longevity and investment
risks on the employee. Additionally, since the employer's contribution is
based on making a profit, the employer enjoys significant financial flexibility and can avoid a fixed obligation to contribute to the plan. If stock
price appreciation and dividends earned in the profit sharing retirement
plan are insufficient to finance a participant's retirement, then the
employee must find other sources of retirement income.
   Profit sharing retirement plans funded with company stock are aimed
at achieving alignment. Presumably, the interests of the owners of the
company and the employees are linked, and positive employee behaviors
toward achieving higher profits are a possible outcome of this design.[99] As
we have discussed, however, an effective communication plan by the
employer demonstrating the connection between the employee's work
and the company's profits is essential. A profit sharing retirement plan is
ideally suited to an employer who wants to base the funding of his retirement plan on company results. Companies like The Procter & Gamble
Company have used this type of plan for years and it has served its human

---

up to a total of 25 percent of company stock that was acquired by the ESOP
after December 1986. After six years, they may diversify up to 50 percent of
their company stock. The Pension Protection Act of 2006, Section 901, provides
for diversification rights that must be made available with respect to employee
contributions to a company stock fund. For those with three years of company
service, they must be permitted to diversify their company stock from employer
contributions over a three-year phase-in period beginning in 2007. It also requires
the plan to offer at least three investment choices.

99. See the profit sharing plan Web site at http://www.psca.org. Once again, we
see the possibility of designing benefits to positively affect behaviors.

resources strategy well by attracting and retaining loyal employees, aligning their interests with the shareholders, and creating substantial retirement accounts for many as they left the company. A similar objective can be found in a related retirement plan called an employee stock ownership plan (ESOP).[100]

EMPLOYEE ALIGNMENT—THE EMPLOYEE STOCK OWNERSHIP PLAN

> Tom Meyer, VP of human resources at Kugler Markets, has a problem. His company's employees are represented by a union, and their wages and benefits are much higher than those offered by their competitors. Kugler is unable to pass these high labor costs on to its customers in the form of higher prices without losing market share, so they must find a way to reduce labor costs and avoid price increases. Meyer knows the union will resist wage rollbacks or benefit cuts, but he has an idea. What if the union agreed to exchange a cut in pay for higher pension benefits? And what if the pension plan was totally funded by company stock? Meyer thought his plan might achieve several objectives, such as reducing labor costs, keeping its prices competitive, and creating a new loyalty and alignment among the workforce. Perhaps the answer is an employee stock ownership plan (ESOP).

There is an obvious human resources strategy with ESOPs. Namely, put a lot of stock in employee retirement accounts and achieve a strategic link between owners and employees. In an ESOP there is no requirement for an employer contribution, but if one is made, it is company stock. The contribution can be made regardless of profits but, like the profit sharing plan, stock is allocated to employee accounts on a tax-favored basis, and taxable distributions will be made upon reaching retirement age. The standard ERISA rules and design features with respect to eligibility, establishment of a trust fund, vesting, coverage, reporting, and disclosure apply. Similar to the profit sharing plan, the total amount contributed to an ESOP cannot exceed 25 percent of the total payroll. Social Security integration or offsets are not permitted in an ESOP.

---

100. For a revealing look at ESOPs, see the ESOP Association Web site at http://www.esopassociation.com/. See also the U.S. Labor Department's definition of an ESOP at 29 CFR 2550.407d-6 (2005), and also see 401(a) of the Internal Revenue Code.

A unique opportunity available to an employer sponsor of an ESOP is the ability to borrow money to fund the plan. This is called a leveraged ESOP. Typically, the company arranges for a loan from a financial institution or bank and then purchases shares of its own stock. As it pays off the loan, the company allocates the shares of stock to the participants' accounts based on a compensation formula used in a profit sharing plan. The employer can deduct the payments on the loan.

This brings us back to Tom Meyer. Kugler could propose employee wage rollbacks in order to survive a particularly difficult competitive period. The rollbacks would be considered a loan by the employees that, over time, would be paid back in the form of company stock placed into a retirement ESOP. If the stock price increases, so does the value of the employees' accounts. The employees' sacrifice would be compensated by an increase in retirement benefits. In this case the leveraged ESOP could be used to facilitate a major cost reduction for the employer, yet provide a potentially substantial and fair return to the employees.

There is a downside to an ESOP. First, it has an adverse impact on existing shareholders. Their ownership interest in the company is diluted by the distribution of new shares, even though the shares are purchased with lower labor costs and higher productivity made possible by the employees' actions. Second, the employees are forced to have all their eggs in one

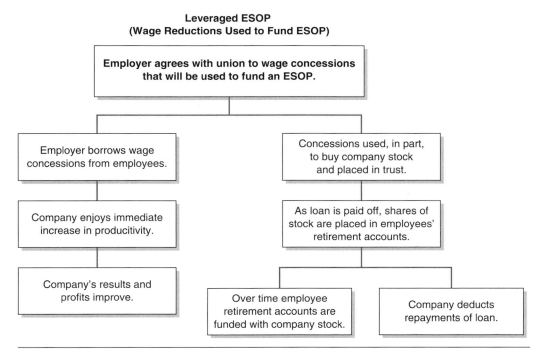

Figure 4.8   Example of a Special Leveraged ESOP Designed for a Collective Bargaining Environment

basket. This presents a real investment risk to the employee. The employer, on the other hand, can achieve significant flexibility in its funding of the plan, reduce its pension expense, and take advantage of additional deductions by borrowing. As with the profit sharing plan funded exclusively with company stock, participants over age 55 who have participated in the plan for more than ten years can diversify their ESOP account by selling up to 25 percent of their company stock over a five-year period.[101]

Evolution and the Small Employer

A variety of employer-sponsored retirement plans have evolved over the years. Each plan design is unique and new employer benefit strategies can be achieved by adjusting design features of a previous generation of benefit plans. The evolutionary process has been driven by the need to provide more cost-effective plans and to offer plans that are consistent with the external competitive labor market of the employer and the demographics and lifecycle needs of the workforce. Size of the employer is also relevant to this evolution. What about smaller employers: Are the traditional designs described above too complex to administer or beyond their financial capacity to support? In the following chapter, we will discuss retirement plans for smaller employers as well as some general strategies and principles relating to retirement planning.

Chapter Exercises

1. A prime objective in creating ESOPs and other DCPs, which facilitate company stock ownership, is to create alignment among the participants. The question is, does this happen? How would you assess and measure the impact such plans have on alignment? What research would you initiate and how would you go about evaluating the efficacy of employee ownership plans?[102]

2. Contact a parent, sibling, relative, or friend and ask him to describe his employer, job position, and retirement plan at his place of employment. In your discussion with him, identify all the relevant features of the plan, including the precise type of benefit plan, eligibility, vesting, retirement age, any supplemental plans,

---

101. See footnote 98, supra.

102. See the research and statistics compiled by the National Center for Employee Ownership at http://www.nceo/org/.

the relative financial strength or experience of the plan, investment options, and other design issues. Then determine whether there have been any events or circumstances that have affected your relative or friend's plans for retirement. Explain them. Finally, briefly discuss how the retirement plan fits into the company's business strategy.

3. Your company currently offers a defined benefit plan using the following formula for retirement benefits at age 65: final average pay, years of service, and a 2 percent replacement income factor. There is a 2 percent actuarial reduction per year for retirement between the ages of 55 (the earliest date on which one can retire) and 65. There is no actuarial cost for the mandatory 50 percent spouse option arising from age variations between the spouses. Your CFO considers the plan too costly. You decide to keep the DBP as is for your current employees, but offer a modified DBP for new hires. The new hire plan will continue to encourage long and productive service, but will reduce the cost to the company. Briefly identify and describe three appropriate design changes you would make for the new hire plan that would best generate these results.

4. An executive of a company that offers a traditional and qualified defined benefit plan is now 65 years old and applies for retirement. His average final pay is $150,000 and his average final bonus is $75,000. The DBP uses a 2 percent income replacement factor, credits for all years of service, and allows for full retirement at age 65. The executive has 30 years of service and is fully vested. Calculate the pension he will receive from the qualified defined benefit plan.

5. Check the features of ESOPs and profit sharing plans at http://www.esopassociation.org, and http://www.psca.org, and the National Center for Employee Ownership, http://www.nceo.org/, and describe the features and differences between the two types of retirement plans.

6. You are a 62-year-old executive considering early retirement. You participate in a defined benefit plan that uses the average of the high three out of the last five years' final pay. Pay includes bonuses representing about 50 percent of your salary when results are good. For the last two years, however, business results have been poor and you have received no bonus in this period. You expect next year to be the same. The company uses a 3 percent actuarial reduction per year for retirement before age 65. Briefly describe the pros and cons of retiring now.

7. Check the University of California (U.C.) Web site at http://atyourservice.ucop.edu. Under U.C. Retirement Plan Benefit Estimator (go to the Web site, select retirement calculators, and choose U.C. Retirement Plan Benefit Estimate), select three different sets of variables in the boxes provided and do the same for the section on survivors. Describe the outcomes of your calculations and briefly summarize your analysis and conclusions.

8. Under the same U.C. plan, check the Summary Plan Description for the retirement plan and answer the following questions: What would happen if you died before retiring under this plan? How is sick leave credited to the pension? If a person elects a lump sum payout, what is forfeited under the plan? What is the benefit formula in this DBP? Is there a COLA? How does it work? What is the age factor? Then look at the Summary Plan Description of the University's DCP, the 403(b) plan. Who is eligible to participate in the 403(b)? Does U.C. match employee contributions? Can a participant borrow money from his 403(b)? What happens when one distributes the 403(b) savings? What happens if a participant dies before the 403(b) fund is distributed?

9. Your company has a DBP. You have just learned, however, that the company provides a supplemental retirement plan to executives in addition to a DBP. The formula for both plans is identical. What is the most likely reason the supplemental plan exists? Explain.

10. An employee has come to you, the benefits manager, for advice. He is planning to retire at age 67 and will receive unreduced retirement income from the company's final average pay-type DBP. He has asked about alternative distribution options, and specifically, whether he should request a level income option. What is your response? Explain.

11. Your company offers a 401(k). Employee participation and amounts deferred in the plan are relatively low. Identify and briefly explain four appropriate 401(k) design changes that might increase participation and deferrals.

12. You are the benefits manager of the University of California's DBP. A faculty member has requested a disability retirement, explaining that his chronic low back pain has made it impossible to continue teaching. The U.C. plan treats disability retirement similarly to most basic DBPs. What advice would you give the faculty member with respect to the requirements, definitions, and retirement income available under the university's disability retirement plan?

13. You are a financial consultant and have been asked by a married couple about the joint and survivor annuity option available to the

spouse under her DBP. The question is, should her husband waive the option? Identify the three most likely reasons why the spouse might choose to make such a waiver.

14. Go to http://www.bls.gov/ and check surveys, including Employee Benefits in Private Industry and Employer Costs for Employee Compensation. You can see the relative cost of benefits as a percentage of total compensation. How would you use this information in determining which benefits to offer your employees?

15. Identify several reasons why a spouse might waive the joint and survivor pension annuity option required to be included in a DBP.

16. Some employees who retire elect to defer their retirement benefit. Why do you think they would do this? Would a deferral of the benefit increase the amount eventually received?[103] Why?

17. Should a company that wants to retain older workers consider an actuarial increase for those who work beyond normal retirement age? Is the benefits model relevant here? Think about the factors that are used in calculating a formula-based DBP.

18. Should there be a maximum age when an employee will be required to receive benefits? Would the type of plan make a difference with respect to a mandatory distribution of benefits? Who would have an interest in this issue?

19. Should an employer permit a person to retire under a DBP and then come back to work? Check the University of California's Web site at http://www.atyourservice.ucop.edu/. Review the Summary Plan Description for the DBP and determine how they provide for this opportunity.

20. Suppose two persons retire from the same company and are participants of the same DBP. Their calculated annuities are the same, but when they elected instead to receive lump sums, the amounts were different. What is the most likely reason for this difference?

21. What would happen if an employer sponsoring a final pay DBP refused to bridge the service before and after a break, but instead calculated and paid two pensions to the same employee? Would the sum of the two pensions be more or less than the pension that was calculated based on total years of service?

---

103. It should because by deferring the benefit, the employee will receive fewer annuity payments during his remaining lifetime.

Pension Plans for Small Employers and Retirement Planning

5

Evolution Reaches the Small Employer and the Self-Employed

In general, the menu of retirement plan choices, which used economies of scale for large employers, was not affordable for small to medium sized employers.[1] They were looking for plans that required less administrative resources, continued favorable tax treatment, and limited legal and tax compliance rules. One suggestion was the individual retirement account (IRA), that would be owned and managed by the employee and would require minimum administrative resources of the employer sponsor. Before looking at employer-sponsored plans that use the IRA as the repository of retirement funds, it might be helpful to know some background on IRAs.

Individual Retirement Account (IRA)

The IRA[2] is a retirement savings account with set limits that is funded by the individual.[3] It is not related to employment. A traditional IRA offers

---

1. The percentage of employees covered by a retirement plan and working in firms with fewer than 10 people was 18 percent, and with 10–24 employees, 32 percent. In total, only 27 percent of workers in businesses with 1–100 employees participated in employer-sponsored retirement plans. See *Employment-Based Retirement Plan Participation.* (October 2005). Employee Benefits Research Institute, Issue Brief #286, p. 13. Small employers, obviously, need special, more cost-effective retirement plans if they hope to be competitive in their labor market.

2. See IRC Section 219(a) et seq. and Section 408A.

3. The limits for 2008 are from $53,000 (single IRS filers) to $85,000 (joint). If earnings do not exceed these amounts, an individual can contribute to an IRA even if he participates in an employer-sponsored retirement plan.

pretax contributions, and earnings are tax deferred until the funds are distributed. While the contribution limit for an IRA is low,[4] if a contribution involves a lawful rollover of funds from a tax-deferred retirement account, such as a 401(k), the limit does not apply.

A Roth IRA is an after-tax personal savings instrument. The allowable contribution is similar to the traditional IRA, but there are higher adjusted gross income limits and one is not excluded from contributing if he also participates in a qualified retirement plan.[5] In addition, since contributions comprise after-tax monies, the distribution of funds and earnings at retirement is tax-exempt.[6]

The Roth 401(k) is a plan that must be sponsored by an employer in order for an individual to participate. Employer matches cannot be made to a Roth 401(k). If the employer chooses to match an employee's contributions, the match must be placed in a special, pretax account. When the money is later withdrawn, it will be taxed as ordinary income. The contribution limits are the same as those applicable to the 401(k), and there are catch-ups permitted for employees over age 50. As in the case of the Roth IRA, the distribution of funds is tax-exempt provided the employee has had the account for more than five years and is over 59.5 years old when the distribution is received.[7] Let's discuss some plans that use IRAs as their centerpiece.

Savings Incentive Match Plan for Employees of Small Employers (SIMPLE)

One plan that has best met the needs of smaller employers is the savings incentive match plan for employees. Available to employers with no more than 100 employees,[8] its basic design features are:

- Eligible employees must have minimum earnings per year in order to participate.[9]

- The employer establishes an IRA for each participant.

---

4. For 2008, the contribution limit is $5,000, but $6,000 for an individual over the age of 50.

5. The 2008 adjusted gross income limits are $101,000 for single taxpayers and $159,000 for joint filers. For persons earning above these amounts, the IRA allowable contribution is proportionately reduced.

6. Distributions cannot be made before age 59.5 without a tax penalty; for Roth IRAs there are no required minimum distributions at age 70.5.

7. See, generally, IRC Section 402A.

8. The SIMPLE was created by the Small Business Job Protection Act of 1996, IRC §408(p).

9. For 2007, the minimum earnings are $5,000.

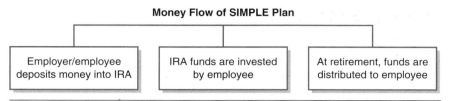

Figure 5.1 General Structure and Money Flow of the SIMPLE Plan
NOTE: IRA used as funding vehicle.

- The employee directs the investments in the IRA.

- The employee can contribute 100 percent of his compensation up to a designated annual maximum, and it is fully vested. The maximum contribution is adjusted for inflation and changes each year.[10]

- The employer must match up to 100 percent of the employee's deferral up to a limit of 3 percent of the employee's salary. Or, the employer must contribute 2 percent of every employee's salary, whether or not they elect to participate in the plan.

- Vesting is immediate for both the employer and employee contributions.

- The account is portable.

- There are catch-up contribution opportunities for employees over age 50.

- The SIMPLE provides favored tax treatment for both employer and employee.[11]

The SIMPLE plan is ideal for the small employer.[12] Compliance with ERISA and the IRC is relatively uncomplicated. There is no discrimination testing required, so the employer does not have to conduct annual tests to assure the IRS that there is no disparate rate of participation in contributions between nonhighly compensated and highly compensated employees in his workforce.[13]

---

10. In 2008, the maximum employee contribution was $10,500. It is indexed annually for inflation in $500 increments.

11. For a concise explanation of SIMPLE, see the U.S. Labor Department's explanation at http://www.dol.gov/ebsa/publications/easy_retirement_solutions .html#section3/; also see Retirement Plans FAQs, regarding SIMPLE IRA Plans (2005), Internal Revenue Service, at http://www.irs.gov.

12. For employers with more than 100 employees, 56 percent offer some type of retirement plan.

13. See Chapter 9 for a detailed discussion of discrimination testing.

Simplified Employee Pension (SEP)

As we look across the pension plan landscape, we see a variety of other plans that are better suited for adoption by smaller employers who are looking for less complex approaches to retirement plans. One such plan is the simplified employee pension plan (SEP). In this plan only the employer can contribute on a pretax basis, unless the plan was adopted prior to 1997 when employee deferrals were permitted. Further, all employees over the age of 21 who have worked a prescribed period and earned minimum compensation must be covered.[14] The essential design features of an SEP[15] are:

- The maximum allowable contribution that can be made by the employer is 15 percent of the employee's compensation per year with an annual indexed cap.

- The employer contribution is immediately vested.

- The account is portable.

- The employer contribution is made to an IRA and the investments are self-directed by the employee.

- The employer may elect not to contribute in a given year; there is no fixed contribution rate imposed.

- A self-employed individual can establish an SEP.

The SEP is not immune from discrimination testing; however, because it only permits employer contributions in plans initiated after 1997, testing the rate of participation among employees would not be too difficult. Since the contributions are made to an IRA, administrative costs are quite low. There are no catch-ups for participants over age 50.

For employers with more than 100 employees, who for a variety of strategic reasons want to offer a retirement plan to their employees, the SEP is an attractive and cost-effective design. Our evolution of pension plan designs includes additional retirement income plans that are more suited for small employers and the self-employed.

---

14. The minimum compensation for purposes of coverage is indexed and currently is $500. The 2008 maximum total contribution is 25 percent of up to $230,000 in salary or $46,000, whichever is less.

15. For a comprehensive explanation and design features of a SEP, see Small Business, Internal Revenue Service (2005), http://www.irs.gov/publications/. See IRC §408(k).

Money Purchase Plan

A money purchase plan, also called a targeted benefit plan, is a DCP in which employer contributions are expressed as a percentage of pay and must be made annually.[16] Similar to a DBP, the employer makes a contribution that is designed to pay a targeted benefit at retirement. While there's an intention to pay the participant, there is no guarantee or obligation to pay this benefit. Thus, the investment risk lies on the participant. The amounts contributed are considered pretax and tax deferred, and the employee participant assumes the investment and inflation risks.

Why would an employer offer such a plan? It bears some resemblance to a DBP; therefore, it gives participants a more secure idea of what they might receive at retirement age, more so than a 401(k). As a DCP, however, a money purchase plan allows portability, imposes limits on contributions, and is governed by the IRC's early and mandatory distribution rules. From a business strategy standpoint, the benefit does not encourage longer service; it only commits the employer to make a contribution, not guarantee a stated benefit. The plan is subject to the requirements of ERISA and must conform to the nondiscrimination provisions of the IRC.

The Keogh

A Keogh is ideally suited for the self-employed. A business owner can fund his own DBP or DCP plan. The compensation and benefit limits relating to a DBP and the contribution limits for DCPs under §415 are applicable.[17] One special advantage to the owner of the business is the deductibility

---

16. For a concise explanation of Money Purchase Plans, see Choosing a Retirement Plan: Money Purchase Plan (2005), Internal Revenue Service, at http://www.irs.gov. There are others; for example, a thrift plan is a type of DCP that is similar to a profit sharing plan but participants are required to make contributions. The employer sponsor matches these in whole or in part, and the contributions are placed in a trust fund and invested. Contributions are limited to 25 percent of compensation with a current maximum of $46,000 per year. The employee participant has an account representing his share of the fund, much like a profit sharing plan, and is paid this amount when he retires.

17. The contribution limits, however, use earned income instead of compensation. For 2008, the limit is 25 percent of earned income of the business or $46,000, whichever is less.

Table 5.1   Examples of Business Factors That Can Affect the Selection of Certain Retirement Plans by Employers

Factor	DBP	401(k)	Profit Sharing	Cash Balance	ESOP	SIMPLE	SEP
Young workers		X		X		X	
Mature workers	X		X				
Competition industry	X	X	X	X	X	X	X
Few employees						X	X
Many employees	X	X	X	X	X		
Cost a major issue		X		X	X	X	X
Affect behavior			X		X		
Financial flexibility			X		X		
Simple administration						X	X

of the funds deposited in the plan trust. Lawful contributions are tax deductible and the interest and investment returns on these amounts are tax deferred until the retirement funds are distributed. There are early distribution limits before age 59.5 and mandatory minimum distribution requirements beginning at age 70.5.[18] In the case of a money purchase Keogh, which is essentially a DCP, the sponsor must contribute annually and meet the funding requirements of ERISA. In a profit sharing Keogh, the contribution is discretionary and can change each year.

We will discuss Social Security and multi-employer plans, which are jointly managed by a union and an employer pursuant to a collective bargaining agreement, in Chapters 12 and 14, respectively. We have not specifically discussed the various types of retirement plans sponsored by

---

18. Keogh plans can include employees of the firm as well as the owner. The administrative expense, however, increases disproportionately in such cases and the employer might be better off choosing a SIMPLE or 401(k) plan. Whole life insurance can be used to fund benefits in a Keogh, but that portion of the premium applicable to the payment of a death benefit is not tax deductible. See IRC Sections 4975(f)(6), 404(a)(3)(A), 401(a)(7), 415(c)(1), and 402(g)(8). For a simple explanation of Keogh plans, search http://www.quicken.com/. Keoghs and other retirement plans for the self-employed and small employers can be purchased from various investment companies. See, for example, T. Rowe Price's products and services at http://www.troweprice.com/.

public employers, such as 403(b) and 457 plans. They are nearly identical to the traditional DCPs we discussed in Chapter 4.[19] Curiously, DBPs have continued to survive in the public sector. Although some are experiencing some funding problems for the same reasons we find in the private sector, there has been no mass exodus toward DCPs in the public sector. We discuss this phenomenon below, but first let's examine some of the circumstances that might lead an employer to select one type of pension plan over another. Here is a table that might be useful in identifying these circumstances and factors.

Contemporary Issues in Retirement

MIGRATION FROM DBPs TO DCPs

There are a number of current issues creating some concern, particularly among participants of employer-sponsored retirement plans. First, there is a decline in the number of DBPs being offered, particularly by private employer sponsors. Many plans that were affected by lower than expected investment returns experienced a funding crisis necessitating significant cash replenishments of their funds. Others simply froze existing accrued benefits in their DBP, or terminated their plans altogether and converted all future benefits to a DCP.[20] Some employers are pointing to the new and more aggressive minimum funding requirements of the Pension Protection Act of 2006 as a reason they are migrating from DBPs to DCPs.

While the funding crisis has not been entirely averted among public employer plans, we have not seen a similar move from DBPs to DCPs in the public sector.[21] There are many reasons for this. First, benefits have been the hallmark of public employment and have an important role in attracting and retaining schoolteachers and city, state, and county

---

19. For an excellent comparison of these public plans, see Retirement Plan Comparison Chart (2007), Ice Miller, LLP, at http://www.icemiller.com/publications/.

20. There are three approaches to freezing a plan: (1) all accrued benefits are vested, but there are no future accruals; (2) no new employees are enrolled in the plan, but current employees continue to accrue future benefits; (3) future accruals are ceased, but the benefit calculation at retirement is based on final pay at retirement, not at the time of the freeze. See Pension Freezes (2007), Pension Rights Center, at http://www.pensionrights.org/.

21. It should be noted that many public employee retirement plans are funded with both employer and employee contributions, making them somewhat financially stronger than a typical DBP.

employees whose salaries and wages are perceived to be below those of similarly situated employees in the private sector. Thus, there is a cultural factor driving the perpetuation of certain benefits such as DBPs. Researchers have suggested that many public employees are older, less mobile, and more risk averse. This type of worker is not comfortable with DCPs in which key risks are placed on the participant. Also, unions represent many public employees, making it impossible for employers to make substantial pension plan changes without submitting their proposal to collective bargaining.[22]

SPECIAL EARLY RETIREMENT PLANS

Employers seeking to downsize their workforce have used their defined benefit plans to finance early retirement incentives, further weakening the long-term funding of these plans.[23] And many active employees who are involved with merging or acquired companies have found the integration of benefits often results in a change of retirement plans and a lowering of their total pension benefits.[24] Moreover, the aging and longevity of the workforce and an accompanying weakening of capital markets have adversely affected the funding while increasing the liabilities of many DBPs. This has put a serious financial strain on the Pension Benefit Guarantee Corporation (PBGC) the agency that insures benefits for employees affected by a plan's insolvency.[25]

Others have converted their participants from a DBP to a cash balance plan (CBP). With the passage of the Pension Protection Act of 2006, which clarified some of the legal issues concerning CBPs and increased the

22. Munnell, A., Haverstick, K., & Soto, M. (December 2007). *Why have defined benefits survived in the public sector?* Center for Retirement Research at Boston College, http://www.bc.edu/crr/. The authors also point out that public employer plans are not covered by some provisions of ERISA, which requires more rigorous funding levels and other administrative compliance.

23. The impact may be indirect, as we have seen in the auto industry where legacy benefits including expensive retiree health care benefits have impeded the employer's ability to finance his retirement plans. Some have transferred their entire retiree health care obligation to a special fund, called a voluntary employee benefit plan (VEBA), by depositing the present value of their liability into the fund.

24. In the case of mergers, a significant objective is to integrate a variety of processes including compensation and benefit plans. This can mean moving one group out of their current retirement plan into a more cost-effective plan.

25. See Lowenstein, R. (2005, October 30). The end of pensions. *New York Times Sunday Magazine*, p. 56. See Ghilarducci, T., & Jeszeck, C. (2007). Retirement, pensions, and managing one's own money. *Contemporary Issues in Employment Relations* (D. Levin, Ed.)., Ithaca, NY: ILR Press, pp. 223–249.

funding obligations of DBPs, one might expect a new wave of interest in CBPs among employers. The majority of employers, however, who are looking to change their pension obligations, have moved to 401(k) plans as their exclusive retirement plan.[26] This presents a new problem.

PERSISTENT LOW SAVINGS RATES AND HIGHER LIVING COSTS

The erosion of DBPs and conversion to DCPs has not sparked the anticipated savings rate increases among U.S. participants. There are consistently low participation and savings rates among employees and, to remedy this problem, many employers are moving to unilateral or non-elective enrollments. It is estimated that 66.6 percent of workers who are 55 or older have saved, on average, less than $50,000.[27] Some employers are reducing their DCP matches even though matches are critical to encourage participation.[28] Further, since the financial market adjustments of early 2000, the expected returns on DCP investments are lower than those experienced in the pre-2000 market. Consequently, it takes more savings to generate sufficient retirement income. Meanwhile retirement expenses are rising.

This is all occurring in an environment where employers are terminating retiree health care and placing the burden on their retirees to find ways to insure their pre-Medicare eligibility years and to pay for Medicare supplemental insurance.[29] So, with lower retirement benefits, longer life expectancies, and higher potential living costs,[30] the employee may decide to delay retirement or retire and take another job.[31]

---

26. According to some commentators, with a consistent contribution of 15 percent of earnings by the employee, a 100 percent match by the employer, and a reasonable investment return, a 401(k) can generate about 75 percent of the value of a standard DBP. See Quinn, J. B. (2006, July 3). A requiem for pensions. *Newsweek*, http://www.msnbc.com/.

27. See http://www.bizjournals.com/, Washington Bureau. (2006, July 17). American City Business Journals, Inc.

28. Even, W., & Macpherson, D. (2005).

29. See *Yolton v. El Paso Tennessee Pipeline Co.*, 435 F.3rd 571 (6th Cir. 2006).

30. For example, between the years 1985 and 2005, for persons between the ages of 65 and 74, housing expenditures rose by 22.5 percent, while health care spending rose 40 percent. This was substantially higher than the same expenses for lower age groups. See *Consumer spending by older Americans, 1985–2005.* (2007, September 24). Congressional Research Service.

31. *Working after retirement: A gap between expectations and reality.* (2006). New York: Pugh Research Center.

SOME IDEAS TO SIMPLIFY EMPLOYER-SPONSORED PLANS

There is an obvious need to simplify the legal and administrative burdens imposed on employer sponsors of pension plans. Propelled by a series of legislated tax policies, we have a crazy quilt of plans that seem to overlap each other or fill some special occasion. This quilt is accompanied by a complex set of rules with respect to plan designs, income and contribution limits, and circumstances permitting their use. We should consider simplifying retirement plan designs. There are current legislative proposals to produce a single, tax-favored DCP retirement plan with common design features and minimal legal restrictions and rules. This would simplify the administration of plans and perhaps lead to a willingness among small and medium sized employers to offer a retirement plan to their employees.[32] There are more fundamental, value-driven approaches to consider.

1. Defined benefit plans that require both employer and employee contributions often can maintain a more sound financial footing, generate higher pension benefits, and mitigate the heavy cost to the sponsoring employer.[33] We rarely see such funding approaches, except in the public sector.

2. There is some inherent, economic inefficiency in offering DCPs where each participant makes savings rate, allocation, and investment decisions. Contrast this splintered process with the investment activities of a DBP where professional money managers decide where and how to invest.

3. We should consider eliminating opportunities among participants or sponsors to use plan funds for any purpose other than to finance a retirement benefit. This means to put very tight restrictions on loans and hardship withdrawals.

4. Most benefits should be distributed through deferred, inflation-adjusted annuities that cover spouses and other beneficiaries. This

32. The Bush administration proposed a comprehensive reform approach consolidating all the various tax-qualified DCPs into three types of plans: the employee retirement savings account (related to employment only and based on 401(k) and 403(b) rules), the retirement savings account (a personal savings vehicle using a Roth-type tax treatment and a $7,500 limit per year), and a lifetime savings account (limit of $7,500 per year), all of which would have common and simplified design features and limited legal restrictions and limits. For an analysis of the Bush proposals, see *Administration's Retirement Savings Proposals.* (2003, August 13). American Academy of Actuaries.

33. See, for example, the Arizona State Retirement System, a multi-employer plan requiring equal contributions from both employer and employee, at http://www.azasrs.gov. It is well funded and provides generous benefits.

approach would simplify, better secure, and satisfy the retirement needs of the workforce on a cost-effective basis.[34] These issues have made planning for retirement more difficult for many. What follows is a brief review of some of the retirement planning issues and strategies that might be helpful to both plan sponsors and participants.

Retirement Planning—Will Your Employee Have Enough to Retire?

PRINCIPLES AND STRATEGIES FOR RETIREMENT PLANNING

"During those morning commutes, I secretly agonized over whether I had enough money socked away to be so casually employed. I was worried about the Number. . . . What are the chances you will live out your days in comfort? What happens if you don't make it to your Number?"[35]

Perhaps the most often asked question among those contemplating retirement is, "Will I have enough money to retire?"[36] For nearly all of Chapter 4, as well as this chapter, we have discussed how to aggregate retirement funds in DBPs, DCPs, and individual investment accounts. From the early years of employment up to retirement, an individual accumulates sources of retirement income, hoping he has enough. Then, when he does retire, the process is reversed and he begins to disaggregate those funds. In this section we will talk about how you know if you have sufficient funds to retire, and how best to disaggregate the funds you have accumulated (see Figure 5.1). But first, when do you want to retire, and what are your objectives in retirement? Following are some points to consider.

1. Most of the tax deferrals a person has enjoyed on the run up to retirement will disappear. As one begins to receive his pension, he

---

34. See editor comment, Rethinking employee benefits, Part 3: Should pensions be voluntary? (2006, Spring). *Benefits Law Journal, 19*(1).

35. Eisenberg, L. (2006). *The number.* New York: The Free Press, pp. xi, 3. This is a comprehensive and thought-provoking book, taking the reader through a step-by-step process in determining whether one has enough retirement income to comfortably retire and illustrating how one can arrive at "the number" needed to achieve such a result.

36. For a comprehensive and enlightening discussion of this issue and how it can be managed, see Richardson, A. (2003, September/October). Retirement Blues. *Contingencies*, pp. 19–29. The author discusses life expectancy risk, investment risk, and inflation risk and reviews the pros and cons of buying an annuity.

will be taxed at ordinary income rates; thus, it is important to view pension assets and funds on an after-tax basis. Also, one should consider minimizing the adverse tax consequences of fund disaggregation as much as possible.

2. Calculating the sufficiency of one's retirement assets should take into consideration life expectancy, which may be longer than one thinks.[37] The most common mistake people make is not to realize they may outlive their retirement benefits.

3. The expected investment returns on pension savings should exceed the expected inflation rate; otherwise, the benefit will be consumed by inflation. So, while one may become somewhat more conservative in investing near or during retirement, some solid returns are necessary in order to avoid degrading your funds.[38]

4. The retirement income that one needs is often expressed as a percentage of final pay. This is not entirely true. The amount a person really needs in retirement should be calculated by estimating projected expenses in retirement, determining the rate of inflation, and projecting how long one is going to live.

5. With respect to investing one's funds in a DCP or in a personal investment account(s), following are some simple approaches: (1) the prospective retiree should have a properly balanced portfolio, continually adjusting allocation of equity and fixed income investments; (2) make a practice of reinvesting dividends and interest earned on this portfolio during the aggregation phase; (3) become familiar with, and possibly utilize, the variety of retirement instruments, such as IRAs, bonds, and trusts, that shelter savings from taxes.

6. There are a number of taxable and tax-deferred investment strategies that also should be considered. For example, some investment vehicles offer significant growth opportunity and flexibility and are subject to a lower tax rate. While there are significant advantages to a 401(k) due to the tax deferral feature, when the distribution of

---

37. This life expectancy factors include age, sex, medical history, and lifestyle.

38. A Hewitt study showed that a minimum 6 percent of pay savings rate, an investment return of 4 percent over inflation, and long service at one employer resulting in a high payout of the company's DBP were three key factors contributing to a successful retirement, defined as providing 95 percent replacement income. See Total Retirement Income at Large Companies—The Real Deal. (2003). Hewitt Associates, LLC. Other financial planners suggest that properly balanced investment portfolios including seven asset classifications can generate acceptably low volatility and respectably high returns. Laise, E. (2008, January 16). Protecting your nest egg in volatile times. *The Wall Street Journal*, D1.

funds occurs all monies are taxed as ordinary income. This is so even though much of the growth of the 401(k) has involved capital gains and dividends that are currently taxed at 15 percent. Also, in a private investment account, the owner is free to invest in any fund or security and is not limited by the options made available by the employer sponsor. Thus, there is a danger of overstuffing one's 401(k). This is especially true when the employer does not offer a match to the employee's contribution.

7. Timing is everything. Is the person emotionally ready to retire? Are earnings at a point where one can gain significant value from a DBP or a DCP by retiring now? Are there better years ahead that might warrant postponing retirement?[39]

8. It is vital for the prospective retiree to develop an updated estate plan to make sure that dependents, survivors, and heirs are taken into consideration.[40]

9. It is a good idea to consider a rollover of your 401(k) assets into an IRA at retirement. In most cases when accomplished in accordance with IRA rules to preserve the tax-qualified status, such a move affords more investment choices and more flexibility in transferring the assets at death.

10. It is prudent to place taxable assets, such as corporate bonds, stocks, and other mutual funds into the IRA in order to shelter them from taxation until withdrawal.

With these basic principles in mind, we can now answer the questions, "Do I have enough to retire?" and "Am I saving enough to finance my retirement later?" Also, there are a number of free Web site calculators that can help you find the answers. (See Chapter Exercises at the end of this chapter.) For now, let's discuss some of the issues pertaining to disaggregating your retirement funds.

The prospective retiree should think about how and when to start receiving payments from his DBP and liquidating the assets in his DCP, personal investments, and savings. Some principles that apply:

---

39. Some retirement planners have established ratios that should be met at various age levels in a future retiree's work life. These ratios involve minimum savings accumulations to income, savings rates as a percentage of earnings, and limitations on debt as a percentage of earnings. Most planners are urging future retirees to save from 12 percent to 15 percent of their annual income. See Opdyke, J. (2006, July 1). Will you be able to retire? *The Wall Street Journal*, B1.

40. The estate plan should include consideration of issues such as the available marital deduction, possible joint ownership of assets, the use of irrevocable inter-vivos trusts, and direct transfers of assets to beneficiaries.

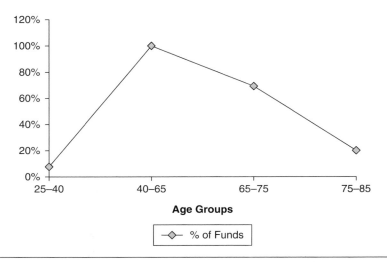

Figure 5.2   Phases of Aggregation and Disaggregation of Retirement Funds

1. Consider the best strategy with respect to taxation. As monies are taken out of the retirement accounts, the retiree should be on guard to exploit the minimum tax impact by knowing his tax bracket, being aware of the timing of the distribution, and taking advantage of tax offsets and deductions.

2. There is a well-publicized Rule of 5 (in some cases, Rule of 3 or Rule of 4) that encourages the disaggregation of funds at no more than 5 percent of the remaining balance in the accounts each year. Presumably, the funds continue to earn returns; inflation is still influencing the purchasing power of these distributions. The Rule of 5 takes these factors into consideration and allows an orderly disaggregation without running a serious risk of depleting the retirement funds before the retiree's passing.

3. Consider calculating the value of the retirement accounts as an annuity[41] and, perhaps, converting some lump sum distributions into a purchased annuity. The tools found in the Chapter Exercises include various methods used to calculate aggregate savings as annuities and expressed in terms of replacement income. For

---

41. A related option might be a bond ladder that comprises an assortment of corporate or municipal bonds, expiring at different times. The ladder allows the owner to diversify interest rates based on the current market conditions and terms of the bond, and also to generate a stream of what could be pension income for the owner retiree.

example, the Sharpe annuity worksheet[42] uses the age and sex of the saver and his beneficiaries, the expected investment returns on the savings, the appropriate discount rate used to convert an aggregate amount to a present value, the saver's expected retirement age, applicable tax rates, and expected salary increases to predict an annuity to be received in retirement. It is expressed as a percentage of final average annual pay.

ANNUITIES

Unlike life insurance, where one protects against dying too young, an annuity protects against living too long. There is an assortment of products one can purchase, but the basic economic concept is rather straightforward:

1. The prospective retiree uses part or all of his retirement savings to buy a guaranteed annual payment.

2. The payment will made during the life of the annuitant.

3. The annuity is calculated by applying the life expectancy of the annuitant as well as the expected investment returns of the purchase price or lump sum offered. The higher the earnings expectation, the larger the annuity. Similarly, the longer the life expectancy, the lower the annuity payments.

4. The cost of the annuity includes a risk premium payable to the issuer of the annuity. Why is there a premium? Where is the primary risk and who is assuming it?

5. Since there is an expected series of payments promised for the future, the fiscal soundness of the sponsoring insurance company should be a paramount consideration of the person considering the purchase of an annuity. Let's briefly discuss annuities.

There are many different kinds of annuities available. One that is popular is the immediate annuity, where the retiree simply deposits his savings and immediately starts receiving an annuity. There is a way to estimate how much you will need in order to buy an immediate annuity. It is called the Rule of 13. So, if he wants an immediate annuity of $50,000 he would have to pay $650,000 (13 × $50,000) in order to purchase it. Another is a period certain annuity that ensures there will be some residual payments made to heirs or beneficiaries in the event of a premature death. A variable annuity is one in which a person purchases the annuity well in advance of retirement; the actual investment returns on the funds, which vary based on

---

42. See http://www.wsharpe.com; worksheets, retirement worksheets.

market conditions, are applied to the amount in the years before the annuity is received. Thus, the present value of the annuity is not known until then. This minimizes one of the risks assumed by the issuing company. There are many more, and you can find references and some case problems on annuities in the Chapter Exercises at the end of this chapter.

There are many tools available to accomplish good planning. The rules, principles, and ideas outlined above should serve as a foundation, enabling employers and employees to facilitate positive retirement results for their organization's human resources.

RETIREMENT AND CONTINUED UTILIZATION OF OLDER WORKERS

Recent articles concerning the funding "crisis" among employer sponsors of retirement plans have suggested that perhaps the "new retirement" will be "to continue working." While this view may be exaggerated, it does prompt a quick review of some of the assumptions surrounding the retirement process. For example, what is magic about age 65 normal retirement? This age was set in the 1930s when Social Security was initiated and life expectancies were in the low 70s. Pension payments were made over a much shorter period of time. Now for a male age 65, there is a 47 percent chance he will live until age 85, and for a female there is a 60 percent chance. The pension liability spans a much longer period than assumed in the 1930s.

There is also a shortage of workers in the United States. When an older worker leaves his or her employment, it takes a longer period of time to replace that level of productivity. Should we be encouraging retirement at age 65? There have been numerous "early retirement windows" used by employers seeking to reduce the number of employees and cut costs. Should there be a more concerted effort to utilize the talent and experience of older workers who might want to continue working or to undergo a gradual, phased retirement? What types of employer-sponsored plans might best serve this goal?[43]

43. See Johnson, R., & Steuerle, E. (2003). *Promoting work at older ages.* Pension Research Council working paper, http://www.pensionresearchcouncil.org. The authors argue that the traditional DBP penalizes workers who continue work beyond the normal retirement age and argue that hybrid plans might be a better choice for companies searching for ways to elicit more labor supply from older adults. Also, the opportunity for more flexible work arrangements among older workers might serve employers who want to retain the talent and experience of senior employees and avoid adverse affects on productivity and economic growth. See *Older workers: Demographic trends pose challenges for employers and workers.* (2001, November). U.S. General Accounting Office, http://www.gao.gov/, Document No. GAO-02-85 Older Workers.

Table 5.2   Review of Pension Plan Design Features

	DBP	401(k)	Profit Sharing	ESOP	Hybrid	SIMPLE	SEP	Money Purchase	Keogh
Vesting	5/7	3/6	3/6	3/6	3				
Fund	Trust	Trust	Trust	Trust	Trust	IRA	IRA	Trust	Trust
Funding	ER	ER/EE	ER	ER	ER	ER/EE	ER	ER	ER
Limits	§415	§415	§415	§415	§415	§415	§415	§415	§415
Catch-ups	N/A	Yes	N/A	N/A	N/A	Yes	N/A	N/A	N/A
Portable	No	Yes	Yes	Yes	Yes	Yes	Yes	Yes	N/A
Longevity risk	ER	EE	EE	EE	EE	EE	EE	ER	ER
Nominal account	No	No	No	No	Yes	No	No	No	No
Real account	No	Yes	Yes	Yes	Yes	Yes	Yes	Yes	No
Final pay	Yes	N/A	N/A	N/A	N/A	N/A	N/A	N/A	Yes
Career pay	No	N/A	N/A	N/A	N/A	N/A	N/A	N/A	N/A
Accrued benefit	Yes	N/A	N/A	N/A	ER	N/A	N/A	N/A	Yes
Investment risk	ER	EE	EE	EE	ER	EE	EE	EE	ER
Inflation risk	EE	EE	EE	EE	EE	EE	EE	EE	EE

NOTE: This table shows some of the key characteristics of the most popular retirement plans. "ER" and "EE" mean employer and employee, respectively. Vesting is described in short "5/7" which means five-year cliff and seven-year graduated. The limits are all contained in §415, but refer to salary and benefit limits in a DBP, and to income deferral and total contributions that can be made in a DCP. Hybrid means the cash balance plan. Keogh plans can be DBPs or DCPs, but in the chart we refer to them as DBPs.

Some of our current tax and pension laws and pension plan designs serve as barriers to this opportunity. For example, the Internal Revenue Code requires that a worker's retirement benefits be suspended during the period when they return to work. He must also begin again to receive service credit under the pension plan for the time worked. Also, a worker who wishes to continue working, but on a reduced basis, would receive a smaller benefit if the DBP uses final average pay in the pension formula. The Pension Protection Act of 2006 has dealt with some barriers, such as Social Security benefit offsets for those who work after retirement, and these are discussed in Chapter 9, Benefit Legal Compliance, but there is more to be done.

Conclusion

There are many factors influencing the offering of employer-sponsored retirement plans. The need to be competitive, an interest in providing an important life event benefit, and tax policies are key among them. Our tax policies also encourage employee savings. Many DBPs are disappearing from the employment landscape, and one questions if they will even exist in ten years. More emphasis is being placed on employee savings, even though data suggests that employees simply are not saving enough to finance their own retirements.[44] The third leg of retirement, Social Security, is a vital element but is in need of fiscal reform. The foundations of our retirement system, and the hopes and dreams of many to leave their employment with sufficient income to enjoy in their later years, are in jeopardy. And this is coming as expenditures for health care, housing, and long-term care are increasing rapidly. It may be that the sources of retirement funding will change over the years. Some predict that with the aging workforce, the pendulum may swing back toward defined benefit plans because they encourage longer service, provide more secure retirement income, and, with their use of final average pay, offer higher benefits for longer service employees.[45] The benefits model, particularly as it relates to the employer's ability to recruit and retain workers and to motivate them

---

44. Opdyke, J. (2006) reports on recent surveys that show 22 percent of workers are not saving at all, and 40 percent have less than $50,000 put aside for retirement. Forty-five percent of working age adults will be unable to maintain their preretirement standard of living.

45. See EBRI Data Book on Employee Benefits, Chapter 1. (2006), Employee Benefits Research Institute, http://www.ebri.org/. But see Johnson, R., & Steuerle, E. (2003), who argue that hybrid plans best serve the retention of older workers.

to higher levels of productivity, will continue to be relevant to the design of pension plans.

Chapter Exercises

1. Check Northwestern Mutual's Web site at http://www.nmfn.com/. Select Learning Center and then Calculators, and do an exercise on the savings needed for college. What is the relevance of this exercise to retirement? What are the factors relevant to making this calculation?

2. On the same site, go to the Longevity Game and alternate some variables to see what factors affect one's life span. How is this relevant to the cost of an employer-sponsored retirement plan?

3. Check out the Power of Tax Deferral at the Northwestern Mutual site, and Double your Money to see how tax deferral and interest rate assumptions can affect your accumulation of wealth.

4. Determine the percentage of replacement income you can expect in retirement by checking http://www.wsharpe.com. Check the retirement worksheet to determine the replacement income an annuity purchased at retirement would generate. (Go to the Web site, select worksheets, and then select retirement.) Choose three different sets of variables in the boxes provided to see how these affect your replacement income percentage. Write up a summary briefly discussing your conclusions. Then check http://www.prudential.com/ (Products and Services, Investments, Annuities) and provide a recommendation with respect to the purchase of an annuity as a guarantee of retirement income. Explain your recommendation.

5. Go to http://www.money.com and select Calculators, then Retirement Planner, and determine whether your hypothetical situation will produce enough money to retire.

6. Go to http://www.bloomberg.com/ and go to calculators. Determine how much you can accumulate in your 401(k) when you include employer matches and disciplined savings.

7. Check http://www.prudential.com/ and Products and Services, Investments, and Annuities. Determine the annual retirement income generated by hypothetical savings based on several assumptions. Do the same with http://www.immediateannuities .com/.

8.   Assume you have contributed to your 401(k) for 30 years and have an account accumulation of $800,000. What annual income would this yield for the remainder of your lifetime when you retire next month as age 65? What are your assumptions?

9.   What is a Roth IRA and how does it differ from an IRA? Check http://www.ira.com/ for the answers and be prepared to discuss why and when you would select one or the other.

10. With respect to retirement planning, we must remember there are three legs to the stool and one is Social Security. How much can you expect to receive from Social Security? Check http://www.ssa.gov/ and go to Benefit Calculators. Then calculate your hypothetical Social Security benefit at the appropriate retirement age. Also, be prepared to discuss average indexed monthly earnings, primary insurance amounts, bend points, and monthly benefit amounts.

11. You are a small employer with 85 employees. Recruiting and retention factors lead you to conclude that you should offer some type of retirement plan for your employees. Identify and briefly describe an optimal plan that would best support your HR objectives and minimize your administrative expense.

12. Your friend indicates he has opened an IRA account and funded it with tax-free municipal bonds. Is this a good strategy? Explain. What should his investment strategy be with respect to an IRA? Would it be different for a Roth IRA? What are the adjusted gross income limits for regular and Roth IRAs? (See http://www.dol.gov.)

13. Your older friend is considering retirement and wants to know if and when she can get the green light to notify her employer. Go to http://www.choosetosave.org/ballpark/ and select Interactive Ballpark. Make two sets of assumptions for each category. Describe what you did and discuss the different results.

Health Care 6

Mike Stoll is the director of benefits for Plastic Products, a 300-employee firm in the Midwest that produces injection molds for dashboards and decorative plastic interior auto parts. The company provides health insurance for its full-time employees. Mike just received the premium schedule from the health insurance company, announcing an increase of 12.5 percent for next year. This is the fastest growing expense in the company, and Mike wonders if they will be able to generate sufficient sales to cover this significant incremental cost. As he prepares to discuss the matter with the general manager, he is determined to find some way to pass the extra cost on to the employee participants in the plan, reasoning it is either that or no pay increase.

Introduction

There are many lifecycle events, such as birth, illness, and disability, that cause people to rely on some form of insurance or financial assistance to reimburse their medical providers. In the United States, for those employed individuals and their dependents, the most common system for reimbursement involves an employer-sponsored health care plan.[1]

---

1. About 60 percent of the population in the United States is covered by employer-sponsored health care. Nearly 10 percent is covered by private health care policies. *American health demographics and spending of health care consumers* (pp. 162–163). (2005). Ithaca, NY: New Strategist Publications, Inc. However, only 47 percent of U.S. workers are covered by employer-sponsored plans. See Allegretto, S., &

For those who are unemployed, or who have income below certain poverty levels, a federal and state program called Medicaid is available. For Social Security participants, particularly those over the age of 65, the Medicare program provides health coverage. For certain military veterans, the Veteran's Administration offers comprehensive health care benefits.[2] We will discuss the government-sponsored health care programs later in Chapter 12.

In this chapter we will discuss employer-sponsored health care programs. As you will see, the structure and design of such programs are substantially replicated in the government-sponsored plans. You will learn the motivation for employer-sponsored plans, as well as the basic principles and design features of health plans in general. While state and federal laws in the United States do have some application to the administration and features of an employer-sponsored health care plan, in most states[3] an employer is not required to offer such a plan to his employees.

Employer-sponsored health insurance is a relatively new phenomenon. Until the late 1940s and early 1950s, health care for the most part involved a direct contractual relationship between the provider and the patient and, in some limited cases, between several large employers and providers.[4] Often, when the patient was unable to pay all or part of the provider's fee, there was an adjustment made to either discount or forgive the amount owed. Public hospitals followed the same process.[5]

During World War II and the Korean Conflict, and in the early 1970s, the U.S. government imposed price and wage controls to curb inflation. As a substitute for wage increases, employers offered and enhanced employee benefits, particularly health care, since they were not covered by the wage

---

Bernstein, J. (2006, January 27). *The wage squeeze and higher health care costs.* Economic Policy Institute, Issue Brief 218, http://www.epi.org.

2. About 12 percent (46 million) of the U.S. population under age 65 is covered by Medicaid programs. Medicare covers 40 million people, and the U.S. military programs cover about 10 million. *American Health Demographics and Spending of Health Care Consumers.* (2005). New Strategist Publications, Inc. We will discuss these government-sponsored plans in some detail in Chapter 12.

3. The federal law, Employee Retirement Income and Security Act (ERISA), and a variety of state insurance laws do control some aspects of health insurance plans once they are offered. As we will see in Chapter 9, some states now mandate health care coverage.

4. Cunningham, R., III, and Cunningham, R. M. (1997). *The blues: A history of the Blue Cross and Blue Shield system* (pp. 35, 50–51). N. Ill. University Press. For a basic history and description of health care plans in the United States, see *Fundamentals of employee benefit plans.* (2005). Washington, DC: Employee Benefits Research Institute, Chapter 20, http://www.ebri.org/.

5. These were called prepayment plans, whereby employers and individuals purchased insurance on a prepaid basis. Cunningham (1997), p. 89.

Health Insurance 6.1%
Wages and Salaries 82.1%
Other Benefits 11.8%

Figure 6.1   U.S. 1996 Employer Compensation by Category as a Percentage of Total Compensation

NOTE: Data obtained from the *Employer Health Care Costs in the U.S.* (2007). California Health Care Foundation.

control system.[6] Accordingly, the concept of employer-sponsored health care as an essential component of the total reward system expanded during this period.[7] Also at this time benefit costs were relatively low, and there was little health care inflation. Thus, they came to be called fringe benefits. Circumstances today are vastly different. Employer-sponsored health care costs have increased dramatically. As a result, the health care system itself over the last 15 to 20 years has undergone a fast-paced evolution.[8]

Today's health care cost inflation is impinging on the employer's ability to offer health care to his employees. Maintaining health care as a benefit is clearly competing with wages. Employees often are faced with having to choose between paying a larger share of their own health care benefit and accepting a pay increase.[9] We discuss this principle of compensating differentials in Chapter 2, but the data reveals that as the percentage of

6. See http://www.yourdoctorinthefamily.com/grandtheory/section3_1.htm/. This site contains a well-written history of health care in the United States. In Section 3, Health Care 2000—How It Got This Way, the writers point out that after World War II, unions began to demand health care as a benefit; government encouraged this by providing favorable tax treatment which in effect subsidized health care by providing deductibility to the employer sponsor and not considering the benefit to be taxable income to the employee participant.

7. See http://www.yourdoctorinthefamily.com/grandtheory/section3_1.htm/.

8. Cunningham (1997), pp. 181–201.

9. As an example, in 2003–2004 the longest work stoppage in the history of the food industry was caused by a dispute over an employer proposal to require employee health care contributions. Three major food chains in southern California and seven United Food and Commercial Workers Union locals, representing 21,000 employees, were involved in the strike that lasted nearly four and a half months. See *Work Stoppages 2003,* Bureau of Labor Statistics, http://www.bls.gov/.

Health Insurance 8.2%
Wages and Salaries 79.5%
Other Benefits 12.3%

Figure 6.2   U.S. 2005 Impact of Increased Health Care Costs on Employer Compensation by Category as a Percentage of Total Compensation

compensation paid as health insurance increased, the share of compensation paid as wages and salaries fell.

For many without employer-sponsored care, purchasing comprehensive health insurance on an individual or family basis is extremely costly.[10] Those who are covered by Medicaid and Medicare have serious concerns because the funding of these plans appears to be in jeopardy.[11] In spite of spiraling costs, many employers who wish to remain competitive in their labor market continue to offer health care benefits.[12] They have been in a frantic search for new plan designs that will break the inflation cycle. Finding no such silver bullet solution, many simply are shifting more costs to their employees.[13] Part of the problem with the health care system in the United

10. To see the various health insurance plans that are available and to get a quote for the purchase of insurance, go to http://www.wizardofhealthinsurance.com/.

11. In 2007 the amount spent on Medicare and Medicaid represented about 19 percent of the federal budget. This was 2 percent less than what was spent on Defense and Security. U.S. Office of Management and Budget (2007). See Samuelson, R. (2006, September 18). The monster at our door. *Newsweek, 148*(12), 51. According to the Trustees report of March 2008, the Medicare fund will be exhausted by 2019. See *2007 Annual Report of Board of Trustees of The Federal Hospital Insurance and Federal Supplementary Medical Insurance Trust Funds.* U.S. Department of Health and Human Services, http://www .cm.hhs.gov/.

12. Initially, employers paid nearly 100 percent of the cost of sponsored health care plans. Today, however, costs have been shifted to the employee participants. Employers in general will be paying about 62 percent of the total cost of a plan, leaving the employee with a 38 percent financing obligation. See Mincer, J. (2006, July 5). Health care costs to hit workers, retirees harder. *The Wall Street Journal,* D3.

13. Health care premiums increased 7.7 percent in 2006, outpacing both wage and price inflation. The trend for 2007 was nearly 8 percent more than double the cost

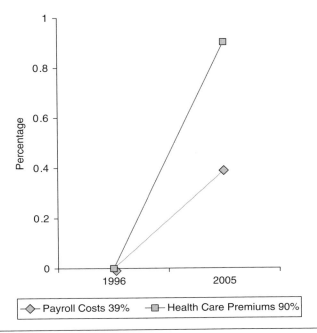

Figure 6.3   Shows the Percentage Increase (0 to 100%) in Payroll Costs
Compared to the Increase in Health Care Premium Costs
Incurred by Employers in the United States

NOTE: Data obtained from the *Employer Health Care Costs in the U.S.*
(2007). California Health Care Foundation.

States is, according to critics, that there is no system. Who are the participants in the United States who have a direct involvement in health care?

Parties and Interests Involved in Health Care

The health care system in the United States has a number of active constituents that add expense to the system and make it difficult to reach a
consensus on how, if at all, the system should be changed, such as:

- Providers that include hospitals, medical professionals, and
  specialized facilities

of living indices and wage increases. See 2007 Segal Health Plans Cost Survey at
http://www.segalco.com/publications/. While the increase is substantial, it is far
below the 14 percent increase in 2003. Fuhrman, V. (2006, September 26). Health
care premiums rise. *The Wall Street Journal Online*, http://www.wsj.com/.

- Researchers and pharmaceutical companies who are searching for better treatments, cures, and vaccines

- Suppliers of health products used in the family physician's office, diagnostic center, and operating room

- Employers who pay for the health care of their employees

- Employees and their dependents who are covered by employer-sponsored plans

- Large labor unions that not only negotiate health care benefits but also, in many cases, administer health care plans along with their cosponsoring employers

- Insurance companies (third-party administrators or TPAs) that either insure health care plans or administer networks of providers who are reimbursed indirectly by employer sponsors

- State agencies that regulate insured health care plans, and the state and federal government agencies that sponsor health care plans for eligible persons and their dependents

- People who are neither covered by public plans nor insured by employer-sponsored plans—the uninsured

- Large endowments administered by trustees that financially support hospitals, medical research efforts, and specialized clinics and are indirectly involved in the administration of certain aspects of our health care system

- A variety of legal systems such as worker's compensation programs and the negligence and personal injury litigation processes that reimburse health care providers for accidental injuries.

These disparate and dispersed parties create a complex landscape for the efficient offering of health care benefits. They also represent a special challenge in the United States to those seeking major reform of the system in order to make it more affordable, accessible, and efficacious. Some estimate this crazy quilt of health care plans adds about 15 percent of redundant administrative expense.[14] Accordingly, they argue that by

---

14. Many health experts have opined that our fragmented health care system adds significant cost to employer-sponsored plans. Anderson, G., Reinhardt, U., Petrosyan, V., & Hussey, P. (2003). It's the prices stupid. *Health Affairs, 22*(1), 89–105. Also, a study in the *New England Journal of Medicine* demonstrated that the United States could save approximately 15 percent of its total health care expenditures by moving to a single payer nationally sponsored system. The authors compared the United States to Canada and calculated redundant

simply consolidating our health care into one universal system, we could reduce the excessive administrative expense and make health care more affordable and accessible. Acknowledging this complexity is an important step toward understanding the driving forces and the evolution of health care plan design in the United States. To fully understand the current health care system in the United States, one must consider the impact our tax and health care financing systems, market factors, and inflation have on the design on various health care plans.

Employer-Sponsored Plans— Taxes, Financing, and Market Factors

In the United States, when an employer offers health care to his employees, he is partially subsidized by the government. The employer can deduct the cost of providing a health care plan, and neither the economic value nor the actual cost to the employer is taxed to the employee as income. On the other hand, the actual amounts paid by individuals for health care premiums are not tax deductible, except in certain limited situations.[15] Some argue this disparity is unfair. So while no employer wants to increase his expenses unnecessarily, the tax deductibility of the health care expense makes such increases more tolerable. One can safely argue that were it not for this tax treatment, many employers would not offer health care as an employer-sponsored benefit. Some argue that by eliminating the exemption from taxation and letting employees deduct all health care expenses including premiums, there would be a significant change in participant behavior. They would act more like real consumers of health care.[16] As we point out below, they do not behave in this manner at present. We will discuss this issue more in Chapter 7.

---

administrative costs in the United States that are attributable to our fragmented system(s). See Woolhandler, S., Campbell, T., & Himmelstein, D. (2003). Cost of health care administration in the U.S. and Canada. *New England Journal of Medicine, 349,* 768–775.

15. A person may deduct expenses paid for health care providers or services provided the costs equal or exceed a specified percentage of their total income. Premiums for health insurance are not deductible by the individual. Publication 502, Medical and Dental Expenses. (2005). Internal Revenue Service.

16. See *Reforming the tax treatment of employment-based health insurance.* (2005, June 27). Galen Institute & Heritage Foundation, http://www.galen.org.

Max is a driver for United Packages. The company provides a health care benefit for family coverage that costs United $800 a month per employee. Under U.S. tax laws, United is permitted to deduct this expense and the government does not consider the cost of the plan as taxable income to Max. In essence, the government is partially subsidizing the cost of United's health care plan, so the real cost of the plan to the company is less than $800 per month. What would happen if the situation were reversed and the IRS considered the cost of the health care plan as earned income by Max? To avoid paying income tax on the $800 per month health care policy, Max could encourage the company to give him the cash and let him buy a health care policy at a lower cost. If the value of the policy were taxed at a 20 percent rate, Max would have $640 a month he could put toward purchasing health care insurance. If he found something cheaper, say for $400 a month, he could pocket the difference of $240 and deduct the premium, freeing up an additional $80 for him per month. The incremental value to Max in purchasing his own health care is $320 per month.[1] The implications are twofold: (1) the deductibility of the health care expense, since it is partially subsidized, motivates employers to offer the benefit, and (2), since the cost is not taxed as income to the employee, the average employee is happy to continue the arrangement. The richer the plan, the better.

---

1. The assumption here is that Tom would be reasonably satisfied with the health care plan he purchases on his own, which may require more cost sharing, such as higher deductibles and less generous benefits.

The reason most employers would not do what is described in the above vignette is competition—their competitors do not structure their health care in this manner. Also, because of their size they believe they have more leverage than Tom to purchase a better and more cost-effective plan for their employees.

Financing

Typically, an employer-sponsored health care plan is either offered on an insured or self-insured basis. With respect to the former, an insurance company (third-party administrator or TPA) not only administers the

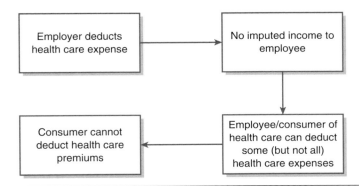

Figure 6.4   Tax Treatment of Employer-Sponsored Health Care

plan but also assumes the risk of paying all the claims in a given time period. The sponsoring employer pays a risk premium as well as the administrative costs to finance his plan in this manner.

Alternatively, larger and more financially robust employers may choose to self-insure their health care plan and, in doing so, assume the risk of paying all employee and dependent claims. In such cases the employer usually selects a TPA to administer the network of providers and plan of benefits. We will discuss some detailed issues pertaining to insured and self-insured approaches later in this chapter.

Depending on the type of plan and the cost sharing arrangement between the employer and the employee, on average the current total allocation of financing costs in employer-sponsored plans is around 60 to 70 percent incurred by the employer and 30 to 40 percent by the employee. In the past, the employer's share was much higher. With the advent of spiraling medical care inflation, more employers are shifting a larger percentage of the financing costs to their employees. This has been accomplished by changing the plan design, as we will discuss below.[17]

Capital markets are implicated in the financing of employer-sponsored health care plans because the plan sponsors or their TPAs need to have some financial reserves that will guarantee their ability to cover fluctuating health expenses that exceed the monthly premium contributions. These

17. According to several recent studies by Milliman, Inc. and Watson Wyatt Worldwide, U.S. workers should expect to pay more for their employer-sponsored health care plan. For example, in 2006 the average total costs to pay for health care, including employee out-of-pocket costs, will rise 9.6 percent. Employers are expected to pay 62 percent of the total cost of a plan leaving the employee with a 38 percent cost obligation. Mincer, J. (2006, July 5). Health care costs to hit workers, retirees harder. *The Wall Street Journal*, D3.

reserves are frequently invested in short-term markets. An aggressive investment strategy with higher returns enables the employer sponsor to reduce his own funding liability to the plan. Conversely, poor market performance of invested health reserve funds can lead to a call for higher premium contributions.

Market Conditions[18]

In a typical service market we find several opposing dynamics at the point of sale. These would include direct relationships between the consumer and the provider, and negotiations between the two with respect to the price and quality of the service. Both provider and consumer in this instance maintain considerable control over the quantity and conditions of the service being offered. Volume discounts are frequently offered to customers and disclosure of certain consumer information prior to purchase of the service is provided. Competition and marketing among providers typically abound in a true marketplace. When the supply of service opportunities is high as compared to demand, prices decrease until the supply adjusts. New products, facilities, services, and research and development are usually driven by the desire to increase revenue and profits. So, how does this compare to the health care market?

> You are a participant in an employer-sponsored health care plan at work. Your lower back hurts and you have numbness in your right leg; you see your family physician. You know nothing about the doctor except he is on your insurance company's list, a friend has told you the doctor has previously shown some warmth and concern, and it is not difficult to get an appointment. The doctor examines you and concludes that you might have a herniated disk. You do not ask him if it could be something else, since he appears to be quite sure. He recommends that you have an MRI. You do not ask if there are alternatives to the MRI, and you also do not ask what the MRI will cost

18. It should be noted that while many competitive factors relate to the offering of health care services, there are some organizational issues pertaining to health care that could be considered anticompetitive and in violation of antitrust laws. Greaney, T. (2006). Antitrust and hospital mergers. *Journal of Health Politics, Policy and Law, 31*(3), 511–529. Most of the anticompetitive issues have involved consolidations of provider organizations, and the separation of lab, diagnostic services, imaging, and medical practices to avoid referrals by the provider that may constitute a conflict of interest.

because the insurance company is paying for it. You leave and make an appointment at the imaging center the doctor recommended. You do not get an itemized bill from the doctor or the imaging center; they are sent directly to the insurance company.

Later, the doctor calls you to report that the radiologist who examined your MRI concluded you have a herniated disc at the L3, L4 vertebrae. You do not know who the radiologist is or, specifically, how he formed his opinion. Your doctor says the radiologist recommends that you see a neurosurgeon. The doctor concurs and he gives you a name. You do not ask about the basis for this recommendation; you only wonder if this neurosurgeon is the best. You make an appointment with the neurosurgeon who, upon looking at the MRI, says you need surgery. He explains how the surgery will work. You do not ask if there are alternatives, or how many of these surgeries he has performed, or if he will provide a warranty of good service. You do not even bother to ask the results of patients under his care; and it certainly never occurs to you to ask what the procedure will cost.

The neurosurgeon tells you when the surgery will be conducted and at which hospital. You know nothing about the hospital, its clinical record with respect to back surgeries, its number of postsurgical infections, or the appropriate length of stay for this procedure. The only thing you know for certain is your cousin was there and described the room and food as pretty good. You leave the neurosurgeon's office with a piece of paper explaining where to go.

So, how does this affect the employer sponsor who is paying for the surgery? The role of the third party distorts what we might find in a true market. In our example, the provider initiates services, but the consumer has been neutralized as a market player because he does not pay for the service. In our scenario, there is no discussion of alternative services or choices, no discussion of price, no guarantees, no detailed information on the service he is buying, no available record of the service provider's past clinical outcomes, and no consideration of competitors offering the same service. While some hospitals do advertise their services and promote their reputation, there is no claim that competition is driving improved quality of their medical services.

Certainly, there is an imbalance of expertise that may inhibit some patients from challenging the provider, but this same imbalance exists when a person who knows little about car mechanics or home construction purchases a car or selects a home improvement company. Let's say a homeowner who knows nothing about stonewall construction wants to hire a stonemason. The homeowner would probably get comparison bids, ask questions, check references, seek guarantees, discuss the date of completion, and negotiate the price. And, until the work is done to proper satisfaction, the homeowner would not pay the bill in full.

When we closely examine the employer-sponsored and other publicly financed health care plans, these market activities are rarely found. The system is distorted and unresponsive to initiatives to optimize market incentives.[19] Prices are not responsive to demand, information about services and outcomes are not available to the consumer or the financing entity, and the ultimate consumer has a proportionately small financial stake in the transaction. As we examine the evolution of health care design and its recent efforts to confront health care inflation, we see attempts at introducing traditional market factors in plan designs. The question is, are we doing enough? The other question is, what is driving this inflation?

Inflation

Recently, a health care executive with General Electric told me a story about his 72-year-old neighbor who had rotator cuff surgery to enable his continued enjoyment of golf. He pointed out that as a result of better surgical techniques and equipment, many more people are having this expensive surgery and, in fact, it has become common among 70-year-olds. Not so long ago, the only persons who had rotator cuff surgery were major league baseball pitchers. Incidentally, the rotator cuff surgery costs in excess of $20,000.

The widening accessibility of medical innovation and new technology to a larger percentage of our population has helped to drive health care inflation. In the United States, health care inflation has far exceeded the rate of our cost of living increases.[20]

There are other attributed causes to this inflation. They include new and costly prescription drugs, longer life spans, and the increased and intensive utilization of health care resources, particularly at end of life.[21] Also, sedentary and poor nutritional lifestyles as well as malpractice

---

19. Porter, M., & Teisberg, E. (2006). *Redefining health care: Creating value-based competition on results.* Boston: Harvard Business School Press.

20. Over the past five years, health care cost inflation has exceeded the CPI by as much as nearly 200 percent. Since 2005, the gap between the two has narrowed. U.S. Bureau of Labor Statistics, U.S. Department of Commerce.

21. For the latest analysis of health care spending in the United States, see Keehan, S., et al. (2008, February 26). Health spending projections through 2017: The Baby Boom Generation is coming to Medicare. *Health Affairs,* 145. The authors point out that spending increased by 6.7 percent in 2007, the largest percentage occurring in public spending for health care, while GDP increased by 4.7 percent. This means that health spending is outpacing economic growth and placing health plans in the private and public sectors in jeopardy.

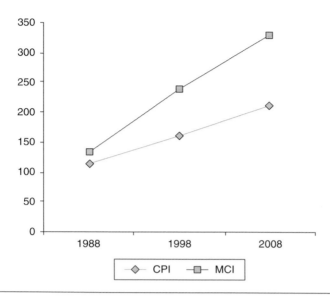

Figure 6.5   Rate of Inflation Comparison—U.S. CPI and MCI

NOTE: This data compares the rate of inflation of the U.S. Consumer Price Index (CPI) and the Medical Care Index (MCI). The MCI includes both medical commodities and medical services by providers. (Data obtained from the U.S. Bureau of Labor Statistics.)

claims, which increase a provider's cost of doing business and in some instances cause defensive medicine procedures, have contributed to inflation. It is estimated that 35 percent of all health care is inappropriate, meaning it is incorrect, insufficient, or too much care.[22] The consolidation of medical practice groups and hospitals has created new leverage among providers in negotiating their fees and generated new rounds of higher provider fees. The lack of dynamic market factors and the presence of a crazy quilt of fragmented health care administrative structures have made it difficult to respond effectively to this inflation.[23] Thus, it has persisted

22. See Wennberg, J., & Cooper, M. (1999). *Quality medical care in the U.S.* Chicago: American Health Association Press. Called the Dartmouth Study, Wennberg discovered extreme variations in medical treatments and inconsistent outcomes among Medicare patients. The variations were not based on acuity of the patient, effective treatments, or patient preferences. They were based on the geographic availability of services and medical facilities.

23. Michael Porter, in his new book, points out that we need a totally new architecture for health care which will transform insurance companies into health care plans, specialty practices, and integrated health practices, and move toward a business unit model that will better ensure "value creation." Porter, M., & Teisberg, E. (2006), p. 9.

and is a major factor in making health insurance inaccessible to many Americans. But let's look deeper.

Suppose you decide to have lasik surgery to improve your vision. More than likely your health insurance will not cover this procedure and you will pay for it yourself. As a result you investigate the doctors in your community who perform lasik surgery. You find some people who have had the surgery, assess their results, and you get the names of their doctors. You also find out what each doctor charges. As more doctors have entered the lasik field, open competition has taken place among providers and fees have dropped, sometimes precipitously. You decide to hold off for a while. One year later, you discover a significant increase in the number of ophthalmologists performing lasik surgery and, indeed, the prices have declined further. They also are offering warranties, promising to redo the procedure if eyesight is not substantially improved. You make an appointment.

Medical procedures typically not covered by health insurance have not experienced the same rate of inflation as those procedures that are covered by health insurance plans. In fact, the cost for lasik surgery has declined in the last ten years due to real, market-based price and quality competition. Similarly, the increase in cosmetic surgery costs, another noncovered medical procedure, has significantly lagged behind the increases in the Consumer Price Index (CPI).[24]

Factors that help drive inflation are not apparent to some parties in the health care system when market factors are absent. Why? Because when someone else, like a TPA, is paying for a substantial part of your health care, the incentive is to consume health care resources until they reach your maximum cost sharing amount. When we pay the entire health care dollar, or a substantial part of it, we behave like real consumers, and services like lasik surgery assume the traditional attributes of a market. This has led researchers to conclude that the real culprits in health care inflation are Medicare, the third-party health insurance system, and the tax-subsidized employer spending on health care.[25] We will come back to this later.

---

24. Herrick argues that the third-party payment system, where someone else pays the bill, is a critical cause of health care cost inflation. Herrick, D. Update (2006, September 21). *Why are health costs rising?* National Center for Policy Analysis, No. 572; Bodenheimer, T. (2005). High and rising health care costs. *Annals of Internal Medicine, 142,* 847–854.

25. Finkelstein, A. (2005). *The aggregate effects of health insurance: Evidence from the introduction of Medicare.* Cambridge, MA: The National Bureau of Economic Research, Working Paper No. 11619. Article submitted to *Quarterly Journal of Economics.* The author finds the introduction of Medicare is responsible for about half of the real per capita increases in health care spending. Her conclusion is based in part on the introduction of a large government purchaser of health care that has caused providers to invest more extensively in capital expenditures increasing utilization and prices. See also Herrick (2006).

Table 6.1   Drivers of Health Care Inflation

Medical technology
New prescriptions/drugs
Life expectancy
Lifestyles
Malpractice insurance costs and defensive medicine
Inappropriate care
More leverage among newly consolidated providers
Inefficient administration/organization
Lack of controls on the utilization of health care resources
Higher compensation levels and prices for goods and services

Evolution of Health Care Plan Design—Some Principles

Employers typically offer benefits to satisfy employee needs during life-cycle events and to compete in the recruitment and retention of employees in their respective labor market. Moreover, employers understand that by offering health care benefits they can maintain healthy and productive workers. In the United States, many employers who sponsor health care offer several alternative plans from which employees can choose. The types of plans offered depend on a variety of factors.

Suppose as a new employer, in order to compete in your product market and geographic labor market among those who offer health care as a benefit, you must do so as well. There are numerous health care plan designs available, so which one do you select?

There are several steps to take and analyses to apply in choosing the right health care plan. First, the employer determines what kind of plans his competitors are offering. Next, an assessment is made with respect to the demographics of the employer's workforce—are they younger, older, mostly men or women, and do they have families? What is the nature of the work at the place of business? Is it dangerous? What plan would be a good fit for this workforce? The employer must determine what he can afford. What are the cost alternatives of the various plan designs, and what is the cost structure of the employer's business? Is the employer's product price sensitive? What if the employer tries to pass on all of the added cost of the health care benefit to his customers? Will the employer lose sales?

The Benefits Model—Health Care

These inquiries reflect, in part, an underlying set of design principles we call the benefits model,[26] which is discussed in some detail in Chapter 2. There are four features of the benefits model that should be used as a template by employers who are selecting and designing a health care plan: (1) maintain internal fairness among the workforce so that one benefit does not disproportionately favor one group of employees over another; (2) be aware of what your competition is offering; (3) include incentives that positively affect behaviors among plan participants; and (4) make sure the plan is cost-effective and well administered. Let's apply these to an employer-sponsored benefit plan.

What if a health care plan provides 100 percent reimbursement to medical providers for management and office employees, but only 50 percent for plant workers who have to make up the 50 percent difference out of their own pockets? Does this violate the principle of internal equity?

Yes, it does violate the principle of internal fairness, and it probably is also illegal.[27] It would be inappropriate to design a health care plan that offers special benefits to some but not other similarly situated employees. What if an employer offers a health care plan for single employees and the same plan for employees with large families? They all pay the same premium and have identical plan features. Would this be fair? The answer is no. How would an employer deal with the issue? We will see that plan design and features typically found in employer-sponsored plans provide the opportunity to ensure internal fairness.

An employer must decide on a benefit strategy. Should he meet, exceed, or lag his labor market competitors with respect to his benefit package? There are some choices. For example, he could lag competition in cash compensation, but lead in benefits. Why would an employer want to do this? Is there a segment of employers, perhaps those involved in public

---

26. The pay model is described by Professor George Milkovich and his coauthor, Professor Jerry Newman, in their book, *Compensation* (8th ed.). 2005. New York: Irwin McGraw-Hill. The authors applied the model in establishing wage, salary, and bonus compensation. In this book we have transposed the concept to apply to benefit designs.

27. There may be a variety of discrimination issues here, but the Health Insurance Portability and Accountability Act of 1996 prohibits differences in premiums and other out-of-pocket costs based on health status. See Chapter 9, Benefit Legal Compliance.

Inputs	Processes	Outcome
• Tax Policy • Human Resource Strategy • Degree of Market Competition • Benefits Model	• "Values" of Sponsor • Financing Mechanism • Admin. of Plans • Plan Design	• Improved Recruitment and Retention • Healthy Employees • Cost-Effective Care

Figure 6.6   Workflow of Health Care

education, who traditionally do this? How about offering higher pay than their competitors, but a less generous health care plan?

Can an employer design a benefit plan that affects behaviors? Yes; for example, the average prescription drug benefit frequently offers financial incentives to participants who choose a generic over a patented drug; the co-pay is less. This kind of incentive achieves the effect of steering participants to choose the less costly generic drug.

Finally, a health care plan must be affordable and well administered. The plan sponsor must try to keep his plan affordable and also establish a formula to share some of the costs with his employees. We will see how plan design affects this issue.

If you ask a typical employee what feature of the health care plan he would be less willing to change, his answer would probably be the family physician. As health care plans have evolved, most sponsors have acknowledged the preservation of choice among plan participants. Quality and cost of plan designs are equally important factors, and we will take a look at how tax policy, market conditions, and financing alternatives play significant roles in the evolution of plan design.[28]

As we consider here the role of our benefits model as well as some of the above-described factors that lead employers to offer health care plans, the "workflow" of health care might look similar to Figure 6.6.

We have reviewed some principles and factors relevant to the employer sponsor's selection of a health care plan design. Now, let's go back into our

---

28. Employer sponsors also designed their plans to avoid the assumption of unnecessary risks, such as adverse selection and cost shifting. They avoided adverse selection by limiting enrollment times to prevent employees from changing their choices because of some newly discovered health risk. Lazear (1998) describes adverse selection as a process that selects the wrong workers, or less profitable buyers and customers or less profitable sellers, as suppliers. It has a more specific application in insurance, but in the context of benefits it essentially involves loss-producing buyers of services (p. 530). The other health care dynamic is called cost shifting. This occurs when one party with low health care risk winds up subsidizing another party with high health care risks. It will be discussed later under insuring health care plans, but it motivates employers to pursue special design features to avoid its occurrence.

rather short history of health care benefits and look at the major medical or indemnity plan, which remains a fundamental benchmark in the evolution of employer-sponsored health benefits.

Design Features of the Major Medical or Indemnity Plan[29]

The indemnity health insurance plan, also called a major medical or fee-for-service plan, provides participants partial reimbursement of covered medical expenses. Provided physician or hospital fees are reasonable, it typically pays up to 80 percent of the expense, and the participant retains the freedom to choose the provider.

Any employer considering the sponsorship of an indemnity plan for his employees must consider some preliminary questions: (1) What is your human resources management strategy and how will the plan help drive the strategy? (2) Who will be covered? Do you want to cover full-time and part-time employees and include the dependents of your employees? (3) What are your values and how will they fit within the plan? (4) What do your employees need and want? (5) Which medical, psychological, and other procedures will be covered? (6) Should your employees share in the cost? (7) Should your plan encourage the most cost-effective treatments? What about quality? (8) Should the right to choose one's provider be a valued criterion in your plan? (9) What is your health care market, and how do you determine who the best providers and TPAs are? (10) Should your plan encourage more healthy lifestyles?

The answers to these questions will serve as a guide for the employer in his examination and selection of the most efficient, cost-effective benefit plan that provides top-quality care. Efficient and cost-effective care are not mutually exclusive. Rather, they are harmonious and work together. The employer, through his TPA, must find a network of health care providers that do both. Figure 6.7 is a matrix that demonstrates the point.

First, let's examine the design elements of the indemnity plan. By understanding the plan, one can readily comprehend the evolution of diverse health care plans that have appeared over recent years. An indemnity plan provides for the partial or full reimbursement of health care providers for treatment of covered employees and their dependents. Most often, it is a simple fee-for-service plan. The provider is reimbursed for each service rendered to the participant. The plan usually includes the following design features.

---

29. For a comprehensive discussion of health care plans, see Beam, B., & McFadden, J. (2001). *Employee Benefits* (6th ed.), pp. 221–309. Dearborn, MI: Real Estate Education Company. See also EBRI (2005).

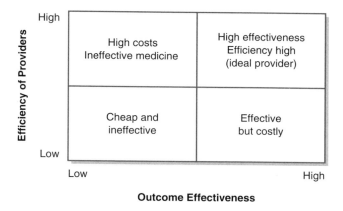

Figure 6.7   Health Care Matrix

NOTE: A matrix of high and low efficiency and effectiveness, as well as the appropriate mix of a high-quality plan that meets the employer's test of affordability (upper-right quadrant).

COVERAGE

The employer[30] and his TPA must first decide which employees and which of their dependents are covered by the health plan. Will the plan cover all full-time employees but exclude part-time workers? Will it cover the employee's dependents? The employer may consider such issues as expense, internal equity, labor market competition, and other factors when determining coverage provisions of his plan.

ELIGIBILITY

The issue of eligibility to receive benefits involves a number of questions. Did the employee actually enroll in the plan? Has he paid his share of the monthly premium? Does the plan require some period of employment before the employee is eligible to receive health care benefits? Do the

---

30. The employer has considerable control over which design features will be included in his health care plan. The control, however, usually involves shopping the health care market to see what plans are being offered by TPAs. Since it is the employer who pays the cost of the health care plan either on an insured or self-insured basis, the employer has a significant interest and role in choosing these design features.

employee and his dependents fit the coverage definitions of the plan of benefits?

We see several compensation and human resources principles applicable here. Why not cover an employee immediately after employment? What is the purpose of excluding part-time employees? How will the design of the plan help in recruitment and retention? Is the plan useful to ensure union avoidance and internal equity? Does the availability of coverage for full-time employees motivate part-time employees to perform better in order to become full-time?

WHICH MEDICAL PROCEDURES ARE COVERED AND FOR HOW MUCH?

In an employer-sponsored health care plan, the employer must decide which health conditions or procedures are covered and what the provider reimbursement levels will be. With respect to the former, employers and their TPAs—again, motivated by cost, fairness, and labor competition—typically decide whether or not to exclude procedures such as cosmetic surgery, treatments that are not medically necessary, certain diagnostic procedures that do not have a reasonable financed return, or experimental medical treatments and drugs.

Additionally, the employer must determine whether or not to pay the entire cost of the treatment or to reimburse only reasonable and customary (also referred to as usual and customary) fees. In a traditional indemnity plan, where the providers have not agreed in advance with the employer or his TPA on a specific reimbursement schedule, the participant patient would have to pay the difference between the provider's fee and the employer's fee schedule of reasonable and customary.

The participant, unlike most consumers of services, has very little role in determining how much the provider should reimburse. The only aspect the participant does control is when to initiate a request for services. As we discuss the evolution of health care plans, we will see efforts on the part of employer sponsors to control this activity.

UTILIZATION REVIEW

To combat the potential abusive utilization of health care resources by the employee or his provider, some indemnity plans introduced a design feature that requires preapproval or precertification of medical services or hospital admissions. This is done by the TPA and usually involves some communication with the treating physician. The criterion on which preapproval is determined may include medical necessity, clinical appropriateness of the procedure, an issue of coverage, and availability of alternative and less costly interventions. Failure to obtain preapproval can result in a denial of the claim by the TPA. In this case payment to the provider becomes the sole responsibility of the participant patient. In utilization reviews we see some effort on the part of the sponsor of the plan to interdict the demand for services.

EMPLOYEE COST SHARING

Giving the participant a financial stake in his medical care is considered to be an important incentive to creating a more judicious use of the health care benefit.

First there is the *deductible*. This is a fixed dollar amount the participant and his dependents, if any, must pay annually for covered health care procedures or treatments before the health care plan reimburses the provider. Depending on the size of the deductible, it generally serves two purposes: (1) to reduce the cost of the plan to the employer sponsor by partially shifting the plan's financing onto the employee; and (2) to affect the employee's behavior—the employee faced with the payment of a deductible becomes better informed in his health care and may decide to forgo a particular treatment or look for a more economical alternative. Only treatments that are covered by the health plan qualify as a deductible expense. When the deductible is exhausted, the plan will then reimburse the participant's providers based on its coinsurance obligations. For example, when an employee has paid $500 of his own money in the plan year for covered treatments, thereby exhausting his deductible, the plan will pay 80 percent of the medical charges (called the "coinsurance") incurred from that point forward during the remaining year.

The deductible can be designed to implicate certain elements of the benefits model, in particular, internal fairness and behavior incentives. Higher deductibles are common for employees with more dependents. This reflects an interest on the part of the sponsoring employer to maintain internal fairness within his workforce. In some plans, the sponsor utilizes tiered deductibles. These are variable deductibles that apply to specific treatments and involve an effort to affect the behavior of the employee. For example, why would a plan waive a deductible for an annual physical? In such cases the plan immediately pays its full coinsurance obligation, or 80 percent of the claim. The plan is obviously trying to affect the behavior of the participant. By offering a financial incentive to have a physical, the employee's physician could possibly detect a potentially life-threatening or chronic disease. This discovery could save the employer considerable expense in the long run, prevent a protracted hospitalization and absence from work, and save the life of the employee.

In other cases there may be varying levels of deductibles that are designed to motivate the employee to choose treatments that are more effective and efficient. The employer sponsor is betting on the value of a smaller and earlier investment in preventive care versus the higher costs of a later catastrophic health event. Conversely, the employer may want to discourage trips to the hospital emergency room, or other inefficient or inappropriate uses of health care resources, by imposing a higher deductible when such services are used. The deductible represents a plan design feature that can be effectively used to achieve internal equity, shift some of the cost of a plan to the participants, and encourage more cost-effective behaviors.

Coinsurance represents the percentage amount of the provider's charges the sponsor will pay after the participant fulfills his deductible. Typically, the percentages are 80 percent to be paid by the employer and 20 percent by the employee; however, they can vary among health care plans. The employer sponsor may be trying to affect the behavior of his employee. For example, he may be trying to encourage more cost-effective behaviors among his employees. He may offer a higher coinsurance for employees who go to certain medical providers because they have agreed to offer discounts or they may be more proficient in their medical specialty.[31] So, instead of an 80 percent coinsurance, in this case he may pay 90 percent. In cases where the employer offers several plans for his employees, the coinsurance among the plans may vary substantially. For example, in order to encourage the employee to choose what the employer believes to be the most cost-effective plan, the coinsurance could be as high as 100 percent (employer) and zero (employee).

In some cases, incentives are far-reaching and strategic. For example, some firms continue to offer retiree health care to those employees retiring before they are eligible for Medicare. This encourages early retirement and opens up opportunities in the workplace for younger and perhaps lower paid employees. If, however, no retiree health care is offered, or if the cost sharing rests heavily on the early retiree, the employer is sending a clear message to the employee—if you want a more generous health care plan, stay employed until you are 65 and eligible for Medicare.[32]

---

31. See the discussion of Preferred Provider Organizations in the next chapter.

32. There are two types of retiree health care: coverage before Medicare and supplemental coverage after the retiree qualifies for Medicare. Many employers are currently reconsidering whether they should offer any retiree health care plan either at early retirement or as a supplement to Medicare. Others are considering a defined contribution approach to retiree health care, whereby they simply promise to fund a health care account by contributing a fixed amount for the purchase of insurance and allow the employee to assume the responsibility to pay the remainder as well as inflationary increases. For those employees retiring before reaching Medicare eligibility and without employer-sponsored health care, the premium is about twice as much as the cost for an employer-sponsored plan. Chaikind, H. (2006, March 28). *Health insurance coverage for retirees.* Congressional Research Service.

The *premium* is the amount the employee must pay per month to be eligible to participate in the employer-sponsored plan. It usually represents some percentage of the monthly expense the employer has accrued in a self-insured plan, or the actual monthly premium paid to the TPA in an insured plan. Premiums usually will vary based on the number of the employee's dependents covered under the plan. The employer in such cases is acknowledging the principle of internal fairness. In some employer-sponsored plans, the premium is also determined by the employee's income. The more one makes, the higher premium co-pay. What do you think of this practice? Does this violate or support internal equity? The premium is a very important feature of the plan design. It can affect which plan an employee chooses, and it may affect the decision as to whether or not the employee will actually enroll in the employer's health care plan.

How is the premium determined? Usually the employer and his TPA will calculate the overall expense of the health care plan and then factor in all the various cost sharing measures such as deductibles, coinsurance, and point-of-service co-pays. This will enable the employer to determine a targeted goal that represents the percentage of the total cost of the plan to be financed by the employees. For example, the employer may decide that employees will pay about 60 percent of the total health care expense.[33] Premiums will be determined in accordance with the employer's formula.

Office *co-pay* is a design feature that requires the participant patient to pay a nominal fee to the provider at the time or point of service. Higher co-pays might be required for specialists. Again, the purpose is threefold: (1) the employee is helping to finance the health care plan and reduce the employer's cost; (2) there is a modest incentive to the employee to utilize health care resources more judiciously; (3) varying co-pays may encourage certain positive behaviors. For example, the employer may have a significant co-pay for visits to the emergency room in order to encourage more cost-effective medical care, such as a visit to the family physician or an urgent care facility.

OUT-OF-POCKET MAXIMUM

Indemnity plans typically include a maximum amount of coinsurance the employee must pay annually, called the *out-of-pocket maximum*. When an employee's coinsurance payments (not including the deductible and

---

33. Milliman, Inc., a health care consulting firm, reports that employees in 2006 paid about 40 percent of the total cost of an employer-sponsored plan covering a family of four. About 56 percent of this amount represents premium co-pays and 44 percent deductibles and point-of-service, or office co-pays. Mincer, J. (2006, July 5). Health care costs to hit workers, retirees harder. *The Wall Street Journal Online.*

Table 6.2   Cost Sharing Features of Typical Health Care

Feature	Example	Impact
Deductible	$100–$1,500	Share cost, affect behavior
Office co-pay	$20–$30	Share cost, affect behavior
Premium	$50–$250	Share cost, internal fairness
Coinsurance	80%/20% or 90%/10%	Share cost, direct plan choice
Out-of-pocket maximum	$2,500	Limit cost sharing
Lifetime maximum	$1 million	Limit sponsor liability

office co-pays) reach a prescribed level, the employer pays 100 percent of all eligible and covered medical expenses with the exception of point-of-service co-pays. Of course, the higher the out-of-pocket maximum, the less costly the plan will be to the employer. If an employer were searching for ways to slightly modify his plan design and shift more costs to his employees, the out-of-pocket maximum feature would serve this end. This design feature recognizes that employees do have some upward limits to their financial ability to pay for their medical care.

LIFETIME MAXIMUM

Similarly, the employer may want to set a limit on the amount of payments it will make on behalf of an employee and his dependents during their lifetime. This amount, usually set at one or more million dollars, is unlikely to be reached, but it does cap the employer's liability. Let's take a look at how this works. Suppose a participant in the health care plan has a severe illness that requires frequent hospitalizations, expensive drug therapy, and sustained medical treatments. At some point, the *lifetime maximum* may be reached and the health care plan will no longer reimburse the providers of this participant. A devastating thought, but it can happen. It would leave the participant in a situation where he would be forced to pay for his health care out of personal savings, or navigate through the various support systems to see if some other public program might provide assistance. In those few cases when the lifetime maximum is close to being exhausted, the employer sponsor and the TPA often take steps to manage the disease more aggressively, and try to postpone or avert the triggering of the maximum. From the employer's perspective, however, the lifetime maximum places a predictable financial limit on the total medical expense that will be incurred by a participant.[34]

Coordination of Benefits

Consider this scenario: a husband and wife work full-time at two different companies. Both are eligible and do participate in their respective health care plans; however, the husband also includes his wife in his plan. What happens when his wife files a claim? Who pays the bill? What if the husband, whose plan has significant co-premiums, a higher deductible, and higher co-pays, decides to decline coverage at his company and be included in his wife's plan? Can he do this? Why should his wife's employer cover him when he could be covered at his own company?

Since employer-sponsored health care is based on employment status, a frequent issue arising in the administration of this benefit involves how to coordinate the reimbursement of providers when both the employee and his dependent are covered by separate benefit plans, but the wife, for example, is also covered by her husband's plan. In this example, since she is actively employed, her employer's plan will be considered the primary plan and will process her claims first. Then, if her husband's plan would have paid benefits on a more generous basis, she can be reimbursed for the difference in the two amounts. The husband's plan becomes a supplemental or secondary plan paying what her plan did not cover.

What happens in the case where both spouses have the opportunity to be covered by their employer's plan but, instead, one declines coverage and elects to be covered as a dependent by the spouse's plan? The plan must cover both spouses. Obviously, this creates an additional liability on the part of the plan sponsor, and some employers who find themselves in similar situations—covering both spouses—have increased premiums or added surcharges as a means of dissuasion.

What happens if an employee has retiree health care as a benefit? She retires and then gets a job with another company that offers health care. She enrolls in that plan but remains in her former company's retiree health care plan. When she goes to the doctor, who pays the provider? The third-party administrators of both plans must determine, based on the terms of the plan designs, which one is primary and which is secondary. Usually the plan covering the employee who is in active service is the primary plan and will reimburse providers. The secondary plan, as in the

---

34. A current trend among plan sponsors is to offer an unlimited lifetime maximum for those employees choosing what the employer believes to be his most cost-effective plan.

earlier example, might allow more generous reimbursements and will pay the balance of the charges remaining after the primary insurance plan has fulfilled its obligations.

Bundling and Unbundling Plans

There are many instances where an employer-sponsored health care plan includes several types of coverage; for example, dental, optical, and prescription. Separate third-party administrators who specialize in assembling special provider networks might offer these plans. Depending on their structure, they might be integrated into the health care plan, bundled, or offered as separate plans that can be elected by the employee unbundled.

Employers have discovered cost savings in unbundling their plans. An example would be when a dependent of an employee has health care coverage at his employment, but the plan does not include dental or optical coverage. The dependent might choose to decline coverage at his employment and become a dependent participant in the employee's plan. This adds expense to the employer with the bundled benefit plan. By separating out each plan, the same dependent could select basic health care coverage from his employer, but choose dental coverage at the employee's place of employment. This has the effect of reducing the health care expense of the dependent's employer.

Conclusion

These are the basic design features of an indemnity plan. As we now examine the evolution of new plan designs, you will see that all health care plans have their design roots in the indemnity plan. Each evolutionary step involves an attempt to introduce more market features into the plan designs, thereby overcoming some of the structural weaknesses in the employer-sponsored health care system. The driving force behind this evolution has been mounting health care inflation. It will become apparent, however, that each of the following plan designs maintained many of the basic design elements of the original indemnity plan except where noted.

As we will discuss in Chapter 10, Employee Benefits and Metrics, employers should view their benefit plans as drivers of their business and human resources management strategies. With respect to health care, not only can it help recruit and retain good employees, it also can create measurable value. Effective health care can reduce absenteeism, limit distractions from work caused by illness, and mitigate the occurrence of critical

Select best providers	Focus on preventive care
Share costs with employees	Engage employees in healthier lifestyles

Figure 6.8   Value Matrix for Health Care Plan

health care problems. It can help develop a strong and healthy workforce that will, ultimately, improve productivity, reduce costs, and drive sales and profits.

In blending the interests of the employees and the owners of the business, a health care plan should use quality medical outcomes measures to identify the best providers, facilitate their accessibility, afford participants the opportunity to choose their provider, encourage employee participation in their own health awareness, and maximize medical interventions at preventive care intervals. By following this type of matrix, one serves to ensure a more healthy and productive workforce, a high satisfaction level among employees with respect to their health care plan, and a cost-effective and efficient plan for the sponsor.

Finally, with respect to interventions at opportune intervals, it is important to understand that some resources spent on diagnostic practices and preventive care can lead to positive human resources and cost results. Plan sponsors should be looking for ways to provide incentives for their employees to utilize health care resources that serve to detect certain chronic or acute conditions early on and prevent them from having a major impact on the employee's health in the future.

Chapter Exercises

The following exercises should be completed as written or prepared for discussion as directed by the instructor.

1. Contact a parent, sibling, friend, or relative and inquire about their employer-sponsored health care plan. Determine the type of plan, the relevant design features including cost sharing, as well as the

choices of alternative plans offered by the employer. If there are several plans offered, how do the premiums compare among the plans? Why did your contact choose a particular plan? Does the employer offer retiree health care? What have the trends been with respect to co-pays, deductibles, premiums, and coinsurance over the last five years? Can you determine from analyzing the plan what the employer's business strategy and values are?

2. Check the Web sites at http://www.dol.gov/ and http://www.bls .gov/ and review the types of health care plans offered in private employment, the relationship of the industry, union status, type of worker, geographic area, and wages to the employer sponsor of a health care plan.

3. Your company offers an indemnity health care plan that provides for a $200 annual deductible ($300 per family), 80/20 coinsurance, $5 co-pay for prescriptions, and all the other design features of typical indemnity plans. Your plan is more than competitive in your industry and you must substantially reduce your costs. You have decided to change the plan but want to preserve choice and quality and still be cost-effective. Identify and briefly explain a range of possible plan design changes you could make that would be consistent with your goals.

4. We know that health care cost increases have outpaced both consumer inflation and wage increases. One ratio that might be relevant to the issue of health care costs is the ratio of an employee's average monthly health care premium to his monthly earnings. How does the present ratio compare to five years ago? Has there been an erosion of earnings? What are employer sponsors doing to control the increase in health care costs? How does size matter? What are smaller employers doing about the increased cost of health care? See *2007 Employer Health Benefits Survey.* (2007, September 11). Kaiser Family Foundation and Health Research and Educational Trust, http://www.kff.org/.

5. Do younger employees subsidize older employees in a company-sponsored health care plan? Explain. Is this something that should be avoided? How could the employer sponsor design his offering of plans to minimize the possibility of subsidization?

The Evolution of Health Care Plan Designs 7

Introduction

In the previous chapter we set out the "raison d'être" of employer-sponsored health care. We also outlined some of the complexities of our health care system, as well as the significant health care inflation that continues to make it more difficult for employer sponsors to continue coverage for their employees. Finally, we described the basic indemnity (fee-for-service) plan and its design features, and briefly discussed the lack of traditional market features in the delivery of health care in the United States.

We spoke about an evolution of health care plan designs beyond the indemnity plan, and in this chapter we will be covering the types of plans that have evolved in the last 20 years in the United States. As the evolution unfolds, you will see an incremental insertion of market features into the basic indemnity plan. Each new plan takes on a new identity, but the core of the indemnity plan remains. We will explore the intended and actual impact of these changes on the employer's ability to meet his goal of sponsoring quality and cost-effective health care while respecting the important feature of choice—the ability to choose one's providers.

Preferred Provider Organization (PPO)[1]— Discounts and Volume

An inherent problem for employers offering the traditional fee-for-service indemnity plan is that the medical provider unilaterally determines which

---

1. PPO network providers typically agree to prescribed cost controls and offer services to subscribers at less than usual charges. Cunningham R., III, & Cunningham, R. M. (1997), p. 261.

health care resources to prescribe. The only exception is in special instances where some form of utilization review is applied. From a market standpoint, this places the provider in the unique position of determining not only the services to be rendered, but also the revenue the service will generate. In the late 1980s, a new plan design evolved that offered a partial solution: the preferred provider organization (PPO). Let's take a look.

The TPAs and sponsoring employers decided to select some providers in a geographic area who would offer a discount for their services in exchange for an increase in number of patients; a simple volume discount concept. The TPA agreed to place the name of the provider on a preferred list.[2] The participants were given a financial incentive in the form of a lower coinsurance amount if they would select health care services from among those appearing on the list. For example, if the participant used the preferred provider, the coinsurance might be 90 percent paid by the employer and 10 percent by the employee, instead of the traditional 80/20 percent. Since choice remained an important value in most plans, the decision by the participant to use a network provider was voluntary. There was only a financial incentive to do so. If the participant chose a provider not on the list, the coinsurance remained at its original 80/20 percent level. It was called a preferred provider organization (PPO). Except for the incentive to see a physician in the network, the PPO retained all of the basic features of the indemnity plan.

Although this appeared to be an inventive introduction of market features, there were several flaws. First, participants are highly motivated by choice and often believe their doctor is the best. And second, was a 10 percent change in coinsurance sufficient incentive to move large numbers of participants to the providers on the preferred list? In many cases the providers were disappointed in the lack of increased volume.[3]

From the sponsor's perspective, while the provider did offer discounts for those participants in the PPO plan, there were no real disincentives to increase the volume of health care resources for each patient. So the risk was that more services, albeit discounted, would be provided and the plan sponsor would wind up paying less per procedure, but more in total.[4] Evidence of this began to appear.

There were virtually no limitations on the referral of a participant to a specialist whose treatments ordinarily cost more. While there were

---

2. A substantially large percentage of persons in the United States is covered by PPOs. For an interesting history and review of health care programs in the United States, see *Fundamentals of employee benefits programs.* (2005). Part Three, Health Benefits, Chapter 20, Health Benefits: Overview. Washington, DC: Employee Benefits Research Institute (EBRI).

3. See EBRI (2005), p. 10.

4. Beam, J., & McFadden, J. (2001), pp. 189–220.

some specialists included in the preferred provider network, the partici-pant was largely free to decide when and who to see, even though the condition might have been treated in a more cost-effective way by a family physician.

Point-of-Service (POS) Plan—Management of Referrals

So, the idea was advanced. Why not create a PPO with added control over the utilization of health care resources, and put that control in the hands of a medical provider versus a TPA?[5]

Suppose you have a sore elbow and want to go to an orthopedic surgeon for treatment. Instead, you visit your family physician and she tells you it is not necessary to see a specialist at this time. She recommends regular icing of the elbow, gives you the name of an over-the-counter, anti-inflammatory drug, and tells you to see her again in three weeks. If the symptoms persist, she will refer you to an orthopedic specialist. The objective is to avoid unnecessary additional health care resources and to secure effective treatment of your elbow.

Controlling the utilization of health care resources was the objective of the new point-of-service (POS) plan. The design included unique features that modified the indemnity and the PPO plans by creating a new role for the family physician, or primary care physician (PCP), who became a gatekeeper. Certain financial incentives were offered to the PCP by the TPA to control medical resources by following protocols and controlling the referral to a specialist. This initially involved trying the most conservative approach in responding to a patient's symptoms, followed by an incremental transition to more complex therapies if the need was demonstrated. The PCP, hoping for additional patients under this plan, discounted his fees, but also was offered financial incentives to control the use of medical resources. The PCP was the only person who could refer the patient to a specialist. If the patient chose to bypass the PCP and go directly to a specialist, then either no coverage or less generous coinsurance would result. So, we now had an indemnity plan, but with a network and a gatekeeper.

Next we see a further introduction of market factors. Discounts, expectation of additional volume, financial incentives to the consumer and provider, and additional effort to manage care and costs all represent important elements in the POS design. While this new design achieved some success in curbing health care cost inflation, it was insufficient to significantly impact the spiraling costs generated by the use of health care

---

5. Cunningham, R., III, & Cunningham, R. M. (1997), p. 260; EBRI (2005), p. 13.

resources.[6] Also, the administrative costs in establishing the gatekeeper's role offset some of the savings attributable to the reduced utilization of specialists. TPAs and employers began to embrace a plan design that had been legislatively acknowledged by Congress some years earlier. The original intent was to provide every employee covered by an employer-sponsored health care plan the opportunity to participate in an alternative design. It was called a health maintenance organization (HMO).

Health Maintenance Organization[7] (HMO)— More Managed Utilization and Care

In the HMO, choice was no longer an option. Suppose you had a deep cough and wanted to see a doctor. You look at the list of doctors in your employer-sponsored plan, but would rather see a pulmonary specialist who is not on the list. You expect your decision will result in a less generous coinsurance payment, 80/20 percent, instead of the plan's normal 90/10, but are willing to pay the difference. When the pulmonary specialist's bill is submitted, however, the TPA pays nothing. That is how the HMO works. There is no out-of-network reimbursement.

The design concept behind the HMO is straightforward; if you go out of network to a physician not on the list, your treatment is not covered and the TPA will not reimburse your provider. The expectation was HMOs would lead to the creation of highly integrated, multispecialty networks. These units usually offered primary or ambulatory care, as well as a variety of specialists that would effectively control the utilization of health care resources by its participants.[8] The network would have access to a common set of medical records, adding efficiency to the treatment

---

6. Beam, J., & McFadden, J. (2001), p. 294. In 2004, 90 percent of Americans with employer-sponsored health care participated in an HMO, PPO, or POS plan. EBRI (2005).

7. See the Federal Health Maintenance Organization Act of 1973, 42 USC §303, which required all plans covered by the Employee Retirement Income Security Act to offer, as an alternative to the prescribed employer-sponsored plan(s), the right of an employee participant to elect an HMO as an alternative. For purposes of this discussion, we focus on group HMOs that involved integrated physician groups from primary care to specialties that could offer a comprehensive set of health care services.

8. The PPO, POS, and HMO designs are commonly called "managed care plans." These plans control the delivery of services, they can involve gatekeeper functions, and they monitor physician decision making. The HMO was the ultimate design in this evolution and still today holds the prospect of providing excellent care at reasonable costs. Cunningham, R., III, & Cunningham, R. M. (1997), p. 259

process, and coordinate referrals to its colleague specialists on a more cost-effective basis. With significant disincentives imposed on those participants who chose providers outside the network, the expectation was there would be a large increase in patient volume for HMO providers. The bargain was modified and discounts and stronger management of health care utilization were afforded to the sponsor in exchange for a higher volume of patients who were given an ultimate incentive to come. They no longer had a choice to go anywhere else. The HMO is an indemnity plan with a network and no option or choice of providers.

TPAs often reimbursed HMO physician groups based on the number of participants they treated, referred to as a capitation basis, creating an opportunity to realize a profit if the capitated fees exceeded the providers' actual expenses. A financial risk existed, however, in the event treatment costs exceeded their per capita fees.[9] The old fee-for-service reimbursement plan was no longer applicable. With capitated fees there was a clear financial risk for inefficient providers. Because of the prospect of increased volume, however, they were more willing to offer deep discounts for their services.

Many aspects of the health care delivery system were controlled or managed in an HMO. In fact, the HMO is the centerpiece of a category of plans, including the PPO and the PPS, referred to as managed care. Primary care and early preventive care were emphasized. There was an interest in avoiding catastrophic and costly health care events among their participants. Less costly outpatient treatment was encouraged and, indeed, facilitated. Treatment protocols were followed by the providers, referrals to specialists were controlled, and prereviews of health care treatments were increased. Practice patterns of physicians were closely monitored. So both care and cost were more intensively managed in an HMO. In order to encourage higher HMO enrollments, employer sponsors, who offered several choices of plans to their employees, provided for lower deductibles, coinsurance, and premiums. In many instances, the coinsurance for an HMO was 100 percent employer paid.

With such a strident interest in cost containment, there was concern that HMOs would create new health care risks; for example, a proliferation of cheap medicine in their networks. This did not happen.[10] HMOs increased the utilization of diagnostic procedures that were designed to

---

9. In some cases, individual physicians within a multispecialty, integrated group were paid on a salary basis.

10. According to a recent report by a group that measures quality practices and outcomes and accredits managed care networks, particularly HMOs, the quality of care provided has significantly improved. *Measurement improves health care quality for 70 million Americans.* (2006). National Committee for Quality Insurance, http://www.ncqa.org. Additionally, a report by the *Journal of the American Medical Association* (1996, October 2) indicated there were no differences in quality of care between traditional fee-for-service and HMO plans.

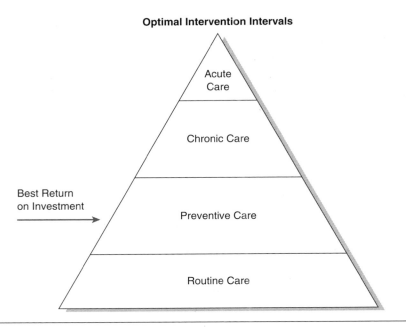

Figure 7.1   The Hierarchy of Medical Care and the Importance of Preventive Care

identify early symptoms of acute illnesses. Clearly, with a capitated reimbursement scheme, there is a higher financial return on such practice patterns for both sponsor and provider. For the first time, the market incentives for both were congruent. Figure 7.1 makes this point.

During the 1990s when HMO plans were very popular, having achieved success in reducing health care cost inflation and creating the opportunity for more volume, providers agreed with HMOs to significantly reduce their reimbursement levels. Likewise, employers reduced their employee cost sharing design features to encourage additional enrollment. Even Medicare offered HMO alternatives to its participants. HMOs, however, had created an appetite among participants for full coverage with minimal cost sharing. Providers began to consolidate their practices, creating area markets with more leverage to negotiate higher reimbursements.[11] When a market has many providers and is fragmented, the resulting extensive market competition allows TPAs to reduce reimbursement levels. Thus, providers in managed care plans such as HMOs were so competitive they were willing to reduce reimbursement levels to get the business. When markets consolidated, TPAs and employer sponsors lost their bargaining leverage and reimbursement levels in most plans increased. This change

11. Grembowski, D., Cook, K., Patrick, D., & Roussel, A. (2002). Managed care and the U.S. health care system. *Social Science and Medicine, 54,* 1167–1180.

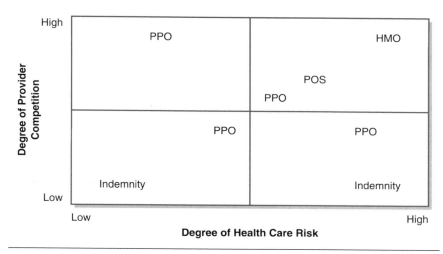

Figure 7.2   Health Care Market and Appropriate Health Care Plan

caused employers either to lose interest and discontinue their HMO or to move to higher cost sharing with the participants.[12] They could no longer afford 100 percent coinsurance, low premiums, and no deductibles as an incentive for their employees to join the HMO. When the incentives began to dissipate, employees were less willing to give up their right to choose providers by participating in an HMO.

Figure 7.2 shows how the degree of competition in a given geographic area will control the suitability of certain types of health care plans. HMOs can exist only where there is strong competition and a high incidence (risk) of medically complex health care. Where there is little competition and low risk care, discounts and managed care efforts are unlikely to be attractive to providers. Consequently, the indemnity model is more suitable.

HMOs also created the need for significant administrative activity by TPAs, further raising the costs of such plans to employers. These factors, combined with some negative anecdotal publicity concerning the controlled utilization of health care resources by HMOs, caused them to lose their competitive advantage. Though a decline in HMO enrollment followed, they still exist today.[13] Employer sponsors began to gravitate back

---

12. Enrollment in HMOs declined in 60 percent of the United States from 2004 to 2005. Walker, T. (2006, August 1). Top 20 states by HMO enrollment. *Managed Healthcare Executive*, http://www.managedhealthcareexecutive.com/.

13. It is universally agreed that HMOs offered too much to participants; the financial incentives to enroll were too generous. Cost sharing between the sponsor and the participant were largely out of balance and the cost of offering the plans became unacceptable to plan sponsors. Generally speaking, however, HMOs were accepted by participants, and surveys showed high degrees of customer satisfaction.

to more simple forms of plan designs such as the PPO. Reducing the cost of administration seemed to be a more prudent course.

During this evolution, we see economic incentives being introduced in order to affect behaviors, reduce costs, and achieve quality health care for employees. Despite HMOs' success in achieving these results,[14] new approaches continued to evolve as employers searched for more cost-effective designs. Perhaps the problem was the TPA. Why not simply contract directly with the providers?

Direct Contracting and Capitation[15]

Except to a certain extent in the case of HMOs, one of the troubling design elements of the previous cadre of health care plans is that providers are reimbursed for all services rendered. There is no financial or performance-based risk placed on them. Do the work and you will get paid. With managed care there is the network creation, fee negotiation, claims processing, and efforts to control care, all of which generate a lot of administrative expense.

To address these problems, a new concept was tested. Why not eliminate the traditional role of the TPA and allow the employer sponsor of the plan to contract directly with the providers?[16] This would have the effect of eliminating the excessive administrative costs of traditional plans. Moreover, if the providers would accept a per capita annual fee from the

---

14. During the period 1985–1993, hospitals in areas with high concentrations of HMOs had a 3 percent lower inflation rate than hospitals in low penetration areas. Estimates of the cumulative impact of HMOs on hospital inflation alone during this period was $56.2 billion. See Gaskin, D., & Hadley, J. (1997). *The impact of HMO penetration on the rate of hospital cost and inflation, 1985–93.* Washington, DC: Institute for Health Care Research and Policy, Georgetown University Medical Center.

15. Although we discuss this alternative design in the context of modern employer-sponsored plans, capitation and direct contract between employers and providers were included in the initial health plan designs offered by employers in the 1930s. See Cunningham (1999), p. 35.

16. Several large companies like Purdue Farms, Inc., Caterpillar, Inc., and Cisco Systems, Inc. have eliminated the TPA and instituted direct contracting with their own networks of providers. Wessel, D., Wysocki, B., & Martinez, B. (2006, December 29). As healthy middlemen thrive, employers try to tame them. *The Wall Street Journal*, A1. Also see Terry, K. (2002, March 8). Cut out the insurance middleman? *Medical Economics*, http://www.medicaleconomics .modernmedicine.com/.

employer that would cover all the participants' health care services, the financial risk could be shifted from the employers to the providers. Naturally, the providers also would have the opportunity to achieve a good return should revenue from the capitated fees exceed the costs of the services rendered.

Except for some type of accounting audits, the administrative costs would be minimal. A simple and straightforward approach—participants receive treatment and there are no claim forms, reimbursement squabbles, or prereviews. Treatment becomes the sole business of the providers. Demographic information, actuarial and underwriting analyses, and periodic reviews of financial and clinical performances would have to be undertaken, but the comparative administrative costs would be less than the indemnity, PPO, HMO, and other TPA-administered health plans.

The provider has an incentive to improve efficiency and quality of medical services, since better and more efficient treatments will create a surplus of revenue. We see a more direct market relationship between the payer of the services and the provider. The employer can decide which providers to use based on some evidence of quality practice, accessibility, or other factors. Yet, the consumer of the services remains above the fray and is not directly involved in paying or contracting for the medical services.

Direct contracting did not draw a significant number of providers or employers. The providers were fearful of the financial risks, and the employers were reluctant to select and deal directly with providers. Hence, the design is hardly used in the employer-sponsored market.[17] Nevertheless, the concept and its components are worth noting as we continue to examine the evolution and search for new health care plan designs. Placing health care in a true market context was the continued goal. Before going further, let's review our health care evolution. Figure 7.3 takes us through the health care plan evolution from indemnity plan right up to the latest designs: consumer-driven health care and wellness programs.

---

17. Capitation is often used by HMOs in the United States and in some European countries that sponsor single-payer, national health systems. In Europe it is used to create global budgets for health care delivery systems and hospitals. Additionally, in the 1980s Medicare began using a Prospective Payment System (PPS) to compensate hospitals. The payment is essentially a per capita fee for treating patients with a given illness, regardless of the actual utilization of health care resources. The PPS was found to have no adverse impact on the quality of care. Draper, D., & Kahn, K. L. (1990). Studying the effects of the DRG-based PPS on quality of care, design, sampling, and fieldwork. *Journal of the American Medical Association, 264*(15), 1956–1961.

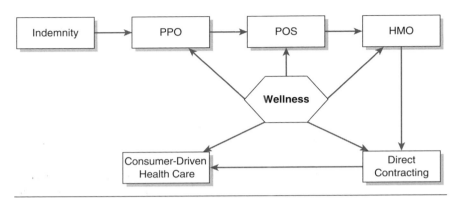

Figure 7.3   The Evolution of Health Care Plans

Consumer-Driven Health Care

We have seen a variety of plans that have included the basic indemnity plan features. The evolution advanced the idea that, by introducing market factors, plans would be more cost-effective. But with each iteration, the employee participant—the consumer—remained largely a passive recipient of services. He had no particular market role. This was considered by many to undermine any effort to introduce effective market incentives that would lead to higher quality, more cost-effective health care in the United States. The saying went, "If the consumer had skin in the game, we would see different behaviors and more equilibrium." Of course, the consumer did participate indirectly by paying premiums and point-of-service fees, but the employer sponsor and the TPA were the key financial and administrative participants in the plans. The consumer's impact was not apparent.

The first effort to increase the role of the consumer was the flexible spending account (FSA).[18] Here the participant could deposit, on a pretax basis, a fixed amount of compensation that would go toward paying annual health care expenses. The amount was in the range of $2,000 to $3,000, and had to be spent within the calendar year or it was forfeited back to the employer. Using pretax money to pay for health care expenses represented some financial advantage to the participant. Provided the money was used on health care (not including premiums), the participant made the final decision on how and where the money would be spent. There was something for the employer as well. By facilitating the

18. For a comprehensive and helpful source of information on FSAs, see http://www.fsafeds.com/. The publication tracks the IRC and the IRS regulations on FSAs.

establishment of FSAs, the employer did not have to pay Social Security or Medicare taxes on income placed in the employee's account. Though still popular, since the plan was basically a tax incentive and included the "use it or lose it" feature, the FSA was not considered to have a major impact on health care costs or participant behaviors. After all, it was called a *spending,* not a *savings,* account, and it did just that.

In order to replicate truer market conditions, the participant had to have access to a larger account for health care spending, the choice on how and when to spend it, and the opportunity to carry it over if it was not consumed in a given year. It was argued that putting the consumer in charge would cure the problem of inefficiency and high inflation in our employer-sponsored system. The solution was for the IRS to allow the funding of a spending account with pretax income, to permit it to be carried over into subsequent years if not spent, and require that it be used solely for medical expenses. But who would fund this account?

There were several different approaches. First, Congress authorized certain smaller employers to pilot a medical savings account (MSA) plan that would allow for a large deductible in a traditional medical plan.[19] On a pretax basis, the consumer employee would defer compensation equaling the deductible into an account used to pay medical bills. He would then use his deductible amount in the MSA to pay expenses as they were incurred. After the deductible amount was exhausted, the traditional indemnity or PPO plan would kick in to reimburse providers. When paying for health care expenses still within the deductible period, the employee would pay only the reimbursement amount authorized by the TPA under the relevant health care plan. Unspent amounts in the deductible would carryover into the following year. Congress limited the use and availability of the MSA and decided to wait and see if the employee's health spending behaviors changed. More specifically, Congress wanted to determine if the new consumer in the MSA used more informed discretion in the utilization of health care resources, and if the cost of health care decreased without affecting quality.

While the MSA was being tested, some employers adopted a slightly different plan design, the health reimbursement account (HRA).[20] Here the employer funds the spending account for his employees. The account is treated like a large deductible that could be used by the participant for the reimbursement of providers. No employee participant dollars can be contributed to the account. The participant can carry over any unspent funds each year. The expectation was the employee would behave like an

---

19. Formally called the Archer Medical Spending Account, it was authorized by the IRC. For a clear and excellent description of the MSA, see *Health savings accounts and other tax-favored health plans.* (2007). Internal Revenue Service, Publication No. 969.

20. *Health savings accounts and other tax-favored health plans.* (2007). Internal Revenue Service.

informed consumer and use health care resources more judiciously. The funding of the HRA by the employer does not constitute taxable income to the employee provided the monies are used for health care expenses.[21]

There are advantages and disadvantages to the employer who adopts an HRA. If the employer uses an insured instead of a self-insured plan, he can reduce his overall premiums because the plan design includes a large deductible and the TPA's projected risk of paying large health expenses is mitigated. In such instances, the employer is obligated only to fund the HRA as actual deductible expenses occur. The disadvantage to the employer using an HRA, however, is that it could have the effect of increasing expenses because he has assumed the liability to pay the deductible. Although the employee could carry over unspent funds to the following year, it was not his money.

For employers who sponsor a self-insured plan, the HRA seems like a less favorable step because they would not be taking advantage of lower premiums. And if an employer chooses to fund an HRA regardless of whether the employee incurs health care expenses, it would seem to be an even less attractive plan. Some employees have little or no medical expenses in a year, while others are just the opposite. Hence, if the employer sponsor funds the HRA for all his employees, he is significantly increasing his benefit expenses. What was really needed in the evolution of plan designs was a cost-effective design that triggered constructive and positive consumer behaviors among its participants. The most likely plan design to achieve this is one with high deductibles, where the employee spends his own money but has the opportunity to save his account for future health care needs.

That brings us to the latest iteration of the consumer-directed health care model, the high-deductible health care plan (HDHCP) with a health savings account (HSA).[22] This is simply a legislatively authorized plan that involves pretax funding of an account by the employee and, in some cases, the employer. For calendar year 2008, the amount of the account could not exceed an annual contribution of $2,900 (single) or $5,800 (family).[23] For participants over age 55, there is an allowable catch-up, with an additional contribution of $900 in 2008 and indexed to a cap of $1,000.

The HSA is a HDHCP typically linked with a PPO. The minimum deductible amount currently ranges from $1,100 (single) to $2,200

21. *Health savings accounts and other tax-favored health plans.* (2007). Internal Revenue Service.

22. *Health savings accounts and other tax-favored health plans.* (2007). Internal Revenue Service. During the course of our discussion we will refer to this type of plan as an HSA or an HDHCP or "Consumer-Driven Health Care." They have identical meanings are used interchangeably in the practice.

23. *Health savings accounts and other tax-favored health plans.* (2007). Internal Revenue Service.

Table 7.1   The Added Expense for a Funded HRA

HRA Contribution of $1,000	Annual Health Care Expenses of Company Before HRA	Annual Health Care Expenses of Company With HRA
Employee A (healthy)	$0	$1,000
Employee B (unhealthy)	$1,500	$1,000
Total Health Care Expenses	$1,500	$2,000

NOTE: The assumption here is that the health care expenses are covered by the HRA account. There would, of course, be additional reimbursements by the health care plan after the deductible was exhausted. This table simply questions whether a company should prefund an HRA, as some do before any expenses are incurred. If so, total expenses will rise, because they are funding an accour for a person who has no or very little health care plan utilization.

(family), up to a maximum of $5,500 (single), $11,000 (family).[24] The money in this account can be withdrawn on a tax-free basis provided it is spent on eligible health care expenses. Any earnings on the HSA are tax deferred, and if spent properly, they are tax-free.

After the annual deductible is exhausted, the plan's PPO will begin to reimburse the employee's providers applying all the traditional plan features including coinsurance. For example, the employee pays the plan premium, office co-pays, and his share of the coinsurance, say 20 percent. The sponsor would pay 80 percent. Once the out-of-pocket maximum is met, the sponsor would pay a coinsurance of 100 percent.

The employee can carryover unspent funds up to retirement age, when the money can be used to pay for retiree health care premiums. There is no "use it or lose it" requirement. An HSA encourages saving, not spending, and it is portable.

The underlying design concept is to cause the employee to behave like a consumer, making decisions about when and where to utilize health care resources. He now has skin in the game. There is also a strong incentive to save the dollars in the HSA and build a large reserve for later.

Since there are tax advantages, the IRS restricts the type of health care expenses that can be paid using the account. For example, one cannot use the HSA to pay premiums for health insurance unless the person is unemployed. The funds can be used, however, to pay for retiree health care, Medicare premiums, and long-term care. In order to encourage preventive and diagnostic care, HDHCPs are permitted to exclude certain preventive care practices from the deductible expenses. These exceptions can

---

24. The maximum also includes other eligible out-of-pocket expenses. The out-of-pocket maximum for these plans is the same.

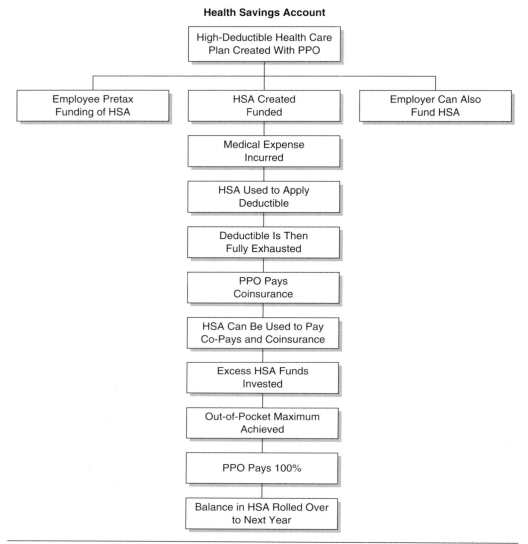

Figure 7.4   The Basic Process and Flow of a Health Savings Account (HSA)

include annual physicals, certain blood work, colonoscopies, and mammograms, all of which are designed to detect a serious condition early and prevent the employee from encountering serious or catastrophic conditions later. Employer sponsors, however, are not permitted to unbundle certain elements of their health care plan, such as prescription care, in order to exclude drug expenses from the deductible.

Employers offering HSAs usually ascribe a lower premium as an incentive for employees to choose what is considered a more cost-effective plan. Most large employers offer their employees a choice of either an HMO, a lower deductible PPO, or an HSA. Typically, the HSA will have the lowest premium. There are some other points to consider about HSAs and the whole consumer-driven health care program.

- First, from an economic standpoint, each $1 spent out of the HSA goes to pay the provider. There are no administrative or TPA fees.

- The high deductible provides an immediate lowering of the employer sponsor's costs because they are shifted to the employee. Since the employer sponsoring an HSA can expect about a 20 to 25 percent reduction in health care claims costs, most employers offer lower monthly premiums to those who enroll. Also, no FICA taxes are paid on contributions to the HSA.

- The tax-free status of the contribution, as well as the opportunity to invest the funds without tax, represents a real value to the employee.

- It remains to be seen how many employees will enroll in these plans when they have a choice of more traditional plans to choose from, and to what extent participants under such plans will behave like real consumers.

Let's go back to our friend in Chapter 6 who had the herniated disk. With a large deductible and a funded HSA, a portion of the charges for the back treatment would be paid by the participant. Would he behave differently than our compliant character in the vignette? Let's review.

Perhaps with his own HSA, our friend might be inclined to ask whether there were some other, less expensive tests to assess the nature of his back problem. Perhaps a simple neurological exam would provide a less definitive, but probably more accurate, determination. He also might ask if there was a chance the pain and loss of sensation in his leg might resolve itself with some exercises or conditioning. Perhaps he would be told that some core body exercises, physical therapy, and weight loss could help stabilize the spine and mitigate his condition. Or maybe an over-the-counter, anti-inflammatory drug would reduce the swelling in his protruding disk and relieve the pressure on the nerve that runs down his leg contributing to his pain and numbness. He might also want to find out more from the spine surgeon. What are his prices, how many back surgeries has he completed, and with what results? What exactly should he expect in recovery? He would conduct the same research on the hospital and, instead of reviewing hotel-like conditions, find out its record on spine surgery, postsurgery infections, and costs. Finally, he probably would ask the spine surgeon if there are less invasive treatments that might be tried before surgery. If he did, he probably would find out that an injection of steroids could help. This would be cheaper and involve no time off from work, and certainly would be worth a try.

Obviously, in order for the HSA to be effective in terms of encouraging quality care, more judicious utilization of health care resources, and reduced costs, the consumer must take charge of his care. There are some concerns.

How does the average health care consumer access reliable information about the propriety or efficacy of certain health care treatments? Can he get access to best practices? Can he position himself to ask the right questions about alternative medical treatments or the skill and performance levels of the providers? With the advent of the Internet, WebMD, and Google, one can find a lot of information about health care conditions, providers, and treatments. This should not necessarily serve as a means to second-guess the medical provider, but it can put the participant in the position to ask relevant questions that can lead to more informed decision making.[25]

Since there is a correlation between education, economic status, and health status, it is more likely that younger and healthier participants and those at higher income levels will enroll in an HSA, as opposed to others who have higher health care risks.[26] Will this type of plan really have a significant impact on the cost of health care, or will it simply distort the risk pool by causing healthy persons to move to the HSA, leaving the higher risk, lower income participants in other health plans? If this does occur, the premiums for the other plans could increase dramatically, leading to an eventual forced migration of employees into an HSA. Of course, this would reduce employee choice, but it probably also would reduce overall employer costs.

There are more issues. Will deductibles be spent on routine versus chronic, severe, or acute health care needs? This might happen because the employee would be more informed about routine care as opposed to more serious conditions. If this is the case, will the employer's savings be confined to reducing the utilization of less serious health care conditions that are not as costly? Will the consumer participant ignore treatment of health care conditions that could become chronic or acute?[27]

With early detection, a potentially deadly medical condition that can go unnoticed until it becomes severe or acute can be reversed or cured. As more health care plans exempt preventive care diagnostics and treatments from the deductible, these early detections will become even more prevalent, saving lives and, ultimately, reducing health care expenses. From an administrative expense standpoint, since the patient with an HSA is

---

25. See Condon, K. (2006, July). The financial case for integrating direct advice programs into consumer-directed health plans. *Employee Benefit News*, http://www.benefitnews.com/. The author discusses the daunting medical education challenge among prospective enrollees in a consumer-driven plan and urges employers to offer direct advice to their employees.

26. *Consumer-directed health care plans—Early enrollment experience with health savings account and eligible health plans.* (2006, August). General Accountability Office (GAO – 06-798).

27. Some argue that HSAs have a positive impact on the choice of treatments and early interventions among the chronically ill. *HSAs and the chronically ill.* (2006, July). Council for Affordable Health Insurance, No. 136, http://www.cahi.org/.

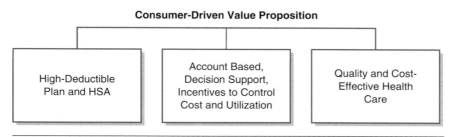

Figure 7.5   The Basic Value Proposition and Workflow of the HSA

responsible for keeping track of his expenses, the role of the employer sponsor in substantiating health care claims becomes extinct. If there is an IRS audit, the employee patient must verify how his HSA account was used to pay for health care expenses, further reducing the time and expense related to plan administration.

Will lower premiums and the opportunity to build one's account be sufficient incentives to attract large numbers of employees into HSA plans? Thus far, the enrollment in HSAs by employees in the United States has been quite small, about 3 percent.[28] Will employers move to reduce the number of health care plan choices and try to nudge more employees into the HSA?

What we see with HSAs at a significantly higher level than we saw with other plan designs is a combination of tax and financial incentives, consumer engagement, and the need for quality information about products and services. Employer sponsors of HSAs, however, need to provide guidance and support as employees navigate their way through the Web and other sources to become more informed about their health care issues. Also, it remains to be seen what impact HSAs will really have on health care inflation and quality. Perhaps it is enough that the HSA allows the consumer to know what the health procedure costs.[29] That may just stir enough inquisitiveness by the employee patient to start down the road for more information, and that is a big first step.

As we have pointed out, a big issue with respect to HSAs is how will the accounts be spent, and will they change the behavior of patients to seek less costly but good quality care. There is a new player in the health care scene

28. National enrollment in HSAs is still relatively small. Many employers, however, are indicating a keen interest in introducing them. Some have experienced major increases in enrollment as employer contributions to the HSA increased. (Interview of Michael Stoll, Vice President of Benefits, The Kroger Co., April 2008.)

29. Jenkins, H. (2006, September 20). No, consumer theory isn't a cure-all for health care. *The Wall Street Journal,* A27. Also see Albeson, R., & Freudenheim, M. (2006, November 4). Rolling the health care dice. *The New York Times,* http://www.nytimes.com/2006/11/04/business.

that might be relevant to this question: the "Mini Clinic."[30] It is gaining momentum and might be a good fit for an HSA participant. The Mini Clinic's business plan is to reduce wait time and costs for an appointment with a medical provider and to create a retail approach to consumer health care. They can be found in shopping malls and pharmacies. Many are going into Wal-Mart. Visits cost about $50–$60, prescriptions can be filled next door, and Medicare and many insurance companies are now covering these expenses. Patients sign in, are given a beeper, and return when called. Most often they are staffed by nurse practitioners. More complex conditions are referred to a doctor. Clinics are striving for uniform standards to overcome the patients' desire to see their familiar doctors. They just may be the answer to offering more cost-effective care, particularly as it relates to the low end of the acuity level. With HSAs we see another example of the relevance of the benefits model. The employer is introducing market features, particularly incentives, to positively influence the behavior of his employee participants. What are some other issues an employer must deal with in selecting a particular health care plan?

Choice of Plans—What Should the Employer Sponsor Offer?

GENERAL CONSIDERATIONS

Many, if not most, employer sponsors of health care plans offer several types of plan designs to their employees. The underwriting and pricing of the various plans are designed to have an impact on their respective enrollments. Demographics of the workforce, health care expenses of the employee group, and the health care market where the employer does business will affect the types of plan choices offered. Also, deductibles, office co-pays, and coinsurance will vary within an assortment of plan offerings, and each will have different premiums the employee must pay. One can easily ascertain the employer's overall evaluation of his plans by looking at plan premiums. By selecting different premiums for different plans, the employer attempts to lead the employees to select what he considers to be his most cost-effective plan.

As we have seen, the health care market where the employer operates may have an impact on the type of plan chosen. The degree of competition and complexity of health care risks will determine whether it is appropriate for a simple indemnity plan or a managed care approach. A consumer-driven plan is probably best augmented by a PPO or POS plan because the employee has incentives to search the market for good treatment opportunities.

There are some additional issues an employer sponsor must address. Should he consider taking steps to encourage healthier lifestyles among his

---

30. McClinics. (2007, April 14). *The Economist*, 78–79.

employees? Should he offer health care to his retirees? Will his plan be insured or self-insured? How does he go about selecting a TPA?

EMPLOYER-SPONSORED WELLNESS PROGRAMS

Wellness programs are designed to impact long-term health positively. They increase the opportunities for preventive health care by using health care assessments and changes in lifestyle. They create incentives to initiate and maintain good health habits and consistent treatment of chronic conditions. They often are included as part of a health care plan administered by a TPA or can be a supplemental plan initiated and managed by the sponsoring employer.

In general, there is a sequence of events that should occur as a wellness program is designed and implemented. First, the employer should assess what health conditions are leading to the highest utilization of health care resources and expenses among his workers. For example, let's say the employer and his TPA examine his health care claims and learn that cardiovascular and low back problems, as well as chronic diabetes and asthma conditions, are generating 80 percent of the claims costs.

Next, the employer will want to make some assessment among his workers, usually by a survey, to determine what potential lifestyles or behaviors might be driving these conditions. For example, he may find there are a number of workers who smoke or fail to take their blood pressure medicine on a regular basis; there may be others who are obese or physically unfit, who have extremely unhealthy diets or are not managing their diabetes or asthma conditions, or are simply failing to follow orthopedic guidelines on lifting or are not following through with physical therapy for their low back problems.

This step might be followed by some independent screenings by the TPA to further assess hypertensive conditions, body mass indices, tobacco use, the extent of diabetic and asthmatic conditions, and stenosis of the spine, as well as other diagnostic steps.

The employer and his TPA should consider how best to address these ailments and whether expanding the use of diagnostic and treatment provisions in the employer-sponsored health care plans would be helpful.[31] Are the right incentives included to encourage early medical

---

31. For example, screenings and diagnostic procedures typically include colonoscopies to detect colorectal cancer for participants over a certain age or with certain medical histories, diabetes screenings and aggressive management of this chronic and often acute disease, PSA blood tests and other related tests to provide for the early detection of prostate cancer in men, mammograms to detect breast cancer in women, cholesterol and hypertension screening and control programs, asthma and other pulmonary disease management programs, and pap tests to detect cervical cancer in women.

diagnoses and treatments? Are the physicians in the network able and willing to secure better compliance with their patients to follow the treatment regimens prescribed? They should closely identify the key risk factors leading to the health care problems. For example, smoking does lead to heart problems and stroke. What can be done to cause employees to cease smoking? Obesity does lead to diabetes, cardiovascular, and orthopedic problems. Can the employer do something to control the waistlines of his employees? Better diet can reduce fat and cholesterol and curb cardiovascular and a variety of other conditions. What can be done here?

Now the employer and his TPA should develop a series of incentives and programs that, ultimately, could change the behaviors leading to poor health. For example, the employer could offer cash contributions to an employee's FSA if he successfully completed a smoking cessation program and quit smoking.[32] Alternatively, the employer could introduce higher cost sharing in the health care plan for those who continue to smoke. Similar approaches could be taken with regard to compliance with treatment regimens, chronic disease management, and obesity. Some believe the carrot is a better incentive than the stick, but both can work.[33] And the U.S. Labor Department has issued guidelines on wellness incentives, including penalties, that do permit both approaches with some limitations.[34] Whatever the choice, the wellness initiative should include communications and informative materials that can be easily accessed by workers to support their changes in behavior. It is important that wellness initiatives reward results, not activities.

---

32. The Cincinnati Employers' Health Care Alliance surveyed 300 employers and found that some have initiated surcharges and many others are giving the idea serious consideration (May 2006).

33. For example, an employee enrolled in a wellness program could be assessed to have excess body weight, calculated as body mass index (BMI). The employee would be advised of the health risks inherent in such a condition, and given targeted BMI reduction goals as well as a specific diet and exercise program to achieve results. As the BMI is monitored and shows measured progress, financial credits would be contributed by the employer to the employee's FSA. These contributions can be used by the employee to pay for out-of-pocket medical expenses incurred during the year. The administration of such plans can involve medical professionals who monitor compliance and progress. It is important that the employer makes sure there will be a financial return on his investment in wellness programs.

34. See the U.S. Department of Labor Guidelines on HIPAA and Wellness Programs at http://www.dol.gov/ebsa/. The specific conditions are that the reward cannot be more than 20 percent of the total cost of coverage, it must promote health or prevent disease, must be available to all in the plan, and alternatives must be available to those who cannot meet the standard. Some states specifically prohibit premium surcharges under their health insurance laws.

The employer should take baseline measures of his claims occurrences, costs, the extent of the targeted conditions, and the specific risk factors and behaviors that are driving up his expenses. For example, how many workers smoke, how many are overweight, and what is the extent of non-compliance with treatments. He should also determine reasonable goals for each of these measured items, as well as a hypothetical financial return (less the fully loaded accounting costs of the wellness program) should the goals be achieved. The employer should not ignore productivity losses and potential gains attributable to the targeted problems.

Once the program is underway, good controls and interim reviews should be undertaken to identify any barriers or problems that are interfering with its progress. When certain timetables are reached, measurements of the risk factors, targeted behaviors, related health care utilization and expenses, and changes in health care conditions should be taken and compared to the baselines to see what, if anything, has been achieved. The financial implications of these results should be calculated in the format of a return on investment or other appropriate metric.

There are several important considerations in designing a wellness program. First, participation must yield measurable results. The employer should avoid rewarding participants for mere activities. Simply joining

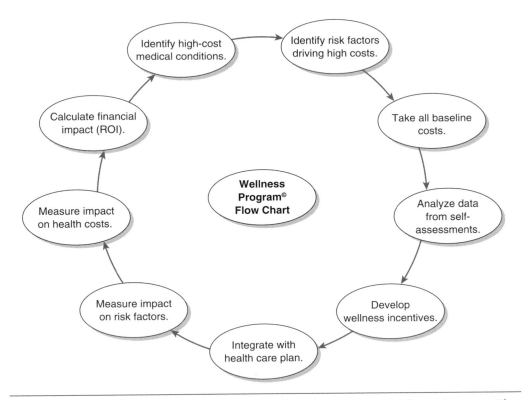

Figure 7.6   The Basic Step-by-Step Process of Implementing a Wellness Program That Is Designed to Affect the Drivers of High Health Care Costs

a fitness center does not warrant a financial reward. Specific health or physiological-related goals for all wellness participants should be the key to reward.

Next, a wellness program should be an initiative among employers whose human resources strategy encourages long service. Though changes in risk factors may occur in a relatively short period, the overall improvement in health status and lowering of health care claims and costs may take years.

In general, a wellness program has the potential to improve the health and productivity of workers and to reduce the level of health care utilization and claims costs.[35] Most programs focus on changing risk factors and underlying lifestyles and behaviors. Employers should not ignore the idea of integrating a wellness approach into their health plans. A program that broadens health assessments, screenings, diagnostics, treatment, and compliance efforts can have a major impact on enhancing the overall health of the workforce and reducing health care costs.

RETIREE HEALTH CARE

Another health care program employers may consider offering is retiree health care. There are two approaches: (1) a plan designed to provide full benefits during the period when the employee is eligible to retire under the employer's retirement plan, at age 55 or 60, but too young to qualify for Medicare, which typically occurs at age 65; and (2) a Medicare supplemental health care plan designed to reimburse expenses not paid by Medicare. In many companies employers offer both plans to their retirees.

As with other benefits, there is no legal obligation on the part of the employer to offer this. Moreover, unlike retirement benefits provided by a defined benefit plan, the employer sponsor is not obligated to prefund retiree health care and, with some exceptions,[36] can discontinue the

---

35. See Loeppke, R., & Hymel, M. (May 2006). Good health is good business. *Journal of Occupational and Employment Medicine, 48*(5), 533–537. This study showed that absenteeism and low productivity generated more costs than health care claims.

36. ERISA provides no such obligation and the courts have basically held that when an employer's benefit summary plan description clearly states that the company reserves the right to modify and cancel its retiree health care plan for current retiree participants, the company may cancel the plan and further decline to offer it to future retirees. There is currently a conflict among U.S. circuit courts as to how and when an employer subject to a collective bargaining agreement may modify or cancel retiree health care. See *Yolton v. El Paso Tennessee Pipeline Co.*, 435 F.3d 571 (6th Cir. 2006). Also, the law seems to be well settled that coordinating Medicare and employer-sponsored retiree health care does not violate the Age Discrimination in Employment Act. Equal Employment Opportunity Commission, 29 CFR 1625 and 1627 (2004).

benefit to newly retired persons, and cancel existing retiree health care plans for those who retired when the benefit was offered. Current accounting rules, however, do require the employer to show his retiree health care liability on his financial statements.

Why would the employer sponsor even bother to offer either type of retiree health care? Once again, the reason is in order to remain competitive in its labor market and to enhance recruitment and retention. Also such a plan generally encourages loyalty and longer service among the workforce. By offering retiree health care, the employer actually facilitates retirement at age 55, or at whatever age the pension plan allows. Without retiree health care, many employees would remain employed until they qualify for Medicare.[37] Employers believe that early retirement opens career opportunities for younger employees who otherwise might be compelled to wait longer for promotions. If the wait is too long, they may leave the firm. Also, early retirement offers the employer the opportunity to replace higher paid workers with lower paid ones, thereby enhancing productivity. So it serves a number of purposes. But there is often a heavy financial burden associated with sponsoring retiree health care. This has caused many to discontinue offering the benefit.

Those employers who do continue to offer retiree health care have changed their plan designs to deal with the higher health care costs associated with an older workforce and increasing life expectancies. When they leave the firm and participate in a separate retiree health care plan, the costs of this plan are based on a higher utilization of health care resources. They are no longer subsidized by premiums paid by the younger workforce who uses less health care resources. The resultant higher costs[38] are passed on to the retirees in the form of new plan designs that require cost sharing in the form of higher out-of-pocket payments and premiums.[39] This is especially true for prescription care plans that may be part of the retiree health care package.

Increasing numbers of employers are shifting many of the costs to the retirees or discontinuing their plans altogether.[40] The message being sent

---

37. When the retiree becomes eligible for Medicare, his dependent can continue in the employer-sponsored retiree health care plan until he becomes eligible for Medicare.

38. From an economics standpoint, there are no higher costs. The employer incurs the same amount of costs with the retirees in an active plan as he would when they are in a retiree plan. It is simply a different allocation.

39. See Chaikind, H. (2006, March 28). *Health insurance coverage for retirees.* Congressional Research Service, The Library of Congress.

40. Chaikind, H. (2006). It should be noted there are a number of legislative initiatives in the United States that would extend Medicare coverage, for example, to those retiring between the ages of 55 and 65, or would prohibit employers from changing their previously offered retiree health care for those who have retired.

is if you want to retire before you are eligible for Medicare, you either will have to find a position that offers health care or buy your own. In the latter case, the cost to the retiree can become excessive. In the former, if the employer terminates retiree health care, the retired employee will have to procure and pay for some type of plan to supplement the reimbursement gaps of Medicare.[41] Now that the newly adopted Medicare Part D includes reimbursements for some government prescription care, the need for employer-sponsored supplemental insurance may be less compelling.

FACTORS AFFECTING THE COST OF THE EMPLOYER-SPONSORED PLAN

Whether a plan is insured or self-insured, the prevailing concern of employer sponsors is health care inflation.[42] The employer must closely examine the basic cost elements of health care: administrative fees for the TPA, past health care claims, and added risk premiums and pooling charges for insured plans that predict the number of claims for the coming year. Then he can take a number of steps to control his expenses, including:

- Negotiate an acceptable administrative fee and performance contract with his TPA

- Get more aggressive discounts for services from his health care providers

- Impact the utilization of health care resources by including various types of behavioral controls in the plan design

- Shift more costs to participate by changing the coinsurance, deductibles, and out-of-pocket maximums

- Direct the focus of employees to the most cost-efficient plan by charging lower premiums or deductibles

---

(See HR 2072 and HR 1322.) See also Mincer, J. (2006, July 5). Health care costs to hit workers, retirees harder. *The Wall Street Journal*, D3. According to Mincer, the vast majority of employers surveyed by two large benefits consulting firms are planning to curtail medical plans for current and future retirees. In fact, according to the report by Mincer, 14 percent of the surveyed companies plan to eliminate retiree health care for future retirees and 6 percent plan to eliminate it for retirees over 65 years of age.

41. This is commonly called Medigap insurance and can be purchased individually by the retiree.

42. For a discussion of the magnitude and purported causes of this inflation, see Herrick, D. (2006) and Bodenheimer, T. (2005).

The most difficult aspect of cost containment relates to utilization. How can an employer and his TPA control inpatient and outpatient hospital services, physician treatments, outpatient services at special facilities, and the use of prescription drugs? The utilization review processes included in some plans are somewhat effective, but also require intense administrative services and are considered to be inefficient. Wellness programs have some efficacy but generate long-term returns and are not consistent with the current trend away from long-term employment.

For now, most employers are simply finding ways to shift the cost of health care to their participants using the standard out-of-pocket features of typical plans. Others are considering dropping health care as a benefit.[43] A few, however, are searching for health care plans that involve networks of both efficient and effective providers, and are studying "pay for performance" contracts where the appropriateness of care is better ensured.[44] As we look at the incentives among our varied participants in the health care landscape, an effort to join these diverse interests is imperative. Employers and their TPAs should insist on receiving value, providers should compete on the basis of their cost and demonstrated quality outcomes, and the participants should be engaged as real consumers. We will discuss this in more detail in Chapter 8.

Insured Plans

For small and medium sized employers who do not have the financial resources to risk paying for large health care claims, an insured plan is the appropriate solution. Insurance, of course, is simply a device to spread the chance of financial loss among a larger number of people. When a smaller company buys health insurance, it is sharing the risk and reducing the chance of a catastrophic health care event among a number of similarly situated employers. The larger number of employers in a group, the more predictable the number of future losses.

43. See Porter, M., & Teisberg, E. (2006). *Redefining health care: Creating value-based competition on results* (p. 506). Boston: Harvard Business School Press. They argue that employers are "feeding the health care cost beast" by not insisting on more results-based deliverables from third parties and providers.

44. "Bridges for Excellence" is an employer-initiated coalition that is demonstrating the connection between health care quality and reduced health care costs. It is encouraging providers to use and publish quality measures in the practice regimens and to offer pay for performance programs. Lau, G. (2005, December 5). Pay for performance gains in popularity. *Investors Business Daily*, A14.

The prediction of loss will control the premium charged by the insurance company. These are called community or manual ratings. As the employer's number of employees increases, the more the employer's own health care claims experience for the previous year will control his premium for the next year. The underlying concept relates to the "Law of Large Numbers": the higher the numbers, the higher the probability of a predicted outcome.[45]

The premium charged by the insurance company includes this prediction, as well as a retention fee that is the insurance company's profit margin. It comprises administrative costs, risk charges, taxes, and commissions. The underlying risks included in the premium charge are based on experience ratings. Larger companies can usually insist that their own experience, and not that of the community, as well as negotiated retention rates be used to determine the renewal premium rates. They are taking some chances here since their numbers are smaller. However, if they have had a relatively healthy workforce and low claims cost, they can significantly reduce their health care premium expense by causing the insurance company to base their premiums on the employer's actual experience rating.[46]

Third-Party Administrator (TPA) Selection

While we will discuss benefit care metrics in more detail in Chapter 10, the issue of vendor selection should involve a quantitative and qualitative evaluation. What are the employer's performance expectations of TPAs and their medical provider networks? In most cases, the selection process begins with the employer issuing a request for proposal (RFP) to a variety of TPAs. The RFP solicits information such as the identity and access to providers in the TPA's network, provider discounts, claims processing performance of the TPA, general customer service rankings, reporting content, and other TPA responsibilities, such as communication programs, enrollment assistance, and claims analysis. It also may include certain performance guarantees with respect to claims processing, cost containment, or general customer service guarantees. The National Council on Quality Assurance rates the performance of TPAs and its

---

45. See Coates, R. (1956). *The law, the world of mathematics* (R. Newman, Ed.), (p. 305). New York: Simon & Shuster.

46. For certain medium sized employers, the premium and renewals will be based on a "blended" rate that comprises, for example, 60 percent based on actual experience and 40 percent based on the manual or community rating.

Table 7.2   Old and New Criteria Applied by Employer Sponsors as They Select New
Health Care Plans

Old Measures	New Measures
Quality providers	Measure clinical outcomes of providers
Access to hospitals and physicians	Health plan can create value
Preserving choice of providers	Transparency in cost and pricing
Cost-effective plan	Pay providers for performance
	TPA performance contracts
	Consumer is engaged in health care

reports are available to employers.[47] Moreover, the employer will examine the various plan designs offered by the TPA and their respective total premium costs.

For self-insured plans, details concerning TPA networks, plan choices, administrative costs, and choice of services are solicited; for insured plans, cost factors relating to the risk elements of the total premium would be studied. A very important element in the relationship between the TPA and the sponsoring employer is the development of cumulative participant data. Can the TPA provide detailed utilization data that will enable both parties to find opportunities to reduce health care expense? The bottom line for the employer sponsor is the formula: (*Utilization* × *Price*) = *Total Cost*. Reduce the price and the utilization and costs will go down. How does the prospective TPA compare to others when considering this formula?

In an effort to acquire more sophisticated administration in certain benefit areas, some employers have engaged specialists such as pharmacy management companies that assume a TPA role only for the prescription drug program. This is called a carve out, and specialized TPAs are currently

47. As we will see in Chapter 10, Employee Benefits and Metrics, the Health Plan Employer Data and Information Set (HEDIS) is a group of performance measures designed to ensure that purchasers and consumers have sufficient information to compare managed care networks. HEDIS is sponsored by the National Committee for Quality Assurance, http://www.ncqa.org/, that also accredits managed care networks.

managing dental, vision, COBRA,[48] and retiree health care. Carve outs
enable the employer to utilize highly specialized companies who are more
aware of provider networks, have better information systems, and can be
held more accountable for performance-based results.

Another initiative designed to improve the cost-effectiveness of the
health care benefit is the employer alliance. Here groups of similarly situated employers join together to collaborate on health care issues, survey
employers' health care practices, look at new designs and approaches to
health care, and, in some cases, use their aggregate size to improve their
leverage in buying health insurance products from TPAs.[49] Some TPAs are
now offering new insured plan products for small employers that are more
responsive to their cost limitations. These products have limited benefits,
high deductibles, and lower lifetime or annual maximums.

Conclusion

The U.S. health program comprises employer-sponsored and government-
sponsored health care, Medicare, and Medicaid. When combined, they
have produced some impressive results.[50] Life expectancy of Americans and
infant mortality have shown dramatic improvements. There are, however,
too many people in the United States who are not covered by an employer-
sponsored plan and do not meet the income tests of Medicaid or the coverage requirements of Medicare. As we look at the growing numbers of
uninsured in the United States, we must ask ourselves, should the employer-sponsored health care plan continue to be a centerpiece of our health
care system?[51] Should we consider some form of national health care to
resolve this problem?

48. The Consolidated Budget and Reconciliation Act (COBRA) is a law allowing
employees who experience certain life events, such as loss of job, to continue
their employer-based health care plan for up to 36 months. It is discussed in
Chapter 12.

49. See, for example, the Employers' Health Care Alliance of Cincinnati at http://
www.cintiehca.com/ and the National Business Coalition on Health at http://
www.nbch.com/, a national affiliation of regional employer groups.

50. Health improvements from 1970 to 1999 have added $1.5 trillion in reduced
work days missed. Bhattacharya, J., & Lakdawalla, D. (2005). *The labor market
value of health improvements* (pp. 1–21). Rand Forum for Health Economics and
Policy.

51. According to the Dartmouth study, the United States does not really have a
"system." Wennberg, J. & Cooper, M. (1999).

It is far more complicated than simply repotting our current compo-nents into a comprehensive, single, national program. There are some fundamental and prerequisite issues to address. If a significant barrier to increasing access and coverage among the uninsured is cost, should we first look at ways to make our current health care system more affordable and cost-effective? Are there viable quality incentives that will cause our providers to get it right the first time? Will the introduction of more mar-ket factors enhance access and higher quality? Is it possible to create a high performance health care system in the United States without moving to a national health care system? How does our health care match up to those in other developed countries where other systems are used? What metrics should we use to make the comparisons? What can we learn from them? We will see this in Chapter 13, Global Benefits.

Now that we understand the basic designs and approaches to health care plans, we move to Chapter 8 to look more intensely at the question of improved access to quality health care and health care reform.

Chapter Exercises

1. Check the American Health Value Web site at http://www .americanhealthvalue.com, as well as some articles on consumer-driven health care, and be prepared to explain the essential design differences among an HRA, HSA, and FSA. Then describe how and under what circumstances an employer might provide all three plans for his employees.

2. How does the consumer-driven HDHCP approach fill a missing market element to traditional health care plans? What is needed to make HSAs achieve their intended purpose? How would you ensure this is included in your own company's strategy to introduce an HDHCP with an HSA?

3. What are the long-term prospects, if any, for consumer-driven plans in reforming health care in the United States? What would you think of a Universal Health Savings Account funded by the employer and employee that would allow the employee to buy a policy anywhere in the health insurance market that would be totally portable?

4. Look at Figure 7.2 and determine in which quadrant you would put an HSA.

5. You are single and a new employee looking at the health care offerings of your employer. The employer offers two health care

plans, an HMO and an HDHCP with an HSA to which it
contributes $75 per month. The deductible for the plan is $1,500
per year. The premium for the HDHCP is 50 percent less than the
premium for the HMO. The deductible for the HMO is $250
(single); the HMO has virtually identical office co-pays, and
coinsurance of 90/10 percent, the same as the HDHCP. Your total
out-of-pocket health care expenses for the last year were $600.
Identify the factors, not necessarily precise numbers, you would
use in calculating the usefulness of choosing the HSA over the
other plans. Don't forget to consider, among other items, the
pretax value of your HSA.

6. Your company currently offers a traditional indemnity-type retiree
    health care plan, as well as a supplemental Medicare policy for its
    retirees. The health care provider market in your community is
    somewhat competitive. Inflation for your retiree plans have
    exceeded national averages and your CEO, while sympathetic to
    her former employees, has demanded that something be done to
    control the costs. Identify and briefly explain a range of possible
    solutions that are responsive to your CEO's demand, and
    recommend a specific and optimal solution that will resolve the
    CEO's concerns and meet legal requirements.

7. Your CFO asks you what benefits you receive as a company by
    offering health care to your employees. Identify the factors you
    would include in your list to the CFO. How would you calculate
    the financial contribution the plan can make to the firm?

8. Assume you are uninsured and wish to buy a health policy on your
    own. Check the following Web sites, get a quote, and identify what
    factors appear to determine the pricing of such plans. See http://
    www.insure.com/ and http://www.ehealthinsurance.com/.

9. Assume you are purchasing health insurance for a medium sized
    employer (300 employees) and want to send out a request for
    proposal to several TPAs. What information would you request in
    your RFP?

10. Suppose you are the CEO of a major hospital with a full array of
    medical services, including a level-three trauma center. A new
    quality and clinical outcomes-based health care data system
    indicates that your hospital significantly lags behind your
    competitors in heart, pulmonary, and orthopedic patient care. On
    the Internet or in the library, check some outcomes-based
    measures that are typically utilized by organizations measuring
    clinical outcomes and then develop an outline of a plan, including
    the steps you would take and the groups you would involve that

could be used to improve your reported results. Include in your plan, among other items, how you would focus on business process changes (workflow) to help drive quality outcomes.

11. The Alliance Health Care Network, a large TPA in your area, has announced it will reward its medical providers with reimbursement bonuses provided they adopt and comply with certain evidence-based medicine or clinical protocol measures recommended by the Health Plan Employer Data and Information Set (HEDIS). Research and become generally familiar with such measures and then advise, as a prospective employer-customer of Alliance, your evaluation of this new approach. Will it create value for your health care program? Explain.

12. You are the HR director of a firm that produces consumer products. You are responsible for all aspects of human resources services, including benefits. Your firm employs 8,000 workers who are located in three manufacturing plants in various locations in the United States. Your health care plan is self-insured and comprises several choices for the employees—a high deductible HSA, two PPOs with different deductibles, coinsurance, out-of-pocket maximums, and premiums. You have received a notice from your TPA, who administers all three plans, that for an extra fee you can include a patient advocate in one or all of your plans. You want to discuss this with your CEO, but first must check into what a patient advocate does, learn how its services are priced in your community, and make an evaluation as to whether such a service would add value to your overall HR and business plans. Do some research on this subject and develop some discussion points you will use in your upcoming meeting with the CEO.

13. Your company just began operating in a rural area where medical provider competition is negligible. Your new workforce is basically young and healthy. You have been asked by your CEO to offer a health care plan that ensures quality and provides choice, but maximizes cost efficiency. Identify and briefly describe the design elements of an optimal health care plan based on these criteria.

14. You have read in the newspapers that the answer to the health care crisis in the United States is to establish the following guiding principles and apply them to our system: "value purchasing, pay for performance, consumerism, and transparency." Do some research and determine what these principles really mean, how they would apply to health care plan design, and how they would help resolve the problem of inefficient and inappropriate care in the United States.

15. Review the following Consumer-Directed Health Care Plan
    (Table 7.3) and comment on its potential efficacy in causing
    employee engagement, enhancing overall health status, and
    reducing claims costs for the employer sponsor. The PPO is the
    accompanying health care plan to the HSA. Is the employer
    sponsor of this plan too generous in giving both a unilateral $250
    contribution, as well as a 100 percent match up to $1,000? What is
    the advantage to the company here?

Table 7.3   Consumer-Directed Health Care Plan

	HSA	PPO
Deductible	$1,100 (single) $2,200 (family)	
Employee contributions (HSA)	$2,900 (single) $5,800 (family)	
Employer contributions	$250 for all accounts and match of 100 percent up to $1,000 (HRA)	
Out-of-pocket maximum		$2,500 (single) $5,000 (family)
Lifetime maximum		Unlimited
Coinsurance after deductible		80/20 percent in network, 60/40 percent out of network
Premium compared to standard PPO with $350 deductible		HDHCP premium is 20 percent of premium for standard PPO
Preventive features		Variety of diagnostic procedures; annual physicals are 100 percent paid by plan, no deductible

Improving Access to Quality Health Care— Do We Need Reform? 8

Janice and her husband own a tile installation company where, until recently, she had been working as an installer. With household bills and two children, they could not afford to purchase a health care plan for themselves or their employees. The premium for them alone is 100 percent of the cost of the plan. For a while they took their chances and then their daughter broke her leg. They took her to the emergency room of an area hospital where she received initial treatment before being transported to an orthopedic surgeon who placed her leg in a cast. Not long after this incident, they received bills from the hospital, the emergency room physician, and the orthopedic surgeon. They were shocked at the amounts, and had to arrange for installment payments to the providers.

Some months later, Janice left the family business and started working at Starbucks in order to get health care insurance for her family and herself. She tells her friends the insurance premium and other co-pays are very reasonable,[1] and that while she preferred working with her husband, they needed the insurance coverage and could not afford it unless she worked at Starbucks.

In the United States, some employees of small, medium, and even large companies choose not to participate in their company's health care plan because, in their opinion, the premium is too expensive for them. Their decision forces them into the ranks of the uninsured and subjects them to the risk of significant medical liabilities. The above scenario is not unique.

---

1. Starbucks offers health care to both full-time and part-time employees to attract applicants who need health care coverage, but can work only limited hours a week. This arrangement works well for Starbucks and generates a positive return. Obviously, the candidates they attract meet their service orientation job requirements and raise the overall level of service in their stores.

There is a health care crisis occurring in the United States. In 2007, total average costs for family coverage under an employer health care plan rose to $12,106 per year.[1] Nevertheless, the rate of increase is slowing. It was 6.1 percent in 2007, which is the lowest since 1999, and this lower rate is expected to continue.[2] While 98 percent of companies with more than 200 workers still offer some form of health insurance, only 60 percent of smaller companies do, compared with 66 percent just five years ago.[3] Those that do offer coverage are shifting more of the costs to the employee participants.[4] On average, an employee pays about 28 percent of the premium costs;[5] however, when you add in co-pays, deductibles, and coinsurance, that employee's share of the total health care expense is closer to 50 percent.[6]

As a result, some employees are declining coverage because they cannot afford it or want to spend their money on other things.[7] Others have no opportunity for coverage and cannot afford to buy a health insurance policy on their own. For example, the Bureau of Labor Statistics reports that in 2007, the average premium paid by an employee to obtain coverage was $81 (single) and $312 (family).[8] Regardless of the circumstances, those who decline coverage and those who are not covered comprise the

1. This cost represents an increase of 72 percent since 2002. See *2007 employer health benefits survey*. (2007, September 11). Kaiser Family Foundation and Health Research and Educational Trust, http://www.kff.org/.

2. *2007 employer health benefits survey*. (2007, September 11).

3. Kaiser Family Foundation and Health Research and Educational Trust (2007).

4. Part of the fallout on our high costs is that some bankruptcies in the United States are a result of health care costs the debtor cannot pay. See Himmelstein, D., Warren, E., Thorne, D., & Woolhandler, S. (2005, February 2). *Illness and injury as contributors to bankruptcy*. Health Affairs, http://www.healthaffairs.org.

5. See Kaiser Family Foundation and Health Research and Educational Trust (2007); Fuhrmans, V. (2006, September 26). Health care premiums rise 7.7 percent, outpacing wages and inflation. *The Wall Street Journal Online*, http://www.wsj.com.

6. See Kaiser Family Foundation/Health Research and Educational Trust (2007). The report indicates premiums for family coverage among U.S. employer-sponsored plans to be 28 percent, without considering office co-pays, deductibles, and coinsurance. Since out-of-pocket maximums (that are based on coinsurance and deductibles paid by the employee in a year) average about $2,500, or 20 percent of the total average health care cost, the total percentage of cost sharing for employees would amount to about 47 percent of the total cost of the plan.

7. See Fuhrmans (2006). The share of workers covered by health insurance through their own employer has fallen to 59 percent from 60 percent last year and 63 percent in 2000.

8. *Employee benefits in private industry*. (2007, August). *Bureau of Labor Statistics*. It should be noted, however, that the rate of annual premium increases have been declining since about 2002. See *Sources of health insurance and characteristics of the uninsured* (p. 9). (2007, October). Employee Benefit Research Institute (EBRI).

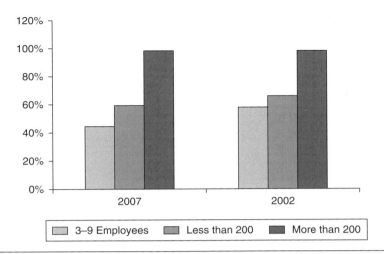

Figure 8.1   Percentage of Employers Offering Health Care Based on Their Size

SOURCE: Kaiser Family Foundation (2007).

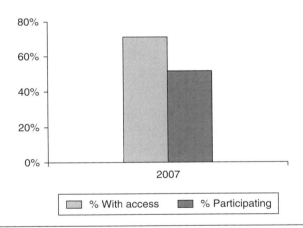

Figure 8.2   Percentage of Employees in Private Sector With Access to Employer-Sponsored Health Care and Percentage Actually Participating

SOURCE: 2007 National Compensation Survey, Bureau of Labor Statistics.

uninsured. But the crisis is not the uninsured; they are simply the collateral damage of a health care system that is bulging with excessive costs and the resulting lack of affordability.[9]

---

9. Health insurance premiums increased 100 percent from 2000 to 2007, while consumer inflation increased 24 percent and wages grew 21 percent. See *Health insurance cost.* (2008). National Coalition on Health Care, http://www.nchc.org/.

We have discussed in Chapters 6 and 7 the apparent drivers of health care inflation. We also have discussed how employer sponsors are searching for ways to make their health care plans more affordable. For the most part, this has involved shifting costs to their employees by increasing deductibles, co-pays, and premiums.[10] In this chapter we will examine the systemic causes of excessive costs, and explore a range of approaches to improve and reform the health care delivery systems. The goal of the chapter is to chart a course toward affordable health care that will make it accessible to all in the United States.

Underlying Problems of Cost and Affordability— Value and the Lack of Quality

"The U.S. health care system is on a dangerous path, with a toxic combination of high costs, uneven quality, frequent errors, and limited access to care."[11] There is a large gap in public and private health care plans through which a significant number of people "fall between the chairs." They are the uninsured and they number about 45.7 million people in the United States.[12] The number decreased from 47 million in 2006. Providing free or uncompensated health care benefits to the uninsured is estimated to cost Americans about $41 billion per year.[13] Although there are public

---

10. Read an interesting story about how an unexpected five-month stay in the hospital for an infection caused a California employee with health insurance to exceed his $1.5 million lifetime maximum, leaving him with the responsibility to pay $1.2 million to the hospital: Carreyrou, J. (2007, November 29). As medical costs soar, the insured face huge tab. *The Wall Street Journal*, A1.

11. Porter, M., & Teisberg, E. (2006). *Redefining health care, creating value-based competition on results* (p. 17). Boston: Harvard Business School Publications. See also the recent Dartmouth report that chronicles uneven health care treatments for those suffering from chronic illness. *The Dartmouth Atlas of Health Care 2008: Tracking the care of patients with severe chronic illness.* The Dartmouth Institute for Health Policy & Clinical Practice.

12. See U.S. Census Bureau, Health Insurance Coverage: 2007. (2008, August). The number of uninsured had, however, increased about 3.4 million people between 2004 and 2006. Most of this increase was attributable to a decline in employer-sponsored health care plans. Holahan, J., & Cook, A. (2008, February 20). The U.S. economy and changes in health insurance coverage, 2000–2006. *Health Affairs, 27*(2).

13. Hadley, J., & Holahan, J. (2004). *The cost of care for the uninsured.* The Kaiser Commission on Medicaid and the Uninsured, Issue Update, 2004. Many hospitals provide "free care" or "uncompensated care" to persons who cannot afford health care. They are sometimes partially reimbursed by local government tax levies.

programs for the elderly and poor, such as Medicare and Medicaid, many of the uninsured do not qualify.[14] Anyone, regardless of their insured status, however, can receive treatment for certain urgent or emergency health conditions. Hospital emergency rooms often serve as the venues for persons with such conditions and they offer care without regard to the patient's coverage. The emergency room, however, does not dispense preventive care and it is expensive.[15] So the uninsured remain vulnerable to untreated, chronic, and acute health problems. Primary and preventive care are the centerpieces of any health care system and without them a person will eventually experience a decline in overall health.[16]

If the underlying problems of the uninsured are high costs and lack of affordability, then what can we do to reform the health care system to change this? Among employers offering health care insurance, there is a clear shifting of costs to the participants, which threatens their ability to pay the premiums and the other cost sharing obligations. Health insurance coverage has become a significant public policy issue among Americans.[17]

Later in this chapter we will discuss a number of approaches to reform the health care financing and delivery systems, ranging from single payer, national systems to enlarged coverage of public programs, and employer or individual mandates. Since the main cause of the problem is high cost and a lack of affordability, we will first explore this issue.

---

14. About 60 percent of the U.S. population is covered by employer-sponsored or other privately sponsored health insurance; 29 percent receives health care coverage from a government-sponsored health plan such as Medicare, Medicaid, Veterans Administration Health Care, or the State Children's Health Insurance Program; the remainder are uninsured. See *Framework for a high performance health system for the United States*. (2006, August). The Commonwealth Fund, Commission on a High Performance Health System, http://www.cmwf.org/.

15. Hospital emergency rooms are also crowded and in recent years the wait times have increased from a median 22 minutes to 30 minutes. *Health Affairs* (2008, January 15).

16. Baker, D., Sudano, J., Albert, J., Borawski, E., & Dor, A. (2001, October 11). Lack of health insurance and decline in overall health in late middle age. *New England Journal of Medicine*. For example, persons in late middle age without health care coverage have an increased risk of a decline in overall health.

17. See Schoen, C., et al. (2006, August). *Public views shaping the future of the U.S. health system*. The Commonwealth Fund, http://www.cmwf.org/publications/. In this study, 75 percent of adults surveyed said the U.S. health system needs fundamental change or complete rebuilding. Expanding insurance and controlling costs are top priorities. The top concern keeps shifting as new developments occur, but health care, the economy, war in Iraq, and immigration consistently have been in the top four among U.S. voters. NBC poll. (2007, November). *The Wall Street Journal*.

Stating the Underlying Problem—High Costs of Health Care

Why is health care so expensive in the United States, and are there some ways to make it more affordable? It is important to point out that the United States has some of the best facilities and providers in the world, and leads the world in medical research and technology. While longevity and infant mortality statistics are somewhat better in other developed countries, it is generally accepted that, if one is severely ill, the United States is the place to be.

There are flaws in our system that lead to its high costs and lack of affordability. Currently, the United States spends 16.7 percent of is gross domestic product (GDP) on health care. It is expected that this will rise to close to 20 percent by 2017.[18] Our key neighbors in Europe, France, the U.K., and Germany spend on average about 30 percent less on health care.[19] Our prices for care are too high, the system lacks transparency, often we experience inappropriate care, and we have little or no data available to determine which providers offer the best clinical outcomes. We also suffer under the weight of unhealthy lifestyles, poor health education, and lack of patient compliance and engagement.[20] How can we resolve these issues and avoid embedding any new broad reform programs with deficiencies that would impede their effectiveness?

The argument that our higher costs deliver the best system depends on how one defines "best." We compare other countries' health care systems to the United States in Chapter 13, but here are a few important statistics:

- The United States has the highest patient survival rate for cancer in the world. Fewer persons with cancer die in the United States than anywhere else.[21]

- Wait times for elective surgeries are the lowest in the United States among five key countries including Canada and the U.K.[22]

18. Keehan, S. et al. (2008, February 26). Health spending projection through 2017: The baby-boom generation is coming to Medicare. *Health Affairs*, w.145–155, Web exclusive, http://www.healthaffairs.org/.

19. *Health care spending in the U.S. and OECD countries*. (2007, January). Kaiser Family Foundations, http://www.kkf.org.

20. Porter, M., & Teisberg, E. (2006), p. 1; *Crossing the quality chasm*. (2003). The Institute of Medicine, National Academy of Sciences; Davis, K., et al. (2004, January). *Mirror, mirror on the wall*. The Commonwealth Fund; The Commonwealth Fund, Commission on a High Performance Health System (2006).

21. Tanner, M. (2007, September 10). *Cancer Society's deadly medicine*. The Cato Institute, http://www.cato.org/; Health care quality indicators project 2006. (2007, October 30). OECD, Working Papers No. 29.

22. *Tackling excessive wait times for elective surgery: A comparison of policies in twelve OECD countries*. (2003, July 7). OECD, Working Paper No. 6. The five countries

- Americans are diagnosed and treated for chronic illnesses more often than most major developed countries. These include diabetes, hypertension, chronic lung disease, asthma, arthritis, and others.[23]

- Most people living in developed countries have easier access to primary care than in the United States.[24]

- The United States leads the world in medical research and development, contributing more medical innovation than any other country.[25]

The United States has allowed financial barriers to care to exist and has relatively more coordination of care problems.[26] So, are we getting appropriate returns on our massive health care investment?[27]

Health Care Investment and Efficacy

While the United States lags behind many other countries in longevity, infant mortality, access to primary care, and quality of life expectancy,[28] some of these variations may be due to lifestyle differences between the United States and its European counterparts.[29] Others appear to be the result of the structure of the health care delivery system.[30]

---

included Canada, Australia, the Netherlands, Spain, and the U.K. Germany, France, Belgium, Austria, and Japan reported no significant wait times.

23. Thorpe, K., Howard, D., & Galactionova, K. (2007, October 2). Differences in disease prevalence as a source of the U.S.–European health care spending gap. *Health Affairs*, 678–686.

24. *First report and recommendations of The Commonwealth Fund's international working group on quality indicators.* (June 2004). The Commonwealth Fund.

25. Tanner, M. (2007, September 10).

26. The Commonwealth Fund (June 2004).

27. See Chapter 13, Global Benefits.

28. See Starfield, B., & Shi, L. (2002). Policy relevant determinants of health: An international perspective. *Health Policy, 60,* 201–218. The authors found that a strong, primary care infrastructure led to better health results and lower costs of long-term health.

29. For example, the U.S. leads the comparator countries in obesity. See Docteur, E. (2003). *U.S. health system performance in an international context.* Organization for Economic Cooperation and Development (OECD). Presentation at Academy Health Research Meeting (2003, June).

30. Comparative statistics reveal that measures such as the supply of health care services including beds, physicians, specialists, and hospital discharges are higher in the comparator European countries than in the United States. On the other

Higher spending in the United States did increase life expectancy, but the cost of such progress was exceptionally high.[31] As noted previously, the United States leads the world in medical research and innovation, with 75 percent of all medications discovered and first used in the United States.[32] The United States also leads all developed countries in biomedical research and innovation. And we spend more on and obtain the superior performance among our research facilities.[33] The conclusion is inescapable. While the United States has experienced positive improvements in health results, our access to care and comparative costs are not favorable and lead one to question whether we could be doing a lot better.[34]

It should be noted that basic measures such as life expectancy and infant mortality do not conclusively reflect on the overall efficacy of the U.S. health care system. They are general epidemiological statistics. Are we getting good comparative value for the prices we pay? We could answer this question more accurately if we were using more precise benchmark measures, such as how effectively are health care practices delivered, or what are the clinical outcomes of a given system?[35] The Organization for Economic Development (OECD) is working on these comparisons. They

---

hand, length of stay for acute care and treatment wait times are lower in the United States, while inpatient surgeries are higher in the U.S. Docteur (2003).

31. We know, for example, that each year of added life expectancy at birth, which climbed from 69.9 in 1960 to 76.9 for a baby born in 2000, cost approximately $20,000. The cost per added year of life expectancy in other OECD countries was far less. Lee, C. (2006, August 13). Study finds health care a good value. *The Washington Post*, A14.

32. See Gambardella, A., Orsenigo, L., & Pammolli, F. (2000, November). *Global competitiveness in pharmaceuticals, a European perspective.* Report for the Enterprise Directorate-General of the European Commission; *Securing the benefit of medical innovation for seniors, the role of prescription drugs and drug coverage.* (2002, July). U.S. Department of Health and Human Services. As of 1994, the United States contributed 45 percent of 152 globally marketed drugs; Tanner, M. (2007, September 10), who points out that American scientists played a key role in 805 of the most important medical advances in the last 30 years.

33. Cowen, T. (2006, October 5). Poor U.S. scores in health care don't measure Nobels and innovation, *The New York Times.*

34. See Lee, C. (2006, August 31). Study finds health care a good value. *The Washington Post*, A14.

35. For example, the survival rate for breast cancer in the United States is higher than in the U.K., France, Germany, and Canada. The same is true for colorectal cancer, prostate cancer, and indeed most cancers. Tanner, M. (2007, September 10). The Commonwealth Fund (2004, June) is currently comparing survival rates for cancers, organ transplants, heart attacks, stroke, vaccination rates, nonsmoking rates, asthma survival rates, accessibility to medical care, financial barriers to care, and patient–doctor communications.

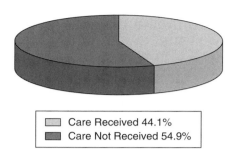

Care Received 44.1%
Care Not Received 54.9%

Figure 8.3   The Gap Between Recommended Care Received and Care
Not Received

SOURCE: McGlynn, E., Asch, S., Adams, J., Keesey, J., Hicks, J., DeCristo-
faro, A., et al. (2003, June 26). The quality of health care delivered to adults
in the U.S. *New England Journal of Medicine, 348*(26), 2635–2645.

intend to contrast clinical outcomes arising from cardiac care, diabetes
care, primary care and prevention, mental health care, and patient safety
among member countries.[36] For now, however, we can examine one of the
internal problems leading to our high costs—inappropriate care.

Inappropriate Care and Clinical Quality Measurements

One of the basic tenets of good management is Deming's "get it right the first
time."[37] Unfortunately, this has not been the case in the U.S. health care
system. About 35 percent of health treatments in the United States are

36. See OECD Health Care Quality Indicators Project. (2004, October). OECD,
http://www.oecd.org/; van der Maas, P. (2003). How summary measures of
population health are affecting health agendas. *Bulletin of the World Health
Organization, Health Care, 81*(5). The WHO bulletin indicates that more precise
metrics will identify the inputs that are driving the epidemiological differences
among compared countries. We do not, however, have comparative clinical outcomes data that would provide a clearer picture of efficacy. For example, there are
no reliable comparative metrics to determine successful and unsuccessful clinical
outcomes and costs of medical procedures, the length of stay for comparable
patients and medical procedures, the rate and success of medical innovation, the
rate of inappropriate care, the acuity adjusted mortality rate of patients among
various providers, quality of life, and the redundant administrative costs of systems expressed as a percentage of total health care costs. Due to competitive pressures, more and more providers in the United States are agreeing to provide data
that would show how they compare in clinical outcomes and many of the above
measures. van der Maas, P. (2003).

37. Deming, W. E., http://www.deming.org/.

inappropriate.[38] Major U.S. studies of health care outcomes and procedures reveal that many patients experiencing similar conditions receive either too much or not enough care.[39] Several years ago, the Dartmouth study[40] showed that millions of Americans do not receive proven, effective medical interventions that can save lives and prevent disabilities. It also revealed poor quality in clinical decision making, frequent failure to apply a scientific basis for clinical practice, and substandard medical skills, all of which result in unnecessary mortality, morbidity, and excessive costs. The studies have found an overuse of procedures particularly in end-of-life acute care periods, an underuse of proven preventive care measures, and significant and irrational variations in health care spending depending on geographic location.

Since these reports were issued, many health care providers, employer sponsors, and TPAs have become very interested in quality measurements. They have implemented medical protocols that lead to better quality outcomes when followed by providers. For example, providing immunizations, giving life-saving drugs after a heart attack, testing for diabetes, and controlling high blood pressure are among the standards and protocols used by the National Committee for Quality Assurance to evaluate provider networks.[41] As a result, the United States has seen some improvements in clinical outcomes over the last several years.[42] The focus, however, has been on process compliance. Measuring and comparing actual clinical outcomes achieved by hospital and medical providers is in a nascent stage in the United States. Since inappropriate care increases the costs of health

---

38. Davis, K., Schoen, C., Guteman, S., Shih, T., Schoenbaum, S., & Weinbaum, I. (2007, January 29). *Slowing the growth of U.S. health care expenditures: What are the options?* The Commonwealth Fund, Vol. 47, http://www.commonwealthfund .org. Kohn, L., & Corrigan, J. (1999). *To err is human: Building a safer health system.* Washington, National Academy Press; Wennberg, J., & Cooper, M. (1999). *Quality medical care in the U.S.* Chicago: American Health Association Press.

39. *Crossing the quality chasm.* (2003). The Institute of Medicine, National Academy of Sciences. Davis, K. et al. (2004, January). *Mirror, mirror on the wall.* The Commonwealth Fund.

40. Wennberg (1999). The 1999 Wennberg findings are consistent with the most recent Dartmouth study that shows poor coordination of treatments and diagnostic procedures, and excessive and unnecessary care. "The quality of care for Americans with chronic disease is remarkably uneven. Most patients receive episodic care from multiple different physicians who rarely coordinate the care they deliver." See *Dartmouth Atlas of Health Care.* (2008). Center for Healthcare Research and Reform, Dartmouth University, http://www .dartmouthatlas.org/.

41. See *The state of health care quality 2006.* Washington, DC: NCQA, http://www .ncqa.org/.

42. See *Measurement improves health care quality for 70 million Americans but gaps remain.* (2006, September 27). NCQA, NCQA News.

care, it is imperative that the United States embraces and implements a system to measure the clinical outcomes of our providers.[43]

Reporting outcomes will facilitate value-based competition that allows sponsors and consumers of health care to determine which providers are achieving the best results and where their health care dollars are being spent. It will also provide a systemwide basis for assessing the causes of and developing corrections for our quality problems. Getting it right the first time can lead to a significant reduction in costs and be a big step toward enhancing affordability.

Errors Increase Costs

The U.S. system experiences too many medical errors that result in severe human and economic consequences. Post-hospital admission infections result in the deaths of 100,000 patients in the United States each year. An acute infection costs a hospital about $40,000 in uncompensated expense, adds to the length of stay, requires the consumption of more health care resources, and results in higher costs for the sponsor of the patient's health care plan.[44]

Medication errors account for another 100,000 deaths annually. An estimated 907,600 medication errors occur each year in our nation's hospitals. A recent Commonwealth Fund study showed the United States ranked last among five English-speaking countries in patient safety. The measurements included medication errors and other medical mistakes.[45] The Leapfrog Group, an organization that compares quality indicators among hospitals, estimates that implementing better safety and quality practices could save up to 65,341 lives each year and $51.3 billion in unnecessary expenses.[46] Errors arise in both diagnosis and treatments, and

43. See Murphy, T. (1995, Winter). Creating market conditions for the delivery of health care. *Human Resource Management, 34*(4). The National Committee on Quality Assurance, http://www.ncqa.org, for example, is actively responding to demands for new quality health care initiatives among U.S. providers.

44. Dr. Richard Shannon, Chairman of the Department of Medicine at Allegheny Hospital in Pittsburgh, has indicated that an average city hospital loses approximately $10 million per year treating post-admission infections. *Remaking American medicine.* (2006, October 11). Public Broadcasting System, http://www.pbs.org/remakingamericanmedicine/.

45. Davis, K., et al. (2004). *Mirror, mirror on the wall: Looking at the quality of American health care through the patient's lens.* The Commonwealth Fund, http://www.cmwf.org.

46. See Leapfrog Group Fact Sheet (2006), http://www.leapfroggroup.org.

they generate billions annually in added expense.[47] Improvements in patient safety could reduce medical costs and improve the affordability of health care in the United States.[48]

There is a systemic deficiency that plays a significant role in contributing to medical and medication errors—the lack of access to accurate and updated patient information and records.[49] While there are incremental enhancements that can be made in the way we maintain medical records, there is a comprehensive solution on the horizon. A single, computerized medical record with a patient's complete medical history, accessible by any medical provider, could eliminate many errors and reduce the overall costs of health care in the United States.[50] A unified medical record could also improve the overall quality of care, if it is fully integrated with the treatment process.

Our Culture, System, and Prices

A lack of outcomes data and quality-based competition, better patient safety, and more consistent treatments all contribute to our high health care costs. But there are other factors. Lifestyles, demographics, and culture, as well as our health care infrastructure, all perpetuate high costs and the lack of affordability. Here are some examples:

- Our aging population and its heavy utilization of health care procedures and medicines, particularly in the final months of life.[51]

47. Porter, M., & Teisberg, E. (2006), p. 26

48. Some insurers and Medicare are beginning to refuse payments for conditions caused by medical errors. The patient as well would not be liable. See Fuhrmans, V. (2008, January 15). Insurers stop paying for care linked to errors. *The Wall Street Journal*, D1. The errors include leaving surgical equipment inside the patient following a procedure, administering wrong blood type, operating on wrong limb, performing wrong procedure, and hospital-acquired bedsores and infections.

49. See The digital hospital. (2005, March 28). *Business Week Online*, http://www.businessweek.com/print/magazine/

50. Only a small percentage of providers are using electronic health records. See Jha, A., Ferris, T., et al. (2006, October 11). How common are electronic health records in the U.S.? A summary of the evidence. *Health Affairs, 25*(6), 496–507. A recent finding of the Dartmouth group illustrates the need for better medical records, "Most patients receive episodic care from multiple different physicians who rarely coordinate the care they deliver. *Dartmouth Atlas of Health Care* (2008). France is currently at work placing a memory chip in each person's health card that includes his entire medical history.

51. Americans approaching retirement age utilize an average of about 50 percent more health care resources. See Chaikind, H. (2006, March 28). *Health insurance coverage for retirees.* Congressional Research Service.

- An increase in sedentary lifestyles, poor health habits, chronic diseases, and widespread obesity.[52]

- Poor health awareness, education, and a lack of patient compliance with prescribed health practices.[53]

- The administrative waste associated with processing claims under our fragmented health care system is as much as three times the cost experienced in countries with national health care plans,[54] and has been aptly referred to as "the most nattily cumbersome administrative system in the world."[55]

- High pharmaceutical costs that are expected to increase due to the cost of research and innovation, increased use, and the protracted FDA approval process.[56]

---

52. Thirty-four percent of U.S. adults age 20 and over are obese. In 1976 the rate was 15 percent. See Centers for Disease Control and Prevention, U.S. Department of Health and Human Services. See also Docteur, E. (2003); Thorpe, K., Howard, D., & Galactionova, K. (2007, October 2). Differences in disease prevalence as a source of the U.S.–European health care spending gap. *Health Affairs*, http://www.healthaffairs.org/. This study indicates that the United States has a higher prevalence of a number of chronic diseases as well as the requisite treatments and this is a major driver of the gap in spending.

53. See Cerise, F. (2005). *How do health care systems recover?* United Health Foundation, America's Health Rankings. In this article, the Secretary of Louisiana's Department of Health and Hospitals reflects that "Louisiana ranks 49th in health status among the 50 states. One in five citizens is uninsured. We have high rates of obesity and tobacco use. Poverty and lack of education are barriers to health improvement in both our state and region." Also, see *Key Facts Race, Ethnicity, & Medical Care.* (2007, January). The Kaiser Family Foundation; Porter, M., & Teisberg, E. (2006), p. 341.

54. See Himmelstein, D., Woolhandler, S., & Wolfe. (2004). Administrative waste in the U.S. health care system. *International Journal of Health Services, 34*(1), 79–86; Woolhandler, S., Campbell, T., & Himmelstein, D. (2003, August 21). *Cost of health care administration in the U.S. and Canada. The New England Journal of Medicine, 349*(8), 768–775.

55. Wessel, D., Wysocki, B., & Martinez, B. (2006, December 29). As health middlemen thrive, employers try to tame them. *The Wall Street Journal*, A1, http://online.wsj.comm/article/.

56. See an interesting article from MIT about how our drug prices that are the highest in the world can be reduced. The interviewees argue that U.S. drug companies devote too many resources to make modest improvements in existing drugs that further increase prices, yet offer minor returns in efficacy. Wright, S. (2008, March 17). How drug prices can be reduced. *MIT News*, http://www.mit.edu.

- An abundance of imaging services and other new medical technologies and their increased utilization in the United States.[57]

- Prices for most health care services in the United States are simply higher than those found in our OECD counterpart countries.[58]

Are these immutable factors that will hobble any reformed health care system, or should they be the initial focus of reform? Some conclude that certain proposed reforms, such as a national single-payer system will automatically correct them. But, public systems that sponsor health care for the poor and the aged are experiencing the same problems—spiraling costs and pending deficits.[59] Thus, it is clear that public sponsorship does not, in and of itself, immunize a health system from the cultural and structural drivers of excessive costs.[60] An argument can be made to attack the underlying

---

57. Medical Cost Reference Guide (2005).

58. These are the result of higher provider reimbursement and compensation, higher equipment and drug costs, less controlled purchasing of high technology equipment, reduced bargaining power among private sponsors of health care for the purchase of health care services, which has apparently resulted from recent consolidations and mergers of providers in the United States. Anderson, G., Reinhardt, U., Hussey, P., & Petrosyan, V. (2003). It's the prices, stupid: Why the U.S. is so different from other countries. *Health Affairs, 22*(3), 89–105. Public sponsors, on the other hand, like Medicare and Medicaid have maintained significant strength in negotiating provider reimbursement levels. Bodenheimer, T. (2005). High and rising health care costs. *Annals of Internal Medicine, 142*, 932–937.

59. Health expenditures increased 32 percent per person between 2000 and 2004; by 2013 it is expected the U.S. health expenditures as a percentage of GDP will rise to 18 percent. Bodenheimer, T. (2005). The impact of these costs affect the ability of employers to continue sponsoring health care to their employees and put the current delivery system in jeopardy. They also lead to increased numbers of persons who are uninsured. *Sources of health insurance and the uninsured.* (2006, October). Employee Benefits Research Institute, EBRI Issue Brief No. 298.

60. Medicare, for example, is on the cusp of a deficit and it is expected that participant cost sharing of its doctor and prescription drug care programs will rise from the current 29 percent of the average Social Security benefit to 53 percent in 2040, to 73 percent in 2080. Munnell, A. (2007, October). *Medicare costs and retirement security.* Center for Retirement Research at Boston University, No. 7-14. See also the U.S. Department of Health and Human Services, Centers for Medicare and Medicaid Services at http://www.cms.hhs.gov/. Medicare expense is expected to rise significantly through 2017 as "baby boomers" apply for benefits. In part, as a result, the percentage of our GDP spent on health care will rise from 16.3 percent in 2007 to 19.5 percent in 2017, almost one-fifth of the U.S. economy. For an excellent summary of the potential areas and degrees of growth in the Medicare, see Keehan, S. et al. (2008, February 26). We should note that most states, local governments, and individual hospitals have programs to provide medical assistance for the poor who do not qualify for Medicaid or Medicare. These programs are often privately funded or supported by local tax levies; however, they do not provide consistent, preventive

causes of high costs in our system first, before or concurrent with any undertaking to restructure its delivery and financing. The menu of opportunities has been outlined above; possible solutions are set forth below.

While we discuss Medicare and Medicaid in detail in Chapter 12, in order to facilitate some discussion of health care reform, here is a brief synopsis of both programs.

Medicaid is available to 56 million low income and low net worth individuals. Federal and state laws establish benefit and eligibility standards. Essentially, it is a fee-for-service plan that directly reimburses providers. Both state (43 percent) and federal (57 percent) governments finance it. Depending on a particular state's laws, participants may be asked to pay a small part of the cost (co-payment) for some medical services. In certain circumstances, Medicaid provides nursing home care and other long-term assistance programs for persons with physical or mental handicaps.[1]

Medicare was created in 1966 as a national health care plan for the disabled and persons over 65. It is a fee-for-service indemnity-type plan that covers hospitalizations of participants who also can elect to enroll in physician reimbursement (Medicare Part B) and prescription care (Medicare Part D) programs.[2] There are 42.5 million elderly and disabled persons covered by these programs.[3] Medicare is financed by a payroll tax on the employee and employer.

1. See the U.S. Department of Health and Human Services, Centers for Medicare and Medicaid Services at http://www.cms.hhs.gov/. Medicare expense is expected to rise significantly through 2017 as "baby boomers" apply for benefits. In part, as a result, the percentage of our GDP spent on health care will rise from 16.3 percent in 2007 to 19.5 percent in 2017, almost one fifth of the U.S. economy. For an excellent summary of the potential areas and degrees of growth in Medicare, see Keehan, S. et al. (2008, February 26). *Health spending projection through 2017: The baby-boom generation is coming to Medicare.* Health Affairs, w.145-155, Web exclusive, http://www.healthaffairs.org/.

2. Medicare has contracted with private insurance companies to provide coverage for Part B (Physicians) and Part D (Prescriptions) coverage through an HMO or PPO-type plan. In such cases the company receives its premium from Medicare.

3. See the U.S. Department of Health and Human Services, Medicare Web site at http://www.medicare.gov/.

care opportunities or access to a primary care physician despite clear evidence that indicates this is the single most important factor in delivering quality, long-term health care. In 1986, the U.S. Congress passed a law that prohibited emergency rooms from refusing emergency treatment for the uninsured. See the Emergency Medical Treatment and Labor Act, 42 U.S.C. §1395dd, 42 C.F.R. §489.2.

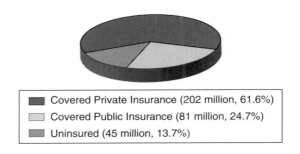

> ■ Covered Private Insurance (202 million, 61.6%)
> ▢ Covered Public Insurance (81 million, 24.7%)
> ▨ Uninsured (45 million, 13.7%)

Figure 8.4   U.S. Health Insurance Coverage

SOURCE: *Income, Poverty, and Health Insurance in the United States: 2007.* (2008, August). U.S. Census Bureau.

Profile of the Uninsured[61]

In spite of programs to cover persons who are elderly, poor, unemployed, or cannot afford to pay the premiums for their employer-sponsored health plan, the number of those without coverage in 2007 totaled 45.5 million.[62] This number is unacceptable. Who are those persons who have no health insurance from either a public program or from their employer? Here is a profile:

- About 17.2 percent of the nonelderly (under age 65) population is uninsured at any one point in time.[63] The total percentage of uninsured among the U.S. population is 15.3 percent. The number is constantly changing as people come off or go on a particular health care plan.

---

61. For a comprehensive statistical survey of the uninsured in the United States, see Sources of health insurance and the uninsured. (2008, September). Employee Benefits Research Institute, EBRI Issue Brief No. 321. Also see *Income, poverty, and health insurance coverage in the U.S.* (2008, August). U.S. Census Bureau. Although the rate of health premium increases has declined in the last several years, a number of employer sponsors have shifted costs onto covered workers, who have experienced a 143 percent increase in premiums and a 115 percent increase in deductibles, co-pays, and coinsurance between the years 2000 and 2004. See National Coalition on Health Care (2004).

62. See EBRI (2008, September); *Changes in employees' health care coverage, 2001–2005.* (2006, October). The Kaiser Family Foundation, Issue Paper.

63. *Who are the uninsured? A consistency profile across the country.* (2006, August). The Kaiser Commission on Medicaid and the Uninsured. The percentage of employed persons who were uninsured increased from 13.7 percent in 2001 to 16.6 percent in 2005.

- The number of uninsured declined from 47 million in 2006 to 45.5 million in 2007 due largely to an increase in coverage under government programs.[64]

- The aggregate number of nonelderly persons covered by health insurance has increased from 82.1 percent in 2006 to 82.8 percent in 2007.[65]

- There were 202 million persons covered by private insurance and 81 million covered by public programs in the United States in 2007.[66]

- The percentage of persons covered by employer-sponsored health care dropped from 62.7 percent in 2005 to 62.2 percent in 2007.[67]

- About 83 percent of the uninsured live in families headed by a worker.[68]

- 8.1 percent of children under the age of 18 are uninsured.

- Persons who buy health insurance on their own comprise 6.8 percent of the nonelderly population.[69]

- Public programs such as Medicaid, Medicare, SCHIP, and military-related health insurance cover about 17.5 percent of the nonelderly.[70]

- Approximately 71 percent of workers had access to health insurance, but only 52 percent participated in a plan.[71] Of those employees who did not participate, 7.2 percent had incomes between $50,000 and $59,999 per year, 5.7 percent earned between $60,000 and $69,000 per year, and more than 8 percent made over $70,000 per year.[72]

64. *The uninsured.* (2008, September). Employee Benefits Research Institute (EBRI), Issue Brief No. 321, p. 1

65. U.S. Census Bureau (2008, August).

66. U.S. Census Bureau (2008, August).

67. EBRI (2008, September). See also Bureau of Labor Statistics, Employee Benefits in Private Industry (2008, August).

68. EBRI (2008, September).

69. EBRI (2008, September), p. 4

70. EBRI (2008, September).

71. See also Bureau of Labor Statistics, Employee Benefits in Private Industry (2007, August).

72. EBRI (2008, September).

- Of the 20 percent of the uninsured who are eligible for coverage by a health insurance plan, most choose not to participate because it is considered too expensive.[73]

- About 35 percent of those who were uninsured have been uninsured for over a year.[74] Similarly, 50 percent represent low-income families.[75]

- About 67 percent of the nonelderly uninsured are employed, but the same percentage have no college education, while 25 percent have no high school diploma.[76]

- Over 90 percent of the nonelderly uninsured claim they are in excellent, very good, or good health.[77]

- Most (60 percent) of the uninsured are young, between the ages of 18 and 44.

- As many as 30 percent of persons who were eligible for public programs such as Medicaid and the special children's program, State Children's Health Insurance Program (SCHIP), chose not to enroll. They are included among the uninsured.[78]

- About 8 percent of the uninsured have started their own business and choose not to include health care as a benefit for themselves or others.[79]

- While the number of Blacks and Hispanics covered by health insurance increased, they are twice as likely as Whites and non-Hispanics to be uninsured.[80]

- The factors that relate to the question of whether a person is covered or not are the type of industry in which the person works,

---

73. EBRI (2008, September), p. 16.

74. EBRI (2008, September), p. 28.

75. *Who are the uninsured?* (2006, August). Low income is generally defined as having income under 200 percent of poverty level.

76. *Who are the uninsured?* (2006, August).

77. *Who are the uninsured?* (2006, August).

78. See *Health coverage issues: The uninsured and the insured.* (2005, December). American Academy of Actuaries, Issue Brief.

79. See *The uninsured.* (2003, March). National Institute for Health Care Management.

80. Ibid. And see U.S. Census Bureau (2006); EBRI (2008, September), p. 15.

Table 8.1   Sources of Health Care Coverage of Persons Under Age 65
From 1994 to 2006

Source of Health Care	1994	2000	2007
Percent insured (employer)	64.4%	68.4%	62.7%
Percent public coverage	17.1%	14.6%	18.2%
Percent uninsured	15.9%	15.6%	17.2%

SOURCE: Profile and Demographics of the Uninsured; see EBRI, Issue Brief 321 (2008, September), *Nonelderly population (under age 65) with selected sources of health insurance coverage 1994–2007.*

NOTE: This chart does not include most persons who are covered by Medicare and are eligible after reaching 65.

the size of the company, the person's income status, and the state in which the person lives.[81]

Based on the profiles and statistics above, we can conclude that the uninsured is a diverse group comprised of mostly poor individuals, but also some who can afford health insurance but choose not to buy it. Most live in families where the head of household is working, but even among those who are working and whose firms offer health insurance, some simply cannot afford it. Our public programs such as Medicaid and Medicare provide a real health care safety net, but a portion of the uninsured that are eligible do not enroll. The lack of health insurance disproportionately affects racial and ethnic minorities.[82] It would seem, however, that cost and affordability are the driving forces leading to the large number of uninsured.

The uninsured compels a public policy concern. They are less likely to receive basic health care services, have fewer ambulatory visits to the

81. EBRI (2008, September), pp. 12, 13, 16.

82. *Key facts race, ethnicity, & medical care.* (2007, January). The Kaiser Family Foundation. Health status is a function of access to care, insurance coverage, education, occupation, income, genetics, and personal behavior. These factors disproportionately affect racial and ethnic minorities who have the poorer health status and higher death rates attributable to common causes among Americans. For example, infant mortality, heart disease, diabetes, and obesity disproportionately affect racial and ethnic minorities.

doctor, and more trips to the emergency room.[83] Their health status is believed to be lower than those who are insured, and they are less productive in the workplace.[84] As providers who treat them do so without reimbursement, more costs are shifted to insured payers.[85] Their mortality rate is higher, and uninsured children suffer from delayed development.[86]

What Are Some Possible Solutions?

Before looking at other reform proposals that involve both changes in the delivery and financing of health care, let's first examine some principles and values that should apply to all potential reform approaches.[87]

- Make health care accessible to all in the United States by making it less costly and more affordable

- Preserve and enhance the primary care function so as to focus resources on preventive medicine

- Encourage a continuation of robust medical research and innovation

- Enhance health, quality of life, and longevity by promoting access to high-quality care that is effective, efficient, safe, and timely

- Promote value and results-based competition among providers

Preserving a set of values and principles should help guide the health care reform process; however, since cost and affordability are causing the current crisis in health care, let's look at some approaches that address the cost issues discussed above. Perhaps we can see how we might significantly reduce the cost of health care by focusing on quality.

---

83. EBRI (2007, October 2007), p. 17.

84. EBRI (2007, October 2007), p. 17.

85. Hadley, J., & Holahan, J. (2004, May 10). *The cost of care for the uninsured*. The Kaiser Family Foundation, Issue Update. The cost is measured as uncompensated care. It is estimated that $41 billion is spent in the United States treating the uninsured. However, if you add in the costs of diminished health care and shorter life spans of the uninsured, the total ranges from an additional $65 billion to $135 billion per year. Total expenditures for those covered by programs like Medicaid are about $125 billion per year. See also the Institute of Medicine (2003).

86. EBRI (2007, October), p. 17

87. See, for example, *Insuring America's health: Principles and recommendations.* (2004, January 14). Institute of Medicine, http://www.iom.edu/.

IMPROVING ACCESS TO QUALITY CARE— MAKING HEALTH CARE AFFORDABLE

The following measures can be taken regardless of the approach selected to reform the delivery and financing of our health care system. As we look closely at the profiles of the uninsured, it is apparent that cost is the underlying problem of our system. By reducing the inefficiencies, errors, and other factors previously discussed that lead to high costs and lack of affordability, health care can be more affordable. To accomplish this requires a program national in scope led by employers, health care providers, TPAs, and the government. It would involve transforming the current system into one that fosters quality and efficiency-based competition among health care providers. This competition can compel providers to flush out the obstacles to affordable health care.[88] As we point out in Chapters 6 and 7, lasik surgery, an increasingly popular process that is not typically covered by health insurance, has demonstrated improved clinical outcomes yearly and the cost for the procedure has dropped appreciably due to its position in a true market. This could happen in other areas of health care.[89] Following are some ideas.

ELECTRONIC MEDICAL INFORMATION SYSTEMS

All health care providers should be required to use an effective electronic information system that is designed to track and record the health care history, medications, drug interactions, and medical interventions of all their patients, and connect patient records with treatment protocols.[90]

---

88. Many of the national health care systems in Europe have opted to simply reimburse providers for health care services and establish budgets for hospitals without examining quality outcomes measurements and latent inefficiencies in their systems. As life expectancies increase and tax revenues decline, these systems are burdened with excessive costs and delays in treatment. Many of their citizens who are unwilling to wait months for free medical procedures are opting to have medical services performed by private providers who are paid directly by the patient or their own insurance company. See Docteur (2003).

89. While it is clear that prices have dramatically dropped for lasik surgery, in spite of the bundling of prices by the surgeons, the ability of the consumer to get quality data is not clear. Most rely on word-of-mouth referrals. See Fuhrmans, V. (2007, February 6). *The Wall Street Journal*, D4. We discuss how to access clinical outcomes data and measure quality in Chapter 10, Employee Benefits and Metrics.

90. See Jha, A. et al. (2006). They indicate the introduction of electronic health care records has the potential to reduce costs and enhance the quality of care.

This would lessen the possibility for medical errors or inappropriate care and, ultimately, reduce costs.[91]

France, Germany, and Japan are developing individual health care cards. Each card contains a chip with the complete medical history of the patient and is accessible by the medical provider, thus enabling a more timely and efficacious treatment. If we had this kind of information system in the United States, it is likely that we could reduce medical errors by 60 percent, save lives, and reduce the cost of the U.S. health care system by 6 percent per year, or $140 billion by the year 2014.[92] This does not include the cost savings that could be realized through more timely and accurate treatments, and eliminating costs associated with erroneous treatments that do not result in mortality or increased morbidity.

Moreover, this system would enable patients and providers to link specific medical histories with existing medical protocols and deliver a menu of treatment options with high success potentials. More effective mining of patient data provides an opportunity to analyze where and when certain medical conditions are occurring, how they are being treated, and with what results. This would allow longitudinal analyses of the efficacy of health care practices among patient care professionals as well as epidemiologists. Government and employer sponsors could provide the political push for a patient record and medical information system, and some government financing of the system development would help make it a reality.

QUALITY-BASED COMPETITION AMONG PROVIDERS

What could happen if competition among providers were based on their demonstrated clinical outcomes? Employer sponsors of health care plans would no longer reimburse providers for merely rendering services, but would insist on performance-based results.[93] They or their TPAs would send their employees only to those providers who demonstrated

---

91. There is proposed legislation in the U.S. Congress to fund grants for Health Information Technology grants and to create the Office of the National Coordinator for Health Information Technology, that will drive the development and implementation of a nationwide convergence of medical data and treatments.

92. The digital hospital. (2005, March 28). *Business Week* online, http://www .businessweek.com/print/magazine/content); Hillestad, R. et al. (2005). Can electronic medical systems transform health care? *Health Affairs, 24*(5), 1103–1117.

93. See Miller, H. (2007, September). *Creating payment systems to accelerate value-driven health care: Issues and options for policy reform.* The Commonwealth Fund, http://www.commonwealthfund.org/.

the best clinical outcomes.[94] In fact, risk premiums could be paid to providers for high acuity patients.

The current reimbursement system does not adequately reward providers for preventive care and many employer sponsors have no incentive to invest in long-term health. Instead, there are reimbursement incentives for providers to perform more services than are necessary.[95] It has been said that the "most powerful instrument in health care is the doctor's ordering pen." Certainly, the reimbursement system fosters this inefficiency and leads to higher costs. Quality competition requires the disclosure of clinical outcomes data. This is a challenge.

There have been efforts among employer and government sponsors to obtain quality clinical data and use it to select or reward providers. Some years ago an employer-led project in Cincinnati, Ohio, obtained and measured data showing clinical outcomes of 14 hospitals.[96] Severity adjusted medical records of Medicare patients were analyzed by the employer sponsors and the hospitals. The resultant data enabled the employers to determine which hospitals were performing at the highest levels in a number of health categories such as heart, pulmonary, and orthopedic conditions. The premise was to stimulate hospital competition based on their clinical results. The early findings showed significant differences among the hospitals in cost, length of stay, mortality, and the occurrence of post-discharge complications and hospital readmissions. Following is an example of what happened.

> After examining its clinical outcomes records, Hospital B in Cincinnati learned that the average length of stay for its pneumonia patients was considerably longer than other hospitals in the area. It assumed that its patients were more seriously ill and this was the reason for the

---

94. For example, patients treated at the Minnesota Cystic Fibrosis Center have an average life span of 46 years versus the national average of 32 years (HBS, Michael Porter).

95. Miller, H. (2007). The author also points out that there are few incentives to coordinate care among providers, current performance bonuses are too small to serve as an incentive, and sometimes tend to encourage short-term cost reductions instead of looking at long-term costs and care.

96. See Murphy, T. (1995). The U.S. Department of Health and Human Services has taken a new interest in quality outcomes and pay for performance in its Medicare and Medicaid programs. See *Premier hospital quality incentive demonstration project, project overview and findings from one year.* (2006, April 13). HHS, Centers for Medicare and Medicaid. The first year of the project showed marked improvement and quality scores in five major diagnostic areas.

discrepancy; however, the records were acuity adjusted so it was an apples-to-apples comparison.

When hospital administrators looked into the problem, they acknowledged that treatment of bacterial pneumonia requires early detection of the precise type of bacteria causing the condition. This is assessed by taking a sputum sample and sending it to the lab for analysis. Developing a culture and identifying the bacteria may take several days so the sooner the staff gets the sample, the quicker the diagnosis, enabling the administration of a precise antibiotic treatment. The hospital examined the workflow relating to the admission of patients who present with pneumonia symptoms and found that in many cases the sputum sample, through inadvertence, was not taken until several days after admission. They changed the procedure and workflow, got the sputum sample immediately on admission, and cut their length of stay for pneumonia patients in half.[1]

Obviously, the lesson is that clinical outcomes records together with competitive pressures compelled the hospital to provide better treatment management that, ultimately, lead to lower costs and better quality.

1. Murphy, T. (1995).

Similarly, other Cincinnati hospitals responded to their nonconforming data by examining all aspects of their treatment regimens and work processes to find out why, for example, they compared unfavorably to the others in a particular diagnostic-related group. This experiment, with the disclosure of clinical outcomes and the competitive responses that followed, had the effect of creating value for the purchasers, providers, and consumers of health care.

Another facet of quality competition is to determine which providers are adhering to certain medical protocols that most often lead to better quality outcomes. The value of focusing on quality outcomes is evident in a recent Medicare project. Premier, Inc., a coalition of nonprofit hospitals working with the U.S. Centers for Medicare and Medicaid Services, completed a study of 224,000 patient records and concluded that adherence to basic medical treatment guidelines significantly improves clinical results, saving lives and medical costs. The report tracked Medicare patients with pneumonia, heart bypass surgery, heart attack, hip and knee replacement, and congestive heart failure. The conclusion was that 5,700 deaths, 8,100 complications, and 10,000 readmissions could have been avoided by following simple treatment guidelines. As an example, the study showed that when pneumonia patients were given oxygen assessments, a blood culture, and, in certain cases, the right antibiotics, their clinical results were significantly improved, resulting in cost savings of $2,275 per case.[97] The study projected that nationally the potential savings attributed to these simple, clinical steps would be $1.35 billion per year. Giving participants, sponsors, and TPAs access to records that tell them which providers follow treatment protocols would go a long way toward achieving more quality-based competition among providers. Those who do the best job earn the business and perhaps even more.

United Health Care, Inc., is financially rewarding providers in its networks who follow certain evidenced-based medicine protocols. Providing financial incentives to such providers can improve quality outcomes and reduce the overall cost of health care.[98] The key here is to insert traditional market incentives to both providers and TPAs who will be rewarded by having the best performers in their networks.[99] A fundamental axiom of effective management is to "get it right the first time." Following this axiom can result in quality competition that leads to lower costs and more affordable health care.[100]

Insisting that providers disclose clinical quality performance records, including clinical outcomes, as well as their compliance with recommended quality protocols, is absolutely essential to achieving quality-based competition. Health care should no longer be considered a commodity.[101]

97. See Premier, Inc. (2006). Centers for Medicare and Medicaid Services (CMS), Premier Hospital Quality Incentive Demonstration Project: Findings from Year One, Charlotte, NC.

98. See, for example, Miller, H. (2007, September). *Creating payment systems to accelerate value-driven health care: Issue and options for policy reform.* The Commonwealth Fund, http://www.commonwealthfund.org/.

99. Ultimately, however, pay for performance should be based on outcomes not following rubrics. Results-based systems create the real value in a health care system.

100. Porter, M., & Teisberg, E. (2006). The methodology of comparing health care clinical outcomes is discussed in some detail in Chapter 10, Employee Benefits and Metrics.

101. For an excellent discussion of value-based competition among providers with a total focus on the patient, see *Building the cornerstones: Recommendations, actions steps, and strategies to advance health care reform,* The Mayo Clinic Health Policy Center, http://www.mayoclinic.org/healthpolicycenter.

REDUCING ADMINISTRATIVE EXPENSE[102]

Provide incentives to simplify and standardize claims processing. There is a potential $35 billion in reduced administrative expense among health care plans that could be captured with some type of reform by:[103] (1) having a single-payer, national system; (2) integrating advanced information technology in the treatment, medical recordkeeping, and claims processing systems; and (3) requiring plan participants to be directly responsible for minor, insignificant health care expenses, and to maintain their own record of these treatments. Claims processing by providers and TPAs adds a costly burden to our current system and we should be looking for opportunities to reengineer this administrative responsibility.

PREVENTIVE MEDICINE

Make primary care the centerpiece of any health care reform initiative. This means providing incentives for consumers to use their primary care physicians for the early diagnosis of conditions, and to reward providers appropriately for effective preventive care. The current system does not do this; it rewards doctors for ordering procedures.

Wellness programs have a role here as well. In the United States there is no question that lifestyle, diet, smoking, poor health education, and patient compliance have a major impact on our overall health. A recent study in *Health Affairs* indicates that Americans are diagnosed with and treated for several chronic diseases more often than their European counterparts, which, in part, explains why health care costs are higher in the United States.[104] Through a combination of wellness programs to reinforce lifestyle changes and better disease management, we can improve overall health, lessen the incidence of chronic disease, and reduce costs. By integrating wellness programs with the health care plan and providing patients and providers with incentives to embrace disease management, to comply with provider recommendations, and to control lifestyle risk factors, we can lower claims costs, improve health, enjoy more fulfilling lives, and return

---

102. See Woolhandler, S., Campbell, T., & Himmelstein, D. (2003, August 21). Cost of health care administration in the U.S. and Canada. *The New England Journal of Medicine, 349*(8), 768–775. The authors found the administrative costs of the U.S. health system were $1,059 per capita and $307 per capita in Canada.

103. Davis, K. et al. (2007, January 29); Himmelstein, D., Woolhandler, S., & Wolfe (2004); Woolhandler, S., Campbell, T., & Himmelstein, D. (2003).

104. Thorpe, K., Howard, D., & Galactionova, K. (2007, October 2).

real value on our investment.[105] We discussed wellness in some detail in Chapter 7, but taking it to new levels beyond sponsoring health walks and encouraging low-fat diets can effectively address these risk factors.

BROADENING COMPETITION AMONG TPAs

Currently, one cannot buy a health insurance plan from another state unless that plan complies with all of the legal requirements of the home state, including coverage and treatment mandates. By removing this legal barrier and encouraging broader geographic competition among TPAs, we could increase the availability of plans designed to provide cost-effective and positive health outcomes for participants.[106] Whether we continue the health care system we have now in the United States or move to a mandated universal plan, we should consider eliminating the power of states to limit competition among TPAs. There is currently proposed legislation in Congress (HR 2355) that would allow residents of one state to purchase a health care plan from another state. The present system of state insurance laws has created an assortment of 1,800 specific mandated health care treatments that increase the cost and limit the accessibility of health care plans.[107]

TAX CHANGES

Some agree that we should change the tax treatment of employer-sponsored care that currently exempts health care costs from taxation.[108]

---

105. For example, Miami University's management department recently participated in a quantitative study with a large municipal employer who is tracking the health impact of assessments and wellness programs and calculating the ROI of such programs. See Schwarz, J., & Murphy, T. (2008, April). Human capital metrics: An approach to teaching using data and metrics to design and evaluate management practices. *Journal of Management Education, 32,* 164–182.

106. The view here is that health insurance costs vary significantly among states. The apparent reason relates to a variety of health benefit mandates imposed by various states on the insurance offerings. The "reform" idea is to allow competition among states for the purchase of health insurance without regard to the mandates. The goal would be to reduce the cost of health insurance.

107. See Mathews, M. (2005, December 27). *Bush's unheralded health care agenda.* Council for Affordable Health Insurance, http://www.cahi.org/ and go to News Room.

108. Cogan, J., Hubbard, R., & Kessler, D. (2004, December 8). Brilliant deduction, *The Wall Street Journal,* A12, http://online.wsj.com/article/. Other related proposals would cap the costs of employer-sponsored health care that can be exempted from income tax if the plan exceeds the cap.

The exemption would be eliminated and the costs of employer-sponsored health care would be considered taxable income, but all health insurance expenses, including employee premiums and co-pays, would be tax deductible. The idea here is to reduce health care expense by making higher cost insurance less attractive and lower cost programs with high deductibles and co-pays more attractive. Employees would want to avoid taxable income attributable to high cost health care plans and, instead, find more cost-effective plans and deduct the costs. Proponents argue such a change would reduce expenses without significant adverse consequences to health care. Since the uninsured and others who would choose to purchase health care could deduct their premiums and out-of-pocket expenses, as many as six million persons could be removed from the ranks of the uninsured. This is because a large number of this group work and pay taxes. Finally, as employers' costs are reduced, the savings can shift back to workers in the form of higher wages.[109]

TORT REFORM

Many urge the United States to initiate a comprehensive state-by-state tort reform program that will reduce escalating malpractice insurance costs to providers. It also would serve to mitigate the practice of "defensive medicine" that results from an overuse of health care resources among providers trying to avoid any possibility of a malpractice claim.[110]

---

109. Cogan, J. et al. (2004). See discussion of the principle of compensating differentials discussed in Chapter 2.

110. See *Limiting tort liability for medical malpractice, economic and budge issue brief.* (2004, January 8). Congressional Budget Office. The study found that malpractice premiums charged to providers have increased dramatically over a nine-year period (120 percent), as have insurance payments for claims (300 percent). However, malpractice costs amount to only 2 percent of the U.S. total investment in health care, so a 25 percent reduction in malpractice costs would not materially affect the total costs of health care. The study did not conclusively examine the issue of "defensive medicine," which many say is the real cost culprit in the malpractice environment. Defensive medicine involves the utilization of additional health care resources that are not medically indicated but are applied to remove any possibility of a malpractice claim. Another recent study indicated that malpractice liability does not change the way medicine is practiced except it does increase the use of imaging services. See Baicker, K., & Chandra, A. (2005). *The effect of malpractice liability on the delivery of health care.* Rand Forum for Health Economics and Policy.

ENCOURAGING INTEGRATED HEALTH CARE PRACTICES

The potential integration of health care practices[111] that are focused on total patient care and not just conditions requiring a specialist can enable a more effective and lean administrative system for reimbursements and medical tracking. The recently heralded quality and efficiency successes of the Veterans Administration are largely based on the concept of an integrated system.[112] Groups of specialists within a single organization allow efficient referral and consultation processes, and focus on the total health care needs of the patient. Such integrated practices produce better and more efficient outcomes, as evidenced with the experience of integrated HMOs. The administrative savings potential also could be significant.

CONSUMER-DRIVEN HEALTH CARE

The high deductible health savings account approach discussed in Chapter 7 is not a panacea that will resolve the problem of the uninsured in the United States. It does, however, engage the patient in the process of utilizing health care resources. And, as we pointed out, it places a major emphasis on preventive care by excluding a number of diagnostic early-warning procedures from the deductible. A recent independent study of consumer-driven plans found that higher deductibles lead to lower utilization of health care resources, lower claims costs, and the plans are chosen by younger, healthier participants. The true dividends of consumer-driven plans await the availability of clinical outcomes data: *"... **until members can truly compare and shop for providers based on quality and cost, realized CDHCP savings are likely to remain limited to the reduced utilization expected from high deductible plans."*[113]

---

111. See Porter, M., & Teisberg, E. (2006). See also *Dartmouth Atlas of Health Care* (2008).

112. *Leadership by example: Coordinating government roles in improving health care quality.* (2002, October 30). The Institute of Medicine, http://www.nap.edu/catalog/10537.html. The report indicates the VA system, with its application of performance standards, is one of the best quality health systems in the United States.

113. Burke, J., & Pipich, R. (2008, April). *Consumer driven impact study.* Milliman, Inc., http://www.milliman.com. There is an interesting article about how outcomes data might be available from individual practitioners. The author acknowledges that such a collaborative approach to securing such information will lead to better quality and lower costs. See Milstein, A., & Lee, T. (2007, December 27). Comparing physicians on efficiency. *The New England Journal of Medicine, 357*(26), 2649–2652. Hospital report cards designed for consumers

Many researchers agree that the three foundations of an effective consumer-driven approach are: (1) transparency with respect to the disclosure of quality information from providers, (2) a system of uniform provider data requirements, and (3) public education and decision support tools concerning health care quality and cost variability. And further, researchers agree that having these will facilitate the creation of a real health care market.[114] Regardless of the shape of health care reform, consumer engagement is vital to the goal of making health care more affordable.[115] Designing a health care plan to be more focused on disease prevention and consistent treatment, as consumer-driven plans do, instead of a program that simply reimburses providers for each doctor visit, could make the process of patient engagement more effective. It is also quite possible to reorient our health care system to accept the idea that insurance is designed to protect the low-risk, high-liability problems. Thus, it is consistent with the view to maintain relatively high deductibles in most health care policies. This would have a major impact on health care expenditures by sponsors.[116] Studies by Rand and others show that such deductibles do not generally affect the quality of health care except

---

are relatively new even though accrediting organizations have collected this data for years. Goff, V. (2004, May 14). *Consumer cost sharing in private health insurance: On the threshold of change.* National Health Policy Forum, Issue Brief No. 798.

114. Goff, V. (2004, May 14).

115. Many European countries that long ago moved to a single-payer system are experiencing significant financing problems and are using point-of-service co-pays and triage-based deferrals of noncritical treatments. These forced engagement efforts are intended to mitigate the patient's demand for health care services. See Donatini, A. (2001). *Health care systems in transition, Italy* (p. 46). European Observatory on Health Care Systems.

116. It is estimated that doubling the average deductible of $250 to $500 would reduce the health plan sponsors' total annual expense by $43 billion. See Buntin, M., et al. (2006). *Consumer-directed health care: Early evidence about effects on cost and quality.* Health Affairs, http://www.healthaffairs.com/. The cost savings are projected to be around 2 to 7 percent arising out of lower utilization. Other early studies reflect higher cost savings of 20 percent, treatment for chronic care was not abated and participants were more value conscious, asking questions more attentive to wellness and prevention, and more likely to use more efficient health care facilities such as urgent care instead of the emergency room. See Turner, G. (2005, August 11). *Consumerism in health care: Early evidence is positive.* The Galen Institute, Health Issues, http://www.galen.org/.

among the very poor and elderly.[117] Much of these projected savings come from actions taken by the consumer.

> There is a clear tradeoff as patient coinsurance amounts rise. On the one hand, coinsurance can induce patients to use care more efficiently. With no coinsurance costs, patients have no financial disincentive to forgo care, even if it has dubious value; but once patients bear some of the economic costs of receiving medical care, they are more likely to use only those health care services that are worth the additional cost they must pay. On the other hand, coinsurance amounts that are too high can lead individuals to avoid medical care that is actually necessary to their health and/or imposes a substantial financial burden. Very high levels of coinsurance may undermine one of the primary reasons that people insure themselves in the first place— which is protection from financial ruin if they become seriously ill. Moreover, high coinsurance amounts place a financial burden on the poorest and sickest members of society.[118]

The lesson here is to allow participant choice on the size of the deductible. Then, build into the health plan a number of preventive care procedures that are proven to be effective and place them outside the deductible, as many plans now do.

True engagement, however, will require public policies that support transparency of price and quality outcomes data.[119] Further, the availability of the new medical information technology and its convergence with medical treatments could make the engagement of the patient more meaningful. Consumers will be better prepared to ask the right questions and to evaluate the answers.

PUT IT ALL TOGETHER

The aggregate impact of the reforms outlined herein—from better health information systems to quality-based competition among providers—would have a significant and positive impact on the problems of

---

117. Gruber, J. (2006, October). *The role of consumer copayments for health care: Lessons from the Rand Health Insurance experiment and beyond.* The Kaiser Family Foundation.

118. Gruber, J. (2006, October).

119. Goff, V. (2004, May 14). *Consumer cost sharing in private health insurance: On the threshold of change.* The National Health Policy Forum, Issue Brief No. 798, George Washington University.

Table 8.2   Summary of Cost Reduction and Reform Proposals

Changes Affecting Cost and Affordability	Reform of Financing and Delivery of Health Care
Uniform electronic medical records	Universal single-payer system
Quality and value-based competition among providers facilitated by making clinical outcomes data available	Employer-mandated and subsidized coverage for those who cannot afford it
Uniform claims processing systems	Individual mandated and subsidized coverage for those who cannot afford it
Expand consumer-driven health care programs	Expand eligibility for Medicaid
Encourage integrated health care delivery	Tax changes to encourage utilization of consumer-driven health care plans
Tort reform	
Tax changes	
Interstate competition among TPAs	
Focus on preventive care and wellness	

inadequate access, excessive costs, and the general level of health in the United States.[120]

Some advocate that all of these changes should be taken before or concurrent with the introduction any new health delivery and financing system whether it involves mandates, a universal single-payer program, or something else. By providing affordable health care, the above steps alone may be sufficient to resolve both the problems of having so many uninsured, as well as having a very fragile employer and government sponsorship of health care. To ignore them would allow our current system laden with excessive costs, spiraling inflation, and inconsistent efficacy to be imbedded into a new system. Its administrators will experience a new financial crisis and begin a

---

120. As we saw with the lasik surgery example in Chapter 7, market competition based on outcomes and price has had the effect of reducing prices and improving quality. Prices in some communities have dropped 90 percent in the last 10 years for lasik surgery. Meanwhile, quality and outcomes have improved. Many ophthalmologists are offering warranties and free "redo" surgeries. (Unofficial survey of Cincinnati-area lasik surgery prices and practices.)

frantic search for expedient measures to reduce health care utilization and expense. Eventually, we could face the rationing of health care services and lack of funding for medical research that have been the experiences of other nations.[121] When we examine the factors that are driving the high costs and resultant lack of affordability, a concerted public effort to impede these drivers will enhance the likelihood of success of any broad-based reform.

New Health Care Delivery and Financing Systems—Health Care Reform

The case for changing health care is compelling. How we accomplish it is not so clear. There are a number of approaches summarized here involving reform of the financing and delivery of health care. In each case we should examine whether the reform will accommodate more cost-effectiveness, provide a higher degree of quality care, and improve the overall health of the nation.

ENLARGE COVERAGE OF PUBLIC HEALTH CARE PROGRAMS

First, we can "rifle shoot" the problem of the uninsured by enlarging the coverage and eligibility provisions of Medicaid, for example, to include a broader definition of the poor. The income levels now applicable would be changed so that persons presently not covered by Medicaid and who cannot afford health care will be covered. Since it appears that about 60 percent of the uninsured are poor, we can assume about 24 million persons will be added to the Medicaid roster. Nothing else would change and we would continue our current employer- and government-sponsored programs.

UNIVERSAL OR SINGLE-PAYER PROGRAM

A second approach would be to convert all health care programs into one single-payer, universal system financed and managed by the federal

---

121. Pharmaceutical research and development spending in the United States far exceeds Europe. For example, 78 percent of biotechnology research funds are spent in the United States compared to just 16 percent in all of Europe. One reported result is that the annual death rate from cancer in the United States is 196 per 100,000 compared to 235 in Britain, 244 in France, 270 in Italy, and 273 in Germany. See Capezzone, D. (2007, August 3). *The Wall Street Journal*, A9. See also the discussion in Chapter 13, Global Benefits.

government. It would operate like Medicare, but would include all U.S. citizens and residents and eliminate the need for employer- or privately sponsored health care plans.[122] The government would establish the basic plan of benefits, coverage requirements, set reimbursement levels, cost sharing requirements, means testing, and probably establish treatment protocols for a variety of health conditions.

In order to ensure some fiscal predictability, the government also may establish a prospective payment system or even budgets for large providers such as hospitals. There would no longer be a diverse array of insurance claims processing systems or administrative distinctions relating to the source or cause of illness or injury, such as worker's compensation, disability claims, simple illnesses, and preventive care. Whether one is over 65, poor, or in need of long-term care, the plan would cover all or some of the expense. There would be one fund and one billing system.[123]

A related choice is for the government to employ all medical providers and pay them a fixed salary for providing covered treatments to their citizens and residents.[124] The government would have to decide whether to allow its providers to work outside the system and be reimbursed by the patients or their insurance companies. In effect there could be two systems.

EMPLOYER MANDATE

Another approach would be to mandate large employer coverage of all employees and their dependents. Employers who do not provide health insurance must contribute toward their employees' health care coverage or the public plans. The government would establish certain standards and coverage requirements and would outline the specifications for plan designs. This might take the form of copying the Federal Employees Health Benefits Program. Small employers would receive tax incentives to provide coverage. Persons who are not covered by their employers or one of the public programs, and cannot afford to purchase a plan on their own, will be covered by a new public plan.

The employer mandate approach traditionally calls for health care institutional reform that includes technology advancement, particularly

---

122. This is essentially the Western European and Canadian system design.

123. See Physicians Working Group for Single-Payer National Health Insurance. (2003, August 13). *Journal of the American Medical Association, 290*(6), 798. The group estimates that a single-payer system would eliminate $200 billion of unnecessary expense annually. As we will see in Chapter 13, some European countries with this type of plan have experienced serious funding problems and patient treatments are frequently subject to long delays.

124. This parallels the system in the U.K.

with respect to medical records, quality care initiatives, and an emphasis on preventive care. The politically endorsed mandates also call for increasing TPA competition by creating a national health insurance clearing-house that controls the dispensing and standardization of plans, ensuring affordable and "fair" premiums, and allowing only minimal co-pays and deductibles.[125]

MANDATING INDIVIDUAL COVERAGE

Mandating the individual to purchase health care is an alternative. Here, like automobile liability insurance, all individuals would be compelled to purchase a government-designed health insurance plan. Employers could continue to sponsor health care for their employees and there could be some requirement to remit a special tax penalty to the government should they choose not to offer a health care plan to their employees.[126] Employer paid insurance would continue to be tax-exempt for the participant, provided the cost does not exceed certain levels deemed to be excessive. Small employers would receive tax incentives to offer health care to their employees.

Every individual must obtain health insurance. They could keep their existing coverage, or obtain it from either the same health care plan available to members of Congress or choose a public plan option such as

---

125. In the early years of the first Clinton administration, the President proposed a managed competition program that mandated employer coverage and subsidized those who could not afford it. It uniquely attempted to foster competition among TPAs. Third-party administrators would participate in regional health purchasing cooperatives and offer a variety of plan choices to the employers. Nonemployed individuals and small employers who could not afford health care would be subsidized by the government and participate in the same program. All participants and sponsoring employers presumably would have some choices as to the type of plan they wanted. It was never presented to Congress for approval.

126. There are a variety of state and local approaches to covering the uninsured. Massachusetts now mandates each resident to obtain health care. Persons who cannot afford it are subsidized. Maryland mandates large employers to cover their employees, as does Hawaii, while Vermont subsidizes coverage for those not covered by employer plans, Medicaid, and Medicare. California's statewide plan was invalidated in the courts, and there are a variety of county and city programs that currently seek to cover the "uninsured." Similar coverage legislation is pending in other jurisdictions such as Wisconsin. The primary legal issue surrounding these programs is whether they are in conflict with ERISA §514 (29 USC §1144) preemption provision. See Butler, P. (2006). *ERISA implications for state health care access initiatives.* National Academy for State Health Care Initiatives, http://www.nashp.org.

Medicare. Insurance rules across the country would be standardized and refusals to cover individuals, as well as excessive fees, would be banned. The government would subsidize the purchase of such insurance for those who could not afford it. They would do so by providing refundable tax credits. Participant costs would be limited based on a percentage of income. There would have to be standards and specifications for minimum or base plans. To enable continuing affordability, the government would take steps to make all plans more reasonable by controlling the pricing and reimbursement levels of providers. Savings from the plan are expected from more efficient administration, higher quality care, and the modernization of health care services.

In 2006, Massachusetts passed a mandated health care plan whereby those earning below the federal poverty threshold could purchase a plan without premiums and with only small deductibles and co-pays.[127] Others with higher earnings up to three times the poverty level could purchase partially subsidized policies. Employers who do not provide health care to their employees would be required to pay a penalty to the state. Residents who do not have a policy would be treated by providers, but would be assessed a penalty by the state as well.

MARKET-BASED REFORM

Finally, there is a legislative proposal to encourage broader acceptance of consumer-driven plans.[128] Employer-sponsored benefits would continue to be tax-exempt to the employee, provided the cost does not exceed a certain amount. However, premiums for HDHCPs with an HSA in the nongroup plan market would be tax deductible and small tax credits would be offered.[129] For low-income persons, tax credits would be awarded to enable the individual purchase of HDHCPs. The central idea

---

127. See Fahrenthold, D. (2006, April 5). Mass. bill requires health coverage. *The Washington Post*, p. A01.

128. Fronstin, P. (2006, June). *The tax treatment of health insurance and employment-based health benefits*. Employee Benefit Research Institute, Issue Brief No. 294; Gruber, J. (2006, February 15). *The cost and coverage impact of the President's health insurance budget proposals*. Center on Budget and Policy Priorities. This plan also includes tax credits for those who choose an HSA plan personal tax credits for low-income persons, but the model used does not show any appreciable reduction of the number of uninsured.

129. Currently persons can deduct health care expenses including premiums only if they exceed 7.5 percent of adjusted gross income and they can only deduct the amount exceeding 7.5 percent.

is to subsidize both premiums and contributions to HSAs and cause a migration from more full coverage plans to consumer-driven plans. There is also an element of fairness in the proposal because it permits individuals who are not covered by a group plan to deduct their premiums. The assumption is that persons will become more discrete purchasers of health care and become engaged in their consumption of health care services.[130]

OTHER APPROACHES

There are other ideas circulating. Eliminating the TPA and allowing the employer or employer group to directly contract with providers is still an idea that has some life.[131] A related concept is to de-emphasize the linkage between employment and insurance and encourage more direct relationships between employees and integrated health plans that require payment for benefit not service.[132] Such plans do not exist at present.

Also, several states have passed health care laws intending to expand coverage that include a variety of facets discussed above. Others are considering such approaches.[133] It remains to be seen how it will work.

All of the above-described solutions are workable. There are details that need to be sorted out and impacts on the current system that should be considered carefully. What will they cost? How well will they deliver quality health care? Over the long term, will we be healthier and live longer, quality lives? We should pay attention to the values outlined earlier in this chapter. We should also understand that whatever solution is chosen, we first should take the steps to make our system less costly and more affordable.

---

130. For an interesting article condemning our "commercialized" health care system and opposing any market-based reform, see Kuttner, R. (2008, February 7). Market Based Failure—A Second Opinion on U.S. Health Care Costs. *The New England Journal of Medicine, 358*(6), 549–551.

131. See Wessel, D., et al (2006, December 29).

132. See Conversation with Michael L. Millenson. (2006, December). Health care reform has only scratched the surface. *Managed Care*, http://www.managedcaremag .com/archives/.

133. Individual mandates to increase health coverage may top state reform strategies for 2008. (2008, January 15). *AIS Health Business Daily*, http://www .aishealth.com/. This story includes a summary of states that are considering such legislation and reports on the Massachusetts plan that is expected to end its first year $150 million over budget.

Conclusion

The U.S. problem of 45.5 million uninsured is a challenge that simply must be resolved. It is not acceptable. Also, the current system of employer-sponsored health care is nearing a crisis because of the expense,[134] and a shifting of costs to the consumers of health care is not a solution.[135] Further, a looming financial crisis is apparent in the government-sponsored programs.[136]

Whatever choices are made to reform our system, we must not ignore the prerequisites—to make our system more effective, efficient, and affordable.[137] Employers, government, providers, unions, and the consumers of health care can make this happen with the right leadership and coordination.[138]

---

134. Mincer, J. (2006, July 5). Health care costs to hit workers, retirees hard. *The Wall Street Journal*, D3.

135. It is estimated that nearly one-half of all personal bankruptcies in the United States are filed because of medical expenses. Christie, T. (2006, July 6). *The Register Guard*, Eugene, OR. Himmelstein, D., Warren, E., Thorne, D, & Woolhandler, S. (2005, February). Illness and injury as contributors to bankruptcy. *Health Affairs Web Exclusive* W5–63.

136. Some argue that the whole idea of employer-sponsored health insurance is outmoded. As one commentator said, employers will be "pit stops," not "permanent homes," for young people entering the job market. We are "moving from employer-managed work lives to self-managed work lives in which workers must figure out on their own how to maintain work and lifecycle issues like health insurance and retirement." Stern, A. (2006, July 17). Horse and buggy health care coverage. *The Wall Street Journal*, p. A10.

137. Government can help by funding the Health Information Systems programs and implementing a vigorous clinical-based outcomes requirement for the providers who are reimbursed under the various federal programs such as Medicare and the federal employees' health insurance program. The Health and Human Services Department now has some limited provider performance data available on its Web site at http://www.hospitalcompare.hhs.gov/. See also http://www.healthgrades.com/ for comparisons of health procedure pricing. Also, on August 22, 2006, President Bush issued an Executive Order requiring federal health sponsoring programs, such as Medicare, the federal employees' plans, and the Veterans Administration to provide by January 1, 2007, cost and quality information of health care providers to beneficiaries so they can compare providers.

138. As an example, in August 2006, President Bush issued an Executive Order requiring health care price and quality information to be available to government workers covered by the federal health care system. Miller, H. (2007, September 24). *Creating payment systems to accelerate value-driven health care: Issues*

Some Perspectives on the Bureaucratic
Barriers to Health Care Reform

Societies often organize their political systems to create welfare programs that distribute cash to broad socioeconomic groups. In the case of health care, the apparent assumption in the United States has been that the employer-sponsored system works well until one is either unemployed or underemployed and not making sufficient income to participate in the various cost sharing schemes found in health insurance. Perhaps, as our policymakers say, we should do something about the poor and provide health care. In such cases we have a wealth transfer from the employed to the unemployed.[139] While somewhat of a subtle conflict, the dichotomy does not serve to energize the political efforts to reform our social welfare systems as we have observed in the U.S. Congress. As we examine various health care issues that seem to be ripe for reform, we must be mindful of inherent political subterfuges that make change more difficult.[140] The U.S. health care system, in spite of its apparent problems, has been amazingly resilient in avoiding major changes and reform. As one writer put it, "Underestimating the system's resiliency risks may lead reform astray again, but what exactly should be done is far from clear. No one knows exactly how to infuse moral urgency into the push for universal coverage, make the system's medical style markedly less expensive, and thrust reform to the top of the agenda for powerful interest groups."[141]

This is occasioned by the instinct to quickly examine the problem of the uninsured and then jump to a grand solution. Reform also has powerful opponents and there are political implications that make them difficult to

---

and options for policy reform. The Commonwealth Fund, Vol. 72, http://www .commonwealthfund.org/publications/.

139. See, generally, Persson, T., & Tabellini, G. (2000). *Political Economics– Explaining Economic Policy* (pp. 123–158). The MIT Press.

140. It is interesting to note that in 1912, Theodore Roosevelt, campaigning for president, endorsed compulsory health insurance as part of his platform. At the same time, the American Association for Labor Legislation promoted the idea of making health insurance mandatory for workers who earned less than $1,200 per year (about $25,000 today). The employer, the employee, and the state would share the cost of the premiums. A coalition of unions, pharmacists, insurance companies, doctors, and the politics of WWI joined together to defeat the proposals. Crossen, C. (2007, April 30). Before WWI began, universal health care seemed a sure thing. *The Wall Street Journal*, B1.

141. Brown, L. (2008, January 24). The amazing noncollapsing U.S. health care system: Is reform finally at hand? *The New England Journal of Medicine, 358*(44), 325–327.

legislate. The more we rely on a relevant and critical analysis of the deep-rooted causes of the problems, as well as the complexities and unique value of our system, and use metrics and data-driven processes to carefully design effective responses to these problems, the more likely we will be able to achieve true and sustainable reform.

Chapter Exercises

1. Form a team and prepare a presentation concerning health care reform in the United States. Review this chapter and also Chapter 13, Global Benefits, and examine the various possible approaches to reform, including those under active consideration by the U.S. Congress. Choose a solution that, in your judgment, best fulfills the principles and values mentioned earlier in this chapter or others that you consider to be vital. Be as specific as possible in describing how your solution will work, how much each element will cost, how you would measure the relative cost of the proposal, how much each element might reduce current spending and costs, how it will affect the current delivery system, how it will be financed, how it will be administered, and how the American public can be convinced to support it.

2. You are the senior HR officer of General Motors. Your company is saddled with extraordinarily high medical care costs for your employees, who are represented by the United Auto Workers Union. Your health care costs for active employees are almost twice that of your nonunion competition. Toyota, for example, requires significantly more employee cost sharing in its plans. GM also pays more than its competitors for retiree health care. These excessive costs make it difficult to compete in the United States. Your CEO has asked you to prepare a policy statement that GM can publish regarding health care reform in the United States. She believes that such reform might reduce GM's health care costs or "level the playing field." Do some independent research and prepare a report and proposed policy statement for review and approval by your CEO.

Benefit Legal Compliance 9

Employee Retirement Income and Security Act (ERISA), Internal Revenue Code (IRC), and the Pension Protection Act of 2006 (PPA)

Isabella and her coworkers work at Silver Lining Company, a subsidiary of Carta Foglia Paper Mills. Silver Lining makes paper boxes for department stores. The company has a collective bargaining agreement with the Paper Workers' Union that requires it to contribute to a defined benefit plan. All employees including Isabella are covered; the pension plan has a five-year vesting requirement. Last month the company announced it was closing the Silver Lining plant and subcontracting the work to another company. The new company has no collective bargaining agreement and only offers a 401(k) to its employees. Isabella and her coworkers are separated from Silver Lining, but she and many others are offered positions at the new company. She suspects the real reasons for Carta Foglia's actions were to avoid paying pensions and to reduce their expenses. The issues presented here and their resolutions will be discussed in the following pages.

History

Prior to 1974 in the United States, many employers sponsored retirement plans for their employees. In some instances employees were not guaranteed a pension until they met all service and other requirements and then reached retirement age, usually 65. Even after reaching retirement age and meeting all the requirements for a pension, some employers retained the right to terminate all pension entitlements if the employee conducted himself in a manner not consistent with the standards of the employer.[1]

Some of the abuses common during this period included terminating an employee just prior to his reaching retirement age and completing all the service requirements for a pension. The purpose was simply to deny the employee a pension and avoid the pension expense. In other cases, if a participant later worked for a company that competed with his previous employer, the company sponsoring the retirement plan would cancel the pension payments for reasons of improper conduct. Employers would offset and reduce pension payments by applying a claim for money that might have resulted from the employee's conduct at the workplace or some payments he might be receiving from another program such as worker's compensation.

In many cases, vesting did not exist. An employer had complete freedom to fund the pension plan in whatever manner he chose, to discontinue pension payments for any reason, or to retain complete discretion as to how a pension plan would be designed.[2] There was no transparency, so participants had no idea what rights, if any, they had under the plan or how the plan was funded or managed. There were instances where plans were simply terminated by the employer and participants with many years of service and high expectations of future retirement income were left with nothing. Other examples of mismanagement that left prospective pensioners with no pension at retirement age include plans that were not properly funded, plan sponsors engaged in self-dealing with service providers, and accrued pension benefits that were assigned to others.

This all changed in 1974 with passage of the Employee Retirement Income and Security Act (ERISA) that was last amended by the Pension Protection Act of 2006 (PPA).[3] In this chapter we will discuss ERISA, as well as provisions of the Internal Revenue Code of 1986 (IRC) that are relevant to the administration of both retirement and welfare (e.g., health) plans.[4] The IRC sets certain conditions with respect to the design and function of a benefit plan because of the favorable tax treatment extended

---

1. See 29 USC §1001 (ERISA, Congressional Findings and Declaration of Policy, 1974). (Note: References to ERISA will include parallel cites to the ERISA sections, e.g., 29 USC §1001 is the same as ERISA §2.)

2. The employee participant could pursue a "breach of contract" claim against the employer in some instances, but there were no regulatory or federal standards pertaining to pension administration.

3. 29 USC §1001 et seq. and the PPA of 2006 that amended a number of provisions of ERISA (PL 109-280, August 17, 2006).

4. See, for example, IRC §105, 106, et seq.

to both sponsors and beneficiaries.[5] Plan contributions made by the sponsor can be tax deductible; plan assets can grow without being taxed; and plan accruals for participants are tax deferred until received. Both laws have gone a long way to create obligations and standards that guarantee predictability, transparency, inalienability, and fiduciary and financial accountability for retirement and welfare plans sponsored by employers in the United States. Some of the specific provisions of the laws will be discussed in more detail in other chapters.

For example, IRC §415, among other things, sets maximum levels of contributions and benefits that a qualified plan may allow. It also establishes maximum income and benefits that can be used to calculate and pay retirement income from defined benefit plans. These were pointed out in Chapter 4, as were certain Safe Harbor provisions relating to the avoidance of disproportionate participation of highly compensated employees (HCEs) in defined contribution plans. In addition, COBRA, HIPAA, FMLA, and other mandated benefit laws are discussed in Chapter 12. For now, we will focus on the basic provisions of ERISA, the PPA of 2006, and the IRC of 1986; to cover all the provisions that apply to pension and welfare plans in detail would require an entire text.[6]

The purpose of this chapter is to describe the basic principles and objectives of these laws, to illustrate how and when they apply, and to stress the importance of legal compliance. The teaching objective is to give you, the students, a quiver of red flags. Thus, when you are working in a company that sponsors benefits and potential legal issues arise, you will have the cautionary "red flag" at your disposal to alert that benefits counsel be consulted.

Getting back to the vignette and Isabella and her coworkers. Does she have a case? Is there a provision in ERISA that might be applicable to her situation? The answer is yes. Section 510 of ERISA[7] makes it unlawful for an employer to discharge a participant of an employee benefit plan for the purpose of "interfering with the attainment of any right to which the participant may become entitled under the plan." If she and her cohorts can show this was the motive for the change, she could prevail in a legal action

---

5. Some examples of tax treatment for pension and health care plans include the deductibility of plan contributions by employers and the deferral of income and earnings among participants, all of which are discussed in Chapters 4 and 5. Compliance with the IRC results in the particular plan being designated as "tax qualified" and eligible for favored tax treatment.

6. See, for example, *Employee Benefits Law*, 2nd ed. (2006). Washington, DC: American Bar Assn., Section of Labor and Employment Law.

7. 29 USC §1140 (§510 of ERISA).

against her employer.[8] What issues might Isabella raise in arguing this point? What might be the arguments put forward by the company?[9]

What if Isabella is discharged one month before completing five years of service and becoming fully vested under Silver Lining's pension plan? What are the issues here and how would you resolve them? Isabella would have to show that her discharge was motivated by the employer's intent to prevent her from attaining a vesting right under the pension plan. The company would be obligated to come forward and show that her discharge was based on poor performance or some other legitimate business reasons. Then Isabella would be obligated to show that the reasons put forth by the company were pretextual.

Prior to the passage of ERISA, Isabella would have had a difficult time prevailing in either case. These illustrations demonstrate how ERISA can be used to protect the rights of participants who are expecting retirement income from an employer's pension plan, but are denied the opportunity to attain such rights. As you can see, however, proving a claim of wrongful discharge requires proof that the sponsor's action was designed to interfere with attaining vesting or other rights under the plan.

The Basic Provisions of ERISA

COVERAGE

> Sam has run a small box manufacturing business for ten years. His workforce comprises 20 employees, and sales have been growing for the last eight years. Recently, his employees talked with him about the possibility of getting a pension plan in the shop. Sam offers a

---

8. 29 USC §1140 (§510 of ERISA) specifically prohibits anyone from interfering with the attainment of any right to which a participant may be entitled under a pension or other plan. Under ERISA, however, when a participant brings a legal action, no compensatory or punitive damages are permitted. Thus, many lawyers are reluctant to pursue such cases because of the rather limited relief available. It should also be noted that if Isabella wants to pursue a state court action alleging that her employer improperly denied her pension rights, the action likely would be "preempted" by ERISA and dismissed. See *Inter-Modal Employees Association v. Atchison, Topeka, and Santa Fe Railway Co.*, 520 U.S. 510 (1997); *Pilot Life Insurance v. Dedeaux*, 481 U.S. 41 (1987). The *Inter-Modal* case involved a wrongful termination issue and the *Pilot Life Insurance* case involved a decision where a state claim for improper denial of plan benefits was held to be preempted.

9. See *Inter-Modal Employees Association v. Atchison, Topeka, and Santa Fe Railway Co, supra.*

health care plan, but never seriously considered a pension plan. The process of studying such a proposal is daunting because of the variety of plans from which to choose and all the legal requirements. He decides to contact his accountant for some ideas. He asks her if his plan has to meet all the requirements of ERISA.

ERISA neither requires an employer to provide retirement or health care benefits nor prescribes the level or amounts of benefits offered. It does, however, cover an employer or employee who is "engaged in" or "affecting commerce," and who establishes a pension plan.[1] Thus, any plan that provides income or allows a deferral of income that is paid at the termination of employment would be considered a pension plan covered by ERISA.[2]

Recognizing that Sam wants a plan for his workers, the accountant explains that, because his company engages in or affects commerce, the plan must meet at least some, if not all, of the specific requirements of ERISA.[3] She goes on to tell him that ERISA applies to all retirement plans except those sponsored by state or government entities that have special exemptions for certain titles of the law.[4]

---

1. 29 USC §1003 (§4 of ERISA).

2. 29 USC §1002(1), (§3 of ERISA). Section 905 of the PPA permits participants to receive retirement benefits from the participant's employer-sponsored plan and continue working on a phased retirement basis after age 62. Thus, the requirement that a participant must be terminated from employment is no longer universally applicable to the definition of a pension plan.

3. Government plans and certain executive plans do not have to comply with Part 1 (Reporting and Disclosure) of ERISA. A plan, such as a governmental plan, church plan, or one created outside the United States with non-U.S. participants, which is exempt from certain of the provisions of ERISA, such as Part 1 (Reporting and Disclosure) and Part 2 (Vesting and Participation), means that benefits could be forfeitable, unsecured, and may not be backed by irrevocably committed assets in a trust fund. There are also certain executive deferred income plans or excess plans that are similarly exempt from certain provisions of ERISA. If such plans are properly constructed, the participants' deferrals will not be taxed until they are paid out. If a covered plan is not in compliance, however, it could mean that no tax advantages are available.

4. There are numerous state and local employee and educator pension funds partially exempt from ERISA that are currently underfunded and awaiting state or local taxpayer relief to liquidate their debt. See McMahon, E. (2006, August 21). Public pension price tag. *The Wall Street Journal*, A10.

If full protection such as secured benefits and tax advantages are desired, all relevant provisions of ERISA must be followed. Similarly, the IRC applies to pension and welfare plans that are intended to gain favored tax treatment.

We have seen in the Silver Lining vignette where an employer sponsor whose intent was to abrogate a right under a pension plan could use ERISA to challenge a participant's discharge. What other protections and obligations exist in ERISA?

REPORTING AND DISCLOSURE[10]

ERISA requires plan sponsors to provide participants with detailed information about the plan, including how it is funded, the various plan features, and how entitlements accrue. It also requires the plan to submit reports to the Department of Labor and the Internal Revenue Service that include actuarial and financial information. The sponsor must make some of these documents accessible to participants. It also must provide the participants, without charge, a "Summary Plan Description" (SPD) setting forth the basic provisions of the plan, eligibility and participation requirements, the method for calculating benefits, how vesting works under the plan, how benefits are distributed, and the participant's rights under the plan to appeal any adverse decision with respect to his claim for benefits.

> Mary, a DBP participant, elects to receive her benefit in a lump sum instead of an annuity. The employer sponsor complies and sends her a check representing the lump sum. Mary requests that the company disclose information as to how it computed the lump sum. For example, how did they calculate the future value of the annuities and what discount rate did they use to calculate the lump sum? The company responds by sending Mary some general plan information about benefits, but refuses to send any information about the computation of the lump sum.

Is this information important to the participant? Yes. The assumptions the company made in calculating the lump sum can have a significant effect on the amount of the lump sum. In a lawsuit filed against the

---

10. See ERISA, 29 USC §1021–1031 (§§101–111 of ERISA). See also §§501–509 of the PPA that includes a new provision allowing the electronic display of annual report information.

Table 9.1   Types of Retirement Plan Information Legally Available From Sponsor

Type of Document	Where to Get It
Summary Plan Description (SPD)—written for participants, the SPD describes the benefits and the basic operation of the plan.	Plan sponsor or U.S. Department of Labor
Summary Annual Report—summarizes the financial activities and status of the plan.	Plan sponsor or U.S. Department of Labor
Individual Benefit Statement—is for the participant and describes his accrued benefits.	Plan sponsor once each year
Notice of Underfunding—must be sent out if the plan is less than 90 percent funded; it also describes PBGC guarantees.	Plan sponsor

SOURCE: U.S. Department of Labor. Participants also can obtain copies of plan applications for a determination of tax-qualified status filed with the IRS. See 29 USC §1025(c).

sponsor by a participant, the Court held the sponsor's refusal to provide information on the calculation of the lump sum violated the sponsor's duty to provide information to participants under Part 1 of ERISA.[11]

The Pension Protection Act[12] says that a plan sponsor has a duty to provide retirement participants with a benefits statement more frequently than in the past. For a DBP, this statement would include the participant's specific nonforfeitable benefit accruals, as well as an estimate of retirement income at certain ages.[13] These must now be distributed at least every three years and the sponsor must notify the participant of the availability of such statements every year. For DCPs, pursuant to the PPA, in cases where the participant directs the investments, a statement of investment accounts and current balances must be distributed quarterly to the participants. Further, this benefit statement must include the value of the

---

11. See *Maiuro v. Federal Express Corp.*, 843 F. Supp. 935 (D.N.J. 1994). See §1025(a) of ERISA.

12. The PPA (PL 109-280, August 17, 2006) amended ERISA and the Internal Revenue Code and its provisions have been integrated into both laws. See §503 and §508 of PPA.

13. Where a pension plan sponsor refused to give a participant any requested information about her pension account, saying simply she had no pension, the Court held the sponsor had violated the reporting and disclosure provisions of ERISA. *Cromer –Tyler v. Teitel*, 41 EB Cases (BNA) (M.D. Ala. 2007).

participant's investments, as well as information regarding the importance of investment diversification.[14] Transparency and the duty to inform are basic to protecting a participant's retirement or other benefit entitlements. There are other considerations, however.

FIDUCIARY RESPONSIBILITY

ERISA created new legal obligations among plan sponsors; one was the sponsor's duty to assume a fiduciary role toward the participant.[15] ERISA requires that plan fiduciaries act solely in the interest of plan participants and their beneficiaries. The fiduciary must act for the exclusive purpose of providing benefits and defraying reasonable administrative expenses, and with the skill, prudence, and diligence of a sensible person familiar with such matters.[16]

The plan must be in writing, and its administrators must follow its terms and conditions. The plan cannot simply provide a benefit, for example, to a friend of the sponsor and ignore the plan provisions pertaining to eligibility for a benefit.

In tax-qualified plans, plan assets must be held in a trust. Plan investments must be diversified and managed so as to minimize the risk of significant losses, unless the plan qualifies as an Employee Stock Ownership Plan (ESOP). In addition, the sponsor of the plan must be careful to avoid mixing plan and nonplan assets of the fund and, further, cannot borrow from the fund.[17] These are called prohibited transactions and they fulfill the purpose of better securing the assets of the fund by avoiding conflicts of interest. These rules also prohibit the fund from holding more than 10 percent of the employer sponsor's stock.

Frequently, the sponsor of a retirement plan can delegate certain fiduciary responsibilities to named fiduciaries. These would include the trustee, who may be charged with collecting and distributing the assets of the fund, and the investment managers, who develop the investment strategies and direct the trustee to make specific purchases and sales of investments. The plan administrator is another fiduciary that is responsible for

---

14. The U.S. Labor Department has been charged with the responsibility to design model benefit statements for plan sponsors that can be used as guides for compliance. See http://www.dol.gov/ebsa (Field Assistance Bulletin No. 2007-03).

15. 29 USC §1101–1114 (§§401–414 of ERISA)

16. Ibid.

17. Specifically, transactions between the plan and a party in interest, the plan and a fiduciary, and the transfer of property to a plan by a party in interest are considered to be "prohibited transactions." See 29 USC §1106 (§406 of ERISA).

implementing the provisions of the plan, distributing benefits, and fulfilling the reporting and disclosure requirements of ERISA. Let's look at an example of how the fiduciary responsibility works.

Suppose a plan sponsor has contracted with an annuity provider who will assume the responsibility of paying benefits to the sponsor's participants. The sponsor intends to terminate its pension plan. The plan is overfunded and the sponsor expects to receive a reversion of funds after the annuities are purchased and all benefit liabilities are met. The sponsor considers several providers, but selects the one with the lowest bid, which would enhance the prospects for a larger reversion of funds back to the sponsor after the annuities are purchased. The selected provider has an unusually large amount of high-yield, low-quality bonds in its investment portfolio, enabling it to be the low bidder in the sponsor's search for an annuity provider. The sponsor signs a contract with the provider. Now, the participants must rely on the provider to pay off their pension benefits by way of annuities.

After a relatively short period, the provider's investments in low-quality bonds results in a billion dollar loss, causing the provider to go into receivership. The annuity payments to beneficiaries in the sponsor's terminated plan are reduced. The beneficiaries file a lawsuit, arguing that selecting an annuity provider who was the lowest bidder was not a proper exercise of fiduciary responsibility. They argue that making the choice on the basis of lowest cost is not an adequate reason and the sponsor has not met its fiduciary duty. Moreover, the plan sponsor should have done more to evaluate the overall risks and rewards of a number of providers because, under §404 of ERISA, the sponsor was a fiduciary owing a duty of care and loyalty to its participants. As such, the beneficiaries argued that the sponsor was obligated to conduct a more thorough investigation into various annuity providers. In particular, the sponsor should have been very cautious about a company that had 50 to 60 percent of its portfolio invested in low-quality bonds. The court agreed with the participants and found the employer sponsor guilty of violating its fiduciary duty. The sponsor was liable to make up the reduction in annuity payments sustained by the beneficiaries.[1]

1. *Bussian v. RJR Nabisco, Inc.*, 233 F.3d 286 (5th Cir. 2000). The Court also notes that a plan sponsor has a duty to diversify its own pension assets. The U.S. Labor Department has published "Tips for Selecting Service Providers," http://www.dol.gov/ebsa, which plan sponsors might find helpful in exercising their fiduciary duties.

Plan sponsors of DCPs also have similar fiduciary responsibilities. These types of plans are a little different from a DBP because DCPs must allow participants to choose their own investments.[18] For example, the sponsor must make sure the participant's investment choices are implemented in a timely manner, and must make prudent decisions with respect to the choice of investment alternatives.[19] It should have a variety of investment options (at least three other than the sponsor's securities) that are reasonably diversified.[20] The PPA provides some protection for the employer sponsor of a DCP when the employer automatically enrolls the employee and then makes an investment selection on his behalf.[21] Further, in cases of automatic enrollment and deferral of the employee's wages into the plan, as long as the sponsor follows the Safe Harbor provisions of ERISA (described in Chapter 4), the sponsor is afforded reasonable protection from fiduciary liability.[22]

The PPA also incorporates some Safe Harbor rules to insulate the employer from discrimination violations arising from the automatic enrollment of his employees in a DCP. To achieve this protection, in 2008 the employer must make sure that his nonelective deferral of the non-highly compensated employee's (NHCE)[23] salary does not exceed 10 percent per year, but is not less than a prescribed schedule ranging from 3 percent of compensation to 6 percent in the fourth and subsequent years.[24]

---

18. This obligation is included in the PPA, §901.

19. See, generally, §404(c) of the IRC.

20. §901 of the PPA. For example, participants of Sprint Nextel Corp.'s 401(k) plan brought an action against the company arguing the company stock was not a prudent investment to be included in the 401(k), and that they were not adequately informed about a new strategic direction of the firm that affected the price of the stock. The company paid $29 million to settle the suit, although it vigorously denied any violation of its fiduciary responsibilities. See Kansas City Star (2006, August 10), http://www.kansascity.com/.

21. See §624 and §902 of PPA. In such involuntary enrollments, the employers use of certain age-based, risk-based, and target date funds will give the employer protection against fiduciary liability.

22. See ERISA §404(c)(5), §624 PPA. The PPA provides that such automatic or involuntary enrollment provision preempts any state or federal law that proscribes garnishment or wage reductions. The U.S. Labor Department has issued guidelines that, if followed, absolve the sponsor from such liability. See http://www.dol.gov/ebsa, 29 CFR 2550 Default Investment Alternatives Under Participant Directed Individual Account Plans; Proposed Rule (September 27, 2006).

23. For 2008 a HCE is one who makes $110,000 per year or more. The amounts are indexed annually. See http://www.irs.gov/ (Pension Plan Limitations for 2008).

24. §902 of the PPA.

In such default participation schemes, the employer can either make a contribution on behalf of all NHCEs of a minimum of 3 percent of salary or, if the employee's salary is involuntarily deferred, he must make a matching 100 percent contribution based on the deferral of up to a maximum of 1 percent of salary. For deferrals in excess of 1 percent and up to 6 percent of salary, the employer must match 50 percent of the salary deferral. In all cases where the Safe Harbor plan is adopted, the employer contributions or matches must be 100 percent vested within two years.[25]

There had been some potential fiduciary liability among employer sponsors who provided investment advice to participants; however, the PPA clarified this practice. Now, plan sponsors can avoid potential prohibited transaction and conflict of interest violations under ERISA if, under certain circumstances, they permit their investment advisor to provide advice to the participants.[26] The investment advisor can be paid a fee for rendering such advice.[27]

In spite of some welcomed changes relating to fiduciary responsibilities included in the PPA, plan fiduciaries remain personally liable for a variety of missteps.[28] For instance, if they fail to deposit a participant's designated deferred compensation into his 401(k) or 403(b) account,[29] or purchase excessive amounts of company stock in a DBP, or fail to exercise prudence in the selection of the investment options for a 401(k) or 403(b) plan, or fail to monitor the service charges of the trustee or other service providers of a plan, they can be liable.[30] For these reasons, most fiduciaries purchase

---

25. §904 PPA, §411 IRC.

26. §601 of the PPA. As we noted in Chapter 4, those few DCPs who do not allow employees with the freedom to invest their plan assets must do so. §901 PPA.

27. See §601 PPA, §4975, and §408(b)(14), §408(g) of the IRC. The plan must also give notice to the participant of his right to divest employer securities held, for example, in an ESOP or Profit Sharing Plan after attaining age 55 and working five years. See §507 PPA, and §502(c)(7) of ERISA, and §401 of IRC.

28. See 29 USC §1105 (§405 of ERISA).

29. See, for example, the Labor Department's publication, Ten Warning Signs That Your 401(k) or 403(b) Contributions Are Being Misused, which includes items such as your statement is consistently late, your account balance does not appear to be accurate, unauthorized investments on your account statement, the employer failed to transmit your contribution and others. See http://www.dol.gov/ebsa.

30. The fiduciary duties test the action of the fiduciary by applying a hypothetical "prudent man" standard. ERISA also allows the sponsor to nominate "named fiduciaries" who have special responsibilities and accountabilities, such as investing assets of the fund. See 29 USC §1104 (§404 of ERISA).

liability insurance protecting them against such risks; to protect the victims, named fiduciaries must be bonded.[31]

PARTICIPATION AND VESTING

ERISA imposes certain minimum participation standards. For example, any person covered by a plan must begin participation when he turns 21 and completes one year of service. Generally speaking, one year of service means the completion of 1,000 hours of work over a 12-consecutive-month period.[32] Thus, a part-time employee who works 1,000 hours or more over a 12-consecutive-month period would be entitled to participate in the plan. Further, once an employee whose position is covered by a retirement plan reaches age 21 and begins participation, all years of service prior to 21 and after the attainment of age 18 will be counted for vesting purposes.

Vesting is a mechanism that ensures a nonforfeitable benefit. If one has served in the company for the required minimum period of time, the employer sponsor cannot alienate or forfeit one's benefits. The sponsor may require that you reach a certain age (e.g., 55) in order to receive a benefit payment but, once you are vested, the entitlement cannot be forfeited. While the employer sponsor is free to determine how many years of service will be required to make benefits nonforfeitable, ERISA mandates certain maximum vesting periods for both DBPs and DCPs.[33] As discussed in Chapter 4, vesting under ERISA can be graduated or cliff. For defined contribution plans, the maximum allowable vesting schedule under ERISA is a three-year cliff vesting or a six-year graduated vesting schedule. In cases where the employer sponsors a Safe Harbor DCP, the employer's contributions must be vested either immediately or, in the case of automatic enrollment, not later than two years.[34]

---

31. 29 USC §1112 (§412 of ERISA).

32. There are several methods permitted for both counting hours and the one year of service provision: the general method, the equivalency method, and the elapsed time method. See 29 USC §1052–1053 (§202 of ERISA).

33. The Economic Growth and Tax Relief Reconciliation Act of 2001 (EGTRRA) modified and reduced the required vesting periods for DCPs. See Summary of EGTRRA and recent law provisions, 2001, http://www.irs.gov/pub. The Act also amended the IRC and ERISA with respect to distributions, plan benefit and contribution limits, and other provisions.

34. Of course employers are free to make their plans more generous with respect to vesting.

Table 9.2   ERISA Maximum Vesting Schedules Effective After 2002*

Defined Contribution Plans (DCP, Employer Contributions)**
Three-Year Cliff

After Year(s)	1	2	3
Percent vested	0%	0%	100%

Six-Year Graduated

Year	1	2	3	4	5	6
Percent vested	0%	20%	40%	60%	80%	100%

Defined Benefit Plans (DBPs)
Five-Year Cliff

After Year(s)	1	2	3	4	5
Percent vested	0%	0%	0%	0%	100%

Seven-Year Graduated

	0–3 Years	3–4 Years	4–5 Years	5–6 Years	6–7 Years	7 Years
Percent vested	0%	20%	40%	60%	80%	100%

*   See earlier vesting schedules at www.dol.gov/ebsa.
**   Employee contributions are immediately vested. For SEPs and SIMPLEs, see Chapter 5; employer contributions are immediately vested.

For defined benefit plans, the maximum allowable vesting schedule is a five-year cliff or seven-year graduated vesting period.[35] For cash balance plans, the PPA provides that the employer's contribution must vest after three years.

An ERISA issue relating to vesting is "breaks in service." Does a person who leaves the company but then returns forfeit his prebreak vesting service, or is it bridged and counted with his postbreak service?

_____

35. 29 USC §1053 (§203 ERISA).

> Suppose A works for company X for three years that are counted for vesting purposes. Company X sponsors a DBP with five-year cliff vesting. A returns to X after a two-year break in service. Is the company obligated to bridge or count her previous three years of service? When will she be vested? The answer is, A must complete two years of service after her return. She can then bridge her previous three years of service with the two years and will be completely vested. In all cases involving breaks in service, the plan is permitted to provide that the employee must work one year after the break before the prior service is bridged.
>
> What happens if A works for two years at the company, leaves, and then returns four years later? Can A's previous service be bridged to her subsequent years of service? The answer is, it depends. The plan can provide that if the break exceeds the years of previous service or exceeds five years, the employer is not legally obligated to bridge the previous service. However, if A left the company with a vested benefit, including graduated-vested years, and then returns, the previous service cannot be forfeited and must be bridged to the service after the break.[1]
>
> ---
>
> 1. 29 USC §1053(b)(3)(A), (B), (C), and (D). (ERISA §203).

It is obvious why a returning employee would want to have his previous service bridged and added to his new service. If he meets the requirements of the "breaks in service" rule, he will vest earlier and also receive an accrual of benefits for each of the prebreak years of service.[36]

---

36. 29 USC §1053(b)(3)(A), (B), (C), and (D). There is some question as to whether the "break-in-service" rules apply only to vesting service or should also include accrued benefit service. Of course, if a person is not vested, the issue of benefit service is moot. But let's say an employee works for three years and then has a four-year break in service. Under the ERISA rules, if the plan provides, he could not bridge those previous three years of service. But what if he resumes working as a participant under the retirement plan and later becomes vested? In calculating his benefit, should those prebreak service years be counted as benefit accrual years and included as "years of service" under the plan's formula? The U.S. Court of Appeals for the 2d Circuit held that they could be included in the formula. It found that the break-in-service rules for "vesting" involve determining how many years of service a participant might have that would render his benefit nonforfeitable. This, the Court said, does not appear to be applicable to the crediting of accrued service, which is used to calculate the benefit. The Court sent the case back to the lower court for further consideration, but pointed out that ERISA (29 USC §1054) outlines the obligation of a plan to credit "all years of service" for purposes of calculating benefit accruals and is silent with respect to "breaks in service." It noted that 29 USC §1053 delineates how vesting years should be counted

Table 9.3   ERISA Break-in-Service Rules

- When prebreak years of service equal cliff or graduated vesting, sponsor must recognize service. No exceptions.
- When prebreak years of service are less than cliff or graduated vesting, sponsor must recognize prebreak service unless the break in service is greater than the prebreak years of service, or the break in service is greater than five years.
- Before the prebreak service can be recognized, the employee must complete one year of service after the break.

Compliance with basic ERISA rules is key to preserving the tax-favored status of a benefit plan. There are some special rules of the IRS and the IRC of 1986, however, that augment ERISA and provide special added requirements to attain tax-qualified status.

BENEFIT ACCRUAL REQUIREMENTS[37]

While the employer sponsor of a DBP is free to determine the amount of benefits his participants will receive, there are obligations with respect to how benefits are accrued in a retirement plan. Whatever formula is selected, a participant's benefit accumulates or is allocated as he earns additional years of service under the plan. For example, if the benefit formula is in part based on years of service, as these years lapse, one can calculate the accrued benefit as of any particular date. The accrued benefit under ERISA cannot be forfeited or reduced.[38] Future benefits, those that have not yet accrued, can be reduced.[39]

---

and does include a "break-in-service" provision. See *McDonald v. Pension Plan of the NYSA-ILA Pension Trust Fund*, 320 F.3d 151 (2d Cir. 2003).

37. See ERISA at 29 USC §1054 (§204 ERISA).

38. The precise and complete listing of all the rules pertaining to benefit accruals is not discussed in this book. There are a couple of issues worth noting, however. Let's say a plan changes its benefit formula to apply "final average pay," but only after a participant works 25 years. This and other practices that unfairly delay the attainment of benefits under a plan are considered "back loading" and are not permitted. There is also a restriction on plan amendments that adversely affect accrued benefits and optional forms of distribution. This is called an "anti-cutback" rule. See IRC §411(d)(6), 29 USC §1054(g) (§204 ERISA). Early retirement benefits, optional forms of benefits, accrued benefits, and other provisions of a plan cannot be eliminated or "cut back." Similarly, it is illegal to provide for significant increases in pension calculations at retirement and benefit increases during a plan bankruptcy.

39. The PPA has provided some special fiduciary responsibilities of the plan sponsor and its named fiduciaries during a merger or acquisition. See §702 PPA.

Let's look at an example. Let's say the DBP formula comprises years of service multiplied by final average pay, multiplied by 2 percent. A fully vested employee who has accumulated ten years of service and whose final average pay currently equals $80,000 would have an unadjusted benefit accrual or retirement benefit of $16,000 per year.[40] This amount, payable when the participant reaches normal retirement age, cannot be reduced unless the plan is terminated and financially unable to pay benefits, or if the employee is subject to an actuarial reduction due to his age at retirement. A plan sponsor sometimes decides it can no longer afford the benefits offered by its plan and looks for an alternative, less costly plan design. It may legally "freeze" its current plan and current or new employees into a new plan. The benefits under the old plan, however, that were accrued by participants who had completed the age and service requirements up until the date of the freeze are fixed and cannot be reduced.

BENEFITS DISTRIBUTION

Spouses

ERISA requires that a defined benefit plan must include an option for the surviving spouse to receive a benefit equal to 50 percent of the participant's benefit.[41] Under the PPA, this mandatory benefit has been broadened to include an optional 75 percent joint spouse survivor benefit, if such an option is available to other contingent, nonspouse beneficiaries under the plan.[42] This benefit will be received unless the spouse specifically waives it.[43] Why would the spouse waive it? If there is an actuarial reduction imposed on the participant because of the spouse election, this reduction in benefits would affect the level of income received over the life of the participant. Thus, the spouse might not elect the joint spouse survivor benefit, so that they may enjoy higher income during the participant's life. If the net worth of both is significant, or if they purchase a life insurance

---

40. This, of course, does not include any actuarial adjustments for early retirement or beneficiary selection.

41. The PPA mandates an offering of a 75 percent spouse survivor option under certain circumstances. See PPA §1004.

42. The PPA also now allows nonspouse beneficiaries of a defined benefit plan participant to "roll over" their distribution to a tax-qualified plan and defer taxation. See PPA §824.

43. What is the applicable time period for making the waiver of survivor benefit? The participant and spouse may only waive the joint and survivor annuity option during the 180-day period ending on the date that a plan is under an obligation to begin making pension payments. *Shields v. Reader's Digest Association, Inc.*, 331 F.3d 536, (6th Cir. 2003).

policy on the life of the participant, then a continuation of adequate income over the life of the successor beneficiary is ensured.

LUMP SUMS AND DBPs

Lump sum is an alternative form of benefit distribution a participant can choose instead of an annuity. There is a problem that has persisted with respect to which interest rate assumption ("discount rate") should be used to determine the present value (or "lump sum") stream of annuity payments. The choice can have a major impact on the amount of the lump sum. See the following vignette for an example.

Mary participates in her company's defined benefit plan and is close to full retirement age. The plan allows the participant to elect a lump sum payout instead of an annuity.[1] Mary would like to consider an annuity, but is unsure how it is calculated. In most cases the plan sponsor adds up the expected annual annuity payments over the projected life span of the participant, applies an interest appreciation rate, and calculates the future value of the pension. Next it calculates the lump sum value of this stream of payments by determining its present value, and then applies an assumed interest rate return and "discounts" the total stream of annuity payments and their appreciation to a present value. If the plan sponsor chooses an aggressive interest rate return, then the lump sum will be smaller than if a more conservative assumption had been selected. So, Mary must determine what assumption the company is using to calculate her lump sum and also what life expectancy (mortality tables) they are using. Obviously, she would argue that the company use a smaller, more realistic interest rate and assume a shorter life expectancy.

---

1. The PPA, §303, and IRC §415(b), as well as IRS Notice 2007-7, provide some specific guidance on the appropriate discount rate to be used in such instances. There are several policy issues with respect to lump sums. If the purpose of a retirement plan is to provide retirement income, should we allow potential spendthrift participants to take all of their benefits and use them as they see fit? The answer thus far has been yes, although there were some proposals to mandate 401(k) sponsors to offer an annuity distribution option to all participants. The PPA does not include such a provision. Of course there are a variety of annuity products one can buy when they receive their lump sum and continue to enjoy tax deferral. Also, participants who elect a lump sum distribution can further defer income taxes on the benefit by rolling the distribution over into a tax-favored instrument such as an IRA.

Investment return and life expectancy assumptions have been contentious for some time. The PPA has helped to clarify the issues by requiring plan sponsors to use the same three-segment yield curve applicable to the minimum pension funding obligations of sponsors as described later on.[44] Instead of discounting the annuity aggregation by using a 30-year Treasury bond interest rate, the sponsor must use different rates covering different time segments.[45] It also requires the sponsor to use a standard mortality table in the calculation of life expectancy. Thus, these two important variables are now standardized and arbitrary assumptions have been removed from the calculation of a pensioner's lump sum estimate.

MINIMUM FUNDING STANDARDS

You will recall in Chapter 2 we used the analogy of how much to save for college to illustrate the considerations relevant to an employer's funding of a DBP. There are many variables the employer must consider: (1) What is the estimated longevity of his workforce? (2) What investment assumptions should be made about the assets of the fund? (3) Since stocks and bonds vary from day to day, how does the employer value the assets of a fund? (4) How far ahead must the employer fund the plan to ensure he can pay accrued benefits? These variables are critical in determining how much money must be put into the pension trust each year.

ERISA and the PPA have provided some certainty and predictability with respect to funding a DBP. The objective is simple—to make sure the plan can deliver the promised benefits. On some occasions in the past, it was possible for the plan sponsor to misuse investment assumptions and mortality tables by plan sponsors. Either one could have had a major effect on the amount of annual contributions a plan sponsor was obliged to make. For example, if the sponsor assumed a higher than realistic investment rate, it would overstate the potential earnings of the fund and understate the contributions needed to fund the benefits. Similarly, if a sponsor uses mortality tables that understate life expectancy, it will understate the years its participants will live and receive benefits and the plan eventually will be underfunded. Why would an employer do this? In most cases, the employer was attempting to correct a business shortfall by shorting the pension fund. Sometimes, however, the shortfall became a long-term problem, which had significant implication on the pension fund.

---

44. §§301–303 of the PPA, §415 IRC. The PPA also provides for rate assumptions in calculating the §415 maximum benefit limitations implicit in the calculation of the lump sum.

45. The IRS is providing some guidance on this issue. See, for example, IRS Notice 2007-7.

The PPA now requires that DBPs use standard mortality tables so the longevity issue cannot be manipulated to affect funding.[46] It also requires that investment return assumptions be predicated on corporate bond rates using 0- to 5-year, 5- to 15-year, and over 15-year returns, representing a set of more realistic and predictable investment assumptions for plan actuaries calculating funding obligations. It also significantly limits wide and perhaps unrealistic assumptions that improperly reduce funding in the short run, but place the plan in jeopardy in the long run.

In addition to standardizing interest rate and mortality assumptions, ERISA and the PPA require that defined benefit plans be fully funded over a seven-year period. The plan's annual contributions must equal the present value of benefits earned by participants during the current year, and be sufficient to amortize any future funding shortfall over the next seven years.[47]

The PPA recently clarified how to value assets in the trust consistently. Previously, fund assets used a "smoothing" process that took into account temporary market volatility. As a result, wide, short-term variations in the value of fund assets could be adjusted or, in some cases, ignored, which could allow for overstated assets. Now the PPA permits less flexibility to plan sponsors in smoothing such market fluctuations, which should result in more predictable and realistic plan asset valuations.[48]

Can the retirement plan be used to fund other benefits? For example, can a pension plan sponsor use pension assets to finance retiree health care? Due to a change in accounting rules requiring the inclusion of retiree health care liabilities on an employer's financial statements, this issue is very timely. According to the PPA, if the plan is 120 percent funded (or more), it can use pension funds to finance retiree health care for a maximum of ten years.[49]

PREEMPTION—PENSION PLANS[50]

What if a company sponsors a retirement plan that fully complies with ERISA but is in conflict with a state law regulating pensions? State and local laws that relate to pensions and other welfare plans are preempted by ERISA. When there is a conflict, ERISA will "supercede any and all state laws insofar as they may now or hereafter relate to any employee benefit plan."[51]

---

46. §111, §112 of PPA; §412, §430 of IRC.

47. See 29 USC §1081–1086 (§301 of ERISA).

48. See §111–112, PPA.

49. See §481, PPA.

50. 29 USC §1144 (§514 ERISA).

51. Ibid.

The preemption provision recognizes a state's right to regulate the administration of insurance and insured plans, in particular, certain welfare or health plans. Retirement plans are a different story. Generally, there is a two-prong test to determine whether a case should be preempted: (1) Does the claim address an exclusive area of federal concern? (2) Does the claim affect traditional ERISA entities, such as sponsors, participants, and fiduciaries?[52] Let's look at an example.

Suppose a nonparticipant spouse beneficiary of a pension plan decided to transfer by testamentary instrument (last will or trust) an undistributed portion of her pension benefit. This action was done pursuant to state law, and was thought to be perfectly legal; however, it was challenged in court by the participant's spouse. The complainant contended that the transfer was in conflict with the nonalienation provisions of ERISA. Moreover, the complainant argued that the right of a surviving spouse to receive 50 percent of the participant's pension, as well as the right of a divorcing spouse to take a financial interest in the pension pursuant to a Qualified Domestic Relations Order (QDRO), would be undermined by allowing the participant to make a testamentary transfer. These are specific rights and privileges under ERISA that would be undermined and in direct conflict with a state law that allows or condones the disposition of undistributed pension benefits. What was the result? The Court held that the state law was preempted by ERISA and it was invalid.[1] The transfer was invalidated.

Can a plan participant sue in state court, challenging the decision of a pension administrator who denied his claim for a disability pension?

A plan participant sued under state law, arguing that the denial of his disability retirement claim by the pension plan sponsor was improper and caused him loss of income and also emotional distress. Implicit in the complaint was a claim alleging breach of the plan administrator's fiduciary duty. A resolution of the claim would involve an interpretation of the terms of the plan and the administrator's application of these terms. The Supreme Court held the action was preempted by ERISA. It could not be litigated under other state laws, and was dismissed.[2]

1. *Boggs v. Boggs*, 521 U.S. 1138 (1997).
2. *Pilot Life Insurance v. Dedeaux*, 481 U.S. 41 (1987).

52. See *Miara v. First AllAmerica Financial Life Insurance Co.*, 379 F. Supp 2d 20 (D. Mass. 2005).

Preemption issues could arise with auto or involuntary enrollment in 401(k) or other DCPs. In such cases, the employer can auto enroll an employee in a DCP and then defer a portion of his earnings into his account. There are, however, state and federal garnishment laws that prohibit or limit certain claims on a person's wages by creditors. The PPA, in endorsing the concept of auto enrollment and nonelective contributions, provides that ERISA preempts such garnishment laws in such cases.[53]

PREEMPTION—HEALTH CARE

After suffering a severe reaction from pain medication, the plaintiff was hospitalized. The treating physician recommended extensive treatment and extended hospital stay. The plaintiff's group health care insurance plan, however, did not permit an extended stay and denied coverage. Accordingly, the plaintiff left the hospital but experienced complications and was readmitted. She argued the refusal to approve the extended stay violated state law that imposed a duty on insurance companies to exercise ordinary care when making health care treatment decisions. The Court, however, agreed with the insurance company defendant who argued the state statute and claim of plaintiff were preempted by §502(a) of ERISA. The Court found that ERISA intended to ensure that benefit plan regulation is an exclusive federal concern, and the law established a comprehensive scheme of rights that can be pursued under the statute. It also found that in enacting ERISA, Congress had excluded certain rights and remedies. Thus, the Court said we cannot allow state law claims that duplicate, supplement, or supplant the ERISA set of remedies. To do so would conflict with congressional intent to make ERISA the exclusive source of such remedies. The claim was preempted.[1]

---

1. *Aetna Health Insurance, Inc., v. Juan Davila*, 542 U.S. 200 (2004). The Court ruled that the claim was preempted by §502(a)(1)(B), 29 USC §1132(a)(1)(B).

ERISA intended to create some predictability for businesses sponsoring benefits including health and welfare plans. As we can see, the preemption doctrine can apply here. Some state laws mandate employee welfare plan

---

53. See §902, PPA.

designs or benefits; they are generally considered to be preempted.[54] But the collision between health care plans and the preemption doctrine is somewhat curious, since ERISA does not provide any significant control over the design features of health care plans as it does with retirement plans. There are disclosure rules, but no vesting requirements.[55] There are no minimum funding standards, but there are fiduciary responsibilities for employer sponsors. There is also a clear distinction between plans that are insured through contracts and those that are self-insured by employer sponsors. The former are subject to state benefit mandates and other terms of the contract. This is considered to be a lawful exercise of insurance regulation reserved to the states. Self-insured plans, however, are not subject to a variety of state mandates and controls. They are given a broad veil of protection by the preemption provision of ERISA.

There is another front on which preemption may have some application: ERISA and state health care reform.[56] Preemption may become a real barrier to a variety of recently enacted mandatory health care insurance schemes by states such as Massachusetts. ERISA is clearly hanging over the heads of policymakers trying to legislate plans where employers and others, for example, are required to purchase health care plans for their employees or themselves.[57] The current issue could be subject to the axiom of previous cases; insurance mandates for self-insured are preempted.[58] Thus, state mandates requiring hospice care, mental health care, and required clinical tests, among others, are subject to challenge by self-insured plan sponsors, unless it can be shown the mandate is a lawful exercise of the state's right to regulate insurance. If not, it will be preempted. Thus, there are some serious doubts about the new state health care reform initiatives.

Tax Treatment of Retirement Plans

Generally speaking, with respect to retirement plans, the IRC's objective is to make sure that such plans do not discriminate in coverage, disproportionately provide a tax-favored refuge for highly compensated employees,

---

54. *Arizona State Carpenters Pension Trust Fund v. Citibank*, 125 F.3d 715 (9th Cir. 1997).

55. The major "vesting" issue involves a contract theory whereby a company seeking to terminate or modify a retiree health care plan is challenged. The retirees argue that the benefits were promised, not that ERISA mandates them.

56. EBRI (1995) ERISA and Health Plans, Issue Brief No. 167 (1995, November). Also see EBRI, Issue Brief No. 193 (1998).

57. See *ERISA could prevent efforts to expand health care access, according to the Christian Science Monitor*. (2007, September 27). http://www.kaisernetwork.org.

58. EBRI (1995).

or allow employees to exclude excessive amounts of earned income from taxation. If a plan complies with the relevant IRC provisions and ERISA, it will be considered tax qualified.[59] Without this designation, in many, but not all, cases the benefit values or accruals could be considered taxable income to the participant and not be deductible as an expense by the employer. The following is a brief discussion of several unique provisions of the IRC that affect the design and application of retirement plans whose sponsors wish to maintain tax-qualified status.

As indicated earlier in this chapter and in Chapter 4, to accomplish the objective of nondiscrimination, the IRC requires defined contribution plans to test the degree of concentration of deferrals made by highly compensated employees versus nonhighly compensated employees.[60] If there is a disproportionate rate of deferrals among the HCEs, the IRS will require the plan sponsor to adjust prior deferrals until the proper balance is achieved. This process is called nondiscrimination testing. To avoid the problem of having too few lower income employees participating in the company's DCP, employers are now providing for nonelective enrollments of all eligible employees or introducing the the IRS Safe Harbor rules into their plans.[61]

Avoiding discrimination and not permitting retirement plans to significantly reduce tax revenues can be seen as objectives of the IRC §415 limits pertaining to total annual deferrals and contributions to defined contribution plans.[62] There also are §415 limitations on the amount of income that can be used in the formula to calculate a retirement benefit under a defined benefit plan and that limit the total amount of pension one can receive from a tax-qualified DBP. One must keep in mind that while tax policy can and does have a profound effect on the design of retirement plans, the ultimate objective of the IRC is to provide a legislative framework

---

59. To obtain "tax qualified" status, the plan must conform to the various provisions under ERISA, such as minimum participation, funding requirements, fiduciary rules, distribution requirements, protection of accrued benefits, nonalienation of benefits, and vesting provisions.

60. The IRC provides that an HCE is either at least a 5 percent owner of the company, or has income equal to or more than $105,000 per year (2008). This is indexed and increases $5,000 per year. Further, the employer can elect to identify an HCE as a person whose income places him in the top 20 percent of compensation in the firm. This calculation would exclude certain new workers or those who work a minimal number of hours per week.

61. These are discussed in Chapter 4 in some detail.

62. Since the limits are indexed, updates can be found at http://www.benefitsattorney .com/ or at http://www.irs.gov/. See Table 9.4 in this chapter.

for the collection of tax revenue; thus, there are limitations.[63] The 2008 limits are shown in Table 9.4.

The nondiscrimination policy of the IRC could be circumvented if the plan sponsor designed its plan coverage to cover only certain groups of employees within the enterprise. Why not just sponsor a plan that covers the highly paid? There are rules concerning nondiscrimination in coverage.[64] Following is an example of a case where an employer tries to construct a plan with features that favor certain groups.

> Art Jones and his brother, Sam, own three companies in Kentucky and Indiana. One provides property management services (company "A"), another sells commercial property (company "B"), and the third provides cleaning and landscaping services (company "C"). Art comes to you, a benefit consultant, and tells you he wants to set up a retirement plan. Specifically, it will be a DBP for the management employees of companies A and B; nonmanagement will not be covered. He wants to reward only loyal, key, and long-service employees, and does not want any plan for company C, because retirement plans are not common in C's labor market.
>
> Although the DBP will use a final average pay formula to determine benefits, the brothers would like to have the discretion to add bonus monies for certain covered employees at the end of the year. The allocated monies in the plan will be invested and controlled by them. In fact, they want to invest a portion of retirement plan assets into a new real estate development venture they are pursuing.
>
> Art specifies that employees must work three years before participating, and will not be entitled to a benefit until they have completed ten years of service. Benefits are to be distributed upon an employee's termination, provided they meet early or full-age retirement of 55 and 65, respectively. He wants the plan contributions to be deductible by the company, and accrued benefits for covered employees to be tax deferred. What would you advise Art? Following are the issues and how they would be resolved.

63. IRC provisions require the participant in a DCP to start receiving benefits after age 70.5, and prohibit early distributions before age 59.5. The consequence here is taxation of the benefits; noncompliance results in a further tax penalty. The IRC also provides that a person will lose the tax-deferred status of his retirement benefits if they are distributed and not immediately "rolled over" to another tax qualified plan.

64. See IRC §410(b).

Table 9.4   IRS Summary of §415 Limits for Retirement Plans

Limitation	2008 Amount
Maximum annual compensation for DBP benefit formula	$230,000
Maximum elective deferrals for 401(k)	$15,500
Maximum contributions for SIMPLE plan	$10,500
Definition of HCE	$105,000
Catch-up contributions for 401(k)	$5,000
DBP pension limit	$185,000
401(k) total contribution limit	$46,000

SOURCE: Internal Revenue Service. The IRS Commissioner adjusts these amounts for inflation each year.

- Is this a retirement plan covered by ERISA and the IRC? Yes, the employer is engaged in commerce, or their activities affect commerce, and benefits are paid upon termination. Therefore, it qualifies as a retirement plan and must comply with the provisions of ERISA and the IRC.

- Does it satisfy the minimum participation standards? No, an employee under ERISA only has to work 1,000 hours in one year to qualify, and must be 21 years of age to be a participant. This plan requires three years of service.

- Does the plan violate the vesting rules of ERISA and the IRC? Yes, since this is a DBP, vesting must be achieved in either five years (cliff) or seven years (graduated). This plan requires ten years to be vested, which is in violation of ERISA.

- Does the plan violate the nondiscrimination rules with respect to benefit allocation? Yes, the employer does not have the discretion to allocate whatever he wishes to an employee's benefit. The allocation must be based on some generally applicable and reasonable formula prescribed by the plan document.

- Does the plan violate the fiduciary rules of ERISA and the IRC? Yes, the sponsor cannot invest funds in a project where there is a conflict of interest. The use of fund assets to support the owners' new real estate development project would be a prohibited transaction and illegal.[65]

- Can the plan exclude the employees of company C? Probably not. First, one must determine if the various businesses are within a controlled group. If not, the employer is free to have different plans or no plans for certain businesses. A controlled group is one in which a person or group owns at least 80 percent of the other entity. In our case, Art and his brother own 100 percent of all three companies.[66] Thus, it is a controlled group, and an aggregation of employee groups may be used to test whether the plan is discriminatory because it does not cover company C. There is an exception to the controlled group rule when the various companies represent qualified separate lines of business (QSLOB). The exception recognizes that separate lines of business may have distinct competitive needs or are operating in distinct geographic areas that would justify separate or different benefit plans. In order to meet the QSLOB rules, however, the employer must clearly show the businesses are indeed separate profit centers that have distinct workforces and management.

- Can nonmanagement employees of companies A and B be excluded from coverage under the plan? Since the employer is not obligated legally to establish a plan, under ERISA or the IRC, the law basically provides that it is not required to include every employee in a plan. It is not that simple, however.

- What if the plan's coverage rule(s) discriminate(s) in favor of highly compensated employees (HCEs)?[67] Would this be relevant to

---

65. See *Patelco Credit Union v. Sahni*, 262 F.3d 897 (9th Cir. 2001) where a fiduciary bought insurance coverage for a benefit plan, but personally received a commission for the purchase.

66. Generally, when there is a close familial relationship among or between owners, such as brother and sister or husband and wife, one must apply the minimum coverage test for all of the units as if they are "commonly owned."

67. For example, in *Bauer v. Summit Bancorp*, 325 F.3d 155 (3d Cir. 2003), the Court found a pension plan that covered salaried but not hourly paid employees did not violate ERISA or the IRC. In this case, however, the Court pointed out that the plaintiff did not allege that the designated coverage discriminated in favor of HCEs. Without such an allegation, the Court found the coverage of salaried only as lawful. Similarly, in *Schultz v. Texaco*, 127 F. Supp. 2d 443 (S.D. N.Y. 2000), the Court held that a plan that excluded temporary employees and independent contractors was not in violation of ERISA or the IRC. The Court in *Bauer v. Summit Bancorp*, supra, held that a plan that excluded hourly employees but

the determination of whether one can exclude nonmanagement from coverage? Yes. A resolution involves the application of a three-part nondiscrimination test: (1) A DBP must cover at least 50 employees or, if less, at least 40 percent of all employees.[68] (2) The plan must benefit a minimum number of nonhighly compensated employees (NHCEs).[69] (3) The plan's formula or features cannot discriminate in favor of HCEs.[70]

- With respect to a defined benefit plan, we can assume the plan does cover 50 employees or 40 percent of all management and nonmanagement employees. So, it passes the first test.

- Does the plan benefit a minimum number of NHCEs? Possibly. The percentage of NHCEs who benefit under the new plan must be no less than 70 percent of the HCEs who benefit. (Without more precise numbers involving the classifications of management and nonmanagement and how these relate to the definitions of HCEs and NHCEs, we cannot answer the question.) A sponsor also must show that the relevant classification is not artificial and inherently discriminatory. This can be demonstrated with particular facts and circumstances that support the distinction between management and nonmanagement employees.[71] Can you identify what some of these facts and circumstances might be? Finally, this test requires the ratio of actual benefits accrued by the NHCEs be at least 70 percent compared to those accrued by the HCEs. So, one has to show that participation and benefit levels between HCEs and NHCEs is not discriminatory.

- Do the benefit features of the plan discriminate in favor of HCEs? This is the third test. For example, does the benefit formula use a different and more favorable formula for HCEs? If the formula used is the same for all—the calculation of final average pay is applied uniformly and there are uniform definitions for age and service—the plan will generally be considered to be in compliance with the benefit features discrimination rules. In our case, however,

---

designated salaried employees as participants did not violate ERISA or the IRC unless it was shown that it unlawfully discriminated in favor of highly compensated employees. It pointed out that the IRC does not presume a plan is discriminatory merely because it is limited to salaried employees. The relevant section of the IRC is §401(a)(5)(A) and Treasury Reg. §1.401(a)(5)-1(b).

68. IRC §401(a)(26).

69. IRC §410(b).

70. IRC §401(a)(4).

71. See *Bauer v Summit Bancorp*, supra.

Art and Sam would not meet the requirements of the test if they intend to add bonus monies on a discretionary basis to certain employee accruals for the purpose of calculating annual income under the plan formula.

As we see in the example of Art and Sam's new pension plan, many of the proposed features do violate ERISA and the IRC. The plan must be changed in order to be tax qualified. Determining whether certain groups of employees can be included or excluded is more complicated.[72] This discussion should give you some analytical template to test the owners' decision to differentiate management and nonmanagement coverage. Moreover, it should give you some idea as to when it might be prudent to "raise the red flag" and summon legal counsel.

Generally speaking, an employer sponsor can exclude union employees, independent contractors, and even hourly workers from pension plan coverage, provided the classification is reasonable and nondiscriminatory.[73] As we can see, the general thrust of the legal interest here is to avoid situations where HCEs disproportionately participate in a pension plan and where the owners artificially segregate groups of employees from participating in the plan.

As you can see, the IRC interacts with some of the basic provisions of ERISA. Together, they provide a formidable set of legal rules that apply to benefit plans. Here are some other ERISA rules.

Nonalienation of Benefits

There is a prohibition against alienation of benefits by a pension plan participant. In other words, a participant in a plan cannot lawfully give away or assign his future benefits to another. What he does with them after they are distributed is not a concern of policymakers. The major exception here is the right of a divorcing spouse to acquire certain pension benefits as a result of a Qualified Domestic Relation Order (QDRO). In such an instance, a domestic relations court can order an ERISA-covered

---

72. For example, there are a number of cases involving whether "leased employees" can be lawfully excluded from a plan. See, for example, *Bronk v. Mountain States*, 140 F.3d 1335 (10th Circ. 1998), and *Wolf v. Coca Cola*, 200 F. 3d 1337 (11th Cir. 2000).

73. See §410(b), §414 IRC. See also an interesting case involving an attempt by Texaco to exclude certain groups of employees from its retirement plans. *Schultz v. Texaco*, 127 F. Supp. 2d 443 (S.D. N.Y. 2000), and *Schultz v. Stoner*, 308 F. Supp. 2d 289 (S.D. N.Y. 2004). See also Allen, E., Melone, J., Rosenbloom, J., & Mahoney, D. (2008) *Retirement plans* (10th ed., pp. 456–457). New York: Irwin McGraw-Hill.

plan administrator to distribute a portion of retirement income to a non-employee divorcing spouse.

Freezes and Terminations

Employers are at liberty to freeze the benefits of their participants. In such cases there are no future accruals of benefits. This occurs if the employer intends to either stop funding a pension plan or wants to switch his employees to a different type of plan on a prospective basis. This is legal under ERISA provided the calculation and entitlement to the accrued benefits are done properly. Employers also may terminate pension plans.[74] Under these circumstances the assets of the plan are used to pay accrued benefits and ERISA mandates that all participants are vested immediately. The practice of terminating a plan, paying out benefits, and reverting the excess plan assets can be a strategy used by a plan sponsor to escape an expensive pension plan and convert the employees to a more cost-effective one.[75]

The popularity of cash balance plans (CBPs), as discussed in Chapter 4, has been met with a number of ERISA and other legal challenges, including age discrimination charges. The PPA of 2006 has provided some clarity on the contentious legal issues pertaining to CBPs. Contrary to several court decisions,[76] the law specifically provides that CBPs created after June 29, 2005, cannot be considered to violate the Age Discrimination in Employment Act provided they meet certain requirements such as providing minimum vesting of three years and applying interest credits of greater than zero but not more than current and relevant market rates.

Cash Balance Plans—Legal

The PPA's ratification of cash balance plans is conditioned upon the plan not using the "wear away" technique when an employer is converting a

---

74. 29 USC §1341 (§4041 of ERISA).

75. See *Shepley et al. v. New Coleman Holdings, Inc,* 174 F. 3d 65 (2d Cir. 1998); the Court held that participants are not entitled to excess assets in a fund and, provided the plan allows it, a sponsor may recoup these excess assets after a plan termination, provided all liabilities of the plan have been satisfied. See 29 USC §1344(d)(1).

76. See, for example, *Copper v. IBM,* holding such plans violate the ADEA because older workers in a CBP do not accumulate retirement funds that are as large as younger workers. The case was reversed by the U.S. Court of Appeals for the 7th Circuit in 2007, 457 F. 3d 636.

DBP to a CBP. So, if the benefit accrual from the DBP credited to an employee's account is more than he would have earned during his career under the terms of the CBP, the employer refrained from making new contributions until the "excess" was "worn away."[77] Similarly, in calculating the participant's opening balance that is being converted from a DBP to a CBP, the employer sponsor can no longer use one interest rate assumption to determine the future value of an annuity stream from the DBP and a different discount rate to calculate the present value of the opening balance. This technique is called "whipsawing" and is now prohibited by ERISA and the new PPA.[78]

Phased Retirement

As mentioned in Chapters 4 and 5, there has been some confusion about phased retirement. Generally speaking, a person who retires and receives benefits cannot continue to work for the employer sponsor and receive his salary. There are exceptions to this, but the general rule blocks the desire of some participants and their employers to gradually relinquish their work responsibilities, while providing the employer with a period of time where the expertise and productivity of the experienced worker can be partially maintained.

There are a number of issues here, including whether the participant retiree should continue to accrue benefit service under the plan. The IRS took the position that benefit payments from the retirement plan would be suspended during the period in which the participant worked. The PPA has established some new standards that allow pension distributions from the plan during a working retirement.[79] The new law allows that persons who retire after age 62 and elect to continue to work at a reduced rate of

---

77. Wear away involves estimating what the opening balance of a CBP would be had the participant been covered during his career. The present value of the participant's accrued benefits from the DBP is then placed in the CBP account as an "opening balance." If, however, this amount is greater than what the participant would have accumulated if he had been covered by the CBP during his career, no annual contributions are made going forward until this "excess balance" "wears away." See *Lyons v. Georgia Pacific,* 221 F. 3d 1235 (11th Cir. 2000). See §701 of PPA prohibits wear away and the starting balance in a converted CBP must equal the participant's accrued benefits under the predecessor DBP. We should note that §411(d)(6) of IRC that prohibits reductions in accrued benefits that was the essence of the problem with the wear away approach.

78. For an explanation of "whipsawing," see *Edsen v. Bank of Boston,* 229 F. 3d 154 (2d Cir. 2000). See §§ 301, 302, 303 of the PPA.

79. §905 of the PPA, §401 IRC.

20 percent or more can receive retirement benefits on a proportionately reduced basis.[80] The IRS has the authority to broaden this phased retirement concept to persons who retire after age 59.5.[81]

The PPA addressed the issue of benefit distribution that expanded the use of rollovers from one tax-qualified plan to another. Now after-tax amounts can be rolled over to purchase an annuity contract, and retirement plan distributions can be rolled over into Roth IRAs. Additionally, nonspouse beneficiaries of certain retirement plans can now roll over their distribution to another tax-qualified plan.[82]

Bankruptcy

Generally speaking, the assets of a tax-qualified retirement plan are not subject to the claims of creditors or to trustee action in a bankruptcy proceeding. If the plan is in substantial compliance with the IRC of 1986, the assets may not be subject to creditors' claims. Rollovers to and from tax-qualified plans that are completed within 60 days of a distribution are not subject to creditor claims. There is also protection against claims by creditors for loan amounts or loan repayments arising from the participant borrowing funds from his defined contribution plan.

> Richard and his wife left their respective employers several years ago to start their own business. They rolled over the balances of their respective 401(k) accounts into two IRAs. Subsequently, their business failed and they filed a personal bankruptcy petition. The creditors filed claims against the IRAs, saying they were similar to savings accounts and subject to creditors in bankruptcy. The Trustee agreed. Richard and his wife, however, argued that an IRA was a tax-qualified retirement plan and should not be subject to creditors' claims. Who won? Bankruptcy Code, 11 U.S.C. §522(d)(10)(E), provides that the "right to

---

80. See §905 of the PPA.

81. Some public plans not fully covered by ERISA provide that a person who wants to continue working after retirement at his original place of employment must elect to either suspend retirement benefits while resuming work or waive the accrual of future years of service under the plan. See for example, the University of California DBP at http://www.atyourservice.ucop.edu/.

82. See §404 ERISA, §402 IRC, PPA §822, PPA §824, 829, and IRC §403, 408, 408(A), and 457.

> receive a payment from a stock bonus, pension, profit sharing, annuity, or similar plan or contract . . . on account of age" can be withdrawn from the debtor's estate and is not subject to creditor's claims. The creditor's argued this provision was not applicable to an IRA since the debtor controlled the distribution that was not dependent upon age. The U.S. Supreme Court ruled that since the IRS imposed penalties for distributions from IRAs occurring before age 59.5, and required minimum distributions after 70.5, the IRA was a plan whose distribution of funds was on account of age. Accordingly, the IRAs of Richard and his wife could not be subject to creditors' claims.[1]
>
> 1. *Rousey v. Jacoway*, 544 U.S. 320 (2005). We should note that states have different rules pertaining to protections of savings accounts, in some cases including IRAs against creditors. How would a court rule in the case of a SEP or a SIMPLE retirement plan that are employer-sponsored plans that involve contributions to an employee's IRA? Should the amount of money in an IRA make a difference? The Bankruptcy Code has been amended in 2005, however, to provide that IRAs are not subject to creditors' claims until and unless the annual earnings on such plans exceed $1,000,000. 401(k) plans as well as 457, 403(b), SEP, and SIMPLE plans are not included in the bankrupt's estate. Further, IRAs funded by rollovers from 401(k), 457, and 403(b) plans are totally exempt from creditors no matter what value they have under the new law. See §224, Bankruptcy Abuse Prevention and Consumer Protection Act of 2005 (BAPCPA).

ERISA and IRC Enforcement

The U.S. Labor Department, plan participants, and beneficiaries have the right to file a lawsuit in the U.S. District Courts for injunctive relief or damages and penalties against a benefit plan and its fiduciaries that are in violation of ERISA.[83] There also are criminal penalties for certain violations.[84] There is a requirement that each plan provide an internal administrative dispute resolution process.[85] Moreover, if the plan no longer

---

83. 29 USC §1132.

84. 29 USC §1131.

85. 29 USC §1102(a).

meets the requirements of ERISA and the IRC, the IRS can revoke the tax-qualified status of the plan, render accruals and contributions as taxable income for participants, and deny the tax deductibility of the pension costs to the employer.[86]

Prior to filing a lawsuit, however, a participant or beneficiary is obligated to follow the plan's internal claims procedure and attempt to resolve the complaint. Lawsuits by participants can be filed to enforce rights under the plan, to get access to documents of the plan, to get relief arising out of a breach of fiduciary duty by the plan, to enjoin the plan to stop violating a participant's rights under the plan, and to comply with the plan provisions and ERISA. A winning claim by a participant can result in an award of attorney fees. Similarly, the Secretary of Labor may also sue a plan and its fiduciaries over violations of ERISA.

Insuring Benefits When a Plan Is Terminated

ERISA established the Pension Benefit Guaranty Corporation (PBGC) to provide insured benefits to participants whose defined benefit pension plans are underfunded and terminated, referred to as distress termination.[87] The PBGC must then supervise the distribution of plan assets and determine if there are sufficient assets to pay guaranteed benefits. These are benefits that are nonforfeitable. If there are, the PBGC will supervise the distribution of assets and the plan will terminate. If there are insufficient funds to pay guaranteed benefits, the PBGC will pay the guaranteed benefits using plan assets and its own funds.

Plan sponsors are required to present to the PBGC a number of reportable events that may lead to a plan's insolvency. For example, if the plan sponsor appears to be approaching bankruptcy, such notices must be given to the PBGC. Plan sponsors are required to pay premiums on a per capita basis to the PBGC to finance this insurance. When a defined benefit plan insured by PBGC terminates, all participants automatically become 100 percent vested.

If such a plan has insufficient funds to pay guaranteed benefits, the PBGC guarantees the payment of a fraction of the prescribed benefit, depending on the year the plan was terminated and the age of the

---

86. See §401(a) of the IRC. The General Accountability Office has conducted reviews for Congress reporting under what circumstances violations of the Code have led to a loss of tax-exempt status. See, for example, Pension Plans—IRS Programs for Resolving Deviations from Tax-Exemption Requirements (2000), GAO (GAO/GGD-00-169).

87. 29 USC §1301 et. seq.

participant. For example, the monthly guarantee limit at age 65 for a plan terminating in 2007 is $4,125 per month. So, in many cases the insured portion of the defined benefit earned by the participant is far less than 100 percent. Nevertheless, the PBGC does provide some level of benefits to those participants who would otherwise receive far less, or even nothing, from their insolvent pension plan. In recent years, with economic turmoil in some industries, the PBGC's financial ability to pay insured benefits has come under severe strain and there is serious ongoing discussion regarding how its role might change.[88]

Conclusion

As mentioned earlier in this chapter, there are innumerable legal rules pertaining to benefits that simply go far and beyond the intent of this book, which is to provide the reader with an understanding of the concepts, principles, and strategic designs of the employee- and government-sponsored benefits[89] (see Figure 9.1).

In Chapter 12 we will discuss laws and topics such as COBRA, HIPAA, parity for mental health care benefits, coverage for reconstructive breast surgery resulting from breast cancer, minimal hospital stays for women delivering newborns, as well as pension rights for persons on military leave[90] that are part of the benefit law landscape. Then, in Chapter 14, we will discuss the Multi-Employer Pension Plan Amendments Act (MEPPAA) that applies to joint union and management pension funds. These laws affect the design of employee-sponsored benefits.[91] A recent study by the Employee Benefit Research Institute showed plan design changes are being driven in part by the PPA and its new minimum funding rules, as well as new accounting rules by FASB that require more

---

88. See, for example, *Addressing the insolvency of PBGC.* (2006, June 14). American Enterprise Institute, http://www.aei.org/publications/. The PBGC experienced a $14.07 billion deficit in fiscal year 2007. See PBGC Annual Management Report, Fiscal Year 2007.

89. For in-depth details, one might consult *Employee Benefits Law* (2nd Ed. (2006). The American Bar Association Section of Labor and Employment Law. Washington, DC: BNA Books.

90. Also, the PPA, §827 provides for penalty-free withdrawals from DCPs for those called to active duty for more than 179 days.

91. See *Pension plans face more cuts.* (2007, July 3). http://www.cnnmoney.com. DBP sponsors are looking for ways to make them less generous or to freeze or terminate them altogether and move to more cost-effective retirement plans.

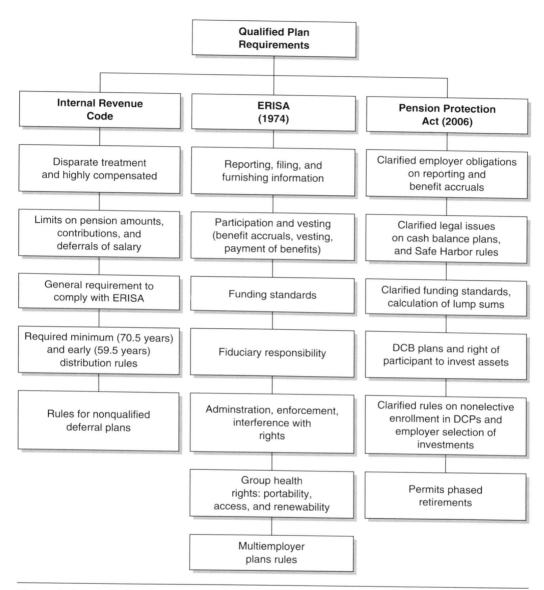

Figure 9.1   Benefit Plan Legal Compliance (Major Provisions)

disclosure of future benefit costs.[92] So, the regulation of benefit plans by ERISA, the IRC, and now the PPA have a significant impact on the employer's decision to offer a retirement plan and which type to offer. The clear shift is toward defined contribution plans.

92. See *Retirement income adequacy after PPA and FAS 158: Part one: Plan sponsors' reactions.* (2007, July). EBRI, Issue Brief No. 307.

Suffice it to say, employers must be aware of the general thrust and purposes of ERISA, to protect retirement income for participants in a pension plan, and the IRC, to prevent benefit plans from becoming the predominant domain of higher-paid persons and executives, and to put limits on the amount of tax deferrals available so as to preserve the integrity of the financing role of taxation.

By now it is hoped that you understand the basic provisions of the laws and how they are applied. Further, with that knowledge you are sufficiently armed with a quiver of "red flags" to be raised when an issue pertaining to a benefit plan might require the assistance of legal counsel.

Chapter Exercises

The following exercises are brief hypothetical fact summaries involving legal issues arising under ERISA, the IRC, or the PPA. You will be asked to identify the legal issues, resolve them, and provide your supporting rationale. This will require you to indicate the probable provision or principle of the law that is relevant, each standard that is applicable, how you would resolve it, and the reasons supporting your decision. At the end of the case there is a citation to an actual case that is similar to the hypothetical. You can access the case through your library, "Indexes and Data Bases," and use the "Lexis/Nexis Legal" database to find the cited case and learn how a court decided the issue. You can also access U.S. Supreme Court cases by going to http://www.law.cornell.edu/supct/; to locate and read sections of ERISA, you can go to http://benefitslink.com/erisa/crossreference.html/) and the Department of Labor has summaries of the PPA in its Employee Benefits Service link at http://www.dol.gov/. You can check IRC provisions by going on its Web site at http://www.irs.gov/.

1. Suppose a municipality in the United States is considering passing an ordinance that would require all employers with more than ten employees to provide a basic health care insurance plan for all their employees. The mayor has asked you, the City Solicitor, to review the proposed legislation. What are the legal issues and how would you resolve them? See *Golden Gate Restaurant Association v. City and County of San Francisco*, 535 F. Supp. 2d 968 (N.D. Cal., 2007).

2. Mary Jones is about to retire. She has participated in a DBP and is considering whether to take a lump sum distribution instead of the annuity payments. Her company is telling her that they are using a 14 percent discount rate and mortality tables developed in 1972. What impact would these assumptions have on her lump sum? Would the PPA be helpful to her in this situation? Explain. What if

Mary were suffering from incurable cancer and the employer knew about it? How would that affect her request for a lump sum instead of an annuity? Can the employer legally take this information into consideration? What if the employer included a COLA adjustment in his retirement annuity? Should that be included in the lump sum? In the case when a participant chooses a lump sum, must the spouse waive the joint survivor benefit? See ERISA, 29 USC §1055(g).

3. You are the plan administrator of a DBP and the investment committee for the plan has generally followed a conservative investment strategy. This has resulted in a slight underfunding of the plan and your CEO has requested that you urge the committee to adopt a more aggressive investment strategy that will, at least for a while, mitigate the funding shortfall. What are the legal issues here and what action should you take with respect to the CEO's request? See *California Ironworkers Field Pension Trust v. Loomis Sayles & Co.*, 259 F.3d 1036 (9th Cir. 2001). See also *U.S. Department of Labor Advisory Opinion*, 2006-08A, http://www.dol.gov/ebsa. What if the suggestion made in 2007 was to invest in subprime mortgages?

4. A participant in your 401(k) claims to have changed her self-directed investment choices about a year ago. Apparently, your administrator failed to make the change and this has resulted in some significant financial losses for the participant. Is the sponsor liable? What legal basis would she likely rely upon? How would the case be resolved in court? See *LaRue v. DeWolff, Boberg & Associates*, 128 S. Ct. 1020 (2008).

5. The owner of a medium-sized company wants to move his plant to an out-of-state location. The purpose is to reduce costs. Most of his current employees are not interested in moving and most file for early or full-age retirement under the company's DBP. The large number of retirees puts a serious financial strain on the DBP, and the administrator of the plan proportionately reduced benefits in accordance with ERISA's guaranteed benefit provisions. The affected employees sue the actuary for damages because it did not change the actuarial assumptions to reflect the large number of retirements that would result from the move. This failure, it was alleged, prevented the employer from adequately funding the plan. What are the legal issues here and how would you resolve them? Check §502(a)(3) of ERISA, and see *Mertens et al. v. Hewitt Associates*, 508 U.S. 248. (1993).

6. A company sponsor of a 401(k) offered several investment options for its participants. It is a self-directed plan. In spite of a steady fall

in the price, and financial and operating problems of the company, the sponsor continued to include company stock as one of the investment choices. Participants who chose this stock suffered serious financial losses in their accounts. Participants in the plan sue the sponsor alleging a breach of fiduciary duty under ERISA. What are the legal issues and how would you resolve them? See §404 of ERISA and *In re Ford Motor Co.* (E.D. Michigan, 2008); also check the Department of Labor's rules on investing pension plan assets ("Investment Duties") and the ERISA fiduciary duty. 29 CFR 2550.404a-1 at http://www.dol.gov/.

7. Several individuals had been employed by Company A as insurance salespersons. They were considered employees and participated in all company benefit plans. Sometime later they were separated and then, shortly thereafter, reinstated in the service of the company as "independent contractors," selling insurance products of Company A and other insurance firms. The ex-employees sued Company A for not including them as participants in the retirement and other plans. They claimed they were improperly discharged by A in order to affect their retirement rights, and they also argued the independent contractor arrangement was unlawfully intended to prevent them from participating in A's benefit plans. Check ERISA §502 and §510. What are the legal issues here and how would you resolve them? See *Schultz et al. v Texaco Inc., et al,* 127 F. Supp 2d 443 (S.D. N.Y. 2000); *Nationwide Mutual Insurance Company v. Darden,* 503 U.S. 318 (1992); and *Berger v. AXA Network LLC and Equitable Life Assurance Society of the U.S.,* 459 F.3d 804 (7th Cir. 2006). See Internal Revenue Code 26 U.S.C.S. §3121(d)(3)(B), and 26 C.F.R. §31.3121(d)-1(d)(3)(ii), and http://www.irs.gov/.

8. An employee was injured at home and was totally disabled and unable to work. He contacted his employer about medical coverage. His employer informed him that since he was totally disabled he had been terminated from employment and no longer participated in the company's group insurance plan. Previously, this plan provided that anyone who was permanently disabled would be continued under the long-term disability provisions of the plan until he reached age 65. The company indicated that this change was disclosed and communicated to all participants several months before. The employee claims he received no such notice. He sued and alleged violations of the reporting and disclosure provisions of ERISA, and also argued that his discharge amounted to an interference with his attainment of rights protected under ERISA. What additional information do you need to better identify

the issues? What are the issues and how would you resolve them? See *Custer v. Murphy Oil USA Inc.*, 493 F.3d 626 (5th Cir. 2007).

9. An employee worked for a company for 22 years. When he applied for retirement under the company's DBP, he was told that he had accrued only 3.7 years of service. He was informed that the DBP excluded hourly employees from coverage and, since he had only been a salaried employee for 3.7 years, his pension would be based on that short service. The employee sued under ERISA claiming the plan sponsor could not lawfully exclude hourly employees from coverage. Read the case *Bauer v. Summit Bancorp*, 325 F.3d 155 (3d Cir. 2003). What did the Court hold and what was its rationale? Does the employer sponsor have the right to determine which class of employees is eligible to participate? How would the case have turned out if the plaintiff had alleged that the distinction between salaried and nonsalaried equated to discrimination in favor of highly compensated employees?

10. A company announced it was selling its business. The plaintiff employee was not hired by the new company and was separated. A company HR benefits counselor met with each employee to calculate his accrued benefit and give an estimate of the monthly amount he would receive from the DBP when he reached retirement age. The plaintiff employee was told his monthly benefit would be $2,800. The HR counselor used a "pension calculator" to make the estimate. It included a caveat that it was an estimate and, if there were any conflict between the estimated amount and the actual amount owed under the plan, the latter would control. There was a conflict. The plaintiff learned later that he would receive only $800 per month. He sued the company. What are the legal issues and how would you resolve them? What do you think the plaintiff could seek in his lawsuit? What would be the ERISA basis for his claim? On what basis do you think the company will defend the lawsuit? See *Livick v. Gillette Co.* (U.S. Court of Appeals, 1st Cir., Case No. 07-2108, April 17, 2008).

Employee Benefits and Metrics 10

Blanche Jones is the general manager of a regional office facility in a major Midwestern city. There are approximately 2,000 employees at the location, most of whom are sales and marketing, finance and accounting, management, information systems, and clerical. Several senior managers have talked to Blanche recently about the high turnover rates in the office, and mentioned the feedback they had been receiving pointed to the absence of a daycare facility as the overriding reason for the exit. Further, they believed such an addition would be beneficial and would eliminate some of the distractions related to child care, thereby improving productivity and attendance, enhancing the company's recruitment capabilities, and reducing turnover.

The growing perception of benefits by employer sponsors is that plans should create value and not be viewed simply as additional costs of doing business driven largely by the desire to be competitive in the labor market. Therefore, the prospective daycare center in our vignette should be viewed as a "value proposition." In order to support this view, the company must examine what the projected financial returns might be for this kind of investment and then compare those returns to the costs of introducing such a benefit. This approach involves a completely different perspective from that generally used in the benefit decision-making process.[1]

---

1. Schwarz, J., & Murphy, T. (2008, April). Human capital metrics: An approach to teaching using data and metrics to design and evaluate management practices. *The Journal of Management Education, 32*(2), 164–182; Phillips, J., & Phillips, P. (2005). *Providing the value of HR: How and why to measure ROI.* Alexandria, VA: Society of Human Resource Management.

This chapter provides some insight into the justification of using a metrics and data-driven approach in assessing whether a benefit should be offered and how it should be designed. The allocation of capital within an enterprise is a fundamental and continuing process. How the money should be spent and which projects have the highest likelihood of resulting in success and generating a good financial return are questions that must be answered before capital is allocated.

All human resources practices, including the offering of benefits, require capital and it is incumbent on the advocate of an employer-sponsored benefit to demonstrate what the expected return will be. As we work our way through this chapter, we will explain the methods and the data and measurement tools required to secure the allocation of capital. The process is dependent on reliable and comprehensive data as well as accurate measurements. We begin first with an analytical framework or "template" to support the decision to offer a benefit.

A New Perspective—Benefits Are Not Just Costs

It is well recognized that an enterprise's human capital can be vital to the achievement of a significant competitive advantage.[2] For years, however, the selection and design of appropriate management practices to achieve business goals have been initiated, supported, and sustained based on an executive's intuition and past experience.[3] Demonstrating the financial returns of such efforts has been ignored. The selection and design of benefits have fallen into the same category. We offer them because our competitors do. In the case of health care and traditional pension plans, the employer often focuses on how to shift the cost and risk onto the employees. In today's highly competitive, global marketplace, however, managers need to do more than speculate and tinker. Does a retirement plan really provide adequate retirement income, impact productivity positively, improve recruitment and retention, or encourage employee savings? Does a health care plan reduce absenteeism and disabilities, or improve productivity and deliver a healthier work force? Does an employer-sponsored fitness center enhance the overall health of the workforce and improve

2. Huselid, M., Jackson, & Schuler, R. (1997). Technical and strategic human resource management effectiveness as determinants of firm performance. *Academy of Management Journal, 40,* 171–188.

3. Murphy, T., & Zandvakili, S. (2000, Spring). Data and metrics-driven approach to human resource practices: Using customers, employees, and financial metrics. *Human Resource Management, 39*(1), 93–105; Becker, B., Huselid, M., & Ulrich, D. (2001). *The HR scorecard.* Boston: Harvard Business School Press.

productivity? Ultimately, do these and other benefit plans really improve sales, profits, and total shareholder return?

Properly designed benefit plans should be considered as investments in the enhanced value and contribution of our human capital.[4] Through the use of data and metrics, we can demonstrate the links between the benefit and strategic results and the resultant financial returns. Let's see how this works.

The Metrics Template for Benefits

Let's go back to our proposed employer-sponsored daycare center and put together a metrics template that will help determine whether the benefit should be offered.

Before the general manager can recommend a capital allocation to headquarters, she will need to know all the costs involved in finding a resolution. Unless this can be determined, the solution conceivably could cost more than the problem. Therefore, further analysis must be done. She should appoint a committee to investigate the issues pertaining to daycare and to submit their recommendations to her along with the data they used in reaching their conclusions. The objective in this particular case is to determine if there are alternative, and perhaps more cost-effective, solutions besides employer-sponsored daycare. If there are turnover, absenteeism, or recruitment problems, do they disproportionately involve employees with preschool children? Does the target group reveal any special needs or problems that would be satisfied by a special benefit?

Through interviews, employee surveys, and other data sources, the committee will determine if there are turnover, absenteeism, and recruiting problems, and whether they are unique to the company or in line with the industry's experience. Data from employee surveys should be helpful in revealing the precise causes of the turnover problem, which also could be related to job design, compensation, lack of career opportunities, poor leadership, or insufficient training.

The committee's findings also will include the various design alternatives of a daycare benefit. For instance, should it be an onsite facility and company-run, or outsourced, perhaps subsidized? Should it be a profit center opened to the children of noncompany employees? Maybe employees should be given vouchers to use elsewhere, or the company should

---

4. Chief financial officers of major U.S. corporations are beginning to consider some benefits such as health care as value propositions, not just costs. CFOs take a fresh look at health and productivity. (2003, March 18). *Business and Health* archive, http://www.businessandhealth.com/.

simply provide a list of reliable daycare centers for its employees, but let them pay the cost. What about a credit to the employee's flexible spending account? This would simplify administration of the benefit and, as a pre-tax account, also save some payroll taxes for the employer. Benchmark research could be helpful here.

As part of its data search, the committee will want to look into what other companies are doing and, in particular, what their labor and product or service competitors are doing. As part of the data collection process, requests for proposals (RFPs) should be gotten from various daycare providers, and should include "measurable performance guarantees" as a condition for obtaining the contract.

An important by-product of their study, and certainly not to be ignored, is the need to maintain internal fairness in the compensation and benefit plans. With a daycare center, only a portion of the employees will enjoy the benefit, thus creating an imbalance in the total reward system and, inevitably, causing concern among those who have no need for daycare. Therefore, the committee's report will need to address this issue and recommend a solution. How should the daycare facility be financed? Should the employees who use it pay for some or all of it? Certainly, that would take care of the internal fairness problem.

Along with their recommendation, the committee will need to establish a set of reasonable goals for the daycare center. For example, presumably it will reduce turnover, but by how much and over what period of time? How will it impact absenteeism, productivity, and recruitment, and what is the expected cumulative value of improvements in these areas?[5]

Obviously, the committee's report will include how much a daycare center will cost, what the unit costs per child per month will be, and what the initial capital as well as ongoing maintenance costs will be. For comparison purposes, they should include cost information for the alternatives.

Assuming the committee's work supports a favorable recommendation for a daycare center, the general manager would have adequate data and metrics to demonstrate a sufficient return on investment[6] and to secure an allocation of capital for the project. Initial "baseline" measures have been

---

5. Should the employer create, for example, an "Employee Satisfaction Index" (ESI) or another new database that shows measurable levels of employee perceptions and behaviors that relate directly to turnover, absenteeism, and productivity? Then, after taking current baselines, set goals for incremental improvements in the Index. Or, on a simpler basis, the employer can measure current levels of turnover, absenteeism, and productivity and set these as "baselines." Goals can be established to improve each.

6. Or the general manager might want to use other measures such as Net Present Value, an Internal Rate of Return metric, or show a reasonable "payback period." These will be explained later in the chapter.

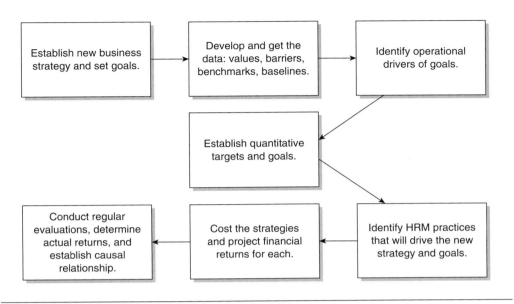

Figure 10.1   Flowchart of Data and Measurement Process

taken on all the factors that will be affected by daycare and will be measured against the data available sometime after implementation.

After the daycare center's installation, the general manager will want to institute measures to regularly monitor the program to make sure that it continues to have its desired effect and financial impact. More surveys and a close analysis of the baseline measures will be extremely useful. There are always design changes to consider.

The Data and Metrics Toolbox—Surveys and Assessments

Sarah Simon is senior vice president of HRM at Star Communications Company. There are three distinct divisions in the company—newspapers, cable TV stations, and Internet sites—that provide customer access to niche selling and buying. In her first tour of the business she observed significantly different groups of employees in each unit. From fairly conservative and relatively older employees in the newspaper companies, to a younger group in the cable TV stations, to people walking around in flipflops and shorts at the Web site division.

A standard DBP and a traditional health care plan were the core of the company's benefit offerings. After seeing the vastly different demographics of the workforce, however, Sarah contemplated taking a closer look at targeting benefits to fit the specific needs and wants of the workforce. Failing to do so, she believed, would not maximize the value of benefits for her employees, as some of the benefits currently being offered might not have much value to certain groups of workers. In the big picture, Star Communications would be wasting its money.

In considering which benefit an employer might sponsor, or whether to sponsor one at all, there are a number of metrics and data tools that can be used. For example, a well-constructed employee survey can examine employee perspectives on benefits, identify barriers to higher productivity, and reveal life events that may demonstrate the need for a particular benefit. Surveys and, in appropriate instances, focus groups, enable the employer to assess how existing benefits are working, and provide some clues as to the most effective benefit design. They can determine the value of enhancing demographically targeted programs. They can help to predict potential employee behavioral responses to certain incentives under consideration for a company-proposed wellness program; for example, or guide the employer in designing a health or retirement plan. Surveys can be useful in deciding whether voluntary employee-paid benefits might be effective in certain instances or in assessing gaps between what employees perceive to be financial security versus how the current benefits actually respond to that perception and the measures taken, if any, to fill in the gaps. According to reports, employers underestimate the impact of benefits on employee loyalty and productivity;[7] surveys can be an excellent assessment tool measuring the strategic role of benefits.[8] Let's look at some practical examples.

Companies can survey their employee participants and measure the quality of their TPA's services with respect to claims administration, participant communications, and the participant's understanding of the benefit. What have been the participant's experiences in getting claims paid and resolved? How prompt is the TPA in responding to participant questions? How effective are the TPA's communications with participants? Does the TPA communication enhance or detract from the participant's

---

7. For a helpful analysis of the value of employee surveys and benefits, see *Study of employee benefits trends, 6th annual national survey.* (2008). MetLife, http://www.metlife.com/.

8. MetLife (2008).

appreciation of the benefit? Does it enable the participant to make impor-tant, self-directed decisions about his benefits? What would be the finan-cial returns on a new benefit communication program? How would you measure this? There are some protocols to follow in using surveys.[9]

First, the enterprise must articulate the "management question." What is it management really wants to know? Let's say it really wants to know if employees understand and fully appreciate their retirement benefit. From this premise, survey managers develop a research question and then a set of investigative questions that will help answer what management wants to know. The research question could be, "What percentage of our employees has a sound knowledge of the key elements of their retirement plan?" The investigative questions, those incorporated in the actual sur-vey, seek to provide more specific data that, when measured, would respond to the "management question." Some investigative questions might be, "Do employees know if they are covered by a health care plan?" or "Do they understand the employer pays 70 percent of the cost of the plan?" Then, actual "measurement questions" are developed for use in the survey.[10] Employees will be asked to respond to the questions.

The survey process requires that management decide the communica-tion mode. Will the questions be asked in person, by way of a focus group, by phone, or by written survey? Should the questioning be dis-guised so participants do not know the ultimate purpose of the inter-view? Asking questions that do not relate to their understanding of benefits can do this.

The process of drafting the measurement questions follows. The employer must test them, determine whether the questions will be under-stood and answered, and make sure the questions contain no particular bias. For example, one might ask, "Do you value a traditional fee-for-service plan or a more cost-effective, consumer-driven health care plan?" By using "cost-effective," the survey question reflects a bias that may dis-tort a proper response. The survey questions can be designed for open-ended, limited, or multiple-choice responses. The sequence of the questions also must be determined. Typically, early questions in a survey are designed to overcome the motivational barrier to answer. Therefore, if controversial questions are asked in the beginning, it may inhibit a free flow of responses later on.

---

9. For an excellent summary of survey protocols, see Cooper, D., & Schindler, P. (2006). *Business research methods* (pp. 242–271). New York: Irwin McGraw Hill.

10. Surveys do require professional preparation, distribution, and analysis in order to ensure accurate data collection. For example, "false negatives" can occur when employees conjecture and fear a possible management reaction to their truthful answer. A set of related questions can determine the likely truthfulness of key answers.

A benefit survey seeking to assess how the employees value certain benefits should use conjointed questions that require the respondents to choose from among several alternative benefits, instead of simply asking them if they would prefer this benefit or that. In this format, there is a cost attributable to a particular benefit and the employee must decide the value of the benefit. This can be helpful as management decides which, among a variety of benefit options, are most important to their employees.

Careful attention must be paid to all steps of the survey process.[11] If the employer intends to take some appropriate action after the survey results are tabulated, the questions, mode, and integrity of the survey must be ensured. In our daycare benefit example, the survey will help determine the underlying reasons for turnover, the degree of interest and possible use of a daycare center among the workforce, and whether offering such a benefit will enhance recruiting, and the level of cost sharing that would be acceptable by users of the plan. These are complex issues that require an expertly designed survey instrument.

Toolbox—Efficiency, Costs, and Productivity

Employer benefit sponsors should consider measuring the efficient administration of certain benefits. What are the costs per employee of health benefits? What do these costs represent as a percentage of the company's sales? What is the cost of benefits as a percentage of total labor costs?[12] How do these costs compare to industry averages? How do the costs of administering the benefit plan compare to the benefits paid out? What are the industry averages?

If these cost measurements are high, what can be done to reduce them? For example, should the employer consider moving from a traditional defined benefit plan to a less costly defined contribution plan such as a 401(k)? What specific design features would be included in the 401(k), and how will they affect the elements of the benefits model? What would be the fully loaded transaction cost in making the change? How quickly will the employer realize the purported lower costs attributable to the 401(k)? If all employees are not required to change, does that add duplicative

11. Cooper, D. (2006), p. 268.

12. Or one could apply the rate of benefit inflation compared to the market or to other types of inflation and determine how the inflation element of the benefit could be leveraged to the participant or someone else. For example, if prescription cost increases were exceeding the Consumer Price Index, perhaps an employee co-pay comprising a percentage of the price of the drug, instead of a flat and nominal co-pay would have this effect.

administrative costs to the new plan? Does it reduce the projected savings? What impact might this have on the quality of hire, productivity of the current workforce, and employee retention? What are the potential costs here? If health costs are too high, can the employer impact the reimbursement levels of providers, reduce the utilization of health care resources by the employees, or simply shift more costs of the health care plan onto the employees by raising copremiums or deductibles? What are the costs, expected returns, and potential behavioral reactions of the workforce?

Evidence of higher costs per employee could merit the application of a Six Sigma[13] or quality and consistency program that would assist in improving the overall efficient administration of the plan. Usually, the issue here is not "should we offer the benefit," but "how can it be offered in a more efficient manner?" Six Sigma breaks down work flow into process segments and studies each to find ways to reduce variation and error relating to output. It then establishes goals relating to the outputs and implements the requisite changes in the work processes that will reduce variation.[14] The following vignette is an example of this process.

> Suppose an audit of the company-sponsored life insurance plan indicates that 15 percent of the employees insured have not named a beneficiary for their death benefit. A work flow and work process analysis shows that newly qualified employees are given a small card by their immediate supervisor to acknowledge that they are aware of the benefit, and are asked to write the name of their beneficiary on the bottom of the card and return it. Many cards are not returned to the supervisors and some are returned but without the named beneficiary. Management decides the work processes should be changed to reduce the error percentage to zero. They note that date of eligibility is the same as the date a new employee finishes the probationary period and is, thereby, entitled to a significantly higher wage. On this occasion a new withholding card is given to the employee to determine the number of dependents he will claim for tax purposes. The return rate of these cards is 100 percent. Management decides to merge the insurance and withholding cards so that the beneficiary

---

13. Six Sigma is a disciplined, data-driven approach and methodology for eliminating defects in any work context—from manufacturing to transactional to service. See http://www.isixsigma.com.

14. For an interesting explanation of the relevance of Six Sigma to human resources, see Heuring, L. (2004, March). Six Sigma in sight. *HR Magazine, 49*(3).

designation and withholding choices are completed simultaneously and are endorsed with one signature. They also place small boxes for the employee to designate the beneficiary by relationship or name. If no designation is made, the form indicates the insurance proceeds will be paid to the employee's estate. This analysis and change in the work process and forms have the effect of raising the beneficiary designation to 98 percent; the remaining 2 percent default to the "payable to estate" choice. Management also decided that as soon as the new Human Resources Management System is installed in two years, this issue would be included in the software design so as to ensure beneficiary designation.

You will recall in Chapter 8, where length of stay for pneumonia patients was dramatically reduced by closely examining the patient admission processes and discovering that sputum samples were delayed in being sent to the lab, thus impeding the diagnosis, treatment, and recovery of the patients. This was a nice example of a Six Sigma approach to improving business results. Another example is DuPont, where they used Six Sigma to find out why it was taking over six months to determine the eligibility of employees applying for long-term disability.[15]

A Six Sigma system would work well to assess the efficiency and effectiveness of plan administration, reduce variation, and lower plan costs by measuring, for instance, incorrect benefit reimbursements, errors in coverage, the selection of plan investment options, or the redundant administrative steps taken to correct dispensed benefits. It is not just an efficiency program; it can identify opportunities for optimizing profitability and growth, and cause benefit plans to generate maximum returns consistent with the four elements of the benefits model.[16] There are other data and metrics approaches to evaluate benefit plans.

Suppose a company is reviewing the efficiency of a plan it administers in-house. Usually, it would develop some unit costs that can be compared to alternative administrative choices. For example, it can determine the number of full-time equivalent employees involved in the administration of a plan of benefits divided by the number of plan participants. It can then compare that to industry averages. Or, an employer sponsor could

---

15. Heuring, L. (2004, March).

16. Gupta, P. (2003). *Six Sigma business scorecard.* New York: McGraw-Hill Professional. In this book, the author merges Six Sigma and the Balanced Scorecard in an effort to go beyond reducing errors and increasing consistency and achieve strategic goals of profitability and growth.

calculate the total benefits paid out by a plan divided by the administrative costs of the plan.

Obviously, the costs of administration can affect the overall competitiveness of the employer and, therefore, are important. Innovations such as electronic self-enrollment in benefit plans have been quite successful in reducing the overall cost of a benefit, and have enabled HR and the benefits departments to spend their time on more value-added activities, such as new benefit design and employee counseling. Outsourcing benefit administration might be a solution to the problem of high benefit costs. Contractors who professionally manage benefits usually have more sophisticated information systems, and can manage benefit updates and legal compliance more reliably. Measuring these outside costs against in-house administration, including a fully loaded analysis of the costs and benefits, will tell the benefit sponsor whether the idea makes sense. In such cases the benefits model should be a template guiding the overall analysis. Often, a switch can lead to an overall lowering of benefit costs and aid the employer in his goal to remain competitive in his markets.[17] A key in any metric system is to "find and mine" the data.

Toolbox—Data Sources for Measurement— Human Resources Management Systems (HRMS)

As an employer considers a new or modified benefit, certain information is important: how many employees will be covered, how many will be eligible, how many will elect to participate, what their demographics are, pay, what the costs will be, and what impact the plan might have on employee behavior. In many cases this information is contained within the existing Human Resources Management Systems, which is key to a data-driven approach to benefits. HRMS also can be a tool to maintain plan legal compliance; for example, to perform discrimination testing for its 401(k) and to generate a variety of helpful reports on cost projections and the demographics of enrollments. HRMS can provide details on how employees respond to various incentives or design changes in a benefit plan. For example, when an employer institutes a new match for 401(k) participation, he can determine quickly in real time the employee response to the incentive. Are more employees enlisting in the 401(k)? What are the

---

17. For an excellent text on valuing management practices that includes a variety of data gathering and measurement approaches, see Cascio, W. (2000). *Costing human resources: The financial impact of behavior in organizations.* Cincinnati, OH: South-Western College Publishing.

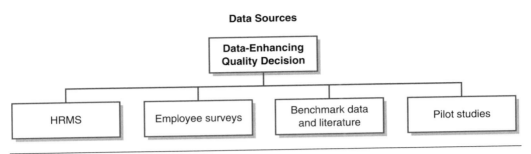

Figure 10.2   Data Sources for Metrics

demographics of the new enrollees? What are their average earnings? What percentage of their income are they deferring?

Or, let's say an employer has just instituted a new consumer-driven, high deductible health care plan and has decided to make a contribution to the health savings accounts of new enrollees. The employer wants to know how many employees are choosing the new plan and what their ages, income levels, and years of service are. Also, what were the company's average total health care claim costs of HSA enrollees last year versus those who chose to remain in the old plan? What are the potential savings to the employer as a result of the enrollment, and how might the plan be changed to encourage higher rates of enrollees?

Since the foundation of the consumer-driven plans is the belief that such plans will cause employee participants to act more like consumers in a real market, the employer can use data to test that assumption. If it is not happening that way, the employer should inquire about designing the plan or its administration to support the desired level of consumer behavior. Are HSA participants using available medical information to become more informed purchasers of health care services? Are HSA participants responding to tiered deductibles, lower co-pays, and more generous co-insurance that encourage preventive care, such as mammography, maternity and prenatal care opportunities, cancer screenings, flu shots, and annual physicals? Do these incentives really work? How does an employer sponsor, perhaps through his TPA, determine whether employees are adopting more healthy lifestyles and complying with recommended treatments for their chronic illnesses? Is it a result of newly introduced employee incentives or, maybe, the new Health Awareness/Wellness Program?

Data can be accessed from the health care plan's TPA to help determine the efficacy of certain plan designs. For example, having access to a provider's clinical outcomes data, professional accreditation, and compliance with health care practice protocols and processes can show the sponsoring employer which providers are providing the best health care. They can then require their TPA to enlist these quality providers into their networks

and encourage their employees through plan designs to use the best providers. This will ensure better and more cost-effective medical outcomes.

Sound Measurement—Validity, Reliability, and Practicality

As employers embark on the measurement of a variety of benefit plan
issues, they must ensure their processes meet the standards of scientific
rigor. If not, the conclusions reached by the research effort have little utility. They also will not support an allocation of capital to be used for a new
benefit or a redesign of an existing benefit plan. Thus, the measurement
process used for a variety of benefit analyses must maintain the standards
of validity, reliability, and practicality.

For example, in our daycare case, how will we know that it was the
daycare center that had a positive impact on absenteeism, turnover, productivity, and recruitment? How does one prove this to be true? Before
you can attempt to show there are corelationships between the new benefit
and the number and quality of new recruits, you must first establish some
working definitions. What criteria will you use to define "better quality
recruitment"? Should they include higher grade point averages of recent
graduates, better results on the company entrance tests, quicker attainment of high productive status on the job, better selling, or higher performance evaluations? And how do we then link the daycare benefit to these
improvements in recruiting? Maybe the improvements are simply a result
of other changes in better management practices or career opportunities,
a new wage adjustment, or more days of continuous sunshine.

The process of linking new benefits or benefit designs to improved
employee behaviors and the resultant creation of new value requires the
application of scientific business methods. More specifically, experimental
design involves an application of the standards of validity, reliability, and
practicality.

"Validity refers to the extent to which a test measures what we actually
want to measure. Reliability has to do with the accuracy and precision of
the measurement procedure. Practicality is concerned with a wide range
of factors of economy, convenience, and interpretability."[18]

In our daycare case, after definitions are agreed upon and data sources
are identified, we must take baseline measures of those items that we
assume will be affected by the new benefit. For example, since we expect
the center will help to attract better candidates, we must get baseline measurements of recent recruits who have been on the job for three to five

18. Cooper, D., & Schindler, P. (2006). *Business research methods* (p. 318). New
York: Irwin McGraw-Hill.

years. Then we accumulate information on new recruits. What are the current grade point averages of our new, college-educated recruits? What are the current average selection scores of new job candidates? How do we define high productivity levels, and how long does it take the average new hire to attain this status? What are the average or mean performance evaluation scores of new employees after 12 months on the job? We must do the same with respect to the other expected results—turnover rates by length of service, absenteeism rates differentiated by age and children, work distractions, and overall company loyalty. These must be done before the new benefit is implemented.

We must establish a statistical method to correlate the changes in any of the baseline measures to the new daycare benefit, thus eliminating the implication of other factors that could have influenced the outcomes. Correlation does not necessarily imply causation. The optimal method for determining causality is to use a pilot program to test the hypothetical effects of the daycare center and to compare changes in the baseline measures that occur in a reasonable time after the program's start. These changes can be compared to a control group that did not participate in the new daycare plan. If positive and significantly different improvements are noted in the pilot group, one can conclude that it was the daycare center that caused the changes.[19] Of course, not all companies have the capacity to do the more sophisticated measurements, but just comparing post daycare numbers to previous baselines would be very helpful in evaluating the program.

Our data collection and measurement process must utilize reliable measures that are consistent and free from error. As an example, if we are measuring changes in performance evaluations, we must use a consistent method of evaluating our recruits and ensure that rater error and bias and other potential inconsistencies are abated so that ultimate measurements are based on reliable data. Similarly, we need to make certain that our selection criteria and standards are administered consistently if we intend to measure changes in job candidate qualifications. Ultimately, we should expect that the same recruit would be given the same performance evaluation regardless of the person doing the evaluation.

As often as possible, the measurement system should use existing data sources in order to minimize the expense of measurement. The evaluation should be designed to allow easy and understandable application so that it can be efficiently administered. In our daycare example, by using existing operational metrics—absenteeism, turnover, productivity, and recruitment—we can make the entire experimental design process practical to

---

19. This is what The Kroger Co. did with a new computer-based employee selection system and computer-based training program. Murphy, T., & Zandvakili, S. (2000).

the organization and not something that adds significant expense and is too complex for most to understand.

Simple software systems such as Microsoft Excel can be used to determine the strength of correlations. By inputting our data, we can determine what relationship exists, if any, between the introduction of the new day-care benefit and the turnover and absenteeism rates, productivity changes, and improved quality recruiting. With care in the design of our measurements, we can be better assured of a probable causal link between the new benefit and the results. Validity, reliability, and practicality help us determine linkage, but how do we calculate the financial value created by this change as compared to its cost?

Measuring the Financial Value of Benefit Plans— Using Capital Budgeting Analysis

When evaluating whether or not to offer a benefit plan, metrics such as net present value, return on investment, internal rate of return, and payback period are all useful tools.[20] These metrics can assist the organization in deciding whether or not to allocate capital to a new or revised benefit plan. By subjecting a proposed benefit plan to this measurement process, the organization puts all allocations of capital—from new warehouses, to new information systems, to a new wellness program—on the same level playing field and can better ensure sustained support for the funded projects.

If one can show, for example, that a new employee stock appreciation rights (SAR)[21] plan can improve productivity in the workforce by 20 percent and cost the employer only a fraction of the return, the employer is likely to embrace the new benefit by funding it and, more importantly, continuing to support it in the future.

RETURN ON INVESTMENT (ROI)

Taking a closer look at these tools, you will find the most common measurement is return on investment (ROI). The formula is: (**Benefits − Costs**) ÷ **Costs** = **ROI**.

---

20. See, generally, Higgins, R. (2001). *Analysis for financial management.* New York: McGraw-Hill.

21. SARs are opportunities for employees to receive the incremental value of the company's stock over a given period. The appreciation is most often awarded in the form of the employer's shares of stock.

Let's suppose the benefits manager wants to introduce a new health care plan design that will encourage employees to optimize preventive care. He proposes having a variety of preventive diagnostic care procedures made available without having to pay a deductible, as a way to create greater interest. This means the employer sponsor's initial costs will increase because the plan's coinsurance will apply to the plan. The benefits manager has argued that this change will reduce health care claims cost for serious illnesses and enhance overall productivity. Further, he expects to see these results in three to five years.

Having determined the positive impact the new health care plan will have on these serious illnesses and productivity, and estimated the resulting financial returns, he will then subtract the cost of the plan and divide that amount by the cost to arrive at a ROI. He also may want to assess whether or not the investment in the new health care plan will meet or exceed some internally established hurdle rates.

NET PRESENT VALUE (NPV)

The net present value is the difference between the market value of an investment and its costs. One estimates the future value of net cash flows generated by the benefit and reduces that by the expenses and costs of the project. Then using the employer's discount rate or opportunity cost of capital,[22] the cash flows are reduced to a present value. If the amount is positive, the investment should be accepted; if it is negative, rejected. The theory is, if the return on the proposal beats that of the company's best use of its capital, then an investment in the benefit is warranted. For example, let's assume productivity increases attributable to the new daycare center amount to $200,000 per year. This particular increase arises from reducing absenteeism and time away from work that preschool parents experience as a result of babysitter absences and minor emergencies arising at home. The duration of this return is estimated, aggregated, and then discounted using a current market rate to a present value. The same total amount is then discounted using the company's cost of capital. If the present value of the productivity returns from the daycare center exceeds that of the cost of capital (by as little as $1) an investment in the daycare center is

22. The opportunity cost is the return one can earn on the next best alternative investment. Higgins (2001), p. 235.

warranted. If not, the daycare center may not be such a good idea.[23] The formula looks like this: **NPV of productivity return from daycare center = (total value of productivity gains over seven years reduced to present value using a market discount rate) – (total value of productivity gains over seven years reduced to present value using the company's cost of capital).**

INTERNAL RATE OF RETURN (IRR)[24]

The IRR is a discount rate at which a program's net present value equals zero.[25] The application of an IRR process is useful when the company must engage in "capital rationing" and choose from among several investment proposals. The IRR is the precise discount rate for a project just prior to the point where the net present value (NPV) changes from positive to negative.[26] It is useful to know the IRR because any return above the rate should warrant an investment, while a rate below would not. So, if the company is allocating its capital by applying a certain discount rate to calculate NPV and that rate represents its cost of capital, then an IRR is a rate where the NPV equals zero. If the IRR were above this cost of capital or discount rate, then an investment would be acceptable; if it were below, it would not be acceptable. If it equals the rate, then the investment at best would be marginal.

The formula is: IRR > cost of capital, invest; IRR < cost of capital, reject; IRR = cost of capital, the investment would be considered marginal. So, if a project's NPV is positive at 12 percent, but negative at 18 percent, we know the IRR is somewhere between 12 and 18 percent. By calculation, the IRR is 15 percent.

THE PAYBACK PERIOD RULE

The payback period calculation could be applied to evaluate a proposed staff reduction plan where severance pay and benefits are used to enhance voluntary separations among workers. For example, suppose a company wants to reduce its labor costs by 15 percent and decides to offer a

---

23. A further example, if one accepts a project with a negative NPV of ($10,000), it is equivalent to investing $10,000 now and receiving nothing in return. The total value of the company would be reduced by $10,000.

24. Higgins, R., pp. 242–244.

25. Higgins, R., p. 265.

26. Higgins, R., p. 242.

generous severance package to encourage voluntary separations.[27] The costs in the first year will be quite high because of the package, but over time the company will be replacing higher paid persons with lower paid entry-level workers. In this case, the employer calculates how many months it will take for the lower labor costs (cash flows) to surpass the costs of the severance plan.

The payback period does not require the use of discount rates or elaborate calculations. It is especially useful when there are two competing proposals. In this case, one proposal may be more generous than the other, or one may involve involuntary separations. The one with the shorter payback period would be the favored option. This essentially means that after the payback period has lapsed, the lower wage rates are creating value for the company.

The formula for the payback period[28] is: **Payback period = (Investment ÷ Annual cash flow).**

Some Perspective

All of these calculations involve judgment and must take into consideration the various risks that might be encountered as the project gets underway. A conservative chief financial officer who applies a high opportunity cost of capital and uses an equivalent high discount rate in calculating the NPV of an investment will raise the bar considerably for project proposals. Whatever measures are applied, management should regard benefits as opportunities to create value.[29] Determining this value requires careful attention to the protocols of measurement and a basic understanding

27. In this instance management will often be called upon to estimate the number of people who will accept the voluntary layoff. The company may have to develop some data and analysis as to how "generous" the program has to be in order to optimize the number of volunteers.

28. Higgins, R., pp. 233–234. Note that this rule does not consider the time value of money.

29. We should note that measuring the financial impact of benefits should also include an analysis of the implied wage contract as discussed in Chapter 2. For example, increasing health costs can be borne by reducing wages. Employee equity benefit plans often add value because the employer's compensation strategy is to substitute their value from salary. With respect to health care, from 1996 to 2005, health insurance costs grew from 6.1 to 8.2 percent of total compensation, while wages and salaries slipped from 82.1 to 79.5 percent. Other benefits rose only .4 percent. *Employer compensation by category.* (2007). California HealthCare Foundation.

of the financial measures used by the enterprise to decide which projects to finance.[30]

Design Principles

There are some existing tools applicable to other management practices that should be in the toolbox. For example, as we discussed in Chapter 2, in designing and evaluating benefits, careful attention should be paid to the benefits model: (1) Does the plan ensure internal fairness or does it apply to only one segment of the employee population? (2) How does the benefit compare to those being offered by your external product or service competitors who are competing for the same labor group? (3) Does the plan include incentives or other design features that can affect employee behaviors positively? (4) Is the plan cost-effective and well administered?

Using the Human Resources Balanced Scorecard[31] to design a benefit plan helps to ensure that the varied objectives of the enterprise are considered. The Scorecard comprises four elements: (1) considering the interests of customers, (2) producing sound financial returns, (3) improving internal business processes, and (4) paying attention to employee learning and growth. Overemphasis on one factor could result in the failure of another, which could result in long-term operational problems.

Let's go back to our voluntary severance program. We have calculated the lower wage costs against the costs of the severance package and attained a desired result. That result, however, may be affected by the departure of experienced employees. Customers must now depend on many short-service, inexperienced workers who know little about the product and are not able to maintain the previous standards of customer service and quality. As a result, customer satisfaction could drop. Therefore, the employer should anticipate this possible scenario as he designs the plan, and take measures to mitigate its impact. For example, when he calculates the ROI of the new early retirement incentive, the employer should estimate the effect poor customer service could have on sales and consider some special employee selection, orientation, training, or rewards that will help maintain high levels of customer service. The bottom line when designing a new benefit plan is to make sure it has a balanced

---

30. See Phillips, J., & Phillips, P. (2005). *Proving the value of HR: How and why to measure ROI.* Alexandria, VA: Society for Human Resource Management; Fitz-enz, J. (1995). *How to measure human resources management.* New York: McGraw-Hill.

31. See Becker, B., Huselid, M., & Ulrich, D. (2001). *The HR scorecard.* Boston: Harvard Business School Press.

Table 10.1   Balanced Value Card for Health Care

Choice of provider is very important.	Use of high-quality, cost-effective providers.
Employee cost sharing will be competitive with external labor market offerings.	Emphasis on preventive care will be included in the design to ensure overall long-term health and lower costs to the employer.

impact.[32] Without this balance, the factors that drive the business may be in jeopardy. Let's look at another example.

A company awards stock options to individual employees who voluntarily enroll in and complete skill-based training. The company's objective is multipurpose—training will enhance workers' productivity and stock options will increase the alignment of interests between hourly workers and owners, causing workers to think and behave more like owners. Ultimately, the company will create a highly productive work environment, reduce product costs, and increase profits. As a result, customers enjoy lower prices and higher quality products and services. The stock option plan also creates opportunities for wealth accumulation among all workers. Overall, this plan would appear to have balance in its design and should lead to adding value to the company.

On a similar level, employers can utilize what might be called a "balanced value" card for a variety of benefits. For example, an employer believes strongly that all health care plans must include the following values: preservation of the participant's right to select his providers, utilization of high-quality and cost-efficient providers, competitive cost sharing of health care expenses by employee participants, and significant emphasis on preventive care. The application of these balanced values will help determine the employer's specific health care plan design. An HMO, for instance, would not be considered because it does not permit choice. Or, in the case of the PPO, the employer may insist that his TPA obtain quality outcomes data for any provider in the network.

Tables 10.1 and 10.2 are offered for illustrative purposes only, and represent templates that can be used by the employer plan sponsor to focus on the potential positive contributions of his benefits plan.

---

32. What does the data show about longer service? Do longer service employees really produce more? How would you measure this? Is the entire premise of our DBP—to encourage longer service—a sound assumption? The employer, using data and metrics, should constantly review and test the assumption that longer service is better service and when the cost of providing a DBP is included in the calculation, should determine whether or not there is a real financial return on the benefit.

Table 10.2   Balanced Value Card for Retirement Plan

Provide design features in the plan that will encourage long and loyal employee service.	Competitive in relevant labor market in offering both traditional and supplemental retirement plan(s).
Employer will assume investment and longevity risks in the basic plan; employee savings and contributions will be encouraged as a supplemental source of retirement income.	Basic plan designed so as to generate an aggregate 60 percent replacement of pretax final average pay for long service and full-age retirement.

Now that we have looked at the various measurement tools, let's examine some examples of how they might be applied to evaluations of retirement and health care plans.

Data, Metrics, and Retirement Plans—Some Examples

The underlying human resources strategy behind an employer's sponsorship of a traditional defined benefit plan is twofold: to encourage longer service and to respond to important employee life events. However, it also provides a total compensation package that is comparable to its competitors, presumably strengthening the employer's ability to recruit and retain good workers. Does it work? When tested by using a data- and metrics-driven approach, the assumptions demonstrate how well the employer's retirement benefits meet these objectives.

Through employee surveys, data mining its HRMS, and benchmark research, a company can determine whether a DBP actually does encourage longer service. By offering an early retirement option at age 55, for example, is the employer encouraging shorter service? What does the data show? And are the best employees—those who have the most confidence in their ability to achieve new successes after leaving the firm—the ones who take advantage of the DBP offering? Should the early retirement age be raised? Is the actuarial reduction before full-age retirement too generous? What is the cost to the company of these early retirements? Are there plan design changes that might reduce their number? Should they be positive or negative incentives? Should there be actuarial increases for people who stay at work beyond a certain age? How would you assess the costs and the benefits of such a change?

There are a number of opportunities for the employer to test assumptions using data and metrics and to determine whether the benefit plans are accomplishing their desired effect. Case in point, does a DBP encourage longer service and at the same time encourage older employees to leave the firm earlier than the employer would desire? Yes. As we discussed in Chapter 4, while the benefit goes up with years of service, at some point the present value of the benefit declines.[33] This is because the period during which the employee will receive pension plan annuities becomes shorter as his life expectancy declines. This is not the case with a DCP in which the employee's aggregate retirement savings appreciate in value with investments, are not subject to actuarial reductions, and can be transferred to heirs and successors at the time of the retiree's death.

Careful research by the company can help determine whether its retirement plans are actually curtailing longer service. What is the estimated cost to the company? Should it allow lump sum payouts for its DBP or find a way to permit phased retirement or full work after retirement as we discussed in Chapter 4? How would the cost of these alternatives compare to the higher productivity gained by retaining older workers?

The calculation of a benefit under a DBP is based in large part on the final average pay of the participant. As income varies over the years, especially in companies with large annual bonus opportunities, a participant is likely to time his retirement based on the calculation of the current average pay versus what he expects in the next few years. How often does this happen and who among your workforce is exploiting this opportunity? Are they among your most productive employees? What data sources would you use to assess this issue? What design changes might mitigate this problem? For example, should you extend the period of "final average pay" from three to five years? How do you think this would help?

Finally, through surveys and a thorough review of his recruitment practices, the employer should determine whether offering a DBP is important to prospective employees. Is it contributing to the overall "quality of new hire"? There is some speculation that a well-designed 401(k) with good matches can actually enhance the quality of hire. This is based on the fact that persons with self-discipline and those willing to delay immediate gratification are better workers. These are the personal characteristics of good savers in a 401(k) plan. Could the employer tout its DCP in its recruiting program to sort better workers?[34]

A data- and metrics-driven analysis could lead the employer to consider freezing his DBP and offering a DCP or a hybrid plan such as a cash balance plan. Generally, both have potentially lower costs and, as we see from the example above, may be more aligned with the interests of new employees who may be more comfortable with retirement account ownership, the

---

33. See Figure 4.4 (Chapter 4).

34. This idea is contained in a yet unpublished PhD dissertation written by a Notre Dame graduate. See Burham, K. (2007). *401(k) as strategic compensation: Align pay with productivity and enable optimal separation.*

opportunity to direct their investments, and the advantage of portability. Besides, they do not expect to work for one company for a lifetime and they understand the inherent investment risk. The employer should constantly test the assumptions that led him to choose a particular retirement plan or health care plan design. Does the plan really do what it was intended to accomplish? Moreover, are the underlying principles and assumptions used to develop the plan still valid? From a fundamental standpoint, does the retirement plan produce sufficient retirement income?

When a company sponsors a DCP, it should project the aggregate savings[35] of its workforce at retirement age and answer the question: Will the DCP really produce sufficient income for the employee to retire comfortably? The answer involves calculating the current savings rate as a percentage of earnings, factoring in expected salary increases, adding employer matches, applying a realistic investment return, and estimating the average year of retirement. The aggregate amount can be converted to an annuity and expressed as a percentage of final pay. It also can be adjusted for inflation or simply be stated in "nominal" dollars. This calculation serves several purposes. First, the employer can test his objective of providing a means to accumulating adequate retirement income against the projections of current employee savings rates. Second, it enables the employer to take timely action to find ways to increase participation and savings rates, to modify his matches, to provide more comprehensive investment education for the participants, or to make other appropriate changes in his plan design.[36]

---

35. The most recent research indicates that nationally employee participants in DCPs will generate less than 50 percent of their final pay. See *Retirement security, Issue guide.* (2006, September). Economic Policy Institute, http://www.epi.org/content/. The EBRI also has found that while 67 percent of workers have access to a retirement plan at work, only 70 percent participate. The Employee Benefit Research Institute's 2006 Retirement Confidence Survey shows that, while 24 percent of U.S. workers are very confident they are saving enough for retirement, 44 percent of the average 401(k) balances of workers over the age of 55 are less than $25,000, and 26 percent are over $250,000. See http://www.ebri.org/. See also Karpel, C. (2006). *The retirement myth.* UK: HarperCollins. The author reports that for many employees the exclusive retirement plan is a 401(k) and they are not saving enough on which to retire. AARP reports that 40 percent of Americans over 60 will experience poverty at some point in their remaining lives. The average 401(k) balance among U.S. workers in 2000 was $42,000, an amount insufficient to support a retiree. See Costello, M. (2002, May 5). *Retirement ready or not here it comes.* CNN/Money, http://www.cnn.com/.

36. The author, together with his students, have performed this function for a very large employer and determined that projected aggregate savings and investments of its 3,000 401(k) participants would provide about 20 percent replacement income. The employer is engaging in communication and educational efforts to improve the savings rates of its employees.

Employers should take an active role in decision support and education with respect to their sponsorship of pension plans. Employees need to know whether they are saving enough, what they should do to achieve their retirement goal, and how they can continually monitor this. "Reverse data," that is, giving the employee the data and metrics to help him navigate the sometimes complicated benefits landscape, can allow the employer to gain an optimal return for his benefit investment. The plans will be appreciated more and will achieve their intended purposes and results. MetLife has some helpful suggestions on improving communications to participants:[37] Targeted messages for individual employees should be included in high-quality employee communications. Extend communications beyond the "big envelope" of traditional printed material.

Employer sponsors of 401(k) plans have had problems getting high participation rates among lower paid employees. The result can be an adverse discrimination finding by the IRS, invalidating the salary deferrals of some higher paid employees. So, employers are looking for ways to increase participation by using nonelective enrollments, direct contributions to the employees' accounts, and increased employer matches of employee deferrals. But is it worth the added expense?[38] Taking baseline measures of the rates of participation by NHCEs before the change was implemented, looking at the costs of legal noncompliance, and factoring in the financial and administrative costs of higher employer contributions and matches can help the employer quantify the value of the new DCP approach. It also can test the working assumption that higher matches will increase participation by using employee surveys.

There are numerous opportunities for employer sponsors to test and evaluate a plan and determine whether it is meeting its strategic objectives. For example, do employees value the plan? Does it affect their behavior at the workplace? What features do employees consider most important? What are the employees' visions of their own retirement plans? Does the plan meet the needs of a multi-generational workforce or are there significant gaps between the plan and the employees' expectations and needs?[39] To ignore these research, data-driven, and measurement

---

37. MetLife (2008).

38. There is considerable research on this topic. The general conclusion is that increased matches increase participation, but not the individual savings rates. As noted in Chapter 4 on Retirement Plans, reputable research indicates the size of the employer's match does affect the rate of participation among employees in a 401(k). Even, W., & Macpherson, D. (2005).

39. Some employers have experience in determining whether a new selection system produces better candidates. The measurement involves linking the new system to improved qualifications of the candidates and their performance levels

opportunities means the employer is willing to potentially waste significant amounts of money and resources on plans that may not be valued by its workforce, and are not linked to the business and HR strategies. The database is there and waiting to be tapped. The metrics and the tools are available and easy to use. The only remaining item is the matter of the TPAs.

The sponsoring employer can evaluate its third-party administrator by using data and metrics. For example, the DCP administrator could be working under a performance-based contract with the employer sponsor requiring certain measured goals be met. The goals could relate to issues such as:

- The overall investment performance of the administrator's investment choices

- How they compare to other third parties and to certain market indices

- The costs of administering the plan and how they compare to other benchmark plans

- The service-level goals provided to the participants; for example, how long participants wait on the phone to have their question(s) answered by the administrator

- The quality of participant communications and investment guidance performed by the administrator

- Whether the TPA is using the latest interactive technology

- How well the administrator upgrades plan provisions to comply with legal changes

Similarly, money managers, trust fund administrators, and actuaries working with an employer-sponsored DBP can be evaluated. Data and metrics play a key role in evaluating the administrator's performance and can significantly affect the effective and efficient operation of the plan, providing the sponsor with a valued benefit among its participants.

As benefit costs occupy a significantly larger piece of the overall cost of employment and as global competition increases, it is vital that the plan sponsor remain price competitive. Thus, the sponsor is constrained to evaluate the strategic effectiveness of its benefit plans. By using a data- and metrics-driven analytical approach, as we have discussed here, the employer can better analyze this efficacy and also make sure that more cost-effective and employee-valued benefit choices are sponsored.

---

after hire. See Cascio, W. (1999). *Costing human resources: The financial impact of behavior in organizations* (p. 192). Cincinnati, OH: South-Western Publishing.

Health Care and Measurement—Plan Design

As we examine the issue of data and metrics and health care, there are two assumptions. First, an employer's primary, strategic purpose for sponsoring a health care plan is to enhance the productive capacity of his human capital.[40] Second, as discussed in Chapter 8, Improving Access to Quality Health Care, health care is not a commodity.[41] There are significant variations in clinical outcomes among various health care providers. These two assumptions should cause an employer sponsor to see his health care plan as a potential value proposition that can be realized through the use of data and metrics.

An employer-sponsored health care plan should help the employer control absences, mitigate physical or mental impairments that interfere with productivity, and avoid catastrophic health events among his workforce. Assessing how effective his health care plan is in accomplishing these events is essential. Let's take a very simple example to illustrate the points.

Suppose the owner of an office supply chain—through simple observation, employee surveys, time records, and an analysis of its health care claims costs—determines a large percentage of absences and disruptions are caused by seasonal flu among workers and their families. Flu shots are currently not covered by the company's health plan. The owner estimates the average cost of these absences and disruptions per employee is five lost days per year. Further, the cost of these five days comprises sick pay, added overtime used to replace the hours, health care claims costs, and the incremental cost of using replacement workers, including their lower productivity. Let's assume

1. We used influenza in this example to simplify the analysis. Almost certainly, an employer would find there is a high productivity and absenteeism cost attributable to such conditions as stress, low back problems, obesity, depression, and chronic illnesses such as diabetes. Similar steps can be taken to analyze and address these conditions.

40. Of course, there are other purposes. One is to be competitive among other employers in your product or labor market so as to enhance recruitment and retention. The employer often has a humanitarian purpose in enabling its employees to deal with illness and other life events requiring medical attention in their families.

41. Porter, M., & Teisberg, E. (2006); Gratzer, D. (2006). *The cure: How capitalism can save American health care.* New York: Encounter Books.

these five days of absence due to sickness and doctor reimbursements cost $1,000 per employee annually. The owner learns that
introducing a plan to provide free flu shots for workers and their
immediate families would cost the company an average of $150 per
employee. This includes the cost of the serum and instruments,
nurses to administer the shots, time away from the work area to
receive the shots, and communication and administrative costs. By
instituting this program, the owner calculates that he can achieve a
60 percent reduction in annual absences.[2] Thus, the cost of the program per employee is $150 with a projected savings of $600 per
employee, or a 300 percent ROI. Is there any doubt the program
should be introduced?[3]

---

2. Of course, this is an estimate, but there appears to be a potentially
positive return even with a lower estimate of reduced absenteeism.

3. Mercer recently refined the methodology for evaluating the overall
ROI of a health care plan. They suggest that population-level trends
be used to estimate future health care costs versus simply looking at
specific plan-level costs. They also suggest longer periods, such as
24 months, to determine baseline measures. Mercer recommends
the employer exclude outliers to make the ROI calculation less sub-
jective to extreme data inputs. It would seem that conducting pilot
programs with a control group also would make the conclusions
from the data more reliable. Serxner, S., & Gold, D. (2006, July).
*Guidelines for analysis of economic return from health management
programs.* http://www.mercer.com.

The formula looks like this:

(Benefits – Costs) ÷ Costs = ROI
$1,000 cost/employee's five-day absence/year
$ 150 cost/employee for flu shot program
$ 600 (represents 60 percent savings in reduced absences)
(600 – 150) ÷ 150 = 300%

This simple analysis shows that a health care plan design can affect
attendance and the human capacity for production. Therefore, it should
not be viewed as a cost but as an investment. In this vignette the employer
refined and modified his health care plan and targeted a specific barrier to
higher productivity. There are differences in health care outcomes that can
be achieved by better designs and there are financial returns to be achieved
by this process. Again, the use of data and metrics empowers the employer
to develop this opportunity. Table 10.3 illustrates a step-by-step approach
to analyzing the potential financial return of a health care plan.

Table 10.3   Metrics and Health Care Step-by-Step Approach

Assumption: Health Care Affects Business Outcomes	
Tasks	
(1) Generate and examine data to see what impacts business results and how it relates to health care	(6) Estimate possible ROI on your health care solution.
(2) Determine cost of this operational problem.	(7) Obtain an allocation of capital to fund your plan.
(3) Hypothesize set of potential health care plan initiatives that could solve problem and estimate their cost.	(8) Implement new health care initiatives and establish a causal or statistical co-relationship between them and the changed business measures.
(4) Identify new goal with respect to business results, e.g., reduce absenteeism by 30 percent; attached financial value to this goal.	(9) Continue to evaluate the program.
(5) Take baseline measures.	

Let's dig a little deeper and examine how refining the design features of a health care plan can produce real financial returns. An employer is considering the cost versus the potential return of introducing several health care screenings to detect conditions that affect worker productivity, such as colon cancer, high blood pressure, breast cancer, and diabetes. By developing some data and research, the employer can estimate the financial returns in claims cost reductions as well as improved productivity resulting from the early detection of these conditions. The alternative is to wait for the catastrophic and more costly events that occur when the conditions develop and become acute. Can the employer introduce employee incentives in his plan design that will enhance the probability of employees taking advantage of these screenings? Yes, he can. For example, exempt the diagnostic charges for screenings from the deductible. The employer sponsor will treat the charges as post-deductible services and reimburse on a coinsurance basis. Thus, employees over the age of 45, for instance, can receive colorectal screening including a colonoscopy every several years; the company will pay 80 percent of the cost, and the employee pays 20 percent. The deductible will not apply.

One can estimate the cost of waiving the deductible against the risk of employees suffering from advanced colon cancer, being off work, and incurring exceptionally expensive claims costs in the future. As we discussed in Chapter 7, the employer sponsor can become even more aggressive in using his health plan to create a healthier, more productive workforce that will, over the long term, incur lower claims costs.

The wellness programs discussed in Chapter 7 provide such an opportunity. Data and metrics should drive the design of the plans. The employer should begin by initiating a health assessment process designed to mitigate negative impacts on productivity. By gathering data that reveals potential or actual health conditions among the workforce, one begins to see a wellness program that incorporates early detection screenings, preventive programs, or special treatments to defend against the onset of certain identifiable conditions. Then, after the employer and his health consultants have analyzed the data from the assessments, several programs are indicated: (1) weight loss, (2) smoking cessation, (3) cholesterol reduction, and (4) diabetes management.

Specific plans and goals are discussed with employees whose assessments indicate they are at risk. Employee surveys tabulating work distractions caused by relevant health conditions should be conducted. Thus, a causal link between chronic health conditions and absenteeism or impeded productivity can be determined, and a remedial or treatment plan is then developed. Incentives such as employer contributions to the employee's Flexible Spending Account could be established and executed only when results are achieved. No incentives are awarded for employee "activity" or "attempts."[42]

Baseline measures for the overall program, such as attendance rates, disability periods, lost-time events, and productivity analyses, should be taken. As the program proceeds, and provided the improvements in these baselines can be attributed to the wellness program, a ROI can be calculated. To make the link between the wellness program and the resultant improvements more obvious, the employer could initiate a pilot program to test it before implementing companywide.

This approach involves the use of data and metrics and is based on a working assumption that health care plan design has real potential for financial returns. Certainly, continuous evaluations including revisions in treatment approaches should be an integral part of the program. The responsibility to follow through and initiate such programs falls on the

---

42. According to the Department of Labor, wellness "rewards" must comply with the following: the reward must not exceed 20 percent of the individual cost of coverage under the plan; the reward must be designed to prevent disease or promote good health; there must be an opportunity to requalify for the award annually; the reward must be available to all similarly situated participants; if the goals are unattainable or medically inadvisable for certain individuals they must be given an alternative standard. *Final Rules Governing HIPAA nondiscrimination and wellness programs*, 29 CFR 2590. (2006, December 13).

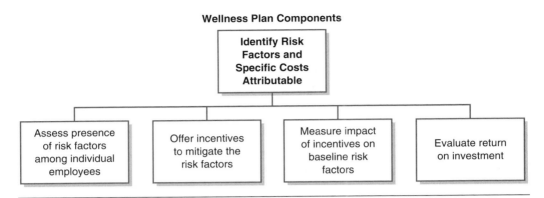

Figure 10.3   The Design Components of a Wellness Program

employer or through his direction on the TPA. It is too important an opportunity to ignore.

We have used a wellness program here to simplify the analysis. Basic health care plan design features, including co-pays, coinsurance, and deductibles, in addition to deciding which conditions are covered by the plan, examining treatment protocols used by providers, using outpatient treatments, and provider reimbursement practices are all health care plan design variables. Moreover, they are all amenable to analysis by the employer and his TPA. Can coinsurance be modified to encourage employees to follow appropriate preventive care opportunities?[43] Or should cost sharing features be used to cause the employee to avoid costly, less efficient services such as going to the hospital emergency room for the flu? Mining the claims data, using surveys, and applying simple metrics can provide the employer sponsor with a variety of plan design approaches that will ensure more effective and efficient health plan utilization. All of this can generate real value.

Evaluating Providers and Their Clinical Outcomes—Sponsors' Efforts

The working assumption is that not all medical providers are equal; and providers who produce the best results—usually getting it right the first

---

43. For example, what behavioral changes occur when certain preventive care measures are "outside" the deductible and substantially reimbursed by the plan? How do co-pays really affect utilization? Further, what are the financial returns on such features?

time—often are the most cost-efficient. The conclusion, therefore, must be that sponsors of health care should insist that their participants be directed to such providers. Once again, we see the importance of data in making well-informed decisions. In Chapter 8, we discuss this issue in detail. The question now, however, is where is the data and how does a sponsor access it?[44] Ultimately, having access to providers' clinical outcomes in which the major diagnostic areas of health are covered is one solution.[45]

In Cincinnati, Ohio, several major employers joined together to obtain and evaluate the clinical outcomes of 14 major hospitals in the metropolitan area.[46] The analysis encompassed most major diagnostic areas (MDA)[47] and made adjustments for severity of the condition and medical history of the patient.[48] The data measures included preventable deaths and mortality, recovery time and charges for treatment, and occasions where the patient was readmitted or visited the emergency room after discharge due to complications. There were wide variations in outcomes. The employers who sponsored the analysis concluded they would purchase health care services from the best providers. They attempted to create a new business model where health care providers competed based on their record of clinical outcomes—quality and value-based competition. In the end, however, such a program requires a broader record base. Medicare records are too narrow in scope because they largely encompass older patients. The employers' efforts to get the providers to share their total clinical data were met with resistance.[49] Nevertheless, there were

---

44. Medicare's Diagnostic Related Groups (DRG) data is public and accessible; private care results are not.

45. It is generally accepted that clinical compliance with certain medical protocols should lead to better clinical outcomes.

46. Murphy, T. (1995). Creating market conditions for the delivery of health care: The Cincinnati experience. *Human Resource Management, 34*(4), 569.

47. An MDA would include groups of conditions such as cardiac, pulmonary, orthopedic, gastrointestinal, and the like.

48. The providers could not argue that their results were below the group average because they treated patients with more severe conditions. The algorithm used in our program adjusted the patient data to account for such issues.

49. The Cincinnati project continues today in the form of an employer–hospital partnership to share clinical data. There are other examples of employers getting access to clinical data and using it to identify the best providers. See, for example, the Leapfrog Group at http://www.leapfroggroup.org. Employer payers for health care are using the data to lobby for patient safety and to reward those providers who offer quality outcomes. CMS and some others are also publishing some outcomes data. As of yet, however, it is not very comprehensive and often involves health protocol compliance instead of actual health outcomes. See Exercises at the end of this chapter.

significant steps taken by various providers whose data showed they were not producing quality outcomes in certain medical areas. They looked deeply into their work processes to find out why they were not doing as well as their peers. The examination of clinical data and the resultant remedial steps by providers directly benefit patients who get better treatment, sponsors who enjoy lower costs, and the community that will have a healthier population.

The U.S. Medicare and Medicaid programs are enormous consumers of health care and are beginning to realize their potential in changing our health care system by bringing about better clinical results. Currently, they are engaged in a study to determine how they can link quality outcomes with reimbursements to providers. Premier, Inc., a coalition of nonprofit hospitals, just completed a related study of 224,000 patient records. They concluded that adherence to basic medical treatment guidelines significantly improves clinical results, saving lives and medical costs. The report tracked Medicare patients with pneumonia, heart bypass surgery, heart attack, hip and knee replacement, and congestive heart failure. The results were conclusive: 5,700 deaths 8,100 complications, and 10,000 readmissions could have been avoided by following simple treatment guidelines. The study projected the additional costs associated with these poor clinical results would be $1.35 billion per year.[50]

The lesson of this data and metrics effort is obvious. As a sponsor of health care, the employer or government agency should take advantage of the same processes it uses in purchasing supplies, raw materials, and services. Who is delivering the best product at the best price? What value am I getting for each dollar spent? What, if any, are the alternatives? The data to make this assessment with respect to health care providers and TPAs exist. Sponsors should use their leverage to insist that it be made available. Significant variations in outcomes can be identified and the data can be used by the plan sponsor to enhance the overall value of its health care plan. It can choose the best performers.[51] The process of using clinical data allows the providers, not the sponsors or TPAs, to deal with the remedial practices and methods that lead to improved outcomes and costs, and to

---

50. See Premier, Inc. (2006). *Premier hospital quality incentive demonstration project: Findings from year one.* Charlotte, NC: Centers for Medicare and Medicaid Services (CMS).

51. The analysis by the providers encompassed such issues as workflow, work processes, medical treatment protocols, drug therapies, staffing, inventories, purchasing, and other relevant data. In part, the effort led to cost savings steps that would ensure improved margins even as reimbursement levels were reduced, new strategic alliances among providers, and the cessation of certain health care services where the provider remained uncompetitive.

reposition themselves within the health care market as one who values quality, not just services rendered.[52]

Conclusion

Supported by a variety of measures used to demonstrate their contribution to the bottom line, benefits have earned their place as value propositions. Using a data and metrics approach, the plan sponsor is able to design better plans and assess their effectiveness. Ultimately, this approach will give the employer sponsor a sustained competitive advantage.

Chapter Exercises

1. Queen City Treating is a metal treating company that hardens prefabricated metal products for automobile accessories, including seat belt buckles, wheel rims, radiator caps, and other items. The company is experiencing some serious cost problems. Foreign competition, which uses better technology and has different cost structures, is taking away some of Queen City's customers by offering lower prices. As a result, Queen City is scrutinizing all of its costs. The CFO has concluded that one area that needs revamping is the high labor cost of the senior workers. The company is considering a voluntary buyout of these workers, in which they would be offered a financial incentive to leave the company before their normal retirement age. Company statistics indicate that 30 percent of the workforce has over 25 years of service and is earning the top rate of pay. The total wage difference among the highest and lowest paid production workers is about $8 per hour, and the company utilizes about two million labor production hours per year. Management believes that replacing these more senior and higher paid workers with persons at lower

---

52. The National Council on Quality Assurance evaluates TPA networks. See http://www.ncqa.org/. The employer sponsor can also evaluate the work of its TPAs and even include certain performance criteria in its contract. For example, who are the providers in the TPA network? What records do we have of their comparative clinical outcomes? Does the TPA insist on having board certified specialists in its network? The board certification is a process that ensures the specialists have completed the training and practice experience that the particular fellowship requires.

rates of pay would significantly improve the costs and productivity of the business.

a. From a labor economics standpoint, are older workers more expensive? What factors would you use to assess this issue?

b. If more senior employees leave the company, could there be a reduction in productivity? How would you calculate productivity? If there is a reduction, how long would it persist? What steps might be taken to mitigate this problem?

c. Are there viable alternatives to the voluntary buyout that would achieve the desired cost reduction? What is a range of possible solutions? How would you measure their effectiveness?

d. Describe in some detail the optimal plan design to encourage voluntary separation of the senior employees.

e. How would you determine the likelihood of your plan succeeding? How would you define success and how would you measure it?

f. What assessments would you make in choosing a method to reorganize and restaff the company after the reduction plan is implemented?

g. How would you financially evaluate and measure the effectiveness of your plan?

2. Wal-Mart has been expanding its construction of super centers, which include major food sections encompassing general grocery items, health and beauty aids, perishable produce, meat, seafood, frozen food, and deli items. The company is nonunion with labor costs at about 7.5 percent of sales versus its organized competitors' 13 percent. This, in part, allows Wal-Mart to offer prices anywhere from 6 to 10 percent below its supermarket competitors. Price sensitivity in the business is important and an overall price difference above 2 percent will cause loss of market share. You work for one of the organized companies and your CEO has directed you to begin an initiative to reduce your wage and benefit costs to be in line with Wal-Mart's levels. You know that negotiating lower wages and benefits with your unions will be a difficult task. While you have not abandoned that idea, you have decided to take a broader approach to reducing overall costs and enabling your company to offer prices that meet Wal-Mart's.

a. Describe a range of possible solutions that does not necessarily involve reducing the level of benefits and wages, but might serve to reduce the ratio of labor costs to sales and would be consistent with the overall business strategy of building sales and profits through top service, competitive prices, and great product variety.

b. What analytical steps, metrics, and assessments would you apply to each?

c. Are there possible total reward solutions that might help to attain your objective? Briefly identify them and explain.

d. How would you measure and evaluate each?

e. Select a comprehensive plan that you believe will enable your company to be price competitive without changing the level of benefits and wages.

f. Describe how you would measure and evaluate your plan.

3. Your company designs and makes electronic counting and control devices for manufacturers. It employs 300 people in the Midwest and has been in business on a privately owned basis for nine years. The industry is competitive, and your company must preserve an edge in getting new products to market faster than others, maintaining a high-quality product, offering good and sustained service to its customers, and selling at a competitive price. The company offers a privately insured health care plan, among other benefits and rewards, for all employees and their dependents. It is a traditional indemnity plan design and the cost as a percentage of total employee compensation has increased from 16 percent to 25 percent over the last two years. There is no cost to the employees for their health care. Your competitors are sponsoring much less expensive plans. Your CEO has asked you for a complete review of the health care plan and to create a design that is in line with the business strategy, is cost-effective, provides employees with choice and quality, and helps recruit and retain employees.

a. What analytical, research, data collection, and assessment steps would you undertake to fulfill this assignment? Explain in detail.

b. Can you link your health care plan to a potential increase in productivity? How? How would you measure?

c. With respect to quality, how would you make sure this element remains an integral part of your plan? How would you measure it?

d. Identify an optimal plan design, including all of its major design features, that you would recommend to the CEO. What factors would you use in measuring its value to the company?

4. Visit the following Web sites and note the differences in their respective approaches to measurement: http://www.hospitalcompare.hhs.gov/, http://www.healthgrades.com/, and http://www.leapfroggroup.org/. Suppose you are an employer in the process of selecting an appropriate health care plan for your employees. You believe that by including only the highest quality providers (doctors, clinics, and hospitals) you can offer the best and most cost-effective plan for your employees. List and briefly explain the optimal set of clinical metrics you would like to have in selecting your list of the best medical providers.

5. You are the benefits manager for a logistics company that employs 550 truck drivers, warehouse, and office employees in the Midwest. You have a standard PPO health care plan and are self-insured. Your CEO, who just returned from a regional leadership meeting, has asked you to evaluate several wellness programs discussed at her meeting. She tells you that the programs would encourage employees to maintain a healthy body weight, reduce cholesterol, quit smoking, become more physically fit, and maintain proper blood pressure levels. She would like to implement such a program at your company. Describe the detailed step-by-step approach you would follow in preparing a response with recommendation(s) to your CEO. In your analysis include: (a) How you would use data and metrics to assess the relevance of such a program for your company; (b) What impact a wellness plan might have on employee health and labor costs; (c) A description of a range of alternative designs with appropriate incentives; (d) Highlight the potential legal issues that might be applicable to your plan and how you would resolve them; (e) Describe how you would determine the prospective financial returns of a wellness program.

6. Your CEO has just returned from an executive conference and wants you to consider introducing a profit match, in addition to the current match, for the 401(k) plan. He believes it will cause employees to work harder and more efficiently. You have decided the issue needs some analysis. What are the issues that you believe need to be studied before embarking on the new plan design, and how would you use data and metrics to evaluate these issues?

7. Your CEO wants you to develop an interactive decision support program for participants in the 401(k) plan. Specifically, he wants to make sure the participants understand the probable percentage of replacement income their accounts will yield at retirement. Describe in some detail: (a) The various factors and variables you would incorporate in calculating their final account balance and relation to final pay; (b) How you would communicate this to

employees; (c) How you might use the results to consider a possible modification of the plan design; (d) What data you might need from the participants to better assess possible plan strategies; (e) What additional data you might provide to participants; (f) How you would assess whether the plan is achieving its intended results, such as enhancing recruitment, ensuring employee satisfaction, and improving overall productivity.

8. Some have argued that a 401(k) plan can sort a highly desirable, productive workforce, supposedly because workers who are willing to deny the immediate gratification of their total paycheck, opting instead to defer some to a DCP, have higher potential to be more productive workers. On the chance there is some truth to this, how would you use data, metrics, and analyses to test its validity in your company? How would you use the plan as a recruiting tool? How would you link the quality of hire and the 401(k)? What factors would be in the numerator of your ROI calculation?

9. Suppose your company offers a broad-based stock option plan for all full-time employees. Your company's stock is publicly traded and has enjoyed growth above industry peer group levels over the last ten years. Institutional shareholders, however, have questioned the usefulness of such option plans and have raised the question with your CEO. He has asked you to prepare a list of talking points he might use with the shareholder group to justify this employee benefit. What would be on your list and how would you use data and metrics to support your conclusions?

10. Here are some other health care data sources that indirectly relate to comparing provider quality. Check them out and comment on their usefulness, for example, to a participant in a HDHCP (consumer-driven) plan: http://www.docinfo.org (license and disciplinary status) and http://www.checkbook.org/ (physician recommendations of other physicians).

Equity Benefits 11

In the late 1980s in the United States, Avis Rental Car Company aired a television advertisement touting that Avis employees try harder because they are number two behind Hertz and because "they own the company."[1] The ad referred to Avis employees' participation in a stock ownership plan that gave them a significant stake in the company.

The inference to be drawn from the ad was that employee ownership can be the ultimate link between employees and shareholders. By owning stock, employees would be more committed to "total shareholder return" (TSR), a combination of stock price appreciation and dividends. More important, they would be focused on the drivers of TSR—increased sales, profits, better customer service, consistent quality, reduced costs, and improved productivity. The advantages for employee ownership, however, proved to require more than just passing out stock to employees. It required a whole new attitude of ownership within the company. And employers understood that even with substantial employee equity they still had to maintain a substantial block of public ownership in the capital markets in order to ensure stock price growth.[2] Thus, their operating

---

1. Avis' first award-winning ad, "We try harder . . . because we are No. 2," ran in 1963. In 1987, the company's ESOP obtained a majority ownership of the shares and the new ads featured employee ownership. See Top 100 Advertising Campaigns, http://www.avis.com, and http://adage.com/century/campaigns.html.

2. Unless there is a large segment of public stock ownership, the price of stock that is held only by employees becomes immune from market dynamics that can have a positive impact on price. Public ownership is driven by the desire to achieve

policies had to appeal to both constituent groups even though, ultimately, the interests of both were aligned.

Motivated by the implications of the agency theory, a labor economics principle endorsing reward practices that link the interests of owners and managers, employers surveyed the landscape of benefits that might have the same impact on large segments of the total workforce. With Avis, broad-based stock ownership became a critical marketing program. For others, stock ownership offered a new approach to business success and they searched for benefit plans that would put more stock in employees' hands.[3]

Retirement Plans and Stock[4]

There are direct and indirect ways that serve the purpose of increasing employee stock ownership. Employer sponsors of profit sharing retirement plans often fund employee accounts with company stock. Employees' shares grow each year as the plan sponsor deposits annual allocations of company stock. The employee participants maintain all the privileges of stock ownership—they receive dividends and have voting rights. Counting on stock price growth to increase their own retirements, employees are perceived to share common interests among executives and other shareholders. They have every incentive to productively apply themselves on the shop floor just "as if they were the owners of the company." Profit sharing plans are a key part of the overall strategy of successful companies like The Procter & Gamble Company (P&G) where all employees accumulate employee stock in their retirement accounts and are focused on stock price growth and the factors that drive it.[5]

---

shareholder return. This desire propels the public demand for stock, which, in turn, drives up the price of stock among those companies who demonstrate positive performance. *The roots of broadened stock ownership.* (2000, April). U.S. Congress, Joint Economic Committee.

3. See, generally, the National Center for Employee Ownership at http://www.nceo.org/, which describes the evolution of benefit plans that included stock as the key asset. See also U.S. Congress, Joint Economic Committee. (2000, April).

4. The expanded stock ownership among the public was directly related to the introduction of IRAs and 401(k) plans. See U.S. Congress, Joint Economic Committee. (2000, April). Retirement plans including profit sharing, 401(k), and employee stock ownership plans are discussed in detail in Chapter 4.

5. P&G actually began its profit sharing plan in 1887. The first plan was designed to let the employees share in the earnings. P&G later converted it to a stock-based

The introduction of 401(k) plans in the mid-1980s offered employers another opportunity to increase employee stock ownership. In the early years of these plans, company stock was one of only a few investment options available to employees.[6] Additionally, employer matches were made in company stock and, in some cases, additional stock matches were paid if the employee chose company stock as his sole investment option. While today's 401(k) plans offer many other investment opportunities, company stock remains a frequent choice among employee participants,[7] and company matches are still paid in company stock. It is estimated the introduction of 401(k), profit sharing plans, and ESOPs increased employee stock ownership to about 35 percent of U.S. employees who work for companies that have stock.[8]

Employee stock ownership plans (ESOPs) became popular in the 1980s and 1990s. In these plans, which were frequently leveraged,[9] the employer

---

profit sharing retirement plan. See information about P&G's program on its 2008 Web site at http://www.pg.com/.

6. See Report on 401(k) plans. (1998, April 13). Department of Labor, Pension and Welfare Benefits Administration, http://www.dol.gov/ebsa/.

7. See 401(k) plans: A 25-year retrospective, Col 12. No. 2. (2006, November). Investment Company Institute, Research Perspective, http://www.ici.org/.

8. See the National Center for Employee Ownership (2008) at http://www.nceo .org/. "New data show that 20 million American workers own stock in their company through a 401(k) plan, ESOP, direct stock grant, or similar plan, while 10.6 million hold stock options. That means that 17 percent of the total workforce, but 34.9 percent of those who work for companies that have stock, own stock through some kind of benefit plan, while 9.3 percent of the workforce, but 18.6 percent of those in companies with stock, hold stock options." Also see Kruse, D., & Blasi, J. (1995, September). *Employee ownership, employee attitudes, and firm performance.* National Bureau of Economic Research, NBER Working paper No. 5227. This research showed some positive relationships between employee ownership and firm results, although ownership did not affect all relevant employee behaviors. "Attitudinal and behavioral studies tend to find higher employee commitment among employee-owners but mixed results on satisfaction, motivation, and other measures. Perceived participation in decisions is not in itself automatically increased through employee ownership, but may interact positively with employee ownership in affecting attitudes. While few studies individually find clear links between employee ownership and firm performance, meta-analyses favor an overall positive association with performance for ESOPs and for several cooperative features. The dispersed results among attitudinal and performance studies indicate the importance of firm-level employee relations, human resource policies, and other circumstances" (Abstract).

9. ESOPs are explained in Chapter 4, Retirement Plans. In many cases ESOPs are leveraged, meaning the employer borrows the money to finance the purchase of

periodically funds the plan by making contributions of company stock to employee accounts.[10] If the ESOP is leveraged, the employer funds the retirement accounts with company stock as the loan is repaid. Like some profit sharing plans, the integrity of the employee's retirement income is based on the continued growth of the company stock. Fearing this might create significant investment risks to the participants, the Internal Revenue Code provides employee participants over age 55 with ten years of service the opportunity to gradually divest their company stock and reallocate their ESOP accounts with other securities.[11]

Stock Purchase Plans

Employers also can take a more direct approach to increasing employee stock ownership by simply facilitating the purchase without a brokerage commission, or offering employees a discount when they buy company stock. Further, employers can include dividend reinvestment plans (DRIPs) where the dividends on the company stock are automatically reinvested to purchase additional stock, thus increasing employee ownership. Stock purchase plans continue to be offered as benefits and in many instances are regarded highly by employees.[12] Employers see these plans as low-cost efforts to increase employee ownership.

American companies are somewhat unique in the world market because of their interest in, and in many instances commitment to, the idea of employee ownership.[13] In the 1970s they started to develop more direct benefit plans that rewarded certain segments of the workforce, particularly

its own stock, deducts the interest expense on the "loan," and then makes deductible contributions of company stock to employee retirement accounts as the loan is gradually paid off.

10. Smiley, R., Gilbert, R., Binns, D., Ludwig, R., & Rosen, C. (2007). *Employee stock ownership plans: ESOP planning, financing, implementation, law and taxation.* San Diego: Beyster Institute, Rady School of Management, University of California.

11. Section 401(a)(28)(B) of the Internal Revenue Code.

12. See Tax Guide for Investors, Overview of Employee Stock Purchase Plans at www.fairmark.com/.

13. Employee equity ownership frequently receives inhospitable tax and policy treatment in many European countries. See Vaknin, S. (2002). *The labour divide V. Employee benefits and ownership.* United Press International. http://samvak.tripod.com/pp131.html. This book generally touts employee ownership as a means to improve firm performance, but generally condemns the issuance of stock options.

executives, with specialized stock ownership plans that included unique features and new incentives. They were called stock options.

Stock Option Plans

A stock option is an offer made by the employer to an employee giving the latter the opportunity to purchase a specified number of shares of company stock at its average market price on the date of the grant. The market price is often referred to as the "strike price." The term of the grant is typically ten years,[14] with a vesting requirement of three to five years. Thus, once the employee-grantee has a vested interest in the options, he has the right to purchase the stock at the strike price for the period of the grant.

The stock option plan also can stipulate graduated vesting. For example, with a five-year graduated vesting requirement, the grantee can exercise 20 percent of the option shares granted after the first year, 40 percent after the second, and so on. Or, the options can be subject to cliff vesting, where the grantee earns the nonforfeitable right to the options after the total vesting period has elapsed.

Options are called long-term incentive plans (LTIPs) because their value usually accrues over a period of several years. The employer's strategy is to provide employees with the opportunity to acquire the same appreciation in stock value as a shareholder except, in the case of the option grantee, there is no requirement at the outset to buy the stock. Unlike the shareholder, the employee has little downside investment risk.[15] Nevertheless, the same agency theory principles designed to create a mutuality of purpose among shareholders, executives, managers, and possibly other employees are apparent with stock options.[16] In offering options, the company mantra is "if we do well, so will you."

---

14. When an employee separates (voluntarily or involuntarily) from the company, he typically will have one year to exercise those options that were vested on the date of separation. The term is cut short. For an employee who retires with vested options, the plans typically allow the employee to exercise the options over the remaining terms of his grants.

15. Stock options are usually the long-term element of an employee's total reward system. The others include salary, a short-term element, and an annual bonus that is considered a mid-term form of compensation. Having these three elements is thought to provide balance to total compensation, thus maximizing an employee's perspective on company goals and performance. See Figure 11.1.

16. The agency theory is discussed in Chapter 2, Human Resources Economics, Principles, and Actuarial Concepts Applicable to Benefits. Also see Eisenhart, M. (1989). Agency theory: An assessment and review. *Academy of Management Review, 14*(1), 57.

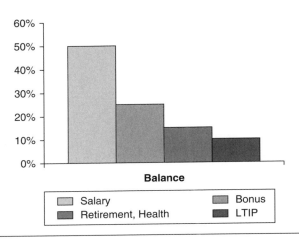

Figure 11.1   The Balanced Approach to Total Rewards

NOTE: The proportional allocation is meant for illustrative purposes only. It varies by firm, industry, and level of employees. The point is to create a reward plan that causes the firm and its workers to focus on short, medium, and long-term business perspectives. Designing rewards with this strategy in mind can fulfill all the elements of the pay and benefit models.

So, the employee is paid a fixed wage or salary and, when performance targets are met and bonus potentials realized, he can earn more. If he owns stock or has options, when the stock price increases, the employee's total compensation could rise significantly above market levels.[17] The employee who receives options is sometimes paying for them through lower, fixed compensation.[18] As commentators debate whether options enhance company performance, it is clear the lower, fixed labor expense associated with option grants does generate higher productivity to the employer.

> **Example of Stock Option and Wealth Accumulation**: An employee receives 2,000 option shares each year for 20 years. The options include a three-year cliff vesting and a ten-year term. The employee exercises each tranche of options as they near their ten-year term. The stock price increases an average 10 percent per year for 20 years.

17. Performance-based compensation in many instances would include an annual bonus that is paid as a percentage of salary and upon the attainment of certain sales, profits, EBITDA, or other targets.

18. This is called the principle of compensating differentials and is discussed in Chapters 2 and 6, Human Resource Economics, Principles, and Actuarial Concepts Applicable to Benefits and Health Care, respectively.

> The first year, the strike price was $20 per share. At the end of 24 years, the stock price has risen to $122.32 and the employee will have accumulated $1.3 million in value. This represents the cumulative differences between the strike price and the market price. It does not include deductions for income taxes. This potential for creating wealth can be optimized by the employer in his effort to recruit, retain, and motivate his workforce.

Studies show that between the years 1992 and 2000, just prior to the stock market's dramatic drop, the cumulative value of options granted by 200 Fortune 500 companies equaled nearly $25 billion. During this period, up to 20 percent of the options were granted to nonmanagement employees.[19]

The mechanics of the exercise process involve several steps. If options are vested, the employee can notify the company that he wishes to exercise. He advances the cash for the shares to the employer, multiplying the strike price times the number of shares to be exercised. The employer then awards the actual shares to the employee. The difference between the strike price and the current market price is called the "option spread."

> **Example of Stock Option Exercise:** 1,000 options shares are awarded to an employee. The strike price is $20 per share, they have a ten-year term, and five-year graduated vesting. The second year after the grant, the employee can exercise 40 percent of his options or 400 shares. The market price of the stock at the end of the second year is $30 per share. The employee exercises by paying his employer $20 times 400, or $8,000. He is granted the 400 shares that have a value of $12,000. The spread for the exercise is $4,000 and it is taxed as ordinary income. His 400 shares have a base of $30 per share and, if he holds the stock for one year or more and sells it at a higher price than $30, the gain on his stock sale will be taxed at the long-term capital gains rate.

In some cases, the employee may not want to expend the cash to exercise the shares. Instead, he can "swap" shares for the options and pay no cash. For example, let's say the employee wants to exercise 1,000 shares with a strike price of $10 per share. The current stock price is $20 per share. The employee can agree to use the value of a certain percentage of

19. Opdyke, J., & Higgins, M. (2002, August 7). What the new options rules mean for your pay. *The Wall Street Journal*, D1.

exercised shares to pay for the exercise, thereby swapping some shares for the transaction. In this example, to exercise the employee must advance $10 multiplied by 1,000 shares, or $10,000. Or, the employee could agree to exercise without advancing any money, but would have to swap or trade 500 shares with a current price of $20 per share in order to receive the remaining 500 exercised shares.

> **Example of Normal Exercise:** An employee has 1,000 vested options with a strike price of $10 per share. Current market price is $20 per share. The employee advances $10,000 and will receive 1,000 shares of company stock.
>
> **Example of Stock Swap:** An employee has 1,000 vested options with a strike price of $10 per share. Current market price is $20 per share. The employee advances no cash, but agrees to give back to the company (or "swap") 500 shares with a value of $20 per share (or $10,000) and will receive only 500 shares of company stock.

In some cases where the option plan permits, the employee can exercise options on a "cashless" basis. In this instance, the employee advances no cash, but simply requests the "spread" be awarded in cash. The employee receives no shares, and the employer simply buys and then sells the shares included in the option, and awards the spread in cash to the option holder minus fees and taxes. Some argue the cashless exercise process undermines the purpose of awarding options, which is to increase employee ownership of company stock. Others argue that the employee is simply put in the same position as a shareholder and, likewise, should be permitted to sell his stock when the price increases. Let's see how this works.

> **Example of Cashless Exercise:** An employee has 1,000 shares of vested options with a strike price of $10 per share and the current market price is $20 per share. He decides to exercise on a cashless basis and notifies the company. The company, or its agent, "lends" the cash to the employee to buy the stock at the current price and then sell it, awarding the employee the $10 per share spread in cash. The employee will pay a small borrowing and transaction fee, and will receive a check, less withholding, amounting to the spread times the number of shares: 1,000 x $10 = $10,000.

This brings us to taxes. There are essentially two types of options: nonqualified stock options (NQSOs) and incentive stock options (ISOs). NQSOs function as described above and comprise the vast majority of options awarded by U.S. companies. The spread is subject to ordinary income tax upon exercise, as well as Social Security and Medicare taxes. There is no long-term capital gains tax on the options. Once the employee owns the stock and keeps it for more than one year, however, any gain on the sale will be taxed as long-term capital gains.[20]

If the employer chooses to offer ISOs, there is no income tax on the exercise. The tax is postponed until the shares are sold. Upon sale of the stock, the employee would pay income tax on the original spread and long-term capital gains on the stock price appreciation occurring after the exercise. The accounting and corporate tax treatment is quite different for ISOs, however, and there is a clear incentive from the employer's standpoint to use NQSOs.[21]

What are the costs of options to the employer? Until recently, the employer did not include the value of options in his financial statements until they were "in the money," at which time they would be reported as a footnote on the income statement. In other words, until there was an actual spread on a grant of options, the employer would not consider or report it as compensation expense. Since there was no cash compensation or other real accounting expense, options were treated by employers as free until the market price of the stock exceeded the strike price.

Because of this perceived low-cost aspect, as well as the compensation rationale, options represented an attractive form of long-term compensation for the employer. Nevertheless, there is a cost or "value." There are several approaches to calculating this value. Since the employee receiving options is able to obtain "a future right of ownership" of company stock without advancing cash to actually buy the stock until the exercise, he saves the "cost of cash." He can preserve his exercise price for up to ten years (or whatever the term of the options is), invest it, and when the options are "in the money," exercise.[22] Thus, the cost or value of the options to the employer can be calculated by imputing the cost of cash savings, or discount value, extended to the employee.

Another approach to determining the cost of options is to measure the dilution cost. When an employee receives options without purchasing the

---

20. See *Taxes on non-qualified options*. (2007). http://www.smartmoney.com/; also see http://www.mystockoptions.com/. The exercise price becomes the new "base" price used to calculate future gain.

21. In most cases the employer cannot deduct the cost or value of the ISOs, and while the employee is not taxed until the sale of the stock, there are strong possibilities that the difference between the strike price and the exercise price will be subject to the dreaded Alternative Minimum Tax. See Learn About Law, The Manager's Guide to Stock Option Plans at www.learnaboutlaw.com/newsletter.

22. The compensation cost to the employer in this case would be the discount rate times the strike price of the options times the number of shares granted. The discount rate should include a calculation relating to the probability of the exercise.

stock, the shareholders' ownership is diluted, as there are more shares issued without any concomitant increase in the value of the company. For example, if the company enjoys annual earnings per share of $3.50 and the company shares are increased by 1,000 due to a grant of options, earnings per share will decrease by .0035 cents per share. If, however, the grant of options preserves cash flows for the company due to the payment of lower cash compensation, there should be offsets to the cost of dilution. With broad-based options grants, or mega grants to executives, this dilution of earnings per share is more apparent, especially to institutional shareholders. And measuring the impact of dilution attributable to options is more easily and precisely calculated.[23]

Despite these varied approaches, there was an aggressive, ongoing move to standardize the costing of options on the date they are granted, and to require the cost to be included in financial statements of publicly traded companies. The underlying rationale among many analysts and institutional shareholders was that stock options involved compensation and had value to the employee and cost to the employer. Therefore, it was incumbent upon U.S. companies to disclose this cost in a uniform and consistent manner. The problem is options values are based on future appreciation of the stock price, and anticipating their value involves some speculation. No one can determine whether the stock price will increase.

The pressure to find a solution continued and accounting experts looked to a formula-based approach using past data and some probabilities that would enable companies to reliably calculate a predicted value of options at the time of grant. They focused on the Black-Scholes method that had been developed and used to value options trades in capital markets.[24] It uses factors such as the current stock price, strike price, time to expiration, volatility of the stock price, and risk-free rate. After much controversy and a push from the international accounting organizations, the Financial Accounting Standards Board (FASB) implemented a new rule (FAS 123R) in 2005 mandating that a "fair value" method be used in calculating the cost of stock options and requiring their inclusion in financial statements. Among the formulas that can be used in assessing the value is Black-Scholes. After June 2005, when a company awarded options, it immediately had to charge them as an expense based on a fair value method.[25]

---

23. Pottruck, D. (2004, March 10). The competitive option. *The Wall Street Journal.*

24. For a good explanation, including illustrations and models of Black-Scholes, see Rubash, K. (2007). *A study of option pricing models.* Bradley University, http://bradley.bradley.edu/~arr/bsm/model.html.

25. The SEC allows a compliance deferral for their version of FAS ("SFAS") 123R until the fiscal year following June 15, 2005. See SEC Final Rule: Amendment to the Compliance Date for SFAS 123R at www.sec.gov/.

Since many companies awarded options broadly across their workforce, it was thought the requirement to expense them at the time of grant would have a significant impact on stated earnings. Many analysts predicted the new FASB rule would cause most companies to simply stop awarding options and find different ways of using equity as a form of compensation.[26] The specific prediction was that companies would switch from options to restricted stock, restricted stock units, performance shares, and stock appreciation rights (SARs).[27] This did happen, but a good number of major employers, such as P&G, continued to offer options.[28] Not surprisingly, many analysts who monitor company performance discounted the impact of the option expense on earnings and continued to look at more relevant financial performance factors connected to the business operation. Also, the stock market rebounded from the 2000 slump and options regained their role as a benefit that could generate new values for employees.[29] Those who abandoned options typically migrated to other equity benefits such as restricted stock and SARs.

---

26. Simon, R. (2004, April 28). With options on the outs, alternatives get a look. *The Wall Street Journal*, D2.

27. Simon R. (2004). Restricted stock units involve a promise to grant shares of the company stock at the end of the vesting period. The grantee, however, does not receive dividends or take on any of the rights of a stock owner until the units vest. Performance shares are simply awards of company shares that vest upon the achievement of company results.

28. According to the National Center of Employee Ownership, in February 2008 there were 3,000 broad-based stock option plans and nine million option holders in U.S. companies. The report also indicates this represents a slight decrease from earlier, recent years, but it is not known how many companies have shifted from options to other equity plans such as restricted stock. See *A statistical profile of employee ownership*. NCEO, http://www.nceo.org. The Bureau of Labor Statistics, however, reported in 2003 that 8 percent of the private workforce participated in stock options. The same report for March 2006 indicated that the number remained at 8 percent. See *Compensation survey of employee benefits in private industry*. (2003, March and 2006, March). U.S. Department of Labor, Bureau of Labor Statistics.

29. Simon, R. (2004, February 10). Stock options make a comeback. *The Wall Street Journal*, D1. This report showed that large percentages of granted stock options were "in the money" as of 2004, which was not the case in the years after 2000. See also *Issue brief: The future of broad-based equity plans*. (2007, January). National Center for Employee Ownership, that found a modest reduction in the number of options issued in general and about one-third of 90 high-tech companies replacing their options plans with restricted stock or restricted stock units.

Restricted Stock

This equity benefit involves a direct award of company stock with restrictions that usually involve the passage of time or vesting. For example, the company awards an employee 300 shares of restricted stock and the restrictions lapse upon the passage of three years. There is no required purchase of stock by the employee and no exercise. During the period when the restrictions are in effect, the employee has ownership rights to dividends and voting. When the restrictions lapse, the value of the stock is taxed to the employee as ordinary income, or he can elect to have the restricted stock taxed at grant based on its current value.[30] The price at grant then becomes the basis for the stock and it is not taxed again until it is sold. Provided it has been held for more than one year, the tax at sale will be treated as long-term capital gains. From a company standpoint, the restricted stock grant is expensed based on the actual value of the stock at the time of grant. There is no need to speculate about the future price or to apply the Black-Scholes method to calculate its value. The grant of restricted stock has even less downside risk for the employee. Its value is not totally dependent on the increased price of the stock as it is with options, because the employee receives the full value of the shares instead of the spread. Thus, there are typically fewer shares of restricted stock granted to employees than options. So long as the stock has some value, the employee's grant does as well. With restricted stock, because fewer options are issued than stock options, there is less dilution for shareholders.[31]

> Example of NQSOs and Restricted Stock:
>
> Employee receives 1,000 shares of NQSOs with a strike price of $10 per share; after vesting the market price is $20 per share.
>
> Value = Spread x Number of Shares ($10 x 1,000 = $10,000)
>
> Employee receives 500 shares of restricted stock with a market price after restrictions lapse of $20 per share.
>
> Value = Number of Shares x Market Price (500 × $20 = $10,000)
>
> The employer awarded half the number of shares of restricted stock, resulting in less dilution, and provided the same value to the employee.

---

30. This is referred to as an Internal Revenue Code §83(b) election.

31. As mentioned earlier, some companies that award restricted stock give "restricted stock units" instead of the shares. This means the employee receives a right to own the described shares of stock when the restrictions lapse. Prior to that time, he has no ownership rights.

Stock Appreciation Rights

Stock Appreciation Rights (SARs) are another long-term incentive benefit that puts equity interests into the hands of employees. They differ from stock options and restricted stock because no stock is actually transferred to the employee. SARs are simply promises by the employer to pay a recipient the value of the difference between the price of the stock on the date of the grant and the price of the stock after vesting. Instead of exercising an option and purchasing the stock at the strike price, however, when the employee "redeems" (or exercises) his SARs, the employer simply awards the difference (the spread) in cash or in company stock.

Thus, no securities or security legal requirements are involved in the grant itself, unless the employer stipulates that the spread must be paid in stock. The FASB accounting rule is applicable to SARs that must be redeemed in stock, so there is an expense for the employer equal to its estimated future value. There is less dilution, however, because the employer redeems fewer shares. Only the equivalent value of the spread is paid to the employee in shares of company stock. SARs carry similar design features as NQSO plans. There is usually a vesting requirement, a term during which the appreciation can be claimed, and employees share an identity with shareholders because they have a common interest to improve the stock price. SARs involve a less complicated transaction than, for example, cashless exercises of NQSOs in that there are no loans to fund the exercise. Also, since the employee is not required to advance any funds to exercise a SAR, there is a better chance he will hold the awarded shares for the long-term because there is no need to swap or finance the exercise.[32]

> **Example of Stock Appreciation Rights:** The employee is granted 1,000 SARs at a price of $10 per share. When the SARs are vested, the market price of the stock is $20 per share. The employee exercises and receives 500 shares of company stock, which represents the value of the $10 spread times 1,000 shares divided by the current market price per share (1,000 x $10) ÷ $20 = 500 shares. The employee's spread is taxed as ordinary income and Medicare and Social Security (if applicable) taxes are also deducted.

32. For excellent insights into stock options, SARs, restricted stock, and other equity awards, see http://www.mystockoptions.com/. Registration is required, but there are some free pages that are both illustrative and informative.

Some Issues Pertaining to Equity Awards

While the stated purpose of options is to align the interests of employees and shareholders, there is some question whether this actually occurs. Typically, options were the exclusive province of the executive group. Senior executives, for example, were thought to have a clearer influence over all the ultimate drivers of the stock price—sales, earnings, cash flows, and good shareholder relations. As companies began to issue options and restricted stock to a broader employee base, however, the link between their work and the stock price became less clear.

The relevant labor economic theory is called line of sight. A stock option has value only if the stock price increases. The line of sight theory questions if the person on the shop floor or in the retail market sees the connection between his work and the stock price, or if the line of sight is too long for him to make the connection. Institutional shareholders have had difficulty with three features of stock options: (1) broad-based option plans diluted their ownership and earnings per share, and had no proven direct impact on the behavior of nonexecutive employees; (2) too many option shares were granted to top executives; and (3) options must be charged as an expense at the time of the grant.[33] This last problem, of course, has been remedied by FASB's new accounting rule.

With respect to their first problem, there is a very long line of sight between the stock price appreciation and the work behavior of mid- and lower-level employees. Can this be bridged? PepsiCo initiated a broad-based option plan in the early 1990s called "SharePower."[34] It used a comprehensive employee communication program to shorten the line of sight. A number of signs and postings constantly reminded option holders to "turn off the lights," "carefully handle product," and "don't waste supplies." The implied consequence: these cost-saving measures can increase profits and help increase your share power. Employees were shown the connection between their work and the potential increase in the value of their options. PepsiCo believed that effective communication programs could impact employee behaviors positively, when the connection between their work and the drivers of stock price appreciation were demonstrated.

Options do have other values to shareholders. As we discussed earlier, they allow the employer to dispense less cash compensation and to benefit from lower labor costs. This occurs when the employer's compensation philosophy is based on paying salaries that are below competitive rates,

33. See Murphy, K., & Hall, B. (2003, Summer). The trouble with stock options. *Journal of Economic Perspectives, 17*(3).

34. See Thornburg, L. (1993, August). Growing up with Pepsi. *HR Magazine*, http://findarticles.com/.

but offering results-based variable compensation such as bonuses and options that could boost the employees' total compensation over competitors' levels. This is particularly noticeable in new or start-up companies that cannot afford high cash compensation levels, but wish to offer the employees an opportunity to accumulate significant wealth provided the company is successful.[35]

The author's professional experience has been that options offer the employer an opportunity to speak with his employees on an entirely different level. Stock price is affected by sales, profits, and the company's competitive position within its industry. Broad equity participation among the workforce allows the employer to communicate with them about sales, expenses, new competition, analyst reports on the company, customer service inputs, raw materials, logistics, marketing, and a variety of other unique business issues, and to share their insights. Ultimately, this new level of exchange inures to the benefit of the employer because his workers not only better comprehend the total business, but can actively participate in discussions about how to deal with its challenges.[36]

Mega grants of options to executives have been problematic for many companies and their shareholders. When an executive receives a stock option grant of 1,000,000 shares with a traditional vesting schedule and term, the slightest increase in stock value can generate an enormous amount of wealth for that executive versus the dilution in earnings per share for the institutional shareholders. Thus, the interests of the shareholders and senior executives are not aligned. An executive whose performance has been less than stellar, perhaps contributing to an anemic total shareholder return, is rewarded with an annual mega grant of options.[37]

---

35. In a nonpublicly traded company, the employer can establish an option plan for his employees. For an excellent discussion on how these options should be valued, see Cron, W., & Hayes, R. (2007, Spring). Valuation of stock options of nonpublicly traded companies. *Mid-American Journal of Business, 22*(1), 11–19.

36. Lublin, J., (2007, April 9). Ten ways to restore investor confidence in compensation. *The Wall Street Journal,* R1. It should be noted, however, that sharing of confidential company information with a broad employee base of option holders could create problems with the SEC's insider trading rules, which limit the trading of company stock by employees who have access to material nonpublic information that could significantly relate to corporate developments. Contrary to popular belief, any employee, not just an executive, can be an "insider." This is called the 10(b)(5) rule. See http://www.sec.gov/, and go to "insider trading."

37. The issue of mega grants and abuses of options granted to executives can relate to how the option plan is administered by the Board of Directors and, in particular, the Compensation Committee. From a corporate governance standpoint, the Board and its delegated committees have the responsibility to approve option plan designs, the total shares to be allocated to a plan, and specific grants to senior

Incentive compensation, such as bonuses and options, should have the clear potential to reward recipients. Yet, there are no guarantees of stock price appreciation for either shareholders or option grantees. Over time, if the stock price does not appreciate and options become worthless, the elements of the benefits model, specifically those dealing with external competition and positive impact on behavior, are not fulfilled. The employee has received less fixed compensation and his hope of gaining value and wealth through bonuses or options has not been achieved. When the strike price of the options continues to exceed the market price, the options are referred to as being "underwater."

When this happens the employer has a few choices.[38] He can do nothing and say this is one of the inherent risks of incentive compensation, thereby putting the options holders in the same shoes as shareholders. Or, he can reissue the same number of options to his employees, but with a lower strike price equal to the current lower market price, which will have a better chance of having some value during their term. In this case the previous grants of underwater options are cancelled. Ordinarily, this solution does not sit well with shareholders, since it results in continued shareholder dilution and is inconsistent with the risks they endure. They cannot turn in their shares and get a second chance to achieve stock price appreciation.

Another solution for underwater options is repricing the worthless options at the current market price. The strike price is reduced to align with the market price. This usually receives a similar negative reaction among shareholders.

In early 2000, Microsoft employees held thousands of underwater options. They were no longer serving to motivate or reward the employees. As a solution to the problem, the company facilitated the purchase of the options from the employees at a cash price estimated to represent their long-term potential value. This "scrap value" was far less than the value that would have been realized had the stock price increased substantially. But their approach returned some value to the employees and had elements of fairness and rationality.[39]

Options which have become valueless for one reason or another have led to some abuses, particularly among company executives who manipulated their grant of options to be "backdated" to a point in time when the market price had declined. The abuse became apparent when a study

---

officers. How effectively these directors manage their responsibilities bears a close relationship to how ethically the plans are administered.

38. See *New technique for handling underwater options.* (2003, August 22). www.morganlewis.com/ (Law Flash).

39. See *New technique for handling underwater options.* (2003).

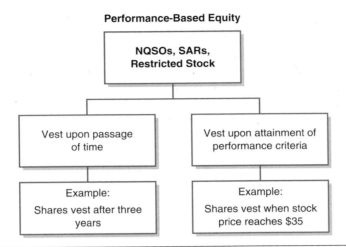

Figure 11.2   Comparison of Traditional Vesting and Performance-Based Vesting of Equity Awards

showed a large number of corporate executives were granted options on a date when the stock had dropped to a very low point. It seemed to be perfect timing, though in many cases the market timing had nothing to do with it; nor did luck.[40] The options were backdated without proper disclosure, giving the executive a disproportionate advantage over other shareholders, and better ensuring a future spread between the strike price and the future stock price. This practice has been investigated by state and federal security agencies and is considered to be illegal.[41]

40. Forelle, C., & Bandler, J. (2006, March 18–19). The perfect payday, *The Wall Street Journal*, A1. It should be noted that "insiders" have the opportunity to dispose of their stock using a pre-established trading plan that identifies the number of shares to be sold on specific dates and based on specific price changes. See SEC Rule 10b5-1. This rule obviates the sale of company stock based on insider information.

41. There are considerable and recurring issues pertaining to executive compensation in the United States. It is considered by many to be excessive. The abuse of options is only one element of this problem. Large severance awards for departing executives, opulent and sometime irrelevant perquisites, substantial retirement benefits far exceeding ERISA and IRS limits, the lack of meaningful performance standards that determine bonus and other compensation elements, and the failure to require shareholder approval of some pay practices have been the targets of executive compensation critics. See Lubin, J. (2007, April 9). The ways to restore investor confidence in compensation. *The Wall Street Journal*, R1.

There are other concerns shareholders have about senior executives abusing stock option programs. One is the temptation to influence short-term results to facilitate quick returns on options. These have led to some proposals for reform. For example, one would require senior executives to retain a high proportion of their options for a longer period before exercising. This could have the effect of causing executives to seek long-term company results and not be tempted to manage short-term results and personal gain by using quick exercises of options.[42] Many of the concerns over stock options and other equity awards can be mitigated with the issuance of performance-based equity.

Performance-Based Equity Awards

What happens if options or restricted stock are linked to the achievement of certain performance goals? This would resonate better with shareholders who are concerned about dilution and "risk-free stock ownership" for executives and others receiving equity awards. Let's take a look at how this would work.

One method is to tie vesting to goal achievement and performance measures instead of the passage of time. Goals can include the achievement of stock price increases at or above industry or market benchmarks. This approach is called "indexing," and it assures shareholders that they will enjoy more significant share price increases before options are vested among employees.[43]

Another way would be to make the vesting of equity—such as options, stock appreciation rights, or restricted stock—dependent upon the achievement of other goals—such as earnings per share, profit and sales, or certain unit business targets. These incentives transform the equity award into a more dynamic, performance-based incentive that can have a shorter line of sight and a better chance of motivating positive employee behaviors. They also "fund" themselves because they are dependent upon real value creation. Such awards are usually well received by shareholders.

---

42. Pottruck, D. (2004, March 10). The competitive option. *The Wall Street Journal.*

43. Indexing means that options (or other incentives) vest based on the attainment of targeted stock prices that are expected by analysts and the employer, according to industry peer group stock performance.

> **Example of Performance-Based Options:** The employee is awarded 1,000 shares of indexed NQSOs, which vest on a date the market price increases of the stock exceed that of its peer group over a given period of time. They also could vest when the market price of the stock exceeds analysts' projections over a given period, or when earnings per share exceed certain levels. The same conditions can apply to restricted stock[1] or SARs. Performance requirements that trigger vesting, or the lapse of restrictions, can be tied to unit profits, sales, or other relevant performance measures.[2]
>
> ---
>
> 1. The accounting for performance-based restricted stock is more complex and less favorable to the employer. The compensation charge will be measured at grant but will be adjusted for grants that do not vest due to turnover or unfulfilled performance conditions, unless the performance condition is based on a target stock price or total shareholder return. See *Last call for preferable stock option accounting*. (2004). Watson Wyatt, http://www.watsonwyatt.com/us/pubs/insider/.
>
> 2. A review of several large cap companies' proxy statements showed performance-based stock options vested upon the attainment of such criteria as EBITDA, net income, operating income, return on shareholders' equity, profit margin enhancements, improvements of capital structure, return on assets, stock price, market share, sales, and others.

Does Equity Compensation Work?[44]

Does equity really have a positive effect on employee behavior?[45] We know it represents a more flexible and, perhaps, less costly form of compensation,

---

44. While some developed and developing countries have issued stock to employees whose organizations have been privatized, generally speaking, equity is not as popular a benefit in other countries as it is in the United States. We will discuss this in Chapter 13, Global Benefits.

45. The general conclusion is that employee ownership can have some positive effects on certain aspects of employee behavior, but there is no proven link between employee ownership and firm results. Kruse, D., & Blasi, J. (1995, September). *Employee ownership, employee attitudes, and firm performance.* National Bureau of Economic Research, NBER Working paper No. 5227. See also Conte, M., Blasi, J., Kruse, D., & Jampani, R. (1996). Financial returns of public

and it allows the employer to communicate with his workforce on a new level. We also know that equity compensation offers the employee an opportunity to accumulate significant wealth over time.[46] Additionally, options can reduce the competitive stress on the employer to enrich cash compensation levels and retirement plans to ensure higher income replacement rates. Further, we know instinctively that stock options and SARs can enhance the recruitment and retention of productive and motivated employees. How do we know this?

The author's experience with respect to a broad-based option plan is that it can cause people to "talk and think like owners." The experience of others with similar plans is the same.[47] Companies like W.L. Gore & Associates, Green Mountain Coffee Roasters, Atlas Container Corporation, Publix Supermarkets, Starbucks, and many others concur that broad-based employee-ownership plans have a positive effect on employee behaviors. The programs, however, must be part of a new management model, one that not only shows employees what activities in their workplace help drive good business results and stock price appreciation, but also illustrates how employee involvement in the business decision-making process can be essential to the enterprise's success.[48] A culture of ownership should pervade the workplace.

ESOP companies: Investor effects vs. manager effects. *Financial Analysis Journal, 52*(4), 51–61. The authors conclude that ESOPs actually reduce financial returns, but the presence of an ESOP remains a good signal for investors to buy the stock. Similar findings were made with respect to cash flows by Ducy, M., Iqbal, Z., & Akhigbe, A. (1997, June). Employee stock ownership plans and cash flow performance of publicly traded companies. *American Business Review*. It should be noted, however, that ESOPs are frequently defensive maneuvers by management to ward off a takeover or to divest a unit of a company. There are often no other significant changes in management practices that would engage the new owner-employees in the strategic business issues facing the company.

46. See Lublin, J. (2007, April 9). Share the wealth. *The Wall Street Journal*, R5. Heartland Payment Systems' CEO has designed unique commission and option plans that have created significant wealth among a large segment of the workforce.

47. According to a Bureau of Labor Statistics study in 2006, about 8 percent of the workforce had access to stock options. Among white-collar worker occupations, 11 percent had access. The percentage was 6 among blue-collar occupations and 3 percent in service occupations. Firms with more than 100 employees made options available to 13 percent of their workers. See *Stock options, national compensation survey update*. (2006). Bureau of Labor Statistics, whttp://ww.bls.dol.gov.

48. Rosen, C., Case, J., & Staubus, M. (2005). *Equity: Why employee ownership is good for business*. Boston: Harvard Business School Press.

According to some contemporary writers, companies with such a culture of equity ownership are improving their competitiveness daily.[49] The employer must do more than just hand out stock. He must communicate and involve his employees in discussions about the company's competitive challenges. He must use equity to cause his workforce to share the same interests in defending and growing their business. Broad-based equity ownership can create an employee group of committed, interested, and involved employees who have the opportunity to gain considerable wealth over a career provided business success is achieved. Equity can be an opportunity to achieve new levels of business success.

The Van Meter Company in Cedar Rapids, Iowa, is 100 percent company owned.[1] Many employees had no idea what stock was or what an employee owner was, and said they would rather have a couple hundred extra dollars in their paycheck. The CFO realized that employee ownership was not just passing out stock and giving employees their annual ownership statements. He and others started a series of programs to cause employees to think about what they could do to increase the price of the stock. First, they made sure the employees understood what stock was and how the employee ownership plan worked. Next, they began to discuss with them how even the smallest changes in the company's operation could affect the stock. Employees were encouraged to find ways to cut costs, and the linkage to results and stock price were demonstrated. The company developed a "Work 10, Get 5 Free" program that showed how stock appreciation and company contributions could equal five years of annual income over a ten-year period of work. Employee committees worked on new approaches to logistics, cost savings measures, and celebrated new participants by giving them a jacket with the words, "I am in." The CFO is convinced their culture of ownership has contributed to higher profits and a steady progression in their stock price. Employee turnover has declined by 60 percent and employees are focused on the business, stock, and their accounts.

---

1. Covel, S. (2008, February 7). How to get workers to think and act like owners. *The Wall Street Journal*, B6.

This vignette clearly demonstrates the potential of equity in the hands of employees. It takes a lot of work and focus, but equity can positively

---

49. See Rosen (2005).

affect employee behaviors, impact the drivers of successful business, and add value to the enterprise.

Chapter Exercises

1. You are the senior HR executive at your company, which provides outsourced HR services to over 100 employers in the United States. Most of your employees work at call centers where the employees of your clients inquire about their employer's benefits and reward practices, make elections in their plans, and enroll and withdraw from various benefit plans. Your company also conducts telephone-based employee surveys and develops Web-based employee selection and performance evaluation systems for its clients. The CEO of your parent company is planning a "spin-off" and issuance of publicly traded stock. She wants you to help decide whether to grant stock options or some other equity benefit for some or all of the employees. Develop a detailed outline you would use in presenting to the CEO. Include such issues as the pros and cons of such a plan, a range of alternative designs, and a method to evaluate possible financial returns of such a measure.

2. Your employer has awarded you 3,000 shares of SARs with a strike price of $20 per share. When SARs are exercised, the company converts the gain and compensates the employee with shares of company stock. The SARs have a five-year graduated and equal vesting schedule and a ten-year term. On the third anniversary of the grant, the market price is $25 per share and you decide to exercise your SARs. (a) Briefly explain the tax consequences, if any, of your exercise. (b) Briefly explain how you would calculate the "spread" owed to you on exercise. (c) Briefly explain how you would calculate the number of shares you would receive.

3. You have received a grant of 2,000 NQSO shares. They vest on a graduated basis over a five-year period. The strike price was $10 per share. It is now three years since the grant and the current price is $20 per share. You decide to exercise on a cashless basis. (a) How many shares can you exercise? (b) What will be your "pretax" gain on the exercise? (c) How will the options be taxed? (d) Assume the price has increased only $0.50 since the grant. What financial reason would there be to exercise now?

4. Your CEO likes the idea of granting performance-based stock options, but she wants to include individual employee performance criteria in your plan. What problems might this cause and how

would you best design a plan that would accommodate her request but ameliorate the problems?

5. Your company is a large multinational enterprise with operations in three developed (host) countries. You utilize a number of expatriates who move to host countries for one to three years and then return to the corporate headquarters (home country). You are aware of a number of different cultural, legal, and taxation differences with respect to equity benefits that exist in your host countries. You would like, however, to provide a consistent package of benefits including stock options to all of your top management, including expatriates, in the home and host counties. Is this a good idea? Why? Is the benefits model relevant here? What are the cultural and legal barriers? How would you overcome them? Choose three host countries and do some research on their legal and tax treatment of stock options. Also, research the potential reaction among host country nationals to such a program. Prepare a list of discussion points you can use in reviewing the issue with your CEO. See http://www.nceo.org/. See also European Commission rules on employee ownership, *The European Federation of Employee Share Ownership* at http://www.efesonline.org. This is an umbrella group promoting employee ownership in Europe.

Government-Sponsored and Mandated Benefits 12

Social Security Retirement Benefit (USA)

Art Jones is about to celebrate his 62nd birthday. He has worked for two companies during his 40-year career as an electrician and, along with his two employers, has contributed a payroll tax to the U.S. Social Security Administration to help finance his retirement benefit. Currently, Art contributes 6.2 percent of his pay up to the maximum annual taxable income of $102,000; his employer contributes the same. With overtime opportunities, his income has reached the maximum on two occasions in the last five years.

Art knows he is eligible to receive an early retirement benefit at age 62; however, if he chooses 62 instead of full retirement age at 66, his retirement income will be actuarially reduced for life. Assuming he will enjoy the same life expectancy under either scenario, early retirement would mean an additional four years of benefits during his lifetime. Also, he has learned that if he continued to work beyond age 62 and earned over a certain amount, his Social Security benefit would be proportionately reduced. Further, even though he contributed to the fund by paying a payroll tax, his benefit also would be subject to federal and state income tax. So, while he would like to retire now and start collecting his Social Security benefit, he is not sure how to go about making the right decision. Should he wait until he is 66 and not incur any offsets to his benefit regardless of earned income, or should he start receiving benefits now?

Before examining Art's question, let's look briefly at how Social Security Retirement[1] works in the United States. It is essentially a defined benefit plan funded by a payroll tax imposed on workers and employers.[2] While there has been a surplus of revenues in the Social Security Trust Fund in the United States for many years, it is a "pay-as-you-go" (PAYGO) program. The Social Security Administration's actuaries calculate, among other items, the amount of reserves needed to pay benefits in the near future. Excess amounts over and above their calculation are considered to be part of the federal budget and the government borrows against the surplus for a variety of expenses and credits the Social Security Trust with bonds that earn a modest interest rate.

Unlike employer-sponsored defined benefit plans, the monies collected for Social Security are not invested in capital markets, even though such investments could increase the financing potential of the fund.[3] It is expected the surplus will continue until 2018, at which time the taxes collected will be insufficient to pay benefits and reserves and bonds will be liquidated to fulfill this purpose. This will continue until 2042, at which time the deficit will render Social Security unable to pay its promised benefits, culminating in benefits being severely cut and taxes rising substantially.[4] The demographic causes for this looming financial failure are lower recent birth rates resulting in fewer workers, a surge of persons nearing

1. The Social Security Act was signed into law in 1935. The benefit is described in the law as "Social Security Old Age, Survivors, and Disability Insurance." It was passed, in large part, due to the devastating economic depression in the United States and was modeled after several European Social Security plans that had been implemented earlier. In addition to retirement income, as the name above implies, the Social Security Act also provides for income benefits to disabled workers at any age, spouses at retirement age, surviving children of deceased participants, as well their spouses caring for the children. There are over 50 million beneficiaries under the system. See *Social Security—A Brief History.* (2005). SSA Publication No. 21-059, http://www.socialsecurity.gov/history/. Social Security is largely a work-related benefit, however, and coverage is dependent upon the participant working in "covered employment" and paying payroll taxes for at least 40 quarters. In this chapter we will discuss the "retirement" benefit of the Social Security system.

2. Currently, the tax is 6.2 percent of earnings for the employer and the employee, respectively, up to a cap of $102,000 (2008) of annual income. SSA adjusts this amount for inflation.

3. There is reluctance among policymakers to allow the government to invest retirement funds in the stock market because of the potential impact it could have on the dynamics of the market.

4. See 2007 Social Security Trustees' Report, http://www.ssa.gov/OACT/TR/; *An actuarial perspective on the 2007 Social Security Trustees' report.* (2007, May). American Academy of Actuaries, http://www.actuary.org/.

retirement age who were born after World War II called the "baby boomers,"[5] and a higher life expectancy resulting in longer retirements. Thus, there are fewer workers paying taxes for a proportionately larger number of retirees who are living longer.

A person is eligible to receive retirement benefits under Social Security if they have worked in "covered employment" for at least ten years (40 quarters) with earnings of at least $870 per year. The employment is considered "covered" if the employer and employee made payroll contributions to Social Security during this period. Currently, most employers are required to withhold payroll taxes on behalf of their workers.[6] The benefit is calculated based on the participant's lifetime earnings history. The more years one works presumably at higher wages, the higher the benefit will be. There is no "nominal account," however, for the worker. The actual amount contributed by the employer and the employee is not directly determinative of the benefit.[7]

Average lifetime earnings occurring during covered employment are calculated using a "wage-based" index ("Average Indexed Monthly Earnings" or AIME), so that earnings from the early years are inflated to reflect more current wage levels. Thus, lower earnings do not substantially diminish the "average." Once average earnings are calculated, the actual benefit is determined by first dividing the average into three brackets from low to high.[8] These are called "bend points." A varying percentage is then multiplied by each of the three levels and the resulting three products are added. This amount will be the "Primary Insurance Amount" ("PIA") or the benefit for the prospective retiree. Here is an illustration of how all this works.[9]

- First, calculate the AIME for the highest 35 years of earnings. Average earnings are increased based on wage inflation up to age of 59. Thereafter, the wages are indexed based on cost of living increases that usually are less than wage indexes.

---

5. See discussion about "baby boomers" at p. 11, infra.

6. Certain public employers and educational institutions are not "covered" for various policy and historic reasons.

7. If an employer and employee contributed payroll taxes up to the maximum income amount for a period of 43 years of employment, the total contributions would have been about $164,000. The present value of a Social Security benefit for the same employee with a life expectancy of 17 years is $440,000. Clearly, the benefit is worth more than the contributions. One cannot help but wonder what the value of the total payroll contributions would have been had they been invested in capital markets. See http://www.ssa.gov/pubs/10035.html/.

8. These "bend point" amounts change each year depending on inflation.

9. See http://www.ssa.gov/pubs/10035.html/. One can do an estimate of his or her own future benefits using several calculators at http://www.ssa.gov/.

- Next, calculate total average monthly earnings over 35 years. Note that we cannot exceed the maximum taxable earnings amount for those years. For example, in 2008, we add 90 percent of the first $711 of the average indexed monthly earnings to 32 percent of the employee's average indexed monthly earnings over $680 up to $4,288; then add 15 percent of the employee's average indexed monthly earnings over $4,288. These three brackets of income that are subject to different percentages are the "bend points."

- The three products are added up and constitute the participant's PIA. Generally, if the participant chooses early retirement at age 62, or sometime before his full retirement age, the PIA will be actuarially reduced up to about 33 percent.[10]

- For example, a person who had maximum taxable earnings in each year since age 22 and retires at full retirement age in 2008 would receive a benefit based on a PIA of $2,100. If this person had retired at age 62 instead, his benefit would have been $1,644 per month.

For many years, unreduced benefits were available at age 65. However, as life expectancy increased and concerns about the financial future of Social Security were raised, the full retirement age was extended for future retirees based on their year of birth.[11] In Art's case, he was born in 1947, so he cannot collect unreduced benefits until age 66. He can begin to collect early retirement benefits after he reaches age 62, but his benefit will be actuarially reduced, and the reduction will be for life. For example, for a person whose full retirement age is 65, but who retires at 62, the annual benefit will be reduced 20 percent for life. At age 63, the reduction will be 13.335 percent, and at age 64, 6.67 percent.

Persons who retire early but continue to earn income also incur an additional reduction in their benefit. The current formula is for every $2 earned above the current earnings limit ($12,960 in the year 2007), the benefit will be reduced by $1. All of the benefit is subject to federal and state income tax.[12]

There is no benefit reduction, however, for those who retire at full retirement age and who have other income.[13] The one exception when

---

10. This reduction will be affected by the participant's date of birth and his full retirement age as well as the number of years before this age that he chooses to retire.

11. This change was made effective in the year 2000. *Social Security—A Brief History* (2005).

12. See *Guide to Social Security and Medicare overview*, 34th ed. (2006). http://www.ssa.gov/.

13. This occurred as a result of the passage of the Senior Citizens Freedom to Work Act of 2000. *Social Security—A Brief History* (2005), http://www.ssa.gov/history/.

there can be a reduction, is the year in which the participant reaches full retirement age.[14] If the retiree has combined income (filing jointly) between $32,000 and $44,000, up to 50 percent is taxed.[15] If income exceeds $44,000, 85 percent is subject to income tax; if it is below $32,000, the benefit is not subject to federal income tax.

Social Security benefits are subject to regular cost-of-living adjustments (COLAs). Since 1975, the increases have been automatic and based on an increase in consumer prices. Over the past several years, the annual increases have been in the 2 to 3 percent range.

If one chooses to retire after the full retirement age, the benefit will be actuarially increased by as much as 8 percent per year up until age 70, at which time there will be no additional increase in the benefit.[16]

So, what should our friend Art do? Knowing now there are some disadvantages under Social Security to taking age 62 retirement benefits, what factors would you apply in helping Art make his decision? What questions would you ask him? For example, what about his interest in continuing to work? What is the state of his health? What is his family's history of longevity? Would investing the early retirement benefit more than make up for the reduction in benefits received at 62 instead of at full retirement? Will his decision affect his survivors? How would you calculate the present value of both choices?

As an example, a person born in 1946, whose early retirement monthly benefit is $1,450 per month, could receive $1,913 per month at full retirement age. If he waited until age 70, he could receive a maximum benefit of $2,538 per month, about 34 percent more than his full-age retirement benefit and 75 percent higher than his early retirement benefit. If one is in the highest income bracket, thereby subjecting up to 85 percent of his Social Security benefit to income tax, and has a family history of longevity, waiting might be a good idea. By waiting until reaching age 70, however, this retiree forgoes receiving a total of

---

14. In this year there can be a reduction in the benefit if annual earnings exceed $33,240 (filing as a single taxpayer). In such cases, the benefit is reduced $1 for every $3 earned.

15. This change was first made in 1983. The technical term for the income is "combined income," which includes all adjusted gross income included in the federal income tax return as well as interest from tax-exempt investments and 50 percent of one's actual Social Security benefit. If you file a joint return, the income limits are $32,000 to $44,000 (one must pay taxes on 50 percent of the benefit), and more than $44,000 (you must pay taxes on 85 percent of the benefit). See *Guide to Social Security and Medicare Overview*, 34th ed. (2006).

16. The annual percentage increases for delayed retirement depends on the year of birth of the retiree. The percentage increases range from 6 percent per year for those born in 1935 or 1936, to 7 percent for those born in 1939 or 1940, to 8 percent for those born after 1942.

$139,200 in retirement benefits that would have begun at age 62. It would take 10.5 years, or until age 80 years and 6 months, for him to collect the deferred money.[17]

Let's do a calculation for Art and see what advice we would give him. Go to the Social Security Online Web site (http://www.ssa.gov/); under "Retirement," select "Calculate Your Benefits." Choose Option No. 1, "Quick Calculator." Using Art's year of birth, 1947, and July 17 as his date of birth, enter $120,000 as his "earnings in the current year." Specify a "future retirement date option" of July 15, 2009. Select "see your benefit" using "today's dollars." Note the benefit in the top left part of the window. Also note what amounts the survivors will receive should Art die. Now enter Art's full retirement age (based on his year of birth) using the same birth dates and income. What is the benefit amount? What is the percentage reduction arising from an early retirement?

Some Social Security Economic and Policy Issues

Some liken the Social Security retirement program to the "third leg" of a retirement stool, the other two being one's employer-sponsored plan(s) and one's savings, be it in retirement plans such as a 401(k), an IRA, or private investments. Putting the three legs together to support a continuation of income at retirement is quite important. For lower income persons, the Social Security benefit is a "lifeline." Of the Social Security beneficiaries, about 65 percent depend on Social Security to provide at least 50 percent of their retirement income.[18]

As in most developed countries, the United States is experiencing a decline in birth rate, longer life expectancies, and workers who want to retire at a relatively early age. The "dependency ratio" measures the number of people working (between ages 18 and 65) to those who are not (below age 18 and above 65). The assumption is that those above 65 are in retirement. It also can be used to measure the "youth dependency ratio,"

17. See http://www.socialsecurity.gov/retire2/agereduction/. Also see *Strange but true: Unusual strategies for claiming a social security benefit.* (2008). The Center for Retirement Research at Boston College. In this article the CRR points out that a retiree can start receiving reduced benefits at age 62, then at full-age retirement return the money received in full, but without interest, and start receiving higher, full-age benefits. In effect, he has received an interest-free loan from SSA.

18. Kotlikoff, L., Marx, B., & Rizza, P. (2006). *Americans' dependency on Social Security.* University of Michigan Retirement Research Center, Working Paper WP 2006-126.

which would compare those working to those too young to work. It is particularly relevant to pay-as-you-go social security systems, since funding the retirees' benefits is dependent upon payroll contributions from active workers and, in the long run, future workers.[19]

Since birth rates have declined in many developed countries and life expectancy has increased, the dependency ratio also has increased. Countries such as France, Italy, Japan, Germany, and the United Kingdom have increasing longevity and decreasing birth rates that are below "replacement rates," which means they have a higher age dependency ratio than, for example, the United States. These countries will be unable to sustain PAYGO entitlement programs that are dependent upon payroll tax revenue. To some, this is alarming. The dependency ratio has been increasing in developed countries for several years. Today in the United States, the age dependency ratio is .19; by the year 2030, it will rise to .30; and .35 in 2050. As you can see from Table 2.5 in Chapter 2, the increases among G7 countries are significantly higher largely because of lower birth rates.[20] In other words, in Japan by the year 2030, there will be only one worker supporting two retirees.[21]

This demographic change has caused actuaries and others to predict a Social Security funding crisis in the United States, at which time Social Security revenues will no longer be sufficient to pay the scheduled benefits.[22] According to the actuaries, by 2017, benefits will exceed tax income and Social Security will begin to use the interest on assets in the fund. As discussed earlier, by 2027, Social Security will need to draw on the assets in the fund to pay benefits and expenses; and by 2042, assets in

---

19. *The dependency ratio.* (2005). International Longevity Center, Alliance for Health and the Future, Issue Brief, The Dependency Ratio, Volume 2, Number 1, http://www.ilcusa.org/). See Table 2.5 in Chapter 2.

20. While wages usually increase with time on the job, the increased revenue resulting from payroll taxes excised on higher income will not be sufficient to overcome the financial impact of the increasing dependency ratio. *The dependency ratio.* (2005). U.S. Congressional Budget Office, Long Term Budgetary Pressures and Policy Options. (1998, May). http://www.cbo.gov/.

21. The International Longevity Center, Alliance for Health and the Future (2005); U.S. Congressional Budget Office (1998, May).

22. Status of the Social Security and Medicare Programs. (2007, April 23). Reports from the Board of Trustees, http://www.ssa.gov/OACT/TR/. The Trustees indicated that they are concerned about the lack of progress in reforming the program that will begin to suffer massive deficits in 2018: "We are increasingly concerned about the inaction on the financial challenges facing the Social Security and Medicare programs. The longer we wait to address these challenges, the more limited will be the options available, the greater will be the required adjustments, and the more severe the potential detrimental economic impact on our nation."

the fund will be exhausted and payroll tax income will be sufficient to pay only 75 percent of the benefits and expenses of the retirement plan.[23] In Chapter 13, Global Benefits, we examine what other countries are doing with respect to their social security funding crisis. The most obvious actuarial solutions are to reduce benefits or increase taxes. There are others, however.

Making a choice to solve the funding crisis involves difficult policy, economic, and political issues. Whatever the range of possible solutions, we must make sure to quantitatively and qualitatively evaluate them before they are implemented. Each proposed reform measure generates behavioral responses and has fiscal results. We must ask the questions: Does the proposed reform generate long-term benefit adequacy and sustained solvency? Does it require supplemental funding from general tax revenue? What impact will it have on income replacement rates at retirement?[24]

We provide a number of calculators and exercises on the issue of Social Security reform at the end of this chapter, but let's look at some possibilities.

- First, the government could increase the payroll tax either by increasing the FICA percentage of 12.4 percent or removing the 2008 cap of $102,000 on the income subject to tax.[25] What would be the economic consequences of this move? Some argue this would have a major economic impact on, particularly, small employers who might reduce their workforce. It also amounts to a significant tax increase on wage earners. An increase of 2.02 percent in FICA tax would provide long-term, but not permanent, solvency.[26] Taking the income cap off the tax would eliminate about 25 percent of the deficit. Taking the cap off the tax, but

---

23. See an interesting analysis by the American Academy of Actuaries: An Actuarial Perspective on the 2007 Social Security Trustees' Report, Issue Brief. (2007, May). http://www.actuary.org/.

24. The various proposals discussed in this section are outlined and analyzed by the Academy of Actuaries in *Quantitative measures for evaluating Social Security reform proposals, Issue Brief.* (2002, April). American Academy of Actuaries, http://www.actuary.org/.

25. The Social Security Trustees have reported that an immediate increase in the payroll tax of 16 percent would bring Social Security into actuarial balance for the next 75 years. See *Status of the Social Security and Medicare programs.* (2007).

26. This means the program would be solvent for about 75 years if the change were done now. *Social Security reform options.* (2007, January). American Academy of Actuaries, Public Policy Monograph.

keeping the limit in calculating lifetime income, would result in long-term, but not permanent, solvency.[27]

- Second, Congress could reduce benefits by further delaying the full retirement age. At present, for example, persons who were born in 1942 must wait until they are age 65 and 10 months to receive an unreduced benefit. The retirement age increases incrementally to age 67 for those born in 1960 or after. What policy argument could one use to support additional postponements in the retirement age? What impact would this have on the actuarial reduction for those retiring early at age 62? Most likely, it would increase. A reduction in benefits equal to 13 percent would result in long-term, but not permanent, solvency.[28]

- Changing the way average indexed monthly earnings are calculated could reduce benefits. By using a cost of living index instead of a wage index, AIME would be reduced in most cases and, therefore, the formula for calculating a benefit would generate a lower benefit. The rationale for this change is that using a cost of living adjustment more accurately reflects the real impact of inflation on purchasing power. The net effect, however, is that people will get lower benefits. Policymakers should assess what financial impact this will have on persons who are dependent upon their Social Security benefit. Such a change would lead to long-term, but not permanent, solvency for the program.[29]

- Congress could apply means testing for benefits at retirement age, similar to what is done for those retiring at age 62. How would this work? Is there a rationale to support this choice? What arguments, pro and con, might there be for this solution? What impact, for example, would this have on the willingness of older persons to continue working after receiving Social Security benefits?[30] Means testing is used in other areas of government benefits. For example,

---

27. *Social Security reform options.* (2007, January). American Academy of Actuaries, Public Policy Monograph.

28. *Social Security reform options.* (2007, January). American Academy of Actuaries, Public Policy Monograph.

29. *Social Security reform options.* (2007, January). American Academy of Actuaries, Public Policy Monograph.

30. For example, in 2000, when Congress repealed the earnings test and resulting benefit reduction for persons who retired under Social Security at Normal Retirement Age, there was an increase in the labor supply among older men with certain educational backgrounds who benefited from the repeal. See Engelhardt, G., & Kumar, A. (2007, May). *The repeal of the retirement earnings test and the*

Medicare premiums gradually increase as one's income goes up. In this case, the idea is that even though a person contributed his entire work life to SSA, because of his wealth status, he really does not need the benefit. Current estimates are that affluence testing would be triggered if family income from SSA exceeds $40,000 per year and the family's total income exceeds $120,000. This could have a positive and long-term effect on solvency.[31]

- What about the finance side of the benefit? Could the Social Security Administration hold and invest the current surplus of Social Security revenue in capital markets, thereby increasing the asset value of the fund? Should the PAYGO design be abandoned? How much would such a move help? Are there some economic policy arguments one might make to argue against such a move? The chief difficulty here is the potential problems that might arise if the government becomes a major investor in the capital markets. Obviously, state pension sponsors invest in the markets without any significant problems. How big would the government's stake in the capital markets be? The American Academy of Actuaries describes it this way: ". . . the vast sums involved under present-law tax rates could have unintended effects on the securities markets. Initially, the trust funds would be major purchasers of equities but later they would become major sellers."[32]

- In Chapter 13, Global Benefits, we discuss the decision of Chile and other countries to allow some diversion of the payroll tax into a participant's personal account over which he would have choices as to how the funds are invested. A similar idea was advanced by the George W. Bush administration in the United States. This would have significant "transitional costs" because there would be a reduction in revenue for the standard benefit. Over the long run, however, the magnitude of the government's liability to pay benefits would be reduced. However, if it were in direct proportion

---

labor supply of older men. Center for Retirement Research at Boston College, Working Paper #2007-1.

31. *Social Security reform options.* (2007, January). American Academy of Actuaries, Public Policy Monograph. There are other ideas concerning reductions in benefits: reduce the COLA, change the benefit formula by limiting the bend point indexing, expand coverage to include those who are currently not covered and thereby increase the revenues, and increase the taxation of benefits. There are others discussed in the American Academy report.

32. *Social Security reform options* (p. 18). (2007, January). American Academy of Actuaries, Public Policy Monograph.

to the reduction of payroll tax revenue, there would seem to be no net reduction in its liability. If the offset is larger than the diversion of taxes, then over time the liability would be reduced and the funding crisis would be resolved.[33] How would you design such a plan and what impact would it have on the funding crisis?

- What if the benefit were completely redesigned to create a nominal account for each participant that would appreciate based on his investment choices (or a variety of choices designated by the government) and be distributed as an annuity or lump sum at retirement? What design features could such a plan have and how would it help the funding crisis? With such a choice, should there be a "guaranteed minimum pension" from the government in the event the account does not produce an adequate retirement?[34] Should participation be voluntary? Should all participants be eligible to participate or just those over a certain age? Should they be required to receive their benefit as an annuity? Should the benefit be provided in lieu of all or a portion of their Social Security benefit, or should it just be a supplemental option allowing SSA participants to invest extra monies, over and above their FICA tax, into a fund and receive payments when the retire.

A strong driver of the funding crisis involves the U.S. "baby boomer generation," comprising 78 million persons who were conceived during the post–World War II "spike in fertility rate." Baby boomers will become eligible for Social Security and Medicare beginning in 2008.[35] The General Accountability Office of the U.S. Congress estimates that in 2040, the U.S. government will be unable to pay for anything more than the interest on public debt and public entitlement programs as a result of the demographic shift as well as increasing longevity. There will be no money for defense, education, or any other federal obligation. According to the GAO, this crisis will be driven by Social Security and, in particular,

---

33. We see in the exercises at the end of this chapter, the Bush proposal on Personal Accounts did provide for an automatic reduction in benefits based on the amount of payroll tax diverted by the employee plus an assumed 3 percent over inflation rate of investment return. So, the benefit offset would be higher than the diversion of the payroll tax.

34. See *Social Security reform options.* (2007, January). American Academy of Actuaries, Public Policy Monograph.

35. *Trustees Report, Old Age, Survivors, Disability Insurance, Report of 2008.* Social Security Administration, http://www.ssa.gov/.

Medicare and Medicaid. The solution, according to the GAO, is a fundamental reform of the health care system in America.[36]

Perspectives on Social Security Reform

Social Security old age and retirement benefits are a key component to financing a worker's retirement. Reducing benefits (either directly or indirectly) as a means to achieve fiscal stability for the Social Security program would have a significant and adverse effect on the elderly. Further, unless sufficient time and advance notice were given for the younger generation to make the requisite changes in their lifestyles, savings patterns, and overall plans for retirement, a cut in their Social Security benefits would have a similar effect on them when they retire.[37]

From a policy standpoint, what is a reasonable objective for the government with respect to this benefit? Before debating a variety of "Social Security Reform" proposals, perhaps we should reexamine the overall objective of the benefit. Should the concept of having three legs supporting the retirement stool be a focus for this reexamination? Which of the three legs has more potential to provide a cost-effective benefit? What are the current and future realities, and actual life events pertaining to retirement in the United States? How are workers in the United States laying the foundation for their retirement and what activities are they pursuing when they actually do retire?

- Are older workers who retire continuing to work in new employment or a completely new career? Should retirement, as we have defined it, continue to exist? For example, one recent study indicated that 77 percent of workers today expect to work for pay after they retire. Most say this will be based on their desire to work and not because they must work.[38]

---

36. Social Security reform, greater transparency needed about potential general revenue financing. (2007, March). General Accountability Office, http://www.gao.gov. Others estimate that national health care spending, as a percentage of GDP, will rise from 16.3 percent in 2007 to 19.5 percent by 2017. This is largely due to the baby boomers spilling into retirement ages. See Keehan, S. et al. (2008, February 26). Health spending projections through 2017: The baby-boom generation is coming to Medicare. *Health Affairs*, 145–148.

37. Kotlikoff, L., Marx, B., & Rizza, P. (2006). *Americans' dependency on Social Security*. University of Michigan Retirement Research Center, Working Paper WP 2006-126.

38. *Working after retirement: The gap between expectations and reality*. (2006). Pew Research Center.

- Many U.S. workers still dream of retiring from their current job at age 55, but expect they will not be able to until they are at least 63. Among European workers, they dream and expect to retire at an earlier age.[39]

- How will younger workers with families save for the university expenses of their children as well as retirement? In Western Europe, higher education is relatively free and saving and investing for retirement is not common. Should we consider changes in the United States that might mirror the European system?[40]

- How much "notice" or time would a generation need to prepare for and react to a reduction in Social Security benefits?[41]

- What percentage of the recently retired workforce has enough retirement income to maintain their desired lifestyles?

- Are there special problems with any particular demographic group that would require special consideration or changes in the way the Social Security benefits are calculated?[42]

---

39. See Presentation, AXA retirement scope—A global survey on life, work, and retirement (2005), http://www.axa.com.

40. According to the Vanguard Retirement Survey, more households are aware of the need to save for retirement, but as many as 40 percent need to save considerably more than they do currently. The conflict is between saving and spending. See *Vanguard retirement outlook for 2006.* (2006, August). Vanguard Center for Retirement Research, http://institutional.vanguard.com/.

41. A 30 percent cut in Social Security benefits would reduce the living standard of a 65-year-old with relatively low income by about 32 percent. Kotlikoff, L., Marx, B., & Rizza, P. (2006), pp. 40–42. The authors show that the impact of a 30 percent cut in benefits is much less significant for younger and higher paid participants.

42. As an example, women workers tend to have more breaks in service due to childbearing responsibilities, they earn less than their male counterparts, have fewer assets, and are more dependent upon Social Security. They are also more likely to be widowed before retirement age, have longer life expectancies, are less likely than men to remarry, and thus must rely heavily on dependent Social Security benefits. As homemakers and family caretakers, women do not earn taxable wages and are more likely to not qualify for Social Security benefits. In some countries, persons are given work credit for some nonwork experiences. Are there potential reforms that come to mind here that are apparent from these statistics? See *Women and Social Security.* (2007, June). American Academy of Actuaries, http://www.actuary.org/. Also see American Academy of Actuaries (2007, January).

- From a political and economic standpoint, should the current working generation be obligated to pay for their predecessors' retirement no matter what the costs?

- How effective are the disability and survivor benefits under Social Security in alleviating the frequent economic crises these lifecycle events create?[43]

- What developments can we expect with respect to employer-sponsored retirement plans? Will defined benefit plans disappear? Will employer-sponsored retirement benefits be exclusively defined contribution plans? DBPs are still very viable in the state and local government-sponsored pension arena.[44] Typically, they produce higher replacement income and are funded by contributions from participants and employers; while some have financing problems, most are fiscally sound.

- How are we doing? What percentage of final pay are the three legs (employer-sponsored retirement, employee savings, and Social Security) currently replacing? We need more data on this, but early

---

43. For example, the research indicates that while the economic status of older persons in the United States has increased over the past years, the status of widows has not improved. In fact, poverty rates for older, nonmarried women is comparatively high. One reason, the study points out, is that under Social Security and employer-sponsored retirement, plan benefits drop for the survivor when the participant dies. See Karamcheva, N., & Munell, A. (2007). *Why are widows so poor?* (2007, June). Center for Retirement Research at Boston College, Issue Brief #7-9. See also American Academy of Actuaries (2007, June), http://www.actuary.org/.

44. See Munnell, A., & Soto, M. (2007, November). *State and local pensions are different from private plans.* Center for Retirement Research at Boston College, No. 1, http://www.bc.edu/crr. In spite of the trend of many employer sponsors of defined benefit plan to switch over to defined contribution plans, there are indications that some employers are having second thoughts about the transition and there are a variety of reasons to keep the DBP. See *The top ten advantages of maintaining Defined Benefit Pensions.* (2007, May). National Conference on Public Employee Retirement Systems, http://www.advisortoday.com/200707/incometax.html/. Some of the arguments here are that DBPs encourage longer service, are more efficient to manage, and they pool the risk among employers instead of assigning the risk onto the employee. We note that many pension plans sponsored by local and state governments are DBPs, usually requiring employee and employer contributions. Their assets are typically invested in capital markets, and in general they are well funded. New accounting rules may have some impact on this, however. We note that 76 percent of the workers in these sectors are covered by a pension plan, most often a DBP, while only 43 percent are covered in the private sector and many private plans are DCPs. Further, state government-sponsored plans are not covered by Title 1 of ERISA [see §4(b) (1) and (2)], and only 70 percent of state and local employees participate in the Social Security pension system while virtually 100 percent of private sector workers are covered. See Munnell, A., & Soto, M. (2007, November).

indications are that relying on employee savings (i.e., personal savings and savings in DCPs) as the primary source of retirement income is not going to be sufficient to retire at typically expected ages.[45] Is it time to consider a reduction in Social Security benefits?

As we explore economic fixes to the problems of aging and inadequate funding of Social Security benefits, one must keep in mind that real and sustainable solutions inevitably will come from political resolutions that should be led by the group that is most likely to benefit from the changes—the elderly.[46] But the longer they wait to pick up the banner and push the establishment for reform, the more costly the reform will be.[47]

Health Care After Retirement—Medicare

Vera Jackson has worked 20 years as a radio advertising salesperson. She has served three broadcasting companies during this period. Next month Vera will be 65. Having worked in covered employment the entire 20 years,[1] she will not be eligible for full retirement age Social Security benefits until she is 66 years old; however, at 65 she will qualify for Medicare.

---

1. Both she and her employer have contributed 12.5 percent of her annual income to Social Security for her retirement benefit. This is called the "FICA" tax, which stands for the Federal Insurance Contributions Act. There is a limited amount of income subject to the tax and SSA adjusts the amount for inflation regularly. The cap on earnings subject to FICA in 2008 is $102,000. They have also contributed 2.45 percent of her annual income to Social Security for Medicare. This payroll tax has no income limits. All income is subject to the tax.

---

45. See Generation X and Y see changing retirement landscape but fail to save enough. (2008, March 19). American Association of Retired Persons (AARP, http://www.aarp.org/. Also see DeVaney, S., & Chiremba, S. (2008, March 16). *Comparing the retirement behavior of the baby boomers and other cohorts.* The Bureau of Labor Statistics, U.S. Department of Labor, http://www.bls.dol.gov. This study explored saving patterns among baby boomers and other cohorts and found age, risk tolerance, and early savings patterns as being most determinative of the adequacy of savings for retirement.

46. Galasso, V. (2006). *The political future of Social Security in aging societies.* Boston: The MIT Press.

47. Munnell, A. (2007, April). *Social Security's financial outlook: The 2007 report in perspective.* Center for Retirement Research at Boston College, Issue Brief #7-6.

Vera retired from active employment two years ago and receives an annuity payment from her employer's defined benefit plan. She has chosen to wait until she is 66 years old before collecting her Social Security retirement benefit. At retirement, she bought an immediate annuity with her 401(k) plan and receives a guaranteed monthly income to supplement her defined benefit.

She also is covered by her employer's retiree health care plan, but this will terminate at age 65 due to her eligibility for Medicare.[2] She has read a lot about Medicare and understands that coverage can include hospital treatments and an optional coverage for doctor treatments, as well as the new coverage for drug expenses. She knows the optional and drug coverage supplements will require her to make premium payments to Medicare.

Vera has been told that because of Medicare's deductibles and various coverage limitations, she would be well advised to buy some type of supplemental or "gap" coverage. Private insurance companies contract with Medicare to provide the full range of benefits from hospitals, to doctors, to drugs. They conduct seminars and invite people like Vera to attend and learn about their Medicare Supplemental, Prescription Drug, and Medicare Advantage plans. Vera wants to make the right decision about this extra coverage and, therefore, is planning to attend one or more seminars to help with her selection.

---

2. See discussion of legal issues concerning this practice later in this chapter.

Medicare is a health care benefit for persons 65 and older. Its basic design comprises the features of a fee-for-service indemnity[48] health care plan with the traditional deductibles, co-pays, coinsurance, out-of-pocket maximums, and for some benefits, employee premiums. It also has a schedule of covered medical services and reimbursement levels for health care provider services. Government-sponsored health care coverage for the elderly was initiated because most persons lost their employer-sponsored health care upon reaching age 65. The U.S. Congress passed

---

48. To be more precise, it is not exactly a "fee-for-service" plan since Medicare imposes reimbursement rates on the providers. In a traditional "fee-for-service" plan, the TPA and plan sponsor pay all "customary and reasonable" fees set by the providers.

this government-sponsored health care plan in 1961 as an amendment to the Social Security Act.[49]

Eligibility for Medicare coverage is available to a U.S. worker 65 years and older who qualifies for a Social Security benefit, including the early retirement benefit.[50] Coverage is distributed among four separate but related plans: Parts A, B, C, and D. Medicare Part A is provided without requiring a premium and covers medical services in hospitals and similar venues.[51] Medicare Part B covers medical services provided by doctors and outpatient care, as well as other medically necessary services and preventive care.[52] A participant pays a premium for Part B, the amount of which is adjusted based on the participant's income.[53] If one cannot afford the premium for Part B, arrangements can be made for a subsidized payment.

Part C includes Medigap and Medicare Advantage Plans. Medigap comprises private supplemental health insurance plans that Medicare beneficiaries can purchase. They are a type of wraparound plan that makes up for the benefit limits in traditional Medicare, and provides coverage for medical expenses, e.g., part of the deductibles, coinsurance, or other costs not covered or only partially covered by Medicare. Medicare Advantage Plans are offered by private insurance companies who contract with Medicare and assume the entire obligation of covering all benefits included in Part A, B, and usually even D. More about these plans a little later.

---

49. Today there are over 40 million people covered by Medicare. *Status of the Social Security and Medicare programs.* (2007, April 23). Reports from the Board of Trustees, http://www.ssa.gov/OACT/TR/. It is administered by the Centers for Medicare and Medicaid Services. See *Social Security—A Brief History.* (2005). SSA Publication No. 21-059, http://www.socialsecurity.gov/history/.

50. Coverage is also extended to certain disabled persons, and those with Lou Gehrig's or kidney disease. Citizens and lawfully admitted aliens who have lived in the United States for five years, but who are not eligible for Part A coverage, can purchase the coverage at a higher premium than otherwise available to covered persons.

51. For example, blood transfusions, home health care, hospice, hospitals, and skilled nursing care up to 100 days after a three-day stay in a hospital.

52. It also covers ambulance services, ambulatory surgical services, blood, bone mass measurement, cardiovascular screenings, chiropractic, clinical lab services, and some clinical trials, as well as medically necessary and preventive services.

53. The premium for 2008, for example, ranged from $96.40 per month to $238.40 per month based on income. By the year 2009, Part B participants will be paying between 25 percent and 80 percent of the actual cost of the coverage depending on their Modified Adjusted Gross Income (AGI plus tax-exempt interest income).

In 2003, Congress added a prescription drug benefit to Medicare. Prior to this, most prescription drugs were not covered and participants had to find other ways to be reimbursed. The drug benefit, effective on January 1, 2006, is called Part D coverage and requires a premium.[54] It is characterized as a stand-alone plan wherein private insurers who have contracts with Medicare administer the drug benefit.[55] Medicare does not procure the drugs covered or negotiate their prices and, while it sets the standards and most design features of Part D, it does not directly administer the drug plan.

The drug coverage is elective and Congress chose to design it by employing market features allowing TPAs and pharmacy providers to compete directly among participants. The criteria one uses in choosing a Part D provider can include the drugs listed in the company's formulary, the premium for the plan, the cost sharing and coinsurance offerings, the services offered such as mail order programs, the accessibility of the plan's pharmacies, or how the plan manages the deductibles including the gap coverage. In most Medicare Advantage Plans, Part D coverage is included in the plan's offerings.[56]

Medicare's prescription drug plan includes an annual deductible of $265. Thereafter, the participant benefits from insurance coverage for drug purchases with some cost sharing. For example, after the plan and participant together have spent $2,400 in drug costs, a coverage gap, sometimes referred to as a "donut hole," is opened. In the coverage gap, the participant pays 100 percent of his drug costs until his yearly out-of-pocket drug expenses (not including premiums) total $3,850. At this

---

54. Under Part D, if one has limited resources, Medicare may allow lower premiums and extra help in paying for Part D costs.

55. Cubanski, J., & Neuman, P. (2007). Status report on Medicare Part D enrollment in 2006: Analysis of plan-specific market share and coverage. *Health Affairs, 26*(1).

56. This "market-based design" has come under other criticism by those who believed the private sector TPAs would not participate in the Part D program. The early reports and evidence, however, suggest that enrollment by participants was larger than expected (23 million), more private companies are entering the Part D program, there was general satisfaction (80 percent) among seniors with the plan, premiums for the program are declining, actual costs of the program were less than budgeted, and seniors are estimating their average net savings to be around $1,200 per year. See Cubanski, J., & Neuman, P. (2007); *HHS Estimates of Prescription Drug Coverage Sources Among Medicare Beneficiaries as of January 2007.* (2007, April 30). Kaiser Family Foundation, http://www.kff.org/medicare/; Capitol Comment, U.S. Senator K. B. Hutchinson (2007, April 20), http://hutchinson.senate.gov/.

point, most of the subsequent prescription drug costs for that year are paid by the plan. Here is how it works.

Sam Terranova has Medicare Part D coverage. His annual prescriptions total about $7,000. Under Part D, Sam pays $31 a month for drug coverage. He pays an initial $265 annual deductible, before Part D reimbursements begin, and then must pay a co-pay and perhaps some coinsurance (for example, 10 to 20 percent of the cost) for each prescription. The amount varies depending on the status of the drug, whether it is a generic or nongeneric, and how it meets the particular drug plan's formulary status. Suppose after six months under Part D, Sam's total drug expenses including the amounts paid by his TPA, his co-pays and deductibles, not including premiums, total $2,400. At this point, Medicare Part D requires a suspension of reimbursements for prescriptions until Sam's total out-of-pocket expenditures for the year reach $3,850. This figure is calculated by adding his annual cost sharing, other than premiums, paid before reaching the $2,400 threshold, together with the drug expenses incurred during the coverage gap period. The period beginning when Sam's total expenses were $2,400 and ending when they reach $3,850 is called the "donut hole." When he is in the donut hole, Sam pays 100 percent of his prescription costs. Upon reaching $3,850, Medicare will resume generous reimbursements at very low coinsurance rates (5 percent) or a small co-payment for each prescription until the end of the year.

Under this scenario, and depending on the particular drugs Sam needs, let's assume his annual expenditures for drugs in the previous year totaled $7,000. During that period he was not covered by any drug plan. If his expenditures for drugs total $7,000 again this year, Sam's out-of-pocket expenditures would be less under Medicare Part D. How much less? Presume his annual deductible, co-pays, and coinsurance before reaching the $2,400 threshold were $700. He is then responsible for 100 percent of his costs until his out-of-pocket expenses (excluding the premiums paid) reach $3,150 ($3,850 less $700). When that occurs, Medicare will resume reimbursing him for the major part of his drug expenses.

Example: Before Medicare Part D, Sam paid $7,000 for annual drug expenses. After enrolling in Medicare Part D, he paid $3,850 plus $360 in premiums, or $4,210. His savings with Part D are $7,000 less $4,210, or $2,790 per year.

> In another example: Max paid $2,500 for his prescriptions before enrolling in Medicare Part D. He now is enrolled and pays a premium of $30 a month. After he pays the first annual deductible of $265, depending on the status of the drugs he needs and the corresponding co-pays and coinsurance, Medicare could pay about 85 percent of his drug costs until the total expenditures reach $2,400. Let's say Max pays $360 in co-pays and coinsurance, a $265 deductible, and $360 in premiums. His annual savings compared to his pre-Medicare Part D coverage would be $2,500 less $985, or $1,515.

Regardless of the savings seen in these two scenarios, Part D of Medicare does provide protection against catastrophic prescription expense. Also, there are several programs under Part D that provide financial assistance for persons with limited income and resources.

A variety of third-party administrators (TPAs), usually health insurance companies with large networks of doctors and hospitals, have entered the Medicare Advantage Plans with Medicare. Their business model is to better manage the plan than traditional Medicare, and to achieve profitable results by offering more efficient plan designs.[57] Medicare Advantage requires the TPA to assume, at a minimum, all of the obligations of the Medicare benefit plan (Parts A and B) and possibly additional features, such as Part D, in exchange for a fee paid to the company by Medicare. They compete with each other in plan design, participant cost sharing, quality, and premiums. In many cases the participant pays no more than the fee that Medicare charges for Plan B.

Medicare Advantage Plans include the traditional private fee-for-service (PFFS), health maintenance organizations (HMOs), preferred provider organizations (PPOs), and point-of-service (POS) plans.

---

57. There is some question about whether Medicare Advantage plans are saving money for the taxpayers and whether too many Medicare beneficiaries are choosing the Private Fee-for-Service (PFFS) plans that are not as cost-effective as HMO, PPO, and POS plans. See Gold, M. (2007, May 15). Medicare Advantage in 2006–2007: What Congress Intended? *Health Affairs*, http://content.healthaffairs .org/. In another recent article, the author pointed out that Medicare Advantage enrollment has increased five-fold in recent years. Yet, largely because of the inclusion of PFFS plans, indemnity type plans, Medicare is paying 12 percent more on Medicare Advantage plans than for its traditional Medicare plans. Lobbyists pushed for the inclusion of PFFS plans in Medicare Advantage in order to avoid cost saving measures and health service cuts for the elderly who need life prolonging treatments. See Zhang, J. (2007, May 8). Growing pains of private Medicare plans. *The Wall Street Journal*, http://www.wsj.com/.

Typically, if the participant chooses an HMO design, he may have to pay only the Medicare prescribed Part B premium to Medicare. If one chooses a PPO or POS plan as his Medicare Advantage Plan, there may be a small premium over and above the Part B fee that is paid to the TPA. Medicare Advantage Plans also can include a traditional or private fee-for-service arrangement usually at a slightly higher premium for the participant, depending on the deductible and cost sharing arrangements.[58]

So what about Vera, from the first vignette, and her choices? As we indicated, she can sign up for Medicare Part A and Part B, pay her Part B premium, select a provider under the drug plan, Part D, and enjoy her health care coverage directly under the original Medicare program. Or, she can select a supplement, or Medigap plan, that will indemnify her for a variety of cost sharing features required under Medicare. Vera must get information on each of these alternatives, check the premiums and plan of benefits, and make a decision. To help her, let's go on the Medicare Web site[59] and see what is available in her area. Pick any major city, go to http://www.medicare.gov/, and select the "Medicare Options Compare" choice. Follow the prompts and you will see what information Vera might have to help make her selection.

Medicare and Medicaid, which are discussed in the next section of this chapter, are experiencing significant annual cost increases and are predicted to run into serious financial problems in the coming years. We will take a look at these problems and issues, and how they might be resolved.

Medicare—Some Important Economic and Policy Issues

It is estimated that Medicare will be unable to sustain its respective obligations to eligible Americans in the years to come. The following is an excerpt from the latest Trustees report on Social Security and Medicare

---

58. Medicare provides a free service on its Web site allowing prospective participants in Medicare Advantage to find out what plans are available in their area and how the plans compare. See http://www.medicare.gov, go to "Compare Health Plans in Your Area."

59. Note that when you go on the Medicare Web site (see previous footnote), simply indicate that you are about to become eligible for Medicare. Do not check any questions concerning letters from Social Security. You must enter your postal zip code, and then determine some defaults concerning design features. Make the selections and run the comparisons. Be prepared to discuss which plan is best for "Vera" and why.

indicating that hospital insurance spending will soon outpace revenues and Medicare will be bankrupt.[60]

> As we reported last year, Medicare's financial difficulties come sooner—and are much more severe—than those confronting Social Security. While both programs face demographic challenges, the impact is greater for Medicare because health care costs increase at older ages. Moreover, underlying health care costs per enrollee are projected to rise faster than the wages per worker on which payroll taxes and Social Security benefits are based. As a result, while Medicare's annual costs were 3.1 percent of GDP in 2006, or about 72 percent of Social Security's, they are projected to surpass Social Security expenditures in 2028 and exceed 11 percent of GDP in 2081.
>
> The projected 75-year actuarial deficit in the Hospital Insurance (HI) Trust Fund is now 3.55 percent of taxable payroll, up slightly from 3.51 percent in last year's report. The fund again fails our test of short-range financial adequacy, as projected annual assets drop below projected annual expenditures within ten years—in 2013. The fund also continues to fail our long-range test of close actuarial balance by a wide margin. The projected date of HI Trust Fund exhaustion is 2019, one year later than in last year's report, when tax income will be sufficient to pay only 79 percent of HI costs. HI tax income falls short of outlays in this and all future years.
>
> The program could be brought into actuarial balance over the next 75 years by an immediate 122 percent increase in the payroll tax, or an immediate 51 percent reduction in program outlays, or some combination of the two. As with Social Security, adjustments of greater magnitude would be necessary to the extent changes are delayed or phased in gradually, or to make the program solvent on a sustainable basis beyond the 75-year horizon.[61]

The basic causes of the problem are the increased number of retirees, increased life expectancy, the high costs of health care in the United States, and insufficient payroll tax revenue. Further, while spending on the new

---

60. *Status of the Social Security and Medicare Programs* (2007).

61. *Status of the Social Security and Medicare Programs* (2007). See also Munnell, A. (2007, October). *Medicare costs and retirement.* Center for Retirement Research at Boston College, No. 7-14. The author notes a projected increase of the Social Security, Medicare, and Medicaid programs from 9 percent of GDP in 2007 to 24 percent in 2080. This would require a 20 percent increase in income taxes by 2040, and out-of-pocket payments for Medicare (deductibles, premiums, co-insurance) will increase from the current 29 percent of the average social security benefit to 73 percent of the average benefit by 2080.

Part D drug benefit has been below expectations, this Medicare obligation has significantly added to the financial burden of the program.[62]

There is, however, an even more insidious fiscal crisis ahead. According to the U.S. Government Accountability Office, the U.S. Comptroller General has indicated that because of the spike in fertility rates which launched the baby boomer generation, there will be 78 million Americans becoming eligible for Social Security and Medicare beginning in 2008. As noted above, by the year 2042 according to the GAO, the federal government will be unable to fund any activities other than health and pension benefits and the payment of the interest rate on the U.S. debt. The GAO believes that unless Medicare and Medicaid undergo a substantial reformation, they will render the U.S. government and many state governments bankrupt.[63]

Let's examine some of the opportunities that are available to stem the spiraling expense. First, we will look at quality and its implications on cost. According to the now famous Dartmouth study led by Dr. John E. Wennberg, there have been wide variations of medical service utilization and health care spending among Medicare patients.[64] Dr. Wennberg also discovered that higher spending did not result in better clinical outcomes. The differences in care seemed to be attributable to the availability of supply-sensitive services.[65] In other words, the available health care resources in a particular geographic area determined the type of care received. According to Wennberg, it is the supply and not the demand that drives the utilization of health care resources.

As an example, Dr. Wennberg showed that a person in Redding, California, was four times more likely to have heart bypass surgery than a person with a similar diagnosis and history who lived in Albuquerque, New Mexico. While Redding had more heart catheterization labs, it did not have more people with heart attacks than Albuquerque. Similarly, a six-fold variation in back surgery among 306 hospitals was apparently due to the weight given to the physician's opinion versus the patient's input.

---

62. See GAO (2007).

63. The GAO also points out the need for an increase in federal revenues and a cap on federal spending, as well as reform of the entitlement programs. See *The Nation's Long-Term Fiscal Outlook.* (2007, January). The Bottom Line: Federal Fiscal Policy Remains Unsustainable, The U.S. Government Accountability Office. See also CBS ("60 Minutes") interview of David Walker, Comptroller General, (2007, July 8, 2007), http://www.cabnes.com/stories/2007/03/01/60 minutes/printable2528226shtml/.

64. Wennberg, J., & Cooper, M. (1999). The Quality of Medical Care in the U.S.: A Report on the Medicare Program. *The Dartmouth Atlas of Health Care.* Chicago: American Health Association Press.

65. Wennberg, J., & Cooper, M. (1999).

Dr. Wennberg called for a major reform of Medicare that included shared decision making, the promotion of Centers of Excellence, the elimination of under-providing health care, and new medical outcomes research that would better facilitate comparisons among providers.[66]

Over the last several years, Medicare has responded to the quality and cost issue. In the past, it reimbursed hospitals based on the actual services rendered to the Medicare patient. It decided to change the reimbursement process by establishing a "Prospective Payment System" that reimburses hospitals a fixed amount based on the diagnosis regardless of the length of stay and type of care received. This created an incentive for hospitals to enhance their efficiencies so that the Medicare reimbursement exceeded the hospital's actual costs. The challenge often heard in many hospital boardrooms was "how can we make money on Medicare?" By closely examining their work processes, medical outcomes, and lengths of stay and hospital charges, hospitals began to find ways to accomplish the goal of providing cost-effective quality health care. Lengths of stay declined, as did hospital charges, without adversely impacting the quality of care.[67] Thus, the prospective pay system is helping to drive down costs and allowed appropriate margins to be realized by hospitals.

The Centers for Medicare and Medicaid Services, the agency that administers Medicare, is also pursuing a variety of quality projects that should affect both outcomes and cost. One such project begun in 2003 is a pay-for-performance plan that pays additional reimbursements to the top performing hospitals. They are among a nationwide group of 235 acute care facilities that demonstrate positive clinical results in five major diagnostic areas: heart attack, heart failure, pneumonia, coronary bypass surgery, and hip and knee replacement. Medicare has established 33 clinical indicators to show results and improvements, and claims there has been an average improvement in these areas of 6.6 percent for 2005.[68] This effort is designed to increase clinical quality and save lives. As the famous industrial consultant, W. Edwards Deming,[69] would say, "If you get it right the first time, you will improve clinical results and reduce costs."

The center also has published a Web-based list of top performing hospitals in various geographic areas that is accessible by the public.[70] The

66. Wennberg, J., & Cooper, M. (1999).

67. *Effect of Medicare's prospective payment system on the quality of health care.* (2000). The Rand Organization, Rand Health, http://www.rand.org/pubs/research_briefs/RB4519-1/index1.html/.

68. Premier Hospital Quality Incentive Demonstration Project. (2006, April 13). Premier, Centers for Medicare and Medicaid Services, http://www.medicare.gov/.

69. For a complete background on Deming, see http://deming.org/.

70. See http://www.hospitalcompare.hhs.gov/. See also Francis, T. (2007, July 10). How to size up your hospital. *The Wall Street Journal*, D1. The article includes

comparisons include the publication of statistics on how well hospitals are complying with key treatment guidelines. Other comparisons include information on medical outcomes—how well comparable patients actually fare after certain types of surgeries or treatments. This type of data is a key not only to improving quality but also to reducing costs. Medical mistakes increase the costs of treatment and often result in patients staying in the hospital longer, returning to the emergency room for remedial treatment, and continuing to suffer acute or chronic medical problems requiring long-term and costly treatments. Some even die.

Based on compliance with treatment protocols and a demonstration of better clinical outcomes, a new emphasis on identifying such hospitals and rewarding them appropriately can have a dramatic and positive impact on quality and cost. It is a key and necessary step for Medicare to take. Should the same be done for physicians? How would this work? TPAs have a lot of claims data that could be mined with appropriate software to disclose clinical outcomes of physicians. Or, physicians could be required to report their own data.

The decision by Medicare to allow competition for the subcontracting of their benefit plans was intended to increase choices among participants, to introduce market features into the Medicare program, and to eventually improve quality and reduce costs. There is some question about whether Medicare Advantage Plans, which involve private fee-for-service designs, have had any positive impact on cost and quality. Some researchers argue the costs of allowing such choice among Medicare Advantage Plans are higher than the cost of simply providing the original Medicare fee-for-service plan.[71]

Other options of Medicare Advantage Plans include more efficient PPO, HMO, and POS plans.[72] Critics say the plan choices are too complicated for participants to understand and to make informed choices. Since the plans are required to be actuarially equivalent and not identical, the variety of benefits and plan designs does create some confusion and

---

references to other Web sites that compare hospital performance: http://www .leapfroggroup.org/, http://www.nahdo.org/qualityreports.aspx./ (National Association of Health Data Organizers), http://www.talkingquality.gov/compendium/ (Agency for Healthcare Research and Quality), http://www.healthgrades.com/, and http://www.dartmouthatlas.com/ (specializing in data on end-of-life treatments).

71. See Gold, M. (2007, May 15). Medicare Advantage in 2006–2007: What Congress Intended? *Health Affairs*, http://www.healthaffairs.org/; Zhang, J. (2007, May 8). Growing pains of private Medicare plans. *The Wall Street Journal*, A9.

72. In 2006 about 25 percent of Medicare participants had enrolled in Medicare Advantage programs. This number is increasing. Most of the MA enrollees chose HMO plans probably due to the fact that the Advantage plans charge little or no extra premiums for HMOs. Less than a million chose a PPO and also less than a million chose a PFFS plan. Gold, M. (2007).

complexity. The same is true for the Part D coverage.[73] It may take time and considerable effort to effectively communicate these choices, but this would seem a better alternative than to simply eliminate them.

From a private insurance company perspective, a possible market-based incentive could be to avoid enrolling unhealthy participants. The TPAs have considerable design flexibility available to them under Medicare Advantage Plans. While they cannot charge different premiums to participants based on health status, they can limit reimbursements for typically high-risk treatments such as hospitalizations, chemotherapy, and certain surgeries. The best way to counter this is for Medicare to allow for risk adjustments for such patient care. This means that Medicare would pay the insurance company more for accepting higher risk patients into their system.

There are other problems. For example, not all regions can offer as wide a variety of Medicare Advantage Plans as those available in large cities. In many areas there is scant provider competition and the only available design is a fee-for-service plan. Thus, residents in rural areas have fewer options. The ultimate question, however, is what impact has Medicare Advantage had on overall cost and quality? The initial reports are not positive. There has been increased spending but this is due largely to the perpetuation of fee-for-service Medicare Advantage Plans. In 2004, for example, Medicare Advantage Plans cost 8.4 percent more than Medicare would have spent had the enrollees remained in the original Medicare (Part A and Part B) plan.[74]

There is a debate as to whether Congress should have designed Part D (the drug plan) to allow for direct procurement of prescription drugs by Medicare. Instead it established a competitive arena for private insurance companies (TPAs) to enter the Part D market and offer drug plans directly to participants. Medicare and many retail pharmacies provide information and assistance to participants in selecting a prescription drug plan under Part D.[75] This requires the participants to examine the alternative plans in their area, assess which plans provide the drugs they are taking, and at what cost.[76] Critics argue that Medicare could have used its purchasing leverage to significantly reduce the costs of the drugs by purchasing them directly from the pharmaceutical companies or other distributors. Why do

---

73. Biles, B., Dallek, G., & Nicholas, L. (2004, December 15). Medicare Advantage: Déjà vu all over again? *Health Affairs*, W4: 586–587, http://www.healthaffairs.org/.

74. Biles, B., Dallek, G., & Nicholas, L. (2004).

75. See, for example, http://www.medicare.gov/ and select "Medicare Prescription Drug Plan Finder."

76. Private plans offering Part D coverage either separately or as part of its Medicare Advantage Plan have wide differences as to which drugs are within their "formulary" and what the co-pays will be for various "tiers" of prescription drugs based on such criteria as generic or brand status.

you think Congress chose the current, competitive model for Part D? What results might occur if Medicare were the chief procurer of drugs under Part D?[77]

There also is an issue with respect to the continuation of employer-sponsored retiree health care after the retired employee becomes eligible for Medicare. Some employers convert their full retiree health care plan to a supplemental plan after their retiree qualifies for Medicare. In many cases, however, employers simply drop retiree health care when the retiree reaches age 65 and is eligible for health care.[78] There are two concerns here. First, since Part D now includes prescription drugs, an important motivation for the employer's continued sponsorship of a Medicare supplemental plan has been eliminated. Congress, however, was concerned about employers dropping their supplemental coverage of retirees after the inauguration of Part D, so an incentive was introduced into the Medicare legislation in 2003. The employer that continues sponsorship of retiree health care including a drug benefit can coordinate coverage with Medicare, thereby, reducing his current prescription care costs and lowering Medicare's liability as well.[79]

The other concern is, does an employer's decision to terminate retiree health care for those retirees who now qualify for Medicare amount to age discrimination? The EEOC and the U.S. Court of Appeals for the Third Circuit have ruled that such a termination does not violate Title VII of the Civil Rights Act and the Age Discrimination in Employment provisions of

---

77. By applying its leverage, the argument goes, Medicare could have delivered lower drug prices to its participants under Plan D. Others argue that such leverage given to the Medicaid program has caused prices for drugs to increase in the private health care sector. See Enthoven, A., & Fong, K. (2006, December 18). Having drug companies and TPAs compete for business from the participants does offer choice and also reduces the administrative burden of the Medicare bureaucracy.

78. The AARP, in a special report, showed statistics that the number of employers offering retiree health care before and after eligibility for Medicare has been declining. This decision to discontinue retiree health care is placing a huge financial burden on retirees, according to the study. See Johnson, R. (2006, September). *Health insurance coverage and costs at older ages: Evidence from the health and retirement study.* AARP Public Policy Institute, Publication: #2006-20, http://www.aarp.org/ppi/. See also Weller, C., Wenger, J., & Gould, E. (2004). *Health insurance coverage in retirement: The erosion of retirement income security.* The Economic Policy Institute and the Center for American Progress. According to this study, the number of employers offering retiree health care has dropped by 50 percent between 1998 and 2002. This has caused, according to the authors, a number of retirees to be at risk because of the lack of coverage and significant expense of purchasing health care.

79. See http://www.medicare.gov/publications/pubs/pdf/10050/pdf, pp. 60–61.

that law. The Court agreed the exemption given by the EEOC to such plans was reasonable and in the proper public interest. Thus, the decision among some employers to discontinue retiree health care at age 65 was upheld.[80]

So, Medicare is going bankrupt! There have been some efforts by Medicare to improve the quality of medical practices among providers, to introduce financial incentives to providers who practice quality medicine, and to inject competitive features such as Medicare Advantage Plans into the program. But, in spite of these efforts, the projections of financial doom are apparent. What else can be done? Here is a range of other possible reform approaches that might positively impact the long-term solvency of Medicare:

- Increase the Medicare payroll tax. The necessary increase is estimated to be 10 percent by 2020 and 60 percent by 2082.[81] Social Security Trustees indicate that an immediate payroll tax increase of 122 percent would make Medicare solvent for the next 75 years. Could the economy sustain such a tax increase?

- Reduce benefits. The Trustees say they must be reduced now by 51 percent.[82] For example, transform Medicare to a simple, high deductible, non-first-dollar-coverage type plan. This would reduce costs and put the consumer of health care in charge of part of his own health spending. The thought of converting Medicare and Medicaid to consumer-driven programs is gaining some traction.[83] How would it work? Can you visualize a plan design here? In any event, a targeted and necessary reduction in benefits will help drive the policymakers' choice of how it should be done.

- Significantly reduce reimbursements to providers. What would be the expected result? Perhaps providers would no longer accept Medicare patients.[84] Or, they might find other ways to make up

---

80. See *AARP v. EEOC*, 489 F.3d 558 (3d Cir. 2007), cert. denied, U.S. Supreme Court (2008).

81. See *Medicare's fiscal future: Getting worse? Getting better?* (2007, April). American Enterprise Institute for Public Policy Research, Summary, http://www.aei.org/events. See also Status of the Social Security and Medicare Programs (2007).

82. *Status of the Social Security and Medicare Programs.* (2007).

83. Herzlinger, R. (2007). *Who killed health care?* (pp. 191, 249–250). New York: McGraw Hill.

84. This does happen, and it has happened to Medicaid because of lower reimbursement levels. Fuhrman, V. (2007, July 19). Note to Medicaid patients: The doctor won't see you. *The Wall Street Journal*, A1.

their losses, such as cutting back on quality or performing more services.

- Introduce competitive market factors into the program. Could any or all of the following be possible new feature perspectives to apply to Medicare—market prices, focus on quality service and outcomes, financial incentives to providers, or the dynamics of consumer demand? They could be the drivers that cause higher quality outcomes and lower costs.[85]

- Some suggest that Medicare could shift to the Federal Employees Health Benefits Program (FEHBP). This program enjoys wide support among participants and providers, and compares favorably to Medicare in cost and quality. It uses competitive forces to drive choice among participants, includes incentives for best practices, but generally allows the TPAs to design plan offerings.[86]

- Make Medicare the provider under a national health care system for all. This would increase efficiencies by eliminating duplicative administrative costs, broaden the risk pool, and simplify the delivery system that comprises our current "crazy quilt" health system in the United States.

Medicare is a vital program serving over 40 million participants. Its fiscal problems relate to the underlying crisis in the U.S. health care system—cost and affordability. There are a variety of reform measures that have been put forward to make health care generally more affordable and at the same time enhance the overall quality of health of Americans. Reform of Medicare must be part of this effort. We must closely examine the causes of growth in health care spending in order to fashion reform. Time is running out for Medicare and comprehensive changes must be considered. As the Trustees of Social Security and Medicare said in its 2007 report:

> Social Security and Medicare both represent daunting fiscal challenges, though Social Security's is far more manageable analytically and dollar-wise. Their fiscal problems are driven by inexorable demographic change and, in the case of Medicare, relentless increases in health care costs, and are

---

85. See Porter, M., & Tesiberg, E. (2006). *Redefining health care, creating value based competition on results* (pp. 366–373). Boston: Harvard Business School Press. Herzlinger, R. (2007). See also the discussion about health care reform in Chapter 6, supra.

86. Francis, W. (2003, August 7). *The FEHBP as a model for Medicare reform: Separating fact from fiction.* The Heritage Foundation, No. 1674.

not likely to be greatly ameliorated by economic growth or mere tinkering with program financing. Prudence dictates action sooner rather than later to address these fiscal challenges.[87]

Medicaid

In the United States there are layers of health care coverage designed to provide health insurance for everyone. We have employer-sponsored and privately purchased health care insurance that covers 201.6 million people, Medicare that covers 42 million over age 65 as well as the permanently disabled, and Medicaid that is designed to cover persons of low income and minimal resources[88] who have no other access to health insurance and cannot afford it on their own. There are 38.2 million people in the Medicaid program. There is also a special program for uninsured children, which is based on the child's status and not that of his parents, called State Children's Health Insurance Program (SCHIP).[89] Additionally, free emergency health care in many counties in the United States is available for those whose income falls below a certain level. The U.S. Veterans Administration runs military veterans health care. There are 10.5 million people covered by military-related health insurance. All told, the government (state and federal) sponsors about 40 percent of the health care received by U.S. residents. According to the 2007 Census Report, there are 46.9 million who have no health insurance.

Unlike Medicare, which is an entitlement program, Medicaid is a social welfare program with federal and state involvement. Medicaid is administered by state governments that receive federal matching funds of 50 percent up to 83 percent of the total cost of the program. The program must follow certain federal guidelines, although eligibility requirements and the scope of medical services provided are established by the states. Medicaid services include physician care, hospital care, preventive medical care, home care, nursing home care, prescription drug coverage, laboratory and x-ray services, and a variety of other comprehensive health care benefits. To qualify, one's income and resource levels cannot exceed those established by the states, or the participant must suffer from certain physical or mental disabilities. Some minimal cost sharing is permitted under Medicaid, and providers are reimbursed by the administering state agency

---

87. *Status of the Social Security and Medicare Programs* (2007), p. 20.

88. Federal law restricts Medicaid coverage for aliens until they are in the country for more than five years. Emergency care, however, is available.

89. For a compelling argument to integrate SCHIP with Medicaid, see Rosenbaum, S. (2007, August 14). SCHIP reconsidered. *Health Reform*, 608–617.

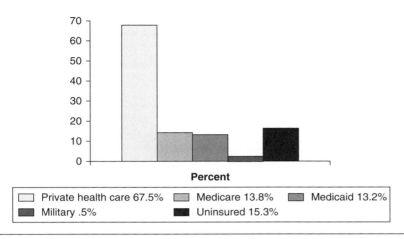

Figure 12.1 Percentage Distribution of Health Care Coverage in the United States (2007)

SOURCE: Income, Poverty, and Health Insurance in the United States, 2007. U.S. Census Bureau. (2008, August).

NOTE: Total exceeds 100 percent due to overlap of people in some categories.

through a fee-for-service or managed care program based on Medicaid-established rates.[90]

Participants in Medicaid number nearly 40 million and outlays have reached close to $300 billion per year. The rapid growth in expenditures has been due to expanded covered populations, higher use of medical resources, the aging population and their need for long-term care, and critical care provided to newborns and older participants. Average payments per participant per year range from around $2,000 for an adult, $1,300 for a child, and approximately $11,000 for an older person. Medicaid payments assist 37 percent of all the births in the United States. The average cost per person for nursing home care is about $22,000 per year. Medicaid finances 60 percent of the care provided in nursing homes. This represents about 1.7 million participants (4 percent) who are generating $37 billion (10 percent) in costs.[91] Adults and children make up about 27 percent of the enrollees in Medicaid but account for only 25 percent of the

90. See Center for Medicare and Medicaid Services, Medicaid Program, Technical Summary, (2007), http://www.cms.hhs.gov/. The managed care programs, such as HMOs often involve per capita fee arrangements with the providers assuming financial risks. Medicaid programs also develop networks of medical providers who are willing to accept the program's established fee schedule.

91. Center for Medicare and Medicaid Services (2007).

Table 12.1   Medicaid Distribution of Costs by Service, FY 2006

Acute care	57.0%
Long-term care	37.0%
Hospital payments	6.0%

SOURCE: Kaiser Family Foundation, http://www.statehealthfacts.org.

spending. The disabled and elderly represent 27 percent of the enrollees and generate 67 percent of the spending.[92]

The State Children's Health Insurance Plan is a federal and state matching fund program that covers targeted low-income children whose parents' income exceeded Medicaid levels, thus, disallowing coverage by Medicaid or other free health insurance programs. There are approximately nine million children who are uninsured, although 75 percent of them qualify for either Medicaid or SCHIP.[93] For 2007 the executive branch of the federal government has allocated $5 billion in matching funds; there are six million children covered by the SCHIP program.[94] The states administer SCHIP and also determine eligibility standards, namely, how high above the poverty level the child's family can be in order to remain qualified for benefits.[95] The required health plan covers inpatient and outpatient hospitalization, physician care, and lab services. It also includes preventive care including well baby and child care and immunizations. The plan can cover abortion as well, but only in the event it is

92. Health Notes. (2006, September 25). The Encyclopedia of Public Health: Medicaid, http://health.enotes.com/.

93. Rosenbaum, S. (2007), p. 608.

94. Estimates are that 20 million children in America are covered by either Medicaid or SCHIP. As of November 2008, there is an indication that the larger Democratic majority in Congress will push for an expansion of SHCIP health coverage for children. This would include allocating more funds for SCHIP and enlarging the eligibility requirements (http://www.medicalnewstoday.com/).

95. For example, 41 states cover children whose families' earnings are at 200 percent of the federal poverty level; seven states allow a 300 percent above poverty level coverage. Rosenbaum, S. (2007), pp. 610–612.

Table 12.2   Medicaid Payments by Enrollment Group, FY 2004

Groups	Percent of Payments
Children	17.2
Adults	11.8
Elderly	26.4
Disabled	40.0
Other	4.6

SOURCE: Kaiser Family Foundation, http://www.statehealthfacts.org.

needed to save the life of the mother or to terminate a pregnancy that resulted from rape or incest.[96]

Perspectives on Medicaid

Medicaid programs have been faced with expanding coverage, increased numbers of participants, and rising health care costs. States must deal with federally imposed mandates for new coverage and in many cases are experiencing fiscal crises arising from their inability to finance the rising overall costs of the program.[97] This has resulted in reduced reimbursements for medical providers that, in turn, have led some providers to drop out of the program. As a result, some Medicaid participants are finding it increasingly difficult to find doctors who accept Medicaid patients.[98] Other providers limit their Medicaid participants to a certain percentage of their practice, or only treat Medicaid patients in clinics. Thus, patients are experiencing delays in getting treatments.[99]

96. State Children's Health Insurance Plan. (2007). Center for Medicare and Medicaid Services, http://www.cms.hhs.gov.

97. Center for Medicare and Medicaid Services. (2007).

98. Bond, M., et al. (2003, February). *Reforming Medicaid*. National Center for Policy Analysis, Policy Report No. 257, http://www.ncpa.org/.

99. Fuhrman, V. (2007, July 19). Note to Medicaid patients: The doctor won't see you. *The Wall Street Journal*, A1. This article explores in some detail the trouble

It is estimated that by 2045, Medicaid costs will total 6.5 percent of GDP.[100] By comparison, France spends 9.7 percent on health care for its entire population.[101] Medicaid currently accounts for 15 percent of all health care spending in the United States, and covers 25 percent of all children, 40 percent of all births, 70 percent of all nursing home resident care, and 50 percent of nursing home costs nationwide.[102]

Taken together, Medicaid, Medicare, and SCHIP have a substantial impact on the health care system in the United States. As major sponsors in our overall health care system, they have an impact on the demand and supply, utilization, cost, and quality of health care resources.[103] The programs do provide essential and comprehensive health care insurance and protection for retired persons, the poor, disabled, and many needy children. But the states and federal government who sponsor such programs are being overwhelmed by their rising costs and expanding coverage and utilization.[104] Many of the Medicare reform issues relating to its financial continuity, as discussed above, are also relevant to the Medicaid and SCHIP programs.[105] But let's look a little closer at one feature of Medicaid that is unique to the program and is having a significant impact on its fiscal integrity. A question that is frequently raised during discussions of

---

Michigan Medicaid patients are having in finding doctors who accept Medicaid patients. It notes that many doctors, who limit their Medicaid "office" practice willingly go to neighborhood clinics where they are salaried and do not have to deal with low reimbursement levels or claims paperwork. According to the article, many Medicaid reimbursements are less than 50 percent of those allowed under Medicare or private insurance companies.

100. Kronic, R., & Rousseau, D. (2007). Is Medicaid sustainable? Projections for the program's second 40 years. *Health Affairs, 26*(2), 271–287. Currently it is 2.0 percent of Gross Domestic Product. See Congressional Budget Office, Long-Range Fiscal Policy Brief (2002, July).

101. International Health Care Comparisons (2005); The Kings Fund (2005, January), http://www.kingsfund.org.uk./.

102. Kronic, R. (2007).

103. Finklestein, A. (2006, April). *The aggregate effects of health insurance: Evidence from the introduction of Medicare.* National Bureau of Economic Research, Working Paper 11619, http://www.nber.org/.

104. Samuelson, R. (2006, September 18). The monster at our door. *Newsweek, 148*(12), 51. Federal spending on the aging is expected to double by 2030, and 75 percent of that spending will be on health care.

105. For example, a study by the National Center for Policy Analysis recommended that Medicaid should pay for results not services, encourage participants to utilize fewer health care resources instead of more, stop paying institutions on a cost basis, thereby paying the most inefficient providers the highest fees for services, and empower state sponsors to manage their own health care dollars, and to experiment and see what works. Bond, M. (2003, February).

the fiscal woes of Medicaid is, what, if anything, can be done about long-term care?

Long-term care for the aged represents a huge and disproportionate share of overall Medicaid spending. Such care involves helping patients with chronic illnesses manage their daily lives. The usual venues for such care are either home or a nursing care facility. About 80 percent receive long-term care at home. Those most in need of long-term care are widows in their 80s who have little income and resources and are suffering from dementia or other mental impairment.[106] It is estimated that nearly 70 percent of those who are 65 years old today will require some long-term care before they die. The average length of time for care is three years; however, around 20 percent continue for five years. The average cost for home care is $34,000 per year and a private room in a nursing home costs about $75,000 per year.[107] These costs could deplete the savings of many Americans.

> These costs far exceed the financial resources of most families. Those who impoverish themselves paying for these services are likely to turn to the government to help finance their long-term care costs. The program they most often turn to is Medicaid, which has become the nation's principle source of payments for professional long-term care services for the elderly and the disabled.[108]

While there are private insurance polices available that cover long-term care, few people have bought them, and only about 7 percent of the costs for such care is currently being paid for by these policies.[109] The problem of Medicaid costs and, in particular, long-term care is especially apparent among the states that spend on average 18 percent (net after federal matching) of their budgets on Medicaid.[110]

In order to qualify for long-term care under Medicaid, an individual must be unable to care for himself and have little income and few resources. Many (about 50 percent) who are not eligible for Medicaid upon their admission to a long-term care facility become eligible after spending down their assets. This, of course, leads us to ask, should

---

106. Gleckman, H. (2007, April). *Medicaid and long-term care: How will rising costs affect services for an aging population?* Center for Retirement Research at Boston College, Number 7-4.

107. Gleckman, H. (2007).

108. Gleckman, H. (2007).

109. Komisar, H., & Thompson, L. (2007, February). *National spending for long-term care fact sheet.* Washington, DC: Georgetown University Long-Term Care Financing Project.

110. Henry J. Kaiser Foundation (2007). State Health Facts, http://www.statehealthfacts.org/.

taxpayers foot the bill for long-term care or should individuals be expected to spend their entire savings until they meet the qualifications for state help under Medicaid?

There is some indication that asset transfers have been employed by persons wishing to qualify for Medicaid. For example, persons who reasonably anticipate eventual nursing home care admission sometimes grant or put all or part of their assets into an irrevocable, inter vivos trust naming their family or others as beneficiaries. Prior to his death, the trustee can spend some of the trust income for the care of the grantor. On the grantor's death, however, the funds are distributed to the beneficiaries. If the trust is created five years before the grantor's admission to a nursing home facility, then none of the assets of the trust can be used to test their eligibility for Medicaid. The state in that case pays the bills for the nursing home. There are a number of suggested solutions for this particular problem, including:

- Encourage the purchase of long-term care insurance by individuals. Congress passed amendments to the Partnership Act in 2006 that allow the possible deduction of long-term care premiums along with medical expenses provided they exceed certain levels. The new law also allows those who purchase long-term care insurance to retain assets up to the face amount of the policy when participating in Medicaid. The results, thus far, have been disappointing because of the high costs of such policies. What else might be done to encourage persons to acquire long-term care insurance? Are there tax or other incentives that might be used? Are there major opportunities to rethink and redesign long-term care that could result in less costly approaches? Should we mandate insurance coverage?

- Expand home-based care. This could be facilitated if Medicaid would make some financial reimbursements for family members who provide such care.

- Since most of the nursing home patients suffer from dementia and Alzheimer's disease, a cure or more advanced treatment of these conditions could have a dramatic effect on Medicaid costs.

- Allow for consumer self-directed choice among participants who receive cash and counseling from Medicaid. This is being tried in several pilot projects in the United States.[111]

111. *Long term care reform, Policy Council document.* (2006, September 28). Center for Medicare and Medicaid Services, http://www.cms.hhs.gov.

Table 12.3   Distribution of Medicaid or Long-Term Care, FY 2006

Intermediate Care Facility for the Mentally Retarded	Mental Health Facilities	Nursing Home	Home Health and Personal Care
11.7%	3.7%	43.8%	40.8%

SOURCE: Kaiser Family Foundation, http://www.statehealthfacts.org.

Table 12.4   Average Annual Growth in Medicaid Spending, FY 1990–FY 2006

1990–2001	2001–2004	2004–2006
10.9%	9.4%	2.8%

SOURCE: Kaiser Family Foundation, http://www.statehealthfacts.org.

How have other countries dealt with the issue of long-term care? What are our values as a society? What are the financial realities of long-term care and Medicaid, and how might they be managed? Medicaid is a vital and significant program that provides needed medical care for the poor and disabled. Its problems of rising costs and utilization are inextricably related to the general health care issues now facing our policymakers. Potential health care reform solutions for the country, no doubt, would include Medicare and Medicaid programs. The problem of long-term care, however, is different and unique. We need to answer the question, should it be provided as part of our structure of social insurance, or as a personal or family responsibility?[112] Like health care, long-term care insurance, albeit expensive, is available to individuals and could be an employer-sponsored benefit. Therefore, we should consider whether the insurance products and plan designs for long-term care might provide a foundation for reform of this important benefit.

Tables 12.3 and 12.4 show how long-term care under Medicaid is allocated and the average annual growth in Medicaid spending.

---

112. Gleckman, H. (2007).

Veterans' Health Care[113]

For most former active duty military veterans, the U.S. government provides inpatient and outpatient hospital care. Those who have experienced combat-related injuries are given a priority for treatment,[114] but all veterans, now totaling 5.8 million, whether they have been in combat or not, are eligible to receive treatment at one of the 1,400 Veterans Administration (VA) facilities throughout the United States. The VA health care plan also covers medical expenses of certain eligible family members in the event the veteran is disabled or deceased. Except in cases where the veteran has combat or other service-related injuries, has been a prisoner of war, or has insufficient income, he is required to make co-payments for treatment. Co-pays range from $8 for prescriptions to $992 for inpatient care. There is no monthly premium for veterans' care arising from service-related injuries or conditions.

At least two years of free medical care is also extended to reservists who were activated and served in a theatre of combat. The reservist can continue coverage after the two years, but will be placed in a different priority group and may be required to make co-payments.

The care available includes a wide variety of preventive care and immunizations, emergency, ambulatory, and diagnostic treatments, hospitalizations, adult day and nursing home care, as well as prescription medications.[115] Care is dispensed at hospitals, clinics, and nursing homes, and the VA employs 14,800 doctors and 61,000 nurses.[116]

Veterans' health care received some interesting attention in the past several years because it compared very favorably to other hospitals and health systems in the United States. The VA had a higher patient satisfaction rate than private institutions, lower mortality rates than Medicare Advantage patients, better clinical ratings for preventive care and chronic disease care such as diabetes, and dispensed care at a lower cost per patient than Medicare.[117] This

---

113. General information about Veterans Health Care can be obtained at http://www.va.gov/.

114. This is a statutory-based priority. Noncombat veterans may have to endure longer waits for their health care needs. Through its various programs about 10 million persons are covered by military health insurance. U.S. Census Bureau (2007).

115. The long-term care benefit requires co-pays of up to $97 per day (after the 22nd day), depending on the veteran's financial status. See http://www.va.gov/.

116. Waller, D. (2006, August 27). How veterans hospitals became the best in health care. *Time*, http://www.time.com/time/magazine/article/0,9171,1376238,00.html/ . See also Asch. S., et al. (2004, December 21). Comparison of quality of care for patients in the Veterans Health Administration and patients in nation sample. *Annals of Internal Medicine, 141*(12), 938–945.

117. Waller, D. (2006). The precise cost difference was $1,500 per year.

favorable performance has continued for several years. In addition, VA facilities received higher health care quality grades from the well-respected Joint Commission on Accreditation of Health Care Organizations.[118] Several reasons are cited for better clinical and patient satisfaction outcomes:

- Since VA patients are typically patients for life, the VA can realize a better return on its investment in preventive care than most other providers and sponsors.[119]

- Since care is integrated, patients can see a variety of specialists all under the VA umbrella, enabling better coordination of care, reducing mistakes, and better tracking of clinical outcomes.[120]

- The VA has a highly sophisticated and integrated medical record system that is available in only a few other private hospitals. This process enhances the quality of treatments and reduces medical errors.[121] Medical records are kept on a system that is routinely accessed by practitioners. Patients receive bar-coded bracelets, and medications are bar-coded as well. If the patient's code does not match the medication code, the medicine will not be released. These records become discrete databases used to test the efficacy of treatments and to maintain a state-of-the-art disease management program.[122]

The Veterans Administration health care system represents an additional opportunity for Americans to receive health care benefits. Care under the VA program is inexpensive for the recipient and in many cases free. The integrated structure of the VA system and the advanced use of medical records technology demonstrates how such reform can enhance the efficiency and reduction in cost of medical care. Unfortunately, it is not all good news at VA hospitals. Recent issues pertaining to the housing of wounded soldiers and veterans at Walter Reed Army Medical Center led to the creation of a Presidential Commission that made a number of recommendations for improvement.[123] Among them, the Commission strongly urged a more aggressive use of post-traumatic stress disorder treatment. In general,

---

118. News Release (2002, May 13), Department of Veterans Affairs. The VA's mean score in 2002 was two points above the national average.

119. Waller, D. (2006). Longman, P. (2007). *Best care anywhere: Why the VA health care is better than yours.* New American Foundation; PoliPointPress.

120. Asch. S. et al. (2004). Asch's research showed also that the VA does a better job of measuring clinical outcomes in its facilities.

121. Asch, S. et al. (2004).

122. Longman, P. (2005, January/February). The best care anywhere. *Washington Monthly.*

123. See http://www.pccww.gov/, (2007, July 25), President's Commission on Care for America's Returning Wounded Warriors (the PCCWW report).

however, the structure, health care delivery system, clinical treatment protocols, and use of integrated medical records at veterans' hospitals could be a point of reference for us all as we search the landscape for models and designs that will make health care in America more accessible, affordable, and available, and cause it to focus on true quality outcomes.

Mandated Benefits (COBRA, HIPAA, FMLA, USERRA)

We turn our attention to several benefits that are mandated by federal statutes. They have been incorporated into mostly employer-sponsored health care plans and leave programs that respond to special life events as we described in Chapter 2.

Max Thomas works for an IT company. Due to an unexpected drop in sales, he has been informed that he will be laid off. Max participates in an employer-sponsored health care plan, and is concerned what will happen to his health insurance as a result of the layoff. The company pays about 80 percent of the cost of the plan, and he pays a monthly premium of $150 plus deductibles, coinsurance, and co-pays. Max visits the human resources department and is told that if he wishes to continue his health insurance, he must file an application according to the Consolidated Omnibus Budget Reconciliation Act (COBRA).[1] COBRA is a law that permits employees, spouses, dependent children, ex-spouses, and retirees to temporarily continue employer-sponsored health coverage at favorable group rates, provided they have experienced a prescribed life event that has caused a loss of coverage.

Does this law help Max? Yes. Being laid off is one of the life events prescribed in COBRA that allows for a continuation of coverage. His complete health care benefit plan must be continued. Whatever benefits were included in the health plan will be extended to Max, and as long as the life event is a layoff, he can continue coverage for 18 months. He can be required to pay up to 102 percent of the full cost of the employer's group plan. In Max's case, this could be much more than the $150 per month he currently pays. He believes this is better than having no coverage at all.

---

1. The Consolidated Omnibus Budget Reconciliation Act of 1986. (Public Law 99-272, April 7, 1986). The law amends ERISA, the Internal Revenue Code, and the Public Health Service Act.

Other COBRA qualifying life events that result in a loss of health care coverage include voluntary termination from employment, involuntary termination except in the case of gross misconduct, reduction in hours, divorce or legal separation, loss of dependent child status, and death of the covered employee. In the case of loss of job or reduction in hours, the employee's spouse and dependent children may continue the health care coverage. The length of time COBRA coverage continues ranges from 18 to 36 months, depending on the life event. Any employer with 20 or more employees must offer COBRA coverage to his workers, and the affected participant must elect COBRA within 60 days of the life event.

> Eric Smith is a senior student at Midwestern University. He has been covered by his mother's employer-sponsored health care plan for many years. His mother has told him that as long as he is a full-time student and is under age 25, he will be covered by her plan. Since he is about to graduate and will no longer be a full-time student, he is concerned about continued health care coverage because he plans to travel around the United States for four months after graduation before looking for a job. Can he continue to participate in his mother's plan? Yes, provided he elects COBRA coverage in a timely manner and pays the 102 percent monthly premium; and in the case of a loss of dependent status, as well as divorce or death of the covered employee, the affected person (Eric) can retain coverage for 36 months.[1]
>
> ---
>
> 1. We should note that since Eric is young and healthy, he could probably find a short-term health insurance policy to buy during this period. The cost of such insurance may be significantly less than what he must pay for COBRA coverage under his mom's policy. See http://www.temporaryhealthinsurance.com/ and http://www.ehealthinsurance.com/.

COBRA requires the employer to notify the plan participant, his dependents, and the health care plan of the opportunity to extend health care coverage. In some cases, however, where the participant has exclusive knowledge of the life event, such as loss of dependent status or divorce, it is incumbent on him to advise the plan sponsor of the change in status. COBRA is a benefit mandated by law and, in that sense, is similar to HIPAA,[124] which mandates health care plans to cover preexisting conditions

---

124. The Health Insurance Portability and Accountability Act, 29 USC §1181 et seq. HIPAA sets standards for the privacy and confidentiality of medical records and information, and also requires special enrollments for spouses who have lost

of new subscribers when certain conditions are met. HIPAA was intended
to mitigate the problem of job lock that results when an employee fears
that changing jobs may result in his loss of health coverage for his preexisting health condition.[125]

> Francie suffers from diabetes. She works at an IT company but has
> been offered a job at a higher salary by a local competitor. She wants
> the job but is concerned the new employer's health care plan will not
> cover her diabetes treatments and medicine because they have a pol-
> icy of excluding coverage of preexisting conditions. Francie has had
> health care coverage with her current employer since her date of hire,
> five years ago, and sees a physician for her diabetes every six weeks.
> She is contemplating turning down the lucrative offer of employment
> because of the potential loss of health care coverage for her diabetes.

HIPAA was intended to help people like Francie. Under HIPAA, an
employer's health care plan can exclude coverage for a preexisting condition, but only for a maximum of one year. Then, coverage must be provided. In many cases the employer's ability to exclude is restricted for a
number of reasons:

- If the employee has not received any care or treatment within six
  months before the enrollment date of the new employer's health
  care plan, he will not be considered to have a preexisting condition
  under the law, and no exclusion of coverage can be allowed.

- If the employee had "creditable" coverage[126] prior to enrolling in
  the new plan, the allowable preexisting coverage exclusion period is
  reduced by the aggregate periods of such coverage.

---

health care coverage to enroll in their spouse's plan. It also provides restrictions
on special rules for eligibility and premiums for persons based on their health
status. It also guarantees coverage under individual plans for certain persons who
have exhausted their COBRA coverage and have no access to group health coverage. See http://www.dol.gov/ebsa/. HIPAA does allow health care plans to vary
offer rewards or impose penalties that exceed 20 percent of the cost of coverage
based on a participant's compliance or noncompliance with a bona fide "wellness
program." See HIPAA Regulations Governing Wellness Programs, effective July
l, 2007. (2006). U.S. Department of Labor.

125. See Frequently Asked Questions about HIPAA. (2007). U.S. Department of
Labor, Employee Benefits Security Administration, http://www.dol.gov/ebsa/.

126. "Creditable Coverage" means a group health care plan, health insurance, a
public health care plan, COBRA, and other types of health coverage. See 29 USC
§1181(c).

- A period of creditable coverage is not counted if the individual was not covered by a plan for 63 or more days prior to the enrollment date of the new plan.[127]

- A health care plan cannot impose any exclusion for newborns and adopted children who were covered by health insurance within 30 days of birth or adoption.[128]

- A health care plan cannot consider pregnancy as a preexisting condition.[129]

> With respect to Francie, should she move to the new job? Let's apply the provisions of HIPAA. Does she have a preexisting condition? Yes, she has been treated within the last six weeks. Can the new employer exclude coverage for her diabetes condition? Yes. How long can they exclude? Without creditable coverage, they can exclude for up to one year. In Francie's case, the period of exclusion is reduced by the period of prior creditable coverage. Since she had such coverage for five years, the period of exclusion will be reduced to zero months. (There would be 60 months of creditable coverage applied to a maximum 12 months of exclusion.) She can go to the new employer and have full medical coverage for all of her conditions, including diabetes, from the outset.

In this vignette, HIPAA is used as an example of a law that facilitates an employee's freedom to move from one employer to another. A similar mandated benefit relates to imposing an obligation on the employer to grant a leave of absence to employees suffering from illness or who are pregnant. It also protects employees who miss work because they are obligated to care for certain family members who are ill. The federal law is called the Family and Medical Leave Act (FMLA).

> Joe Barnard works for Zenith Chemical, Inc., in the Receiving Department. Zenith employs 150 workers. Joe's job is to document the receipt of raw materials from suppliers and to unload and place containers of such materials in specified warehouse slots, where they

---

127. 29 USC §1181(c)(2).

128. 29 USC §1181(d)(1,2).

129. 29 USC §1181(d)(3).

remain until they are mixed, treated, and converted into various fin-
ished products. Joe has worked for Zenith for five years, but has had
a problem with absenteeism. The company has a no-fault attendance
program. Their rules prohibit excessive absenteeism, defined as
incurring more than an average of three absences per month over a
90-day period. This would include an absence without call-in, arriv-
ing late or leaving early regardless of reasons or excuses, or an
absence of more than one day that is not supported by a doctor's
statement indicating the employee suffered from an illness and was
totally incapacitated and unable to perform his job. Employer-
approved leaves of absence are not counted as excessive absences.

Over the last 90 days, Joe has been late for work four times, missed
two days without call-in, and in just the past week has been absent
four days due to the flu. For the latter, he has a doctor's statement
documenting that he suffered from the flu. Due to the doctor's busy
office schedule, Joe never visited the doctor or was examined personally by him, but was prescribed medicine based on symptoms
described by Joe over the phone. The human resources manager just
met with Joe and gave him a written warning stating that his noncompliance with the company's attendance program is unacceptable and
future excessive absenteeism could lead to his discharge. He has
been placed on probation. What are the issues here? Can Joe be
legally disciplined? Let's look a little closer at the Family and Medical
Leave Act (FMLA).

The U.S. Congress passed the FMLA[130] in 1993 to protect the job of an
employee who is absent due to childbirth or adoption, whose serious illness prevents him from working, or who had obligations to care for an
immediate family member suffering from a serious illness.[131] The maximum leave allowed is 12 weeks per year, and the law does not require the
payment of lost salary or wages during this period. It does require the
continuation of health benefits to which the employee was otherwise

130. See 29 USC §2601-2654; also see 29 CFR §825.100-800. Also see http://www
.dol.gov/ ("Leave Benefits").

131. More specifically, unpaid leave not to exceed 12 weeks in a year must be
granted for the birth and care of the newborn child of the employee, for placement with the employee of a son or daughter for adoption or foster care, care
for a spouse, child, or parent with a serious health care condition, and when
the employee is unable to work because of a "serious health condition." 29 USC
§2601 and http://www.dol.gov/, Fact Sheet #28, The Family and Medical Leave
Act of 1993.

entitled, and mandates the employer to restore the returning employee to his original job or to an equivalent job and compensation.[132] The law applies to most employers with 50 or more employees and to an employee with one year of service.[133] The major issues in interpreting the law are:

- What is a "serious health condition"?

- Under what circumstances can the employee take "intermittent leave"?

- When can the employer require the employee to use vacation or other "paid" leave entitlements instead of the unpaid FMLA leave?

- Who has the obligation to notify and designate the leave as covered by the FMLA?

- How does one calculate the 12-week period?

The definition of "serious health condition" is an illness requiring hospital admission or treatment by a health care provider for a condition resulting in incapacity of three or more consecutive days. Would this include a bout of the flu?[134] With respect to "intermittent leave," it cannot be taken for the birth of a child or for adoption purposes without the expressed approval of the employer. Other types of leave relating to serious health conditions can be taken on an intermittent basis when medically necessary.

The employer can require the employee to use his vacation time or accrued sick leave as a substitute for FMLA leave, and must designate it as paid leave when they choose to impose this requirement. When possible, employees are required to give 30 days' advance notice of their need to take a leave.

In designating the leave as covered "FMLA leave," the employer has the responsibility to be sure the employee understands his rights as well as the consequences he might face if he ignores the requirements under FMLA. The employer also must designate how it will calculate the one-year period so the employee understands how his absence will be counted.[135] Finally,

---

132. A "key employee" is a highest paid 10 percent of employees whose absence could cause substantial and grievous economic injury to the employer. Such "key employees" may be legally denied job restoration. 29 USC §2601.

133. The employee must work a minimum of 1,250 hours in the 12 months previous to the leave in order to be considered eligible.

134. 29 CFR 825.114, http://www.dol.gov, Compliance Assistance, FMLA-87, December 12, 1996.

135. See *Bachelder v. America West Airlines*, 259 F. 3d 1112 (9th Cir. 2001), where the Court held the employer must properly disclose in advance which of the four authorized methods of calculating a "year" it will use. It cannot be designated

the employer can require a medical certification supporting the need for leave, as well as second or third opinions and periodic reports on the condition of an employee who is on leave.

So what about Joe at Zenith? Can he be disciplined? It would appear that his late arrivals and early departures as well as his absences without call are not protected by the FMLA. The four-day absence due to the flu, however, caused him to go over the absence limit and must be more closely examined. Is flu a serious health condition? It could be. Can flu symptoms and resulting incapacities continue for more than three days? Yes, provided the doctor or provider certifies the condition and resulting incapacity. Joe did consult with a physician, but did he receive treatment? Would a telephone call qualify as treatment? According to the Department of Labor, no. He must actually see the doctor. So, the four days would legally count as absences and are not insulated from discipline by the FMLA. Joe had better improve his attendance or he soon may be out of a job.[136]

In the FMLA we see a public policy initiative designed to deal with work-life conflicts and to provide job protection for employees who experience lifecycle events.[137] The law does not require compensation, although there are proposals in Congress to add this feature, nor does it prevent employers from offering paid leave for pregnancy or illness, which many of them do.

The current landscape of mandated benefits also includes rights of certain military personnel who are called up for active duty and required to leave their job. How are their jobs protected? The law that provides such protection is the Uniformed Services Employment and Reemployment Rights Act of 1994 (USERRA).[138]

---

after the employee's absences have occurred. The four methods include calendar year, a 12-month leave year such as one based on the employee's anniversary date, a one-year period beginning on the date when the first FMLA leave began, a "rolling" 12-month period looking backward from the date the employee uses FMLA leave.

136. See http://www.dol.gov, Compliance Assistance, FMLA-87, December 12, 1996. In *Miller v. AT&T Corp.*, 250 F.3d 820 (4th Cir. 2001), the Court held that where an employee saw her doctor twice and was absent for four days due to the flu, the employer must consider the absence as protected FMLA leave.

137. In cases where both spouses work for the same company, the couple must combine their leave to total 12 weeks if the time off is for childbirth, adoption, or the care of a parent who has a serious health condition, http://www.dol.gov, Compliance Assistance, FMLA-87, December 12, 1996.

138. 38 USC §4301 et seq.

> Madeline Rose is a staff sergeant in the U.S. Army Reserves. She also works at Allied Metals as a fabricator, Level 1. Her Reserve Unit has been called up for active duty in the Middle East. She provides her company with notice, departs for the Middle East, and returns to Allied after two years of active service. Upon her return, she notices that two other employees who were also in the fabricator Level 1 job have moved up to a higher paying Level 2 position. She asks the plant's human resources manager if she should be placed in the same Level 2 position. What is the obligation of her employer?

Designed to protect the jobs of persons required to serve in the country's uniformed services, and to minimize the disadvantages arising in the workplace as a result of such service, USERRA is a law that applies to every individual employee required to serve and to all employers. It also prohibits job discrimination against persons who have served in the military. Thus, it protects employment and reemployment rights of persons in uniformed services, which includes all military branches as well as the Public Health Service. It applies to training, deployment for active duty, full-time National Guard duty, and disaster response performed by the U.S. Public Health Service. In general, the maximum length of service for which protection is extended is five years. A person who has been discharged from the service under a prescribed list of negative scenarios, namely, the discharge was due to a disqualifying event, is not entitled to the protection under the Act. Persons must report for work[139] within a defined number of days, ranging from eight hours to 90 days after being discharged, depending on the duration of the military service. When the person has incurred a disability during service, the time to report is extended to two years or more depending on the particular circumstances of the disability.

The law includes what is called an "escalator principle," which allows each returning service member to step back onto the seniority escalator at the point the person would have occupied had he remained continuously employed, so long as the person is qualified (to perform the job) or can become qualified after reasonable efforts.[140]

---

139. For an employee whose service extends more than 31 days, he may be required to submit documentation on the date and circumstances of his discharge.

140. See U.S. Department of Labor, Veterans Employment and Training Service, A Non-Technical Guide to USERRA (2003, March).

Aside from the escalator principle, employers are obliged to reemploy returning service members promptly, and must provide reasonable training and/or retraining in the event the employee's skills render them no longer qualified to perform the job due to technological advances. Reasonable accommodations also are mandated for returning service members who have disabilities that were incurred or aggravated due to military service.

Returning service men and women will be continued as participants in the employer's pension plans for both vesting and benefit accrual purposes. Such service members may be required to make contributions to a particular retirement plan if other employees on leaves of absence are so required. Service members can continue to participate in their employer's health care plan for up to 18 months, provided they contribute up to 102 percent of the cost of the plan. Also, upon return to work, no waiting period or preexisting exclusion is applicable with respect to the health care plan. Employers are prohibited from discharging service personnel without just cause for a period of one year after returning to the job, or six months for those whose military service extended from 31 to 180 days. This restriction does not apply to layoffs or reductions in force that occurred and would have included the service member.

Table 12.5 is a summary of the key laws that mandate certain types of benefits. There are others we have not discussed.[141] The chart facilitates a comparison of these laws and an overall view of their basic concepts and intent. As we merge the application of government-sponsored benefits and the laws that mandate certain benefits, we find that a range of lifecycle events is addressed. While there are financing, enforcement, and coverage issues still apparent, nevertheless, there are many people with particular needs who are given protection and support by these benefits. Our challenge is to see if these benefits can be broadened to remedy situations like the 45 million uninsured and others whose circumstances make it difficult or impossible to enjoy retirement, good health, and job security. In

---

141. For example, the Worker Adjustment and Retraining Notification Act (WARN) of 1988 (29 USC 2101 and 20 CFR 639 et seq.) requires advance notice of facility closings and layoffs. See http://www.doleta.gov/. The Pregnancy Discrimination Act protects female employees who are pregnant; the ADEA prohibits age discrimination that extends to benefit design and participation; Title VII of the Civil Rights Act prohibits discrimination with respect to all aspects of employment including benefits; the National Labor Relations Act requires employers to bargain with unions over employee benefits; the Multi-Employer Pension Protection Act requires employers who are leaving a multi-employer pension plan to fund the unfunded vested liabilities before ceasing their participation; and the Security and Exchange Act(s), as well as Sarbanes-Oxley, partially regulate how certain benefits, particularly those involving how company securities are administered and awarded.

Table 12.6   Mandated Benefits

Benefits Law	ER Covered	EE Covered	Life Event	Rights/Privileges	EE Responsibility
COBRA	20 employees	Health care participants	Loss of coverage (loss of job, divorce, loss of dependent status)	Continuation of same coverage, 18 or 36 months	Pay 102% of health care premium
HIPAA	Any group health care plan	Has preexisting condition (treatment within six months)	Change job and apply for new health care coverage	No exclusion of preexisting condition for more than 12 months; creditable coverage offset; pregnancy LOS; private med recs.; parity in pysch. benefits	No "break in service" of coverage of more than 63 days; EE must prove evidence of creditable coverage
FMLA	50 employees	One year of service	Serious illness, pregnancy/adoption, care of family (child, spouse, parent)	Up to 12 weeks of leave/year; restoration of employment rights (except executives); benefits continuation; ER can substitute paid leave (vacation)	EE required to give 30 days' notice; must show evidence of serious condition; limits on intermittent leave for birth or adoption
USERRA	Any ER of covered uniformed service EE	Active or Reserve member of Armed Forces, National Guard, or Public Health Service	Activation of unit for military operations, disasters, riots, training	Reemployment and restoration of all employment rights, unless EE was dishonorably discharged; no discharge within one year without cause	Maximum of five years' leave and EE must return to work within statutory periods

Chapter 13, Global Benefits, we will examine how benefits are financed, designed, and provided in other countries. We will see if there are models for comparison and application in the United States, and also examine comparative labor costs that are affected by employers' benefit sponsorship or funding.

Chapter Exercises

1. Determine a parent, grandparent, or friend's projected Social Security benefit. Go to the Social Security Online Web site (http://www.ssa.gov/) and select under "Retirement," "Calculate Your Benefits." Choose Option No. 1, "Quick Calculator," and select a date and year of birth, average final income, "future retirement date option" at age 62, and the full retirement age of your participant. Select to "see your benefit" using "today's dollars." Note the benefit in the top left part of the window. What is the percentage reduction arising from an early retirement? Also note what amounts the "survivors" will receive should your participant die. What seems to be the most critical variable in your calculation?

2. Go http://www.ssa.com/ and, in particular, the wage indexing found under the page "Average Indexed Monthly Earnings (AIME)," and see how actual wages earned are inflated by the index. Also on the Web site, find the latest "bend points" for a benefit calculation. How would you change the AIME and the bend points to make Social Security less costly? What impact would these changes have for participants?

3. President George W. Bush proposed a Social Security reform idea that would create a personal retirement account owned by the participant. The plan would involve the diversion of some percentage of the FICA payroll tax of certain Social Security participants under age 50 who voluntarily select the personal account option. The monies in this account would be invested in capital markets at the direction of the participant, and the standard Social Security benefit will be proportionately reduced. The eventual retiree will get a partial benefit from Social Security and receive a distribution of the monies accumulated in his personal account. Due to the diversion of payroll taxes, there would be a temporary and rather large Social Security deficit produced by this approach. The hope, however, is that the personal account option, together with the adjusted Social Security benefit, will produce higher total retirement

income for the participant and lower the liability of the Social Security Administration due to the lower benefit owed. See http://www.whitehouse.gov/infocus/social-security/. Over the long term, does the personal account idea improve the fiscal integrity of the Social Security program? Explain. In view of the economic turbulence occurring in the fall of 2008, do personal accounts still have some political viability? Explain. What arguments would you advance to support the idea? What are the arguments against their consideration?

4. Visit the Heritage Foundation Web site at http://www.heritage .org/. On the home page, go to "Browse Heritage Research," and choose "Domestic Issues." In the drop-down box, select "Retirement Income and Social Security," and then "Personal Retirement Account Calculator." Input some assumed ages and income and see how you would fare under this Personal Retirement Account approach. What is the assumed rate of investment return for the Personal Account?

5. Go to http://www.socialsecurity.org/ and see what the Cato Institute has to say about Social Security reform. Select "Cato's Plan" in the left column.

6. With respect to Social Security reform proposals, the Society of American Actuaries suggests that quantitative measures be applied to various proposals. These would include: (1) Does the proposal provide for "long-term" adequacy or is it a temporary solution? The Trustees of Social Security traditionally use a 75-year timeline. (2) Will the trust fund balances remain positive over this projected period? (3) How will the fund ratio (fund assets at the beginning of the year divided by the benefit payments totaled at the end of the year) at the 75th year compare to the 70th year? (4) Will the proposal require shifting of general tax revenue to the Social Security funding? Use these measures and the analysis of the Actuary Society to evaluate the various reform proposals. *Quantitative measures for evaluating Social Security reform proposals, Issue Brief.* (2002, April). American Academy of Actuaries, http://www.actuary.org/pdg/socialsecurity/reform/. How do these criteria apply to the various reform proposals?

7. Review some of the quality efforts and clinical outcomes data programs initiated by Medicare and other organizations that are currently available, as described in this chapter. Then develop a bullet point and comprehensive outline of a national plan for introducing quality into our Medicare system. Include in your outline the concept, goals, design features, implementation steps,

the financial and quality of life impact of your plan, and the
process you would employ to evaluate it.

8. Go to http://www.medicare.gov/ and get some comparative
information on Part D prescription drug plans. Select a zip code,
enter one or two prescriptions and dosages, select preferred
pharmacies, and then compare the costs and the benefit designs of
various plans. For example, do they provide any benefits while the
second deductible ("donut hole") is in place? What are the
performance criteria that you might use to evaluate the various
plans? Should there be more criteria? Choose a plan for a family
member, friend, or yourself and be prepared to discuss the basis
for your decision.

9. David has health coverage through his wife's plan. They are
divorcing. David's employer does not provide health care coverage.
What are David's options with respect to continuing health care
coverage? How long can he maintain this coverage?

10. John was discharged by his employer for falsifying his time card.
He wants to continue the health care coverage provided by his
employer. Can he do this? What are the issues and how would you
resolve them?

11. Anne has been covered by a health care plan for the last three years
provided by her current employer. The plan does not include
dental coverage. She has had some treatment for a problem tooth
within the last two months. She is now changing jobs and the new
employer provides dental coverage. Can the new employer exclude
coverage for her current dental problem? If so, for how long can
the exclusion last?

12. Harry works at a factory that makes molds for plastic products
such as water bottles and other household items. His wife is about
to deliver their first-born and he requests his employer grant him
12 weeks (60 days) of leave so he can help his wife care for the
baby. He would like to take his leave on an intermittent basis (two
days per week) over 30 weeks so as to maximize assistance to his
wife. His employer has declined to grant his request. What are the
issues and how would you resolve them?

13. Mike has worked at a commercial baking company for five years
and has participated in the company's health care plan. He has
been looking for a better opportunity and after several interviews
was offered a position at a food processing company. He suffers
from hypertension, however, and is concerned the new employer
may not provide health care coverage for this condition. He is

thinking perhaps he should stay at his current job. As a benefits consultant, what advice would you give Mike?

14. Mary is a full-time lab technician at a pharmaceutical company. She served four years of active duty in the Army after college and has continued her military service in the Army Reserves. Over the past five years, her military obligation has involved going on brief training leaves and attending weekend meetings once per month. Her employer has been most accommodating. She has just been notified, however, that her unit is being deployed to Iraq for ten months. She comes to you, the benefits manager, with some questions: What will happen to her civilian job? Will she be able to return to her position when the deployment ends? What about the continuation of benefits? Will her husband and two children still be covered under her company's health insurance plan? What answers will you give her?

15. Female spouses of Social Security participants traditionally have lower historical earnings than their spouses. They also traditionally have longer life expectancies. While both are alive, she is entitled to receive benefits based on either her own or her husband's earnings record. Typically, she will choose his. When her husband dies, she is entitled to either a survivor benefit based on his earnings or her own earned benefit, whichever is greater. Based on these assumptions, what are the arguments (pro and con) for the husband to claim pre-full-age retirement under Social Security, say at age 62?[142]

---

142. See Sass, S., Wei, S., & Webb, A. (2008, March). *When should married men claim Social Security benefits?* Center for Retirement Research at Boston College, No. 8-4.

Global Benefits $\mathbf{13}$

In this chapter we will discuss the design and financing of health care systems and government-sponsored pension programs in several European and Asian countries as well as in Canada. This analysis can be important for a number of reasons.

- The dynamics of the global marketplace warrants an examination of these benefit designs because they can affect competitive labor costs, which in turn can impact unit prices of goods and services offered. Certainly, the cost of labor has had and will continue to have some bearing on the decisions enterprises make with respect to where they produce or offer their goods and services.

- As U.S. workers are sent abroad to work in their companies' foreign facilities, an understanding of appropriate compensation and benefit plans for expatriates is important.

- The United States is searching for possible solutions to the uneven health care coverage among its citizens, and is also facing a funding crisis with respect to Social Security retirement and Medicare and Medicaid programs. A review of ways other countries approach publicly funded retirement and health care programs might be helpful.

Let's first take a look at the government-sponsored health and retirement systems in some European countries. We start with France because they are recognized by various groups as having the "best" health care system in the world. Then we look at some typical features of European and developed countries' health care systems. Next we focus on China because of their global competitive situation and their low labor costs. With respect to social security pension systems, we begin with France again, provide some general features of the European system, look closer at China, and, because of its somewhat unique use of social security personal accounts, we take a good look at Chile.

Health Care in Europe

Louis lives in Nice, France. He has been experiencing a chronic sore throat and has made an appointment to see his family's private practice physician. After a full examination, the doctor has concluded that Louis has a digestive problem called "reflux," which results in excess stomach acid flaring up into the esophagus. She prescribes medicine and tells Louis to return in three weeks if the problem is not resolved. The cost of the doctor's services is €60, which is €30 more than the state health care system ("sécurité sociale") has authorized for an office visit. The physician is charging a higher fee ("dépassment") because of the special diagnostic tool she used to detect the reflux condition. Since Louis is a citizen (or legal resident) of France, he has a health care card from the government ("carte vitale") that will pay about 70 percent of the authorized cost. In this case, Louis would receive 70 percent of the authorized fee of €30, or €21, from the state health system, but will have to pay the remaining €39 to the doctor on his own.

Louis has another medical insurance card, a "mutuelle" or "police complémentaire" as the French call it, which will pay most of the costs not reimbursed by the state system. This card is provided by his employer, who pays a substantial part of the monthly insurance premium; Louis pays the remainder of €100 per month. If his employer did not provide this supplemental insurance, Louis would have to buy it himself and pay a significant premium per month, in some cases, depending on his status, as much as €800 per month. However, if he can show that he has insufficient means to buy the insurance, the government will partially subsidize the purchase of the "mutuelle." Louis has read that only a small percentage of French citizens, about 8 to 10 percent, do not have supplemental insurance and must pay all out-of-pocket costs not reimbursed by the state system on their own.[1]

---

1. The national plan covers prescriptions for drugs as well, which now represent about 20 percent of the total cost of the French health care program. The information on the French system is based largely on the following articles: Bellanger, M., & Mosse, P. (2005). The search for the holy grail: Combining decentralized planning and contracting mechanisms in the French health care system. *Health Economics, 14,* 119–132; *Health care in France.* (2004). National Coalition on Health Care, http://www.nchc.org/. It also is based on interviews of French nationals conducted in France in June 2007 by the author.

So the French health care system ("national plan") provides universal insurance to all legal residents of France, covering about 70 percent of authorized medical expenses. It is a government-sponsored, fee-for-service indemnity plan. It is dependent, however, upon persons obtaining—either through their employment, self-purchase, or government subsidy—a supplemental or complementary health insurance plan (mutuelle) to cover the remaining 30 percent. France ranks third behind the United States and the Netherlands among the Organization for Economic Cooperation and Development (OECD)[1] countries in the share of health care financed by private insurance.[2] Dental and optical care are not covered by the national plan.[3]

About 60 percent of French physicians are in private practice; the remainder work for the government or hospitals. Private physicians can accept either the authorized reimbursement levels ("Tarif de Convention")

---

1. The Organization for Economic Cooperation and Development (OECD), an organization comprising 30 countries, provides research and direction to developed countries with a commitment to democracy and a market economy. See http://www.oecd.org/.

2. Buchmueller, T., & Couffinhal, A. (2004). *Private health insurance in France.* OECD, Working Paper No. 12.

3. See Buchmueller, T., & Couffinhal, A. (2004). About 92 percent of French residents obtain the supplemental insurance. In some European countries, the supplemental insurance is used to advance the patient's personal position in the health care delivery system or to obtain, for example, a private room in a hospital.

set by the state system or charge a higher fee (dépassment). In the case of some specialists, the dépassment is considered to be the authorized fee and is reimbursed at the standard 70 percent rate. In other cases, such as mentioned in the vignette, the patient must find a way to pay the remaining 30 percent charge not covered.

The French system is financed through payroll taxes of 20 percent and income taxes,[4] and is administered by the national government (state) and regional health groups. The state establishes the annual health care budget, determines the basic benefits provided under the plan, and engages in certain planning aspects with respect to hospital construction, expansion, and location, as well as the number of students enrolled in medical schools. It establishes the reimbursement percentages shared by the individual and the state. Regional administration groups led largely by industry and unions set the Tarif de Convention and administer provider reimbursements. Private insurance companies manage the mutuelle.

The core of the French health care system is the hospital, where most significant treatments are rendered. Unlike the United States, there are few nonhospital-based outpatient treatment centers and there are not many integrated physician groups.

The French have 3.7 acute care hospital beds per 1,000 of population.[5] The United States has about 2.7.[6] There are no significant waiting times for surgeries, general necessary medical procedures, or elective treatments in France. There are 208,000 physicians (3.1 per 1,000 of population) in France. The OECD's median number of physicians per 1,000 of population is 3.1, while in the United States it is 2.8.[7]

The World Health Organization (WHO) ranked France as the "number one" health care system, based on the fact that approximately 75 percent of the country's health care costs are publicly funded, its residents have a

---

4. The French "social system" (retirement, health, and unemployment programs) has been in the red for some time. Currently, the annual deficit is running about €5.9 billion, and most of this is attributable to health care. It has the second highest payroll tax among OECD countries. The social program deficit is due, in part, to unemployment and soft economic conditions that affect tax revenue as well as its aging population. The new Sarkozy government wants to decrease the payroll tax in order to stimulate hiring among French employers. It would offset this increase by increasing the Value-Added Tax (sales tax) from 19.6 percent to 24.6 percent. See Gauthier-Villars, D., & Walker, M. (2007, July 17). French welfare overhaul focuses on higher consumer sales tax. *The Wall Street Journal*, A10.

5. World Health Organization (WHO) Health Statistics, 2007 (see Table 11C).

6. *Fast facts on U.S. hospitals.* (2006, October 20). The American Hospital Association, http://www.aha.org/.

7. Docteur, E. (2003, June 28). *U.S. health system performance in an international context.* Academy of Health Annual Research Meeting (Presentation).

long life expectancy, and its infant mortality rate is low. Currently, the French are considering some health care program adjustments because of spiraling costs.[8] For example, there is a view that reimbursements to providers should be based on the affliction of the patient instead of a more general set fee criterion.[9] Also, though France has a universal coverage system, the government indirectly subsidizes the purchase of employer-sponsored supplemental health insurance by providing favorable tax treatment. This reduces tax revenue. While the French system is not without problems and challenges, it does seem to work. Let's take a broader view of the French and other European health care systems to see some of the underlying plan designs that might be instructive for a U.S. health reform program.

Some General Principles and Features of European Health Systems

We should note that the concept of universal health care has been present in Europe since the days of Otto von Bismarck, the first Chancellor of Germany, who presided over the passage of the first health insurance law in 1883. Europe has a long history of social welfare programs. There are certain values, principles, and standards that pertain to many national health care programs in key European countries. The key differences are set forth in Table 13.1. The principles include:

- Universal health care access to all residents of the country that is insured by the government. The program should be "equal for all," and not permit variations of health care benefits based on economic status.[10]

- The national health plan should provide a comprehensive set of health care benefits sufficient to alleviate sickness and suffering.[11]

---

8. As noted above, however, France has the third highest health care expense in the world and is financially running a deficit, National Coalition on Health Care (2004).

9. This is commonly called a "DRG" (diagnostic related group) type of reimbursement. In other words, if a patient has pneumonia, and perhaps certain acuity adjustments are considered, there will be a standard fee set by the government for the treatment of the condition.

10. Bellanger, M., & Mosse, P. (2005).

11. Oliver, A. (2005). The English National Health Service: 1979–2005. *Health Economics, 14,* 75–99.

- While there may be cost sharing, particularly based on a resident's means, point-of-service co-payments should not be relevant to the offering of health care services or resources.[12]

- To the extent possible, the plan should guarantee the resident his choice of a physician. Primary care should be the centerpiece of the plan because overall long-term health is best ensured when patients regularly see their primary care physician.[13]

- In order to ensure health protection for EU citizens who are working or traveling to other sister nations, there should be cross-border coordination of health care.[14]

- Plans should ensure accountability, efficiency, and quality.[15]

There are certain design, organizational, and structural features of many European health care systems that appear to have some commonality.[16] Some are quite different, but common basic features that we find include:

- The national government collects taxes, sets budgets, and distributes health funds to the regional administrative health care units.[17]

- The national government sets standards, determines the covered health care benefits, and determines the basic reimbursement percentages to be paid by the plan to the providers.[18]

---

12. Oliver, A. (2005).

13. Grol, R. (2006, March). *Quality development in health care in the Netherlands.* The Commonwealth Fund, Commission on a High Performance Health System, http://www.cmwf.org.

14. EU citizens working in another EU country can receive health care treatment in the host country; similarly, EU citizens or legal residents traveling in EU countries can receive emergency treatment in the host country. Osterle, A. (2007, May). Health care across borders: Austria and its new EU neighbors. *Journal of European Social Policy, 17*(2), 112–124.

15. Maynard, A. (2005). European health policy challenges. *Health Economics, 14,* 255–263.

16. While most EU countries have decentralized some parts of their health care system, the degree varies. Italy, for example, allows regions to collect revenue for their national health care system, while other countries use regional political units to contract with providers and administer the reimbursement system. There is, however, very little use of market forces among the regional units. Saltman, R. (2006). Conceptualizing decentralization in European health systems: A functional perspective. *Health Economics, Policy and Law, 1,* 127–147.

17. See, for example: Canada, France, and the U.K. at Bellanger, M., Mosse, P., & Oliver, A. (2005).

18. See, for example, Italy's system: France, G., Taroni, F., & Donatini, A. (2005). The Italian health care system. *Health Economics, 14,* 187–202.

- The national government establishes capital expenditures for hospitals and the budgeting and award process for medical research.[19]

- Regional health agencies, often comprising employer and labor group representatives, administer the delivery of health care services at the local level.[20]

- In some countries, for example Germany, all employers are required to cover their employees with the prescribed health insurance plan and the government subsidizes the purchase of insurance for those not in the workforce or who cannot afford to purchase it.[21] In such cases they will buy policies from various nonprofit TPAs who compete for the business and administer the plans.

- In countries like France, residents purchase supplemental health insurance to cover the gaps in the national plan. In other countries, residents can buy private insurance to upgrade services guaranteeing amenities like a private room in a hospital or to move up on a waiting list. Still others buy a comprehensive insurance policy to "opt out" of the national system altogether.

With respect to physicians and health care providers, some fairly common features exist:

- In some countries, such as the U.K., a large percentage of doctors are salaried employees of the public health system or hospitals.[22]

- In many other European countries, physicians in private practice contract with the regional health authority with respect to services, reimbursement rates, and fees.[23]

- Some private physicians, such as in Italy, who work on a contract basis with the regional authority or are employed by a government

19. France, G., Taroni, F., & Donatini, A. (2005).

20. Anell, A. (2005). Swedish healthcare under pressure. *Health Economics, 14,* 237–254.

21. See *Health care in Germany.* (2004). National Coalition on Health Care, http://www.nchc.org/; Worz, M., & Busse, R. (2005). Analyzing the impact of health care system changes in the EU member states—Germany. *Health Economics, 14,* 133–149.

22. Schoen, C., Osborn, R., Huynh, P., Doty, M. Peugh, J. O., & Zapert, K. (2006, November 2). On the front lines of care: Primary care doctors' office system, experiences, and views in seven countries. *Health Affairs,* 555–571.

23. Lopez-Casasnovas, G., Costa-Font, J., & Planas, I. (2005). Diversity and regional inequalities in the Spanish "System of Health Care Services." *Health Economics, 14,* 221–235.

authority, may have a private practice where they establish their own fee schedules and arrange for health services totally outside the national system. Patients using this system often purchase their own health care insurance or simply pay for the services with their own funds.[24]

- For the most part, reimbursements are based on a fee-for-service basis, a contracted reimbursement rate, a percentage of the contracted rate, or on a capitation basis. The latter involves paying a physician a per capita fee based on the population in his or her district. In some cases, part of the physician's compensation is based on a combination of fee-for-service and capitation.[25]

- The national government usually controls the number of students training to be physicians.[26]

- There are few integrated practices, as most physicians work solo or in small groups, and there are few market features that serve as incentives to providers to compete on the basis of quality or price.[27]

Financing of Health Care—European Countries

Generally, health care is financed among European countries by employee payroll taxes, income and other general taxes, and the value-added tax (VAT), which is a type of sales tax. In a few cases, regional tax revenues are used to support health care plans. Participants are often expected to bear some of the cost themselves by paying the difference between the percentage reimbursed by the national plan to the physician and the actual fee

24. France, G., Taroni, F., & Donatini, A. (2005).

25. Schoen (2006). The U.K., however, is piloting some "pay-for-performance" plans among their providers and it has attained some success in getting the physicians to comply with clinical guidelines. Fleming, C. (2006, September 6). Under British pay-for-performance initiative quality is unexpectedly high, but so are payments. *Health Affairs.*

26. For a summary of the mechanisms and policies controlling the supply of physicians in OECD countries, see Simoens, S., & Hurst, J. (2006, January 16). *The supply of physicians in OECD countries.* OECD Working Papers. The article also points out that a higher density of physicians tends to result in better health outcomes. For some interesting comparisons of health care systems among EU countries, see Dubois, C., & Mckee, M. (2006). Cross national comparisons of human resources for health—What can we learn? *Health Economics, Policy and Law, 1,* 59–78.

27. Worz, M., & Busse, R. (2005); Annel, A. (2005); Grol, R. (2006).

charged. Point-of-service co-pays are beginning to appear in several countries, for example in Italy, where a resident who is treated at the hospital will incur a very modest "ticket" or co-pay. As previously noted, some participants buy supplemental health insurance to cover health expenses that are partially reimbursed by the national plan. As we see in Table 13.2, the percentage of health care costs borne by private versus public sources is comparatively low in many European countries.

Funds for health care in European countries are, in many instances, allocated to the regional administrative agencies based on the population and demographics of the area. In many cases, prospective budgets for the regional administrative agencies, hospitals, and other provider groups are formulated based on expected DRG (Diagnosis Related Group) case mix and experience. This sometimes will result in a fixed annual budget for the health care unit that limits its flexibility and leads to rationing of health care resources as actual utilization of health care resources exceed the expected consumption. Acuity factors that can have a significant impact on the amount of health care resources used to treat patients with severe complications, however, are not considered in the prospective budgeting process.[28] Table 13.1 illustrates some structural comparisons of European, Asian, Canadian, and U.S. health systems.[29]

---

28. In order to have severity adjusted data, the health system should use some form of DRG-based designations for health conditions and then apply an algorithm to determine how many of the patients in the DRG grouping, either because of age, overall health condition, ancillary conditions, or other reasons, should be placed in a numbered acuity ranking. For example, a 75-year-old male, who presents at the hospital with severe chest pains, is diagnosed with cardiovascular blockage, and is in need of a five-graph heart bypass surgery, has acute kidney disease, emphysema, and liver disease would be rated with a higher acuity number than an otherwise healthy 45-year-old male with the same heart condition. Severity adjusting takes into consideration the inherent risk of the treatment based on the particular medical condition of the patient.

29. The author has used data from and prepared Table 13.1 based on comparative health care systems from *Health Economics, 14,* 1–263. (2005, September). This is a symposium describing 15 European health care systems. For the reader who is interested in some data comparing the efficacy of various health care systems, see the Commonwealth Fund International Health Policy Survey (2005); life expectancy data is available from the U.S. Census Bureau. Healthy life expectancy data is available from the World Health Organization (WHO, Healthy Life Expectancy Tables, HALE, estimates from member states for 2001–2002). U.S. hospital data is available from the American Hospital Association, Fast Facts on U.S. Hospitals, http://www.aha.org/, and the National Coalition on Health Care that provides summary data on foreign health care systems, http://www.nchc.org. Canada's system is analyzed in Esmail, N., & Walker, M. (2006, December). *How good is Canadian health care? An international comparison of health care sstems.* The Fraser Institute Digital Publication, http://www.fraserinstitute.ca/.

Table 13.1 Global Health Care Comparisons

	System of Health Care	Financing	Access	Opt Out	Delivery System
Canada	Single-payer system with regional administration	General tax revenue	100% of population, no co-pays	Very limited	Local provinces
France	All employed and their dependents are covered; all "residents" not employed are covered with basic plan	Employment and social taxes	Universal access, but 85% have supplemental private coverage	Nonparticipating MDs partially paid by government	National government; some regional administration
Germany	Mandatory coverage for employees; free care for unemployed	Payroll and general taxes for capital expenditures and co-pays	90% public coverage; others choose private insurance	Yes, can opt out for private insurance	Regional Sickness Fund
Ireland	Poor and elderly get free health care; nonpoor must pay for some charges up to limit; 30% utilize the free system	Taxes, lottery, co-pays	45% purchase private insurance	Yes, can opt out for private insurance	Centralized
Italy	Largely hospital based, free health care for all	Payroll, VAT, and business taxes (97%) and co-pays (3%)	All are eligible; 15% choose private insurance	Yes, can opt out for private insurance	Shared between national and regional government

	System of Health Care	Financing	Access	Opt Out	Delivery System
Japan	Mandatory coverage by employers; some employee cost sharing; free care for nonemployed	Payroll tax (4.1% employer, 4.1% employee)	All employees must be covered; nonemployees covered by national plan	Not applicable	Occupational societies and national government manage health care
Netherlands	Private health insurance is mandatory; there is competition among TPAs; subsidies for low-income persons	Means-tested premiums for participants and taxes	62% by Sickness Fund, 32% by private insurance	Yes, can opt out for private insurance	Supervisory Board for Health Care Insurance
U.K.	National Health Service offers point of service care with no charge to patient	Tax revenue	100% free for all; co-pays for prescriptions, dental, optical	Yes, persons can seek private care and pay for it on their own	National Health Service
United States	National coverage for elderly and poor; private coverage for employed and others	Payroll, general taxes, employment premiums	45 million have no health care insurance	Not applicable	Federal and state governments and employment

NOTE: Using data from a variety of sources, the author prepared this chart on comparative health care systems. Chief sources: *Health Economics, 14;* 1–263 (September 2005). This is a symposium describing 15 European health care systems. Information on wait times was obtained from the *Commonwealth Fund International Health Policy Survey* (2005).

Current Problems and Issues in European Countries

Like most countries with universal or insurance-based health care coverage, health systems in EU countries are experiencing significant health care inflation. This is due largely to aging populations, the availability of new drugs, and new medical technology. Many European health care systems are running deficits and using other tax sources to cover overruns. The prices and demand for health care services are increasing and putting a strain on the public financing of health care. High unemployment in many of the EU countries and low birth rates are exacerbating the problem of financing social benefits like health care. Members of the "Eurozone" (those countries using the Euro as their currency) are required to limit their budget deficits in order to keep parity among their fellow EU countries. This makes deficit spending for health care quite difficult.[30]

European health care plans over the years have experienced excessive wait times that usually result from the rationing of health care services. This is especially true for referrals to specialists for elective treatments such as orthopedic surgeries, more complex interventions, and diagnostic procedures, particularly imaging. Some countries have effectively mitigated the problem, but some have not. The solutions, however, are often at odds with the financing constraints.[31]

We have discussed some the comparative efficacies of the United States and some European countries in Chapter 8. A comprehensive comparison is beyond the scope of this chapter. Issues such as cost, life expectancy, infant mortality, wait times for elective and nonelective procedures, average length of stay, survival rates for several major diagnoses, and medical quality and clinical outcomes are all relevant measurements. The OECD has produced significant comparative data, as has the World Health Organization and groups such as the Commonwealth Fund. The current data, however, does not present a clear picture enabling meaningful comparisons of quality health care outcomes. We reference some sources for data on this topic in our exercises at the end of the chapter. We will, however, leave a broad analysis to another day. We can show the latest WHO international comparisons that offer a general idea of issues such as longevity, cancer survival rates, expenditures for health care, and the density of medical facilities.

30. Goddard, M., Hauck, K., Preker, A., & Smith, P. (2006). Priority setting in health—A political economy perspective. *Health Economics, Policy and Law, 1,* 79–90.

31. Wilcox, S., Seddon, M., Stephen, D., Edwards, R., Pearse, J., & Tu, J. (2007, July/August). Measuring and reducing wait times: A cross-national comparison of strategies. *Health Affairs, 26*(4), 1078–1087.

Some Perspectives on Costs, Long-Term Health, and Reform

Are labor costs higher because of national health care systems? Is it important to understand the labor cost implications of global benefits? In the long run, of course, the health of a nation will have a significant impact on its ability to be productive and competitive. Providing quality-based and cost-efficient health care is the ultimate test for a nation's system.[32] But, we should measure the impact that benefit costs among various countries have on the ability of business to compete in the global market.[33] We will look more closely at this at the end of the chapter, after reviewing global social security retirement systems. For now, when we consider the relationship of health care to labor costs, it is timely that we examine China.

China's Health Care System[34]

China has a bifurcated health care system—some good programs in the big cities, but some very inadequate systems in rural areas where the vast majority of its population resides.[35] Expenditures for health care in city hospitals, for example, are significantly higher than that in the country.

Most Chinese do not have health insurance and many simply cannot afford to go to a hospital. The average stay in a hospital would cost the patient about one-half of a year's salary. Although 21 percent of the population has access to state medical facilities, outside of the large cities the system is corrupt and in many instances inept. For example, it is common for patients to give a treating physician in a state facility a *"hong boa"* ("red envelope"), which is an illegal payment, intended to facilitate access and

---

32. There are also some significant variations in medical practice protocols among EU countries. These issues are being addressed by advancing "evidence-based medicine" practices and pay-for-performance reward systems.

33. The social costs include government-financed retirement, health care, and unemployment costs. The major differences between the United States and our comparator group, however, relates to the health care systems.

34. Curing China's ailing health care system. (2003, April–June). *The World Bank Group, Beyond Transition, 14,* 4–6, http://www.worldbank.org/. In Beijing, with a population of 13 million, there are more CAT scanners than in the U.K., with a population of 49 million. About three-fourths of the medical spending in China is hospital-based. Staffing, however, is another problem. In many cases, due to staff shortages, relatives nurse and feed their patients.

35. More than 50 percent of China's urban population and 90 percent of its rural population have no health insurance or coverage. This amounts to over 66 percent of the population. There is no viable system to cover these individuals.

Table 13.2 International Comparisons of Core Health Indicators by the WHO

	Canada	France	Germany	Ireland	Italy	Japan	Netherlands	U.K.	United States
Life expectancy at birth (years) males	78.0 (2005)	77.0 (2005)	76.0 (2005)	77.0 (2005)	78.0 (2005)	79.0 (2005)	77.0 (2005)	77.0 (2005)	75.0 (2005)
Life expectancy at birth (years) females	83.0 (2005)	84.0 (2005)	82.0 (2005)	81.0 (2005)	84.0 (2005)	86.0 (2005)	81.0 (2005)	81.0 (2005)	80.0 (2005)
Infant mortality rate (per 1,000 live births)	5.0 (2005)	4.0 (2005)	4.0 (2005)	4.0 (2005)	4.0 (2005)	3.0 (2005)	4.0 (2005)	5.0 (2005)	7.0 (2005)
Age-standardized mortality rate for cardiovascular diseases (per 100,000 population)	141.0 (2002)	118.0 (2002)	211.0 (2002)	214.0 (2002)	174.0 (2002)	106.0 (2002)	171.0 (2002)	182.0 (2002)	188.0 (2002)
Age-standardized mortality rate for cancer (per 100,000 population)	138.0 (2002)	142.0 (2002)	141.0 (2002)	151.0 (2002)	134.0 (2002)	119.0 (2002)	155.0 (2002)	143.0 (2002)	134.0 (2002)
Physicians (density per 1,000 population)	2.14 (2003)	3.37 (2004)	3.37 (2003)	2.79 (2004)	4.20 (2004)	1.98 (2002)	3.15 (2003)	2.30 (1997)	2.56 (2000)
Total expenditure on health as percentage of gross domestic product	9.8 (2004)	10.5 (2004)	10.6 (2004)	7.2 (2004)	8.7 (2004)	7.8 (2004)	9.2 (2004)	8.1 (2004)	15.4 (2004)

	Canada	France	Germany	Ireland	Italy	Japan	Netherlands	U.K.	United States
General government expenditure on health as percentage of total expenditure on health	69.8 (2004)	78.4 (2004)	76.9 (2004)	79.5 (2004)	75.1 (2004)	81.3 (2004)	62.4 (2004)	86.3 (2004)	44.7 (2004)
Private expenditure on health as percentage of total expenditure on health	30.2 (2004)	21.6 (2004)	23.1 (2004)	20.5 (2004)	24.9 (2004)	18.7 (2004)	37.6 (2004)	13.7 (2004)	55.3 (2004)
General government expenditure on health as percentage of total government expenditure	17.1 (2004)	15.4 (2004)	17.3 (2004)	16.8 (2004)	13.7 (2004)	17.2 (2004)	12.4 (2004)	15.9 (2004)	18.0 (2004)
Per capita total expenditure on health at international dollar rate	3173.0 (2004)	3040.1 (2004)	3171.3 (2004)	2617.8 (2004)	2414.4 (2004)	2292.6 (2004)	3092.0 (2004)	2559.0 (2004)	6096.2 (2004)
Hospital beds (per 10,000 population)	36.0 (2003)	75.0 (2004)	84.0 (2005)	57.0 (2004)	40.0 (2004)	129.0 (2001)	50.0 (2003)	39.0 (2004)	33.0 (2003)
Population in urban areas (percent)	80.0 (2005)	77.0 (2005)	75.0 (2005)	60.0 (2005)	68.0 (2005)	66.0 (2005)	80.0 (2005)	90.0 (2005)	81.0 (2005)

SOURCE: World Health Organization Statistical Information System (2007).

to ensure better treatment.[36] The system is plagued by well-publicized cases of medical and pharmaceutical errors, long waits for treatment, rude personnel, lost records, and a lack of privacy.[37]

In the 1960s and 1970s, China experienced major success in improving its health care system and outcomes. During the 1980s and 1990s, however, there was a deterioration due, in part, to the decentralization of medical responsibilities from the national government to the impoverished local governments.[38] Recently, China has begun instituting significant reforms to its system, but it has a long way to go. Following are the chief features of China's health care system, and the problems and challenges arising therefrom.

- There is obvious inequality of health care coverage among Chinese,[39] and most of it is based on where one lives—the city versus the rural areas.

- There is a new initiative to institute a countrywide social insurance plan with personal medical accounts somewhat like the Health Savings Accounts (HSAs) currently touted in the United States.[40] It has not been implemented to any significant extent.

- Government employees and their families are covered by a national government-sponsored health care system. Medical services are provided, in many instances, by designated hospitals or clinics owned by the employing organization.[41]

- The government mandates health coverage for employees and their families of state and collective enterprises. Typically, the enterprises reimburse providers or patients for the cost of health care services

---

36. Bribes or informal payments from patients to secure better treatment are not uncommon in developing countries. In China, however, the percentage of patients making such payments is about 75 percent. This payment represents about one month's average pay. See Lewis, M. (2006, January). *Governance and corruption in public health care systems* (pp. 30–31). Center for Global Development, Working Paper No. 78, http://www.cjdev.org/.

37. Curing China's Ailing Health Care System (2003).

38. Health, Nutrition & Population in China. (2007). The World Bank, http://go.worldbank.org/OOE7NJ8SK0/.

39. Brant, S., Garris, M., Okeke, E., & Rosenfeld, J. (2006, April). *Access to care in rural China: A policy discussion.* International Policy and Development Program, University of Michigan, http://umich.edu/~ipolicy/china/1.

40. Health, Nutrition & Population in China (2007).

41. Wong, B., & Gabriel, S. (2007). *The influence of economic liberalization on urban health care services in the People's Republic of China.* Mt. Holyoke University course paper, http://www.mtholyoke.edu/courses/sgabriel/health.htm/.

out of their own "welfare funds," or provide health care directly to the participants through their own hospitals or clinics.[42] The funds are financed by a 7 percent payroll tax levied on the employer. With the rapid inflation in health care costs, many enterprises have found a 7 percent contribution inadequate to cover their expenses and simply charged the overrun to their general tax revenues.[43]

- The rural health care cooperatives that covered farmers and other nonstate employees have been dismantled. The national government has proposed a new health cooperative for the rural population that will require equal financing by local governments, the farmer, and the national government. The system has not yet impacted any significant percentage of noncovered rural patients.[44]

- Local government's ability to collect tax revenue for social programs is directly related to the geographic area's economic success. This has led to rich economic areas providing better health care than those less fortunate locations.[45]

- There is no national legal requirement for private companies to provide health care coverage for their employees. As China entertains more traditional market-based infrastructure and organizations, there are a vast number of new, private employers with a growing number of employees who have no coverage.[46] The issue of coverage has been left to the local governments to resolve.

- There is no substantial medical insurance industry in China at the present time. Only a small percentage of Chinese have what we understand to be "medical insurance" coverage where a third party is involved.[47]

- There is a significant amount of waste and inefficiency in the Chinese system. The reimbursement process for providers lacks financial discipline, allowing providers to get pretty much what they ask for, and there are few protocols with respect to hospitalization and treatments. Staffing of hospitals is based on the number of beds, giving administrators little leeway to control labor expense. The average length of a hospital stay is three times that found in the United States. Thus, excessive wait times are common in China.

42. Wong, B., & Gabriel, S. (2007).

43. Wong, B., & Gabriel, S. (2007).

44. Health care reform in China. (2005, September 15). *Harvard University Gazette*, http://www.news.harvard.edu/gazette/2005/09.15/09-china.html/.

45. Wong, B., & Gabriel, S. (2007).

46. Wong, B., & Gabriel, S. (2007).

47. Wong, B., & Gabriel, S. (2007).

- Government financing of hospitals is more of a subsidy. Hospitals are expected to generate sufficient revenue to cover about 70 percent of their operating costs.

A quick look at some key indicators of resources and efficacy of the Chinese health care system reflects some interesting comparisons. Per capita health care spending is $277 in China.[48] In the United States, the dollar amount is ten times that amount per person. China spends about 4.7 percent of its GDP[49] on health care, but the recipients pay 63 percent of that cost. In the United States, the GDP rate for health care is 16 percent. In rural areas, where 700 million people live, or 66 percent of the population, patients pay 90 percent of health care costs.[50] In per capita expenditures for health care, China ranks 144th among 191 WHO members. Life expectancy at birth is 71 for males, 74 for females.[51] In the United States, life expectancy at birth is 75 for males and 80 for females. Infant mortality in China is 27 per 1,000; in the United States, 6.3.[52]

In addition to the social and humanitarian issues apparent from this data, it also is obvious that from a global competitive situation the absence of health care for many of China's citizens means lower labor costs for the producers of goods and services.

For now, China has no particular relevance as a health care model for the United States to examine. It does, however, provide producers of goods and services the opportunity to enjoy significantly lower aggregate social costs than many of its global competitors. This is probably a short-term advantage because every country needs a healthy workforce.

Some Conclusions—The United States and Other Countries

In the United States, the core of health care coverage (about 60 percent) is linked to employment. For those who are not covered by their employer, are unemployed, or who meet certain low-income guidelines, there is a state-federal system (Medicaid) that provides health care. For those who meet the requirements for Social Security and have reached the age of 65, a national health care system (Medicare) is provided. Military veterans are covered by the U.S.-sponsored veteran's health care system. Children whose parents do not meet the strict income tests set by Medicaid, but fall

48. Hewitt Global Report (2006).

49. Hewitt Global Report (2006, August). Health Care in China, http://www
.hewittassociates.com.

50. See WHO (2008), http://www.who.int. All data is from 2005.

51. See WHO (2008), http://www.who.int/countries/chn. All data is from 2002.

52. See WHO (2008), http://www.who.int. All data is from 2005.

within expanded poverty guidelines and are without coverage, are covered by a government-sponsored plan called State Children's Health Insurance Program (SCHIP). The structure of the system appears to be sound.

Some people in the United States, however, cannot afford or choose not to pay the premiums or cost sharing obligations of their employer-sponsored health care plan, or cannot meet the eligibility requirements for any of the government-sponsored plans. Some qualify but do not apply. These are the uninsured and they number around 46 million persons. They present U.S. policymakers with a major challenge.

The comparison between systems of some of the developed countries described above and the United States yields this conclusion: In many European countries, basic health care coverage is guaranteed to the individual by the government as a sponsor or based on a mandate and it is essentially equal in terms of the benefits offered. In some countries, however, supplemental health insurance seems to be necessary. In the United States, there is a system with safety nets for those who cannot afford health care, but the scope of the coverage and benefit designs are not universal or equal. Moreover, while no one in the United States is denied health care for critical needs because of income or means, the lack of health care insurance by many results in poor or no access to regular primary care.[53] Primary care has been shown to be the most critically important factor leading to better long-term health. The public policy question is what to do about it. The economic question relates to whether the United States, which has the most expensive system in the world, is thrusting its businesses into a noncompetitive position by clinging to its current system. There are two approaches that were discussed in Chapter 8: (1) change the financing and delivery system in the United States, or (2) reform health care in the United States to make it more affordable. There are also other components of labor expense that should be explored.

In the following section, we will examine the various social security retirement systems among developed and developing countries. Remarkably, we will find more uniformity as we compare the designs.

Social Security—Providing and Insuring Retirement Income

The United States and many developed countries have comparable government-sponsored retirement income plans, often called "Social

---

53. See Starfield, B., & Shi, L. (2002). Policy relevant determinants of health: An international perspective. *Health Policy, 60,* 201–218 (Elsevier, Ireland). The authors show a strong correlation between the availability of various levels of primary care and the level of health, particularly among young persons. Measured health indictors included low birth weights, neonatal mortality, post-neonatal mortality, infant mortality, and life expectancy at various ages.

Security." They are designed to provide a minimum retirement benefit for those who have been employed for a requisite period of time, during which the employee and the employer have contributed a payroll tax to the fund. Most of these plans are financed and their benefits are distributed on a pay-as-you-go (PAYGO) basis. This means that contributions to the plans generated by various payroll and other tax programs are paid out over a short term versus being invested in capital markets to provide long-term growth through investment growth.

The key principle underlying the design of such plans in many European countries is solidarity. This means the working generation will pay the taxes that are currently used to finance the retirement income of those who have retired before them. Retirees are entitled to leave the workforce with a secure source of income for themselves and certain of their survivors.

But solidarity is in trouble. In both the United States and Europe, increased longevity of the population, the "baby boom" generation that is beginning to retire in large numbers, and the decreased number of active workers have led to a perilous funding crisis for all such plans.[54] In France, for example, only 35 percent of employable persons between ages 55 and 65 are actually employed; the remainder is retired. Among the 60- to 65-year-old group, only 10 percent are employed.[55] Meanwhile, the number of children per woman is below 1.5 in Germany and Italy. France has dropped from 2.5 in 1965 to 1.8 today. Similar declines in birth rates are observed in many other European countries.

The dependency ratio is the rate of persons who are working compared to those who are not working either because they are too young or are retired. The higher the ratio, the fewer working people there are to fund the retirement system. This is a direct result of low birth rates and early retirement programs. Currently, the dependency ratio is increasing in many developed countries with social security systems, and there is a looming funding crisis for government-sponsored retirement and health care programs. Almost all of these governments are scrambling to find solutions to ease the funding crisis. These efforts include reducing benefits, delaying the retirement age, or requiring more years of service for future retirees.

For the most part, the social security public retirement systems in developed countries are defined benefit plans that base retirement income on the participant's years of work, years of contributions to the system, average pay in some cases, and age at retirement. One measure of a social security

---

54. Wannell, T. (2007, February). Young Pensioners. *Perspectives on Labour and Income, 8*(2). Also, HSBC's 2008 annual research papers on retirement expectations and the implications of longevity can be found at http://www .hsbc-of-retirement/future-of-retirement-200.com/1/2/retirement/future. Finally, see *Managing Reforms*. (2008). International Social Society Association, http://www.issa.int/aiss/Topics/Managing-reforms.

55. Moreau, Y. (2007, May 21). *The retirement pensions in France.* The Embassy of France in the United States, http://www.ambafrance-us.org.

system's efficacy is to examine the percentage of replacement income it provides at retirement. The higher the percentage, the more effective the system in sustaining income needs to the retiree. A related issue here is how dependent are persons in the country upon social security for their retirement income? In countries where there are fewer employer-sponsored retirement plans, this dependency may be quite high.[56] Let's take a more personal look again at Louis, our Frenchman who is considering retirement.

Louis is now 65 years old and has contributed to the French retirement system for 40 years. He has worked at IBM France for 30 years and wants to retire and collect his pension(s). His age and the number of years of contributions through payroll taxes will entitle him to pensions from the various government- and employer-sponsored plans. Under the French public system, he has contributed about 7 percent of his own earnings up to a limit of what is now €2,589 per month for his retirement and his survivor's benefits. His employer has contributed 8.3 percent of his earnings up to the same limit and also 1.6 percent of pay for his survivor's benefit.[1]

His 40 years of contributions will entitle him to a minimum government-sponsored pension (CNAVTS—National Employees' Old Age Insurance Fund) of €1,100, which is the current maximum per month. He also is entitled to receive a supplemental (AGIRC—General Association of Pensions Institutions for Management Staff)[2] pension

1. See *Social Security programs phroughout the world, Europe* (p. 106). (2006, September). Social Security Administration, SSA Publication No. 13-11801.

2. In spite of its name, "management," or what we in America might call, "541 Exempt Executive, Administrative, and Professional" (from 29 CFR 451 et seq.) the supplemental pension is also available to nonmanagement, or nonexempt personnel. Employers and employee groups administer the supplemental plan jointly. Also, in France and elsewhere, persons who are not employed can still gain service credit if they are, for example, studying in the university, caring for a newborn, caring for a disabled relative, or working abroad. In France, there are also special pension funds for government employees, agricultural workers, miners, and a variety of other occupational groups. See Moreau, Y. (2007, May 21). *The retirement pensions in France.* The Embassy of France in the United States, http://www.ambafrance-us.org.

---

56. A Chartbook of International Labor Comparisons: The Americas, Asia Pacific, and Europe. (2007, June). U.S. Department of Labor, 33, Chart 4.4. Japan has the highest dependency ratio (.51), while the Republic of Korea has the lowest (.39), and the United States is .49.

from the government that is based on his average income over a 25-year period. This will give him an additional €600 per month. As a result of working for IBM France, he also participated in an employer-sponsored defined benefit pension plan. The assets of this plan have been invested by IBM, and it will produce a pension of about €2,000 per month, based on his final average pay and years of service. In all, Louis will receive three pensions that together will replace about 70 percent of his final pay. Add to this amount his personal savings and investments, which include his apartment in Nice, a small mountain vacation home in Chamonix, France, and an apartment he rents out in nearby Menton, France, and his retirement income nearly equals his final average pay.[3]

Louis knows that if he had participated only in CNAVTS, his pension would have been less than 20 percent of his final pay. Adding in the supplemental pension would have raised him to about 30 percent of final pay. Without his IBM pension, he would have to cut corners significantly to live comfortably in retirement. For those earning less, for example €2,000 or €3,000 per month, the two pension plans can provide as much as 76 percent of the last wages. For higher earners, however, the replacement income, without company-sponsored plans, would be significantly lower.[4]

---

3. In France, the Fillon Law recently authorized employees and employers to create tax-favored retirement savings accounts, called "PERCOs." These are becoming more popular. See Watson Wyatt, International Update (2007, June).

4. *Pensions in the European Union.* (2000). Observatoire des Retraites, http://www.observatoire-retraites.org/.

How does all of this compare to other European countries' social security systems? What are the key design features among the countries and what can we learn from them?

Some General Retirement Approaches in European and Other OECD Countries[57]

Here are some of the basic features of social security retirement systems of the OECD and other countries. Also described are a variety of new

---

57. See *U.S. Social Security reform, other countries' experiences provide lessons for the United States.* (2005, October). General Accountability Office, GAO 06-126.

approaches underway that are designed to deal with the financial crisis of pay-as-you-go social security systems.[58]

- Most European and OECD countries' public pension plans are organized on an occupational basis. The pension amount is often based on a retiree's earnings record, years of service, and age at retirement. Some OECD countries have "flat amount" pensions based simply on years of work and age at retirement. Most provide for a type of "means testing" that pays a minimum pension amount regardless of the result of the pension formula calculation.

- Three-pillar plans involve a government-sponsored PAYGO system, supplemented by voluntary employer-sponsored and funded pensions as well as employee-funded savings accounts.[59] Employer-sponsored plans are not as common in OECD countries as in the United States. Some, but not a substantial number of employers, create such plans and the funds are invested in capital markets.[60] Typically, the plans are designed and administered within an industry or regional framework.[61]

- Several countries have introduced partially funded segments in their social security PAYGO system. In other words, part of the payroll taxes collected is invested in markets so as to exploit the opportunity for capitalized growth of the government's pension obligation. This has served to strengthen pension funding, provided that they insulate the funds from other government spending.

---

58. *U.S. Social Security reform* (2005).

59. See Queisser, M., & Whitehouse, E. (2003, August 6). *Individual choice in social protection: The case of Swiss pensions.* OECD. Also Moreau, Y. (2007). See also Byrne, A. (2007, Spring). Employee savings and investment decisions in defined contribution plans: Survey evidence from the U.K. *Financial Services Review, 16*(1), 19–40.

60. See, for example, updates on employer-sponsored plan designs and regulations at http://www.socialsecurity.gov/policy/. This site, International Update: Recent Developments in Foreign Public and Private Pensions, describes changes in public laws regulating private pensions and updates in a country's social security systems. Also, for an interesting review of Canada's employer-based retirement plans and trends with respect to early retirements, see Wannell, T. (2007). Young pensioners. *Perspectives on Labour and Income, 8*(2). In countries such as France, the public social security pension is significantly higher than, for example, in the United States and the privately sponsored pensions are not a substantial factor in funding the employee's retirement. See Ernst, P. (2006). *France: A new landscape for employer-provided retirement plans.* Mercer Human Resource Consulting, http://www .mercerHR.com. In many cases, employer-sponsored pension plans in Europe, in addition to holding a second place position to the income available from the social security system, are not funded but are secured with insurance contracts.

61. Pensions in the European Union (2000).

- A number of Eastern European and Latin American countries have introduced individual account programs that permit the employee to divert some of his social security contribution and invest it in various capital markets so as to supplement future retirement income. In order to mitigate the individual's investment risk, some plans require that the private account represent a rather small amount of the total pension; others guarantee a minimum return for the account. In most of these countries, the individual accounts are an option for the current workers but compulsory for new participants.[62]

- Some OECD countries have mandated employer-sponsored pensions, and have regulated their design and administration.[63] A few have required employers to offer a type of 401(k) defined contribution plan. They are not obligated, however, to provide matches or contributions to such plans. Voluntary employee contributions are made on a tax-deferred basis and are designed to supplement public social security pensions and the employer-sponsored defined benefit plan. In Ireland, Germany, and the U.K., where there are such laws, the new defined contribution plans (also called "personal accounts") are not generating significant participation by employees.[64]

- Italy, Poland, and Sweden have converted to a type of defined contribution approach whereby each retiree has a nominal account based on payroll tax contributions from both the employee and his

---

62. Mexico, for example, has most recently adopted such an option for all of its public employees. Chile has used such a plan for several years. See *International Update.* (2007, May). U.S. Social Security Administration, http://www.ssa.gov/policy/docs. See also *Reforming Social Security: Lessons from thirty countries.* (2005, June). National Center for Policy Analysis, NCPA Study No. 227. This study also points out the importance of maintaining low administrative costs for such programs.

63. See Queisser, M., & Whitehouse, E. (2003). Also Korczyk, S. (2007, January). *Mandatory employer pensions in Ireland, Germany, and the United Kingdom.* AARP Report #2007-03. The Netherlands has authorized employers to convert to "hybrid" plans, called "Cash Balance Plans" that utilize average annual earnings instead of "final pay" to calculate benefits. This approach usually results in lower pensions at retirement than those using final pay in their formula. *The recent evolution of pension funds in the Netherlands.* (2007, April). Center for Retirement Research, Working Paper #2007-9, http://www.bc.edu/centers/crr/wp_2007-9 .shtml/.

64. Byrne, A. (2007). A study of participants in an employer-sponsored defined contribution plan in the U.K. revealed that many have limited interest in and knowledge of their plans.

employer which grows based on investment assumptions and is paid out based on the retiree's life expectancy.

- Almost all OECD countries that are dealing with a pension funding crisis have initiated reforms by either increasing tax contributions or reducing benefits.[65] The reductions have usually involved extending the normal retirement age and service requirements.[66] Other reform measures under consideration or recently enacted in these countries include using a lower inflation adjustment to recalculate average pay, or using a longer period of average pay (for example, stretching the period from the last ten years of earnings to the last or highest average 25 years) to calculate average past earnings.[67] Some countries have simply increased the payroll tax that finances the benefits, while others have equalized the heretofore different retirement age requirements between men and women. Another approach is to reduce the cost of living adjustments to existing pensions, or link adjustments in pensions to such factors as economic growth, longevity, and the ratio of workers to retirees.[68]

- Usually, OECD countries' public pension plans provide for a survivor's benefits and permit work after retirement without penalties, such as pro rata reductions in the social security pension or special taxes on pension benefits.[69] Their social programs also

---

65. The OECD reports that the average level of future pension benefits in 16 member countries has been reduced by 22 percent. See OECD (2007, July 6). People will need to save more as reforms cut retirement income, http://www .oecd.org/. For a general discussion on the causes of the funding crisis of public and pensions in Europe, see *Economist intelligence unit, Europe's pension crisis* (2002, October 16).

66. National Center for Policy Analysis (2005). Also see U.S. Social Security Administration, International Update (2007, May), http://www.ssa.gov/policy/ docs. For example, Germany has just increased the normal retirement date from age 65 to 67, and Spain is considering increasing the service requirements required to earn a pension. See *Global news brief—Europe and Spain.* (2006). Watson Wyatt Worldwide, http://www.watsonwyatt.com/.

67. Moreau, Y. (2007).

68. See OECD (2007, July 6).

69. It is interesting to note that in Japan's labor force, social security or retirement plan participation rates among older workers are the highest among industrial nations. The Japanese simply do not retire early. There are a number of factors leading to this phenomenon; the primary motivation is a desire to maintain their standard of living. The general replacement of final pay in Japan is about 60 percent at full retirement age. Williamson, J., & Higo, M. (2007, June). *Older Workers:*

include paid maternity leaves, unemployment benefits, and disability programs.[70]

- Many OECD countries consider periods of unemployment, including higher education, maternity leave, and other certain lifecycle events, as part of the calculation of an employee's service under the social security laws. There also are minimum pensions available regardless of the years of service. Finally, cost-of-living adjustments often are made to pensions of persons over the age of 65 to ensure they maintain their purchasing power.[71]

- The European Union is working on a pan-European pension plan that will coordinate the taxation and regulations of various occupational, employer-sponsored pensions earned by employees of companies with operations in different EU states.[72]

It might be useful to look at some non-OECD countries that have social security systems to see how they are designed.

China and Social Security Retirement Income

China has moved from a socialist, planned economy to a market economy in the last 20 years. As such, its social security system has evolved in response to the shift to a market-based system. In 2004, the Chinese government introduced the initial phases of a retirement income program as well as unemployment insurance, work-related injury insurance, maternity care, and medical care programs. Here is how the retirement system works.[73]

Lessons from Japan. Center for Retirement Research at Boston College, Series 11, http://www.bc.edu/crr.

70. For an interesting global survey of attitudes toward life and retirement among European and U.S. populations, see *AXA retirement scope, A global survey on life, work, and retirement.* (2005, January). AXA Financial Protection. The conclusions of this study are: retirement is an active and positive stage of life; while most want to retire at age 55, they recognize it probably will not be possible; workers are mentally and financially preparing for retirement; most do not expect any "reform" of pension systems in the near future.

71. Moreau, Y. (2007).

72. See *Guidance note on pan-European pensions.* (2004, January 28). Federation of European Employers, http://www.fedee.com/pensions/.

73. China issues white paper on Social Security. (2004, September). *China Daily,* http://www.chinadaily.com.cn/); China's Social Security. (2004, September). Information Office of the State Council of the People's Republic of China; *Global*

- It mandates coverage for about 2 percent of the total population, including enterprise employees in urban areas. Rural area residents and farmers have no social security program.[74]

- The benefit is designed as a PAYGO, but does include a personal accounts plan. It mandates employer and employee payroll contributions totaling about 28 percent (20 percent from the employer and 8 percent from the employee). Only half of the urban employers, however, make contributions. Self-employed persons must pay 18 percent of their wages to the fund.

- The system is locally managed and financed; a good portion of the payroll contributions are being used to pay legacy costs of persons in the pre-1997 era of pensioners who did not contribute to the fund(s).

- Retirement age is 60 for males and 55 for females.

- There is a minimum contributory service requirement of 15 years of payments.

- The base pension pays about 20 percent of the person's average final pay. The basic minimum benefit for retirees is the equivalent of $75 per month.

- The supplemental element of the pension plan comes from the so-called "personal account." This involves calculating a certain percentage of the gross contributions made to the fund on behalf of the participant. The benefit equals about 1/120 of the person's accumulated contributory payments. The longer one works, therefore, the larger the account and the higher the pension amount.

- The social security plan is available to, but not required of, foreign, private, and other types of enterprises in urban areas.

- Benefits are indexed based on cost of living increases.

In addition to the fact that it does not cover most of the population, some of the structural problems with the plan are that it does not cover persons who have stopped working and do not have the requisite number of years of service under the new plan. Thus, while there are many entitled to legacy pensions not funded by their own contributions, there are many more impoverished elderly who have no chance of receiving a pension.[75]

Action on Aging. (2007). http://www.globalaging.org/pension/world; Pozen, R. (2007, August 6). Insuring China's future. *The Wall Street Journal,* A12.

74. Global Action on Aging (2007).

75. Global Action on Aging (2007).

Also, there are apparently significant differences in pension levels between retirees from government agencies and those from enterprises, as well as differences based on geographic regions due to the decentralized approach to pension funding and administration. There can be as much as an 800 percent difference between pensions awarded in one region to another or from one type of government-supported agency to another.

With a rather porous safety net, the Chinese will continue to be more interested in saving than spending, and the hopes to open a vast and powerful consumer market in China will not be hampered. Thus, while there are signs that China is beginning to move from a producing economy to a consumer economy, there are inherent structural barriers to fulfilling this transition. U.S. producers of goods and services may have some time to wait for the opportunity to sell large amounts of goods and services to Chinese consumers.[76]

Chile and the Personal Account

We look at Chile because they have used a private account approach in their national social security retirement system for some time. This approach has been suggested as a solution to the U.S. Social Security financing problem. We think it is important not only to mention Chile, but also to see in some detail how their unique system works.

Chile began reforming its state-run PAYGO social security system in 1981. The essential design feature of the plan is a private account to which the individual employee contributes through payroll deductions. Benefits are dependent upon contributions made to the account and the overall growth in the account. An overview of the plan follows.

- It requires successful investment of saved funds.

- It subjects participants to investment risks.

- It has the potential to produce wide variations in pension amounts among participants.

- The law does not cover everyone, but noncovered workers can voluntarily contribute.

- It has a relatively high administrative cost because of the unique account feature.

76. India has only a public pension system for government employees. There is no government-sponsored or mandated retirement income plan for the unorganized workers who comprise about 93 percent of the Indian workforce. Global Action on Aging (2007).

Nevertheless, it has been credited with helping to stimulate Chile's economy by reducing employer pension expense, adding new monies to its rather small capital markets, and using the market to help finance benefits.[77] It also has the potential to increase retirement income substantially. Here is a little closer look at how it works.

- The Chilean system produces benefits that are strictly a function of the worker's earnings and the investment returns on his account.[78]

- Each worker is required to contribute at least 10 percent or more of his salary to the plan.[79]

- There is a cap on the total amount of salary that can be contributed.

- The employer is not obligated but may contribute. The accounts receive favorable, deferred tax treatment.

- There is a minimum, guaranteed retirement income plan sponsored by the government, referred to as a "floor plan," that provides a guaranteed pension in the event the accounts are not prudently invested. Contributions made to the old PAYGO plan are recognized and credited to one's account based on the life expectancy of the worker and the number of years worked under the old plan.[80]

Participants currently choose from among six investment funds. Here is a summary of the Chilean plan's investment activities.

- Annual rates of return have ranged from 13 percent in 1982, to 30 percent in 1992, to 17 percent in 1999, and 10 percent in 2003. This parallels the investment returns of the basic capital markets.

---

77. Tamborini, C. (2007, May 17). *Social Security: The Chilean approach to retirement.* The Congressional Research Service, Report for Congress.

78. There are some important differences between the United States and Chile that are worth noting: (1) The population of Chile is aging at a slower pace than the United States. (2) Chile has 16 million in its population compared to 300 million in the United States. (3) Life expectancy is about the same; median age for the United States is about six years higher, but the percent of the population working between the ages of 20 and 64 are about equal. (4) Chile, at the time of conversion from PAYGO to Accounts, had a government budget surplus that enabled them to pay for the transition costs. At the time, however, their PAYGO was insolvent. (5) Chile has a large, informal, "self-employed" worker population (about 27 percent) that does not participate in the plan. Tamborini, C. (2007).

79. Tamborini, C. (2007), p. 14.

80. Tamborini, C. (2007), p. 14.

- The asset mix of the Chilean funds has been moving toward optimal levels. For example, 32 percent of the contributions are invested in foreign instruments.[81] Results for many participants have been excellent.

- There also are age-based investment guides that take into account the age of the prospective retiree and the appropriate investment risk.[82]

- The value of pension funds assets has increased from 0 in 1981 to 60 percent of GDP at the end of 2005.

- With respect to retirement income distributions, the participant can elect an annuity, make predetermined withdrawals, or receive a combination of both.

The government has several roles in the pension system: (1) to oversee the program; (2) to provide a minimum, guaranteed (floor) pension should the accounts not produce sufficient retirement income, which is measured as 75 percent of the minimum wage;[83] and (3) to provide a pension for the aged and poor who do not have enough years of service under the private plan to generate an adequate pension.[84]

While the Chilean system has some problems, particularly with high transition and administrative costs, the general conclusion is that it does work well for employees with stable jobs and consistent contributions. The market growth of the accounts has been better than expected.[85] The concept of individual accounts to supplement retirement income is spreading.

As we discussed in Chapter 12, the United States has considered private accounts as a possible reform to solving the looming financial shortfall in its social security retirement system.[86] It is obvious the Chilean program also includes several design features of the 401(k) that are quite similar to defined contribution plans sponsored by U.S. employers. So, a transition to an individual account approach in the United States might encounter fewer cultural barriers.

There are, however, other countries that have instituted Chilean-like reform in their social security systems. These include Sweden, which

---

81. Tamborini, C. (2007), p. 18.

82. Tamborini, C. (2007), p. 25.

83. Tamborini, C. (2007), p. 22.

84. There are several reform proposals in Chile that would enhance benefits for the aged poor and also facilitate participation in the current plan among self-employed and other noncovered employees and students. Tamborini, C. (2007), p. 24. See also Kritzer, B. (2002). Recent changes in the Chilean system. *Social Security Bulletin, 64*(4).

85. Tamborini, C. (2007), p. 31.

86. See full discussion of Social Security Reform in Chapter 12.

Table 13.3   International Comparison of Social Security Retirement Plans

	Canada	France	Germany	Ireland	Italy	Japan	Netherlands	U.K.	United States
Basic Design	PAYGO (employee contributory and noncontributory for residents)	PAYGO	PAYGO	PAYGO	PAYGO (new employees have notional accounts)	PAYGO (employee contributory and noncontributory for residents)	PAYGO	PAYGO (employee contributory and noncontributory for residents)	PAYGO
Financing	Contributory pension, 4.95% employer, 4.95% employee	Payroll tax 8.3% employer, 6.5% employee	Payroll tax 9.75% employer, 9.75% employee	Payroll tax 8.5% employer, 4% employee	Payroll tax 23.8% employer, 8.9% employee	Payroll tax 7.32% employer, 7.32% employee	Payroll tax 5.4% employer plus government contribution, 17.9% employee	Payroll tax 12.8% employer, 11% employee	Payroll tax 6.2% employer, 6.2% employee
Coverage	Employment and residents	Employed, housewife, and others	Employment plus some nonwork periods	Employment plus credit for care giving	Employment		All persons residing therein	Employment plus credit for child/elderly care	Employment
Retirement Age and Service Requirement	Age 65 plus 10 years' residence or age 60 plus contributions	Age 60 plus 160 quarters contributions	Age 65 plus 5 years' contributions	Age 65 plus 260 weeks contributions	For new workers, age 65 with 18 years' service	Age 65 plus 25 years' contributions	Age 65 plus 50 years' residence	Age 65 plus 44 years' contributions (flat pension) plus earnings-related pension	New workers age 67 plus 40 quarters contributions
Survivor and Disability	Yes	Yes	Yes	Yes	Yes		Yes	Yes	Yes
Salary Cap on Tax	C$41,100/year	€2,589/month	€5,250/month	€4,666/month	€85,478/year (employee only)	¥620,000/month	€29,543/year	N/A	$
Replacement Income (%)	57%	65%	72%	N/A	89%	59%	84%	48%	43%

NOTE: Many of the European countries provide special benefits for a variety of life events, such as family allowances for children, paid maternity leave, sickness leave, long-term care, unemployment, disability leave, and others that are funded by additional taxes (most often payroll taxes), and are not included in this table. This table is based on information obtained from a number of sources under the title *Social Security Programs Throughout the World*, prepared by the U.S. Social Security Administration, http://www.ssa.gov/policy/docs/progdesc/ssptw/index/html/. Information on percent of replacement income is based on: Pension Rights Center, International Pensions (2007), http://www.pensionrights.org/policy/international/pension/html/. Note that each country's policies contain a number of details that are not included in this general survey.

introduced a multi-pillar system with a mandatory individual account; seven countries in Central and Eastern Europe; eight countries in Latin American; and the U.K.[87] These countries either have integrated individual accounts with their PAYGO systems or have abandoned PAYGO by instituting mandatory individual accounts. Germany also inaugurated a new individual account system to supplement their PAYGO system, but requires a guaranteed nominal value of the savings account at retirement.[88]

Some Perspectives on Social Security Reform

All developed countries are experiencing significant financing problems of their social benefits including retirement and health care. There are a myriad of actuarial and economic reform proposals that are being tried and considered. Some, however, argue that the key to reform lies in politics. Galasso argues that the success of any reform proposal depends on political factors rather than economic theory.

> An aging society leads to large increases in pension spending because of the political accountability of the policymakers. Policymakers will likely determine the pension policy in order to favor their aging electorate and hence increase the probability of being re-elected.[89]

He examines the significance of the proportion of retirees in a population, the income redistributive features of each system, and the country's existing retirement policy. He concludes that an aging population will lead to more pension spending; yet, postponing retirement mitigates the impact of this and may be the only politically viable alternative for social security reform.[90] Perhaps, as the United States and its European friends debate social security reform, we will take this lesson into consideration. It is important because there are competitive consequences in our labor markets.

---

87. See *Reform of Social Security.* (2005). Social Security Administration, Office of Policy and Research, http://www.ssa.gov/policy/research.

88. Maurer, R., & Schlag, C. (2002, June). *Money back guarantees in individual pension accounts: Evidence from the German pension reform.* Pension Research Council, Working Paper 2002-11.

89. Galasso, V. (2006). The political future of Social Security in aging socities, Boston: MIT Press, p. 7

90. Galasso, V. (2006). p. 7.

Competitive Labor Costs and Benefits

After looking at a variety of approaches among countries to provide some form of health care and retirement income security for their populace, the question arises of what impact do these programs have on the cost of labor for the respective country's employers. We know, for example, that the United States has one of the highest aggregated costs for health care calculated as a percentage of GDP. But does this necessarily mean that U.S. employers pay more to provide health care to their workers? Or does it mean that taxpayers, employees, and employers' aggregate costs for health care in the United States as a percentage of GDP are higher?

From a global competitive standpoint, the cost of labor is extremely relevant. Table 13.4 displays the cost of social benefits as an employment expense or cost of labor. Although the United States spends more as a country on health care, this table shows that the cost to the employers in the United States is not as great as it is in countries where a single-payer system is largely financed by employment taxes. Where general taxes or value-added taxes are the primary source of benefits funding, for example in the U.K., the labor expenses are lower.[91] This makes sense. The same table shows a comparison of hourly compensation costs for manufacturing among nine countries.

Table 13.4 reflects generally higher labor costs among Western European countries. Also, in most of these countries the percentage of labor costs allocated for social expenditures is higher than in the United States and Japan. We can only imagine what these costs are in China. Clearly, they are well below our levels.

Because benefits in several European countries are funded by general tax revenue and value-added tax, it is not possible to specifically say their rates of pay are higher because of benefit costs. But it appears the principle of compensating differentials is present and European workers are sacrificing a larger portion of their pay for social costs.[92] Also we note that in Germany, for example, there is an employer mandate to provide

91. We should note that higher labor costs, although they represent a large part of product or service costs, do not always impact prices. The price of goods and services may, in some instances, be more affected by the market and what price increases it will bear. In such cases the market drives inflation. See Banerji, A. (2005, May). *The relationship between labor costs and inflation: A cyclical viewpoint.* U.S. Department of Labor, Bureau of Labor Statistics, Economic Cycle Research Institute.

92. Europeans spend less on health care, but they earn less too. Americans earn more than Europeans, and their higher productivity allows them to spend more

Table 13.4   International Comparison of Hourly Compensation Costs for Production Workers (Indexed to U.S. Dollars) and Percent of Labor Costs for Social Expenditures

Country	Percentage of Labor Rate Spent on Social Costs 2006	Indexed Hourly Costs 2006
Canada	19.7 percent	108
France	32 percent	105
Germany	23 percent	144
Ireland	17 percent	109
Italy	30.4 percent	105
Japan	18 percent	85
Netherlands	22.4 percent	136
U.K.	21.3 percent	114
United States	22 percent	100

SOURCE: U.S. Department of Labor, Chart Book of International Labor Comparisons (2007) and U.S. Department of Labor, Bureau of Labor Statistics (2006, November), http://www.bls.gov/fls/hcompsupptabtoc.htm.

health care, and their labor costs and social allocation rate are among the highest.

We do know the United States pays more for health care than any other developed country. The bulk of the funds for social costs in the United States comes from employers, designated payroll taxes, and employee cost sharing. The high costs for health care do not necessarily render the United States uncompetitive, especially among Western European countries. Their labor rates are higher than in the United States. With China, however, it is another story. In the global marketplace, there is a clear opportunity. The United States should be constrained to dramatically lower its health care costs to targeted levels.

on health care, particularly for high technology treatments. See Graham, J. (2007, November 13). The health care myth. *The Wall Street Journal*, A17.

No matter what course the United States takes with respect to health and social security reform, we should always remember that nothing is free. As we learned from the benefits model, benefits must be delivered on a cost-effective basis. The marketplace is no longer isolated and employers cannot be assured of cost parity among their labor, product, and service competitors. There are wide disparities in approaches, all of which must be given close scrutiny. Survival in the global market is at stake.

Expatriates and Global Benefits—Taking Your Business Abroad

An issue related to global benefits is how do employers, particularly with home headquarters in the United States, who want to send their employees to work abroad provide them with health care, retirement, and other benefits?[93] In spite of the cost of assigning expatriates, their numbers are rising and, because of the complexities largely arising from compensation and benefit issues, they often take a disproportionate amount of the corporate staff's time and resources.[94]

> Art Ferguson works for a global home appliance company that has a number of plants all over the world, including a facility in Milan, Italy, that makes washing machines. Art is the HR director for the corporate office located in Harrison, Ohio, and has been asked to facilitate the transfer of a highly valued engineer to the Milan plant. The assignment will last about four years. It is expected that she will transfer new technology to the Milan plant. This particular engineer is regarded as a future executive, and Art's CEO believes that international assignments are a necessary preparation for all executive positions.

---

93. In this section we will not discuss a variety of approaches undertaken by EU countries to facilitate the movement and expatriate assignments of an EU national to another EU country. The tax and benefit issues are explained in Endres, D., Spengel, C., Eischner, C., & Schmidt, O. (2005). The tax burden on international assignments. *Intertax* (Kluwer Law International), *33*(11), 490–502. See also *Guidance note on Pan-European pensions.* (2004, January 28), Federation of European Employers, http://www.fedee.com/pensions/.

94. Latta, G. (2006). The future of Expatriate compensation. *World at Work Journal,* Second Quarter, 42–49, http://www.worldatwork.org/advancesearch/; search for "Expatriate Compensation."

> Currently, the engineer is a production supervisor at the refrigerator plant in the southern United States. The transfer to Milan would involve a next-step promotion for her and improve her status in the company's executive succession plan. She will be assigned as an assistant plant manager in Milan.
>
> She currently makes a pretax salary of $140,000 and has a bonus potential of $45,000. She is covered by a PPO health care plan in the United States and pays a monthly co-premium of $125 for family coverage. She has been awarded stock options each year. Currently, she has 7,000 vested but unexercised shares. The company's current stock price is $60 per share and her previously granted options are in the money. She has 3,000 unvested shares. She participates in a 401(k) retirement savings plan with a 100 percent employer match on the first 3 percent of her salary that she defers, and a 20 percent additional match if she chooses the company stock as her investment option. She has three weeks vacation per year and a company car, lives in an upscale community with average housing values around $650,000. Her children attend private schools, which cost approximately $15,000 per year, and her husband works as a hospital pharmacist and earns $139,000 per year with many of the same benefits.
>
> An Italian national who currently occupies the position to which she would be transferred makes the equivalent of $55,000 (USD) take-home pay. He is a participant in the government-sponsored pension and health care plans. There are no option plans at his level, and he receives six weeks annual holiday leave. He lives in a two-bedroom flat and has a summer home at Lake Garda in Northern Italy. He is not provided a company car, but drives a "motolino" (motorbike) to work. He will move to a similar position at the company's microwave oven plant in Monza, Italy, to make room for her transfer.
>
> How should Art prepare an optimal package of compensation and benefits that will ensure the acceptance of the transfer by the engineer and, ultimately, the success of her assignment?

There are several competing theories about expatriate compensation. One, called the balance sheet approach, is designed to make the employee whole during the assignment. The objective is to offer a compensation package that allows the expatriate to retain his lifestyle and standard of living while working in the host country. The other approach is called the host country (market rate) plan, and it provides the expatriate with the same compensation package as that of the host country nationals working in same or similar positions at the facility or in the comparative external labor market. It is based on the internal fairness concept of the pay and benefits model, which recommends equal compensation for equal work.

Imagine telling an employee who has special expertise not available in the host country or whose career development plan requires a foreign assignment, that she must take a cut in pay, benefits, and other forms of compensation and go to work in another country. In most cases, the employee would not accept the assignment or would do so very grudgingly, thereby enhancing the prospects for failure. So, most U.S. companies follow the balance sheet approach or a modified version thereof.[95]

There are many factors and components to the expatriate's total compensation, including benefits that must be considered. What is his current standard of living? What is the cost of living in the host country compared to the home country? How do you deal with currency value fluctuations? What about schools for children, home leaves, transportation, moving expenses, security, the trailing spouse, income taxes, social security, company-sponsored health care, performance bonuses, stock and stock options, retirement, and life and disability insurance? What, if anything, should be done about the higher costs of many goods in European countries that levy economic value-added taxes? Many of these issues are dealt with by providing allowances in addition to salary and bonuses to compensate the employee.

So, our engineer might receive an allowance for moving special furniture, housing, and transportation in the host country. She also might receive an allowance for her children's education at a private school in the host country, cost of living differences, and other unique expenses to mitigate the added burdens of a foreign assignment.

But what do we do about her health care? In the United States, this is largely a third-party administered, employer-sponsored insurance benefit that provides reimbursements to providers in the same locality as the participant. In many host countries, health care is a nationally sponsored, regionally administered service and is provided to all citizens and legal residents. How does an employer ensure that its expatriates have access to quality health care? If the employer's facility sponsors health care insurance to all of his employees, then the expatriate would be similarly covered. If the expatriate is not able to attain legal residency status and,

---

95. See Konopaske, R., & Werner, S. (2005, July). U.S. managers' willingness to accept a global assignment: Do expatriate benefits and assignment length make a difference? *International Journal of Human Resource Management, 16*(7), 1150–1175. Among the authors' conclusions is that an international health care insurance plan as well as other benefits were very instrumental in causing an employee to accept an assignment. For a view of how smaller companies wanting to make expatriate assignments might offer special benefits to make a good fit with the employee, see Polak, R. (2006, October). The Goldilocks Approach to International Assignments. *Employee Benefit News*, http://www.benefitnews.com.

therefore, is not eligible to participate in a national health care system, the employer could provide an agreement to hold the employee harmless and simply pay for health expenses as they are incurred. A more structured approach, however, would be for the employer to purchase some type of universal or international health insurance for all of his expatriates in this host country as well as others.[96] So, our engineer and her family would use local, host country health care providers often identified by the international insurance company, and they would be reimbursed by the international insurance plan.

What about income taxes? The United States taxes worldwide income but does exempt a certain amount of compensation for expatriate assignments.[97] If the host country and the United States both tax the expatriate's income, then the employee would be at a significant financial disadvantage. The United States has tax treaties with a number of countries, such as France, whereby residents or citizens of foreign countries working in a host country are taxed at a reduced rate or are exempt from taxes on certain items of income received from the host country.[98] Absent a treaty, most global companies provide for tax equalization by guaranteeing the employee will not suffer a reduction in income as a result of the assignment. The employer calculates the taxes owed by the employee in the United States and pays the excess tax owed to the host country. This practice obviously can add significant expense to an expatriate assignment.[99]

Art also must consider Social Security and Medicare. The United States would continue to deduct the payroll taxes for these government-sponsored benefits. The host country may do the same. Again, the employee would be at a disadvantage.[100] Art's engineer would be taxed

96. The employer also usually provides for emergency medical evacuation of the expatriate or family member to facilitate treatment in the United States.

97. The Internal Revenue Code of the United States, Section 911(b)(d)(2), provides for an income tax exemption of the first $82,400 (effective 2006) of salary earned abroad during an expatriate assignment. See also *Foreign earned income exclusion—What is foreign earned income?* (2007). Internal Revenue Service, http://www.irs.gov/businesses/small/international/. There are certain requirements, however, that must be met in order for the exemption to apply. As an example, the expatriate must be physically present in the country for at least one continuous year.

98. See *United States income tax treaties—A to Z.* (2007). Internal Revenue Service, http://www.irs.gov/ and search "businesses/international/article/." The treaty between France and the United States is called "The Convention Between the U.S. and the Republic of France for the Avoidance of Double Taxation and the Prevention of Fiscal Evasion of 1994."

99. See http://www.ssa.gov/ and search "international/agreements."

100. Some countries consider the employer's contribution to an employee's social security program to be taxable income. This further complicates expatriate assignments.

twice for Social Security but, unless she works a substantial number of years in the host country, she would not qualify for a benefit. Her contributions would be lost.[101] To rectify this problem, the United States and 21 countries have treaties that provide for single coverage and single taxation under one system.[102] Thus, if an employee would be covered by two social security systems and subject to two payroll tax plans, the agreements between these countries exempt workers from the coverage of one of the systems.

For those who divide their work careers between the United States and another country, the treaties provide social security benefit protection.[103] In certain cases, for example where the employee has worked a substantial time under two systems but does not qualify for one or the other, totalization agreements exist between countries that allow total years of service and credits to be added, and each country pays a proportionate share of the benefit. Thus, when the employee retires under the home country plan, monies and employment credits retained in the host country's system would be transferred to the home plan to help pay for the social security and other relevant benefits.[104]

Madeline will reach age 65 in 2009. She has worked under two social security systems, one in the United States and the other in Luxembourg. She needs 40 quarters of work and payroll contributions to qualify for a Social Security pension in the United States. She only has 30, but she has 10 quarters of work and contributions under the Luxembourg system. Under a totalization agreement, provided she has a minimum number of six quarters of work credits, she can receive a partial Social Security pension by combining the credits from both countries. Her pension will be based on the proportion of credits she earned (30/40) in the paying country, which in this case is the United States. Depending on the circumstances, Luxembourg could similarly grant her credits for work in the United States if her work credits combined met its eligibility requirements. If she worked enough to qualify under both countries' plans, she could receive proportionate retirement income from both countries.

101. Ibid.

102. See *Social Security systems throughout the world,* http://www.ssa.gov/international/.

103. Ibid.

104. Ibid.

There are a number of different approaches to benefits allowed and their tax treatment in respective countries. Will the host country give favorable tax treatment to contributions made to a defined contribution plan such as a 401(k) or a profit sharing plan administered in the United States? What if they do not recognize the tax-deferred status of these contributions and tax them as income? Again, the tax equalization plan of the employer would make the employee whole in this instance and reimburse him for the taxes on the deferral to the 401(k).

Equity benefits and the concept of rewarding value creation are not as common in European countries as they are in the United States. Those European companies that have options are frequently designing them to be performance-based and they only vest when certain targets are met, such as a large increase in the stock price. The diffusion of stock options to lower-level managers is also starting to accelerate in countries like France.[105] Some countries provide different tax treatment of equity benefits. For example, Belgium taxes stock options at grant. So, let's say a U.S. expatriate working in Belgium receives nonqualified stock options and is taxed on their purported value at the time of grant. If he then moves to Germany, he is taxed again upon exercise of the options. He also would be subject to U.S. tax on his worldwide income. If he is then transferred to France and sells the stock from the earlier exercise, he is taxed on the gain by both France and the United States. Or, suppose he was in Japan when the options vested, but did not exercise until several years after returning to the United States. Japan would claim tax on the proportionate share of gain realized when the options vested there. While tax equalization is the solution, one can see it adds quite a bit of time, recordkeeping, and expense for the employer, not to mention the significant disadvantage to the expatriate. In the United States, nonqualified stock options would have been taxed only on exercise.[106]

The expatriate must decide whether to rent or purchase a residence. There are different tax consequences to this decision in various countries. There also are different rules on the decedent's estate succession. For example, notwithstanding the expressed declaration of the expatriate in a last will and testament in the United States, some countries require a distribution to members of the immediate family.[107] This might be very

105. Ponssard, J. (2001). *Stock options and performance-based pay in France*. The Brookings Institution, Global Politics, http://www.brookings.edu/.

106. See *Policy and business practices: End double taxation of stock options*. (2002, May 9). International Chamber of Commerce, http://www.iccwbo.org/policy/taxation/. See also *Equity incentives*. (2006). Deloitte Tax Solutions, http://www.deloitte.com/.

107. See, for example, a review of French inheritance protocols and taxes at French Property, Services and Information (2007), http://www.france-property-and-information-com/.

important to an expatriate with real estate or a large net worth secured in the host country. Will these assets be subject to inheritance tax, income tax, or some type of more favorable capital gains tax treatment by the host country? What role should the employer play in providing assistance to the expatriate in ameliorating these problems?

There are currency and inflation risks that must be taken into consideration. Currency rates fluctuate and inflation ebbs and flows during an expatriate assignment. How should these variations be handled? What currency will be used to pay the compensation and benefits of the expatriate and where will the payments be made? Some companies compensate their expatriates in both home and host country currencies to mitigate the risks.

In the case of our HR director, Art Ferguson, he will have to review carefully all the financial aspects of the assignment of the engineer. It, obviously, will cost more than her current annual compensation to provide the necessary allowances, and he must assure her that she will not be worse off with respect to benefits and taxes. It all looks pretty complicated. Moreover, the trailing spouse, who normally cannot obtain a work visa, will have to forgo employment in the host country unless Art's company wants to offer him a job at the plant as well.[108] In this case, his income will be lost during the expatriate assignment. Should the company consider some allowance for this loss? Usually it does not. What impact would such a subsidy have on the total cost of the transfer?

Many companies that have large global operations and large numbers of expatriates are developing special, international compensation and benefit packages[109] that are uniformly available to all expatriates. A number of items, particularly the benefits, apply wherever the expatriate is assigned. The cost, however, of sending employees abroad is quite high, and employers are paying more attention to which employees really need to go, and what the likelihood is that the assignment will succeed.[110]

The reality is that the lower the compensation level in the host country, the larger the compensation differential for the expatriate. The engineer's

---

108. "In most cases it is impossible to ensure that the accompanying spouse with a career can continue to practice that career in the assignment location." Latta, G. (2006), p. 47.

109. See, for example, the recent *2007 Towers Perrin health care cost survey* (2007, July), that discusses global benefit strategies among companies with expatriates, at http://www.towersperrin.com/.

110. For an excellent review of issues pertaining to the who, how, and why of expatriate assignments, as well as their general efficacy as a means of knowledge transfer and employee development, see Black, S., & Gregersen, H. (1999, March–April). The Right Way to Manage Expats. *Harvard Business Review*, 52. Usually, a "failure" is defined as a premature return from the host to the home country.

compensation package will far exceed that of the host country's employees. Nevertheless, if companies are investing more in plants and facilities located in less-developed countries, this cost and imbalance in expatriate compensation will continue. It appears the need to fill skill gaps and to provide foreign assignments as part of management development will continue to motivate increased expatriate assignments by U.S. companies.[111] There has been some convergence of compensation and benefits among European Union countries as well as some efforts by global companies to develop an integrated approach to their worldwide compensation and benefit practices.[112] But the task of gaining acceptance of such transfers by key employees, particularly in countries where there are significant differences in the labor markets, may be difficult to accomplish without a customization of the expatriate's compensation and benefit package.

Conclusion and Perspectives—The Global Workplace

I have a friend I have known for 20 years, who was formerly a senior officer of a Fortune 100 company that employed 30,000 employees. He left to become an executive of a small manufacturing firm that makes plastic parts for engines. The parts wind up in U.S.-, Japanese-, and European-made autos. The company has one plant and employs 300 skilled workers, salespeople, and administrative support personnel. It is located in a small Indiana town where most residents have never gone beyond the state lines, much less traveled to Europe or Asia.

My friend's firm, however, is dealing on a daily basis with global customers, navigating through diverse cultures, legal and business systems, and struggling to remain cost competitive. He looks at every aspect of product costs, including labor and benefits, because, as he says, each year his customers expect his prices to decline. His

---

111. There are some experiments being conducted with "virtual" foreign assignments where managers are accountable for certain foreign operations and use technology to exercise their leadership. Also, there are home country nationals who are being asked to accept multiple assignments during their career. This practice facilitates the development of a uniform international package of compensation and benefits. Latta, G. (2006), p. 49.

112. Latta, G. (2006), p. 48.

competitors are in China, Mexico, the United States, and Europe. This is the new reality of globalization; your competitors and customers are no longer down the street, across town, or in the same country. Their "bailiwick" has no national boundaries. They do, however, have different labor costs, and can leverage this advantage to offer lower prices, better service, and higher quality. My friend, and the thousands of similarly situated Americans who are running a business, must be vigilant to closely control his labor costs to make sure he can continue to compete in these new, global markets. A nation's system of health care and retirement can have a significant impact on the ability of an enterprise to compete, and labor cost comparisons can no longer be confined to the company down the street, across town, or even in your own country.

Chapter Exercises

1. How can we better measure the efficacy of various health systems, particularly among developed or OECD countries? What should the measures be? Read the following article and give a constructive appraisal of the measures and methodology used by the authors in comparing the efficacies of the health systems in Australia, Canada, Germany, New Zealand, and the United States. Do these results tell us which system works best? What are the factors used and are they subject to some critical analysis? How do the authors define, for example, quality, efficiency, access, equity, and healthy lives? See Davis, K. et al. (2007, May). *Mirror, mirror on the wall: An international update on the comparative performance of American health care.* The Common Wealth Fund, http://www.commonwealthfund.org.

2. The problem of excessive wait times among OECD countries for elective surgery and other medical procedures is problematic. Are there intrinsic and intractable problems that lead to excessive wait times in single-payer, universal health care systems? What are some practical, supply-side measures that are available to a particular country to solve the problem of wait times? Are there lessons for the U.S. system here? See Hurst, J., & Siciliani, L. (2003, July 7). *Tackling excessive wait times for elective surgery: A comparison of policies in twelve OECD countries.* OECD Health Working Papers.

3. From a microeconomic basis, and assuming other factors are equal, based on the labor cost data shown above, where should cost-conscious employers look to establish manufacturing facilities? What other factors are relevant to making this decision?

4. After comparing the U.S. health care and Social Security systems to other countries, which plan design(s) would appear to be good "fits" for the United States? What are the comparative rates of improvements in health status, risk factors, capacity to provide services, level of service, and access to service among OECD countries? Are these good measures to use? How do length of stay and wait times correlate? Read Docteur, E. (2003, June 28). *U.S. health system performance in an international context*. OECD, http://www.oecd.org. Be prepared to discuss these issues. For an explanation of a new OECD initiative on health care outcomes measurements, see Docteur, E. (2003, June 26). *Reforming health systems in OECD countries*. OECD. Also, check out the OECD Health Care Quality Indicators Project that compares outcomes for cardiac care, diabetes care, primary care and prevention, mental health, and patient safety. Is the OECD on the right track? Where is the status of the outcomes metrics initiative today? How would these measures be relevant in the debate over health care reform?

5. How would you go about calculating the potential savings, if any, in administrative costs the United States might enjoy if it chose a single-payer, uniform health care system for its population? Read this article and be prepared to discuss: Woolhandler, S., Campbell, T., & Himmelstein, D. (2003, August 21). Costs of health care administration in the U.S. and Canada. *The New England Journal of Medicine, 349,* 768–775.

6. With many public pension systems in financial trouble among OECD countries, some have tried investing their funds in capital markets, adjusting pension amounts based on life expectancy, increasing the retirement age, and increasing the minimum years of service to qualify for a pension. What successes, if any, have these reforms achieved? See *Pensions at a glance, public policies across OECD countries,* 2007 edition, OECD, http://www.oecd.org/. Also see James, E. (2005, June). *Reforming Social Security: Lessons from thirty countries*. National Center for Policy Analysis, No. 277.

7. What are the comparative net and gross replacement rates for public pensions in OECD countries, and what is the percent of public spending on pensions? How do these compare to the United States? Is there less reliance in the United States on the public Social Security system? Why? How should this affect reform

proposals in the United States? Should the United States "mandate" employer-sponsored pensions or retirement savings plans as have Ireland, Germany, and the U.K.? *Pensions at a glance, public policies across OECD countries,* 2007 edition. OECD, http://www.oecd.org/. See also *International retirement security survey research report.* (2005, July). Harris Interactive, Inc. and AARP, http://www.aarp.org/ and Korczyk, S. (2007). *Mandatory employer pensions in Ireland, Germany, and the United Kingdom.* AARP, http://www.aarp.org.

Collective Bargaining and Benefits 14

General Obligation to Provide New Benefits Pursuant to Collective Bargaining

Art Juergens is the human resources manager of C&S Logistics, a warehouse and distribution company that employs over 1,400 drivers, warehouse workers, and professional and management staff. The company just experienced an organizing drive by Local 1A of the International Brotherhood of Teamsters, who won a National Labor Relations Board (NLRB) supervised election and now represents the hourly drivers, warehouse workers, and receiving and shipping clerks. The Local has requested a meeting to begin discussions about a collective bargaining agreement. Art is representing management in this first negotiating session.

After a brief opening statement, the Local president hands Art a list of proposals for a new contract. Among the list of items is a call for increases in hourly wages, a seniority system, additional vacation time, more holidays, premium time for certain shifts, and overtime for work on all holidays. The new contract also would include a "successors and assigns" clause meaning that, in the event the company sold or transferred its business, the union contract would apply to the buyer. The proposal includes significant improvements in the current retirement and health care plans, and seeks to place both plans in joint trusts that would be managed by equal numbers of union and company trustees. The company would continue to be the exclusive funding source for the plans. The improvements for pensions include a change in the formula for calculating the defined benefit, an annual cost of living adjustment for all retiree benefits, retiree health care, and mandatory fixed company matches for the 401(k) plan.

The union's proposal includes an elimination of the deductible and the employee premium in the health care plan, as well as a conversion of the current PPO and HMO alternatives to a single fee-for-service indemnity plan with no coinsurance. The plan would pay 100 percent of all costs incurred. It also would require the company to continue to fund the plan's trust so as to maintain these levels of benefits in the future.

Art responds to the union's proposals by asking a number of questions. When he gets to pension and health care, he explains that these company-sponsored plans have been in place for over 30 years, and points out that company management has worked hard to provide generous retirement income to their older workers and to keep all of their employees healthy. He goes on to say that the company employs professional actuaries, accountants, and lawyers to keep both plans in full compliance with ERISA and the Internal Revenue Code, and further states that the insurance company which manages the health care plan has some of the best doctors and hospitals in its network. Both plans compare favorably to those offered by competitors in the industry.

The Local president says that new members will not be satisfied to pay union dues simply to maintain the status quo. The union must win wages and benefits that are significantly better than nonunion competition. Further, in order to get full credit for these improved benefits, they must be channeled through and administered by a joint trust.

Art takes advantage of a coffee break to reflect on what he has just heard. He has a number of questions and issues in his new role as company negotiator, including: Is it necessary to "bargain" with the union over benefits? Will he have to change the pension and health care plans? Will he be required to give up administration of the plans and put them into a joint trust and, if so, won't this forfeiture of control make it impossible to really manage the plans? Will there be added administrative costs? Must he bargain over retiree benefits, especially since no competitor is offering retiree health care? Since labor costs represent a large percentage of the company's total cost of doing business, how can his company remain competitive in their pricing when conceivably its labor costs could far exceed those of its competitors?

It is well established that a company must bargain in good faith over employee benefits.[1] The definition of good faith bargaining is somewhat vague; however, both parties have the mutual obligation to

> meet at reasonable times and to confer in good faith with respect to wages, hours, and other terms and conditions of employment, or the negotiation of an agreement or any question arising thereunder, and the execution of a written contract incorporating any agreement reached if requested by either party, but such obligation does not compel either party to agree to a proposal or require the making of a concession.[2]

Topics such as wages, hours of work, health care, life insurance, break rules, vacation, holidays, free parking, the cost of coffee in the break room, the placement of security cameras in the workplace, and pensions fit into the scope of "mandatory subjects" of bargaining. This means the parties must bargain, but not necessarily agree, over these types of subjects, and a proponent can insist on their acceptance to the point of impasse.[3]

There also are subjects of bargaining that are defined as "permissive." Here the parties are permitted to subject the particular issue to bargaining, but are not obligated to do so. An example of a "permissive" subject of bargaining is a demand that the union submit a detailed bargaining agenda as a precondition of the company's willingness to bargain over a new contract. In this case, the company cannot insist to the point of impasse on a permissive subject of bargaining. If it does, it violates the National Labor Relations Act (NLRA).[4] Also, there are "illegal subjects of bargaining" that impose no obligation on the other side to even discuss the issue and are not even permitted to be included in a labor agreement. An example of an "illegal" subject might be a proposal by the union to include a provision in the agreement that would allow union members to refuse to handle products that were produced by nonunion suppliers. Would it be illegal for the company to propose that several union officials relinquish the office to which they were elected by the membership?[5] Could it insist on such a proposal to the point of impasse?

---

1. See §8(a)(5) of the NLRA.

2. §8(d) of the NLRA.

3. The test is whether the subject is "germane to the working environment and not among those managerial decisions, which lie at the core of entrepreneurial control." See *Brewers and Malsters, Local Union No. 6, I.B.T., v. NLRB*, 414 F.3d 36 (D.C. Cir. 2005).

4. *Vanguard Fire and Supply Co. v. NLRB*, 468 F. 3d 952 (6th Cir. 2006).

5. See generally *Hill-Rom Co. v. NLRB*, 957 F.2d 454 (7th Cir. 1992); *Eddy Potash, Inc.*, 331 NLRB 552 (2000) where the company bargained to impasse and imple-

When the union bargains over benefits, it often requests financial, actuarial, and claims experience and other "relevant" data and information from the company. The obligation to bargain in good faith often carries with it an obligation to disclose information and data in the company's control that is important to the union in developing its position on certain bargaining topics. There are limits to this obligation, such as privacy and confidentiality, but some examples of occasions when the duty to disclose has been enforced include the duty to furnish health care claims data of nonunion employees covered by the health care plan, employee census data, benefit cost data, actuarial information concerning funding, and other benefit plan or demographic information that will assist the union in carrying out its bargaining function.[6]

When an employer is obligated to bargain with a union over benefits, the employer no longer can exercise his unilateral prerogative in designing and offering benefits. The decision with respect to deductibles, co-pays, coinsurance, out-of-pocket maximums, and a variety of other features now must be subjected to collective bargaining with the union and, in Art's mind, the possibility of increased expense for the company.[7] The issues of a defined benefit formula, early retirement age and actuarial

---

mented an illegal "12-hour shift" proposal for underground workers. In *NLRB v. General Teamsters Union Local 662*, 368 F. 3d 741 (7th Cir. 2004), the Court held that a proposal by the company to require certain employees to forfeit their leadership position in the union was a "permissive" subject of bargaining and not "illegal."

6. See generally *St. Clair Die Casting*, 341 NLRB 144 (2004) and *Evergreen America Corp. v. NLRB*, 312 F. 3d 827 (D.C. Cir. 2004). The Supreme Court has held that certain confidential information need not be disclosed to the union in bargaining, see *Detroit Edison Co. v. NLRB*, 440 U.S. 301 (1979). But the Court of Appeals for the District of Columbia recently found that an employer must furnish the union with health care claims histories of nonunion employees when a proper rationale for the disclosure was made. See *U.S. Testing v. NLRB*, 160 F.3d 14 (DC Cir. 1998). In this case the company asserted the need to make a 30 percent reduction in health care costs, and the union requested the disclosure of nonunion employees' claims data. The union's claim was upheld with the stipulation that no employees' names would be revealed.

7. In a recent article by health care plan consultant David Gibson, published by the respected International Foundation of Employee Benefit Plans in their October 2007 issue of *Benefits Compensation*, 44(10), http://www.ifebp.org/, the author identifies the excessive cost differentials among joint health care trust funds that are being expended unnecessarily. He suggests a number of strategies the funds should employ to relieve the inflationary trends that fund leaders indicate will eventually lead to the termination of their plans. Among the author's recommendations is a move to proactive management of medical risks that could reduce health expenses by as much as 40 percent. Making such a move, however, will take union and management cooperation and agreement.

reductions, investment strategy concerning the funding of the plan, as well as the amount of the match and type and number of investment options for the 401(k) are all matters of mandatory bargaining. Let's focus on Art's current situation and illustrate the type of benefit issues that arise in his collective bargaining venue.

What Will Happen to the Current Plans?

If the company would agree to the Local's demands concerning pension and health care, what will it do with management and others not included in the bargaining unit who are in the current plans? Should it simply allow current nonunion employees to move into the "newly negotiated union plan," or should it split off the current plan and allow nonunion employees to remain? Since the current pension plan provides participation and service credit for any employee who works more than 1,000 hours per year, can the union employees be excluded? The company certainly does not want to cover union employees under two plans. Does the company have to bargain over this exclusion or can it unilaterally change the current plan to provide for the exclusion?[8]

Must the Company Bargain Over an Entry Into a Joint Trust?

The answer is yes. In some instances, for example, the selection of a third-party administrator, in most cases the insurance company, of a health care plan may not be a mandatory subject of bargaining.[9] It is clear the design features of the plan would be subject to the "mandatory" bargaining obligation. Assuming, however, the selection of the TPA does not materially affect the employees' participation in a health care plan, it would be a "permissive" subject of bargaining. What about a joint trust? Isn't it the same thing? If the union wants to jointly manage a plan, requiring its

---

8. The company has some legal liberties here. It can create a special plan for employees covered by the collective bargaining agreement or it can change the benefits and administration of the current plan and allow everyone, union and nonunion, to participate. Most employers separate the two groups of employees and create a new plan for the organized workers.

9. Courts have held that the designation of the particular health insurance carrier is not a mandatory bargaining subject, so long as the parties have negotiated over the "benefits, coverage and administration of the plan." *Connecticut Light & Power Co. v. NLRB*, 476 F.2d 1079, 1083 (2d Cir. 1973)

representatives to receive monies from the company to fund the plan, it must utilize a joint trust.

In Section 302(b)(1) of the NLRA, Congress recognized the existence of joint trusts dedicated to the administration of benefit plans. Such a trust is the only legal way a labor organization can receive funds from an employer. Otherwise, employer payments to a union are illegal. The benefit trusts must be jointly managed by an equal number of union and management trustees who are obligated to assume a fiduciary role and act in the best interests of the participants.[10] It is permissible to have joint trusts that include contributions and representation from several employers, usually in the same industry, and these are called "multi-employer" joint trusts. Or, the trusts can simply include one employer and one local union.

Union and employer(s) trustees design benefit plans that will be sponsored by the trusts. They employ a variety of professionals such as actuaries, investment specialists, attorneys, and the day-to-day fund administrators. The trustees establish the contributions the employer(s) must make in order to properly fund the obligations set forth in the plans. Typically, as a result of a written contribution agreement, the employers are then legally obligated to remit such contributions to the trust. The collective bargaining agreement usually only refers to the trust as the administrator for the retirement or health care plan, and then delineates the precise contributions that will be made to the trust during the term of the agreement.[11] Most often, there is no bargaining between the trust and the union or employer. The trust is merely a receptacle for funds that support a specific trust-sponsored health or retirement plan (also called "welfare" plan). The plans, of course, must comply with ERISA and the Internal Revenue Code.[12] They also must make contributions to the Pension

---

10. Selection of their respective trustees is within the exclusive province of the employer and the union. 29 USC § 302(b).

11. There are sometimes disputes between the trustees with respect to investment assumptions and strategies of joint pension plans. On occasion the contributions to the trust and the investment in capital markets by the trustees do yield significant returns that actuarially would permit a suspension of contributions due to "overfunding" of the plan. Unlike a private employer-sponsored plan, however, the employer is obligated by the collective bargaining agreement to continue making contributions to the fund unless his obligation is modified based on a clear agreement with the union. Interview of Michael Stoll, Vice President of Employee Benefits, The Kroger Co. (2007, August 19).

12. Among bargained plans, there are sometimes conflicts about "preemption." Which law—ERISA, NLRA, IRC—governs? For example, if a dispute arises over a benefit issue, should it be resolved pursuant to the NLRA or ERISA? Usually, if the dispute involves an interpretation of the plan, ERISA will preempt any NLRA claim. If, on the other hand, the dispute involves the administration or process of

Benefit Guaranty Corporation (PBGC) to insure benefit payments in the event of a plan's insolvency.

Bargaining over a joint trust-sponsored benefit plan involves control over key issues such as plan designs, funding, and the assumption of important fiduciary roles for both union and company.[13] It also gives the union strategic insights into management's benefit strategies, allowing them to play a more informed role in the bargaining. In cases where there are multi-employers in the same industry contributing to the trust, the union can better guarantee parity of benefits and costs among the participants.[14] Having one fund in industries like construction, where employees move from employer to employer, is important because it allows employees to accrue service and benefit entitlements under one plan.

Theoretically, these multi-employer trusts provide lower administrative expenses, because all contributing employers share in the costs. This, in fact, may be the only way some small employers can sponsor a pension or health care plan. Also, a joint trust gives the union a higher profile among its members.[15]

Joint Trusts—Issues and Challenges

There are challenging issues for employers who take part in multi-employer joint benefit trusts. Participation provides the employer with significantly less flexibility to argue or bargain for plan design changes. For example, if an employer participates in a multi-employer health care trust, his costs may be adversely affected by the health experience of other

---

bargaining, the NLRA will control. See *Felix v. Lucent Technologies, Inc.*, 387 F.3d 1146 (10 Cir. 2004) and *IBEW v. L.G. Philips Display Components Co.*, 32 EB Cases (BNA) 1471 (N.D. Ohio 2004).

13. An example of a controversial labor contract provision relating to health care is the maintenance of benefits clause. It is discussed infra.

14. In some joint trusts, there are several plans that employers and their respective unions can choose during negotiations for a new labor contract. Each optional plan has varying benefit levels and costs, and the union and company negotiate which plan their members and respective employees will be in. In such cases there may not be "parity" among other employers contributing to the trust. It should be noted that multi-employer plans are different from "multiple employer" plans where each employer and his employees have a separate plan and account; liabilities are not pooled. Fund administration is, however, shared, which permits lower administrative costs. *Multiemployer pensions face key challenges to their long-term prospects.* (2004). General Accountability Office (GAO-04-542T).

15. Even though the terms of the plans were agreed to by the union and company and appear in the labor agreement.

employers who have an older workforce, more intense health care resource utilization, or other characteristics that lead to higher health care expenses. In such cases, the employer with a positive health care experience may be forced to pay higher contributions to the trust than he would pay in his own individual plan, thereby subsidizing the higher cost employer. In some cases, employers with exceptionally high health care costs gladly join a trust-sponsored plan to spread their risks and higher costs on to others. The same type of cost shifting can occur among employers in a joint pension trust if one employer has a much older workforce that is likely to retire earlier than a younger workforce employed by another employer. In this case, the second employer would be subsidizing the higher impending costs of retirements of the employer with the older workers.

Another issue pertaining to trusts involves conflicts among the professionals and their respective union and management constituents. It is not uncommon for employers and unions, particularly in large multi-employer trusts, to have their own respective investment adviser, actuary, and counsel. This two-instead-of-one staff adds expense to the administration of the

Table 14.1   Multi-Employer Benefit Structure

Collective Bargaining Agreement	Participation Agreement
Establishes coverage requirements for employees	Signed by the employer and the trust
Identifies joint trust that sponsors the benefit	Incorporates the obligation of the employer to pay for benefits as set forth in the collective bargaining agreement
Sometimes identifies the specific plan of benefits for employee	Sets the time, place, and other details for contributions
Sometimes requires the employer to pay to "maintain" current benefits	Often provides for binding arbitration to resolve any disputes
Requires the employer to sign a participation agreement with the trust	
Provides for specific dollar contributions per hour per covered worker	

fund and often leads to protracted disagreements over such issues as investment strategy, funding status of the plan, and contributions necessary to fund specific benefit plans.[16] For example, the union professionals might want a more conservative investment approach with respect to fund assets. Employer trustees and their professionals might argue for a more aggressive approach so as to maximize investment returns that can help fund the plan. Their hope, of course, is that the higher returns will obviate the need for increased employer contributions to the plan in the future. There are other contentious issues among trustees, but most often the parties resolve them. If not, the dispute must usually be resolved by binding arbitration.[17]

MPPAA—What Happens if the Employer Closes His Operation and Leaves the Joint Trust?

There is a significant problem related to multi-employer benefit trusts involving employer withdrawals from the plan. Let's say an employer does business in Los Angeles and contributes to a joint trust industry pension fund comprising one local union and several employers. The employer's business in Los Angeles is declining and he decides to sell his assets and move to another state. His current employees will remain in the Los Angeles area; however, there are others who are retired or may be eligible to retire under the plan in the near future. As a result, there could be vested but not funded liabilities in the plan attributable to these employees. With no future contributions from the departing employer, the obligation falls on the remaining employers to fund this residual vested liability. Thus, an employer could "escape" a pension liability by simply leaving the plan.

The remedy for this problem came from Congress in the Multi-Employer Pension Plan Amendments Act (MPPAA). Among its provisions, the Act requires the departing employer to pay to the fund all of his unfunded vested benefits (UVB).[18] This payment, called a "withdrawal liability," presumably mitigates the problem of burdening the remaining employers and possibly jeopardizing the solvency of the plan.[19] Issues

---

16. Gibson (2007).

17. 29 USC §302(b).

18. Vested benefits are not subject to forfeiture. Unfunded Vested Benefits are the excess of the present value of a plan's vested benefits over the value of plan assets. See General Accountability Office (2004), p. 5. The MPPAA also requires participating employers to make contributions to the PBGC so as to insure benefits to participants in the event of a plan's failure.

19. See 29 USC §1381 and, more specifically, §1385(b)(2)(a)(1). Withdrawal liability is the departing employer's proportionate share of the UVB. General

concerning the legitimacy and amount of withdrawal liability are subject to mandatory and binding arbitration.[20] Without MPPAA, the remaining employers would have to increase their contributions to the plan in order to fund the UVB of the departing employer.[21]

In the above illustration, if the labor agreement provided that it would apply to a successor to the departing company, then the company who bought the employer's business and continued its operations would be bound by the labor agreement and required to continue making contributions to the plan.[22] In such case, there would be no UVB and no issue of withdrawal liability on the departing employer.[23]

Our friend, Art Juergens, is at the bottom of a new learning curve. The obligation to bargain over benefits creates a significant change for the newly organized employer. Most all benefit issues are no longer within the

---

Accountability Office (2004), p. 5. MPPAA also requires payment to the fund when an employer "partially withdraws" from a multi-employer trust fund. This could arise when the employer has reduced his workforce or ceased operations of a part of his business but remains obligated to continue some contributions to the fund by continuing to operate in the jurisdiction of the collective bargaining agreement. See *Central States Pension Fund v. Schilli Corporation*, 420 F. 3d 663 (7th Cir. 2005).

20. 29 USC 1401. For an interesting case on a fund's untimely efforts to collect the withdrawal liability, see *Board of Trustees North Jersey Welfare Fund and Pension Fund v. Kero Leasing*, 377 F. 3rd 288 (3d Cir. 2004).

21. With the decline of union representation in the United States, many multi-employer plans have suffered recent funding losses, and plan participation by employers has declined. *Multiemployer pensions face key challenges to their long-term prospects.* (2004). General Accountability Office (GAO-04-542T).

22. In *U.S. Generating Company*, 341 NLRB 12 (2004), the predecessor employer sold his assets to a company that continued the operation and was a successor. The union and predecessor, however, had agreed that a successor employer could use its "existing pension plan." The successor recognized the union and assumed the collective bargaining agreement, but it substituted its 401(k) plan for the predecessor's defined benefit plan. The Board held this to be lawful and not a violation of the NLRA.

23. When the labor contract includes a "successors and assigns" clause, it is ordinarily the obligation of the seller to include in the contract of sale an obligation of the buyer to assume the obligations of the labor agreement and the bargaining relationship with a union. Absent such a clause, the courts must interpret the details of the transaction and the buyer's continued operation of the business and determine whether the buyer is indeed a legal successor and obligated to assume the provisions of the collective bargaining agreement. See *United Steel Workers of America v. Cooper-Standard Automotive of Bowling Green, Ohio, et al.*, 175 L.R.R.M. 3249 (N.D. Indiana, 2004).

exclusive province of the employer to decide, such as should the employer sponsor an HMO, a PPO, a high-deductible health care plan, a defined benefit pension plan, or a defined contribution plan and all the attendant design issues. This is now a shared decision-making process.

What if the Company and the Union Cannot Agree on Benefits?

Under the law, if the company and union reach an impasse in bargaining, the company can unilaterally implement its final proposal made to the union.[24] This means there would be no agreement on the mandatory subjects of bargaining, including the benefit plans, but the company is simply going ahead and putting its proposed changes into effect. The union may decide to reject the implementation and strike. For example, when an employer decided to unilaterally implement a change in life insurance benefits, from a whole life policy to a term policy, it was held to be unlawful and the strike that followed was found to be an unfair labor practice strike. During the strike, if the employer had chosen to permanently replace the workers, they would be entitled to reinstatement and back pay when the strike ended.[25] The question as to when an impasse occurs is difficult to assess. The law requires that the parties be "hopelessly deadlocked," but if the company miscalculates the issue and a strike ensues, there could be significant liabilities imposed on the employer.[26]

---

24. The NLRB has defined an impasse to mean a "deadlock." The parties have discussed subject(s) in good faith and, despite their best efforts to achieve an agreement, neither is willing to move from its respective position. When this occurs, the duty to bargain becomes dormant until changed circumstances indicate that an agreement may be possible. See *Advice Memo, General Counsel, NLRB*, Rood Trucking Co., Inc. (2005, May 31). 6-CA-34491.

25. *Allen Storage and Moving Co., Inc. 342 NLRB 44* (2004).

26. Of course, the company also would be ordered to continue bargaining over the benefits and all other mandatory issues. The right to permanently replace has long been supported by the courts. See *NLRB v. Mackay Radio and Telegraph Co*, 304 U.S. 333 (1938), *American Ship Building v. NLRB*, 380 U.S. 278 (1965); the risks of misjudging when an impasse does in fact occur or whether one can unilaterally implement and permanently replace are apparent in *NLRB v. Plainville Ready Mix Concrete*, 44 F.3d 1320 (6th Cir. 1995), where the employer implemented only the negative features of his final offer, which was found to be an unfair and unlawful bargaining practice.

What Happens if the Contract Expires
and There is No New Agreement?

Does the company have to continue making contributions to the benefit plans administered by the trusts or continue funding the negotiated plans sponsored by the employer? If the contract is not extended, then certain obligations such as contributing to a joint trust benefit fund, which is totally dependent upon the existence of a previously agreed labor agreement authorizing such contributions, may terminate as well.[27] But if the plan is a single employer-sponsored benefit, until there is an impasse, the company cannot unilaterally implement any changes in the previously agreed plans.

If there is an impasse, followed by a unilateral implementation by the employer, it does not mean the company can legally cease bargaining with the union. Unless there is a good faith doubt of the "majority status" of the union as the collective bargaining representative,[28] even if the contract is expired, the company must continue to meet and discuss a new contract with the union. But until a new agreement is reached, the terms and conditions of employment will be governed by the contract implemented by the company.[29]

What Happens if the Contract Expires
and the Employees Go on Strike?

Is the company required to continue their participation in the benefit plans? Would the striking employees, for example, lose their health care? If the employees participate in a joint trust-sponsored plan but are not working, the employer would no longer be obligated to submit contributions. If the employees and their dependents, however, lost their health care coverage, it would be a significant hardship and perhaps weaken their resolve to continue striking. So, some solution is needed. The union, the employees, or someone else could make contributions to the joint trust health care plan, and the striking employees would be able to continue participation in the health care plan. What if it was a company-sponsored plan? Would the striking employees be able to make COBRA (Consolidated

27. See *Litton Financial Printing Div. v. NLRB*, 501 US 190 (1991).

28. Or, if the union has been decertified as the collective bargaining representative.

29. The employer must be very careful here to make sure he has presented the same proposals to the union before the impasse and is not changing them in any way. See *NLRB v. Mello*, 172 LRRM 2436 (3d Cir. 2002).

Omnibus Budget Reconciliation Act) contributions to the plan and continue their health care? What are the qualifying events that trigger the availability of COBRA?[30] Would a striking employee qualify?[31]

Bargaining and Retiree Health Care

Many employers are experiencing spiraling "legacy" costs arising from their retiree health care plans. With the baby boomer surge looming, as well as increased life expectancy, these liabilities will only increase. The new standard accounting requirements, stipulating the disclosure of retiree health care liabilities in a company's financial statements, have made the exceptional cost of retiree benefits apparent to investors and have further motivated employers to look for some solution. Also, with the advent of drug benefits under Part D of Medicare, one of the chief reasons for continuing retiree health as a supplement to Medicare has been eliminated and has caused employers to rethink the need to offer the benefit.[32]

The business choices, therefore, are straightforward—increase the cost sharing for current retirees, radically change plan design, reduce benefits, or eliminate the benefit for future and perhaps current retirees altogether. If the employer has no obligation to bargain over benefits, these solutions are more apparent, unless it can be interpreted that the current retirees' health care benefits are vested. Employers who have properly articulated their right to terminate a retiree health care plan in the Summary Plan Description have been permitted to do so even for current retirees who are enjoying the benefit.[33]

---

30. See *IBT Local 120 et al v. Marathon Petroleum* (U.S. Dist. Min.) 38 EBC (BNA) 2797 (2006). Here the Court held that the issue of COBRA compliance was not preempted by the NLRA, and that the employer did not comply with the notice and other mandatory provisions of COBRA for his ex-employees and their dependents in violation of this statute. See *Communication Workers of America, AFL-CIO v. Nynex Corporation,* 898 F.2d 887 (2nd Cir. 1990). The answer to the question in the text is yes.

31. These include voluntary or involuntary job loss, reduction in hours, death, divorce, and loss of dependent status. Do these apply here?

32. Many employers provide retiree health care to their former employees, but only until the retiree qualifies for Medicare. This policy of providing differential benefits on the basis of the retiree's age has been held not to violate the *Age Discrimination in Employment Act.* See 29 CFR §1625.10 (e).

33. See *Sprague v. General Motors Corp.,* 133 F. 3d 3888 (6th Cir. 1998).

What about collective bargaining provisions that promise retiree health care? Is this promise relieved when the contract expires?[34] Generally, the answer is yes. What if there was a specific promise to pay retiree benefits for life? Does this promise expire with the contract? The Courts, generally, have held that in such cases the retiree health care is vested and said no, the employer's obligation to provide retiree health care for the current retirees does not expire with the contract.[35]

There are some broader questions concerning retiree benefits and bargaining. What if the union wants to increase the retiree health care or retirement benefits of current retirees? This is a different issue. It has been held that bargaining over current retiree benefits is a permissive subject of bargaining. This is based on the fact that retirees are no longer employees within the bargaining unit.[36] Thus, the employer has no obligation to bargain over a union demand to increase the pension benefits of current retirees or to reduce the co-pays of the current retirees' health care plan. The benefits for retirees must be established on a prospective basis, and modifications thereafter can be made only if the employer agrees to discuss the subject.

Conclusion and Perspective

Art Juergens has a full agenda in bargaining over benefits with the union. He will find significant tension in this arena because there is a misalignment of objectives. In the past unions promoted health care

---

34. See *Litton Financial Printing Div. v. NLRB*, 501 US 190 (1991).

35. See *UAW v. Yard Man, Inc.*, 716 F.3d 1476 (6th Cir. 1983); *Yard Man* established several tests to determine whether or not there is an unambiguous intent to perpetuate the retiree benefits beyond the contract. See *Golden v. Kelsey-Hayes Co.*, 73 F.3d 648 (6th Cir. 1996) and *McCoy v Meridian Automotive Systems, Inc.*, 390 F.3d 417 (6th Cir. 2004). Where there are clear indications in the communications between union and employer that the retiree health care is not a "lifetime benefit," there is no obligation to continue the plan for the retirees. See *Mauer v. Joy Technologies, Inc.* 212 F.3d 907 (6th Cir. 2000); *Utility Workers, Local 369 v. NSTAR Electric and Gas Corp.,* 317 F. Supp. 3d 69 (D. Mass., 2004); and *Joyce v. Curtiss-Wright Corp.,* 171 F. 3d 130 (2nd Cir 1999). Life insurance and retiree health care for retirees and their dependents was found to continue for the life of the retirees and was not subject to cancellation or modification when the evidence indicated the employer had promised such a permanent benefit. See *UAW, Local 540 v. Beaver Precision Products*, 190 F. 3d 768 (6th Cir 1999).

36. See *Allied Chemical v. Pittsburgh Plate Glass Co.*, 404 U.S. 157 (1971).

plans with no premiums, small deductibles, few co-pays, and all-inclusive benefits. The employers, on the other hand, are interested in offering benefits that are competitive within their industry, will serve to attract and retain the workforce, and are cost-effective. If the union represented employees in most or all of the industry's competitors, their bargaining strategy could lead to parity among most, if not all, employers in that particular industry. Assuming there is little global competition affecting the industry, the union's goals would not jeopardize the employer's market share or competitiveness. However, the reality is that unions only represent the employees of about 8 percent of the nonpublic employers in the United States.[37] Further, unions have varying penetration among global companies in Europe, Asia, and the Americas. Therefore, the unions' bargaining position can lead to a noncompetitive model that will result in benefit costs exceeding industry levels and possibly rendering the employer's labor costs and prices to be higher. In such cases the employer must search for ways to become more productive,[38] or go out of business.

The record is clear. Benefit levels among companies organized by unions are typically more generous than those provided by nonunion companies.[39] Moreover, these noncompetitive benefit levels create conflicts. A review of serious work stoppages among organized employers indicates that benefits are among the key issues at bargaining that precipitate strikes.[40] Many of the veteran employers in key manufacturing industries are struggling to relieve the legacy costs incurred over years of bargaining, which led to generous retiree pension and health care

---

37. About 8 percent of the private sector is represented by a labor organization in the United States. See Statement of Peter J. Hurtgen. (2003, Winter). Federal Mediation and Conciliation Service.

38. This normally involves taking labor out of the business operation through technology or closing unproductive assets and facilities.

39. See Union status and employment based health benefits. (2005, May). *Employee Benefit Research Institute, 26*(5). The EBRI reports that 86 percent of union workers are covered by employer-sponsored health benefits, while 59.5 percent of nonunion workers are covered. See also *Employee contributions to employer-provided medical plans by bargaining status, private industry.* (2005). Bureau of Labor Statistics; the study indicates 57 percent of union employees are required to contribute to their health care fund, while 79 percent of nonunion employees must make such contributions. See also *Table 5, Private Industry, by Major Occupational Group and Bargaining Status.* (2007). Bureau of Labor Statistics, that shows hourly benefit costs among union employers to be nearly $7 per hour higher than those of nonunion employers.

40. Federal Mediation and Conciliation Service (2003).

benefits.[41] Their new nonunion competitors have no such burden, and they work hard to remain "union free."

Additionally, the joint administration of benefits under Section 302 plans has generated internal conflicts between union and employer trustees. There are disputes over how much of the reserves should be set aside in a health care plan, what the investment strategy should be for the pension plan, what the required funding levels for multi-employer pension plans are, and if the company should agree to maintain benefits no matter what the cost. Even when investment results cause the pension plan to be overfunded, the opportunity to suspend employer contributions is often not available. The employer's flexibility and ability to react to new market forces are restricted.

Finally, administrative costs are not necessarily reduced among collectively bargained plans. With a crazy quilt of benefit plans negotiated by various local unions and a single national company, the opportunity of the employer to use his potential purchasing leverage is not apparent.[42] On the other hand, Wal-Mart, a global, nonunion retailer, can negotiate with one TPA to provide health care at very favorable rates for all of its 1.2 million U.S. employees. Its organized competitors, on the other hand, are burdened with redundant administrative costs arising out of their participation in numerous joint union and management trusts.[43]

Collective bargaining is a process that allows employees to have a voice in the establishment and design of their own benefits. Their collective bargaining representatives must understand the rising costs of benefits and the impact on the global competitiveness of the organized employers.

---

41. According to press reports, in their current 2007 negotiations with the United Auto Workers Union, Ford, General Motors, and Chrysler have proposed to shift more than $100 billion in retiree health care benefit liabilities to a special independent trust fund that is, in part, controlled by the union. This will require some careful calculations of the present values of such liabilities that the companies would agree to pay to the fund, and also mandate the companies to make specific promises about future manufacturing venues. See Walsh, T. (2007, September 7). Trade off on jobs, benefits in works. *Detroit Free Press*, http://www.freep.com/. This would have the effect of dramatically improving their financial statements. The same type of transfer was completed by Goodyear Tire and Toledo-based Dana Corporation and their respective unions. See Peterson, K., (2007, September 7). Companies eye trusts for retirees. *The Fort Wayne Journal Gazette*, http://www.journalgazette.net/.

42. For example, The Kroger Co., a national supermarket company, negotiates benefits with numerous United Food and Commercial Workers Union locals and contributes to 40 joint trust funds that administer health and pension benefits. Many have only several thousand employee-participants. Interview of Michael Stoll, Vice President of Employee Benefits, The Kroger Co. (2007, August 19).

43. Michael Stoll (2007).

Likewise, employers must understand the importance of health care and retirement benefits to their workforce and how such benefits will affect the life events their employees will encounter.[44] To achieve success and find solutions to these vexing problems, management and unions must become allies, not adversaries, in providing competitive and cost-effective benefits. This leads us back to Art Juergens and his challenge.

The journey ahead for Art will be far more difficult than anything he has experienced. There are bargaining, legal, and competitive challenges for him as he sits across the table from the union representing his employees, and he must try to resolve them with the union. He cannot simply do it alone. His task will be to develop a unique and firm relationship of mutual trust and respect with his union counterpart. This can lead to more candid and productive discussions of the competitive realities relevant to benefit designs and their impact on labor costs. Together they must find solutions that will provide benefits that deal effectively with the important life events of their employees and members and do so in a cost-effective manner. Creativity and problem solving are the currency of a constructive collective bargaining process, and Art will do well to assume this perspective.

Chapter Exercises

1. A major supermarket chain was sued by the Teamsters' Central States pension plan for not paying hourly pension contributions for certain workers the company has classified as "casual." The labor agreement between the company and the union provided that casual employees were not entitled to pension benefits. The contract did not explicitly define "casual," except to say that they would be hired on a "short-term basis." Read the case, *Central States Southeast and Southwest Areas Pension Fund v. The Kroger Co.*, 73 F.3d 727 (7th Cir. 2005), and answer the following:
   a. What is the source of the employer's obligation to contribute to the pension fund?
   b. What is the nature of the obligation? Must the employer provide a pension plan or just pay the contributions?

---

44. Federal Mediation and Conciliation Service (2003). The author's experience in this area is that unions are recognizing this dilemma and are approaching benefit negotiations with a clearer understanding of their competitive impact on the organized employer. But, they do have commitments and obligations to their members who pay dues for representation and bargaining. Thus, the issue of benefits remains a key agenda item in bargaining and continues to be a major challenge to resolve.

    c. How would you go about defining "casual" and how does your definition comport to that in the labor agreement?

    d. With respect to the designation as "casual," what facts are relevant in determining their status?

    e. What designation did the Court give the disputed employees?

    f. Was there an alternative dispute mechanism the parties could have used to reach some conclusion to the dispute?

    g. What was the Court's disposition?

2. Suppose your CEO has told you that your pension plan and health care expense are much too costly and significantly higher than your competitors. Because a union represents the employees, he understands the company cannot simply eliminate or change the plans. A joint union and employer trust sponsor both plans. The pension plan is a DBP with a 70 percent income replacement at full-age retirement, and the health care plan is a PPO with a small deductible and significant first-dollar coverage for those who stay within the network. The CEO has asked you, the HR vice president, to persuade the union in upcoming negotiations to agree to less costly plan designs. She would prefer some type of DCP to replace the pension plan and a more cost-effective managed care health plan or consumer-driven plan to replace the current PPO. She and the finance department have established some financial goals for cost reduction in labor expense that they are expecting you to achieve in negotiations.

    a. Prepare a list of negotiating goals and optimal replacement plans that you would establish and discuss with the CEO before the first negotiation session.

    b. What arguments would you likely make to the union in trying to persuade them to accept your new plans?

    c. Could some type of choice be included in your proposals so as to facilitate union support?

    d. What direct communication with your employees would you propose in order to get their support for your proposal?

    e. What would you consider success and how would you measure it?

3. The union trustees of a joint trust pension plan (DBP) have proposed a 20-cents-per-hour increase for all plan participants. Pursuant to their collective bargaining agreement, the employers contributing to the fund would pay the increase. The union trustees, with the assistance of the union-retained actuary, have said the plan is not adequately funded to provide the promised level of benefits. You are a company trustee and have asked the management actuary to look into this.

a. What will you tell the actuary as he prepares to test the conclusions of the union trustees?
b. If the conclusions of the union trustees were correct, what is a range of alternative solutions that could be considered to remedy the problem?
c. Should there be some protocols dealing with this issue to resolve similar problems that might arise in the future? What are they?

4. Union and company trustees on a joint trust considered whether the TPA should receive an increase in compensation. The union argued he should get a 25 percent increase; the company said it should be 6 percent. Of course, the company pays for all expenses and benefits under the plan, so an impasse developed. In accordance with the participation agreement between the contributing employer and the fund, the issue was submitted to binding arbitration. The union argued that the arbitrator was free to select any amount of increase and was not bound by the two proposals of the parties. The company argued the arbitrator was limited in his power to choose a new fee for the TPA by the parties' specific proposals. He could not "split the difference." What arguments would you use to support the company trustee's position?

5. A union has been decertified as the collective bargaining representative of employees working at Company A. Previous to the decertification, Company A had an obligation to make contributions to a multi-employer plan. After the decertification, the obligation ceased because there was no longer a collective bargaining agreement or duty to bargain. Company A was obligated, however, to pay a withdrawal fee under MPPAA. It did so. The employees of Company A continued to work for the company and some who qualified under the terms of the multi-employer plan applied for retirement. Their application for retirement benefits was denied because they were still working. The employees argued that the provision in the multi-employer plan's SPD indicated that they could only be denied benefits if they were working for a company that was contributing to the plan. This was no longer the case with Company A. The employees were correct in their argument, so the plan trustees amended the plan to require that employees who had worked at any time for a company that contributed to the plan would have to quit working before they would be entitled to retirement benefits. What are the issues and how would you resolve them? See IRC §411(d)(6) and also *Central Laborers' Pension Fund v. Heinz*, 541 U.S. 739 (2004).

Life and Disability Insurance, Pay for Time Not Worked

15

With help from several investors, Francesca is purchasing a small box company that employs 200 people. The workforce comprises production, quality assurance, accounting, and sales personnel. Shipping is done by outside logistics services. The company makes custom size boxes for customers whose products range from specialty food merchandise to electronic components. It has been in business for 25 years, and Francesca hopes to increase sales among current and new customers, modernize the production process, develop closer relationships with customers, improve the timing of order filling, reduce working capital, and lower the cost of raw materials and supplies. The company has had a comparatively high rate of turnover and the average tenure is about five years. The average age of the workforce is 32 years. The company already provides health insurance and a cash balance retirement plan for its employees. Francesca wonders if other benefits might improve the recruiting and retaining of employees and also better align her with evolving business strategy. In particular, she wonders if some type of life and disability insurance should be included in the benefit package. She also wants to rethink how vacation, sick days, and other paid time off programs might be redesigned to better conform to the vision she has for the business.

How does Francesca decide these issues? First, she should consider whether she wants to encourage long service or mid-level service among her employees. This would depend, in part, on how long it takes an employee's skill level to reach highly productive stages, and how important it is for employees to be able to rotate jobs and develop new skills. If she wants longer service employees, some type of life, disability, and paid time off benefits make sense. She might consider taking an employee survey to find out what her employees think are important benefits and how they affect their productivity, loyalty to the company, and retention. She also should calculate the cost of turnover and hypothesize how these benefits might reduce unwanted turnover and actually generate a financial return to her new enterprise.

Next, she should consider what employee life events her prospective benefits might address. For example, premature death or death before retirement can leave an employee's dependents without an important income stream. Death of a worker's spouse might also place him in some financial jeopardy. There could be a loss of income or services that must be replaced at a cost to the employee. Death of an employee's child, likewise, could result in a loss of supplemental income for an employee and result in some unexpected burial, health care, or related expense.

There is another important life event to consider. What happens to the life insurance policy if the employee retires or separates from the firm? Would the employee have some difficulty in qualifying for a replacement policy? Should Francesca design her life insurance program to deal with this contingency? What about employees who become sick and are off work without a continuation of income? Would they lose their life insurance if premiums were not paid during this period?

Finally, Francesca must determine who would be covered, who would pay for the insurance, when eligibility would become effective, how the policy(s) would be treated with respect to taxes, and what type of insurance should be provided.[1]

---

1. There are numerous opportunities for employers and employees to use life insurance in a variety of ways. For example, certain policies such as whole life or universal life are sometimes offered to executive-level employees. They are funded by the employer and considered a perquisite. They add real value to the retiring employee's net worth. Life insurance can be used to fund certain benefits, e.g., split-dollar insurance is designed so that the employer pays the premiums for the insurance, but part of the death benefit goes to the employer as reimbursement. The promise of the employer to pay for a permanent life insurance policy can be ensured by contract and by the employer placing funds to pay for the promised benefit in a "Rabbi Trust." However, unless the plan is fully funded and meets the IRS requirements as a tax-qualified plan, the money in the Rabbi Trust will be subject to creditors' claims if the company becomes insolvent. An employee can place a whole paid or universal life policy in an irrevocable trust in order to keep

Life Insurance[2]

Life insurance is an important benefit offered by many employers to provide some income security to survivors of an employee who dies while employed. Most often it is a group life insurance plan that pays a lump sum to designated beneficiaries at death.[3] It is linked to the employment relationship and when that is terminated, in most cases, so is the life insurance policy. Under the tax code, an employer can fully pay for and provide a term life insurance policy for an employee up to a face amount of $50,000.[4] In such instances there is no imputed income to the employee. A "term" policy is one that lapses when premiums are discontinued, has no cash or borrowing value, and only provides a payment of the face amount of the policy in the event of the insured's death. Premiums of term policies increase, or the face amount of the policy decreases, as the insured ages.[5]

It is common for employers to procure "supplemental" term policies for their employees in amounts greater than $50,000. In these cases, the face amount of the policy is usually a multiple of the employee's salary.[6] Either the employer or the employee can pay the premium for the policy; however, due to the potential imputed tax liability, usually it is the employee.

---

the policy out of his estate and ensure that his beneficiaries will not incur inheritance and estate taxes. The policy must be in the trust for a minimum of three years in order to escape the estate. Corporate-owned life insurance (COLI) policies can be purchased to insure the life of an important partner or key executive of the company. The death benefit will be paid to the company to offset the financial losses to the company resulting from the executive's death. Some employers have abused COLI policies by insuring a large segment of their workforce without their knowledge or benefit, borrowing money to pay the premiums, deducting the interest and, ultimately, taking the death benefit when the employee dies and using it to pay for company projects. The IRS and some state insurance laws, which require that the policy must provide for an "insurable interest" and the beneficiary must incur some potential loss as a result of the insured's death, have challenged these policies.

2. In this chapter we will deal with employer-sponsored life insurance that is considered to be an employee benefit.

3. See *Fundamentals of employee benefits programs, group life insurance* (Chapter 33, p. 21). (2005). Employee Benefit Research Institute (EBRI). There are also plans that pay monthly payments to survivors, but due to tax regulations they are not very popular.

4. See §79 of IRC and 1.79(a) of U.S. Treasury Department Regulations.

5. Beam, B., & McFadden, J. (2001). *Employee Benefits* (6th ed., p. 152). Chicago: Real Estate Education Company.

6. About 60 percent of employer sponsors use the multiple of salary approach. See EBRI (2005), supra at p. 22.

Due to its purchasing leverage based on its size and the number in the pool of insured employees, a company can buy insurance at more reasonable rates than an individual.[7] After the initial several years, however, for larger companies the rate will be solely dependent upon its own claims experience.

As we have seen with health insurance policies, larger companies can self-insure their employee policies or they can purchase insured policies through a carrier. In either case, usually the employer will use an insurance company to administer its program, assess the risks, review and resolve claims, and calculate premiums.

Generally speaking, a life insurance policy owned by the employee will be included in his estate when he dies. There are significant exemptions applicable to assets in an estate and often the insurance policy is not subject to state and federal inheritance and estate taxes.[8] For example, if the beneficiary of the policy is the deceased's spouse, the policy is not included in the estate. The payment of the face amount of the policy to any beneficiary is not considered taxable income provided it is paid in a lump sum and is not an annuity.

The owner of a life insurance policy can name a person or persons, trust, one's estate, a lender, or other entity as a beneficiary. The owner of the policy can change a beneficiary at any time unless the policy's beneficiary has been irrevocably nominated in an inter-vivos trust. An employee who indicates in his last will or trust that a certain beneficiary will receive the death benefit of a life insurance policy must make sure the policy itself designates his estate or the trust as the beneficiary in order to effect such a disposition. The issues pertaining to life insurance, taxes, estates, and the like should probably be generally communicated to employees so as to optimize the use and value of the benefit and achieve the employer's intended purpose: in this case, to enhance recruitment and retention.

Many employer-sponsored group term policies impose premium rate increases based on age progressions. Usually individual health status will not affect the premiums.[9] Some employers can offer multi-year level premium group policies to their employees, thus ensuring that they pay

7. For example, in 2008 a younger participant of a large employer-sponsored group plan can be covered with a $50,000 term policy for about $50 per year (10 cents per $1,000). Paying for experience simply means the employer sponsor pays the total claims incurred plus fees and profits for the insurance company administering it. For smaller employers the rate may be dependent upon a standard rate table for a longer period of time. See EBRI (2005), p. 22.

8. The federal estate tax is currently being phased out. The tax rate is 45 percent, but the exemption increases from $1 million in 2003 to $3.5 million in 2009, and then in 2010 the tax is repealed. However, in 2011 the tax will be reinstated unless Congress takes appropriate action. See Stevic, G. (2007). *The income tax treatment of life insurance,* http://www.advisortoday.com/.

9. Since there is an increased mortality risk associated with tobacco use, it is possible that some employer sponsors of group life insurance plans will increase the premium for those who smoke. See http://www.insurance.com/FAQs/Life/.

the same premium over a period of fixed years. There is a cost involved in offering such a policy.

Some group employee term policies are convertible during employment or upon separation.[10] This means the employee can elect to convert his term policy to a permanent, whole life policy without having to show insurability. Converting a term policy to a whole life policy enables an employee to avoid the ever-increasing cost of a term policy as he ages. Also, the employer can offer a separating or retiring employee the opportunity to convert and make his life insurance benefit portable. In the case of either whole paid or term life insurance, since the employee is no longer within the employer's pool, the allocated cost of such an opportunity is usually far above that incurred under the employer's group plan. Further, at some renewal point, the individual employee's health status and age would be relevant in determining the premiums for the policy. Thus, most term life insurance policies lapse when the employee separates from employment.

There is a policy that responds to the needs of an employee who is terminally ill and incurring large medical or prescription expenses. The employer sponsor can provide an "accelerated death benefit" ("living benefit") that enables the employee to receive a portion, usually 50 percent, of the death benefit prior to his passing.

Employers frequently offer accidental death and dismemberment insurance (AD&D).[11] These policies are not affected by the health status or age of the insured and the employer has more flexibility in allowing employees to maintain coverage at their own expense when they leave the company. AD&D insurance only pays a benefit when the employee is killed or dismembered as a result of an accident. The death benefit is often a multiple of the term policy in effect. The dismemberment portion pays a scheduled amount for loss of limb(s) or sight. Consequently, the risk is more manageable and there is little room for adverse selection. Many employers permit a departing or retiring employee to continue, or convert, his AD&D coverage on an individual basis. From the employee's perspective, replacing his employer-sponsored term policy with an AD&D policy is attractive and practical. The premiums are reasonable, the risk is low to the insurer, and the employee mitigates the potential for significant loss of income caused by death.

A whole life insurance policy is one where part of the premium is directed into a savings segment that earns interest as the policy matures. It also includes a life insurance segment that will pay a face amount to the deceased's beneficiary. Thus, the policy has cash value and can be collateralized. Such policies usually have a maturity date at which time they are considered paid up. Obviously, whole life plans have higher premiums than term policies unless the term policy participant has reached a considerably advanced age. Some believe whole life policies offer a better value because of their invested

---

10. Beam, B. (2001), p. 163.

11. Beam, B. (2001), p. 163.

cash value, the ability to borrow against the policy, the tax deferral of the cash buildup and earnings, the stability of the premium structure, and the possibility to have lifetime coverage. From an investment viewpoint, they are considered to be very conservative with returns on the cash portion of the policy usually well below typical returns available in the markets. An employer can sponsor such plans as group policies, or it can just facilitate their direct purchase by the employee at some discounted rate.

Universal life policies can be offered to employees instead of whole life policies or as a supplement to the traditional life insurance policies.[12] Here the employee, as well as the employer, can pay the premium costs. If the employer pays for the insurance, there will be income tax implications to the employee. Such plans usually provide the flexibility to increase or reduce the death benefit with corresponding changes in premiums. For example, if the need for insurance increases due to marriage or the arrival of children, the face amount can be increased. If the need for insurance subsides due to financial emancipation of the insured's children or diminished financial dependency among his family members, the face amount of the insurance can be reduced. If the employee has some financial difficulty in meeting the premium requirements, he can reduce the insurance to an affordable cost level. Universal life policies, like whole paid life insurance, have term insurance protection as well as cash value accumulation. The premium for the term element is based on mortality and will increase with age, or the benefit can be reduced as age increases. They are frequently portable.[13]

In some cases universal life insurance is offered exclusively to top managers or executives as supplemental policies. This might be related to the fact their higher total direct compensation often exceeds the limits on group term life insurance offerings. Many universal life policies are designed to be paid up at retirement; this occurs because the cash value is more than sufficient to cover the future premiums. If it is not paid up, the retiree can continue making premium payments and the policy will remain in full force. Another option permits the employee to surrender the policy and receive the cash value or use the cash value to buy an annuity. From a financial planning standpoint, universal life insurance policies can be an important part of the retired employee's net worth.

For example, a universal life policy enables the spouse of the retiree to waive the joint survivor spouse benefit that is required by ERISA, thus allowing the couple to receive a higher unreduced pension.[14] When the

---

12. Beam, B. (2001), p. 155. Laprade, J. (2004, December). *A benefit program that works double duty—Group variable universal life.* Employee Benefit Plan Review.

13. EBRI (2005), supra at p. 26.

14. As we learned in Chapter 4, Retirement Plans, the age of the surviving spouse who is a beneficiary may trigger an actuarial reduction of the benefit. If the

pensioner of a surviving spouse dies, the universal life policy death benefit paid to the spouse essentially replaces the value of the waived joint survivor retirement plan benefit. Further, provided the policy is owned and paid for by the employee, it can be placed in an irrevocable inter-vivos trust.[15] This placement will exclude it from the deceased's estate and permit tax-free distribution after the second to die passes. Thus, if there are funds remaining in the trust when the surviving spouse passes, the surviving children of the deceased employee can receive the balance from the trust without being charged inheritance or estate tax. Placement of the policy into the trust can save up to 40 or 50 percent of the remaining value by avoiding such taxation.

Francesca has decided to offer term life insurance to her full-time employees and those part-time employees who work more than 32 hours per week over a 12-week consecutive period. They must be on the payroll for more than 30 days before they can enroll. She wants the employees to share in the cost of the life insurance and wants the benefit to respond to the serious life events she had identified earlier. Also, she wants to take full advantage of the tax benefits relating to life insurance. Francesca believes that executives should participate in the same benefit plans as all other employees. She wants the life insurance benefit to generate real financial returns for her company by encouraging long and productive service among her employees. Knowing this, and applying the elements of the benefits model,[1] how should her life insurance plan be designed?

---

1. The benefits model is discussed initially in Chapter 2, Human Resources Economics, Principles, and Actuarial Concepts Applicable to Benefits, and includes consideration of internal equity, external competitiveness, positive behavioral impact, and well administered and cost-effective.

Let's look at employer-sponsored life insurance from an employee's perspective. Here we will see how Francesca ultimately designed her plan. Madeline, an employee of Francesca's box company, is reviewing the life insurance offerings by the company. She wants to know how the program meets her current needs and her future life events and how it will fit into her overall financial plan.

---

surviving spouse waives the benefit, there will be no such actuarial reduction based on her status.

15. See *Irrevocable life insurance trusts can skirt taxes, but cost you flexibility.* (2008, January 3). http://www.insure.com/.

Madeline works at Francesca's box company as a shift manager. She
is full-time and has worked there for three years. She also is expecting
her first child next month and wonders about taking advantage of the
company-sponsored group life insurance. The company now offers a
term life policy for all employees. It has a face amount of $50,000 and
there is no cost to the employee. Madeline is eligible to buy additional
term life insurance through the company up to four times her salary.
The price per thousand dollars of coverage is very reasonable, but she
must pay the full premium. She is aware that she can buy an additional
AD&D policy for a rather inexpensive rate as well. She wonders
whether she should take these steps. Her HR manager advises that the
premiums for the supplemental insurance will increase every five
years, but her individual health status will not affect the premiums she
must pay. She is told that the company's life insurance is an insured
plan administered by Global Insurance Company. She checks the Internet and learns that Global is highly rated by "A. M. Best,"[1] and can be
expected to pay any death benefits under their policies. Madeline is
curious as to whether her insurance death benefit will be included in
her estate and whether it will be taxed as income to her beneficiaries.
The HR manager explains that, if she structures it properly, neither her
estate nor her beneficiaries will be taxed when the benefit is paid. She
asks the HR manager if her husband and new child can purchase life
insurance up to a face amount of one times her salary. The HR manager advises that they can be covered under her policy with some
limits. She must, however, pay the premiums for her husband and
child. She reads in the company benefits brochure that the policy is
cancelled when she leaves the company, but she can continue to be
covered by the AD&D policy, provided she pays the premiums. She
asks the HR manager if whole paid life insurance is available from the
company. The HR manager responds that it is not, because the new
CEO does not consider such policies to have good investment values.
Madeline asks what happens if she is disabled and off work. The HR
manager tells her that the obligation to continue paying premiums will
be suspended during the period of the disability and the policies will
remain in full force.

---

1. There are several raters of insurance companies, including Moody's,
Standard and Poor's, and A. M. Best. They assess the financial stability of the company. If a life insurance company goes bankrupt, many
states have guaranteed funds that provide some payments, much like
FDIC for banks.

Madeline is young and has a family who is dependent upon her earned
income. She should give serious consideration to taking advantage of the

maximum face amount of insurance that is available.[16] For instance, how long will it take her surviving beneficiaries to replace the income lost by her untimely demise? What will be the expenses incurred by her beneficiaries over the coming years? Is there a mortgage on her home, a significant debt, or possible health problems? What is the life expectancy of her beneficiaries? Does she need to consider providing income over a long period? What is the likelihood her beneficiary will recover easily from a financial standpoint after her demise? There is a "Rule of Thumb" that says the face amount of the policy of an employed person with dependents should range from five to ten times earnings, depending on the factors outlined above.

The old adage that "life insurance is for persons who might die early, while an annuity is for those who expect to live longer," had some truth to it. Life insurance is an important employee benefit, in that it offers some comfort that an early death will not significantly imperil the employee's dependents. As the dependency increases and a loss of life and income become more perilous, the employee should take optimum advantage of the life insurance benefits made available by his employer. From the employer's standpoint, offering life insurance has some value. It enables the employer to remain externally competitive in recruiting and retaining employees, and can help generate commitment and loyalty to the firm. It also mitigates the distraction and resulting loss of productivity that arises when employees fear that loss of life will thrust their dependents into the proverbial "poor house." It is also a very cost-effective way for employers to provide income protection for their employees. It requires minimal administration and, in part, obviates the need for more expensive benefits, such as overly generous retirement plans that provide income continuation to survivors after the employee attains eligibility. There are other life events that employers can consider as well.

What happens if an employee becomes disabled and cannot work for a significant period of time, or perhaps permanently? Should the employer provide a benefit that responds to this tragic life event?

Disability Insurance

Our new entrepreneur, Francesca, wonders about other employee lifecycle events that might be addressed by an employee benefit. For example, what should the company do if an employee becomes disabled for a short or long period? There could be a significant loss of

---

16. See *Life insurance basics.* (2008, February 9). http://www.insure.com/.

income for the employee and his dependent(s) and it could last anywhere from a few days, to years, or even a lifetime. Francesca is
aware there are government-sponsored plans such as Workers' Compensation and Social Security that provide for income continuation in
the event of a disability. How would her program interact or supplement these government offerings? What happens if an employee dies
because of his work?

There is a story in the *The Economist* about Japanese employees "working
themselves to death." The story involves an employee who worked 80
hours of overtime each month for six months, and collapsed and died of
"karoshi" (death by overwork) at the age of 30. A court held that his family
was entitled to compensation.[17] Usually, workers' compensation cases in
the United States are more straightforward and involve accidents or
trauma where an employee injures his back, arm, or other important area
of his body. Compensable injuries also can involve emotional or psychiatric conditions arising directly from work or work injuries. Workers' compensation is grounded in and dependent upon state law. The origin of
these laws relates to a principle that employers can avoid costly lawsuits by
employees alleging negligence in the workplace by participating in a state-
run program that provides scheduled payments to employees injured at
work.[18] Each employer is required to pay premiums into a state agency
fund that administers payments to injured workers. The state agency also
enforces statutes and rules pertaining to workplace safety. The employer's
premium is based, in part, on his safety record. So, employers have an
incentive to reduce worker accidents by organizing effective safety
programs.

---

17. The Japanese have a reputation for working long and hard hours and, in many
instances, without receiving overtime premium pay. See Jobs for Life. (2007,
December 22–2008, January 4). *The Economist*, p. 68.

18. The principle is often referred to as "The Fellow Servant Rule" and permits
employees to sue the employer for the negligence and resulting injury caused
by the plaintiff's fellow servant. It should be noted that some states allow the
employer to waive workers' compensation participation and protection and, with
the appropriate program, handle all worker injury claims outside the system.
By doing so, they are subjecting themselves to expensive employee lawsuits, but
many employers who participate in such programs believe through aggressive
safety programs and quick and fair resolution of injury claims, they can spend less
than the premiums required by their state workers' compensation program. This
approach is euphemistically called "going naked."

In the case of workers' compensation, if an employee is disabled due to a work-related injury, he can receive reimbursements for medical expenses as well as loss of income. If the disability is total and permanent, the benefit can be for life. If it is partial and either permanent or temporary, the benefit will be apportioned according to the extent and time period of the disability. The disability portion of the payment is based on the potential economic loss sustained by the employee. Frequently, permanent disabilities are resolved by the payment of a lump sum representing the present value of the benefit.

The employer pays for this benefit either on a self-funded basis or by paying premiums to a state workers' compensation program; participation by employers is often mandatory. Negligence of an employer or its "servants," as well as contributory negligence by the claimant, is largely irrelevant to determining the validity or the amount of the claim.[19] The only issue involves whether the injury was job related and what the medical and economic loss is.

Employers who wish to keep their workers' compensation costs low are often found sponsoring and facilitating major employee safety programs, and including safety achievements as part of employee incentives and rewards such as gain sharing. Workers' compensation liabilities can have a significant impact on an employer's financial performance. Often, the financial liability for a partial disability can increase over time due to the aggravation of the injury and age of the claimant. So, a person who is originally judged to be 20 percent permanently disabled can come back later to the state agency and show that the disability is now 30 percent. Appropriate, incremental compensation will be awarded. Some employers compare their long-term workers' compensation liability to the long tail of a lizard that just keeps growing. Thus, it is incumbent upon employers to provide a safe place to work and carefully manage their workers' compensation cases.

Social Security also provides for disability benefits. A person is "disabled" under Social Security when, because of a severe medical (physical or mental) impairment, he is considered unable to do the work he had been performing and cannot adjust to doing other work. Further, a disabled person is expected to have the disability for at least one year and must have sufficient Social Security credits—over 40 quarters of covered work—to qualify. The Social Security definition is quite different from "disability" determinations under other benefit plans, such as private

---

19. There are some states that allow an injured employee to sue in court when the negligence of the employer is regarded as "willful or intentional." Potential damages in a court case could be significantly higher than the allowable scheduled compensation provided by a workers' compensation system. For example, damages could include not only economic loss by the plaintiff, but also damages for pain and suffering, loss of consortium, and possible punitive penalties.

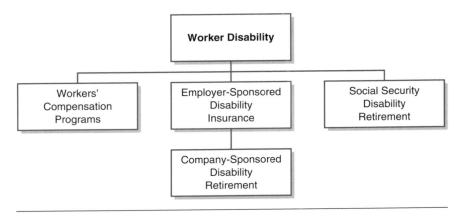

Figure 15.1   Coverage for Disabled Workers

disability insurance. A "disabled" person under Social Security can receive disability benefits in an amount equal to his expected full-age retirement benefit prior to attaining the minimum retirement age. There is a five-month waiting period before benefits are paid. Benefits also are available under Social Security for a disabled person's dependent children, who are under 18 years of age, and spouse, who is responsible for caring for the dependent children.

Francesca now understands that when the disability is "total," an employee has protection under Social Security, and when the injury is work related, the employee has protection under Workers' Compensation laws. She knows that funding for both programs comes, in part, from her company's legally mandated contributions, but there are gaps and she wonders if they should be filled. What about non-work-related illnesses or conditions that are short term but prevent the employee from coming to work? Or conditions that do not necessarily meet the rather strict definition of "disability" under Social Security but, nevertheless, prevent the employee from coming to work over a long period of time? These are serious life events that could be catastrophic to a worker and his family. She has read that with the aging of the U.S. population, persons with disabilities can live much longer than before. Despite medical advances, many will be disabled temporarily or permanently by their conditions. She knows that many of her labor competitors offer such benefits, and believes it could serve her company's interests to provide such protection on a cost-effective basis.

Employers often do provide short-term and long-term disability insurance protection for their employees.[20] Short-term disability is defined as lasting for more than two weeks but less than six months (26 weeks); long-term disability is greater.[21] Most often, the employer pays short-term disability insurance on an out-of-pocket basis; no insurance policy is necessary. The employer simply pays a portion of the disabled employee's earnings. Long-term disability plans usually involve the purchase of insurance by the employee whose employer has applied his leverage to obtain it at a significant discount.[22] It also can be purchased by the employer on a group basis, but funded in part or totally by employee contributions.

Benefits for such programs involve salary continuations amounting to either a percentage of earnings or a fixed amount per month. Long-term disability policies can be "guaranteed nonforfeitable," locking in the premium for the duration of the policy. Or, they can be "guaranteed renewable," allowing premium increases but guaranteeing coverage. Generally, the latter can be purchased at lower costs. Premiums depend on a number of variables and plan features including age, sex, occupation, amount of income being replaced, waiting period before benefits are paid, nature of the guarantee of continued coverage, definition of disability,[23] duration of

---

20. Eligibility usually involves full-time status, an age requirement, and some minimum period of service. Benefits range from 50 to 70 percent of pretax income with some cap. For company-sponsored plans, Titles 1, 2, and 3 of ERISA are applicable to employer-sponsored group plans. In 2006, about 31 percent of all workers were covered by long-term and short-term disability policies. See *National compensation survey: Employee benefits in private industry in the U.S.* (2007). U.S. Department of Labor, Bureau of Labor Statistics.

21. Some states, such as New York, New Jersey, California, Hawaii, and Rhode Island, require an employer to provide short-term (26 weeks) disability protection. See McQueen, M. (2007, December 19). The growing appeal of disability insurance. *The Wall Street Journal*, D1. We note that ordinary sick days are covered under different policies whereby employees are either given credit for so many sick days per year or are paid for incidental days off taken when they are ill. Some injuries, such as self-inflicted wounds, are not covered by the insurance.

22. Similarly, employers are offering their employees the opportunity to purchase long-term care insurance (LTC) at discounted rates. LTC provides for nursing, custodial, or special home care of persons who are physically or mentally disabled. In many cases the employee can buy a policy for himself and his immediate family. Obviously, the earlier the insurance is purchased, the lower the rate. See *Long-term care insurance gains prominence.* (2004). U.S. Department of Labor, Bureau of Labor Statistics, http://www.bls.gov/. For an interesting excursion into the purchasing options for LTC in the employer market, see http://www.johnhancocklongtermcareinsurance.com/.

23. For example, if the definition refers to your own occupation, then it will not require a disability that broadly prevents you from doing any occupation.

the policy, whether the policy has inflation protection that provides cost-of-living increases for benefits, and whether it includes a waiver of premiums during the disability period or a provision that provides a replacement of lost pension contributions, as well as the tax treatment of the benefits. If purchased on an individual basis, the policy can be considered portable and convertible so one can take it to another job. Group coverage provided by the employer with or without employee cost sharing is usually not portable and will terminate when the employee separates. Group policies have the advantage of including guarantees, and no medical exams are required. If the employer pays the premiums, the benefits will be taxed as income to the participant. If the employee pays, there is no income tax imposed when benefits are received.[24]

Other issues involve integration or coordination of benefits, return to work programs, and disability retirement. For example, if a person is receiving disability payments from Social Security or Workers' Compensation, the disability insurance often provides that it would not allow the insured to collect more than a specific percentage of earnings from all sources. What happens if an employee is on disability, but is capable of returning to work on a part-time or light duty basis? In many cases, it is in the interest of the employer to bring the employee back to work and to continue pro rata disability payments. In this case, compensation is being paid for productive work and there is a good chance the disability period can be shortened.

Finally, most employer-sponsored disability plans terminate when the employee is eligible for retirement under the company's pension plan. These DBPs provide for disability retirement when the employee is first eligible to receive benefits under the plan (often at age 55), and qualifies as being disabled under the terms of the pension plan. In such instances, there will be no actuarial reduction for early retirement and the employee will be considered to have retired at the normal retirement age as defined by the plan. At this point, disability payments under the insurance policy will end.

Madeline, our employee at Francesca's company, reviews her benefits statement and finds a new disability benefit. The statement says that when a full-time employee who has worked one year at the firm is medically incapable of performing her work for up to six months, the employer will pay 50 percent of her pretax earnings. The employee does not have to pay anything for this program. The statement also indicates that the employer has arranged for his employees to purchase, on an individual basis, long-term disability insurance that will pay up to 70 percent of pretax earnings for an employee who

---

24. Long-term disability payments (more than six months) are not subject to FICA payments. See IRC §3121(a)(2)(A), 3121(a)(4), 3121(a)(13), and 3121(a)(15).

is disabled and unable to perform his job for more than six months.[1] The plan is coordinated with Social Security and other disability programs, and will continue until the employee qualifies for retirement under the company's plan. The plan is guaranteed renewable.

1. The benefit decreases to 50 percent after five years.

Pay for Time Not Worked—Sick Days, Vacation, and Holidays

We now turn to examine benefits that pay compensation for time not worked. These traditionally include sick days, holidays, and vacations. There is, however, a growing trend among employers to lump entitlements for time not worked into one integrated benefit that the employee accrues with service—"paid time off."

Several years ago, a large French bank opened its first facility in the United States. Vowing to apply the same cultural and social standards followed in France, the bank offered its new employees five weeks of vacation after the first year of work. Top business school graduates and MBAs flocked to the bank's recruiters due, in part, to the generous vacation entitlement. Several years later, the bank compared its head count to U.S. banks of similar size and realized they had significantly more employees. Why? Because they needed more people to cover the work not being performed by their vacationing employees. The large head count resulted in disproportionately higher labor expense and hampered their ability to compete in a price-sensitive market. After several years, the French bank retreated and adopted the U.S. custom—it offered two weeks of vacation to new hires who completed one year of service.

Vacation benefits can be very important to the workforce. The number of weeks offered is usually related to completed years of service. For example, for employees with service from one to three years, the entitlement might be two weeks. It then can increase with service to three, four, and ultimately five weeks. There are some features about vacation that are important to remember:

- Vacation is usually accrued after completing the requisite year(s) or other stated period of service. Thus, the entitlement arises a year (or the required time) after the service begins. Vacation pay equals the rate of the employee's salary or wages.

- Vacation can be taken in days or periods of less than a week. A "week of vacation" means five (not seven) workdays of paid time off.

- Under union contracts, the timing of the vacation may depend on seniority of the employee. Senior workers usually get to choose their vacation period first.

- Since vacation requires making arrangements for replacements, the supervisor must approve the timing.

- The employer can require the employee to take or lose the vacation in the year. Some allow employees to "roll over" their vacation for several years. Others allow employees to "bank" their vacation and take it when they wish, or upon retirement. A few employers simply will pay an extra week of "vacation pay" for those who do not wish to take time off for their vacation. Accrued vacation pay must be paid when an employee separates from employment.

- Lateral appointments involve someone who is recruited from another company. They may have had longer service at the previous company and longer vacation as well. But the question for the recruiting company is should they be treated as a "new hire" for vacation purposes. Often the new company will give the recruit some years of service credit as if the employee worked at the firm for a previous period of time so they can enjoy more vacation.

In addition to vacations that involve paid time off, there are occasions where the employer can choose to pay the employee for time not worked.[25] These include:

- *Paid sick days or disability leave.* About 86 percent of employers surveyed by the Society for Human Resource Management (SHRM) indicated they offer some sort of paid sick leave. The average is 11 days per year, and most permit rollovers to the following year.[26]

- *Paid FMLA leave.*[27] The FMLA mandates a minimum of 12 weeks of leave for serious health conditions or for pregnancy, parental care, or care of an immediate family member. There is no

---

25. The Web site http://www.salary.com/ includes an extensive summary and some analysis of many forms of compensation, including paid time off.

26. See http://www.salary.com/ and also *Survey findings, managing time off.* (2001). Hewitt Associates LLC.

27. FMLA leave, while mandatory, does not require the employee be paid. See Chapter 12, Government-Sponsored and Mandated Benefits.

requirement for compensation, but some employers choose to pay the employee during their leave period.

- *Personal leave or sabbaticals.* Employers permit their employees to take an average of four days per year to take care of personal business such as moving, home repairs, or visiting a doctor.[28] The personal days are paid. A broader program is called a "personal leave of absence," where the employee is permitted to leave work for a maximum of one year and promised the right to return to his previous job. The employee usually must articulate a reasonable and somewhat compelling motive for leaving. There is no pay for personal leaves of absence. A sabbatical, rarely found among private employers, is extended time off work with some pay to complete a project or to undertake some other growth experience. Typically found in university settings, sabbaticals are granted to professors every seven years.

- *Holidays.* While there are ten federal holidays in the United States,[29] there are wide variations among employers with respect to which of these holidays they recognize for purposes of allowing employees to take off work with pay. While most public employers recognize the federal holidays, it is up to the private employer to offer all or only some to his employees.[30] In cases where work is required on holidays, the employer may choose to pay a premium rate for those employees assigned to work.

- *Bereavement leave.* Here an employee who has lost an immediate member of his family is permitted to take about three days off with pay to grieve the loss.

- *Jury duty.* When an employee has been summoned by the Clerk of Courts in his community to serve as a juror, the employer is required to release him from work. The employer may choose also to pay the employee for the lost work. Court systems also pay jurors a nominal fee for each day of duty.

- *Military leave.*[31] The individual's rights are protected by USSERA for leave up to five years and full reemployment rights for uniformed personnel called to active duty or training. Some

---

28. See *Survey of benefits.* (2004). SHRM. See *Survey of paid time off in the United States.* (2004). SHRM.

29. 5 USC §6103.

30. *Fundamentals of employee benefit programs, Chapter 30 (Leave Benefits), 3.* (2005). Employee Benefit Research Institute (EBRI).

31. As pointed out in Chapter 12, Government-Sponsored and Mandated Benefits, the employer is not required to pay compensation during military leaves.

employers, however, choose to provide some compensation to the employee or provide a continuation of health benefits, for example, to his family during the military leave.

Paid time off is being lumped into one integrated entitlement by many employers, sometimes referred to as "paid time off banks."[32] With the completion of certain periods of service, employees begin to accrue paid time off hours or days that can be taken for any reason—sickness, vacation, personal leave, or others.

According to the Society for Human Resource Management (SHRM), the average number of paid days off is 14 workdays after one year of service, 23 days after six years, and 27 days after 15 years of service.[33] This contrasts with the average vacation offering of nine days after one year, 15 days after six years, and 19 days after 15 years of service.[34] Paid time off ordinarily does not include the paid holidays recognized by the employer. These are offered in addition thereto.

There are ten federal holidays in the United States and some states have their own holidays. An employer must reasonably accommodate time off on religious holidays if an employee wishes to observe. The employer is not required to pay for the religious holiday. The attraction of an integrated pay-for-time-off plan is the employee can choose when to take off for whatever reason, provided there are remaining days in his account.

In the case of pay-for-time not worked, the decision of when and how much to offer is typically up to the private employer. Again, the issue connects with the four elements of the benefits model, particularly, "external competition"—what are they doing?—and "behavior"—does it affect retention, productivity, and recruitment?

Life insurance, disability insurance, and pay for time not worked provide an employee facing a serious life event with considerable protection and also support an employer's objective to provide balance between work and personal life.[35] For the most part, these benefits allow the employer to remain competitive in hiring and retention and to enhance the focus and productivity of his workforce.

---

32. EBRI (2005), Chapter 30, p. 6. A variation on this benefit is "donated time," where the employer allows fellow employees to donate their accrued vacation or other time off to an employee experiencing a medical or other life event and who has expended his paid time off.

33. *Survey of paid time off in the U.S.* (2004). Society for Human Resource Management (SHRM).

34. SHRM. (2004).

35. See generally, http://www.salary.com/.

Chapter Exercises

1. Go to http://www.quickquote.com, http://www.quotesmith.com/, and http://www.masterquote.com/, and get estimates on insuring your own life. Choose several different variables in getting your estimates and determine which variables have measurable impact on the cost of your plan. Explain why these variables are relevant to the underwriting of the plan.

2. Do the same for a parent or friend by checking http://www.insure .com/, http://www.evaluatelifeinsurance.com/, http://www .accuquote.com/calculation, http://www.term4sale.com/, and http://www.usaa.com/.

3. How would you calculate the Return on Investment to the employer who decides to provide company paid, term life insurance of up to $50,000? Think about the benefits model and the financial impact such a plan might have.

4. Your CEO wants to consider offering life, disability, and AD&D insurance to your employees and possibly their dependents. She has asked you, as benefits manager, to come up with a recommended package of such benefits. Do some research and write a brief summary of the current trends among employers offering life insurance as a benefit. Refer to publications by the Employee Benefits Research Institute (http://www.ebri.org), SHRM, http://www.salary.com, Employee Benefit News (http:// ebn.benefitnews.com/), and others. What types of life insurance are typically offered? Who pays? What percent of employers offer life insurance and disability insurance? Make your recommendation to the CEO.

5. Your client is 65 years old and has a $750,000 whole paid life policy in effect. He originally purchased it through his employer and has maintained it after retiring. He is receiving a retirement benefit from his former employer, as well as a pension from Social Security. His spouse is the same age and both are in good health. He earns a sizable amount of income each year from his investments. He comes to you and wants to know if he should keep his life insurance in effect or "cash it out." What facts would you need to know in formulating advice to this client?

6. Go to the Social Security Web site (http://www.ssa.gov/) and then to "calculators." Do a quick calculation of a disability pension for a person who has completed 40 quarters of covered employment, was born in 1975, earns $120,000 per year, and has a spouse and

one dependent child. What would be the benefit in current dollars if the person worked to full-age retirement? Change the variable and run another estimate. What factor(s) seem to have the most significant impact on the benefit amount?

7. You are the HR director of a company with a "no-fault" attendance program. The program provides for progressive discipline for individuals who miss ten days of work during a three-month period. The progressive discipline scheme involves a written warning, then probation, and then discharge for repeated offenses. You are concerned about whether your plan is subject to legal challenge. What are the potential effects the following laws could have on your plan: Pregnancy Protection Act, the Family and Medical Leave Act, and the Americans with Disabilities Act? Do some research on each law. Outline the potential issues that could amount to a conflict between the laws and your program. Are any modifications of your policy warranted?

8. Outline the optimal design elements of an integrated paid time off plan for a medium sized employer.

9. Identify and briefly explain the pros and cons of offering sick days that accumulate and can be rolled over all the way up to retirement. If the person retires with accrued sick days, should they be added to the years of service factor in the DBP formula? What is the HR policy issue here?

10. What is a disability retirement under an employer-sponsored plan? Go to the University of California system, at http://atyourservice .ucop.edu/, and find the Retirement Handbook for the University's Retirement Plan (UCRP). Identify the basic eligibility requirements for a disability retirement. How does this compare to the requirements under Social Security? What is the level of benefits compared to a full-age retirement when the Retirement Age Factor is .0250? What happens if the employee has enrolled in the Supplemental Disability Plan?

11. In this chapter we discuss short- and long-term disability benefits sponsored by an employer. Assume your CEO is interested in sponsoring such benefits. How would you go about calculating the potential financial returns to the company?

Convenience and Accommodation Benefits, Benefits Administration **16**

Convenience and Voluntary Benefits

While working as a senior HR officer of a Fortune 50 company, Tony Vairo's responsibilities included managing billion dollar benefit plans, supervising the negotiation and administration of over 300 collective bargaining contracts, and handling the traditional human resources functions, such as employee selection, training, development, succession planning, compensation, equity awards, and employee relations. When he left the company, his expectations were that some of the HR group's accomplishments in these arenas would be recognized and remembered. In reality, however, the HR practice that received the highest acclaim was the decision to allow casual business attire to be worn throughout the workweek.

The concept of "total reward" emphasizes the importance of all aspects of a company's work environment and not just pay, health insurance, and pension. It also includes a variety of customized employee relations practices that can help drive employee motivation, morale, and commitment. These practices, called "convenience" or "accommodation benefits," can have a positive impact on worker productivity and serve to reduce costly employee turnover. The caveat, however, is to avoid simply loading up on too many of these types of benefits when they do not produce tangible and positive returns in the workplace. It is not uncommon to see a company receive public acclaim for some extraordinary and unique benefit, such as free daycare centers or college scholarship credits for the children of its employees, only to learn later that the company has either abandoned the plan or gone out of business. A review of our previously discussed benefits model reminds us of the four issues relevant to the design of any benefit:

- Does the benefit ensure internal equity?
- Is it competitive in the labor market?
- Does it positively affect employee behaviors?
- Is it well administered and cost-effective?

It is incumbent upon employers to examine the demographics of their workforce, the geography of their workplace, and the relevant labor market. They must measure and be aware of the effectiveness of their benefits in increasing sales and improving profits (see Chapter 10, Employee Benefits and Metrics). We see this in companies like Starbucks that recruit a mature, part-time service corps through offerings of health care and flexible schedules. Other companies aggressively recruit on college campuses, offering graduate school tuition reimbursements to match the special interests and ambitions of this segment of their workforce, while others work to create more of a family atmosphere, recognizing the connection between their workforce and local community issues. They encourage their employees to pursue a variety of causes, for example, on behalf of a new park, a scholarship fund for children of fallen or injured military veterans, or a general United Way campaign. Facilitating these endeavors can produce favorable results—an enhanced employee commitment and loyalty to the company, as well as a positive public persona for the employer in the community. This said, however, companies need to be attentive in evaluating the costs of such programs and estimating their financial returns.

Making the Benefits Fit the Workplace

Brunello Cucinelli designs and makes cashmere sweaters in Solomeo, Italy, located in the region of Umbria.[1] He operates his company out

1. Binkley, C. (2007, November 29). Style showdown: $1,000 sweater faces $100 rival. *The Wall Street Journal*, D1.

of a 17th-century castle where his 1,500 employees arrive each day for work at 8:00 a.m. Each employee has a key to the factory, and is free to join his family at home for lunch from 1:00 to 2:30 p.m. For those employees who choose to stay at the plant, a three-course meal is prepared and served by several company cooks who shop each morning for fresh vegetables, meat, fruits, and cheeses. Employees return to work at 2:30 p.m. and end their workday at 6:00 pm. The employees craft beautiful, sophisticated designs; 25 percent of the workforce works in quality control to ensure the quality of the ultimate product. The company has been involved in Solomeo community projects, such as restoring the town piazza (square), building a local school, and constructing a town theater. What is the return on Signore Cucinelli's personal investments in the work environment? It is hard to say. Nevertheless, the Cucinelli sweater is one of the finest in the world due, in part, to the skill and attention of 1,500 workers. Sweaters sell for around $950, and company sales were $163 million in 2007.

Signore Cucinelli has taken into consideration the culture and work environment of his workforce, has carved a product niche for his top-quality, handmade sweaters, and has grown his sales and output over the years since the company was founded in 1978. If he were making sweaters of lesser quality without the sophisticated design, using machines and unskilled labor, and selling his product for $100, he probably would not be serving free lunches and building schools. His employee relations practices are geared toward his town, his employees and their skill levels, and his unique product. The mistake many companies make is to ignore their own particular circumstances, jump on the proverbial bandwagon, and adopt others' HR practices. There must be a fit.

As noted in Chapter 3, Lifecycle Events, benefits are designed to correspond and accommodate a variety of life events that occur among the workforce. Convenience benefits go outside an employee's critical needs, such as health and retirement, and can be defined as plans that relieve the employee of time-consuming, incidental distractions. They draw on the purchasing leverage of the employer, who can assess and procure benefits paid for by the employee but at a lower cost than he would be required to pay on his own. Another group of convenience benefits includes plans that assist the employee in coping with lifecycle events that could affect his work productivity, tenure, and general well-being. Let's look at some of these benefits.

Concierge Benefits

Bianca works at a regional cellular phone company. She is a single mother, and each morning drops her two preschool-age children off at the company's daycare center. She uses her flexible spending account and other funds to pay a discounted rate for the child care service. As she reaches the nearby office building, she passes the company concierge and hands him a laundry bag of clothes that need to be sent to the dry cleaning company. The concierge makes sure the cleaner's driver picks up the bags each morning; he will send Bianca an e-mail when her items are returned. She also hands him a list of groceries she needs to have by 5:00 p.m. He will enter the items on a supermarket company's Web site, the market will charge Bianca's account, and the items will be delivered to the phone company's refrigerated storage boxes just below the lobby before 5:00 p.m.

As Bianca sits at her desk, she remembers that she has forgotten to get tickets for her family to see the community's annual "Nutcracker" production. She sends the concierge an e-mail asking him to order three tickets in the center orchestra section of the music hall for a Saturday or Sunday afternoon performance. At noon, in the midst of a rush project for her department, Bianca chooses to have a quick lunch with her project team in the company's dining center, where lunch is provided without charge to its employees. Later, she contacts the company travel agent and asks her to get airline tickets and a hotel for her business trip to Cincinnati, Ohio. She also asks the agent to get her some choices of flights and hotels for a vacation trip to an amusement park with the kids next month. At 3:00 p.m., Bianca heads to the employee health lounge, where she gets her flu immunization shot and has her blood pressure checked by the company physician's assistant. She has been taking medication on a regular basis for a while now, and is pleased to find out that her blood pressure is under control.

At 5:00 p.m., Bianca grabs her company-provided Blackberry and laptop computer, passes the concierge desk, where she picks up her dry cleaning and laundry from a previous day, and is handed an envelope with her three "Nutcracker" tickets. She proceeds to the company garage grocery pickup station to get her groceries. Five minutes later, she retrieves her two children from the daycare center and heads home. After dinner and reading some stories to the kids before bed, she checks her e-mail on the Blackberry and sits down with the laptop to continue her work on the project. It is 9:00 p.m.

It is obvious from this example that Bianca's company, with its host of convenience benefits, is enabling her to undertake an incredibly busy work schedule. By enhancing her productivity and relieving some of the frustration in balancing her personal and professional life, the convenience benefits can generate real financial returns for the company. This is why companies offer on-the-spot therapeutic massages, employee lounges and media rooms, breast-feeding lounges for nursing mothers, fitness centers, cafes, flexible schedules, and a variety of other benefits. These kinds of benefits mitigate stress caused by the conflict between work and personal life, and the desire to do both well. The benefits remove a number of personal tasks from the employee's agenda that, in turn, permit a more focused concentration on work.

Chapter 2, Human Resources Economics, Principles, and Actuarial Concepts Applicable to Benefits, covered one of the reasons employers provide benefits instead of just paying their cash value to employees. The employer often has significant purchasing leverage, which can be used to negotiate lower rates for the service or product. The employer also can use his resources to perform due diligence in selecting a preferred provider of services or products for his employees. Ultimately, however, it may be the employee who "funds" some of the benefits. These might include discounted daycare facilities, fitness centers, long-term care insurance products, life and accidental death insurance, disability insurance, legal services, pet insurance, travel insurance, homeowners' insurance, medical procedures not covered by the health care plan such as lasik surgery, and financial or preretirement planning.[1] An employer can also use his presence in a community to help employees navigate through public or nonprofit bureaucracies that handle, for example, adoptions or provide special services for their aged parents.

Providing these types of benefits can produce loyalty among employees, relieve distractions from work, and provide real financial value to them.[2] Unlike health care and retirement benefits, there is less administrative burden on the company and fewer issues of legal compliance. At most, the company assumes an obligation to make payroll deductions or facilitate flexible spending account contributions by the employee to fund the benefit.

---

1. One of the most daunting financial challenges for many employees is financing their children's higher education. The employer can remind his employees of the importance of saving and, perhaps, using §529 plans to finance this education.

2. If the employer does offer them, he would probably select a cafeteria-type benefit plan that permits employees to pick and choose which benefits they want with allocated costs for each benefit and a monthly employee total benefit allowance. This ensures internal equity and limits costs.

Flexibility

According to a number of studies, many employees want flexibility in the workplace, meaning the traditional nine-to-five schedule does not fit their needs. Face time, requiring the employee to spend long hours at the office, is no longer an unwritten company requirement. The new mantra is "do your work and do it well and in a timely manner."[3] To accommodate a need for flexibility, a number of approaches can be offered:

- *Flextime schedules*—where employees, usually based on their personal preferences, are permitted to work varying schedules outside the normal workweek. This could include different hours, days, or special shifts.

- *Telecommuting*—where employees work at home instead of the office. They use their home computers as well as other forms of telecommunication and electronics to integrate their working relationships with coemployees at the workplace. They complete research, make calls, write up projects, and use their computers to contact coworkers, customers, and others via video and audio media. Often, they are required to spend one day a week or every other week at the office to attend meetings and maintain close relationships with fellow workers.[4]

- *Part-time work for managers and professionals*—more companies are allowing managers and professionals with significant personal obligations to work part-time. This is a major shift from previous practices, where such a move might be permitted but would result in the employee being taken off the promotable list. The rationale is to enhance recruitment and also to recognize that the family or personal circumstances preventing them from working full-time now may indeed change over several years, allowing them to become fully engaged in the future. There are important issues to be resolved with respect to part-time managers and professionals. Should they be entitled to full benefits, career development training, and the opportunity to attend management meetings? How should they be paid? Should they participate in company bonus plans, be assigned to company committees, and be slotted into the company's succession plan? These are issues the employer must resolve, usually with good communication and some explicit policies so as to avoid

---

3. Shellenbarger, S. (2007, November 15). Good news for professionals who want to work at home. *The Wall Street Journal*, D1.

4. See Demerath, N. (2002, April 1). Telecommuting in the 21st century. *All Business,* http://www.allbusiness.com/.

the notion that exceptions are unlimited and apply to special people. There are potential internal fairness conflicts resulting from full-time employees resenting the special treatment afforded to the others. In the end, however, the employer who is interested in recruiting and retaining the best workforce should consider work flexibility as one important means to that end.

- *Combined work schedules (work sharing)*—this is similar to the part-time approach, but involves two part-time managers or professionals combining their work schedule, making it a 40-hour, or full-time, workweek. With work sharing, we have the same compensation, benefits, career issues, and rationale as discussed above with respect to part-time employees.

As discussed in Chapter 12, Government-Sponsored and Mandated Benefits, the Family and Medical Leave Act (FMLA) requires covered employers to grant up to 12 weeks annual unpaid leave for childbirth, adoptions, serious illnesses, and care of an immediate family member who may be ill or in need of assistance. Some companies offer additional leave time and partially or fully compensate their employees, thereby exceeding their obligations under the FMLA.

Some employers, in addition to offering generous vacation benefits, allow longer service employees to take extended sabbatical leave to pursue personal interests,[5] or temporarily lend their managers to community nonprofit groups to provide them with skilled leadership for a particular event.

Employee Assistance Plan (EAP)

Max Thomas works for a national accounting firm performing financial audits of client companies. Max's wife of ten years has filed for divorce and is requesting alimony, child support, and child custody. Max has moved out of the couple's home and is living in a furnished apartment. The divorce, which is expected to take about a year to

---

5. There are a number of studies that indicate stress, overwork, under-utilization of vacation days, and very long workweeks are quite common in the U.S. workplace. They all have an impact on labor costs and productivity. See Key Organization Systems, http://www.keyorganization.com/.

resolve, is proving to be a major distraction for Max. He is having difficulty concentrating on his work and feels that his life is coming apart. Meanwhile, he is trying desperately to maintain a close relationship with his children. Max knows the company provides an employee assistance program (EAP) for its employees who are experiencing difficult life events. He calls the EAP number and makes an appointment to see one of their psychologists. He is told the company will pay 100 percent of the fees for the first six visits. He is under no obligation to advise his supervisor of his actions, and is aware that the company will not have access to the confidential records generated by his visits to the psychologist. After four visits, Max's perspective on the pending divorce has changed. He is experiencing less guilt, has a better understanding of how to continue his relationship with his children, and has a good idea how to approach a reconciliation using professional counselors.

Many employers offer employee assistance plans. These programs provide professional counseling, enabling employees to get through difficult emotional events such as divorce, loss of a loved one, or some other traumatic event.[6] The purpose is to minimize the distractions these life events cause and to allow the employee to refocus on work and the core direction of his life. In most cases the assistance is free with limits on the number of uses.

While some programs provide a number to call and talk to a counselor, most offer personal visits with a licensed counselor. The assistance is not designed to render medical or psychiatric treatment. Confidentiality is an important feature of EAPs. While a supervisor might suggest to the employee that he utilize the program, referrals and sessions most often are independently initiated by the employee and are confidential. They are considered to be outside the employer-sponsored health care plan. As with other benefits, it is the obligation of employers to evaluate the effectiveness of such programs, making sure they achieve their intended purpose and add value. Including such programs among the benefit offerings often enhances the employee's perception of the employer as one who is concerned for his overall well-being.

---

6. These are not to be confused with health care plans that provide mental health benefits on a full parity basis with medical benefits and involve treatment on an ongoing basis as opposed to short-term counseling that is the mainstay of EAP. See Ridgely, S., Burnham, A., Barry, C., & Hennessy, K. (2006). Health plans respond to parity: Managing behavioral health care in the federal employees health benefits program. *Milbank Quarterly, 84*(1), 201–218.

Company-Sponsored Educational Benefits

An important interest among many new employees is their opportunity to grow, learn, develop, advance, and pursue a career within the organization. How and if this happens can depend on the availability and quality of training and education in the company. One way to accomplish this is to include training and education as features of a company's benefits plan. With the help of the U.S. Tax Code,[7] some companies reimburse employees taking courses at accredited educational institutions or professional organizations. Areas of study can include special technical or leadership courses, advanced degrees such as an MBA, or certification programs offered by professional organizations in a variety of disciplines such as human resources, compensation, and benefits. In many cases financial assistance is dependent upon the course being relevant to advancement within the organization, as well as the employee's successful completion of the course.[8] In laying the groundwork for advancement within the organization, some companies select employees for training courses in specific areas such as creativity, facilitative leadership, finance, or team building.

A note of caution to offering this opportunity—because it is exclusive to only certain employees, it can create an internal fairness problem. An easy solution would be to offer a cafeteria plan, in which there are a variety of benefit choices, each with a prescribed financial value and a total dollar limit per employee.[9] The IRS does not, however, offer favorable tax treatment for educational financial assistance included in cafeteria plans. So, the employer must consider this option for other benefits that might have particular appeal to a certain segment of his workforce. In general, the employee can choose which benefit he wants, but is limited by the total value of his choices. For an example of how such a plan might work, see Table 2.2 in Chapter 2.

As we look at these convenience or accommodation benefits, as well as voluntary benefits[10] that might be funded by the employee, we are

---

7. See Tuition Reimbursement at http://www.salary.com. The IRC allows the employer to reimburse the employee for a portion ($5,250 each year) of the employee's tuition expense without it being considered as ordinary income and taxable. See Employer Provided Educational Assistance, Publication 970, (2007), Internal Revenue Service, http://www.irs.gov/publications/.

8. For example, the employer often requires the attainment of certain grades before reimbursement is made. For a complete summary of the IRS rules on employer-sponsored educational assistance programs, see Publication 970, (2007), at http://www.irs.gov/.

9. See Silva, C. (2007, June 1). All benefits to all people. *Employee Benefit News.*

10. See Chapter 15, Life and Disability Insurance, Pay for Time Not Worked. A popular benefit procured by the employer but fully funded by the employee is

reminded of the importance of total rewards in an organization. Benefits, including those facilitated by the employer but funded by the employee, can be highly regarded by the workforce and can enhance commitment, alignment, loyalty, and productivity. As pointed out in Chapter 10, Employee Benefits and Metrics, however, the employer must constantly evaluate their effectiveness—is there a fit with the needs and wants of your workforce and do they create value?

Administration of Employer-Sponsored Benefits

> Sam works for a management consulting firm. He has a 401(k) and regularly contributes the maximum allowable percentage of his salary to the plan. A number of investment options are available to participants and Sam has given the plan manager specific instructions on how to invest his income deferrals. The manager, however, has ignored Sam's instructions and placed Sam's money in less successful investments. As a result, Sam's account suffered a loss in appreciation of $150,000. He sues his employer alleging a violation of ERISA.[1]
>
> ---
>
> 1. See *La Rue v. DeWolf*, 128 S. Ct. 1020 (2008). The question involves whether ERISA can be read to protect an individual participant's rights affected by a breach of the plan's fiduciary responsibility, or whether it applies to breaches that involve losses to an entire retirement plan. The U.S. Supreme Court held for the participant; the fiduciary was legally responsible for the mistake. There are about 50 million participants in private employer-sponsored 401(k) plans and $5.5 trillion invested. Richey, W. (2007, November 26). Can you sue if your 401(k) nest egg is mishandled? *The Christian Science Monitor*, http://www.csmonitor.com/.

This serves as an excellent reminder that unless a plan is efficiently and effectively administered, the anticipated value it provides to the sponsor will be lost. This is the fourth element of our benefits model and its

---

long-term care insurance that pays for future nursing home or home care services the employee or his family might incur as a result of a debilitating illness. For a review of the variety of voluntary benefits being offered, see http://www.voluntary.com/.

importance should not be ignored. Employees are not happy when their 401(k) deferrals are sent to the wrong investment option, or when they are enrolled in the wrong health care plan, or when they do not understand how much their retirement income will be under the employer's plan. Some basic principles that apply to good plan administration are:

- Plans should be simple and easy to understand.

- Sponsors should control the administrative expense of plans.

- Where possible, allow employee choices to be part of the overall plan.

- Sponsors should strive to allow employees to administer their own plans by introducing information systems that enable benefit selections and provide information and enrollment.

An essential element of good benefit plan administration is an accurate and current human resources management system (HRMS). This enables employer sponsors to understand who is eligible, who is enrolled in which benefit programs, who the dependents are, and how much to withhold from pay for policy premiums or salary deferrals.

Before going into some of the details of administration, keep in mind that the employer sponsor has a number of legally imposed administrative obligations. For example, he must report and disclose certain information to plan participants, as discussed in Chapter 9, Benefit Legal Compliance. Further, the employer has a fiduciary obligation to run his retirement and welfare plans in the best interests of the participants and to make judgments applying reasonable care and diligence. Under ERISA, the employer also has to provide an internal appeal process for employees who believe their benefits were improperly denied.

ERISA allows the employer sponsor to delegate certain aspects of the plan administration to fiduciaries with special competencies. Certain administrative responsibilities can be delegated to internal or external groups that enroll participants, hold plan assets in trust, invest salary deferrals in accordance with the participant's directions, and develop communications and documents that aid the participant's understanding of his particular plan. For example, in a defined benefit plan, the investments of plan assets can be delegated to persons who have expertise in capital markets and investing. Ultimately, however, the overall accountability for the administration and the selection of fiduciaries lies with the sponsors and their boards of directors. In Figure 16.1 we outline the basic administrative duties that would apply to most benefit plans. In today's world, the employer sponsors are retaining the responsibility to design the plan, determine coverage and eligibility, and, in some cases, enroll the participants. Specialized third-party administrators (TPAs) are doing the rest.

Outsourcing Administration

Dr. DiMauro is a primary care physician. When she sees a patient, certain codes are entered into an electronic patient record that includes information about the patient, his condition, and the treatment rendered. This data is transmitted online to the health insurance company sponsored by the patient's employer. It passes through the insurance company's software that automatically evaluates the claim. The insurance company's software already has received online data from the sponsoring employer with eligibility information about the patient and the particular benefit plan in which the employee has enrolled. If the data conforms to the benefits and coverage requirements of the employer's plan, the system creates data for an explanation of benefits (EOB) statement, which will be sent to the employee, and a reimbursement check to the physician.[1]

---

1. Increasingly, employers are asking their health care TPAs to examine their claims data to determine the most prevalent drivers and risk factors of health care expense. See Elswick, J. (2005, April 25). Technology helps firms define health cost drivers. *Employee Benefit News*, http://www.eba.benefitnews.com/.

For the most part, employer sponsors of benefit plans recognize the value of placing plan administration in the hands of the experts—those who have the systems, expertise, and capacity to do the work. In many cases the employer can delegate all of the responsibilities listed in Figure 16.1 except the design and eligibility functions. For example, employers often outsource health care plan administration to a TPA, the prescription care plan to a pharmacy benefit specialist, and the administration of retiree health care and COBRA to other specialized third-party administrators. These outside parties are specialists who have the systems, call service centers, and expertise to administer a specific aspect of the plan more effectively and efficiently than the plan sponsor.

Employers sponsoring retirement plans outsource or delegate investment strategy, trust administration, employee communications, legal compliance, and enrollment to third parties. The employer simply establishes eligibility and may adjudicate internal claims regarding the denial of benefits. These actions free up the employer's benefits department to work on strategic initiatives such as exploring new benefit designs, evaluating their current plans, and getting participant inputs that can add real value to the company's financial success.

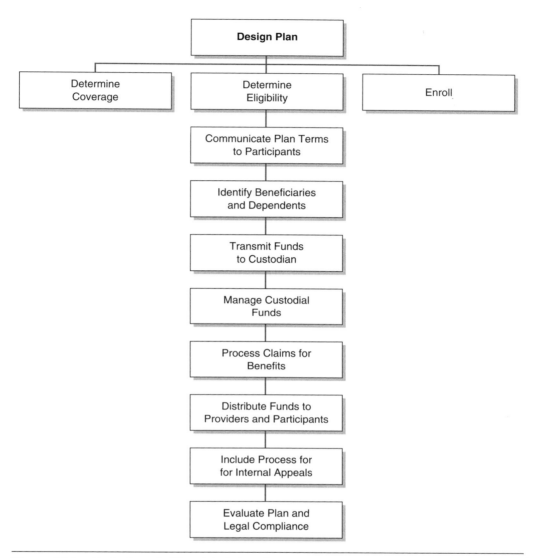

Figure 16.1   Basic Benefit Plan Administration

From the administrator's perspective, it is estimated that 90 percent of health claims are processed without any claims adjudicator.[11] Coded data is transmitted electronically from provider to TPA, algorithms determine the appropriateness of care, and reimbursement is facilitated. The plan sponsor makes the final decision on eligibility and plan design,

11. Interview of Michael Stoll, Vice President of Employee Benefits, The Kroger Co. (2007, December).

and the third party administering a health care or pension plan takes care of the rest.[12]

Information Systems for Benefits

In today's world, newly hired employees enter personal and human resources information on a terminal that is immediately integrated into the company's HRMS.[13] It becomes the basis for determining when the employee becomes eligible for certain benefits. Thereafter, these employees are summoned to their terminal, computer, or a kiosk on the shop floor to make their open enrollment choices for health care, to elect beneficiaries for their life insurance, and to make choices of investments for their 401(k) plans.

Gone are the days where the HR manager scheduled meetings with each employee and personally shepherded these choices. While the employer must delegate and outsource such functions carefully so as to ensure accurate and cost-effective administration, many employers, through the use of technology and online systems, have basically shifted the responsibility of administration to the employee participant and benefit administration specialists.

Plan Optimization and Communication

Consider these final thoughts regarding benefit plan administration. First, employers are finding their multigenerational workforce has different needs and interests. Second, the workforce wants some guidance from their employers with respect to the optimization of benefit choices that will meet their own needs. This is a real opportunity for employers to engage employees in their benefit decisions and to get more credit for the benefit offerings. Thus, the opportunity to gain loyalty and commitment can be linked to the employer's benefits. Technology and effective plan administration make this all possible. Many companies find the new mixed

---

12. Technology is also being used in the selection of benefits and providers. Many employer sponsors are using online bidding processes to get the best deals for their employees. For example, if the employer wants to find a good voluntary life insurance policy for his employees at a very competitive price, he can use an online bidding service, similar to eBay, to find the best value for his employees.

13. See Silva, C. (2007, September 4). Employers making strides in streamlining HR tech systems. *Employee Benefit News*, http://www.ebn.benefitnews.com/.

demographics of their workforce means that some rewards and benefits simply do not fit with many of their workers. Some employees would prefer defined contribution plans; others expect to be with the company long term and consider a retirement plan that rewards long service more desirable. Similarly, varied perspectives are found with respect to health care, life insurance, work flexibility, and other benefits. Previously, offering two or more plans and giving employees a choice was not practical. So, one plan was made available resulting in a limited optimization of the benefit. Some employees did not prefer or even want a particular benefit. The employer in those cases was giving away a benefit that had no value. Today, with technology and the outsourcing of benefit administration, it is possible for employers to offer an assortment of retirement, health care, and other plans that are responsive to a diverse and multigenerational workforce.

The employer should provide help to his employees as they navigate these benefit choices and try to find ways to maximize their short- and long-term goals. Educational assistance with respect to benefits can enhance employee retention and cause employees to better appreciate their benefits. Again, using third parties and technology can facilitate this process. Giving employees an envelope with all their benefit materials once a year does not meet this objective. Just like stock options, the employer cannot expect that handing them out will cause a positive change in behavior. Employers should seize the moment and provide the roadmaps that employees need to make the right benefit choices and plan for their own futures. This process must continue throughout the year and not just occur on open enrollment day. Such an aggressive communication and benefit educational process can have a lasting effect in the workplace and make benefits a real value proposition.[14]

Chapter Exercises

1. You are the HR director of a 5,000-employee electrical supply company. The company currently offers a variety of standard benefits, such as health care, retirement, and life insurance. You would like to enrich the offerings by adding several voluntary benefits. One in particular is long-term care. (a) What research would help you determine the need for such a benefit among your employees? (b) What design alternatives are available in your respective area for long-term care? (c) What plan design do you think would be most appropriate for your company? Describe the

14. See *Study of employee benefit trends (sixth annual)*. (2008). MetLife, http://www.metlife.com/.

plan of benefits in some detail. (d) How would you go about marketing the plan to your employees? (e) What type of information support would you provide to your employees to better inform them about the program? (f) What would be the optimal way to finance such a program?

2. Contact a parent, relative, or friend who works for an employer who sponsors a retirement plan. Ask them some questions relating to their understanding of their plan, their long-term goals and plans for financial security and retirement income, and what information they would like to have about accomplishing these goals that they currently are not receiving. Assume you are the benefits director for this employer. From the foregoing conversation, develop some talking points that you would present to the CEO of the employer sponsor concerning possible communication and educational opportunities. Also identify the optimal format you would recommend to facilitate this process. How would these opportunities generate more value to the employer?

3. You are the benefits manager of a call center with 350 employees. It is one of seven in your company. The center is located in a large midwestern town. You have quite a few employees with preschool-age children. You cannot afford an onsite daycare center or a program where you would pay for such services. Instead, you would like to offer your employees the opportunity to have reliable information on quality centers in the area. The employees who use it would pay for the service. You want to convince your employees that you have performed due diligence to select appropriate providers, that you have used your leverage to obtain the best discount, and that you will support the employees in obtaining quality service. Outline a step-by-step approach you would take in developing your plan and how you would go about meeting the employees' expectations. How would you measure the apparent effectiveness of the program?

4. Go to http://www.voluntary.com/ (or a source of your choosing) and do some research on elder care. Would this be a possible voluntary benefit that a company could offer? Why? Would there be some specific workforce demographics that might warrant such a benefit? Be prepared to discuss the nature of the benefit in class and discuss why it might be particularly attractive to a workforce. What are some available design alternatives and how would the sponsoring employer financially justify the administrative expense of offering it to his employees?

5. International adoptions are growing in the United States and often involve complicated, expensive, and drawn-out processes. Do some research on the issue and write up some talking points you would use to explain to your CEO why this is a possible benefit that might be extended to your workforce. Be sure to include the data on which you would base a recommendation, the assumptions you would make, financing alternatives, and the various plan designs and alternatives typically offered. Identify the possible returns to the employer for offering such a benefit. Use the benefits model in developing your presentation.[15]

---

15. See a list of companies that offer such benefits in Shellenberger, S. (2007, August 7). For some, job benefits ease growing hassles of adoption. *The Wall Street Journal*, D1.

Index

About the Author

Thomas E. Murphy graduated from the University of Cincinnati with a degree in economics and a Juris Doctorate in law. He subsequently served as a trial attorney with the U.S. Department of Labor. He returned to the University of Cincinnati College of Law, becoming an associate professor of law and later associate dean. He left the University of Cincinnati to join The Kroger Co., where he served as senior labor counsel, vice president and senior counsel, and senior officer and group vice president of human resources and labor relations. At Kroger, among other duties, he was responsible for the company's benefit plans covering nearly 300,000 employees. Upon leaving Kroger, he was awarded a Fulbright Scholar Fellowship and worked on economic development projects in Jordan. He is currently an executive professor in the Farmer School of Business at Miami University in Oxford, Ohio, where he teaches courses in benefits, negotiation and conflict resolution, human resource management, human capital metrics, employment law, and employee compensation. He also has served on the faculty of the International University of Monaco, and taught special programs at the University of Genoa, Italy; Lebanese American University in Beirut, Lebanon; and Vienna University of Economics and Business Administration in Vienna, Austria. Professor Murphy has published articles on health care, human capital metrics, employment law, and human resource management in the Middle East. He has lived and worked in Europe, the Middle East, and the United States.

  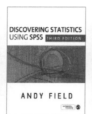